Basic and Clinical Science Course 1999-2000;
Section 2

Fundamentals and Principles of Ophthalmology

1999-2000

(Last major revision 1997-1998)

LIFELONG
EDUCATION FOR THE
OPHTHALMOLOGIST

American Academy of Ophthalmology

The Basic and Clinical Science Course is one component of the Lifelong Education for the Ophthalmologist (LEO) framework, which assists members in planning their continuing medical education. LEO includes an array of clinical education products that members may select to form individualized, self-directed learning plans for updating their clinical knowledge. Active members or fellows who use LEO components may accumulate sufficient CME credits to earn the LEO Award. Contact the Academy's Clinical Education Division for further information on LEO.

This CME activity was planned and produced in accordance with the ACCME Essentials.

The Academy provides this material for educational purposes only. It is not intended to represent the only or best method or procedure in every case, nor to replace a physician's own judgment or give specific advice for case management. Including all indications, contraindications, side effects, and alternative agents for each drug or treatment is beyond the scope of this material. All information and recommendations should be verified, prior to use, with current information included in the manufacturers' package inserts or other independent sources, and considered in light of the patient's condition and history. Reference to certain drugs, instruments, and other products in this publication is made for illustrative purposes only and is not intended to constitute an endorsement of such. Some material may include information on applications that are not considered community standard, that reflect indications not included in approved FDA labeling, or that are approved for use only in restricted research settings. The FDA has stated that it is the responsibility of the physician to determine the FDA status of each drug or device he or she wishes to use, and to use them with appropriate patient consent in compliance with applicable law. The Academy specifically disclaims any and all liability for injury or other damages of any kind, from negligence or otherwise, for any and all claims that may arise from the use of any recommendations or other information contained herein.

Each author states that he or she has no significant financial interest or other relationship with the manufacturer of any commercial product discussed in the chapters that he or she contributed to this publication or with the manufacturer of any competing commercial product.

Basic and Clinical Science Course

Thomas A. Weingeist, PhD, MD, Iowa City, Iowa
Senior Secretary for Clinical Education

Thomas J. Liesegang, MD, Jacksonville, Florida
Secretary for Instruction

M. Gilbert Grand, MD, St. Louis, Missouri
BCSC Course Chair

Section 2

Faculty Responsible for This Edition

Ramesh C. Tripathi, MD, PhD, *Chair*, Columbia, South Carolina

K.V. Chalam, MD, Columbia, South Carolina, *Pharmacology*

Gerhard W. Cibis, MD, *Consultant*, Kansas City, Missouri

Randy H. Kardon, MD, PhD, *Consultant*, Iowa City, Iowa, *Anatomy*

Brenda J. Tripathi, PhD, Columbia, South Carolina, *Embryology*

F.J.G.M. van Kuijk, MD, PhD, *Consultant*, Galveston, Texas,
Biochemistry and Metabolism

Richard G. Weleber, MD, Portland, Oregon, *Genetics*

Martin Wand, MD, Hartford, Connecticut
Practicing Ophthalmologists Advisory Committee for Education

Recent Past Faculty

Robert E. Anderson, MD, PhD
H. Dwight Cavanagh, MD, PhD
Emily Y. Chew, MD
Richard B. Einaugler, MD
Frederick L. Ferris III, MD
Gerald A. Fishman, MD
Mitchell H. Friedlaender, MD
Edward K. Isbey, Jr, MD
Henry J. Kaplan, MD
Sidney Lerman, MD
Richard A. Lewis, MD

Joel S. Mindel, MD
Kenneth H. Musson, MD
Paul F. Palmberg, MD, PhD
James M. Richard, MD
Morton E. Smith, MD
Elise Torczynski, MD
David L. Verlee, MD
Stephen R. Waltman, MD
Thomas A. Weingeist, MD, PhD
Norman F. Woodlief, MD

In addition, the Academy gratefully acknowledges the
contributions of numerous past faculty and advisory
committee members who have played an important role in
the development of previous editions of the Basic and
Clinical Science Course.

American Academy of Ophthalmology Staff

Kathryn A. Hecht, EdD
Vice President, Clinical Education

Hal Straus
Director, Publications Department

Margaret Denny
Managing Editor

Fran Taylor
Medical Editor

Maxine Garrett
Administrative Coordinator

American Academy of Ophthalmology
655 Beach Street
Box 7424
San Francisco, CA 94120-7424

CONTENTS

GENERAL INTRODUCTION

The Basic and Clinical Science Course (BCSC) is designed to provide residents and practitioners with a comprehensive yet concise curriculum of the field of ophthalmology. The BCSC has developed from its original brief outline format, which relied heavily on outside readings, to a more convenient and educationally useful self-contained text. The Academy regularly updates and revises the course, with the goals of integrating the basic science and clinical practice of ophthalmology and of keeping current with new developments in the various subspecialties.

The BCSC incorporates the effort and expertise of more than 70 ophthalmologists, organized into 12 section faculties, working with Academy editorial staff. In addition, the course continues to benefit from many lasting contributions made by the faculties of previous editions. Members of the Academy's Practicing Ophthalmologists Advisory Committee for Education serve on each faculty and, as a group, review every volume before and after major revisions.

Organization of the Course

The 12 sections of the Basic and Clinical Science Course are numbered as follows to reflect a logical order of study, proceeding from fundamental subjects to anatomic subdivisions:

1. Update on General Medicine
2. Fundamentals and Principles of Ophthalmology
3. Optics, Refraction, and Contact Lenses
4. Ophthalmic Pathology and Intraocular Tumors
5. Neuro-Ophthalmology
6. Pediatric Ophthalmology and Strabismus
7. Orbit, Eyelids, and Lacrimal System
8. External Disease and Cornea
9. Intraocular Inflammation and Uveitis
10. Glaucoma
11. Lens and Cataract
12. Retina and Vitreous

In addition, a comprehensive Master Index allows the reader to easily locate subjects throughout the entire series.

References

Readers who wish to explore specific topics in greater detail may consult the journal references cited within each chapter and the Basic Texts listed at the back of the book. These references are intended to be selective rather than exhaustive, chosen by the BCSC faculty as being important, current, and readily available to residents and practitioners.

Related Academy educational materials are also listed in the appropriate sections. They include books, audiovisual materials, self-assessment programs, clinical modules, and interactive programs.

Study Questions and CME Credit

Each volume includes multiple-choice study questions designed to be used as a closed-book exercise. The answers are accompanied by explanations to enhance the learning experience. Completing the study questions allows readers both to test their understanding of the material and to demonstrate section completion for the purpose of CME credit, if desired.

The Academy is accredited by the Accreditation Council for Continuing Medical Education to sponsor continuing medical education for physicians. CME credit hours in Category 1 of the Physician's Recognition Award of the AMA may be earned for completing the study of any section of the BCSC. The Academy designates the number of credit hours for each section based upon the scope and complexity of the material covered (see the Credit Reporting Form in each individual section for the maximum number of hours that may be claimed).

Based upon return of the Credit Reporting Form at the back of each book, the Academy will maintain a record, for up to 3 years, of credits earned by Academy members. Upon request, the Academy will send a transcript of credits earned.

Conclusion

The Basic and Clinical Science Course has expanded greatly over the years, with the addition of much new text and numerous illustrations. Recent editions have sought to place a greater emphasis on clinical applicability, while maintaining a solid foundation in basic science. As with any educational program, it reflects the experience of its authors. As its faculties change and as medicine progresses, new viewpoints are always emerging on controversial subjects and techniques. Not all alternate approaches can be included in this series; as with any educational endeavor, the learner should seek additional sources, including such carefully balanced opinions as the Academy's Preferred Practice Patterns.

The BCSC faculty and staff are continuously striving to improve the educational usefulness of the course; you, the reader, can contribute to this ongoing process. If you have any suggestions or questions about the series, please do not hesitate to contact the faculty or the managing editor.

The authors, editors, and reviewers hope that your study of the BCSC will be of lasting value and that each section will serve as a practical resource for quality patient care.

OBJECTIVES FOR BCSC SECTION 2

Upon completion of BCSC Section 2, *Fundamentals and Principles of Ophthalmology,* the reader should be able to:

☐ Identify the bones making up the orbital walls and the orbital foramina

☐ Identify the origin and pathways of cranial nerves I–VII

☐ Identify the origin and insertions of the extraocular muscles and use CT and MRI studies to point out the extraocular muscles, optic nerve, and lacrimal gland in axial and coronal views of the orbit

☐ Describe the distribution of the arterial and venous circulations of the orbit and optic nerve

☐ Summarize the structural-functional relationships of the outflow pathways for aqueous humor of the eye

☐ Delineate the events of early embryogenesis that are important for the subsequent development of the eye and orbit

☐ Identify the roles of growth factors, homeobox genes, and neural crest cells in the genesis of the eye

☐ Describe the sequence of events in the differentiation of the ocular tissues during embryonic and fetal development of the eye

☐ Recognize and characterize congenital anomalies of the eye that arise as a result of genetic factors or environmental effects during development

☐ Review the stages in the development of the eye and the correlation between congenital ocular disorders and the timing of an insult to the embryo

☐ Appreciate how the human genome is organized and the role of genetic mutations in health and disease

☐ Explain how DNA can be manipulated in the laboratory to map and to clone genes, identify genes from surrounding DNA, and create transgenic and knockout animals

☐ Demonstrate how appropriate diagnosis and management of genetic diseases can lead to better patient care

☐ Assess the role of the ophthalmologist in the provision of genetic counseling

☐ Identify the biochemical composition of the various parts of the eye and its secretions

☐ Review new concepts regarding the interaction between membrane proteins and G proteins and how this affects ocular functions, such as rhodopsin with transducin in the conversion of "light-stimulus" to "electric-signal"

☐ Discuss the biochemical derangements in diabetes and how they lead to its ocular complications, such as diabetic retinopathy and cataract formation

☐ List the varied functions of the retinal pigment epithelium such as phagocytosis and vitamin A metabolism and their relationship to retinal diseases

☐ Summarize the role of free radicals and antioxidants

☐ Recognize the features of the eye that facilitate or impede drug delivery

☐ Cite the basic principles underlying the use of autonomic therapeutic agents in a variety of ocular conditions

- List the indications, contraindications, mechanisms of action, and side effects of various drugs in the management of glaucoma
- Describe the mechanisms of action of antibiotics, antivirals, and antifungal medications: their indications, dosages, and side effects
- Discuss the anesthetic agents used in ophthalmology, their dosages and adverse effects
- Recognize therapeutic drugs on the horizon and in the process of being introduced into clinical practice in the immediate future

INTRODUCTION TO SECTION 2

The renowned science historian Derek deSolla Price addressed the growth of scientific knowledge in his Pegram Lecture at the Brookhaven Laboratory in 1962. Since 1660, when modern scientific societies were established, periodicals, rather than books, became the accepted source for inquiry. By measuring published papers, Price concluded that scientific knowledge has been doubling every 10 years since the mid-17th century. Recent reports have shortened the doubling time to every 5 years or even every 2 years. However, the exact number of years in the doubling time is not as important as the result, as we all know only too well: it is now very difficult, if not impossible, to keep up with this information explosion.

There are currently over 23,000 members of all categories in the American Academy of Ophthalmology. About two thirds of the members finished their training 10 or more years ago. Using the conservative 10-year doubling time, the majority of Academy members find that more than half of the current scientific, and presumably medical, knowledge had not even been conceived during their training.

Comprehension of many journal articles now requires a sound knowledge of cellular and molecular biology and genetics. To benefit fully from the complete 12-volume Basic and Clinical Science Course, the reader must be familiar with the ever-growing fundamental block of scientific knowledge. That is why Section 2, *Fundamentals and Principles of Ophthalmology,* is perceived as the foundation of the BCSC series. To keep pace with this exponential growth of information, Section 2 has been extensively rewritten and brought up to date. The highlights of each of the five parts of Section 2 are touched on briefly below.

Anatomy While anatomy has not undergone major discoveries, newer diagnostic techniques have allowed better anatomic visualization and three-dimensional correlation of the ocular, orbital, and extraorbital structures. The illustrations, which are critical to any anatomic text, have been reworked to provide clearer and better figures and, where appropriate, use newer imaging techniques. This new edition presents the illustrations interspersed within the text, making conceptualization easier.

Embryology The embryology section has been completely rewritten, incorporating new information on the role of growth factors, homeobox genes, and neural crest cells as determinants in the genesis of the eye. Instead of merely giving a chronological description of anatomical changes, these chapters emphasize the molecular and cellular basis for such changes. The Glossary has been expanded and moved to the front of this part for handy use.

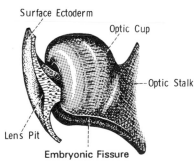

*Development of the optic cup.
See Part 2, Embryology.*

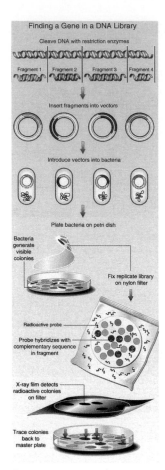

Finding a Gene in a DNA Library

Cleave DNA with restriction enzymes

Fragment 1 | Fragment 2 | Fragment 3 | Fragment 4

Insert fragments into vectors

Introduce vectors into bacteria

Plate bacteria on petri dish

Bacteria generate visible colonies

Fix replicate library on nylon filter

Radioactive probe

Probe hybridizes with complementary sequence in fragment

X-ray film detects radioactive colonies on filter

Trace colonies back to master plate

Screening a DNA Library.
See Part 3, Genetics.

Genetics   Genetics has undergone an explosion of knowledge that perhaps may be dwarfed by what is yet to come. A Glossary of important genetic terms introduces these revised chapters, which represent, essentially, a stand-alone primer on basic genetics as well as the genetics of ocular diseases. The chapter on molecular genetics reviews the structure of DNA, genes, and chromosomes and the processes of transcription, translation, replication, and DNA repair. Also covered are imprinting, X-chromosomal inactivation, and gene regulation, as well as techniques of DNA amplification, manipulation, and analysis within the laboratory and the search for genes in specific diseases. These substantially expanded chapters also incorporate several new illustrations to complement and explicate the text.

Biochemistry and metabolism   The biochemistry and metabolism section has undergone major revision as well to keep abreast of recent developments. For example, free radicals and antioxidants, subjects barely touched upon in the last edition, receive extensive discussion, clarifying recent theories of antioxidants as factors in cataract formation and the pathogenesis of age-related macular degeneration. More than half of the illustrations in the chapters are new. The references have also been updated and selected to stress clinically relevant publications.

Ocular pharmacology   Since the last edition, ocular pharmacology has seen many new medications introduced, and they have all been included here. For example, latanoprost, the first major antiglaucoma medication in 20 years, became available as this edition began its revision, and the literature concerning this agent has been reviewed and distilled. New information has also been included to reflect recent therapeutic advances in antiviral therapy with special emphasis on pharmacotherapy of HIV-related infections. Gene therapy is discussed in the pharmacology chapters for the first time, and almost all of the illustrations and tables are new.

Summary

New to this edition is a list of Objectives to inform the reader of the scope of each part. Compared to previous editions, this revision has almost doubled the number of Study Questions, which should help readers to assess their understanding of the information presented. Explanations have been added to many of the answers as a further review of the text.

This group of authors has worked with exceptional cognizance and effort on this edition. They have consulted with eminent clinicians and scientists in their areas. We trust that Section 2 will help curious and concerned ophthalmologists and ophthalmic professionals keep abreast of the information explosion, while enjoying the experience.

The authors would like to thank the following institutions for their assistance to the faculty: University of South Carolina, School of Medicine, Columbia; National Eye Institute (NIH), Bethesda, Maryland; University of Kansas, Kansas City; University of Iowa, Iowa City; University of Texas Medical Branch, Galveston; Oregon Health Sciences University, Portland; University of Connecticut, Hartford.

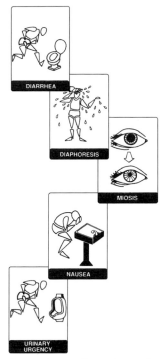

Some adverse effects observed with cholinergic drugs. See Part 5, Ocular Pharmacology.

Ramesh C. Tripathi, MD, PhD, FACS, FRCOphth
Chair, Section 2, BCSC

Martin Wand, MD
Practicing Ophthalmologists Advisory Committee for Education

PART 1

ANATOMY

The classic reference books listed below are especially useful in the study of ophthalmic anatomy. Rather than being cited repeatedly in the text, these works are listed here for the reader's general reference. Other references are interspersed throughout the text where relevant.

Beard C, Quickert MH. *Anatomy of the Orbit: A Dissection Manual.* 3rd ed. Birmingham, AL: Aesculapius Publishing Co; 1988.

Duke-Elder S, ed. *System of Ophthalmology.* Vol II. *The Anatomy of the Visual System.* St Louis: Mosby; 1976.

Dutton JJ. *Atlas of Clinical and Surgical Orbital Anatomy.* Philadelphia: Saunders; 1994.

Fine BS, Yanoff M. *Ocular Histology: A Text and Atlas.* 2nd ed. Hagerstown, MD: Harper & Row; 1979.

Hogan MJ, Alvarado JA, Weddell JE. *Histology of the Human Eye.* Philadelphia: Saunders; 1971.

Mausolf FA. *The Anatomy of the Ocular Adnexa.* Springfield, IL: Charles C Thomas; 1975.

Miller NR, Newman NJ, eds. *Walsh and Hoyt's Clinical Neuro-Ophthalmology.* 5th ed. Baltimore: Williams & Wilkins; 1997.

Reeh MJ, Wobig JL, Wirtschafter JD. *Ophthalmic Anatomy.* San Francisco: American Academy of Ophthalmology; 1981.

Snell RS, Lemp MA. *Clinical Anatomy of the Eye.* Boston: Blackwell Scientific Publications; 1989.

Tasman W, Jaeger EA, eds. *Duane's Clinical Ophthalmology.* Philadelphia: Lippincott; 1994.

Zide BM, Jelks GW. *Surgical Anatomy of the Orbit.* New York: Raven Press; 1985.

CHAPTER I

Orbit and Ocular Adnexa

Orbital Anatomy

Periorbital Sinuses

The eyes lie within two bony cavities, or *orbits,* of the skull located on each side of the root of the nose. Each orbit is shaped like a pear with the optic nerve representing the stem. The medial walls of the orbits are almost parallel. They border the nasal cavity anteriorly and the ethmoidal air cells and the sphenoid sinus posteriorly. In the adult the lateral wall of each orbit forms an angle of approximately 45° with the medial plane at the orbital apex. The lateral walls border the middle cranial, temporal, and pterygopalatine fossae. Superior to the orbit are the anterior cranial fossa and the frontal and supraorbital sinuses. The maxillary sinus and the palatine air cells are located inferiorly.

The periorbital or nasal sinuses may offer a route for the spread of infection. Mucoceles occasionally arise from the sinuses and may confuse the clinician in the differential diagnosis of orbital tumors. The locations of the paranasal air sinuses and their relation to anatomical features of the skull are shown in Figures I-1 and I-2. Figure I-1 also shows the distribution of pain originating from sinusitis.

BCSC Section 7, *Orbit, Eyelids, and Lacrimal System.*

Doxanas MT, Anderson RL. *Clinical Orbital Anatomy.* Baltimore: Williams & Wilkins; 1984:232.

Orbital Volume

The volume of each adult orbit is slightly less than 30 cc. The orbital entrance averages about 35 mm in height and 45 mm in width. The maximum width occurs about 1 cm behind the anterior orbital margin. In adults, the depth of the orbit varies from 40 to 45 mm from the orbital entrance to the orbital apex. Both race and sex affect each of these measurements.

Bony Orbit

Seven bones make up the bony orbit (Fig I-3):

- Frontal
- Zygomatic
- Maxillary
- Ethmoidal
- Sphenoid
- Lacrimal
- Palatine

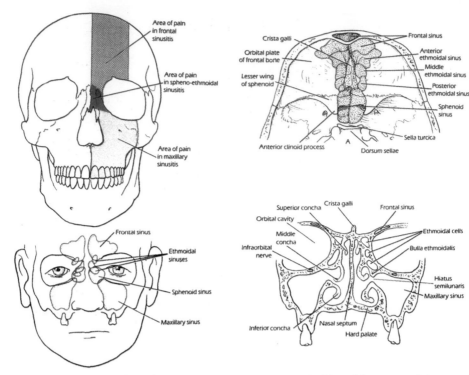

FIG I-1—*Top,* Bones of the face, showing regions where pain is experienced in sinusitis. *Bottom,* Positions of paranasal sinuses relative to the face. (Reproduced with permission from Snell RS, Lemp MA. *Clinical Anatomy of the Eye.* Boston: Blackwell Scientific Publications; 1989.)

FIG I-2—*Top,* Position of the paranasal sinuses relative to the anterior cranial fossa, in axial view. *Bottom,* Coronal section through the nasal cavity, showing the ethmoidal and maxillary sinuses. (Reproduced with permission from Snell RS, Lemp MA. *Clinical Anatomy of the Eye.* Boston: Blackwell Scientific Publications; 1989.)

Orbital Margin

The orbital margin forms a quadrilateral spiral (Fig I-4). The superior margin is formed by the frontal bone, which is interrupted medially by the supraorbital notch. The medial margin is formed above by the frontal bone and below by the posterior lacrimal crest of the lacrimal bone and the anterior lacrimal crest of the maxillary bone. The inferior margin derives from the maxillary and zygomatic bones. Laterally, the zygomatic and frontal bones complete the spiral-shaped rim.

Orbital Roof

The orbital roof is formed from both the orbital plate of the frontal bone and the lesser wing of the sphenoid bone (Fig I-5). The fossa for the lacrimal gland, lying antero-laterally behind the zygomatic process of the frontal bone, resides within the orbital roof. Medially, the fovea trochlearis, located on the frontal bone approximately

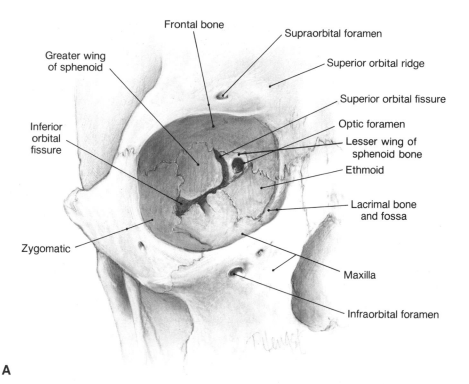

A

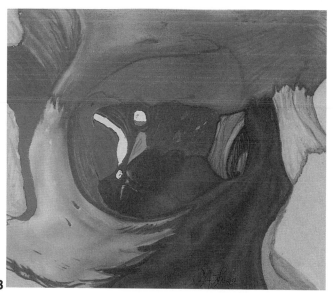

B

FIG I-3—*A*, Frontal view of bony right orbit. (Reproduced by permission from Doxanas MT, Anderson RL. *Clinical Orbital Anatomy.* Baltimore: Williams & Wilkins; 1984.) B, Bony components of the right orbit: maxilla (*orange*); zygoma (*beige*); greater wing of sphenoid bone (*light blue*); lesser wing of sphenoid bone (*dark blue*); palatine bone (*light green*); ethmoid bone (*purple*); lacrimal bone (*pink*); frontal bone (*green*). (Reproduced by permission from Zide BM, Jelks GW. *Surgical Anatomy of the Orbit.* New York: Raven Press; 1985.)

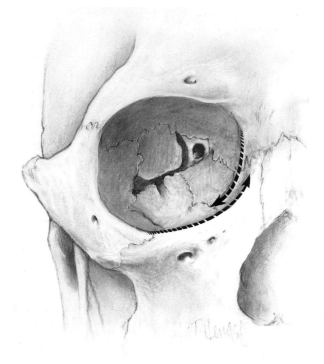

FIG I-4—Right orbital margin. Note the relationship between the anterior lacrimal crest of the maxillary bone and posterior lacrimal crest of the lacrimal bone. (Reproduced by permission from Doxanas MT, Anderson RL. *Clinical Orbital Anatomy.* Baltimore: Williams & Wilkins; 1984.)

4 mm from the orbital margin, forms the pulley of the superior oblique muscle where the trochlea, a curved plate of hyaline cartilage, is attached.

> Helveston EM, Merriam WW, Ellis FD, et al. The trochlea. A study of the anatomy and physiology. *Ophthalmology.* 1982;89:124–133.

Medial Orbital Wall

The medial wall of the orbit is formed from four bones: the frontal process of the maxillary, the lacrimal, the orbital plate of the ethmoidal, and the lesser wing of the sphenoid (Fig I-6). The ethmoidal bone makes up the largest portion of the medial wall. The lacrimal fossa is formed by the frontal process of the maxillary and the lacrimal bone. Below, it is continuous with the bony nasolacrimal canal, which extends into the inferior meatus of the nose. The paper-thin structure of the medial wall is reflected in its name, *lamina papyracea.*

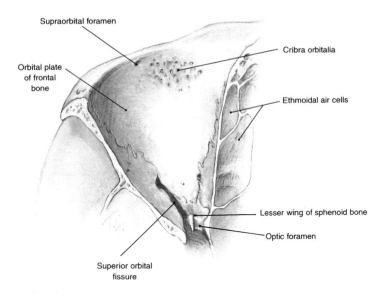

FIG I-5—View from below looking up into orbital roof (superior orbital wall). (Reproduced by permission from Doxanas MT, Anderson RL. *Clinical Orbital Anatomy.* Baltimore: Williams & Wilkins; 1984.)

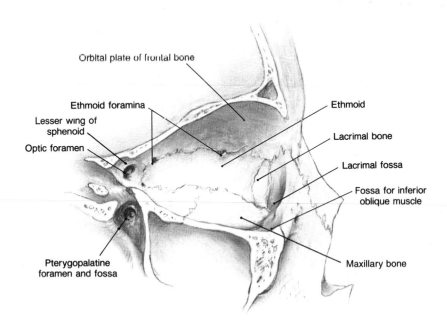

FIG I-6—Right medial orbital wall as viewed from lateral side. (Reproduced by permission from Doxanas MT, Anderson RL. *Clinical Orbital Anatomy.* Baltimore: Williams & Wilkins; 1984.)

Orbital Floor

The floor of the orbit, which is the roof of the maxillary antrum, or sinus, is composed of three bones: the maxillary, the palatine, and the orbital plate of the zygomatic (Fig I-7). The infraorbital groove traverses the floor and descends anteriorly into a canal. It exits as the infraorbital foramen below the orbital margin of the maxillary bone. Arising from the floor of the orbit just lateral to the opening of the nasolacrimal canal is the inferior oblique muscle, the only extraocular muscle that does not originate from the orbital apex. The floor of the orbit slopes downward approximately 20° from posterior to anterior.

Blunt trauma to the soft tissues of the orbit may cause a dehiscence of the fragile bony floor. Clinical features of this *blowout fracture* may include diplopia, enophthalmos, hypoesthesia in the distribution of the infraorbital nerve, entrapment of orbital tissues, a positive forced duction test, and radiographic evidence of a fluid level or cloudiness of the maxillary sinus.

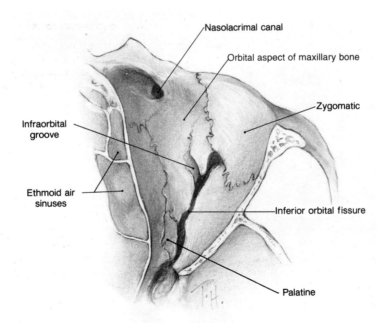

FIG I-7—Right orbital floor and inferior orbital fissure. (Reproduced by permission from Doxanas MT, Anderson RL. *Clinical Orbital Anatomy.* Baltimore: Williams & Wilkins; 1984.)

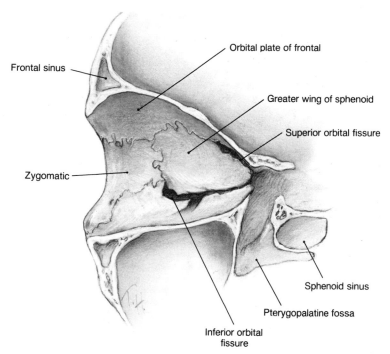

Frontal sinus

Orbital plate of frontal

Greater wing of sphenoid

Superior orbital fissure

Zygomatic

Sphenoid sinus

Pterygopalatine fossa

Inferior orbital
fissure

FIG I-8—Right lateral orbital wall as viewed from medial side. (Reproduced by permission from Doxanas MT, Anderson RL. *Clinical Orbital Anatomy.* Baltimore: Williams & Wilkins; 1984.)

Lateral Orbital Wall

The lateral wall of the orbit is the thickest and strongest of the orbital walls, and it is formed from two bones: the zygomatic and the greater wing of the sphenoid (Fig I-8). The lateral orbital tubercle (Whitnall's tubercle), a small elevation of the orbital margin of the zygomatic bone, lies approximately 11 mm below the frontozygomatic suture. This important landmark is the site of attachment for the following:

- Check ligament of the lateral rectus muscle
- Suspensory ligament of the eyeball
- Lateral palpebral ligament
- Aponeurosis of the levator muscle

Orbital Foramina, Ducts, Canals, and Fissures

Foramina   The *optic foramen* leads from the middle cranial fossa to the apex of the orbit. It is directed forward, laterally, and somewhat downward and conducts the optic nerve, the ophthalmic artery, and sympathetic fibers from the carotid plexus (Figs I-9, I-10). The optic foramen passes through the lesser wing of the sphenoid bone. The *supraorbital foramen,* or notch, is located at the medial third of the superior margin of the orbit. It transmits blood vessels and the supraorbital nerve, a branch of the ophthalmic division (V_1) of cranial nerve V (trigeminal). The *anterior ethmoidal foramen* is located at the frontoethmoidal suture and transmits the anterior ethmoidal vessels and nerve. The *posterior ethmoidal foramen* lies at the junction of the roof and the medial wall of the orbit and transmits the posterior ethmoidal vessels and nerve through the frontal bone. The *zygomatic foramen* lies in the lateral aspect of the zygomatic bone and contains zygomaticofacial and zygomaticotemporal branches of the zygomatic nerve and the zygomatic artery.

Nasolacrimal duct   The nasolacrimal duct travels inferiorly from the lacrimal fossa into the inferior meatus of the nose.

Infraorbital canal   The infraorbital canal continues anteriorly from the infraorbital groove and exits 4 mm below the inferior orbital margin, where it transmits the infraorbital nerve, a branch of V_2, the maxillary division of cranial nerve V.

Fissures   The *superior orbital fissure* is located between the greater and the lesser wings of the sphenoid bone and lies below and lateral to the optic foramen. It is approximately 22 mm long and consists of two parts: The *superior part* transmits the lacrimal and frontal branches of cranial nerve V_1, and cranial nerve IV (trochlear). The *inferior part* is divided from the superior part by the origin of the lateral rectus muscle. The superior and inferior divisions of cranial nerve III (oculomotor), the nasociliary branch of cranial nerve V_1, cranial nerve VI (abducens), the superior ophthalmic vein, and the sympathetic nerve plexus pass through the inferior portion of the superior orbital fissure.

The *inferior orbital fissure* lies just below the superior orbital fissure between the lateral wall and the floor of the orbit. It transmits the maxillary and pterygoid parts of cranial nerve V and a nerve arising from the pterygopalatine ganglion. The inferior ophthalmic vein passes through its lower portion before entering the cavernous sinus.

Cranial Nerves

Six of the twelve cranial nerves of the body (CN II–VII) directly innervate the eye and periocular tissues. Because certain tumors affecting cranial nerve I (olfactory) can give rise to important ophthalmic signs and symptoms, familiarity with the anatomy of this nerve is also important for the ophthalmologist. (Chapter IV discusses the central and peripheral connections of cranial nerves I–VII.)

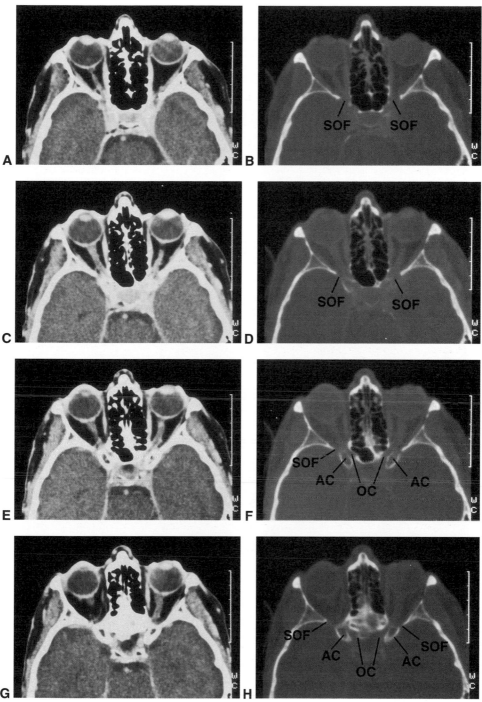

FIG I-9—Series of axial CT scans. Each compares tissue and corresponding bone window density through the optic canal (*OC*) and superior orbital fissure (*SOF*). The superior orbital fissure passes above and below the plane of the optic canal and is commonly mistaken for the optic canal. The optic canal lies in the same plane as the anterior clinoid processes (*AC*) and may be cut obliquely in scans so that the entire canal length does not always appear in one section. Four different planes of section are shown in this series: *A–B,* Plane one is below the canal; *C–D,* Plane two is just under the canal; *E–F,* Plane three is at the canal; *G–H,* Plane four is just at the top of and above the canal.

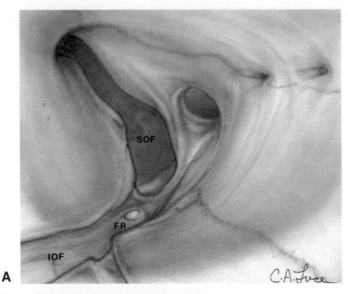

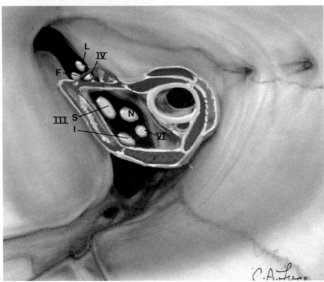

FIG I-10—*A*, The superior orbital fissure (*SOF*) widens medially where it lies below the level of the optic foramen. Its total length is 22 mm. Note the foramen rotundum (*FR*) just inferior to the confluence between the SOF and inferior orbital fissure (*IOF*). *B*, The common tendinous ring, or annulus of Zinn, divides the SOF. The extraocular muscles arise from this common ring. The portion of the annulus that is formed by the origin of the lateral rectus muscle (*blue*) divides the SOF into two compartments. The area encircled by the annulus is termed the oculomotor foramen, which opens into the middle cranial fossa and transmits cranial nerve III (*III*), superior (*S*) and inferior (*I*) divisions; cranial nerve VI (*VI*); the nasociliary (*N*) branch of cranial nerve V_1; ophthalmic veins; the orbital branch of the middle meningeal artery (occasionally); and sympathetic nerve fibers. Above the annulus, note cranial nerve IV (*IV*) and the frontal (*F*) and lacrimal (*L*) branches of cranial nerve V_1. It is important to realize that the frontal and lacrimal branches of the ophthalmic division of cranial nerve V and cranial nerve IV enter the orbit outside the muscle cone. (*A* and *B* reproduced by permission from Zide BM, Jelks GW. *Surgical Anatomy of the Orbit.* New York: Raven Press; 1985.)

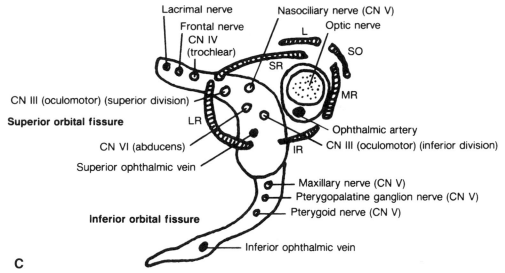

C

FIG I-10 (cont.)—*C,* Orbital apex, superior and inferior orbital fissure. (*MR*) Medial rectus; (*IR*) inferior rectus; (*LR*) lateral rectus; (*SR*) superior rectus; (*L*) levator; and (*SO*) superior oblique. Note that cranial nerve IV and peripheral divisions of cranial nerve V lie outside the muscle cone. (Illustration by Thomas A. Weingeist, PhD, MD.)

Ciliary Ganglion

The ciliary ganglion is located approximately 1 cm in front of the annulus of Zinn, the site of origin of the extraocular muscles, on the lateral side of the ophthalmic artery between the optic nerve and the lateral rectus muscle (Figs I-11, I-12). It receives three roots:

□ A long *sensory root* arises from the nasociliary branch of cranial nerve V_1. It is 10–12 mm long and contains sensory fibers from the cornea, the iris, and the ciliary body.

□ A short *motor root* arises from the inferior division of cranial nerve III, which also supplies the inferior oblique muscle. The fibers of the motor root synapse in the ganglion and carry parasympathetic axons to supply the iris sphincter.

□ The *sympathetic root* comes from the plexus around the internal carotid artery. After it passes through the inferior portion of the superior orbital fissure, it enters the orbit, passes through the ciliary ganglion, and innervates blood vessels of the eye and possibly the dilator fibers to the iris.

Branches of the Ciliary Ganglion

Only the parasympathetic fibers are thought to synapse in the ciliary ganglion. Sympathetic fibers from cell bodies in the superior cervical ganglion and sensory fibers from cell bodies in the trigeminal ganglion carry sensation from the eye, the

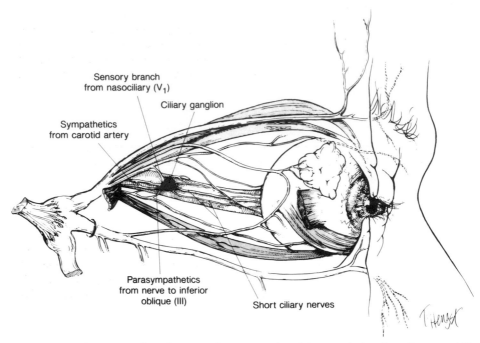

FIG I-11—Contributions to the ciliary ganglion. (Reproduced by permission from Doxanas MT, Anderson RL. *Clinical Orbital Anatomy.* Baltimore: Williams & Wilkins; 1984.)

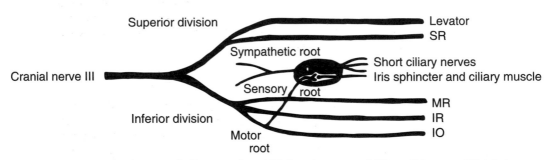

FIG I-12—Cranial nerve III and ciliary ganglion. (*SR*) Superior rectus; (*MR*) medial rectus; (*IR*) inferior rectus; (*IO*) inferior oblique. (Illustration by Thomas A. Weingeist, PhD, MD.)

orbit, and the face. All pass directly through the ciliary ganglion without synapsing. Together, the nonsynapsing sympathetic and sensory fibers and the postganglionic parasympathetic fibers form the short ciliary nerves.

Short Ciliary Nerves

Two groups totaling 6–10 short ciliary nerves arise from the ciliary ganglion. They travel on both sides of the optic nerve and together with the long ciliary nerves pierce the sclera around the optic nerve. They pass anteriorly between the choroid and the sclera into the ciliary muscle, where they form a plexus that supplies the cornea, the ciliary body, and the iris.

Extraocular Muscles

Knowing the anatomic location, origin, and insertion of the extraocular muscles is important to understanding the action of these muscles on the globe. These features are shown in Figures I-13 to I-16.

Extraocular Muscle Insertions

The four rectus muscles insert on the anterior portion of the globe in a configuration called the *spiral of Tillaux* (Fig I-17). The medial rectus muscle inserts nearest to the limbus, and the superior rectus muscle inserts farthest from the limbus (Table I-1). The relationship between the muscle insertions and the ora serrata is clinically important. A misdirected bridle suture passed through the insertion of the superior rectus muscle could perforate the retina.

Extraocular Muscle Distribution in the Orbit

Figures I-15 and I-16 show the arrangement of the extraocular muscles within the orbit. Note the relationship between the oblique intraocular muscles and the superior, medial, and inferior rectus muscles.

   The location of the extraocular muscles within the orbit and their relationship to surrounding nerves and bone is illustrated in coronal, cross-sectional view (Figs I 18, I 19) and correlated with a coronal MRI of the orbit (Fig I-20). Longitudinal, axial views are shown in Figures I-21 and I-22.

Extraocular Muscle Origins

The annulus of Zinn consists of a superior arching ligament and an inferior arching ligament. The superior portion has also been called the *superior orbital tendon* or the *upper tendon of Lockwood*; the inferior portion is called the *inferior orbital tendon* or the *lower tendon of Zinn*. The lateral and medial rectus muscles originate from the upper tendon while the inferior rectus arises from the lower tendon.

   The superior oblique muscle originates from the periosteum of the body of the sphenoid bone, above and medial to the optic foramen. Only the inferior oblique muscle does not originate from the orbital apex; it arises from a shallow depression in the orbital plate of the maxillary bone at the anteromedial corner of the orbital floor near the lacrimal fossa. The inferior oblique muscle passes from its origin posteriorly, laterally, and superiorly before inserting in the globe.

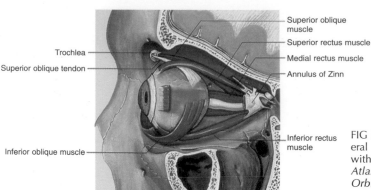

Superior oblique muscle

Trochlea

Superior oblique tendon

Superior rectus muscle

Medial rectus muscle

Annulus of Zinn

Inferior oblique muscle

Inferior rectus muscle

FIG I-13—Extraocular muscles, lateral composite view. (Reproduced with permission from Dutton JJ. *Atlas of Clinical and Surgical Orbital Anatomy.* Philadelphia: Saunders; 1994.)

Superior oblique tendon

Trochlea

Medial rectus tendon

Levator palpebrae superioris muscle

Superior rectus tendon

Lateral rectus tendon

Inferior rectus tendon

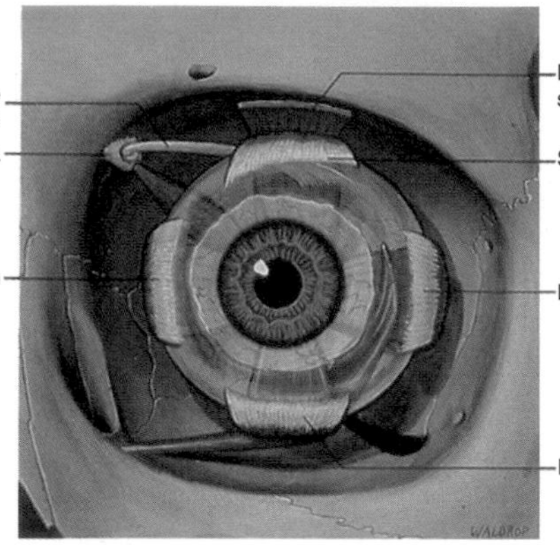

FIG I-14—Extraocular muscles, frontal composite view. (Reproduced with permission from Dutton JJ. *Atlas of Clinical and Surgical Orbital Anatomy.* Philadelphia: Saunders; 1994.)

Superior oblique muscle

Lateral rectus muscle

Annulus of Zinn

Levator palpebrae superioris muscle

Superior rectus muscle

Superior orbital fissure

Lateral rectus muscle

Inferior oblique muscle

Inferior rectus muscle

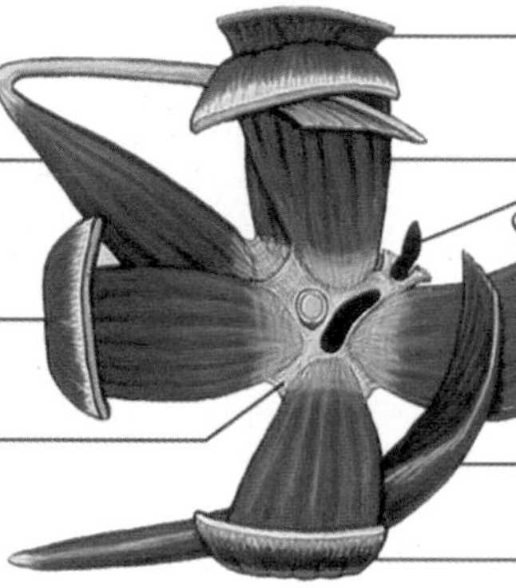

FIG I-15—Extraocular muscles, frontal view. (Reproduced with permission from Dutton JJ. *Atlas of Clinical and Surgical Orbital Anatomy.* Philadelphia: Saunders; 1994.)

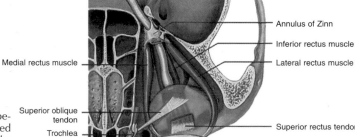

Medial rectus muscle

Superior oblique tendon

Trochlea

Annulus of Zinn

Inferior rectus muscle

Lateral rectus muscle

Superior rectus tendon

FIG I-16—Extraocular muscles, superior composite view. (Reproduced with permission from Dutton JJ. *Atlas of Clinical and Surgical Orbital Anatomy.* Philadelphia: Saunders; 1994.)

TABLE I-1

COMPARISON OF EXTRAOCULAR MUSCLES

MUSCLE	ORIGIN	INSERTION	BLOOD SUPPLY	SIZE
Medial Rectus	Annulus of Zinn	Medially, in horizontal meridian 5.5 mm from limbus	Inferior muscular branch of ophthalmic artery	40.8 mm long; tendon:3.7 mm long, 10.3 mm wide
Inferior	Annulus of Zinn at orbital apex	Inferiorly, in vertical meridian 6.5 mm from limbus	Inferior muscular branch of ophthalmic artery and infraorbital artery	40 mm long; tendon: 5.5 mm long, 9.8 mm wide
Lateral Rectus	Annulus of Zinn spanning the superior orbital fissure	Laterally, in horizontal meridian 6.9 mm from limbus	Lacrimal artery	40.6 mm long; tendon: 8 mm long, 9.2 mm wide
Superior Rectus	Annulus of Zinn at orbital apex	Superiorly, in vertical meridian 7.7 mm from limbus	Superior muscular branch of ophthalmic artery	41.8 mm long; tendon: 5.8 mm long, 10.6 mm wide
Superior Oblique	Medial to optic foramen, between annulus of Zinn and periorbita	To trochlea at orbital rim, then inferior and under superior rectus posterior to center of rotation	Superior muscular branch of ophthalmic artery	40 mm long; tendon: 20 mm long, 10.8 mm wide
Inferior Oblique	From a depression on orbital floor near orbital rim (maxilla)	Posterior inferior temporal quadrant at level of macula	Inferior branch of ophthalmic artery and infraorbital artery	37 mm long; no tendon: 9.6 mm wide at insertion

Blood Supply to the Extraocular Muscles

The inferior and superior muscular branches of the ophthalmic artery, lacrimal artery, and infraorbital artery supply the blood for the extraocular muscles. Except for the lateral rectus muscle, each rectus muscle receives two anterior ciliary arteries that communicate with the major arteriole circle of the ciliary body. The lateral rectus muscle is supplied by a single vessel derived from the lacrimal artery. The vascular supply and drainage of orbital structures is discussed on pp 41–45.

Hayreh SS, Scott WE. Fluorescein iris angiography. I. Normal pattern. II. Disturbances in iris circulation following strabismus operation on the various recti. *Arch Ophthalmol.* 1978;96:1383–1400.

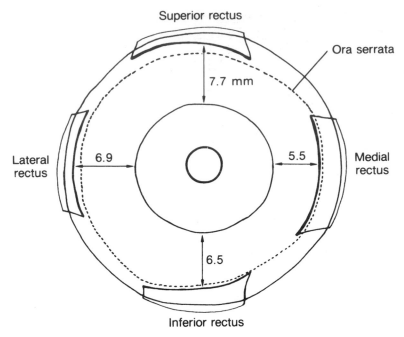

FIG I-17—Anterior view of right globe. Spiral of Tillaux is a curve connecting the anterior margins of insertions of rectus muscles; ora serrata is represented by the dotted line. (Illustration by Thomas A. Weingeist, PhD, MD.)

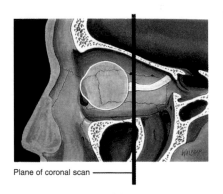

FIG I-18—Location of the plane of section shown in Figure I-19. (Reproduced with permission from Dutton JJ. *Atlas of Clinical and Surgical Orbital Anatomy.* Philadelphia: Saunders; 1994.)

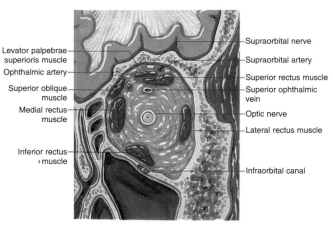

FIG I-19—Coronal section through the central orbit just posterior to the globe. (Reproduced with permission from Dutton JJ. *Atlas of Clinical and Surgical Orbital Anatomy.* Philadelphia: Saunders; 1994.)

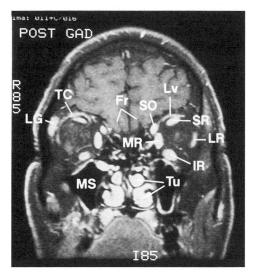

FIG I-20—Coronal MRI with fat suppression and gadolinium enhancement through midorbit in a patient with Graves disease. All of the muscles are enlarged and show normal enhancement. (*SR*) superior rectus; (*Lv*) levator; (*SO*) superior oblique; (*MR*) medial rectus; (*IR*) inferior rectus; (*LR*) lateral rectus; (*TC*) Tenon's capsule; (*LG*) lacrimal gland; (*Tu*) turbinates; (*MS*) maxillary sinus; (*Fr*) frontal lobe of brain. This is the same plane of section shown in Figures I-18 and I-19.

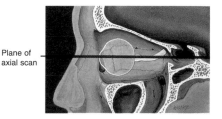

FIG I-21—Location of the plane of section shown below in Figure I-22. (Reproduced with permission from Dutton JJ. *Atlas of Clinical and Surgical Orbital Anatomy.* Philadelphia: Saunders; 1994.)

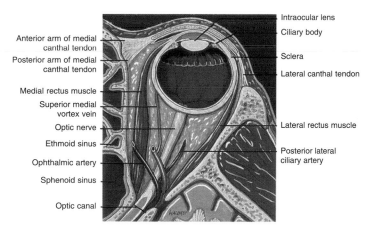

FIG I-22—Axial section through the midorbit at the level of the optic nerve. The third portion of the ophthalmic artery is seen crossing the nerve in the posterior orbit. (Reproduced with permission from Dutton JJ. *Atlas of Clinical and Surgical Orbital Anatomy.* Philadelphia: Saunders; 1994.)

TABLE I-2

EXTRAOCULAR MUSCLES

	FIBRILLENSTRUKTUR	FELDERSTRUKTUR
	"fibril" (fast, twitch)	"field" (slow, tonic)
myofibrils	well defined	poorly defined
sarcoplasm	abundant	sparse
sarcomere	well developed	poorly developed
T-system	regular	absent, or aberrant
Z-line	straight	zigzag course
M-line	well marked	absent
nuclei	located peripherally	located centrally or eccentrically
innervation	thick; heavily myelinated	thin
neuromuscular junction	en plaque (single)	en grappe (grapelike)
synaptic vesicles	agranular	granular/agranular
acetylcholine	poor response	good response

Structure of the Extraocular Muscles

The extraocular muscles are striated muscle cells (*myofibers*) built of repeating groups of myofibrils called *sarcomeres*. Unlike most other skeletal muscles, the extraocular muscles contain two types of muscle cells: Fibrillenstruktur and Felderstruktur (Table I-2). Each motor neuron supplies relatively few muscle fibers.

Fibrillenstruktur muscle fibrils are thought to produce fast, or twitch, movements. Their individual neuromuscular junctions have many postjunctional folds that respond poorly to acetylcholine. *Felderstruktur* muscle fibers are thought to be responsible for slow, or tonic, movements. Their multiple grapelike neuromuscular junctions with poorly developed postjunctional folds exhibit a brisk response to acetylcholine. Additional subtypes of these muscle fibers have been defined by histochemical methods, but little is yet known about the functional significance of these findings.

Eyelids

The interpalpebral fissure is the exposed zone between the upper and lower eyelids. Normally, the adult fissure is 27–30 mm long and 8–11 mm wide. The upper eyelid, more mobile than the lower, can be raised 15 mm by the action of the levator muscle alone. If the frontalis muscle of the brow is used, the interpalpebral fissure can be widened an additional 2 mm. The levator muscle is innervated by cranial nerve III, and the orbicularis oculi muscle is its antagonist. Clinically important changes in the eyelid fissure occur in thyroid disease, myasthenia gravis, congenital ptosis, levator disinsertion, Horner syndrome, facial palsy, and third nerve palsy (Fig I-23).

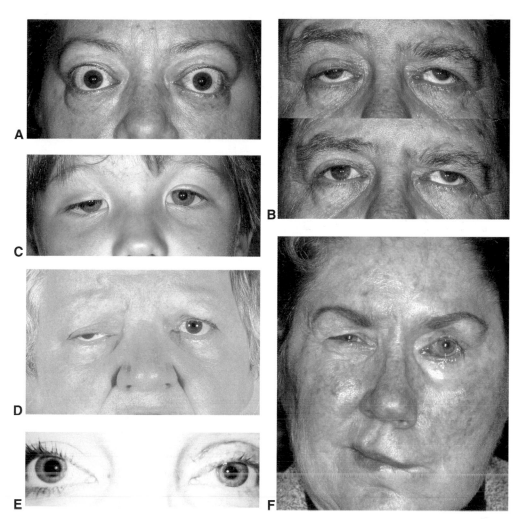

FIG I-23—Changes in the eyelid fissure. *A,* Graves disease; *B,* myasthenia gravis (top: right eye ptosis before Tensilon; bottom: ptosis gone after Tensilon); *C,* congenital ptosis of right eye; *D,* levator disinsertion; *E,* Horner syndrome or oculosympathetic denervation of left eye; *F,* left seventh (facial) nerve palsy. (Photographs courtesy of Jeffrey Nerad, MD.)

Anatomy

The upper eyelid can be divided into eight anatomical segments from the dermal surface inward (Figs I-24 to I-27):

Skin   The skin of the eyelids is the thinnest in the body. It contains the usual adnexal structures: fine hairs, sebaceous glands, and sweat glands. An eyelid fold is usually present near the upper border of the tarsus, where the levator aponeurosis establishes its first insertional attachments, except in individuals of Asian descent. The aponeurosis of the levator forms its firmest attachments on the anterior aspect of the tarsus about 3 mm superior to the eyelid margin.

Margin   This margin contains several important landmarks. A small opening, or *punctum*, from the canaliculus exits at the summit of each lacrimal papilla. The upper punctum, normally hidden by slight internal rotation, is located more medially. The lower punctum is usually apposed to the globe and not normally evident unless the eyelid is everted.

Along the entire length of the free margin of the eyelid is a delicate pigmented line, the so-called gray line, or intermarginal sulcus. The eyelashes, or cilia, arise anterior to this line. Posterior to the line are the openings of the tarsal, or *meibomian, glands*. The mucocutaneous border occurs at the level of the orifices of the meibomian glands. The gray line corresponds histologically to the most superficial portion of the orbicularis muscle, the muscle of Riolan.

Wulc AE, Dryden RM, Khatchaturian T. Where is the gray line? *Arch Ophthalmol.* 1987;105:1092–1098.

The eyelashes are arranged in two or three irregular rows along the anterior dermal edge of the eyelid margin. They are usually longer and more numerous on the upper than the lower eyelid. The margins contain the glands of Zeis, holocrine glands (modified sebaceous glands) associated with the cilia, and the glands of Moll, which are apocrine glands of skin (Table I-3). There are some 30–40 meibomian gland orifices in a single row in the upper eyelid but only 20–30 similar openings in the lower.

Subcutaneous connective tissue   The loose connective tissue of the eyelid contains no fat. Fluid from edema or hemorrhage can accumulate beneath the skin and result in rapid and dramatic swelling of the eyelids.

Orbicularis oculi muscle   The orbicularis muscle, which is arranged in several concentric bands around the interpalpebral fissure, can be subdivided into orbital and palpebral parts.

The *orbital part* inserts in a complex way into the medial canthal tendon and into other portions of the orbital rim and the corrugator supercilii muscle. The orbital portion acts like a sphincter and functions solely as a voluntary muscle.

The *palpebral portion* of the orbicularis functions both voluntarily and involuntarily for normal and reflex blinking. The preseptal and pretarsal portions unite along the superior palpebral furrow. The pretarsal muscle is firmly adherent to the tarsus.

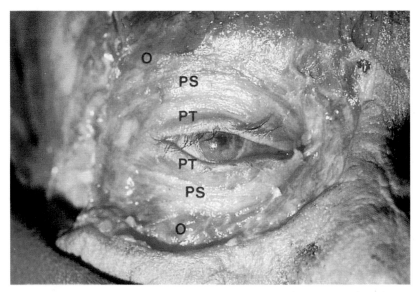

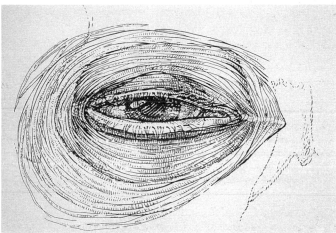

FIG I-24—The periorbital skin has been removed in the top photograph, exposing orbicularis oculi muscle that is innervated by cranial nerve VII. This muscle acts as an antagonist to the levator palpebrae superioris muscle innervated by cranial nerve III. The orbicularis muscle is divided into the palpebral and orbital (*O*) portions. The palpebral portion is further subdivided into pretarsal (*PT*) and preseptal (*PS*) portions. The bottom diagram depicts the arrangement of muscle fibers of the orbicularis muscle. (Reproduced by permission from Zide BM, Jelks GW. *Surgical Anatomy of the Orbit.* New York: Raven Press; 1985.)

Orbicularis fibers extend to the eyelid margin, where there is a small bundle of striated muscle fibers called the *muscle of Riolan*. Disinsertion of the lower eyelid retractors from the tarsus may result in laxity of the lower eylid, followed by spastic entropion.

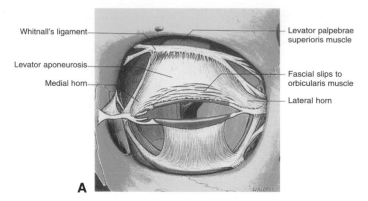

Whitnall's ligament

Levator aponeurosis

Medial horn

Levator palpebrae
superioris muscle

Fascial slips to
orbicularis muscle

Lateral horn

A

FIG I-25—*A,* The upper and lower tarsal plates and their attachments to the levator aponeurosis and to Whitnall's ligament. (Reproduced by permission from Dutton JJ. *Atlas of Clinical and Surgical Orbital Anatomy.* Philadelphia: Saunders; 1994.) B, The three-dimensional organization of the upper eyelid. For convenience, the upper eyelid may be divided into anterior and posterior lamellae. The anterior lamella consists of the skin and orbicularis muscle and its associated fascial and vascular structures. Note the marginal artery (*lower arrow*) approximately 3.0–3.5 mm above the eyelid margin. The posterior lamella consists of the levator aponeurosis (*L*), tarsus (*blue*), Müller's muscle (*M*), and conjunctival lining (*C*). At a variable height above the superior edge of the tarsus, the orbital septum (*OS*) forms the anterior border of the preaponeurotic fat space. The peripheral arterial arcade is situated (*upper arrow*) at the level of the superior edge of the tarsus posterior to the levator aponeurosis within the so-called pretarsal space. The levator muscle usually becomes aponeurotic at the equator of the globe in the superior orbit. The aponeurosis courses anteriorly to insert onto the lower two thirds of the anterior tarsal plate. The levator muscle provides origin to Müller's muscle (*M*), the nonstriated, sympathetically innervated elevator of the upper eyelid, which inserts into the

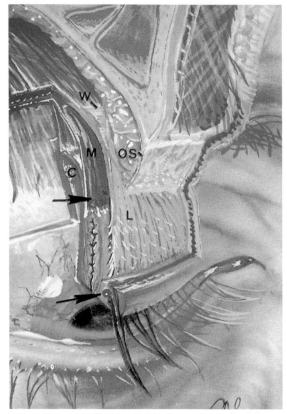

B

superior edge of the tarsus. The superior transverse ligament of Whitnall (*W*) is noted as a fascial condensation along the upper aspect of the levator muscle. This ligament attaches to the trochlear fascia medially and the fascia of the orbital lobe of the lacrimal gland laterally. (Reproduced by permission from Zide BM, Jelks GW. *Surgical Anatomy of the Orbit.* New York: Raven Press; 1985.)

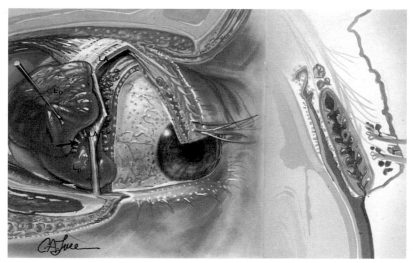

FIG I-26—The lacrimal secretory system is divided into basic and reflex secretors. The *basic secretors* are divided into three groups: (1) conjunctival, tarsal, and limbal mucin-secreting goblet cells (*green*), which produce a mucoprotein layer covering the epithelial surface of the cornea; (2) accessory lacrimal exocrine glands of Krause and Wolfring, present in the subconjunctival tissues (*blue*); these glands produce the intermediate aqueous layer of the precorneal tear film; (3) oil-producing meibomian glands and palpebral glands of Zeis and Moll (*pink*). The *reflex secretors* consist of the orbital lobe of the lacrimal gland (*Lo*) and the palpebral lobe of the lacrimal gland (*Lp*), which are separated by the lateral horn of the levator palpebrae superioris (*LA*). The tear ducts (*arrow*) from the orbital portion traverse the palpebral portion. (Reproduced by permission from Zide BM, Jelks GW. *Surgical Anatomy of the Orbit.* New York: Raven Press; 1985.)

TABLE I-3

GLANDS OF THE EYE AND ADNEXA

GLANDS	LOCATION	SECRETION	CONTENT
Lacrimal	orbital gland	eccrine	aqueous
	palpebral gland	eccrine	aqueous
Accesory lacrimal	plica, caruncle	eccrine	aqueous
Krause	eyelid	eccrine	aqueous
Wolfring	eyelid	eccrine	aqueous
Meibomian	tarsus	holocrine	oily
Zeis	follicles of cilia	holocrine	oily
	eyelid, caruncle	holocrine	oily
Moll	eyelid	apocrine	. . .
Goblet cell	conjunctiva	holocrine	mucous
	plica, caruncle	holocrine	mucous

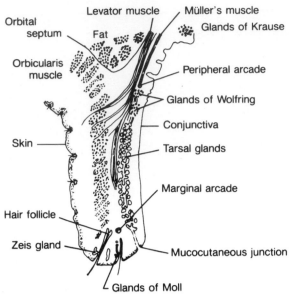

Levator muscle Müller's muscle

Orbital septum Fat Glands of Krause

Orbicularis muscle Peripheral arcade

Glands of Wolfring

Conjunctiva

Skin Tarsal glands

Marginal arcade

Hair follicle

Zeis gland

Mucocutaneous junction

Glands of Moll

FIG I-27—Cross section of upper eyelid. Note position of cilia, tarsal gland orifices, and mucocutaneous border. (Illustration by Thomas A. Weingeist, PhD, MD.)

Orbital septum   A thin sheet of connective tissue called the orbital septum encircles the orbit as an extension of the periosteum of the roof and the floor of the orbit (Fig I-28). It also attaches to the anterior surface of the levator muscle. Posterior to the orbital septum is orbital fat. In both the upper and lower eyelids, the orbital septum attaches to the aponeurosis. The orbital septum thus provides a barrier to anterior or posterior extravasation of blood or the spread of inflammation. The intramuscular orbital septa can be identified in coronal MRI studies with fat suppression and gadolinium enhancement.

    Superiorly, the septum is attached firmly to the periosteum of the superior half of the orbital margin. It passes medially in front of the trochlea and continues along the medial margin of the orbit, along the margin of the frontal process of the maxillary bone, and on to the inferior margin of the orbit. Here it also delimits the lateral spread of edema, inflammation, or blood trapped anterior to it and is seen clinically as a dramatic barrier to these processes.

Levator muscle   The levator palpebrae superioris muscle originates from a short tendon that blends with the superior rectus and the superior oblique muscles at the apex of the orbit. The body of the levator muscle overlies the superior rectus as it travels anteriorly toward the eyelid. Whitnall's ligament results from a condensation of tissue surrounding the superior rectus and levator muscles. Near Whitnall's ligament the levator muscle changes direction from horizontal to more vertical, and it divides anteriorly into the aponeurosis and posteriorly into the superior tarsal (*Müller's*) muscle.

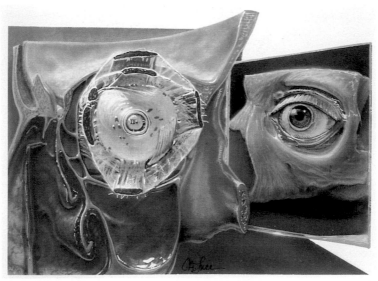

FIG I-28—The orbital septum. More posteriorly, the intervening intramuscular septa are thinner and may become discontinuous, thus opening the muscle cone. Tenon's capsule continues posteriorly adherent to the globe to eventually encircle the optic nerve, which penetrates it. More anteriorly, as the intermuscular septa thicken, the connective mass between the inferior oblique and inferior rectus muscles forms the inferior suspensory ligament of Lockwood (*green*). Similarly, a thickening or condensation of fascia (i.e., Whitnall's ligament) may be noted superiorly overlying or surrounding the levator muscle. (Reproduced by permission from Zide BM, Jelks GW. *Surgical Anatomy of the Orbit.* New York: Raven Press; 1985.)

The *aponeurosis* inserts into the anterior surface of the tarsus and by medial and lateral horns into the canthal tendons. The fibrous elements of the aponeurosis pass through the orbicularis muscle and insert subcutaneously to produce the eyelid crease or fold. The aponeurosis also inserts into the tissue of the trochlea of the superior oblique muscle and into the fibrous tissue bridging the supraorbital notch. Attachments exist with the conjunctiva in the upper fornix and with the orbital septum as well.

The levator muscle and tendon are 50–55 mm long. The muscle, which elevates the upper eyelid, is 40 mm long and is innervated by the superior division of cranial nerve III.

Tarsus The tarsal plates consist of dense connective tissue, not cartilage. They are attached to the orbital margin by the medial and lateral palpebral ligaments (Fig I-29). The length (29 mm) and thickness (1 mm) of the upper and lower tarsal plates are similar. The upper tarsus is more than twice as wide (11 mm) as the lower (4 mm).

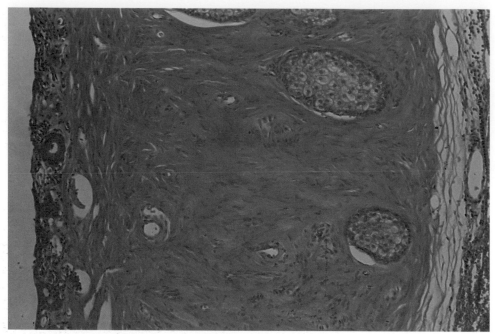

FIG I-29—Palpebral conjunctiva and meibomian glands within the tarsus of the eyelid (H&E ×32). (Photograph courtesy of Thomas A. Weingeist, PhD, MD.)

The meibomian glands (Fig I-30) are modified holocrine sweat glands that are oriented vertically in parallel rows through the tarsus. Their distribution and number within the eyelid can be observed using infrared transilllumination (Fig I-31). Their oily secretion passes through small orifices into the tear film at the mucocutaneous border of the upper and lower eyelids.

The hair bulbs of the cilia are located anterior to the tarsus and the meibomian gland orifices. Misdirection in the orientation of the eyelashes (*trichiasis*) or aberrant growth through the orifices of meibomian glands (*distichiasis*) may occur as either a congenital or an acquired defect and may occasionally be hereditary.

Müller's muscle Müller's muscle originates from the undersurface of the levator muscle in the upper eyelid and from the capsulopalpebral head of the inferior rectus in the lower eyelid. It attaches to the upper border of the upper tarsus and to the lower border of the lower tarsus. This smooth (nonstriated), sympathetically innervated muscle gives rise to important clinical signs in thyroid ophthalmopathy and Horner syndrome.

Conjunctiva The palpebral conjunctiva is a transparent vascularized membrane covered by a nonkeratinized epithelium that lines the inner surface of the eyelids. Continuous with the conjunctival fornices (cul-de-sacs), it merges with the bulbar conjunctiva before terminating at the limbus.

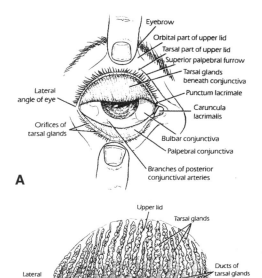

A

Eyebrow
Orbital part of upper lid
Tarsal part of upper lid
Superior palpebral furrow
Tarsal glands beneath conjunctiva
Punctum lacrimale
Caruncula lacrimalis
Bulbar conjunctiva
Palpebral conjunctiva
Branches of posterior conjunctival arteries
Lateral angle of eye
Orifices of tarsal glands

B

Upper lid
Tarsal glands
Ducts of tarsal glands
Lateral angle of eye
Anterior margin of lid
Posterior margin of lid
Lower lid

FIG I-30—*A,* Complete eversion of the upper eyelid of the right eye, made possible by stiffness of the superior tarsal plate; the lower eyelid is pulled downward. Note the orifices of the tarsal (meibomian) glands and the punta lacrimalia; note also the branches of the posterior conjunctival arteries. *B,* Posterior view of the eyelids with the palpebral fissure nearly closed. Note the tarsal glands with their short ducts and orifices. The palpebral conjunctiva has been removed to show the tarsal glands in situ. (Reproduced with permission from Snell RS, Lemp MA. *Clinical Anatomy of the Eye.* Boston: Blackwell Scientific Publications; 1989.)

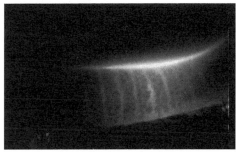

FIG I-31—Distribution of the meibomian glands in the lower eyelid as revealed by infrared transillumination of the eyelid. The glands appear as dark gray linear structures. (Photograph courtesy of William Mathers, MD.)

Vascular Supply of Eyelids

The blood supply to the eyelids is derived from the facial system, which arises from the external carotid artery, and the orbital system, which originates from the internal carotid artery along branches of the ophthalmic artery (Fig I-32). The superficial and deep plexuses of arteries provide a vast blood supply to the upper and lower eyelids. The facial artery becomes the angular artery as it passes upward, forward, and lateral to the nose, where it serves as an important landmark in dacryocystorhinostomy (DCR) surgery.

The marginal arterial arcade is located 3 mm from the free border of the eyelid, just above the ciliary follicles. It is located either between the tarsal plate and the orbicularis or within the tarsus. A smaller peripheral arcade runs along the upper margin of the tarsal plate within Müller's muscle.

The venous drainage of the eyelids can also be divided into two portions: a superficial, or pretarsal, system that drains into the internal and external jugular veins; and a deep, or posttarsal, system that eventually flows into the cavernous sinus.

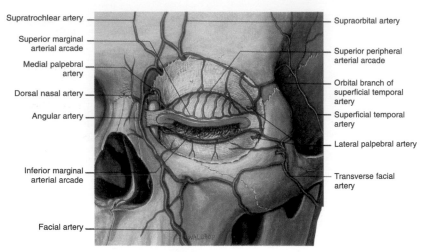

Supratrochlear artery —

Superior marginal arterial arcade —

Medial palpebral artery —

Dorsal nasal artery —

Angular artery —

Inferior marginal arterial arcade —

Facial artery —

— Supraorbital artery

— Superior peripheral arterial arcade

— Orbital branch of superficial temporal artery

— Superficial temporal artery

— Lateral palpebral artery

— Transverse facial artery

FIG I-32—Periorbital and eyelid arteries, frontal view. (Reproduced with permission from Dutton JJ. *Atlas of Clinical and Surgical Orbital Anatomy.* Philadelphia: Saunders; 1994.)

Lymphatics of Eyelids

Aside from the conjunctiva, no lymphatic vessels or nodes are normally found in the orbit. Lymphatic drainage from the eyelids parallels the course of the veins. Two groups of lymphatics exist: a medial group of vessels that drains into the submandibular lymph nodes and a lateral group that drains into the superficial preauricular lymph nodes.

Accessory Eyelid Structures

Plica semilunaris   The plica semilunaris is a narrow, highly vascularized, crescent-shaped fold of the conjunctiva located lateral to and partly under the caruncle. Its lateral border is free and separated from the bulbar conjunctiva, which it resembles histologically. The epithelium of the plica is rich in goblet cells. Its stroma contains fat and some nonstriated muscle. This vestigial structure is analogous to the nictitating membrane, or third eyelid, of dogs and other animals.

Caruncle   The caruncle is a small, fleshy, ovoid structure attached to the inferomedial side of the plica semilunaris. As a piece of modified skin, it contains sebaceous glands and fine, colorless hairs. The surface is covered by nonkeratinized, stratified squamous epithelium.

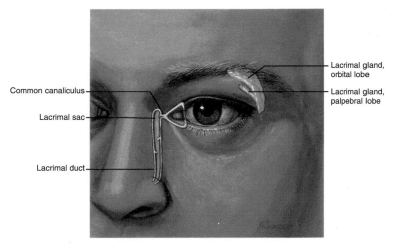

Common canaliculus

Lacrimal sac

Lacrimal duct

Lacrimal gland, orbital lobe

Lacrimal gland, palpebral lobe

FIG I-33—Lacrimal system. (Reproduced with permission from Dutton JJ. *Atlas of Clinical and Surgical Orbital Anatomy.* Philadelphia: Saunders; 1994.)

Lacrimal Gland and Excretory System

Lacrimal Gland

The lacrimal gland is located in a shallow depression within the orbital portion of the frontal bone. The gland is separated from the orbit by fibroadipose tissue and divided in two parts by a lateral expansion of the levator aponeurosis (Fig I-33). The smaller *palpebral gland* can be seen in the superolateral conjunctival fornix when the upper eyelid is everted. An isthmus of glandular tissue occasionally exists between the palpebral lobe and the main *orbital gland.*

A variable number of thin-walled excretory ducts, blood vessels, lymphatics, and nerves pass from the orbital into the palpebral lacrimal gland (Fig I-34). The ducts continue downward and empty into the conjunctival fornix approximately 5 mm above the superior margin of the upper tarsus. Because the lacrimal excretory ducts pass through the palpebral portion of the gland, biopsy of the lacrimal gland is usually performed on the orbital portion to avoid sacrificing the ducts.

The lacrimal glands are exocrine glands, and they produce a serous secretion. The body of each gland contains two cell types: *acinar cells,* which line the lumen of the gland; and *myoepithelial cells,* which surround the parenchyma and are covered by a basement membrane (Fig I-35). The lacrimal artery, a branch of the ophthalmic artery, supplies the gland. The gland's neuroanatomy governs both reflex and psychogenic stimulation and is extremely complex. See BCSC Section 5, *Neuro-Ophthalmology.*

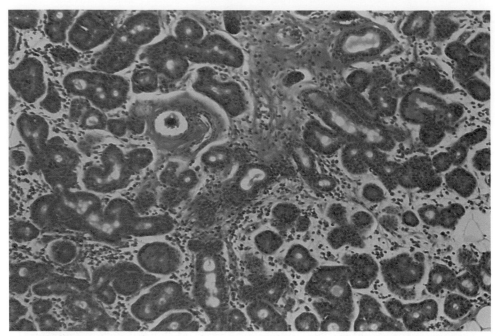

FIG I-34—Orbital lacrimal gland and ducts (H&E ×32). (Photograph courtesy of Thomas A. Weingeist, PhD, MD.)

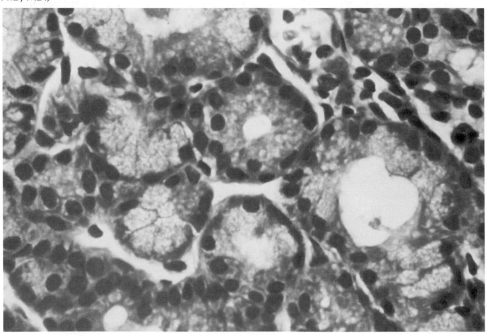

FIG I-35—Higher magnification of lacrimal gland lobules. Note that the acinar cells forming the lobules are surrounded by myoepithelial cells that contain flattened nuclei (H&E ×64). (Photograph courtesy of Thomas A. Weingeist, PhD, MD.)

Accessory Glands

The accessory lacrimal glands located in the eyelids, the glands of Krause and Wolfring, are cytologically identical to the main lacrimal gland but much smaller. They appear to be under sympathetic control and furnish basal tear secretion.

Lacrimal Excretory System

The lacrimal drainage system includes the upper and lower canaliculi, the tear sac, and the nasolacrimal duct (Figs 1-36, 1-37). The lacrimal papillae are located on the posterior edge of the eyelid margins between the openings of the meibomian glands and the eyelashes. Each tiny opening, or lacrimal punctum, is 0.3 mm in diameter. The inferior punctum is 6.5 mm from the medial canthus; the superior punctum is 6.0 mm. These openings lead to the lacrimal canaliculi on to the lacrimal sac and finally through the nasolacrimal duct to the nose. In 90% of subjects both canaliculi join to form a single common canaliculus. In about 30% of full-term neonates the outlet of the nasolacrimal duct is closed and may remain so for up to 6 months. Occasionally, massage or blunt probing may be necessary to allow adequate outlet for tears into the sac and nose. BCSC Section 7, *Orbit, Eyelids, and Lacrimal System*, discusses these issues in detail.

The lacrimal puncta and the canaliculi are lined with stratified squamous epithelium that merges with the epithelium of the eyelid margins. Near the lacrimal sac the epithelium changes to two layers: a superficial columnar layer and a deep, flattened cell layer. Goblet cells and occasional cilia are present. In the canaliculi, the substantia propria consists of collagenous connective tissue and elastic fibers. The wall of the sac resembles adenoid tissue and has a rich venous plexus and many elastic fibers. The angular vein and artery, important surgical landmarks in dacryocystorhinostomy surgery, can be seen 3–4 mm medial to the inner canthus.

Conjunctiva

The conjunctiva can be divided into three geographic zones: palpebral, forniceal, and bulbar (Fig 1-38). The *palpebral* portion begins at the mucocutaneous junction of the eyelid and covers its inner surface. This portion adheres firmly to the tarsus. The tissue becomes redundant and freely movable in the *fornices,* where it becomes enmeshed with fibrous elements of the levator aponeurosis and Müller's muscle in the upper eyelid. In the lower eyelid fibrous expansions of the inferior rectus muscle sheath fuse with the inferior tarsal muscle, the equivalent of Müller's muscle. The conjunctiva is reflected at the cul-de-sac and attaches to the globe. The delicate *bulbar conjunctiva* is freely movable but fuses with Tenon's capsule and inserts into the limbus.

Anterior ciliary arteries supply blood to the conjunctiva. Its innervation is derived from the ophthalmic division of cranial nerve V. The conjunctiva is a mucous membrane consisting of nonkeratinizing squamous epithelium and goblet cells on its surface and a thin, richly vascularized substantia propria, which contains lymphatic vessels, occasional accumulations of lymphocytes, plasma cells, macrophages, and mast cells.

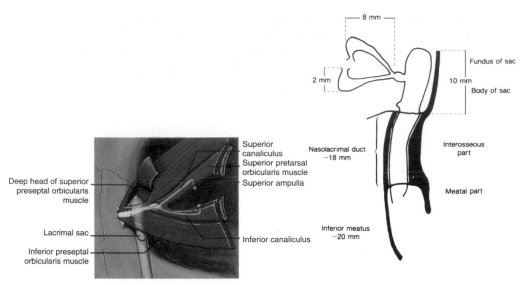

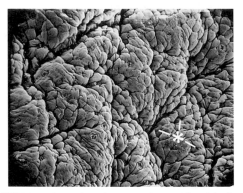

Deep head of superior
preseptal orbicularis
muscle

Lacrimal sac

Inferior preseptal
orbicularis muscle

Superior
canaliculus
Superior pretarsal
orbicularis muscle
Superior ampulla

Inferior canaliculus

8 mm

2 mm

Nasolacrimal duct
~18 mm

Inferior meatus
~20 mm

Fundus of sac

10 mm

Body of sac

Interosseous
part

Meatal part

FIG I-36—Lacrimal drainage system and the orbicularis muscle. (Reproduced with permission from Dutton JJ. *Atlas of Clinical and Surgical Orbital Anatomy.* Philadelphia: Saunders; 1994.)

FIG I-37—Lacrimal excretory system. (Illustration by Thomas A. Weingeist, PhD, MD.)

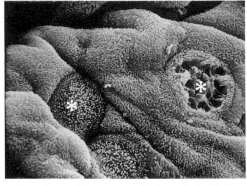

FIG I-38—Scanning electron micrographs of bulbar conjunctiva. *Left,* Low magnification. *Right,* higher magnification showing nonkeratinized epithelium with interspersed goblet cells (*) at different stages of secretion. Before secreting, the goblet cell surface has many microvilli, which are lost as mucin accumulates within the cell in preparation for secretion.

The conjunctival epithelium varies from two to five cells in thickness. The *basal cells* are cuboidal and evolve into flattened polyhedral cells as they reach the surface. The *goblet cells* (unicellular mucous glands) are concentrated in the inferior and medial portion of the conjunctiva, especially in the region of the caruncle and plica semilunaris. They are sparsely distributed throughout the remainder of the conjunctiva and are absent in the limbal region.

Tenon's Capsule

Tenon's capsule is composed entirely of compactly arranged collagen fibers and a few fibroblasts. Anteriorly, it fuses with the conjunctiva slightly posterior to the corneoscleral junction. Posteriorly, it is perforated by the optic nerve sheath and the posterior ciliary vessels and nerves (see Figure I-28). The vortex veins pass through it near the equator of the globe. Tenon's capsule and intermuscular fibrous membranes surrounding the four rectus muscles fuse to form a type of fibrous sling or support.

Koornneef L. *Spatial Aspects of Orbital Musculo-fibrous Tissue in Man.* Amsterdam: Swets & Zeitlinger; 1977.

The suspensory ligament of Lockwood is a fusion of the sheath of the inferior rectus muscle, the inferior tarsal muscle, and check ligaments of the medial and lateral rectus muscles. It supports the globe and attaches to the medial and lateral retinacula. The retinacula are formed from thickened periosteum attached to the zygomatic bone in the lateral canthal region and to the lacrimal bone in the medial canthal area.

Vascular Supply and Drainage of the Orbit (Figs I-39 to I-44)

Anterior and Posterior Ciliary Arteries

Approximately 20 short posterior ciliary arteries and 10 short posterior ciliary nerves enter the globe in a ring around the optic nerve (Figs I-39, I-40, I-41). Usually, two long ciliary arteries and nerves enter the sclera on either side of the optic nerve close to the horizontal meridian. The course of these structures can usually be followed for a short distance in the suprachoroidal space. The posterior ciliary vessels originate from the ophthalmic artery and supply the whole uveal tract, the cilioretinal arteries, the sclera, the margin of the cornea, and the adjacent conjunctiva. Occlusion of the posterior ciliary vessels, such as in giant cell arteritis, may have profound consequences for the eye and usually results in anterior ischemic optic neuropathy.

Hayreh SS, Baines JA. Occlusion of the posterior ciliary artery. I. Effects on choroidal circulation. II. Chorio-retinal lesions. III. Effects on the optic nerve head. *Br J Ophthalmol.* 1972;56:719–764.

The anterior ciliary arteries also arise from the ophthalmic artery and usually supply (in pairs) the superior, medial, and inferior rectus muscles (Fig I-43). A single anterior ciliary vessel enters the lateral rectus muscle from the lacrimal artery. The anterior and posterior ciliary vessels usually anastomose with the long posterior ciliary vessels to form the intramuscular circle of the iris from which branches supply

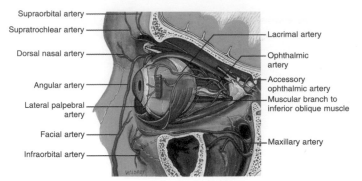

Supraorbital artery

Supratrochlear artery

Dorsal nasal artery

Angular artery

Lateral palpebral artery

Facial artery

Infraorbital artery

Lacrimal artery

Ophthalmic artery

Accessory ophthalmic artery

Muscular branch to inferior oblique muscle

Maxillary artery

FIG I-39—Orbital arteries. *Left,* Lateral view with extraocular muscles, composite view. *Below,* Central dissection. (Reproduced with permission from Dutton JJ. *Atlas of Clinical and Surgical Orbital Anatomy.* Philadelphia: Saunders; 1994.)

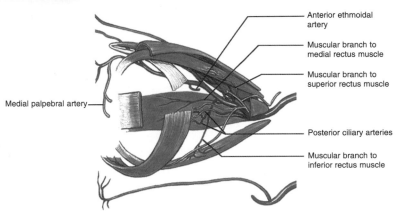

Anterior ethmoidal artery

Muscular branch to medial rectus muscle

Muscular branch to superior rectus muscle

Medial palpebral artery

Posterior ciliary arteries

Muscular branch to inferior rectus muscle

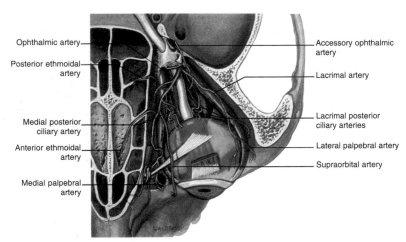

Ophthalmic artery

Posterior ethmoidal artery

Medial posterior ciliary artery

Anterior ethmoidal artery

Medial palpebral artery

Accessory ophthalmic artery

Lacrimal artery

Lacrimal posterior ciliary arteries

Lateral palpebral artery

Supraorbital artery

FIG I-40—Orbital arteries, superior composite view. (Reproduced with permission from Dutton JJ. *Atlas of Clinical and Surgical Orbital Anatomy.* Philadelphia: Saunders; 1994.)

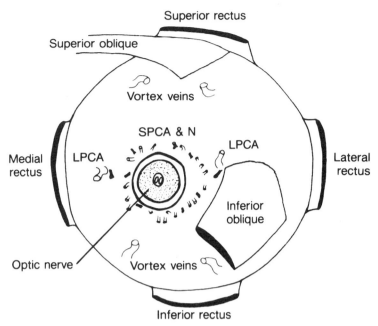

FIG I-41—Posterior view of right globe. (*LPCA*) Long posterior ciliary arteries; (*SPCA & N*) short posterior ciliary arteries and nerves. (Illustration by Thomas A. Weingeist, PhD, MD.)

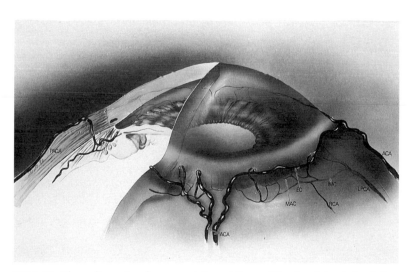

FIG I-42—Three-dimensional representation of the multilevel collateral circulation in the primate anterior uvea in both surface and cutaway views. (*ACA*) Anterior ciliary artery; (*LPCA*) long posterior ciliary artery; (*PACA*) posterior perforating anterior ciliary artery; (*RCA*) recurrent ciliary artery; (*EC*) episcleral circle; (*IMC*) intramuscular circle; (*MAC*) major arterial circle. To the left, in cross section, perforating branches of the anterior ciliary artery are shown as they pass through the sclera to supply the intramuscular circle and major arterial circle. (Reproduced by permission from Morrison JC, van Buskirk EM. Anterior collateral circulation in the primate eye. *Ophthalmology.* 1983;90:707.)

FIG I-43—Orbital arteries, frontal view with extraocular muscles. (Reproduced with permission from Dutton JJ. *Atlas of Clinical and Surgical Orbital Anatomy.* Philadelphia: Saunders; 1994.)

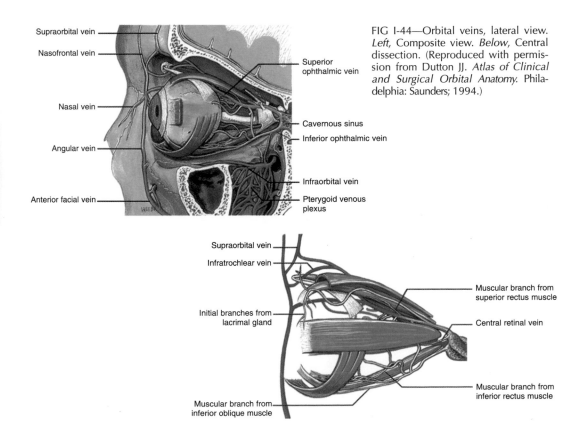

FIG I-44—Orbital veins, lateral view. *Left,* Composite view. *Below,* Central dissection. (Reproduced with permission from Dutton JJ. *Atlas of Clinical and Surgical Orbital Anatomy.* Philadelphia: Saunders; 1994.)

the major arterial circle (usually discontinuous), iris, and ciliary body. Anterior segment ischemia often results in segmental areas of sphincter palsy in the pupil and in iris atrophy.

Hayreh SS, Scott WE. Fluorescein iris angiography. I. Normal pattern. II. Disturbances in iris circulation following strabismus operation on the various recti. *Arch Ophthalmol.* 1978;96:1383–1400.

Vortex Veins

The vortex veins drain the venous system of the choroid, ciliary body, and iris. Each eye contains from four to seven or more veins. One or more veins are usually located in each quadrant and exit 14–25 mm from the limbus between the rectus muscles. The ampullae of the vortex veins are 8–9 mm from the ora serrata and are visible by indirect ophthalmoscopy. A circle connecting these ampullae corresponds roughly to the equator and divides the central or posterior fundus from the peripheral portion.

Rutnin U. Fundus appearance in normal eyes. I. The choroid. *Am J Ophthalmol.* 1967;64:821–839.

Rutnin U, Schepens CL. Fundus appearance in normal eyes. II. The standard peripheral fundus and developmental variations. *Am J Ophthalmol.* 1967;64:840–852.

CHAPTER II

Topographic Features of the Globe

The adult human eye averages 24 mm in diameter. The normal anteroposterior diameter varies between 21 and 26 mm. This measurement is characteristically smaller in hypermetropia and larger in myopia and buphthalmos. The anteroposterior diameter is approximately 16 mm at birth but reaches about 23 mm by 3 years of age. Its maximum size occurs by puberty. The transverse vertical diameter is less variable.

Important surface features of the globe not discussed below are the vortex vessels, the posterior ciliary arteries and nerves, and the optic nerve and its surrounding meningeal sheaths. They appear in illustrations in chapter I.

Cornea

The cornea occupies the center of the anterior pole of the globe. Since the sclera and conjunctiva overlap the cornea anteriorly, slightly more above and below than medially and laterally, the cornea appears elliptical when viewed from the front. In the adult it measures about 12 mm in the horizontal meridian and about 11 mm in the vertical meridian. From behind, the circumference of the cornea appears circular. The limbus, which borders the cornea and the sclera, is gray and translucent. The extraocular muscles insert at various distances posterior to the limbus, as shown in Figure I-14 in chapter I. Also see Table I-1.

Sclera

In contrast to the transparent cornea, the sclera is opaque and white. It is thinnest at the insertions of the rectus muscles (0.3 mm) and increases to about 1 mm thick posteriorly. The sclera becomes thin and sievelike at the lamina cribrosa, where the axons of the ganglion cells exit to form the optic nerve.

The insertions of the extraocular oblique muscles can be seen from the posterior aspect of the eyeball, as shown in Figure I-41. The inferior oblique muscle has little, if any, tendon. Its medial border inserts near the fovea and its lateral border inserts more anteriorly. The superior oblique muscle inserts mostly posterior to the anatomical equator of the eye and temporal to the vertical meridian. The muscle passes anteriorly beneath the superior rectus muscle on its way to the trochlea (see Figure I-15).

CHAPTER III

The Eye

Precorneal Tear Film

The anterior surface of the cornea is covered by the tear film, which is composed of three layers:

- A superficial oily layer produced predominantly by the meibomian glands and the glands of Zeis and Moll in the eyelids
- A middle watery layer produced by accessory lacrimal tissue and the lacrimal glands
- An inner mucous layer derived from the secretion of goblet cells within the conjunctiva

Maintenance of the precorneal tear film is vital for normal corneal function. In addition to lubricating the surface of the cornea and conjunctiva, tears produce a smooth optical surface, provide oxygen and other nutrients, and contain lysozyme and immunoglobulins. Aberrations in the tear film or its adherence result from a variety of diseases and may profoundly affect the function of the eye.

Cornea (Fig III-1)

Characteristics of the Central and Peripheral Cornea

The cornea and the aqueous humor together form a positive lens of about 43 D in air and therefore constitute the main refractive element of the eye. The central third of the cornea is nearly spherical and measures about 4 mm in diameter in the normal eye. Because the posterior surface of the cornea is more curved than the anterior surface, the central cornea is thinner (0.5 mm) than the peripheral cornea (1.0 mm). The cornea becomes flatter in the periphery, but the rate of flattening is not symmetrical. Flattening is more extensive nasally and superiorly than temporally and inferiorly. This topography is important to understand for contact lens fitting. BCSC Section 8, *External Disease and Cornea,* discusses the cornea in detail.

Epithelium and Basal Lamina

The anterior surface of the cornea is derived from surface ectoderm and is made up of nonkeratinized, stratified squamous epithelium. The epithelium consists of a basal columnar cell layer attached to its basement membrane (basal lamina) by hemidesmosomes (Fig III-2). Recurrent corneal erosions may occur because hemidesmosomes are not properly formed after a corneal epithelial abrasion.

Arising from the basal cell layer of the corneal epithelium are two or three layers of polygonal cells. Because the lateral extensions of these cells are thin and wing-

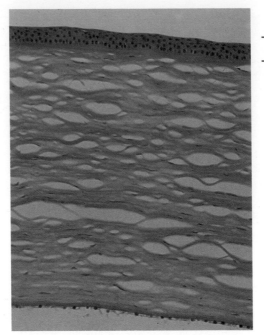

See Figure III-2 below for diagram of this portion

FIG III-1—Cornea. The empty spaces in the stroma are artifactitious (H&E ×32). (Photograph courtesy of Thomas A. Weingeist, PhD, MD.)

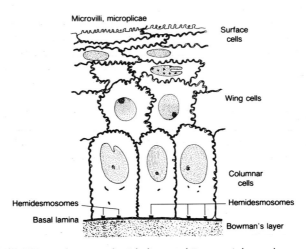

FIG III-2—The corneal epithelium and Bowman's layer, showing hemidesmosomes along the basal lamina. (Illustration by Thomas A. Weingeist, PhD, MD.)

like, they have been described as wing cells. The superficial corneal epithelial cells become extremely long and thin. Microplicae and microvilli make their apical surfaces highly irregular; however, the precorneal tear film renders the surfaces optically smooth. Although all the epithelial cells are firmly attached to one another by multiple desmosomes, they appear to migrate continuously from the basal surface toward the tear film into which they are shed.

> Fine BS, Yanoff M. *Ocular Histology: A Text and Atlas*. 2nd ed. Hagerstown, MD: Harper & Row; 1979:163–168.

Nonepithelial Cells

Nonepithelial cells may appear within the corneal epithelial layer. Wandering histiocytes, macrophages, lymphocytes, and pigmented melanocytes are frequent components of the peripheral cornea. Langerhans' cells have also been described, but their function is unknown.

Bowman's Layer

Beneath the basal lamina is Bowman's membrane, or more correctly, Bowman's layer. *Bowman's membrane* is an antiquated term used by light microscopists to describe this structure. More correctly, electron microscopists refer to it as *Bowman's layer*, since it consists of randomly dispersed collagen fibrils and is 8–14 μm thick. Its posterior border merges with the corneal stroma. Unlike Descemet's membrane, it is not replaced and may become opacified by scar tissue following injury.

Stroma

The stroma constitutes about 90%, or 500 μm, of the total corneal thickness in humans. It is composed of collagen-producing fibroblasts (keratocytes), ground substance, and collagen lamellae. The collagen fibrils form obliquely oriented lamellae in the anterior third of the stroma and parallel lamellae in the posterior two thirds. The corneal collagen fibrils are remarkably uniform in size and probably extend across the entire diameter of the cornea. The macroperiodicity of the fibrils (640 Å) is similar to typical collagen.

The ground substance of the cornea consists of mucoprotein and glycoprotein. It fills all of the space not occupied by the fibrils and cells in the corneal stroma. The keratocytes lie between the corneal lamellae. Electromicroscopic studies reveal that keratocytes have most of the characteristic features of fibroblasts. They are believed to synthesize both collagen and mucoprotein.

Descemet's Membrane (Fig III-3)

The basement membrane of the corneal endothelium, Descemet's membrane, is periodic acid–Schiff (PAS)–positive like the lens capsule, but it has unusual thickness. At birth it is 3–4 μm thick, and thickness increases throughout life to the adult level of 10–12 μm. Descemet's membrane is composed of an *anterior banded zone* that begins to develop in utero and a *posterior nonbanded zone* that is laid down by the corneal endothelium throughout life (Fig III-4).

In a sense, the layers of Descemet's membrane can be looked upon as a historical record of one aspect of endothelial cell function. Excrescences of Descemet's

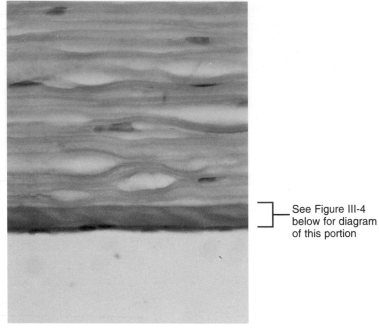

See Figure III-4 below for diagram of this portion

FIG III-3—Posterior cornea. Note the appearance of Descemet's membrane and the corneal endothelium (H&E ×64). (Photograph courtesy of Thomas A. Weingeist, PhD, MD.)

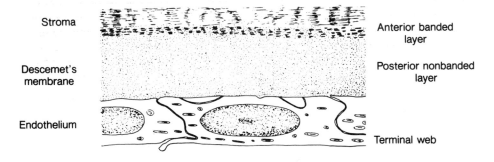

Stroma

Descemet's membrane

Endothelium

Anterior banded layer

Posterior nonbanded layer

Terminal web

Anterior chamber

FIG III-4—Corneal endothelium and Descemet's membrane. (Illustration by Thomas A. Weingeist, PhD, MD.)

membrane in the peripheral cornea known as Hassall-Henle warts are common, especially among elderly individuals. *Cornea guttata*, central excrescences (guttae) in Descemet's membrane, may occur with increasing age, often with an autosomal dominant pattern of transmission. In Fuchs endothelial dystrophy large numbers of these deposits may be associated with endothelial cell loss and with stromal decompensation.

Murphy C, Alvarado J, Juster R. Prenatal and postnatal growth of the human Descemet's membrane. *Invest Ophthalmol Vis Sci.* 1984;25:1402–1415.

Endothelium

The corneal endothelium is neither endothelium nor a mesothelium as some authors have suggested in the past. The best recent evidence shows that the corneal endothelium is derived from the neural crest and is therefore neuroectodermal, not mesodermal.

Johnston MC, Noden DM, Hazelton RD, et al. Origins of avian ocular and periocular tissues. *Exp Eye Res.* 1979;29:27–43.

A single layer of mostly hexagonal cells forms the corneal endothelium (Fig III-5). The size, shape, and morphology of endothelial cells can be observed by specular microscopy using a slit lamp. The apical surfaces of these cells face the anterior chamber; the basal surfaces abut Descemet's membrane. Typically, young endothelial cells have a large nucleus and abundant mitochondria. These organelles play an important role in active transport and maintenance of deturgescence of the normal corneal stroma. Mitosis of the endothelium seldom occurs in humans, and the overall number of endothelial cells decreases with age.

Adjacent endothelial cells interlock and form a variety of tight junctions, but desmosomes are never seen between normal cells. In cross section, pinocytotic vesicles, a terminal web (a thin meshwork of fine fibrils that increases the density of the cytoplasm), and numerous tight junctions can be seen toward the apical surface of the corneal endothelium. Injury to the endothelium from surgery, from raised intraocular pressure, or from other disease processes may destroy endothelial cells. In the absence of mitosis, destruction of cells results in decreasing density of cells and ultimately endothelial decompensation, edema, and clouding of the cornea.

Iwamoto T, Smelser GK. Electron microscopy of the human corneal endothelium with reference to transport mechanisms. *Invest Ophthalmol.* 1965;4:270–284.

Sclera (Fig III-6)

The sclera covers the posterior four fifths of the surface of the globe with potential openings anteriorly for the cornea and posteriorly for the optic nerve. The tendons of the rectus muscles insert into the superficial scleral collagen. Overlying both the sclera and the rectus muscles anteriorly are Tenon's capsule and the bulbar conjunctiva, which make firm attachments near the limbus.

The sclera is thinnest (0.3 mm) at the insertion of the rectus muscles and thickest (1.0 mm) at the posterior pole. It measures 0.4–0.5 mm at the equator and is 0.6 mm thick anterior to the muscle insertions. Because of the thinness of the sclera, care must be taken during placement of bridle sutures and of scleral sutures in strabismus and retinal detachment surgery. Scleral rupture following blunt trauma can

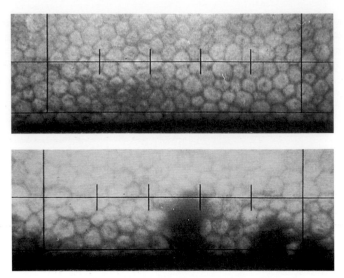

FIG III-5—Specular micrographs of the corneal endothelium. *Top,* Normal patient. *Bottom,* Patient with Fuchs endothelial dystrophy. Both are taken at the same magnification. Bottom micrograph shows larger, more irregular cells (polymegethism); the three dark areas toward the bottom are cornea guttata. (Photographs courtesy of David Palay, MD, and David Litoff, MD.)

RETINA CHOROID   SCLERA   EXTRAOCULAR
                                                       MUSCLE

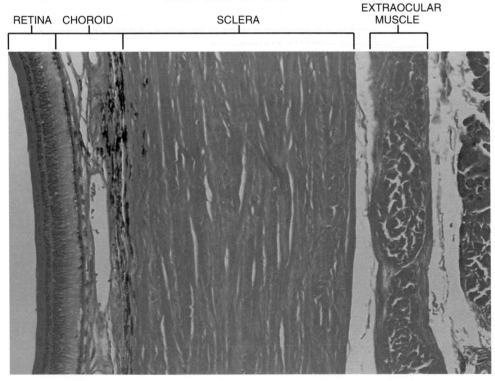

FIG III-6—Retina, choroid, sclera, and extraocular muscle (H&E ×8). (Photograph courtesy of Thomas A. Weingeist, PhD, MD.)

occur at a number of sites: in a circumferential arc parallel to the corneal limbus opposite the site of impact, at the insertion of the rectus muscles, or at the equator of the globe. The most common site is the superonasal quadrant near the limbus.

The sclera, like the cornea, is essentially avascular except for the superficial vessels of the episclera and the intrascleral vascular plexus located just posterior to the limbus. A large number of channels, or emissaria, penetrate the sclera for the passage of arteries, veins, and nerves. Extraocular extension of malignant melanoma of the choroid often occurs by way of the emissaria.

Branches of the ciliary nerves that supply the cornea sometimes leave the sclera to form loops posterior to the nasal and temporal limbus. These nerve loops are often pigmented and have been mistaken for uveal tissue or malignant melanoma. They are painful when touched, and if they are mistakenly excised, the cornea may become anesthetic in the area they supply.

Anteriorly, the episclera consists of a dense vascular connective tissue that merges with the superficial scleral stroma below and with Tenon's capsule and the conjunctiva above. The scleral stroma is composed of bundles of collagen, fibroblasts, and a moderate amount of ground substance. Collagen bundles of the sclera vary in size and shape and have been shown to taper at their ends, indicating that they are not continuous fibers as in the cornea. In general, the outer scleral collagen fibers have a larger diameter (1600 Å) than the inner collagen fibers (1000 Å). The inner layer of the sclera (lamina fusca) blends imperceptibly with the suprachoroidal and supraciliary lamellae of the uveal tract. The collagen fibers in this portion of the sclera branch and intermingle with the outer ciliary body and choroid. Electron-dense bodies, fibroblasts, and melanocytes occur within the bundles of collagen fibers. The opaque, porcelain white appearance of the sclera contrasts markedly with the transparent cornea and is primarily a result of the sclera's greater water content and the less uniform orientation of its collagen fibers.

Limbus

The transition zone between the peripheral cornea and the anterior sclera known as the limbus is defined differently by anatomists, pathologists, and ophthalmic surgeons and clinicians. Although not a distinct anatomic structure, it is very important both because of its relationship to the chamber angle and because of its use as a surgical landmark. The following are the structures included in the limbus:

- Conjunctiva
- Tenon's capsule
- Episclera
- Corneoscleral stroma
- Aqueous outflow apparatus

The transition from opaque sclera to clear cornea occurs gradually over 1.0–1.5 mm and is difficult to define histologically. The corneoscleral junction begins centrally in a plane connecting the end of Bowman's layer and the termination of Descemet's membrane, and it extends posteriorly toward Schlemm's canal for an undetermined distance. Pathologists consider the posterior limit of the limbus to be formed by another plane perpendicular to the surface of the eye, about 1.5 mm posterior to the termination of Bowman's layer (Fig III-7).

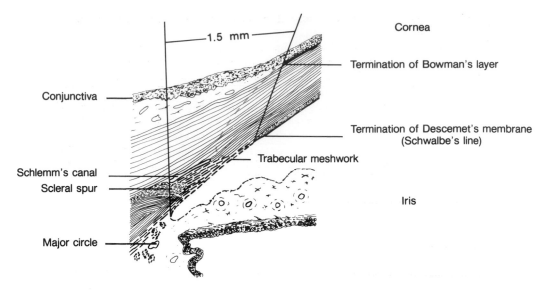

Cornea

Termination of Bowman's layer

Conjunctiva

Termination of Descemet's membrane
(Schwalbe's line)

Trabecular meshwork

Schlemm's canal

Scleral spur

Iris

Major circle

FIG III-7—Anterior chamber angle and limbus, depicting concept of limbus. Solid lines represent the limbus as seen by pathologists; the green dotted line represents the limbus as seen by anatomists. (Illustration by Thomas A. Weingeist, PhD, MD.)

The anatomy of the surgical limbus is approximately 2 mm wide and can be divided conceptually into two equal zones: an anterior bluish gray zone overlying clear cornea and extending from Bowman's layer to Schwalbe's line, and a posterior white zone overlying the trabecular meshwork and extending from Schwalbe's line to the scleral spur or iris root. Familiarization with these landmarks is essential to the surgeon performing a cataract extraction or a glaucoma filtering procedure.

Jaffe NS, Jaffe MS, Jaffe GF. *Cataract Surgery and Its Complications*. 5th ed. St Louis: Mosby; 1990:46–50.

Anterior Chamber

The anterior chamber is bordered anteriorly by the cornea and posteriorly by the iris diaphragm and the pupil. The chamber angle, which lies at the junction of the cornea and the iris, consists of the following structures:

□ Schwalbe's line

□ Schlemm's canal and the trabecular meshwork

□ Scleral spur

□ Anterior border of the ciliary body

□ Iris

The depth of the anterior chamber is variable. It tends to be deeper in aphakia and myopia and shallower in hyperopia. In the normal adult emmetropic eye, the anterior chamber is about 3 mm deep at its center and reaches its narrowest point slightly central to the angle recess.

The anterior chamber is filled with aqueous humor, which is produced by the ciliary epithelium in the posterior chamber. The fluid passes through the pupillary aperture and drains chiefly through the trabecular meshwork into Schlemm's canal. Accessory pathways, including uveoscleral drainage and diffusion into the iris, cornea, and posterior segment, account for less than 10% of aqueous outflow. BCSC Section 10, *Glaucoma*, discusses the anterior chamber and aqueous humor in detail.

A new technology, ultrasound biomicroscopy, allows high-resolution, two-dimensional views of the anterior segment of the eye to be obtained in vivo (Fig III-8). This allows the clinician to view the relationship of the structures in the anterior segment under different pathologic conditions.

Pavlin CJ, Sherar MD, Foster FS. Subsurface ultrasound microscopic imaging of the intact eye. *Ophthalmology.* 1990;97:244–50.

Trabecular Meshwork (Figs III-7, III-9)

The drainage of the aqueous humor is the most important function of the limbal region. The relationship of the trabecular meshwork and Schlemm's canal to other structures is complex, because the outflow apparatus is composed of tissue derived from cornea, sclera, iris, and ciliary body (Figs III-8, III-10).

The trabecular meshwork is roughly triangular in cross section, with the apex at Schwalbe's line and the base formed by the scleral spur and the ciliary body. The trabecular meshwork can be divided into three parts: the uveal portion, the corneo-scleral meshwork, and the juxtacanalicular tissue adjacent to Schlemm's canal. The uveal and corneoscleral meshwork may be divided by an imaginary line drawn from Schwalbe's line to the scleral spur. The uveal meshwork lies internal and the corneoscleral meshwork external to this line.

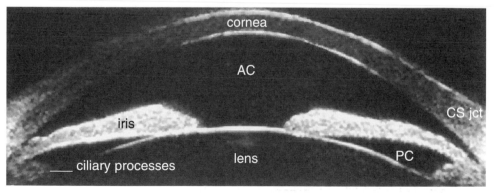

FIG III-8—Ultrasound biomicroscopic composite image of the anterior segment, including the anterior chamber (*AC*). The iris is slightly convex indicating mild pupillary block. The corneoscleral junction (*CS jct*), ciliary processes, and posterior chamber (*PC*) region are clearly imaged. The angle is narrow, but open. Iris–lens contact is small. (Photograph courtesy of Charles Pavlin, MD.)

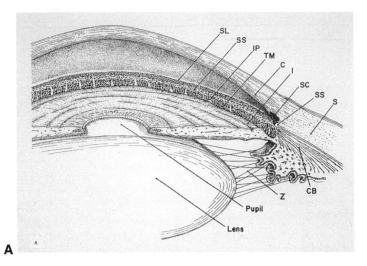

A

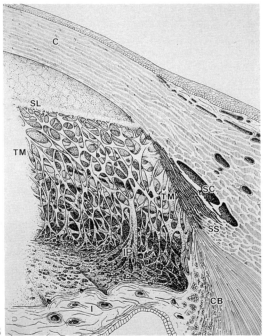

B

FIG III-9—Semidiagrammatic representation of the structures of the angle of the anterior chamber and ciliary body. *A,* Composite gonioscopic and cross-sectional view of the anterior segment of the eye. *B,* Enlarged view. Note the superimposed trabecular sheets with intratrabecular spaces through which aqueous humor percolates to reach Schlemm's canal. (*SL*) Schwalbe's line; (*SS*) scleral spur; (*IP*) iris process; (*TM*) trabecular meshwork; (*C*) cornea; (*I*) iris; (*SC*) Schlemm's canal; (*S*) sclera; (*CB*) ciliary body; (*Z*) zonular fibers.

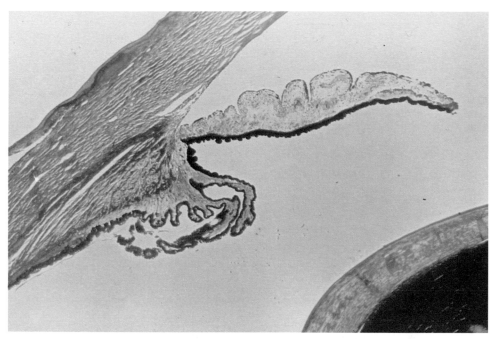

FIG III-10—Anterior chamber angle, ciliary body, and peripheral lens. Note the triangular shape of the ciliary body. The muscle fibers appear red in contrast to the connective tissue. The scleral spur is clearly delineated from the ciliary muscle in the region of the trabecular meshwork. The lens is artifactually displaced posteriorly. (Masson trichrome ×8). (Photograph courtesy of Thomas A. Weingeist, PhD, MD.)

Pigmentation of the trabecular meshwork is variable. It tends to be greater in individuals with brown irides than those with blue irides; however, the only reliable means of determining the degree of pigmentation is by gonioscopy. The lower chamber angle commonly is more pigmented than the upper. The melanin granules located in the trabecular meshwork are structurally identical to those found in the posterior pigmented layer of the iris.

Corneoscleral Meshwork

The corneoscleral meshwork consists of a series of thin, perforated connective tissue sheets arranged in a laminar pattern. These sheets have a central core of collagen and elastic fibrils surrounded by a thin basal lamina and then by a single continuous row of thin endothelial cells with multiple pinocytotic vesicles.

Uveal Trabecular Meshwork

The uveal meshwork varies only slightly from the corneoscleral sheets. It tends to be cordlike and to have fewer elastic fibers. The endothelial cells usually contain pigment granules, and the transtrabecular apertures are less circular and larger than those of the corneoscleral meshwork.

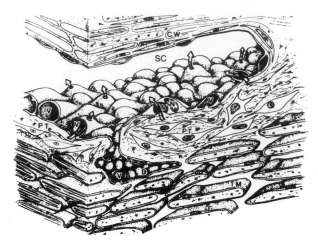

FIG III-11—The walls of Schlemm's canal (*SC*) and adjacent trabecular meshwork (*TM*). The endothelial lining of the trabecular wall of Schlemm's canal is very irregular, and normally the cells show luminal bulges corresponding to cell nuclei (*N*) and macrovacuolar configuration (*V*). The latter represents cellular invaginations occurring from the basal aspect and eventually opening on the apical aspect of the cell to form transcellular channels (*arrows*) through which aqueous humor flows down a pressure gradient. A diverticulum (*D*), its endothelial lining continuous with that of the canal, is shown on the inner wall of Schlemm's canal next to macrovacuolar configurations. Such blind, tortuous diverticula course for a variable distance into the trabecular meshwork but remain separated from the open spaces of the meshwork by their continuous endothelial lining. The endothelial lining of the trabecular wall is supported by interrupted, irregular basement membrane and a zone of pericanalicular connective tissue (*PT*) of variable thickness. The cellular element predominates in this zone, and the fibrous elements, especially elastic fibers, are irregularly arranged in a netlike fashion. Here, the open spaces are narrower than those of the trabecular meshwork. The corneoscleral trabecular sheets show frequent branching, and the endothelial covering may be shared between adjacent sheets. The corneoscleral wall (*CW*) of Schlemm's canal is more compact than the trabecular wall, with a predominance of lamellar arrangement of collagen and elastic tissue.

Schlemm's Canal

A large venous channel that closely resembles a lymphatic vessel, Schlemm's canal is formed by a continuous monolayer of nonfenestrated endothelium and a thin connective tissue wall. The basement membrane of the endothelium is poorly defined. The lateral walls of the endothelial cells are joined by tight junctions. Micropinocytotic vesicles are present at both the apical and basal surfaces of the cells. Larger vesicles (so-called giant vacuoles) have been observed along the internal canal wall (Figure III-11, III-12). These vacuoles are lined by a single membrane, and their size and number are related to the intraocular pressure. Their role, if any, in aqueous outflow is a subject of continuing research.

Collector Channels

Multiple internal and external collector channels arise from Schlemm's canal (Fig III-13). The external collector channels drain into the intrascleral venous plexus, the deep scleral plexus, and then into the aqueous veins, which are visible in the conjunctiva by biomicroscopy.

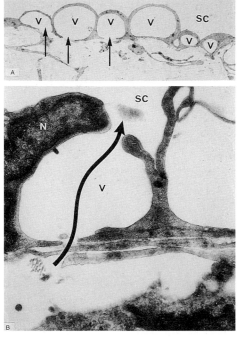

FIG III-12—*Top,* Low-magnification electron micrograph of the endothelial lining of Schlemm's canal (*SC*) shows that the majority of the vacuolar configurations (*V*) at this level of section have direct communication (*arrows*) with the subendothelial extracellular spaces, which contain aqueous humor (×3970). *Bottom,* Electron micrograph of a vacuolar structure that shows both basal and apical openings, thus constituting a vacuolar transcellular channel (*arrow*). In this way, the fluid-containing extracellular space on the basal aspect of the cell is temporarily connected with a lumen of Schlemm's canal, allowing bulk outflow of aqueous humor. (*N*), Indented nucleus of the cell (×23,825).

Gonioscopy of the Chamber Angle—Clinical Anatomy

Much of the chamber angle anatomy may be visualized by gonioscopy. Description here of the chamber angle refers only to the superior angle as viewed through the lower mirror of a gonioprism. The gonioscopist should acquire the habit of looking first at the pupillary margin. Dandrufflike deposits produced by exfoliation of the lens capsule may be noted, as well as posterior synechiae caused by adhesions formed between the posterior surface of the iris and the anterior lens capsule. Small grapelike clusters of blood vessels can sometimes be observed on the anterior portion of the pupillary border; these are normal and should not be confused with iris neovascularization. Anterior neovascularization, as seen in diabetic patients with ocular ischemia or in patients whose ocular ischemia is a result of severe carotid artery disease, appears as a fine network of blood vessels on the iris surface. Or it may be seen in the anterior chamber angle on gonioscopy. The contour of the iris

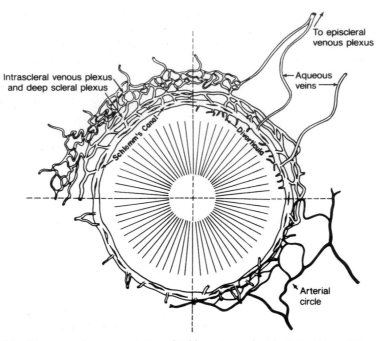

Intrascleral venous plexus
and deep scleral plexus

To episcleral
venous plexus

Aqueous
veins

Schlemm's Canal

Diverticula

Arterial
circle

FIG III-13—Diagrammatic representation of Schlemm's canal and relationships of the arteriolar and venous vascular supply. For clarity, the various systems have been limited to only parts of the circumference of the canal. Small, tortuous, blind diverticula (so-called Sondermann's channels) extend from the canal into the trabecular meshwork. Externally, the collector channels arising from Schlemm's canal anastomose to form the intrascleral and deep scleral venous plexuses. At irregular intervals around the circumference, aqueous veins arise from the intrascleral plexus and connect directly to the episcleral veins. The arteriolar supply closely approximates the canal, but no direct communication occurs between the two. (Reproduced by permission from Tripathi RC, Tripathi BJ. Functional anatomy of the anterior chamber angle. In: Jakobiec FA, ed. *Ocular Anatomy, Embryology, and Teratology*. Philadelphia: Harper & Row; 1982:276.)

plane should be noted and the width of the chamber angle estimated, since this observation is the basis for the classification of both primary and secondary glaucoma into open-angle or angle-closure glaucoma.

The surface of the iris is normally devoid of vessels. In lightly pigmented irides, radial vessels may be observed within the iris stroma. Undulations in the surface of the iris appear as a series of concentric rings as the examiner looks toward the chamber angle. The final iris roll is visible at the beginning of the angle recess, or *iris root,* the thinnest portion of the iris where it joins the ciliary body. Occasionally, iris processes extend from the surface of the iris into the trabecular area. Iris processes should not be confused with peripheral anterior synechiae (PAS), which are formed when the peripheral iris becomes adherent to the peripheral cornea.

The *ciliary body* is visible as a concavity above the iris root. Adjacent and above it is the *scleral spur,* a band of collagen fibers invaginated between the anterior portion of the ciliary body and Schlemm's canal. The scleral spur marks the attachment of the ciliary body and the insertion of its longitudinal muscle fibers. Gonioscopically, the scleral spur (the posterior border ring) is a white line of varying width. Directly above it are the trabecular meshwork and Schlemm's canal, which appears as a faint gray line. If blood has refluxed from the episcleral veins into the collector channels, Schlemm's canal will stand out as a fine red line located between the middle and the posterior third of the trabecular meshwork. The trabecular meshwork terminates at the peripheral margin of Descemet's membrane known as *Schwalbe's line* (the anterior border ring). Schwalbe's line can easily be identified by gonioscopy since the slit beam converges to a point in this location. BCSC Section 10, *Glaucoma*, discusses gonioscopy in depth.

Uveal Tract

The uveal tract is the vascular, middle compartment of the eye. It consists of three parts:

□ Iris

□ Ciliary body located in the anterior uvea

□ Choroid located in the posterior uvea

The uveal tract is firmly attached to the sclera at only three sites: the scleral spur, the exit points of the vortex veins, and the optic nerve. These attachments account for the characteristic ophthalmoscopic findings in choroidal detachment.

Iris (Fig III-14)

The iris is the most anterior extension of the uveal tract. It is made up of blood vessels and connective tissue, in addition to the melanocytes and pigment cells that are responsible for its distinctive color. The mobility of the iris allows the pupil to change size. During mydriasis, the iris is thrown into a number of ridges and folds, while during miosis its anterior surface appears relatively smooth.

The iris diaphragm subdivides the anterior segment into the anterior and posterior chambers. The iris root, the thinnest portion of the iris, may become disinserted from the ciliary body as a result of blunt trauma.

Stroma

The iris stroma is composed of pigmented (melanocytes) and nonpigmented cells, collagen fibrils, and a matrix of hyaluronidase-sensitive mucopolysaccharide. The aqueous humor flows freely through the loose stroma along the anterior border of the iris, which contains multiple crypts and crevices that vary in size, shape, and depth. This surface is not covered by a continuous layer of cells. Instead, it consists of an interrupted layer of connective-tissue cells that merges with the ciliary body.

The overall structure of the iris stroma remains similar in irides of all colors. Differences in color are related to the amount of pigmentation in the anterior border layer and the deep stroma. The stroma of blue irides is lightly pigmented, and brown irides have a densely pigmented stroma that absorbs light.

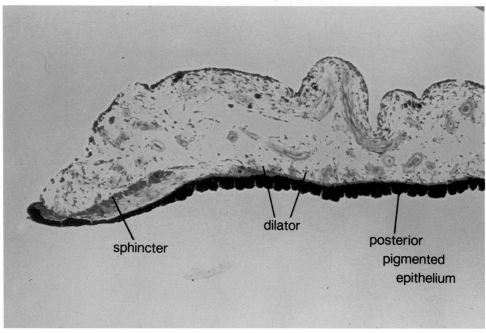

FIG III-14—Iris. Note the relationship between the sphincter and dilator muscles (H&E ×20). (Photograph courtesy of Thomas A. Weingeist, PhD, MD.)

Vessels and Nerves

Blood vessels form the bulk of the iris stroma. Most follow a course radial to the center of the pupil, and additional vessels pursue a concentric course in a corkscrew fashion around the pupil. The diameter of the capillaries is relatively large. Their endothelium is nonfenestrated and is surrounded by a basement membrane, associated pericytes, and a zone of collagenous filaments. The intima has no internal elastic lamina. In the region of the *collarette*, the thickest portion of the iris, anastomoses occur between the arterial and venous arcade; however, no true major iris circle exists. The major arterial circle is located in the ciliary body, not the iris. In humans, the anterior border layer is normally avascular. The development of rubeosis iridis, a complication that occurs in a number of vascular diseases including diabetes mellitus, is evidence of neovascularization.

Myelinated and nonmyelinated nerve fibers serve sensory, vasomotor, and muscular functions throughout the stroma.

Posterior Pigmented Layer

The posterior surface of the iris is densely pigmented and appears velvety smooth and uniform. It is continuous with the nonpigmented epithelium of the ciliary body and the neurosensory portion of the retina. The polarity of the cells is maintained from embryogenesis. The basal surface of the pigmented layer borders the posterior

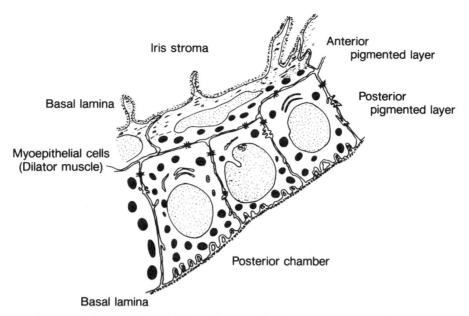

Iris stroma

Anterior
pigmented layer

Basal lamina

Posterior
pigmented layer

Myoepithelial cells
(Dilator muscle)

Posterior chamber

Basal lamina

FIG III-15—Posterior layer of the iris. (Illustration by Thomas A. Weingeist, PhD, MD.)

chamber. The apical surface faces the stroma and adheres to the anterior pigmented layer, the dilator muscle (Fig III-15).

The posterior pigmented layer of the iris curves around the pupillary margin and extends for a short distance onto the anterior border layer of the iris stroma (physiologic ectropion). In certain pathologic conditions (rubeosis iridis) the pigmented layer extends farther onto the anterior surface of the iris (pathologic ectropion). The term *ectropion uveae* is a misnomer, since all of these layers are derived from neuroectoderm.

Dilator Muscle

The dilator muscle arises from the outer layer of the optic cup, which is neuroectoderm. It lies parallel and anterior to the posterior pigmented epithelium of the iris. The smooth muscle cells contain fine myofilaments and melanosomes. The myofibrils are confined mainly to the basal portion of the cells and extend anteriorly into the iris stroma. The melanosomes and the nucleus are located in the apical region of each myoepithelial cell.

Morphologically, evidence suggests a dual sympathetic and parasympathetic innervation. In vitro organ bath experiments on the dilator muscle indicate that it contracts in response to alpha$_2$-adrenergic sympathetic stimulation, but there may be an inhibitory role for cholinergic parasympathetic stimulation.

The first-order neuron of the sympathetic chain begins in the ipsilateral posterolateral hypothalamus and passes through the brain stem to synapse in the intermediolateral gray matter of the spinal cord at cervical level 8 and thoracic level 2. The second-order neuron exits the spinal cord, passes over the pulmonary apex and through the stellate ganglion without synapsing, and synapses in the superior cervical ganglion. The third-order postganglionic neuron originates in the superior cervical ganglion, joins the internal carotid plexus, enters the cavernous sinus, and travels with the ophthalmic division of cranial nerve V to the orbit and then to the dilator muscle.

Sphincter Muscle

Like the dilator muscle, the sphincter muscle is derived from neuroectoderm. It is composed of a circular band of smooth muscle fibers and is located near the pupillary margin in the deep stroma anterior to the pigment epithelium of the iris. Although a dual innervation has been demonstrated morphologically, the sphincter muscle receives its primary innervation from parasympathetic nerve fibers that originate in the cranial nerve III nucleus, and it responds pharmacologically like other parasympathetically innervated structures. The reciprocal sympathetic innervation to the sphincter appears to serve an inhibitory role, helping to relax the sphincter in darkness.

The fibers subserving the sphincter muscle leave the Edinger-Westphal subnucleus and follow the inferior division of cranial nerve III after it bifurcates in the cavernous sinus. The fibers continue along with the branch supplying the inferior oblique muscle, exit, and synapse with postganglionic fibers in the ciliary ganglion. The postganglionic fibers travel with the short ciliary nerves to the iris sphincter.

Ciliary Body

The ciliary body, which appears triangular in cross section, bridges the anterior and posterior segments (see Figure III-9). The apex of the ciliary body is directed posteriorly toward the ora serrata. Its base gives rise to the iris and is partly visible by gonioscopy. The only attachment of the ciliary body to the sclera is at its base, where it inserts into the scleral spur.

The ciliary body has two principal functions: aqueous humor formation and accommodation of the lens. It may also play a role in the uveoscleral outflow of aqueous humor.

Ciliary Epithelium and Stroma

The ciliary body is 6–7 mm wide and consists of two parts: the pars plana and the pars plicata. The *pars plana*, which is 4 mm in width, extends from the ora serrata anteriorly to the ciliary processes (Fig III-16). As its name implies, it is a flat area. The safest posterior surgical approach to the vitreous cavity is by way of the pars plana, which is located 3–4 mm from the corneal limbus. The *pars plicata* is richly vascularized and consists of approximately 70 radial folds, or ciliary processes. The zonular fibers of the lens attach primarily in the valleys of the ciliary processes but also along the pars plana.

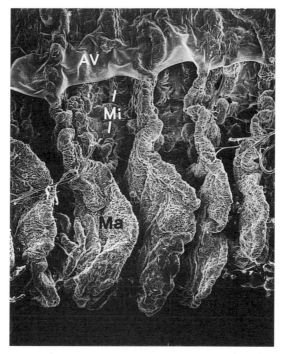

FIG III-16—Scanning electron micrograph of the human ciliary processes showing major processes (*Ma*) and minor processes (*Mi*). Remnants of the anterior vitreous (*AV*) are covering the pars plana (×60).

The capillary plexus of each ciliary process is supplied by arterioles as they pass anteriorly and posteriorly from the major arterial circle and is drained by one or two large venules located at the crest of each process. Sphincter tone within the arteriolar smooth muscle not only affects the capillary hydrostatic pressure gradient but also influences whether blood flows into the capillary plexus or directly to the draining choroidal vein, bypassing the plexus completely. Neuronal innervation of the vascular smooth muscle and humoral vasoactive substances may be important in determining regional blood flow, capillary surface area available for exchange of fluid, and hydrostatic capillary pressure. All of these affect the rate of aqueous humor formation.

The ciliary body is lined by a double layer of epithelial cells, the nonpigmented and the pigmented epithelium. The inner nonpigmented epithelium is located between the aqueous humor of the posterior chamber and the outer pigmented epithelium. The apices of the nonpigmented and pigmented cell layers are fused by a complex system of tight junctions and cellular interdigitations. Along the lateral intercellular spaces, near the apical border of the nonpigmented epithelium, are zonulae occludentes that maintain the blood–aqueous barrier. The basal surface of the nonpigmented epithelium, which borders the posterior chamber, is covered by a basement membrane. The basal lamina is multilaminar in the valleys of the processes. The basement membrane of the pigmented epithelium is more homogeneous than that of the nonpigmented epithelium but thicker.

The pigmented epithelium is relatively uniform throughout the ciliary body (Fig III-17). Its cuboidal shape is characterized by multiple basal infoldings, a large nucleus, mitochondria, extensive endoplasmic reticulum, and many melanosomes. The nonpigmented epithelium tends to be cuboidal in the pars plana region but columnar in the pars plicata. It also has multiple basal infoldings, abundant mitochondria, and a large nucleus. The endoplasmic reticulum and Golgi complex present in these cells play an important role in aqueous humor formation. Occasional melanosomes are present, especially anteriorly near the iris.

The uveal portion of the ciliary body consists of comparatively large fenestrated capillaries, collagen fibrils, and fibroblasts. The main arterial supply to the ciliary body comes from the long posterior and the anterior ciliary arteries, which come together to form a multilayered arterial plexus consisting of a superfical episcleral plexus, a deeper intramuscular plexus, and an incomplete major arterial circle often mistakenly attributed to the iris but actually located posterior to the anterior chamber angle recess in the ciliary body. The major veins drain posteriorly through the vortex system, although some drainage also occurs through the intrascleral venous plexus and the episcleral veins into the limbal region.

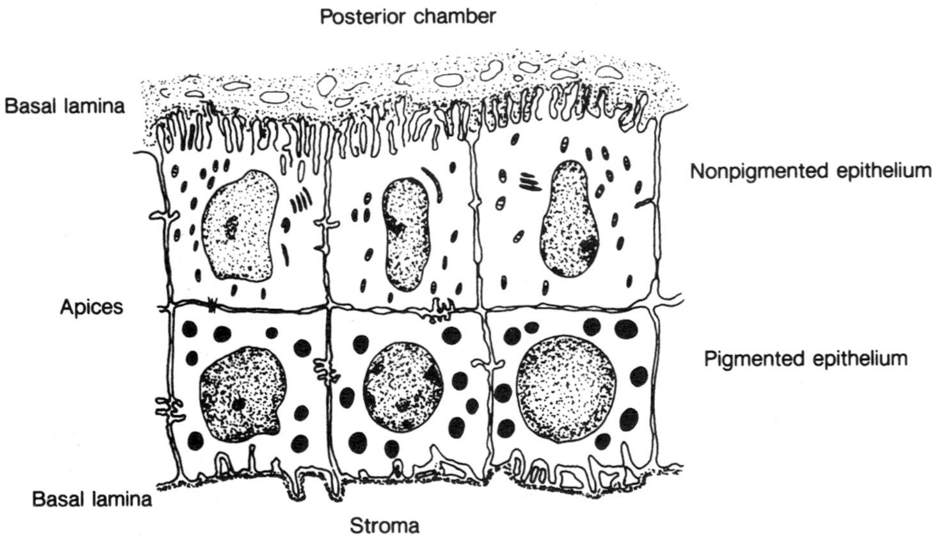

FIG III-17—Ciliary epithelium. (Illustration by Thomas A. Weingeist, PhD, MD.)

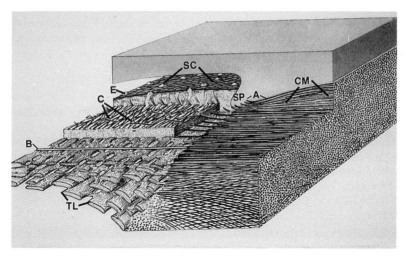

FIG III-18—Schematic drawing of the ciliary muscle–tendon attachments. Type A tendons (A) connect the anterior ciliary muscle tips to the sclera and scleral spur. Type B tendons (B) traverse through the entire trabecular meshwork and insert into the corneal stroma. Type C tendons (C) appear brushlike and fan out at 90° angles at their terminal ends. They become continuous with the cribriform meshwork of elastic fibers underlying Schlemm's canal that connect to the endothelial cells lining the canal. (CM) Ciliary muscle; (E) endothelium of Schlemm's canal; (SC) Schlemm's canal; (SP) scleral spur; (TL) trabecular lamellae. (Reproduced by permission from Rohen JW. The evolution of the primate eye in relation to the problem of glaucoma. In: Lütjen-Drecoll E, ed. *Basic Aspects of Glaucoma Research.* New York: FK Schattauer; 1982:21.)

Ciliary Muscle (Fig III-18)

Descriptions of the ciliary muscle suggest that it has three layers of fibers: longitudinal, radial, and circular. Most of the ciliary muscle is made up of an outer layer of longitudinal fibers that attach to the scleral spur. The radial muscle fibers arise in the midportion of the ciliary body, and the circular fibers are located in the innermost portion. Clinically, the three groups of muscle fibers function as a unit. Presbyopia is related to aging changes of the lens, which is discussed below, rather than of the ciliary muscles.

The ciliary muscles behave like other smooth, nonstriated muscle fibers. Ultrastructural studies reveal that they contain multiple myofibrils with characteristic electron-dense attachment bodies, mitochondria, glycogen particles, and a prominent nucleus. The smooth muscle cells are surrounded by a basal lamina separated from the cell membrane by a 300 Å space.

Both myelinated and nonmyelinated nerve fibers are observed throughout the ciliary muscle. Innervation is mainly derived from parasympathetic fibers of cranial nerve III. Sympathetic fibers have also been observed, but their function is not understood. Miotics contract the ciliary muscle. Since some of the muscle fibers form tendon attachments to the scleral spur, their contraction increases aqueous flow presumably by changing the configuration of the trabecular meshwork and/or Schlemm's canal. Because these muscle-tendon attachments are not well formed in infants, miotics have only a minor influence on aqueous outflow in this age group.

Choroid

The choroid, the posterior portion of the uveal tract, nourishes the outer portion of the retina (Fig III-19). It averages 0.25 mm in thickness and consists of three layers of vessels: the *choriocapillaris*, the innermost layer; a larger middle layer; and a still larger outer layer.

Perfusion of the choroid comes from both the long and short posterior ciliary arteries and from recurrent branches of the anterior ciliary arteries (Fig III-20). The venous blood drains through the vortex system. The blood flow through the choroid is high compared to other tissues. As a result, the oxygen content of the choroidal venous blood is only 2%–3% less than the arterial blood.

CHOROID ——————

CHORIOCAPILLARIS ——————

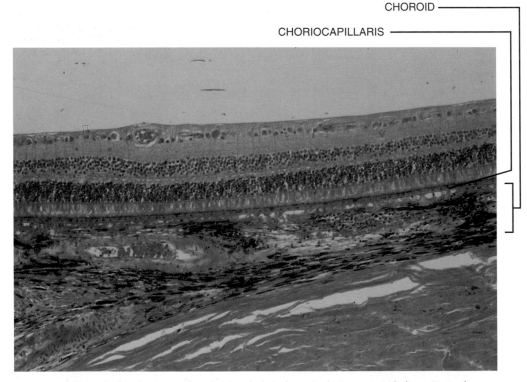

FIG III-19—Choroid. The choriocapillaris lies just below the retinal pigment epithelium. Beneath are a middle and outer vascular layer and multiple dendritic melanocytes (H&E ×32). (Photograph courtesy of Thomas A. Weingeist, PhD, MD.)

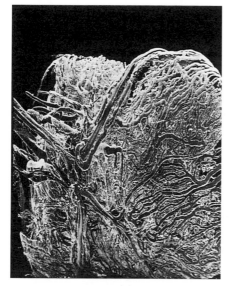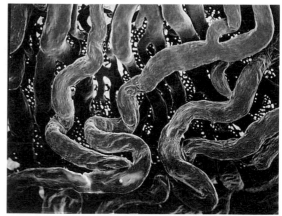

FIG III-20—Scanning electron micrograph of a vascular cast of the choroidal circulation as viewed from the scleral side of the posterior pole. The outer choroid consists of many interweaving branches of the short posterior ciliary arteries and vortex veins. Beneath these vessels, the choriocapillaris layer appears as a sheet or net of capillaries. *Left,* Low magnification; *right,* higher magnification. (Reproduced by permission from Kessel RG, Kardon RH. *Tissues and Organs: A Text-Atlas of Scanning Electron Microscopy.* New York: WH Freeman Co; 1979.)

Bruch's Membrane (Figs III-21, III-22)

Bruch's membrane appears by light microscopy as a PAS-positive membrane but is actually not a true membrane. Electron microscopy shows that this band, which extends from the margin of the optic disc to the ora serrata, has five elements:

- The basal lamina of the retinal pigment epithelium
- An inner collagenous zone
- A thicker porous band of elastic fibers
- An outer collagenous zone
- The basal lamina of the outer layer of the choriocapillaris

Bruch's membrane, therefore, consists of a series of connective tissue sheets that are highly permeable to small molecules such as fluorescein. Defects in Bruch's membrane develop spontaneously in myopia, pseudoxanthoma elasticum and other diseases, trauma, or inflammation. Subretinal neovascular membranes are important sequelae of these defects that can lead to the development of disciform macular changes such as senile macular degeneration and ocular histoplasmosis syndrome.

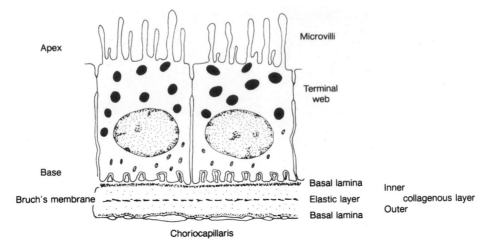

Apex

Microvilli

Terminal
web

Base

Basal lamina — Inner
Bruch's membrane — Elastic layer — collagenous layer
Basal lamina — Outer

Choriocapillaris

FIG III-21—Retinal pigment epithelium and Bruch's membrane. (Illustration by Thomas A. Weingeist, PhD, MD.)

Choriocapillaris

The choriocapillaris is a continuous layer of large capillaries (40–60 μm in diameter) lying in a single plane beneath the retinal pigment epithelium (Fig III-23). The vessel walls are extremely thin and contain multiple fenestrations, especially on the surface facing the retina (Fig III-24). Pericytes are located along the outer wall.

Although in vitro and postmortem injection studies have indicated that the choriocapillaris is a continuous vascular system, ample clinical evidence suggests that, functionally, it acts like an end-arteriole system. In vivo fundus fluorescein angiography reveals that the choriocapillaris, especially in the posterior pole, has a lobular pattern. The central element in the lobule is supplied centrally by a precapillary arteriole that drains peripherally into the postcapillary venule. A mosaic lobular pattern can be demonstrated in the early phases of fluorescein angiography, especially under experimental conditions if fluorescein is injected intra-arterially or with video fluorescein angiography with a fast sampling rate.

Recent studies using corrosion vascular casts and scanning electron microscopy have demonstrated that the angioarchitecture of the choriocapillaris is most dense at the macula and becomes less so toward the periphery (Fig III-25).

Hayreh SS. The choriocapillaris. *Albrecht von Graefe's Arch Klin Exp Ophthalmol.* 1974;192:165–179.

Torczynski E, Tso MO. The architecture of the choriocapillaris at the posterior pole. *Am J Ophthalmol.* 1976;81:428–440.

Yoneya S, Tso MO. Angioarchitecture of the human choroid. *Arch Ophthalmol.* 1987;105:681–687.

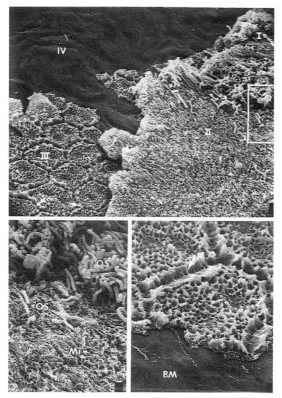

FIG III-22—Scanning electron micrograph of Bruch's membrane and pigmented epithelium–photoreceptor complex. *Top,* View from the inner retinal side, with most of the retina removed, exposes the outer layers: *I,* the layer of the outer segments of photoreceptors; *II,* the microvillous layer of the apical end of the pigmented epithelium; *III,* the cytoplasm and polygonal cell borders of the pigmented epithelium; *IV,* Bruch's membrane. The arrows point to depressions in the cytoplasm where the cell nuclei were removed. The rectangle at right is magnified in the lower left photo. *Lower left,* Relationship of the photoreceptor outer segments (*OS*) (inner segment torn away) to microvilli (*Mi*) of pigmented epithelium. *Lower right,* Basal portion of pigmented epithelial cell in relation to Bruch's membrane (*BM*). Adjacent epithelial cells are joined through junctional complexes (*arrows*). The pigment granules have left small holes in the cytoplasm after tissue preparation, giving the cell a honeycomb appearance at this plane of section. (Reproduced by permission from Kessel RG, Kardon RH. *Tissues and Organs: A Text-Atlas of Scanning Electron Microscopy.* New York: WH Freeman Co; 1979.)

The middle and outer choroidal vessels are not fenestrated. The large vessels, typical of small arteries elsewhere, possess an internal elastic lamina and smooth muscle cells in the media. As a result, small molecules such as fluorescein, which can be expected to diffuse through the endothelium of the choriocapillaris, do not leak through medium and large choroidal vessels. Abundant melanocytes as well as occasional macrophages, lymphocytes, mast cells, and plasma cells appear throughout the choroidal stroma. The intercellular space contains collagen fibers and nerve

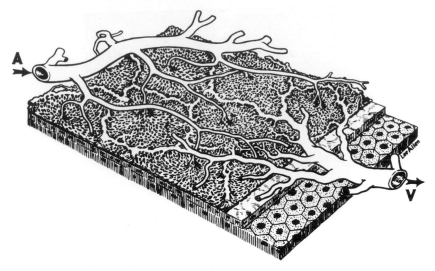

FIG III-23—Lobular pattern of choriocapillaris. Note that the retinal pigment epithelium is below. (A) Choroidal arteriole; (V) choroidal venule. (Reproduced by permission from Hayreh SS. The choriocapillaris. *Albrecht von Graefe's Arch Klin Exp Ophthalmol.* 1974;192:165–179.)

fibers. The degree of pigmentation observed ophthalmoscopically in the ocular fundus is dependent primarily on the number of pigmented melanocytes in the choroid. Melanosomes are absent from the retinal pigment epithelium and choroid of albino individuals. In lightly pigmented eyes, pigmentation is sparse in the choroid compared with darkly pigmented eyes. The degree of pigmentation in the choroid must be taken into consideration when performing photocoagulation.

Lens (Fig III-26)

The lens is a biconvex structure located in the posterior chamber directly behind the pupil. The lens is the second of the two refractive elements in the ocular dioptric system and is weaker than the cornea. The anteroposterior diameter of the lens varies from 4.0 to 5.0 mm in adults up to age 40, and the width increases gradually throughout life. The equatorial diameter varies from 9.0 to 10.0 mm in the adult and remains unchanged. Lens thickness changes during accommodation, and in young individuals the thickness of the lens varies, depending on the degree of accommodation. Relaxation of tension on the zonular fibers resulting from contraction of the ciliary muscles causes the lens to increase in thickness.

The lens has a number of unusual anatomic characteristics. It lacks innervation. After regression of the hyaloid vascular system during fetal life, it depends totally on the aqueous and vitreous for its nourishment. It continues to grow throughout life and is entirely enclosed from embryo stage onward by a basement membrane. BCSC Section 11, *Lens and Cataract,* discusses the lens in depth.

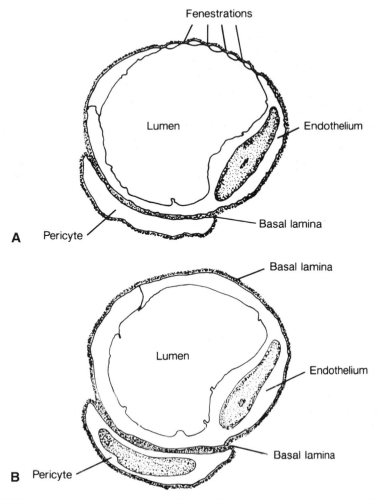

Fenestrations

Lumen

Endothelium

Basal lamina

A Pericyte

Basal lamina

Lumen

Endothelium

Basal lamina

B Pericyte

FIG III-24—*A,* Fenestrated choroidal capillary. *B,* Nonfenestrated retinal capillary. (Illustration by Thomas A. Weingeist, PhD, MD.)

Capsule

The lens surface is covered by a PAS-positive basement membrane, the lens capsule, which is a product of the lens epithelium (Fig III-27). The anterior lens capsule is almost twice as thick as the posterior capsule and increases in thickness throughout life. Cryoextraction of the lens during intracapsular cataract extraction (ICCE) is best achieved if the cryoprobe is placed midway between the anterior pole and the superior equator of the lens where the capsule is thickest.

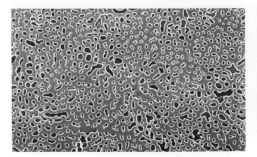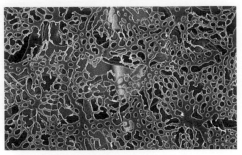

FIG III-25—*Left,* Scanning electron micrograph of a vascular cast of the choriocapillaris at the macula in the posterior pole after tissue digestion, as seen from the retina side. The superficial retinal circulation was removed in this preparation. *Right,* Similar view from a more anterior location, toward the ora serrata. The larger arteries and veins can be discerned underneath it. Anatomically, the choriocapillaris resembles a continuous sheet toward the macula, but the capillary plexus becomes much less dense in the periphery.

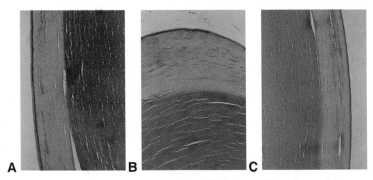

A   B   C

FIG III-26—*A,* Lens: anterior capsule, epithelium, and lens fibers. *B,* Equator of the lens. Note nuclei within the lens bow and the zonular fibers. *C,* Posterior lens capsule. Note absence of lens epithelium (H&E ×32). (Photographs courtesy of Thomas A. Weingeist, PhD, MD.)

Morphologically, the lens capsule consists of fine filaments aligned parallel to the surface. The anterior lens capsule can be distinguished at the ultrastructural level from the posterior capsule by the presence of zonular fibers and fibrogranular material embedded deep within it. The thinness of the posterior capsule creates a potential for rupture during extracapsular cataract extraction (ECCE), particularly by phacoemulsification.

Epithelium

The lens epithelium lies beneath the anterior and equatorial capsule but does not exist under the posterior capsule. The bases of the lens epithelial cells abut the lens capsule. There are no specialized attachment sites between the lens epithelium and the basal lamina. The apices of the cells face the interior of the lens, and the lateral borders are interdigitated with practically no intercellular space. The cytoplasm contains a prominent nucleus but relatively few cytoplasmic organelles.

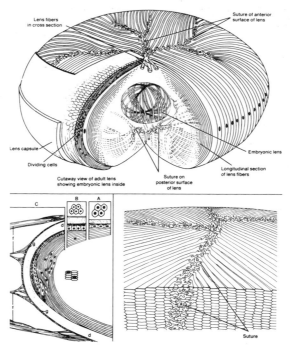

FIG III-27—The organization of the lens. At areas where lens cells converge and meet, sutures are formed. *Top,* The embryonal nucleus has a Y-shaped suture at both the anterior and posterior poles. In the adult lens cortex the organization of the sutures is more complex. At the equator the lens epithelium can divide, and the cells become highly elongated and ribbonlike, sending processes anteriorly and posteriorly. As new lens cells are formed, older cells become displaced to deeper parts of the cortex. The diagram at lower left illustrates the difference in lens fibers at the anterior (A), intermediate (B), and equatorial zones (C) as shown in cross section and corresponding surface view. The lens capsule or basement membrane of the lens epithelium (d) is shown in relation to the zonular fibers (f) and their attachment to the lens (g). Diagram at lower right shows a closer view of lens sutures. (Reproduced by permission from Kessel RG, Kardon RH. *Tissues and Organs: A Text-Atlas of Scanning Electron Microscopy.* New York: WH Freeman Co; 1979.)

Important regional differences exist in the lens epithelium. In the pre-equatorial zone, the cells undergo mitotic division at the germinative zone. As the cells become elongated and descend to the deeper layers of the lens, they are transformed from tall cuboidal cells to slender lens epithelial cells, or so-called fibers. The absence of dividing epithelial cells on the posterior capsule makes it possible to have a clear posterior capsule following ECCE. However, granular opacification of the posterior lens capsule may occur following ECCE as a result of migration and proliferation of lens epithelial cells. Discission of the posterior capsule can be performed by use of either a Zeigler knife or Nd:YAG laser if the opacification is obstructing the patient's vision.

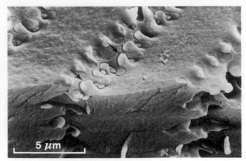

FIG III-28—Scanning electron micrograph of the relationship of lens fiber packing and interdigitation (arrows in right photograph). (Reproduced by permission from Kessel RG, Kardon RH. *Tissues and Organs: A Text-Atlas of Scanning Electron Microscopy.* New York: WH Freeman Co; 1979.)

Fibers

The cortex and nuclear lens fibers are derived from proliferating lens epithelial cells. On cross section, the cortical cells are hexagonal and possess numerous interlocking fingerlike projections (Fig III-28). The cytoplasm is homogeneous and contains few organelles. The *lens sutures* are formed by the arrangement of interdigitations of apical cell processes (anterior sutures) and basal cell processes (posterior sutures). In addition to the so-called Y-sutures located within the nucleus of the lens, multiple optical zones are visible by slit-lamp biomicroscopy because strata of epithelial cells with differing optical densities are laid down throughout life.

Zonular Fibers

The zonular fibers originate from the basal laminae of the nonpigmented epithelium of the pars plana and pars plicata of the ciliary body, and attach chiefly to the lens capsule anterior and posterior to the equator. Each zonular fiber is made up of multiple filaments of collagen that merge with the lens capsule. Accommodation of the lens is controlled by the contraction and relaxation of these fibers.

Retina

The retina is a thin, transparent structure that develops during differentiation from the inner and outer layers of the optic cup. The structure of the outer, pigmented epithelial layer is relatively simple compared with the overlying inner or neurosensory retina. BCSC Section 12, *Retina and Vitreous,* discusses the retina in depth.

Retinal Pigment Epithelium

The retinal pigment epithelium (RPE) consists of a monolayer of hexagonal cells that extends anteriorly from the optic disc to the ora serrata, where it merges with the pigmented epithelium of the ciliary body. Its structure is deceptively simple considering its many functions:

- Vitamin A metabolism
- Maintenance of the outer blood–retinal barrier
- Phagocytosis of the photoreceptor outer segments
- Absorption of light
- Heat exchange
- Formation of the basal lamina
- Production of the mucopolysaccharide matrix surrounding the outer segments
- Active transport of materials in and out of the cells

Like other epithelial and endothelial cells, the RPE cells are polarized. The basal sides are intricately folded to produce a large surface attachment to a thin basement membrane (basal lamina) that forms the inner layer of Bruch's membrane, as shown in Figures III-21 and III-22. The apices have multiple villous processes into which the photoreceptor outer segments are embedded in a mucopolysaccharide matrix. Separation of the pigmented epithelial layer and the neurosensory retina is called a *retinal detachment*.

Adjacent RPE cells are firmly attached by a series of lateral, intercellular adhesions called junctional complexes (Fig III-29). The zonulae occludentes and zonulae adherentes not only provide structural stability but also play an important role in maintenance of the outer blood–retinal barrier. Zonulae occludentes consist of fused plasma membranes forming a circular band or belt between adjacent cells. A small intercellular space is present between zonulae adherentes.

Important regional differences exist in the RPE (Fig III-30). Cells vary from 10 to 60 μm in diameter. The retina is thickest in the papillomacular bundle near the optic nerve (0.23 mm) and thinnest in the foveola (0.10 mm) and ora serrata (0.11 mm). Cells in the foveal area are taller and thinner and contain more and larger melanosomes. These characteristics account in part for the decreased transmission of choroidal fluorescence observed during fundus fluorescein angiography. Cells in the periphery are broader, shorter, and less pigmented. The eye of a fetus or infant contains between 4 and 6 million RPE cells. Although the surface area of the eye increases appreciably with age, the increase in the number of cells is relatively small. In the adult eye, normally, no mitotic figures within the RPE are observed.

The cytoplasm of the RPE cells contains multiple round and ovoid pigment granules (*melanosomes*). These organelles develop in situ during formation of the optic cup and first appear as nonmelanized premelanosomes. Their development contrasts sharply with the pigment granules in melanocytes in the uveal tract, which are derived from the neural crest and migrate into the uvea later.

Lipofuscin granules probably arise from the discs of photoreceptor outer segments and represent residual bodies of phagosomal activity. This so-called wear-and-tear pigment is less electron dense than the melanosomes, and its concentration increases gradually with age. Histologically, it is sudanophilic and exhibits a golden yellow autofluorescence in the fluorescent light microscope.

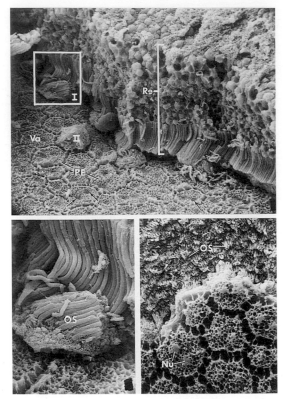

FIG III-29—*Top,* Scanning electron micrograph of the retina (*Re*) in relation to the pigmented epithelium (*PE*). The outer segments (*OS*) of the photoreceptors can be seen attaching to individual pigmented cells at *I* and *II.* The vacuolated appearance (*Va*) of the epithelium is caused by the loss of pigment granules during tissue preparation. *Lower left,* Enlargement of the area enclosed by rectangle in the top picture. *Lower right,* View from the basal aspect of the pigmented epithelium with Bruch's membrane stripped away. Tissue shrinkage during preparation left a space separating the cell borders, and junctional complexes appear as threads bridging this space. Within the cells, nuclei (*Nu*) can be seen among the dissolved granules. (Reproduced by permission from Kessel RG, Kardon RH. *Tissues and Organs: A Text-Atlas of Scanning Electron Microscopy.* New York: WH Freeman Co; 1979.)

Phagosomes represent membrane-enclosed packets of disc outer segments that have been engulfed by the RPE. Several stages of disintegration are evident at any given time. In some species, shedding and degradation of the membranes of rod and cone outer segments follow a diurnal rhythm synchronized with daily fluctuations of environmental light.

Bok D. Retinal photoreceptor-pigment epithelium interactions. *Invest Ophthalmol Vis Sci.* 1985;26:1659–1694.

Young RW. The daily rhythm of shedding and degradation of rod and cone outer segment membranes in the chick retina. *Invest Ophthalmol Vis Sci.* 1978;17:105–116.

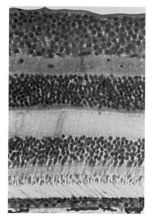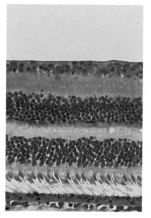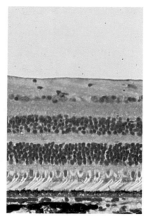

FIG III-30—Regional differences in the retina. From left to right: papillomacular bundle, macula, and peripheral retina (H&E, all same magnification). (Photographs courtesy of Thomas A. Weingeist, PhD, MD.)

The cytoplasm of the RPE also contains numerous mitochondria involved in aerobic metabolism, rough-surfaced endoplasmic reticulum, a Golgi apparatus, and a large round nucleus.

Throughout life incompletely digested residual bodies, lipofuscin pigment, phagosomes, and other material are presumably excreted beneath the basal lamina of the RPE. These contribute to the formation of drusen. Commonly classified by funduscopic appearance as either hard or soft, *drusen* are typically located between the basement membrane of the RPE cells and the inner collagenous zone of Bruch's membrane. They are thought to undergo a cycle of formation and regression, depending on the health of the overlying pigment epithelium. Hard drusen are thought to represent a focal byproduct of cell renewal and may thus be found even in young eyes. Softening with the addition of membranous components may indicate a general decline in cellular function. Drusen are presumed to be derived from the pigment epithelium, but it is not known if other sources exist.

Farkas TG. Drusen of the retinal pigment epithelium. *Surv Ophthalmol.* 1971;16:75–87.

Sarks SH, Sarks JP. Age-related macular degeneration. In: Ryan SJ, ed. *Retina.* 2nd ed. St Louis: Mosby–Year Book; 1994;2:152–165.

Sarks SH. Aging and degeneration in the macular region: a clinico-pathologic study. *Br J Ophthalmol.* 1976;60:324–341.

Neurosensory Retina

The neurosensory retina is composed of neuronal, glial, and vascular elements (Figs III-31, III-32).

Neuronal elements The *photoreceptor layer* consists of highly specialized neuro-epithelial cells called *rods* and *cones.* Each photoreceptor cell consists of an outer and an inner segment. The outer segments, surrounded by a mucopolysaccharide matrix, make contact with the apical processes of the retinal pigment epithelium. Tight junctions or other intercellular connections do not exist between the photoreceptor cell outer segments and the RPE. The factors responsible for keeping these layers in apposition are poorly understood but probably involve active transport.

The *rod photoreceptor* consists of an outer segment containing multiple laminated discs resembling a stack of coins and a central connecting cilium that has a "9 plus 0" cross-sectional configuration, rather than the "9 plus 2" configuration found in motile cilia. The rod inner segment is subdivided into two additional elements: an outer ellipsoid containing a large number of mitochondria and an inner myoid containing a large amount of glycogen that is continuous with the main cell body where the nucleus is located (Fig III-33). The inner portion of the cell contains the synaptic body, or *spherule,* of the rod, which is formed by a single invagination that accommodates two horizontal cell processes and one or more central bipolar dendrites (Fig III-34).

The *extrafoveal cone photoreceptors* of the retina have conical ellipsoids and myoids, and their nuclei tend to be closer to the external limiting membrane than the nuclei of the rods. Although the structure of the outer segments of the rods and cones is similar, at least one important difference exists. Rod discs are not attached to the cell membrane, but cone discs are, and they are thought to be renewed by membranous replacement. The cone synaptic body, or *pedicle,* is more complex than the rod spherule. Cone pedicles synapse with other rods and cones as well as with horizontal and bipolar cell processes. *Foveal cones* have cylindrical inner segments like rods, but otherwise are cytologically identical to extrafoveal cones. *Horizontal cells* make synaptic connections with many rod spherules and cone pedicles and extend cell processes horizontally throughout the outer plexiform layer. *Bipolar cells* are oriented vertically. Their dendrites synapse with either rod or cone synaptic bodies and their axons make synaptic contact with ganglion cells and amacrine cells in the inner plexiform layer.

The axons of the *ganglion cells* bend to become parallel to the inner surface of the retina where they form the nerve fiber layer and later the axons in the optic nerve. The nerve fibers from the temporal retina follow an arcuate course around the macula to enter the superior and inferior poles of the optic disc. The papillomacular fibers travel straight to the optic nerve from the fovea. The nasal axons also pursue a radial course. The nerve fiber pattern is enhanced when viewed ophthalmoscopically using green-only (red-free) illumination.

The overall complexity of the neuronal elements and their connections in the retina is far greater than described. Many types of bipolar, amacrine, and ganglion cells exist. The neuronal elements of more than 120 million rods and 6 million cones are interconnected and processed within the neurosensory retina before entering more than 1 million optic nerve fibers.

Dowling JE. *The Retina: An Approachable Part of the Brain.* Cambridge, MA: Harvard University Press; 1987.

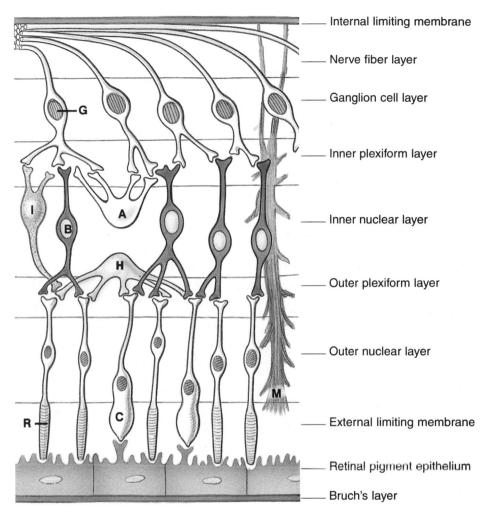

Internal limiting membrane

Nerve fiber layer

Ganglion cell layer

Inner plexiform layer

Inner nuclear layer

Outer plexiform layer

Outer nuclear layer

External limiting membrane

Retinal pigment epithelium

Bruch's layer

FIG III-31—Schematic diagram of cell types and histologic layers in the human retina. The basic relationship between rod (*R*) and cone (*C*) photoreceptors as well as bipolar (*B*), horizontal (*H*), amacrine (*A*), inner plexiform cell (*I*), and ganglion (*G*) neurons is depicted. Note that the Müller's cell (*M*) extends almost the thickness of the retina; the apical processes of Müller's cells form the external limiting membrane while the foot processes of Müller's cells partially form the internal limiting membrane. (Illustration by Christine Gralapp.)

Glial elements *Müller cells,* or fibers, extend vertically from the external limiting membrane inward to the internal limiting membrane. The nucleus in these cells is located in the inner nuclear layer. Müller cells provide structural support and nutrition to the retina together with the other glial elements: fibrous and protoplasmic astrocytes, microglia, and oligodendrocytes that are evident around myelinated nerve fibers of the retina.

FIG III-32—Scanning electron micrograph of the retinal layers diagrammed in Fig III-31, but oriented 180° in the anatomical position with the photoreceptors at the top. (*OS*) Outer segments of photoreceptors; (*IS*) inner segments of photoreceptors; (*OLM*) outer limiting membrane; (*RCB*) rod cell bodies; (*ERF*) external rod fibers (dendrites); (*IRF*) internal rod fibers (axons); (*OPL*) outer plexiform layer; (*MC*) Müller's cell; (*INL*) inner nuclear layer; (*BN*) bipolar cell nuclei; (*) indentation in Müller's cell left by bipolar cells and ganglion cells after removal during tissue processing; (*IPL*) inner plexiform layer; (*GC*) ganglion cell. (Reproduced by permission from Kessel RG, Kardon RH. *Tissues and Organs: A Text-Atlas of Scanning Electron Microscopy.* New York: WH Freeman Co; 1979).

Recent studies have provided further evidence for the important role that Müller cells play in retinal development and metabolism. Immunohistochemistry has shown the presence of cellular retinaldehyde-binding proteins, glutamine, taurine, and glutamine synthetase in these cells. They have also been shown to be involved in the degradation of the neurotransmitter gamma-aminobutyric acid. The presence of messenger RNA coding for carbonic ahydrase II implies that these cells also play an important role in buffering carbon dioxide liberated into the extracellular space by neurosensory elements of the retina. The production of insulin and growth factors by these cells may also play an important role in retinal metabolism.

Tripathi RC, Tripathi BJ. The retina. In: Bron AJ, Tripathi RC, Tripathi BJ, eds. *Wolff's Anatomy of the Eye and Orbit.* 8th ed. London: Chapman and Hall; 1997.

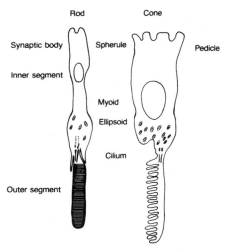

FIG III-33—Rod and cone photoreceptor cells. (Illustration by Thomas A. Weingeist, PhD, MD.)

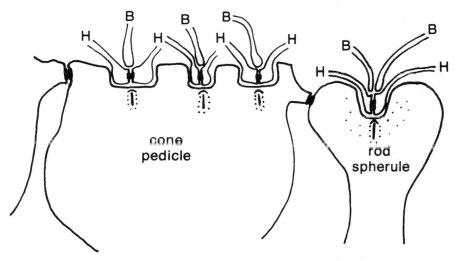

FIG III-34—Synaptic bodies: cone pedicle, rod spherule; (*H*) horizontal cell process; (*B*) bipolar cell process. (Illustration by Thomas A. Weingeist, PhD, MD.)

Vascular elements The inner portion of the retina is perfused by branches of the central retinal artery. In 30% of eyes and 50% of individuals, a cilioretinal artery also supplies part of the inner retina. A cilioretinal artery contributes to some portion of the macular circulation in approximately 15% of individuals, but it may supply any portion of the retina.

Justice J Jr, Lehman RP. Cilioretinal arteries: A study based on review of stereo fundus photographs and fluorescein angiographic findings. *Arch Ophthalmol.* 1976;94:1355–1358.

The retinal blood vessels are analogous to the cerebral blood vessels because they are responsible for maintenance of the inner blood–retinal barrier. This physiologic barrier appears to be the single layer of nonfenestrated *endothelial cells* with tight junctions that are impervious to tracer substances such as fluorescein and horseradish peroxidase. A *basal lamina* covers the outer surface of the endothelium. Within the basement membrane is an interrupted layer of *pericytes,* or mural cells, surrounded by their own basement membrane material.

Müller cells and other glial elements are generally attached to the basal lamina of retinal blood vessels. Retinal blood vessels lack an internal elastic lamina and the continuous layer of smooth muscle cells of other vessels in the body. Smooth muscle cells are occasionally present in vessels near the optic nerve head. They become a more discontinuous layer as the retinal arterioles pass farther out to the peripheral retina. The retinal blood vessels do not ordinarily extend deeper than the middle limiting membrane. Where venules and arterioles cross, they share a common basement membrane. Venous occlusive disorders commonly occur at an arteriovenous (AV) crossing (Fig III-35).

Hogan MJ, Feeney L. The ultrastructure of the retinal blood vessels. I: The large vessels. *J Ultrastruc Res.* 1963;9:10–28.

Hogan MJ, Feeney L. The ultrastructure of the retinal blood vessels. II: The small vessels. *J Ultrastruc Res.* 1963;9:29–46.

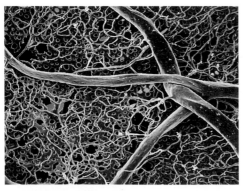 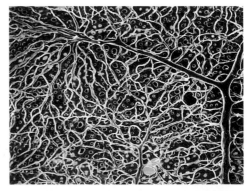

FIG III-35—Scanning electron micrographs of vascular cast of inner retinal circulation. *Left,* An arteriovenous crossing is seen with intervening capillary plexus and underlying choriocapillaris. *Right,* End arteriole is seen supplying the inner retinal capillary plexus.

Stratification of the Retina

The retina can be subdivided into several horizontal layers, as already shown in Figures III-31 and III-32.

The *external limiting membrane* (ELM), or outer membrane, is formed by the attachment sites of adjacent photoreceptors and Müller cells. The ELM is therefore not a true membrane. In the peripheral retina the ELM fuses with the pigment epithelium at the ora serrata. It is highly fenestrated.

The *outer plexiform layer* (OPL) is made up of the interconnections between the photoreceptor synaptic bodies and the horizontal and bipolar cells. The outer plexiform layer is thicker and more fibrous in the macular region, because the axons of the rods and cones become longer and more oblique as they deviate from the fovea. The OPL in this region is known as the *fiber layer of Henle.* At the edge of the foveola, it lies almost parallel with the internal limiting membrane. Accumulation of lipid and other blood products within the fiber layer of Henle accounts for the star pattern observed ophthalmoscopically in some cases of systemic hypertension.

The *inner nuclear layer* (INL) contains nuclei of bipolar, Müller, horizontal, and amacrine cells.

The *middle limiting membrane* (MLM) is formed by a zone of desmosome-like attachments in the region of the synaptic bodies of the photoreceptor cells. It is not a true membrane. The retinal blood vessels ordinarily do not extend beyond the middle limiting membrane.

The *inner plexiform layer* (IPL) consists of axons of the bipolar and amacrine cells and dendrites of the ganglion cells and their synapses.

The *ganglion cell layer* (GCL) is made up of the cell bodies of the ganglion cells that lie near the inner surface of the retina.

The *nerve fiber layer* (NFL) is formed by axons of the ganglion cells. Normally, they do not become myelinated until after they pass through the lamina cribrosa of the optic nerve.

The *internal limiting membrane* (ILM) is also not a true membrane. It is formed by the footplates of the Müller cells and attachments to the basal lamina. The basal lamina of the retina is smooth on the vitreal side but appears undulating on the retinal side where it follows the contour of the Müller cells. The thickness of the basement membrane is variable.

Foos RY. Vitreoretinal juncture: topographical variations. *Invest Ophthalmol.* 1972; 11:801–808.

The overall direction of cells and their processes in the retina is perpendicular to the plane of the RPE in the middle and outer layers but parallel to the retinal surface in the inner layers. For this reason deposits of blood or exudates tend to form round blots in the outer layers where small capillaries are found and linear or flame-shaped patterns if they occur in the nerve fiber layer. At the fovea the outer layers also tend to be parallel to the surface (Henle's layer). As a result, radial or star-shaped patterns may arise when these extracellular spaces are filled with foreign materials.

Macula

The terms macula lutea, macula, posterior pole, area centralis, fovea, and foveola have created confusion among both anatomists and clinicians. Clinical retina specialists tend to regard the *macula* as the area within the temporal vascular arcades. Histologically, it is the region where more than one layer of ganglion cell nuclei can be found (Figs III-36, III-37).

> Orth DH, Fine BS, Fagman W, et al. Clarification of foveomacular nomenclature and grid for quantitation of macular disorders. *Trans Am Acad Ophthalmol Otolaryngol.* 1977;83:506–514.

The description *macula lutea,* which means small yellow spot, is based on the gross anatomic appearance of the central retina in dissected cadaver eyes. The exact chemical composition and the location of the yellow pigment have been subjects of controversy.

Quantitative analysis of the macular pigment from human donor eyes, using high-performance liquid chromatography, has identified two major pigments: zeaxanthin and lutein. In 90% of eyes studied zeaxanthin was dominant; in the remaining 10% lutein was dominant. The proportion of these two pigments has not been found to change appreciably with age. However, the lutein:zeaxanthin ratio does appear to correlate with distance from the fovea (1:2.4 in the central 0.25 mm and greater than 2:1 in the periphery at 8.7–12.2 mm). This variation in pigment ratio appears to correspond to the rod:cone ratio. Lutein is more concentrated in rod-dense areas of retina, and zeaxanthin in cone-dense areas. Lipofuscin granules, which are known to be yellowish in color, have been observed by electron microscopy in the cytoplasm of ganglion cells in the perifoveal region.

> Bone RA, Landrum JT, Fernandez L, et al. Analysis of the macular pigment by HPLC: retinal distribution and age study. *Invest Ophthalmol Vis Sci.* 1988;29:843–849.

> Nussbaum JJ, Pruett RC, Delori FC. Historic perspectives. Macular yellow pigment. The first 200 years. *Retina.* 1982;1:296–310.

The *fovea* is a concave central retinal depression approximately 1.5 mm in diameter, comparable in size to the diameter of the optic nerve head (Fig III-37). Its margins are clinically inexact, but in younger subjects it is evident ophthalmoscopically as an elliptical light reflex that arises from the slope of the thickened internal limiting membrane of the retina. From this point inward the basal lamina rapidly decreases in thickness as it dives down the slopes of the fovea toward the depths of the foveola, where it is barely visible even by electron microscopy.

The masking of choroidal fluorescence observed in the macula during fundus fluorescein angiography is caused in part by xanthophyll pigment as well as the increased pigmentation of the RPE of the fovea, rather than to any peculiarity in the structure or perfusion of the choroidal vessels.

The *foveola* is a central depression within the fovea. Its center is located approximately 4.0 mm temporal and 0.8 mm inferior to the center of the optic disc. It is approximately 0.35 mm across and 0.10 mm in thickness at the floor, or *umbo*. The borders of the foveola merge imperceptibly with the fovea. The nuclei of the photoreceptor cells in the region of the foveola bow forward toward the internal limiting membrane to form the fovea externa. Only photoreceptors, glial cells, and

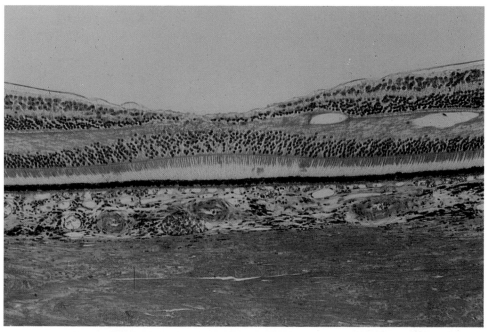

FIG III-36—Light micrograph of the macula. Compare with Figure III-37. (Photograph courtesy of Thomas A. Weingeist, PhD, MD.)

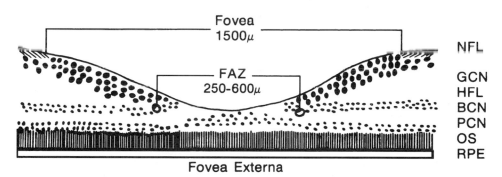

FIG III-37—Fovea, foveal avascular zone, and foveola. (*FAZ*) Foveal avascular zone; (*NFL*) nerve fiber layer; (*GCN*) ganglion cell nuclei; (*HFL*) fiber layer of Henle; (*BCN*) bipolar cell nuclei; (*PCN*) photoreceptor cell nuclei; (*OS*) outer segments; (*RPE*) retinal pigment epithelium. (Illustration by Thomas A. Weingeist, PhD, MD.)

Müller cells are usually present in this area. Occasionally, ganglion cell nuclei may also be observed by light microscopy just below the internal limiting membrane.

The photoreceptor layer of the foveola is made up entirely of cones, which accounts for the fact that this small area is responsible for the most acute vision. The foveal cones resemble rods in shape, but they possess all the cytologic characteristics of extramacular cones. The outer segments are oriented parallel to the visual axis and perpendicular to the plane of the RPE. By contrast, the peripheral photoreceptor cell outer segments are tilted toward the entrance pupil.

The *foveal avascular zone* (FAZ), also referred to as the capillary-free zone (Fig III-38), has become an important clinical landmark in the treatment of subretinal neovascular membranes by laser photocoagulation. Its location is approximately equal to the foveola, and its appearance in fundus fluorescein angiograms is highly variable. The diameter of the FAZ varies from 250 to 600 μm or more, and in many instances a truly avascular or capillary-free zone cannot be identified.

Bird AC, Weale RA. On the retinal vasculature of the human fovea. *Exp Eye Res.* 1974;19:409–417.

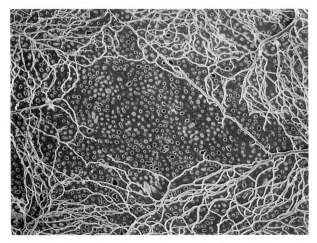

FIG III-38—Scanning electron micrograph of a retinal vascular cast at the fovea showing the foveal avascular zone and underlying choriocapillaris.

Ora Serrata

The ora serrata marks the boundary between the retina and the pars plana. Its distance from Schwalbe's line, or the limbus, is normally between 5.75 mm nasally and 6.50 mm temporally. In myopia the distance is greater, and in hyperopia it is less. Bruch's membrane extends anterior to the ora serrata but is modified as a result of the absence of the choriocapillaris in the ciliary body.

The diameter of the eye at the ora serrata is 20 mm and the circumference 63 mm, compared to a diameter of 24 mm and a circumference of 75 mm at the equator. Topographically, the ora serrata is relatively smooth temporally with a serrated appearance nasally. Retinal blood vessels end in loops before reaching the ora serrata. They do not enter the ciliary body or choroid.

The ora serrata is in a watershed zone between the anterior and posterior vascular system, which may explain in part why peripheral retinal degeneration is relatively common. The peripheral retina in the region of the ora serrata is markedly attenuated. The photoreceptors are malformed and the overlying retina frequently appears cystic in paraffin sections (Blessig-Iwanoff cysts) (Fig III-39).

Vitreous

The vitreous cavity occupies four fifths of the volume of the globe. The transparent vitreous humor plays an important role in the metabolism of the intraocular tissues because it provides a passageway for metabolites used by the lens, the ciliary body, and the retina. It weighs approximately 4.0 g and its volume is close to 4.0 ml. Although it has a gel-like structure, the vitreous consists of 99% water, so the term vitreous swelling is a misnomer. Its viscosity is approximately twice that of water, mainly because of the presence of the mucopolysaccharide hyaluronic acid (Fig III-40).

At the ultrastructural level, fine collagen fibrils and cells have been identified in the vitreous. The true origin and function of these cells is unknown. They have been termed hyalocytes and probably represent modified histiocytes, glial cells, or fibroblasts. The fibrils at the vitreous base merge with the basal lamina of the nonpigmented epithelium of the pars plana and the internal limiting membrane of the retina.

Sebag J, Balazs EA. Morphology and ultrastructure of human vitreous fibers. *Invest Ophthalmol Vis Sci.* 1989;30:1867–1871.

The vitreous adheres to the retina peripherally at the vitreous base. The anterior vitreous base extends 2.0 mm anterior to the ora serrata, and the posterior vitreous base approximately 4.0 mm posterior to the ora serrata. Additional attachments exist at the disc margin, in the perifoveal region, and onto the posterior lens capsule. The potential spaces formed by other sites of vitreous condensation and attachment sport the names of numerous anatomists: space of Berger, area of Martegiani, Cloquet's canal, and Weiger's ligament. Separation of the vitreous from the inner retina

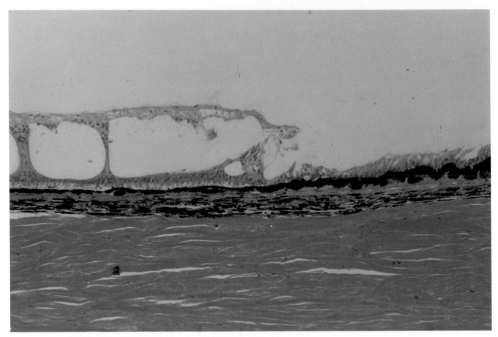

FIG III-39—Ora serrata. Note the malformed appearance of the peripheral retina and the cystic changes at the junction between the pars plana and the retina (H&E ×32). (Photograph courtesy of Thomas A. Weingeist, PhD, MD.)

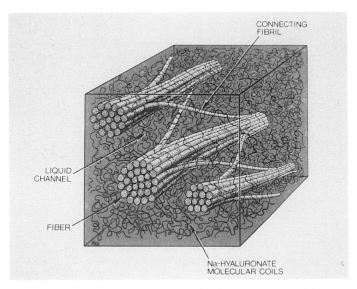

FIG III-40—Three-dimensional depiction of the molecular organization of the vitreous, showing the dissociation between hyaluronic acid molecules and collagen fibrils. The fibrils are packed into bundles, and the hyaluronic acid forms molecular "coils" that fill the intervening spaces to provide channels of liquid vitreous. (Reproduced by permission from Sebag J, Balazs EA. Morphology and ultrastructure of human vitreous fibers. *Invest Ophthalmol Vis Sci.* 1989;30:1867–1871.)

(posterior vitreous detachment, Fig III-41) proceeds with age and is the most common inciting event associated with rhegmatogenous retinal detachment (Figs III-42 to III-44).

Foos RY. Posterior vitreous detachment. *Trans Am Acad Ophthalmol Otolaryngol.* 1972;76:480–497.

Michels RG, Wilkenson CP, Rice TA, eds. *Retinal Detachment.* St Louis: Mosby; 1990.

Sebag J. *The Vitreous: Structure, Function, and Pathobiology.* New York: Springer-Verlag; 1989.

Tolentino FL, Schepens CL, Freeman HM. *Vitreoretinal Disorders: Diagnosis and Management.* Philadelphia: Saunders; 1976:130–154.

During embryonic development, regression of the hyaloid vasculature results in the formation of an S-shaped channel (Cloquet's canal), which passes sinuously from a point slightly nasal to the posterior pole of the lens to the margin of the optic nerve head. Remnants of this fetal vasculature may be observed clinically in the adult (Mittendorf's dot, vascular loops, and Bergmeister's papilla).

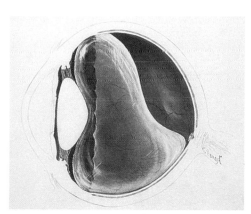

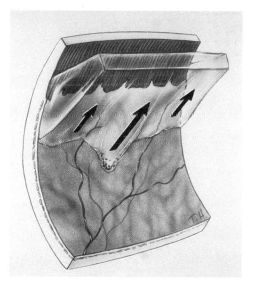

FIG III-41—Typical posterior vitreous detachment. The cortical vitreous initially separates from the retina in the posterior pole and the superior quadrants. The detachment may then progress farther anteriorly until reaching the posterior margin of the vitreous base in the inferior quadrants. (Reproduced by permission from Michels RG, Wilkenson CP, Rice TA, eds. *Retinal Detachment.* St Louis: Mosby; 1990.)

FIG III-42—Localized posterior extension of the vitreous base with firm underlying area of vitreoretinal attachment may result in greater traction in that area (large arrow) than along the adjacent vitreous base (smaller arrows). (Reproduced by permission from Michels RG, Wilkenson CP, Rice TA, eds. *Retinal Detachment.* St Louis: Mosby; 1990.)

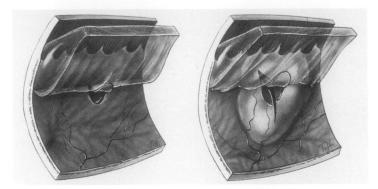

FIG III-43—*Left,* Traction from the posterior vitreous surface on a site of firm vitreoretinal attachment is the usual mechanism causing a retinal break. *Right,* Persistent traction on the flap of the retinal tear and fluid currents in the vitreous cavity contribute to retinal detachment. (Reproduced by permission from Michels RG, Wilkenson CP, Rice TA, eds. *Retinal Detachment.* St Louis: Mosby; 1990.)

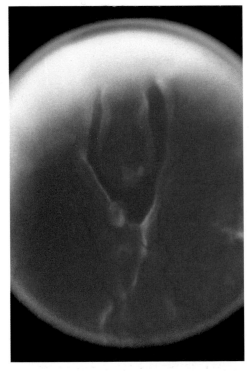

FIG III-44—Fundus photo of a flap retinal tear with associated retinal detachment. (Photograph courtesy of James Folk, MD.)

CHAPTER IV

Cranial Nerves: Central and Peripheral Connections

Cranial nerves I–VI are depicted in Figure IV-1 in relationship to the bony canals and the arteries at the base of the skull. The reader may find it useful to refer back to this figure as each of the cranial nerves is discussed individually below. BCSC Section 5, *Neuro-Ophthalmology*, describes the cranial nerves, their function and dysfunction, in detail.

Cranial Nerve I (Olfactory)

Cranial nerve I originates from small olfactory receptors in the mucous membrane of the nose. Unmyelinated CN I fibers pass from these receptors in the nasal cavity through the cribriform plate of the ethmoid bone and enter the ventral surface of the olfactory bulb, where they form the nerve.

 The olfactory tract runs posteriorly from the bulb, beneath the frontal lobe of the brain in a groove or sulcus, and lateral to the gyrus rectus (Fig IV-2). The gyrus rectus forms the anterolateral border of the suprasellar cistern. Meningiomas arising from the arachnoid cells in this area can produce important ophthalmic signs and symptoms associated with loss of olfaction.

Optic Nerve (Cranial Nerve II)

The optic nerve consists of more than 1 million axons that originate in the ganglion cell layer of the retina and extend toward the occipital cortex. The optic nerve may be divided into the following topographic areas:

- Intraocular portion (nerve head) of the optic nerve: optic disc or nerve head, prelaminar, and laminar portions
- Intraorbital portion located within the muscle cone
- Intracanalicular portion located within the optic foramen
- Intracranial portion ending in the optic chiasm

See Table IV-1 for a summary of regional differences; these are illustrated in the magnetic resonance scans shown in Figures IV-3 to IV-5.

 The optic nerve has a similar organization to the white matter of the brain. Developmentally, it is part of the brain, and its fibers are surrounded by glial and not Schwann cell sheaths. The optic nerve varies in length from 35 to 55 mm and averages 40 mm. Part of the intraocular portion of the optic nerve is visible ophthalmoscopically as the optic nerve head. The *optic nerve head* is oval and measures approximately 1.5 mm horizontally and 1.75 mm vertically.

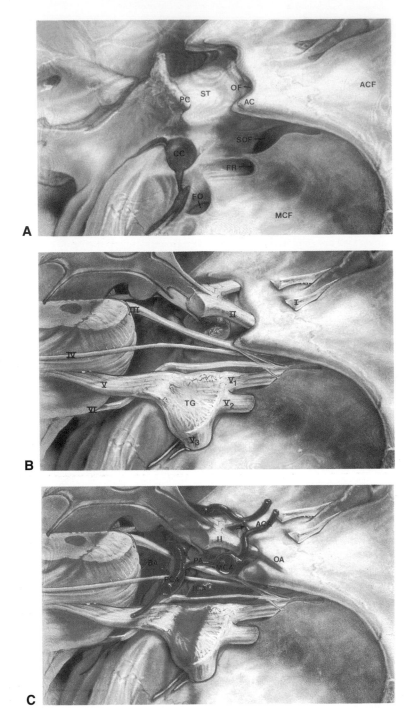

FIG IV-1—View from the right parietal bone looking downward into the skull base showing the relationship between the bony canals (A), nerves (B), and arteries (C) at the base of the skull. The orbits are located to the right out of the picture (the roof of the orbits is just visible). The floor of the right middle cranial fossa is in the lower part. A, (PC) Posterior clinoid; (AC) anterior clinoid; (ST) sella turcica; (OF) optic foramen; (CC) carotid canal; (SOF) superior orbital fissure; (FR) foramen rotundum; (FO) foramen ovale; (ACF) anterior cranial fossa; (MCF) middle cranial fossa. B, (I) olfactory nerve; (II) optic nerve; (III) oculomotor nerve; (IV) trochlear nerve; (V) trigeminal nerve with ophthalmic (V_1), maxillary (V_2), and mandibular (V_3) divisions; (VI) abducens nerve; (TG) trigeminal (Gasserian) ganglion. C, (BA) basilar artery; (PCA) posterior cerebral artery; (PA) posterior communicating artery; (MCA) middle cerebral artery; (ACA) anterior communicating artery; (OA) ophthalmic artery; (arrow) anterior communicating artery; (ICA) internal carotid artery. (Reproduced by permission from Zide BM, Jelks GW, eds. *Surgical Anatomy of the Orbit.* New York: Raven Press; 1985.)

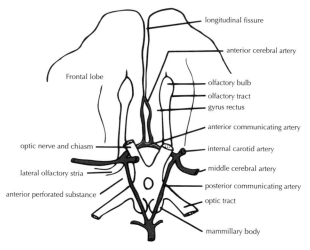

FIG IV-2—Inferior surface of the brain, depicting cranial nerves I and II and surrounding structures. (Illustration by Thomas A. Weingeist, PhD, MD.)

TABLE IV-1

REGIONAL DIFFERENCES IN THE OPTIC NERVE

SEGMENT	LENGTH mm	DIAMETER mm	BLOOD SUPPLY
Intraocular optic disc prelaminar laminar	1.0	1.5 × 1.75	Retinal arterioles Branches of posterior ciliary arteries
Intraorbital	25	3–4	Intraneural branches of central retinal artery; pial branches from CRA and choroid
Intracanalicular	4–10		Ophthalmic artery
Intracranial	10	4–7	Branches of internal carotid and ophthalmic artery

After the axons pass posterior to the lamina cribrosa, they become myelinated. The intraorbital portion of the optic nerve increases to 3 mm in diameter as a result of this myelination of the nerve fibers and the surrounding meningeal sheaths (pia, arachnoid, and dura) (Fig IV-6). The intraorbital portion of the optic nerve is 25–30 mm long. In the primary position, the optic foramen and the insertion of the nerve into the eye are only about 18 mm apart. Thus, the optic nerve runs a sinuous course.

Quigley HA, Addicks EM. Regional differences in the structure of the lamina cribrosa and their relation to glaucomatous optic nerve damage. *Arch Ophthalmol.* 1981; 99:137–143.

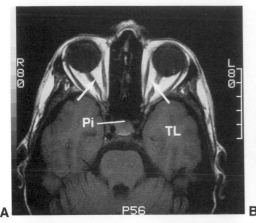
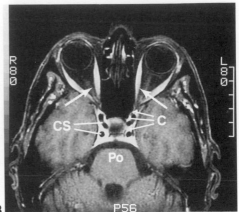

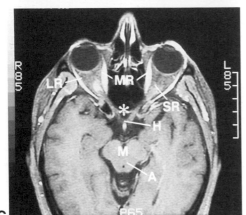

FIG IV-3—Axial MRIs showing course of the optic nerve (*arrows*) as it passes from the orbit to the chiasm (*) (*lower left*). Image at upper left made without fat suppression; ocular muscles and optic nerve appear dark against the bright fat signal in the orbit. Image at upper right made with fat suppression and gadolinium, causing the fat to appear dark with bright, enhancing ocular muscles. Normal optic nerves do not enhance. (*SR*) Superior rectus cut obliquely; (*MR*) medial rectus; (*LR*) lateral rectus; (*C*) carotid arteries; (*CS*) cavernous sinus; (*Po*) pons; (*M*) midbrain; (*A*) aqueduct of Sylvius; (*H*) hypothalamic stalk; (*TL*) temporal lobe; (*Pi*) pituitary.

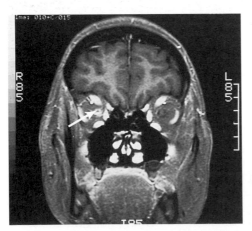
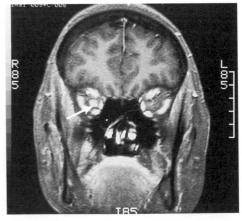

FIG IV-4—Coronal orbital MRI images with fat suppression and gadolinium enhancement in a patient with a right optic nerve meningioma. From left to right, images show successive cuts moving posteriorly. Note the abnormal enhancement of the pia of the right optic nerve (*arrow*) compared to the normal left nerve, and the relationship of the nerve to the extraocular muscles in which enhancement is normal.

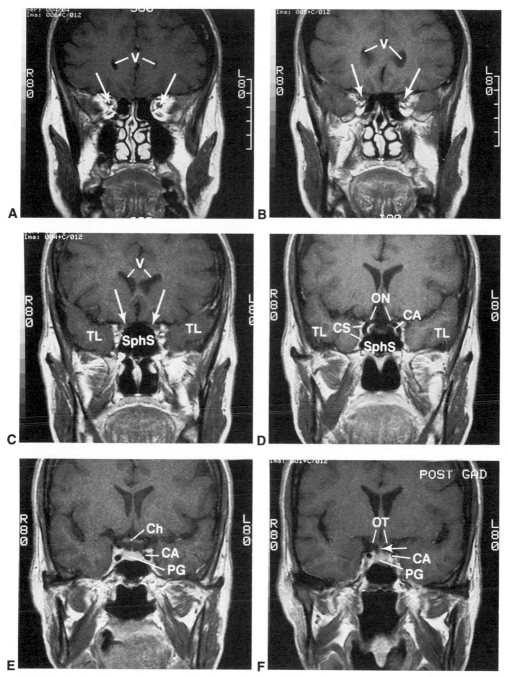

FIG IV-5—Series of coronal MRIs without fat suppression of a normal patient starting at the posterior orbit and moving caudally toward the optic chiasm and optic tracts. The images move more posteriorly from A to F. The white surrounding the central dark optic nerve and peripheral dark muscles represents orbital fat at the orbital apex. A, Posterior orbit at muscle cone; (arrows) optic nerves; (V) ventricles. B, Orbital apex, intracanalicular region. C, Intracranial region; (TL) temporal lobe; (SphS) sphenoid sinus. D, Intracranial portion of optic nerves; (ON) optic nerve; (CS) cavernous sinus; (CA) carotid arteries. E, Plane of section is at chiasm. (Ch) chiasm; (PG) pituitary gland. F, Plane of section is at the optic tracts. (OT) optic tracts; (arrow) infundibulum.

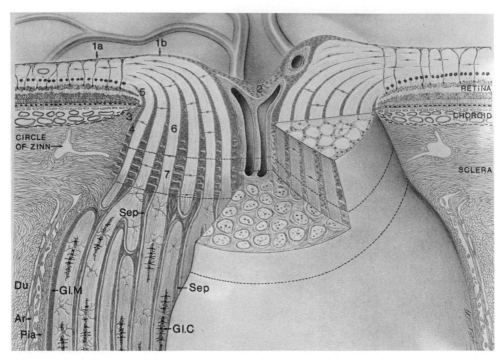

FIG IV-6—Three-dimensional drawing of the intraocular and part of the intraorbital optic nerve. Where the retina terminates at the optic disc edge, the Müller cells (*1a*) are continuous with the astrocytes, forming the *internal limiting membrane of Elschnig* (*1b*). In some specimens Elschnig's membrane is thickened in the central portion of the disc to form the *central meniscus of Kuhnt* (*2*). At the posterior termination of the choroid on the temporal side the border tissue of Elschnig (*3*) lies between the astrocytes surrounding the optic nerve canal (*4*) and the stroma of the choroid. On the nasal side the choroidal stroma is directly adjacent to the astrocytes surrounding the nerve. This collection of astrocytes surrounding the canal is known as the *border tissue of Jacoby,* which is continuous with a similar glial lining called the *intermediary tissue of Kuhnt* (*5*) at the termination of the retina. The nerve fibers of the retina are segregated into approximately 1000 bundles of fascicles by astrocytes (*6*). Upon reaching the lamina cribrosa (*upper dotted line*), the nerve fascicles (*7*) and their surrounding astrocytes are separated from each other by connective tissue. This connective tissue is the cribriform plate, which is an extension of scleral collagen and elastic fibers through the nerve. The external choroid also sends some connective tissue to the anterior part of the lamina. At the external part of the lamina cribrosa (*lower dotted line*), the nerve fibers become myelinated, and columns of oligodendrocytes and a few astrocytes are present within the nerve fascicles. The astrocytes surrounding the fascicles form a thinner layer here than in the laminar and prelaminar portion. The bundles continue to be separated by connective tissue all the way to the chiasm (*Sep*). This connective tissue is derived from the pia mater and is known as the septal tissue. A mantle of astrocytes (*Gl.M*), continuous anteriorly with the border tissue of Jacoby, surrounds the nerve along its orbital course. The dura (*Du*), arachnoid (*Ar*), and pia mater (*Pia*) are shown. The nerve fibers are myelinated. Within the bundles, the cell bodies of astrocytes and oligodendrocytes form a column of nuclei (*Gl.C*). The central retinal vessels are surrounded by a perivascular connective tissue throughout its course in the nerve. This connective tissue blends with the connective tissue of the cribriform plate in the lamina cribrosa; it is called the central supporting connective tissue strand here. (Reproduced by permission from Anderson DR, Hoyt WF. Ultrastructure of intraorbital portion of human and monkey optic nerve. *Arch Ophthalmol.* 1969;82:507.)

Intraocular Portion

The intraocular portion of the optic nerve can be divided into three parts: prelaminar, laminar, and retrolaminar.

Prelaminar portion   The *optic disc,* or optic nerve head, is the principal site of many congenital and acquired ocular diseases, and therefore detailed knowledge of its anatomy is important for the practicing ophthalmologist. The surface of the *prelaminar portion* is visible ophthalmoscopically. It is a 1.5 × 1.75 mm oval with a disc-shaped depression, the *physiologic cup,* located slightly temporal to its geometric center. The main branches of the central retinal artery and vein pass through the center of the cup.

The optic nerve head is made up of nonmyelinated axons from the retinal ganglion cells, blood vessels, and astrocytes that form a thin basal lamina on its inner surface. Myelinated nerve fibers in the retina result from oligodendrocytes that have migrated beyond the lamina cribrosa and have formed a lamellar envelope around ganglion cell axons.

Apple DJ, Rabb MF, Walsh PM. Congenital anomalies of the optic disc. *Surv Ophthalmol.* 1982;27:3–41.

As ganglion cell axons enter the optic nerve head, they become segregated into bundles, or fascicles, by neuroglial cells. The astrocytes that form these continuous circular tubes enclose groups of nerve fibers throughout the intraocular and intraorbital portions of the optic nerve.

When damage occurs to the optic nerve, loss of axons and supporting glial elements can take place, resulting in *cupping* of the optic nerve head, or the formation of a depression, as observed from an ophthalmoscope. This cupping may be the first objective sign of damage from glaucoma. Technologies such as confocal scanning laser ophthalmoscopy and scanning laser polarimetry can help quantify the amount of loss of tissue at the optic nerve head. Such methods may be useful in diagnosing pathologic changes at this location and whether damage has progressed (Figs IV-7, IV-8).

The retinal layers terminate as they approach the edge of the optic disc. The Müller cells that make up the internal limiting membrane, for example, are replaced by astrocytes. The pigment epithelium may extend deeper into the disc, giving rise to an ophthalmoscopically visible pigmented crescent. The relationship of the choroid to the prelaminar portion of the optic nerve accounts in part for the diffusion of fluorescein and the staining of the disc normally observed in late phases of fundus fluorescein angiography. The disc vessels do not leak, but the choroidal capillaries are freely permeable to fluorescein, and the scleral collagen will stain readily with the dye liberated from that level.

The axoplasm of the neurons contains neurofilaments, microtubules, mitochondria, and smooth endoplasmic reticulum.

Laminar portion   The laminar portion of the optic nerve is composed of astrocytes, elastic fibers, collagenous connective tissue from the scleral lamina, and small blood vessels. The lamina cribrosa functions as a scaffold for the optic nerve axons, a point of fixation for the central retinal artery and vein, and a reinforcement of the posterior segment.

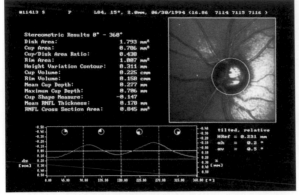
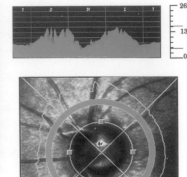
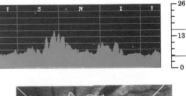

FIG IV-7—A, Confocal scanning laser ophthalmoscopy image (Heidelberg Retinal Tomograph) of the normal optic nerve head. Height variation diagram (bottom) shows normal double hump pattern corresponding to higher nerve fiber layer superiorly and inferiorly. B, Scanning laser polarimetry (Nerve Fiber Analyzer II) image and height variation cross-sectional diagram (top) shows same double hump pattern corresponding to thicker nerve fiber layer in these regions. (Photographs courtesy of Robert Weinreb, MD.)

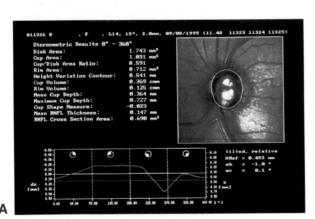
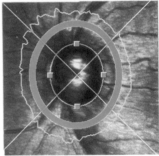

FIG IV-8—A, Confocal scanning laser ophthalmoscopy image (Heidelberg Retinal Tomograph) of the optic nerve from a 58-year-old female patient with glaucoma. Height variation diagram shows depression in the inferotemporal region corresponding to notching of the neuroretinal rim and wedge-shaped nerve fiber layer defect. B, Scanning laser polarimetry (Nerve Fiber Analyzer II) image of the same eye shows similar depression in the infero-temporal region corresponding to thinning of the nerve fiber layer in this region. (Photographs courtesy of Robert Weinreb, MD.)

Retrolaminar portion   The retrolaminar portion extends from the lamina cribrosa to the apex of the orbit. From the lamina cribrosa centrally, the retinal ganglion cells become myelinated, and the cross-sectional diameter of the nerve rapidly increases at the posterior surface of the sclera to approximately 3 mm.

Intraorbital Portion

Annulus of Zinn   The intraorbital portion of the optic nerve lies within the muscle cone. Before passing into the optic canal, the nerve is surrounded by the annulus of Zinn, formed by the origins of the rectus muscles. The superior rectus and the medial rectus partially originate from the sheath of the optic nerve. This connection may explain in part why patients with retrobulbar neuritis complain of pain when moving their eyes.

At the optic canal the dural sheath of the nerve fuses to the periosteum, completely immobilizing the nerve. Blunt trauma, especially to the brow area, is thought to transmit forces to this area, causing a shearing between the dural sheath and its attachment to the periosteum. This, in turn, may cause an interruption to the blood vessels traversing the periosteum and dural sheath of the nerve, producing ischemic nerve damage as a result of the trauma.

Meningeal sheaths: pia, arachnoid, dura mater   The *pial septae,* which originate in the region of the posterior lamina cribrosa, gradually take over and enclose all neurofascicles. The septae continue throughout the intraorbital and intracanalicular portions of the nerve and end in the intracranial portion. They are composed of collagen, elastic tissue, fibroblasts, nerves, and small arterioles and venules (Fig IV-9). They provide mechanical support for the nerve bundles and nutrition to the axons and glial cells. Meningothelial cells cover the pia mater, the innermost layer of the optic nerve sheaths.

The *arachnoid mater* is continuous posteriorly with the subarachnoid space of the brain. Anteriorly, it ends at the level of the lamina cribrosa. It is composed of collagenous tissue, small amounts of elastic tissue, and meningothelial cells, which may give rise to corpora arenacea.

The thick *dura mater* encases the brain and makes up the outer layer of the meningeal sheaths. It is 0.3–0.5 mm thick and consists of dense bundles of collagen and elastic tissue that fuse anteriorly with the outer layers of the sclera.

The meninges of the optic nerve are supplied by sensory nerve fibers, which accounts in part for the pain experienced by patients with retrobulbar neuritis and other inflammatory optic nerve diseases.

Intracanalicular Portion

Within the optic canal the blood supply of the optic nerve is derived from pial vessels originating from the ophthalmic artery. The optic nerve and surrounding arachnoid are tethered to the periosteum of the bony canal within the intracanalicular portion. Blunt trauma, particularly over the eyebrow, can transmit the force of injury to the intracanalicular portion, causing shearing and interruption of the blood supply to the nerve in this area. In addition, optic nerve edema in this area can produce a compartment syndrome, further compromising the function of the optic nerve within the confined space of the optic canal.

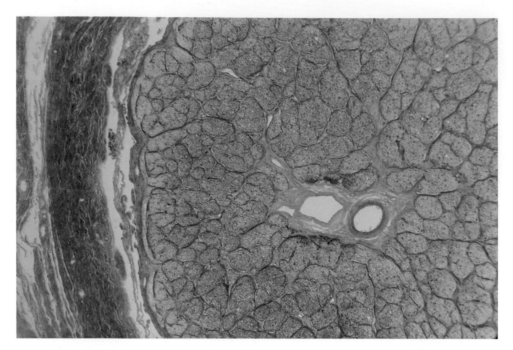

FIG IV-9—Meningeal sheaths. The dura mater, the outer layer, is composed of collagenous connective tissue. The arachnoid sheath is the middle layer made up of fine collagenous fibers arranged in a loose meshwork lined by endothelial cells. The innermost layer, the pia, is made up of fine collagenous and elastic fibers and is highly vascularized. Elements from both the arachnoid and the pia are continuous with the optic nerve septa (Masson trichrome ×64). (Photograph courtesy of Thomas A. Weingeist, PhD, MD.)

Intracranial Portion

After passing through the optic foramen, the two optic nerves lie above the ophthalmic arteries, and above and medial to the internal carotid arteries. The anterior cerebral arteries cross over them and are joined by the anterior communicating artery, which completes the anterior portion of the circle of Willis. The optic nerves then pass posteriorly over the cavernous sinus to join in the optic chiasm. The chiasm then divides into the right and left optic tracts, right and left lateral geniculate bodies, and right and left visual radiations that end in the primary visual cortex. Lesions at different locations along the visual pathway from anterior to posterior can produce characteristic visual field defects (Fig IV-10) that help to localize the site of damage.

Chiasm The optic chiasm makes up part of the anterior inferior floor of the third ventricle. It is surrounded by pia and arachnoid and is richly vascularized. The chiasm is approximately 12 mm wide, 8 mm long in the anteroposterior direction, and 4 mm thick. The extramacular fibers from the inferonasal retina cross anteriorly in the chiasm at Wilbrand's knee before passing into the optic tract. Extramacular superonasal fibers cross directly to the opposite tract. Extramacular temporal fibers

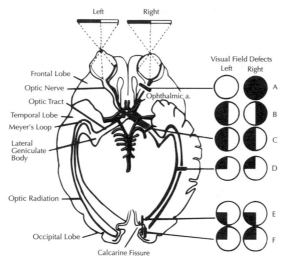

FIG IV-10—The visual pathway and the circle of Willis. (Illustration by Thomas A. Weingeist, PhD, MD.)

remain uncrossed in the chiasm and optic tract. The macular projections are located centrally in the optic nerve and constitute 80%–90% of the total volume of the optic nerve and the chiasmal fibers. The temporal macular fibers pursue a direct course through the chiasm as a bundle of uncrossed fibers. Nasal macular fibers cross in the posterior part of the chiasm. Approximately 53% of the optic nerve fibers are crossed and 47% are uncrossed.

Optic tract   Each optic tract contains ipsilateral temporal and contralateral nasal fibers from the optic nerves (Fig IV-11). Fibers from the upper retinal projections, both crossed and uncrossed, travel medially in the optic tract while lower projections move laterally. The macular fibers adopt a dorsolateral orientation as they course toward the lateral geniculate body.

Lateral geniculate body   The lateral geniculate body, or nucleus, is the synaptic zone for the higher visual projections. It is an oval or caplike structure that receives approximately 70% of the optic tract fibers within its six alternating layers of gray and white matter. Layers 1, 4, and 6 of the lateral geniculate body contain axons from the contralateral optic nerve. Layers 2, 3, and 5 arise from the ipsilateral optic nerve. The six layers, numbered consecutively from below up, give rise to the optic radiations.

Optic radiation   The optic radiation connects the lateral geniculate body with the cortex of the occipital lobe. The fibers of the optic radiation leave the lateral geniculate body and run around the temporal horn of the lateral ventricle, approaching the anterior tip of the temporal lobe (the so-called loop of Meyer). They then sweep backward toward the visual area of the occipital lobe.

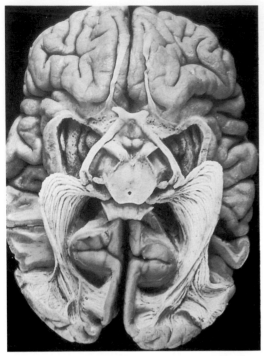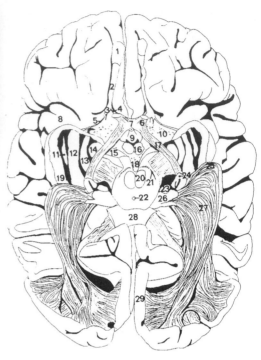

FIG IV-11—Anatomic dissection of the visual radiations. (Reproduced by permission from Gluhbegovic N, Williams TH. *The Human Brain: A Photographic Guide.* Hagerstown, MD: Harper & Row; 1980.)

1. Olfactory bulb
2. Olfactory tract
3. Olfactory trigone
4. Medial olfactory stria
5. Lateral olfactory stria
6. Optic nerve
7. Optic chiasma
8. Limen insulae
9. Tuber cinereum with infundibulum
10. Anterior (rostral) perforated substance
11. Claustrum
12. Putamen
13. Lateral part of globus pallidus
14. Medial part of globus pallidus
15. Basis pedunculi

16. Mamillary body
17. Optic tract
18. Posterior (interpeduncular) perforated substance
19. Cortex of insula
20. Superior cerebellar peduncle
21. Substantia nigra
22. Mesencephalic (cerebral) aqueduct
23. Medial geniculate nucleus
24. Lateral geniculate body
25. Temporal genu of optic radiation
26. Pulvinar of thalamus
27. Sagittal stratum
28. Splenium of corpus callosum
29. Upper lip of calcarine sulcus

Visual cortex The visual cortex, the thinnest area of the human cerebral cortex, has six cellular layers and occupies the superior and inferior lips of the calcarine fissure on the posterior and medial surfaces of the occipital lobes. Macular function is extremely well represented in the visual cortex, and it occupies the most posterior position at the tip of the occipital lobe. The most anterior portion of the calcarine fissure is occupied by contralateral nasal retinal fibers only. The posterior cerebral artery, a branch of the basilar artery, supplies the visual cortex almost exclusively. Anatomical variation in the blood supply to the occipital lobe does exist, however, with the middle cerebral artery making a contribution in some individuals.

Blood Supply of the Optic Nerve

The ophthalmic artery lies below the optic nerve. The central retinal artery and, usually, two long posterior ciliary arteries branch off from the ophthalmic artery once it has entered the muscle cone at the annulus of Zinn.

The blood supply of the optic nerve varies from one segment of the nerve to another. Although the blood supply can show marked variation, a basic pattern has emerged from a multitude of studies.

Hayreh SS. Blood supply and vascular disorders of the optic nerve. In: Cant JS, ed. *The Optic Nerve.* London: Kimpton; 1972:59–67.

Hayreh SS. Structure and blood supply to the optic nerve. In: Heilmann K, Richardson KT, Aulhorn E, eds. *Glaucoma: Conceptions of a Disease.* Stuttgart: Thieme; 1978:78–96.

The prelaminar region and the lamina cribrosa are supplied by branches of the posterior ciliary arteries, while the surface of the optic nerve head is supplied by retinal arterioles, which are branches of the central retinal artery, or by branches of small cilioretinal arteries (Figs IV-12 to IV-14). The posterior ciliary arteries are terminal arteries, and the area where the respective capillary beds from each artery meet has been termed the *watershed zone.* When perfusion pressure drops, the tissue lying within this area is the most vulnerable to ischemia. Consequences can be significant when the entire optic nerve head or a portion of it lies within the watershed zone, as shown by fluorescein angiograms taken during acute anterior ischemic optic neuropathy (Fig IV-15).

The *intraorbital part of the optic nerve* is supplied by intraneural branches of the central retinal artery and multiple recurrent pial branches arising from both the peripapillary choroid and from the central retinal and ophthalmic arteries.

The *intracanalicular portion of the optic nerve* is supplied almost exclusively by the ophthalmic artery.

The *intracranial portion of the optic nerve* is supplied primarily by branches of both the internal carotid artery and the ophthalmic artery.

Central retinal artery and vein The lumen of the central retinal artery is surrounded by nonfenestrated endothelial cells with typical zonulae occludentes like those in retinal vessels. The central retinal artery, however, differs from retinal arterioles, since it contains a fenestrated internal elastic lamina and an outer layer of smooth muscle cells surrounded by a thin basement membrane. The retinal arterioles have no internal elastic lamina and lose the smooth muscle cells shortly after entering the retina. The central retinal vein consists of endothelial cells, a thin basal lamina, and a thick collagenous adventitia.

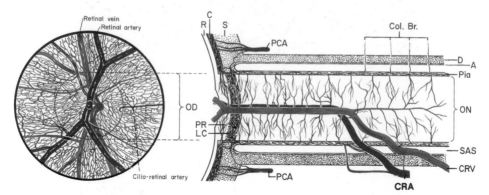

FIG IV-12—Diagrammatic representation of blood supply of the optic nerve head and intraorbital optic nerve. (*A*) Arachnoid; (*C*) choroid; (*CRA*) central retinal artery; (*Col Br*) collateral branches; (*CRV*) central retinal vein; (*D*) dura; (*LC*) lamina cribrosa; (*OD*) optic disc; (*ON*) optic nerve; (*PCA*) posterior ciliary arteries; (*PR*) prelaminar region; (*R*) retina; (*S*) sclera; (*SAS*) subarachnoid space. (Reproduced by permission from Hayreh SS. Anatomy and physiology of the optic nerve head. *Trans Am Acad Ophthalmol Otolaryngol.* 1974;78:240–254.)

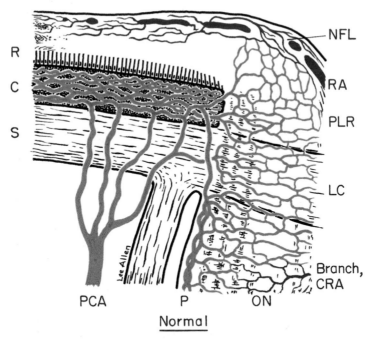

FIG IV-13—Schematic representation of blood supply of the optic nerve head and retrolaminar optic nerve. (*C*) Choroid; (*CRA*) central retinal artery; (*LC*) lamina cribrosa; (*NFL*) surface nerve fiber layer of the disc; (*ON*) optic nerve; (*P*) pia; (*PCA*) posterior ciliary arteries; (*PLR*) prelaminar region; (*R*) retina; (*RA*) retinal arteriole; (*S*) sclera. (Reproduced with permission from Hayreh SS. Structure and blood supply to the optic nerve. In: Heilmann K, Richardson KT, Aulhorn E, eds. *Glaucoma: Conceptions of a Disease.* Stuttgart: Thieme; 1978.)

FIG IV-14—Vascular cast of optic nerve surface capillaries that are supplied by branches of the central retinal artery. The branches of the central retinal artery and vein are shown originating in the center. The retinal surface capillary plexus appears continuous with the optic nerve surface capillaries. In this specimen, the vasculature was filled with a polymer and allowed to harden; the tissue was then digested with alkali; and the cast was viewed by scanning electron microscopy (magnification ×50).

Cranial Nerve III (Oculomotor)

Although cranial nerve III contains only 24,000 fibers, it supplies all the extraocular muscles, except the superior oblique and the lateral rectus. It also carries cholinergic innervation to the pupillary sphincter and the ciliary muscle.

Cranial nerve III arises from a complex group of cells in the rostral midbrain, or mesencephalon, at the level of the superior colliculus. This nuclear complex lies ventral to the periaqueductal gray matter, is immediately rostral to the cranial nerve IV nuclear complex, and is bounded inferolaterally by the medial longitudinal fasciculus (MLF). The CN III nucleus consists of several distinct, large motor cell subnuclei, each of which subserves the extraocular muscle it innervates (Fig IV-16). Except for a single central caudal nucleus that serves both levators, the cell groups are paired. Fibers from the superior rectus cross in the caudal aspect of the nucleus and, therefore, supply the contralateral superior rectus muscles.

The Edinger-Westphal nucleus is cephalad and dorsomedial in location. It provides the parasympathetic preganglionic efferent innervation to the ciliary muscle and pupillary sphincter. The most ventral subnuclei supply the medial rectus muscles. A subnucleus for ocular convergence has been described but not found consistently in primates.

Carpenter MB. *Core Text of Neuroanatomy.* 4th ed. Baltimore: Williams & Wilkins; 1991.

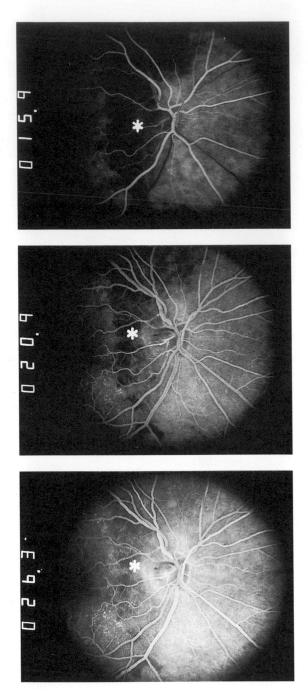

FIG IV-15—Fluorescein angiogram shows sequence of early phase of filling in watershed zone of choroidal filling (*) between the areas of choroid supplied by two posterior ciliary arteries during acute anterior ischemic optic neuropathy. Note that the optic nerve lies within the watershed zone and thus may be prone to ischemic damage from drops in perfusion pressure. The lobular filling pattern of the choroid is also shown.

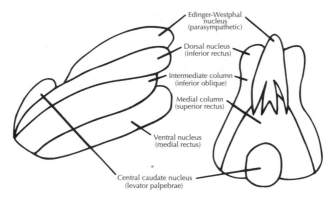

FIG IV-16—Schematic diagram of cranial nerve III (oculomotor) nuclear complex. Muscle innervated by each subnucleus shown in parentheses. (Illustration by Thomas A. Weingeist, PhD, MD.)

The fascicular portion of CN III runs from the nuclear complex ventrally, through the red nucleus, between the medial aspects of the cerebral peduncles and through the corticospinal fibers. It exits in the interpeduncular space. In the sub-arachnoid space, CN III passes below the posterior cerebral artery and above the superior cerebellar artery, the two major branches of the basilar artery (Fig IV-17). The nerve travels forward in the interpeduncular cistern lateral to the posterior communicating artery and penetrates the arachnoid between the free and attached borders of the tentorium cerebelli. Tumors of the oculomotor nerve, such as gliomas, cause an enlargement and thickening that can be easily identified in MRIs (Fig IV-18).

Aneurysms that affect cranial nerve III commonly occur at the junction of the posterior communicating and internal carotid arteries. The nerve pierces the dura on the lateral side of the posterior clinoid process, initially traversing the roof of the cavernous sinus. It runs along the lateral wall of the cavernous sinus and above cranial nerve IV and enters the orbit through the superior orbital fissure.

Cranial nerve III divides into superior and inferior divisions after passing through the annulus of Zinn in the orbit. Alternatively, it may divide within the anterior cavernous sinus. Cranial nerve III maintains a topographical organization even in the midbrain, so lesions almost anywhere along its course may cause a divisional nerve palsy.

Kardon RH, Traynelis VC, Biller J. Inferior division paresis of the oculomotor nerve caused by basilar artery aneurysm. *Cerebrovasc Dis.* 1991;1:171–176.

The superior division of CN III innervates the superior rectus and levator palpebrae muscles. The larger inferior division splits into three branches to supply the medial and inferior rectus muscles and the inferior oblique.

The parasympathetic fibers are located in the periphery of the nerve and course through the same branch that supplies the inferior oblique muscle. After passing through the ciliary ganglion, these fibers emerge as many short ciliary nerves. They

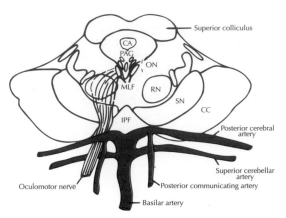

FIG IV-17—Cross section through the midbrain at the level of the third nerve nucleus. Note relationship between cranial nerve III (oculomotor) and posterior cerebral, superior cerebellar, and posterior communicating arteries. (*CA*) Cerebral aqueduct; (*PAG*) periaqueductal gray; (*ON*) oculomotor nucleus; (*MLF*) medial longitudinal fasciculus; (*RN*) red nucleus; (*SN*) substantia nigra; (*CC*) crus cerebri (includes corticospinal tract); (*IPF*) interpeduncular fossa. (Illustration by Thomas A. Weingeist, PhD, MD.)

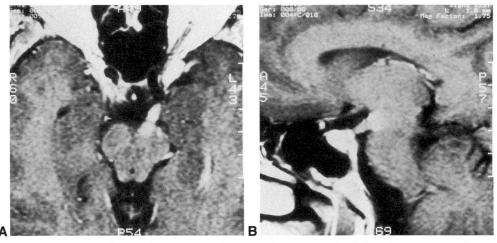

FIG IV-18—*A,* MRI of an axial and *B,* sagittal section of a patient with a left oculomotor nerve glioma, causing a thickening of the nerve as it exits the midbrain. The course of the enlarged nerve can thus be easily discerned.

travel through the sclera and choroid and innervate the pupillary sphincter and the ciliary muscle. The superficial location of these fibers makes them more vulnerable to compression than to ischemia. Pupillary dilation is a sensitive, and commonly an early, sign of compression.

Cranial Nerve IV (Trochlear)

Cranial nerve IV contains the fewest nerve fibers of any cranial nerve, approximately 3400 fibers, but it has the longest intracranial course (75 mm). The nerve nucleus is located in the caudal mesencephalon at the level of the inferior colliculus near the periaqueductal gray matter, ventral to the aqueduct of Sylvius. It is continuous with the caudal end of the CN III nucleus and differs histologically only in the smaller size of its cells. Like the CN III nucleus, it is bounded ventrolaterally by the medial longitudinal fasciculus (Fig IV-19).

The fascicles of CN IV curve dorsocaudally around the periaqueductal gray matter and decussate completely in the anterior medullary velum. The nerves exit the brain stem just beneath the inferior colliculus. Thus, CN IV is the only cranial nerve that is completely decussated and the only motor nerve to exit dorsally from the nervous system. As it curves around the brain stem in the ambient cistern, CN IV runs from beneath the free edge of the tentorium, passes between the posterior cere-

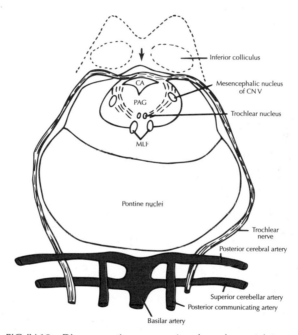

FIG IV-19—Diagrammatic cross section through cranial nerve IV (trochlear) nucleus. Dotted lines show the inferior colliculi (lower midbrain), while remainder of section is through upper pons (no single transverse cut would reveal all of these structures). (*Arrow*) Decussation of fourth nerve fascicles in superior medullary velum; (*CA*) cerebral aqueduct; (*PAG*) periaqueductal or central gray matter; (*MLF*) medial longitudinal fasciculus. (Illustration by Thomas A. Weingeist, PhD, MD.)

bral and superior cerebellar arteries, and then pierces the dura mater to enter the cavernous sinus.

Brodal A. *Neurological Anatomy in Relation to Clinical Medicine.* 3rd ed. New York: Oxford University Press; 1981.

Cranial nerve IV travels beneath CN III and above the ophthalmic division of CN V in the lateral wall of the cavernous sinus. On occasion, communications occur between CN IV, the ophthalmic division of CN V, the sympathetics of the paracarotid plexus, or the lacrimal branch of CN V. These communications are of no known clinical significance. Cranial nerve IV enters the orbit through the superior orbital fissure outside the annulus of Zinn and runs superiorly to innervate the superior oblique muscle. Because of its location outside the muscle cone, CN IV is usually spared following injection of retrobulbar anesthetics.

Brodal A. *Neurological Anatomy in Relation to Clinical Medicine.* 3rd ed. New York: Oxford University Press; 1981:533.

Cranial Nerve V (Trigeminal)

Cranial nerve V, the largest cranial nerve, possesses both sensory and motor divisions. The *sensory* portion subserves the greater part of the scalp, forehead, face, eyelids, eye, lacrimal gland, extraocular muscles, ear, dura mater, and tongue. The *motor* portion innervates the muscles of mastication through branches of the mandibular division.

The CN V nuclear complex extends from the midbrain to the upper cervical segments, often as caudal as C_4. It consists of the following four nuclei, from above downward:

▫ Mesencephalic nucleus

▫ Main sensory nucleus

▫ Spinal nucleus and tract

▫ Motor nucleus located in the pons

Important interconnections exist between the different subdivisions of the fifth nerve sensory nuclei and the reticular formation (Fig IV-20).

Mesencephalic nucleus   This nucleus mediates proprioception and deep sensation from the masticatory, facial, and extraocular muscles. The nucleus extends inferiorly into the posterior pons as far as the main sensory nucleus.

Main sensory nucleus   This nucleus lies in the pons, lateral to the motor nucleus. It is continuous above with the mesencephalic nucleus and below with the spinal nucleus. It receives its input from ascending branches of the sensory root, and it serves light touch from the skin and mucous membranes. The sensory root of cranial nerve V, upon entering the pons, divides into an ascending tract and a descending tract. The former terminates in the main sensory nucleus, and the latter ends in the spinal nucleus.

Spinal nucleus and tract   The spinal nucleus and tract extend through the medulla to C_4. The nucleus receives pain and temperature afferents from the descending spinal tract, which also carries cutaneous components of cranial nerves VII, IX, and

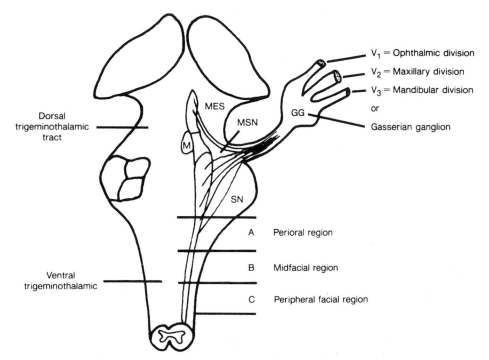

V_1 = Ophthalmic division

V_2 = Maxillary division

V_3 = Mandibular division

or

Gasserian ganglion

Dorsal trigeminothalamic tract

MES

MSN

GG

M

SN

A   Perioral region

B   Midfacial region

Ventral trigeminothalamic

C   Peripheral facial region

FIG IV-20—Cranial nerve V complex (dorsal view of brain stem). (*GG*) Gasserian ganglion; (*MES*) mesencephalic nucleus; (*MSN*) main sensory nucleus; (*M*) motor nucleus; (*SN*) spinal nucleus and tract. *A, B,* and *C* are portions of the caudal spinal nucleus that correspond to concentric areas of the face: (*A*) perioral; (*B*) midface, including eyes; (*C*) peripheral face and scalp. (Illustration by Thomas A. Weingeist, PhD, MD.)

X that serve sensations from the ear and external auditory meatus. The sensory fibers from the ophthalmic division of CN V (V_1) terminate in the most ventral portion of the spinal nucleus and tract. Fibers from the maxillary division (V_2) end in the midportion of the spinal nucleus (in a ventral–dorsal plane), and the fibers from the mandibular division (V_3) end in the dorsal parts of the nucleus.

The cutaneous territory of each of the CN V divisions is represented in the spinal nucleus and tract in a rostral-caudal direction. Fibers from the midfacial region (perioral and perinasal) are thought to terminate most rostrally in the nucleus, while fibers from the peripheral face and scalp end in the caudal portion. The zone between them, the midface, is projected onto the central portion of the nucleus. This "onion-skin" pattern of cutaneous sensation has been derived from clinical studies in patients with damage to the spinal nucleus and tract (Fig IV-21). In other words, damage to the trigeminal sensory nucleus at the level of the brain stem causes bilateral sensory loss in concentric areas of the face with the sensory area surrounding the mouth in the center. When a patient verifies this distribution of sensory loss, the lesion is in the brain stem. Conversely, when the sensory loss follows the peripheral

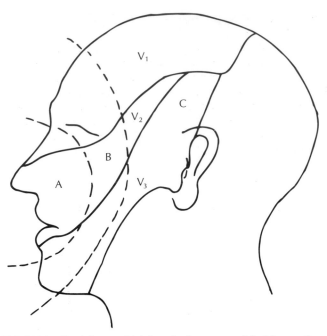

FIG IV-21—Cranial nerve V (trigeminal): pattern of facial sensation. "Onion-skin" distribution from lesions of the trigeminal sensory nucleus in the brain stem (A, B, and C) is delineated by dotted lines. Classes V_1, V_2, and V_3 (solid lines) show the pattern of ophthalmic, maxillary, and mandibular nerves, respectively, from lesions of the peripheral divisions of the fifth nerve. For in-depth discussion, see Brodal A. *Neurological Anatomy in Relation to Clinical Medicine.* 3rd ed. New York: Oxford University Press; 1981:524–529. (Illustration by Thomas A. Weingeist, PhD, MD.)

distribution of the trigeminal sensory divisions (ophthalmic, maxillary, and mandibular), the lesion lies in the fifth nerve after it exits the brain stem.

The axons from the main sensory, the spinal, and portions of the mesencephalic nuclei relay sensory information to higher sensory areas of the brain. The axons cross the midline in the pons and ascend to the thalamus along the ventral and dorsal trigeminothalamic tracts. They terminate in the nerve cells of the ventral posteromedial nucleus of the thalamus. These cells in turn send axons through the internal capsule to the postcentral gyrus of the cerebral cortex.

Motor nucleus This nucleus is located medial to the main sensory nucleus in the pons. It receives fibers from both cerebral hemispheres, the reticular formation, the red nucleus, the tectum, the medial longitudinal fasciculus, and the mesencephalic nucleus. A monosynaptic reflex arc is formed by cells from the mesencephalic nucleus and the motor nucleus. The motor nucleus sends off axons that form the motor root, which eventually supplies the muscles of mastication (pterygoid, masseter, temporalis), the tensor tympani, the tensor veil palatini, the mylohyoid, and the anterior belly of the digastric.

The intracranial fifth nerve emerges from the upper lateral portion of the ventral pons, passes over the petrous apex, forms the Gasserian ganglion, and then divides into three branches. The *Gasserian ganglion,* also referred to as the semilunar, or trigeminal, ganglion, contains the cells of origin of all the fifth nerve sensory axons. The crescent-shaped ganglion occupies a recess in the dura mater posterolateral to the cavernous sinus. This recess, called Meckel's cave, is near the apex of the petrous part of the temporal bone in the middle cranial fossa. Medially, the Gasserian ganglion is in proximity to the internal carotid artery and the posterior cavernous sinus.

Divisions of Cranial Nerve V

The three divisions of cranial nerve V are the ophthalmic (V_1), the maxillary (V_2), and the mandibular (V_3).

CN V_1 The *ophthalmic division* enters the cavernous sinus lateral to the internal carotid artery and courses beneath cranial nerves III and IV. It gives off a tentorial-dural branch within the sinus, which supplies sensation to the cerebral vessels, the dura mater of the anterior fossa, cavernous sinus, sphenoid wing, petrous apex, Meckel's cave, tentorium cerebelli, falx cerebri, and dural venous sinuses. CN V_1 passes into the orbit through the superior orbital fissure, and divides into three branches: frontal, lacrimal, and nasociliary.

The *frontal nerve* divides into the supraorbital and the supratrochlear nerves, which provide sensation for the medial portion of the upper eyelid and the conjunctiva, forehead, scalp, frontal sinuses, and side of the nose.

The *lacrimal nerve* innervates the conjunctiva and skin around the lacrimal gland and carries postganglionic parasympathetic fibers for reflex lacrimation. The pathway for reflex tearing originates in the parasympathetic lacrimal nucleus of the pons, located above the superior salivatory nucleus. Its supranuclear input comes from the cortical, limbic, and hypothalamic systems. Reflex tearing receives input from the fifth nerve sensory nuclei. The preganglionic fibers join the sensory root of cranial nerve VII (the facial nerve), exit the pons with CN VII and VIII, and pass into the internal auditory meatus. They go through the geniculate ganglion in the petrous pyramid and pass forward as the greater superficial petrosal nerve. This nerve runs under the Gasserian ganglion, enters the vidian canal, and joins the deep petrosal nerve to become the vidian nerve. The vidian nerve enters the sphenopalatine ganglion, then passes to the infraorbital nerve of CN V_2, which transmits postganglionic parasympathetic fibers to the lacrimal nerve through the zygomaticotemporal nerve.

The *nasociliary nerve* supplies sensation through nasal branches to the middle and inferior turbinates, septum, lateral nasal wall, and tip of the nose. The infratrochlear branch serves the lacrimal drainage system and the conjunctiva and the skin of the medial canthal region. Long ciliary nerves carry sensory fibers from the ciliary body, the iris, and the cornea and provide the sympathetic innervation to the dilator muscle of the iris. Sensation from the globe is carried by short ciliary nerves. The fifth nerve fibers pass through the ciliary ganglion to join the nasociliary nerve. The ciliary nerves also contain postganglionic parasympathetic fibers from the ganglion to the pupillary sphincter and the ciliary muscle.

CN V_2 The *maxillary division* leaves the Gasserian ganglion to exit the skull through the foramen rotundum, which lies below the superior orbital fissure. CN V_2 courses through the pterygopalatine fossa into the inferior orbital fissure, then runs through the infraorbital canal as the *infraorbital nerve.* After exiting the infraorbital foramen, it divides into an inferior palpebral branch supplying the lower eyelid, a nasal branch for the side of the nose, and a superior labial branch for the upper lip. The teeth, maxillary sinus, roof of the mouth, and soft palate are also innervated by branches of the maxillary division.

CN V_3 The *mandibular division* contains both sensory and motor fibers. It exits the skull through the foramen ovale and provides motor input for the masticatory muscles. Sensation is supplied to the mucosa and skin of the mandible and lower lip, tongue, external ear, and tympanum.

> Williams PL, Warwick R. *Gray's Anatomy.* 38th ed. Edinburgh: Churchill Livingstone; 1995.

Cranial Nerve VI (Abducens)

The nucleus of cranial nerve VI is situated in the floor of the fourth ventricle, beneath the facial colliculus, in the caudal pons. Fibers of CN VII pass over or loop around the sixth nerve nucleus and exit in the cerebellopontine angle. The medial longitudinal fasciculus lies medial to the sixth nerve nucleus. The fascicular portion of the nerve runs ventrally through the paramedian pontine reticular formation (PPRF) and the pyramidal tract and leaves the brain stem in the pontomedullary junction (Fig IV-22).

Cranial nerve VI takes a vertical course along the ventral face of the pons and is crossed by the anterior inferior cerebellar artery. It ascends farther through the subarachnoid space along the surface of the clivus, surrounded by Batson's venous plexus, to perforate the dura mater below the crest of the petrous portion of the temporal bone about 2 cm below the posterior clinoid process. It then passes intradurally through or around the inferior petrosal sinus and beneath the petroclinoid (Gruber's) ligament through Dorello's canal, where it enters the cavernous sinus. In the cavernous sinus CN VI runs below and lateral to the carotid artery and may transiently carry sympathetic fibers from the paracarotid plexus. It passes through the superior orbital fissure within the annulus of Zinn and innervates the lateral rectus muscle on its ocular surface.

> Williams PL, Warwick R. *Gray's Anatomy.* 38th ed. Edinburgh: Churchill Livingstone; 1995.

Cranial Nerve VII (Facial)

Cranial nerve VII is a complex mixed sensory and motor nerve. The motor root contains special visceral efferent fibers that innervate the muscles of facial expression. The so-called sensory root of cranial nerve VII is the *nervus intermedius,* which contains special visceral afferent, general somatic afferent, and general visceral efferent fibers. The special visceral afferent fibers, which convey the sense of taste from the anterior two thirds of the tongue, terminate centrally in the nucleus of the tractus solitarius. The general somatic afferent fibers convey sensation from the external auditory meatus and the retroauricular skin; centrally, they enter the spinal nucleus of CN V. The general visceral efferent fibers provide preganglionic parasympathetic

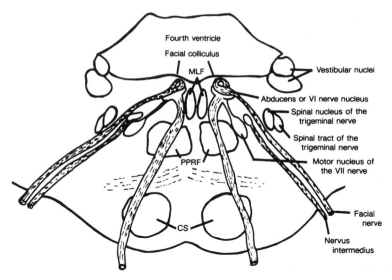

FIG IV-22—Cross section of the pons at the level of the cranial nerve VI (abducens) nucleus. (*MLF*) Medial longitudinal fasciculus; (*PPRF*) pontine paramedian reticular formation; (*CS*) corticospinal tract. (Illustration by Thomas A. Weingeist, PhD, MD.)

innervation by way of the sphenopalatine and submandibular ganglia to the lacrimal, submaxillary, and sublingual glands.

The *motor nucleus* of CN VII is a cigar-shaped column 4 mm in length, located in the caudal third of the pons. It is ventrolateral to the sixth nerve nucleus, ventromedial to the spinal nucleus of CN V, and dorsal to the superior olive. Four distinct subgroups within the nucleus innervate specific facial muscles; the ventral portion of the intermediate group probably supplies axons to the orbicularis oculi. That portion of the nucleus supplying the upper half of the face receives corticobulbar input from both cerebral hemispheres. The lower half of the face is influenced by corticobulbar fibers from the opposite cerebral hemisphere.

Fibers from the motor nucleus course dorsomedially to approach the floor of the fourth ventricle and then ascend immediately dorsal to the sixth nerve nucleus. At the rostral end of the sixth nerve nucleus, the main facial motor fibers arch over its dorsal surface (forming the internal genu of CN VII) and then pass ventrolaterally between the spinal nucleus of the fifth nerve and the seventh nerve nucleus to exit the brain stem at the pontomedullary junction. The bulge formed by the seventh nerve genu in the floor of the fourth ventricle is the facial colliculus (Fig IV-23).

Carpenter MB. *Core Text of Neuroanatomy.* 4th ed. Baltimore: Williams & Wilkins; 1991.

The *sensory nucleus* of CN VII is the rostral portion of the tractus solitarius, sometimes known as the gustatory nucleus. It lies lateral to the motor and parasympathetic nuclei in the caudal pons. Sensations of taste from the anterior two thirds of the tongue are carried by special visceral afferent fibers to this nucleus. The impulses travel along the lingual nerve and chorda tympani and have their cell bodies in

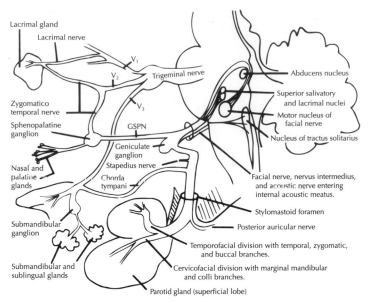

FIG IV-23—Cranial nerve VII (facial) and its components. (*GSPN*) Greater superficial petrosal nerve. (Illustration by Thomas A. Weingeist, PhD, MD.)

the geniculate ganglion. They eventually reach the brain stem through the nervus intermedius.

Cranial nerve VII, the nervus intermedius, and cranial nerve VIII (acoustic) pass together through the lateral pontine cistern in the cerebellopontine angle and enter the internal auditory meatus in a common meningeal sheath. The seventh nerve and the intermedius nerve then enter the fallopian canal, the longest bony canal traversed by any cranial nerve (30 mm).

Cranial nerve VII can be divided into three segments in its course through this canal. After passing anterolaterally for a short distance known as the *labyrinthine segment,* the nerves bend sharply at the geniculate ganglion and are then directed dorsolaterally past the tympanic cavity. This 90° bend, known as the *tympanic segment,* is the external genu of CN VII. Two parasympathetic branches from the superior salivatory and lacrimal nuclei leave the nerve at the tympanic segment: the greater superficial petrosal nerve and a small filament that joins the inferior petrosal nerve.

The third, or *mastoid, segment* of the nerve is directed straight down toward the base of the skull. The stapedius nerve leaves and the chorda tympani joins CN VII in the mastoid segment. The seventh nerve trunk then exits the skull at the stylomastoid foramen and separates into a large temporofacial and a small cervicofacial division between the superficial and deep lobes of the parotid gland. This area of branching is known as the *pes anserinus.*

The *temporofacial division* gives rise to the temporal, zygomatic, and buccal branches, and the *cervicofacial division* is the origin of the marginal mandibular and colli branches. However, numerous anastomoses and branching patterns are seen.

Commonly, the temporal branch supplies the upper half of the orbicularis oculi, while the zygomatic branch supplies the lower half. The frontalis, corrugator supercilii, and pyramidalis muscles are usually innervated by the temporal branch.

The parasympathetic outflow originates in the superior salivatory nucleus and the lacrimal or lacrimopalatonasal nucleus, which lie posterolateral to the motor nucleus. Both probably receive afferent fibers from the hypothalamus. The superior salivatory nucleus also receives input from the olfactory system. The hypothalamic fibers reaching the lacrimal nucleus may mediate emotional tearing, while reflex lacrimation is controlled by afferents from the sensory nuclei of CN V. These preganglionic parasympathetic fibers pass peripherally as part of the nervus intermedius and divide into two groups near the external genu of CN VII. The lacrimal group of fibers passes to the sphenopalatine ganglion on the greater superficial petrosal nerve. The salivatory group of fibers projects through the chorda tympani nerve to the submandibular ganglion.

Postganglionic parasympathetic fibers from the sphenopalatine ganglion innervate the lacrimal gland, the glands of the palate, and the nose. The lacrimal gland parasympathetics are carried in the infraorbital nerve of CN V_2 to the zygomaticotemporal nerve to the lacrimal nerve of CN V_1. Postganglionic fibers from the submandibular gland innervate the submandibular and sublingual salivary glands.

Cavernous Sinus

The cavernous sinus is an interconnected series of venous channels located lateral to the sphenoidal air sinus and the pituitary fossa (Fig IV-24). The cavernous sinus is

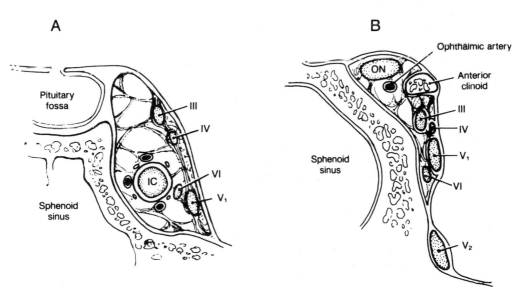

FIG IV-24—Cavernous sinus, coronal sections. *A*, At the level of the pituitary fossa. *B*, At the level of the anterior clinoid process. (*ON*) Optic nerve. (*IC*) Internal carotid artery. (Reproduced by permission from Doxanas MT, Anderson RL. *Clinical Orbital Anatomy.* Baltimore: Williams & Wilkins Co; 1984.)

located just posterior to the orbital apex and lies intracranially. The following structures are located within the venous cavity:

- The internal carotid artery surrounded by the sympathetic carotid plexus
- Cranial nerves III, IV, and VI
- The ophthalmic and maxillary divisions of cranial nerve V

Other Venous Sinuses

The cavernous sinus is only one part of an interconnecting series of venous channels that carry blood away from the brain and drain into the internal jugular veins. Other venous sinuses include the superior sagittal, transverse, straight, sigmoid, and petrosal. The various components of the venous system are depicted in Figure IV-25. Thrombosis in any portion of the venous sinuses can lead to increased venous pressure and may cause intracranial hypertension, which can cause papilledema.

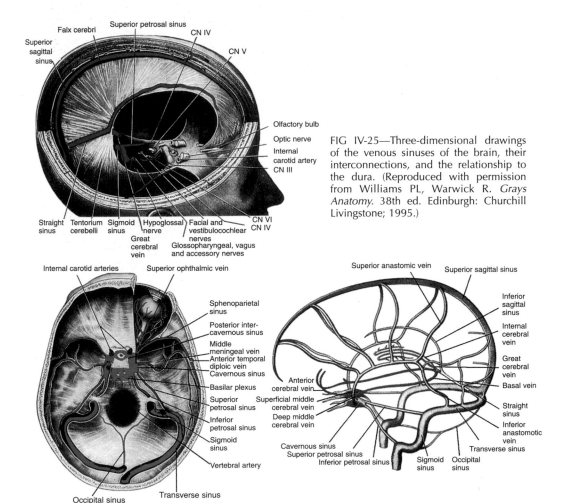

FIG IV-25—Three-dimensional drawings of the venous sinuses of the brain, their interconnections, and the relationship to the dura. (Reproduced with permission from Williams PL, Warwick R. *Grays Anatomy.* 38th ed. Edinburgh: Churchill Livingstone; 1995.)

Circle of Willis

The major arteries supplying the brain are the right and left internal carotid arteries, which distribute blood primarily to the rostral portion of the brain; and the right and left vertebral arteries, which join to form the basilar artery. The basilar artery primarily distributes blood to the brain stem and posterior portion of the brain. These arteries interconnect at the base of the brain at the circle of Willis (Fig IV-26). These interconnections help to provide the distribution of blood to all regions of the brain even when a portion of the system becomes occluded.

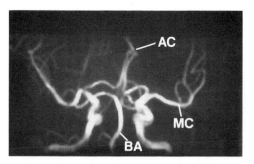 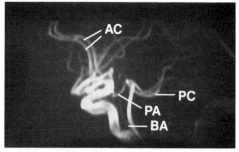

FIG IV-26—*Left,* Magnetic resonance angiogram showing circle of Willis in an anteroposterior view. *Right,* Same patient shown with an oblique view. (*BA*) Basilar artery; (*PA*) posterior communicating artery; (*MC*) middle cerebral artery; (*AC*) anterior cerebral artery; (*PC*) posterior cerebral artery. (Photographs courtesy of T. Talli, MD, and W. Yuh, MD.)

PART 2

EMBRYOLOGY

Glossary

Agenesis   Absence of an organ resulting from failure of its primordium to appear in embryonic development. Aplasia.

Animal cap   Cells of the blastula that originated as a result of regional differences in the fertilized ovum and are destined normally to form epidermis.

Aniridia   Absence of the iris.

Anisocoria   Inequality in diameter of the pupils.

Anlage   Primordium. Primitive tissue from which an organ or part develops (plural, *anlagen*).

Anophthalmos   A developmental defect characterized by absence of the eye.

Aplasia   Lack of development of an organ; frequently used to describe complete suppression or the failure of development of a structure from the embryonic primordium.

Apoptosis   Intrinsically programmed cell death that is characterized by distinctive morphologic changes, especially in the nucleus, and is responsible for physiologic deletion of cells.

Choristoma   A mass of tissue histologically normal for an organ or part of an organ other than the site where it appears.

Coloboma   A fissure of a part or parts of the eye; failure of fusion and subsequent development. May be congenital or acquired.

Cryptophthalmos   A developmental anomaly in which the skin is continuous over the eyeballs without any indication of eyelid formation.

Cyclopia   A developmental anomaly characterized by a single orbital fossa with the globe absent, rudimentary, or single and the nose absent or present as a tubular appendage located above the orbit.

Dermoid   Congenital inclusion of epidermal and associated connective tissue at the line of closure of the fetal cleft.

Dysgenesis   Defective development.

Dysplasia   Abnormal development of tissues or cells with retention of some features resembling normal structures.

Ectoderm   The outermost of the three primary germ layers of the embryo. The epidermis and the epidermal tissues develop from surface ectoderm as the nasal, hair, and skin glands; the nervous system and the external sense organs develop from neuroectoderm. Neural crest cells arise from primitive ectoderm.

Embryogenesis   The earliest stages of development of a new individual from a fertilized ovum.

Evagination   An outpouching of a layer or part. Evagination of the optic anlage forms the optic vesicle.

Fissure   Cleft or groove formed as the optic cup invaginates.

Growth factor   A protein that binds to its receptor and induces up-regulation or down-regulation of specific cell activities.

Homeobox   A sequence of base pairs in the DNA that is very similar in genes of many different species.

Hypertelorism   An abnormal increased distance between two organs.

Hypoplasia   Defective, limited, or incomplete development.

Induction   The stimulatory process whereby one tissue directs a second tissue to develop in a specific direction.

Invagination   The infolding of one part within another; the optic vesicle infolds to form the double-layered optic cup.

Leukoma   A dense white opacity of the cornea.

Mesenchyme   A dispersed population of undifferentiated embryonic cells, stellate-shaped and arranged loosely, that have their embryonic origin from either mesoderm or neural crest cells.

Mesoderm   The middle layer of the three primary germ layers of the embryo, lying between the ectoderm and the endoderm. In the orbit, it gives rise to the vascular endothelium and the myoblasts of the extraocular muscles.

Messenger RNA (mRNA)   Ribonucleic acid that provides the information as triplicate sequences of nucleotides (codons) for the synthesis of protein.

Microphthalmos   A small, disorganized eye.

Nanophthalmos   A rare developmental anomaly in which the eyeballs are abnormally small but are without other deformities.

Neural crest cells   A cellular mass of primitive ectoderm that arises at the peak of the neural folds as they close.

Neural folds   The paired folds, one lying on either side of the neural plate, that form the neural tube.

Neural tube   The epithelial tube that develops from the neural plate and forms the central nervous system of the embryo.

Neurocristopathy   Clinical disorder that results from abnormal induction, proliferation, migration, differentiation, or regression of neural crest cells.

Neuroectoderm   The region of the ectoderm destined to become the neural tube.

Optic cup   The cup-shaped structure of the primitive eye formed by invagination of the optic vesicle.

Optic pits   Indentation of optic primordia at the stage of neural folds.

Optic sulcus   A groove or furrow in the neural plate and folds that is the first identifiable structure destined to become the eye.

Optic vesicle   Saccular structure of the embryonic eye formed by evagination of the optic pit.

Organogenesis   The development or growth of organs; period of development after embryogenesis; begins about the fourth week in ocular development.

Placode   A platelike structure, especially a thickened plate of ectoderm in the early embryo from which an organ, lens, or glands develop.

Pluripotent   The capacity to differentiate into any one of several cell types.

Posterior embryotoxon   A congenital opacity of the margin of the cornea; also called *arcus juvenilis*.

Primordium   The earliest discernible indication during embryonic development of an organ or part. Also called *anlage* or *rudiment*.

Progenitor cell   An ancestral or parent cell.

Somite   One of a pair of mesodermal cell masses situated on either side of the embryonic neural tube.

Synophthalmia   Form of cyclopia in which parts of the two eyes are joined at the midline.

Teratogen   An agent or factor that produces physical defects in the developing embryo.

Teratoma   A true neoplasm made up of various types of tissue, none of which is native to the area in which it occurs.

Tunica vasculosa lentis   The vascular envelope that encloses and nourishes the developing lens of the fetus. Normally, this structure regresses and disappears shortly before birth.

CHAPTER V

Ocular Development

Introduction

Experimental studies conducted during the last three decades have revolutionized our understanding of ocular development. Consequently, the original treatises on the growth and differentiation of the eye have been modified. The classic germ layer theory depicted the epithelium of the cornea, the retina, and the neural components of the uveal tract as derived from ectoderm, and the remainder of the ocular structures from mesoderm.

Although this general schema is still used, it is currently recognized that the embryonic and fetal development of the human eye involves a series of sequential events that include inductive interactions and the morphogenetic movement of cells from distant regions of the embryo. The primary tissues involved in these processes are the head epidermis, neuroectoderm, and mesenchyme. Three elements have been identified as making important, if not pivotal, contributions to the genesis of the eye:

□ Growth factors

□ Homeobox genes

□ Neural crest cells

Each is described separately below, but interaction between these elements is also crucial. Part 3 of this volume, Genetics, also discusses some of the concepts reviewed in chapters V and VI.

Growth Factors

The process of *induction* is mediated by tissue communication by way of macromolecules that act as chemical signals. Growth factors are now known to be active in the earliest stages of embryonic development. They are a class of trophic substances that participate in the control of normal development by modulating the migration, proliferation, and differentiation of cells. These molecules act at nanomolar concentrations by binding with high affinity to specific receptor sites localized in the plasma membrane of the target cell.

The embryonic genome is not transcribed until the stage of midblastula transition, which takes place several hours after fertilization. The messenger RNAs (mRNAs) for the growth factors involved in the earliest aspects of the growth and differentiation of the fertilized egg are endogenous and are supplied from maternal sources until the embryonic tissues develop the capacity to synthesize them de novo. These growth factors include

□ Fibroblast growth factor (FGF)

□ Transforming growth factor–beta (TGF-β)

□ Insulin-like growth factor–I (IGF-I)

Experimental studies have revealed that exposure of cells of the animal cap to FGF induces their differentiation into posterior mesoderm that is destined to form tissues of the caudal region. However, TGF-β induces animal cap cells to differentiate into mesoderm that forms structures in the head region, including the eye.

Growth factors also regulate the levels of expression of homeobox genes, which function as a mechanism for controlling the establishment of the overall arrangement of the eye as an organ. Visual acuity necessitates a precise spatial arrangement of the tissues of the eye, and it is therefore critical that the homeobox genes be expressed at the appropriate level and time.

Some growth factors, especially TGF-β, have a crucial role in directing the migration and developmental patterns of cranial neural crest cells by influencing the synthesis and degradation of the extracellular matrix. Various components of the extracellular matrix act as morphogenetic factors that facilitate a complex series of integrated tissue interactions, movements, and shape changes, especially during the earliest stages of morphogenesis of the optic vesicle and lens.

Differentiation of the various ocular tissues appears to be controlled, at least in part, by a variety of growth factors. For example, the FGFs induce the neuroectodermal cells that line the inner wall of the optic cup to develop as neural retina and are responsible for certain aspects of lens epithelial differentiation as lens fibers. However, the differentiation of lens epithelial cells immediately anterior to the equator as well as their mitotic activity is promoted by the IGFs. The synergistic action of multiple trophic factors appears to be a significant regulatory tool for initiating cellular activities and for limiting the occurrence of abnormal development.

Tripathi BJ, Tripathi RC, Livingston AM, et al. The role of growth factors in the embryogenesis and differentiation of the eye. *Am J Anat.* 1991;192:442–471.

Homeobox Genes*

Homeobox genes contain a distinctive segment of deoxyribonucleic acid (DNA), 180 base pairs in length, which shows similarity in the sequence of the nucleotides. This region is termed the *homeobox* (from the Greek *homoios* = like, resembling; box = the extent of the conserved sequence). The homeobox encodes an almost identical sequence of approximately 60 amino acids, the *homeodomain,* in the protein products of these genes. Because they control the activity of many subordinate genes, homeobox genes are considered "master" genes. Conserved evolutionarily, these genes are present throughout the plant and animal kingdoms. Individual homeobox genes are identified based on their original characterization in the fruit fly; for example, the paired box, or *PAX,* genes. Homologues of the fruit fly genes are also recognized; for example, the antennapedia genes are designated *HOX* genes in mammals.

The function of homeobox genes is mediated by the homeodomain, which recognizes and binds to specific DNA sequences in the subordinate genes, thereby activating or repressing their expression. Thus, these genes act as transcription factors. On the basis of the pattern of homeobox gene expression, which is restricted both spatially and temporally during the earliest stages of development, the vertebrate

---

* Because many genes contain a conserved sequence of nucleotides or homeobox region, those responsible for the segmental development of the embryo are more correctly referred to as *homeotic* genes. However, the terms *homeobox* and *homeotic* are used interchangeably in the literature.

embryo can be subdivided anteriorly to posteriorly into fields of cells that have different developmental capacities. This organizational plan precedes the formation of any specific organ or structures. The fact that homeobox genes are located on the chromosomes in the same order as they are expressed along the anteroposterior axis of the embryo indicates that they are activated sequentially.

The same homeobox genes are expressed again later in embryogenesis, apparently to specify the identity of a particular cell. Experimental evidence suggests that homeobox genes are activated not only by growth factors, especially FGFs and TGF-βs, but also by retinoic acid.

Recent investigations in several vertebrate species have revealed the involvement of specific homeobox genes in the development of the eye. For example, expression of the PAX6 gene marks the location of the lens-competent region in the head ectoderm before the optic vesicle can be recognized. During the early stages of eye development, two HOX genes are expressed with a distinct spatial and temporal relationship: expression of the HOX8.1 gene occurs in the surface ectoderm in a region destined to form the corneal epithelium and in the optic vesicle where the retina will differentiate before invagination occurs. HOX7.1, which is expressed after the formation of the optic cup, marks the region of the future ciliary body. Subsequently, the PAX6 gene has a role in the expression of tissue-specific genes in the eye; for example, it induces both differentiation of progenitor cells into neurons in the retina and the expression of zeta crystallins in lens epithelial cells.

Mutations in homeobox genes are known to produce congenital ocular abnormalities. Patients with aniridia or Peters anomaly have a mutation in the PAX6 gene, and a mutation in PAX2 can produce coloboma of the optic nerve. Often the mutation results from the deletion or insertion of a single nucleotide that causes a frameshift in the coding region. Exposure of the developing human embryo to excess amounts of retinoic acid causes malformation of the retina and optic nerve and probably reflects the anomalous involvement of homeobox genes. Future investigations will identify additional roles for homeobox genes in normal development and their aberrant expression in abnormal ocular development.

Grindley JC, Davidson DR, Hill RE. The role of Pax-6 in eye and nasal development. *Development.* 1995;121:1433–1442.

Li HS, Yang JM, Jacobson RD, et al. Pax-6 is first expressed in a region of ectoderm anterior to the early neural plate: implications for stepwise determination of the lens. *Dev Biol.* 1994;162:181–194.

Matsuo T. The genes involved in the morphogenesis of the eye. *Jpn J Ophthalmol.* 1993;37:215–251.

Monaghan AP, Davidson DR, Sime C, et al. The Msh-like homeobox genes define domains in the developing vertebrate eye. *Development.* 1991;112:1053–1061.

Sanyanusin P, Schimmenti LA, McNoe LA, et al. Mutation of the PAX2 gene in a family with optic nerve colobomas, renal anomalies and vesicoureteral reflux. *Nat Genet.* 1995;9:358–363.

Neural Crest Cells

Neural crest cells arise from neuroectoderm located at the crest of the neural folds at about the time the folds fuse to form the neural tube. They are a transient population of cells: after they migrate to different regions of the embryo, differentiation occurs. The contribution made by crest cells to the tissues of the developing embryo was recognized in experimental studies. Grafts of neural crest primordia or paraxial mesoderm from Japanese quail were transplanted into host chick embryos, or vice versa. The presence of a heterochromatin condensation in the cell nucleus of the quail, which replicates with each mitotic division, provided a marker not possessed by the chick cells and allowed the origins of specific tissues to be identified throughout development. Studies in mice using tritiated thymidine as a nuclear marker have confirmed the observations in chick/quail chimeras. Although exact labeling is not possible in human embryos, the similarity in the basic developmental patterns in vertebrates supports the conclusion that comparable events occur.

Most mesenchymal cells of the facial primordia are derived from the neural crest. Crest cells do not arise from the region of the forebrain. However, neural crest cells from the diencephalic, mesencephalic, and rhombencephalic regions migrate anteriorly along the dorsum of the embryo. Crest cells that originate from the posterior midbrain form the maxillary primordia, and those from the hindbrain form the mandibular primordia. The crest cells from the diencephalon contribute to the tissue of the frontonasal mass; later they are joined by cells from the anterior midbrain that migrate to and settle around the optic vesicles. The anterior flexure of the embryo aids the migration of neural crest cells ventrad and cephalad.

The extracellular matrix has a significant role in directing the migration of neural crest cells. Molecules such as fibronectin promote migration, whereas others such as proteoglycans are inhibitory. The positive and negative cues that the crest cells encounter during migration appear to guide the cells along the correct pathways to the appropriate destination. Because the synthesis and secretion of extracellular matrix molecules such as collagen, fibronectin, and proteoglycans can be influenced by growth factors, especially TGF-β, cytokines also have a role in regulating the migration of crest cells.

Early in development, neural crest cells are pluripotent, and local factors have a considerable influence in their final differentiation. Crest cells from the hindbrain normally form the connective tissue of the visceral arch and contribute to the formation of the cranial sensory ganglia. However, if these hindbrain neural crest cells are grafted in place of the posterior diencephalic and mesencephalic crest population, they will differentiate appropriately into ocular, orbital, and facial tissues.

Neural crest cells make a major contribution to the connective tissue components of the eye and orbit. Notable exceptions include the striated fibers of the extraocular muscles and the endothelial cells that line all blood vessels of the eye and orbit. Both of these exceptions arise from mesoderm (Table V-1).

Neurocristopathy   Congenital and developmental anomalies that involve cells derived from the neural crest have been grouped together under the term *neurocristopathies.* Most of these abnormalities result from defects in either the migration of neural crest cells or their terminal differentiation. Craniofacial and dental malformations; middle ear deafness; and malformations of the skull, shoulder girdle, and upper spine are seen frequently in combination with ocular defects, especially those of the anterior segment. Primary cleft palate can be produced by extirpation of the neural folds prior to crest cell migration. The median face malformation (severe orbital hypertelorism) is believed to result from an impaired midline coalescence of the frontonasal process.

Johnston MC, Noden DM, Hazelton RD, et al. Origins of avian ocular and periocular tissues. *Exp Eye Res.* 1979;29:27–43.

TABLE V-1
DERIVATIVES OF EMBRYONIC TISSUES

ECTODERM

Neuroectoderm
Neurosensory retina
Retinal pigment epithelium
Pigmented ciliary epithelium
Nonpigmented ciliary epithelium
Pigmented iris epithelium
Sphincter and dilator muscles of iris
Optic nerve, axons, and glia
Vitreous

Cranial Neural Crest Cells
Corneal stroma and endothelium
Sclera (see also mesoderm)
Trabecular meshwork
Sheaths and tendons of extraocular muscles
Connective tissues of iris
Ciliary muscles
Choroidal stroma
Melanocytes (uveal and epithelial)
Meningeal sheaths of the optic nerve
Schwann cells of ciliary nerves
Ciliary ganglion
Orbital bones (all midline) and inferior orbital, as well as parts of orbital roof and lateral rim
Cartilage
Connective tissue of orbit
Muscular layer and connective tissue sheaths of all ocular and orbital vessels

Surface Ectoderm
Epithelium, glands, cilia of skin of eyelids and caruncle
Conjunctival epithelium
Lens
Lacrimal gland
Lacrimal drainage system
Vitreous

MESODERM

Fibers of extraocular muscles
Endothelial lining of all orbital and ocular blood vessels
Temporal portion of sclera
Vitreous

Lallier T, Leblanc G, Artinger KB, et al. Cranial and trunk neural crest cells use different mechanisms for attachment to extracellular matrices. *Development.* 1992; 16:531–541.

Noden DM. Periocular mesenchyme: neural crest and mesodermal interactions. In: Jakobiec FA, ed. *Ocular Anatomy, Embryology, and Teratology.* Philadelphia: Harper & Row; 1982.

Tripathi BJ, Tripathi RC, Wisdom JE. Embryology of the anterior segment of the human eye. In: Ritch R, Shields MB, Krupin T, eds. *The Glaucomas.* 2nd ed. St Louis: Mosby; 1996;1.

Embryogenesis

In the 2 weeks after fertilization, the impregnated ovum undergoes a series of repeated cell divisions and, through repositioning and reorientation of the cells, becomes sequentially *morula, blastula,* and *gastrula* (Fig V-1). Only the inner cell mass, a small number of cells derived from the fertilized ovum, differentiates subsequently

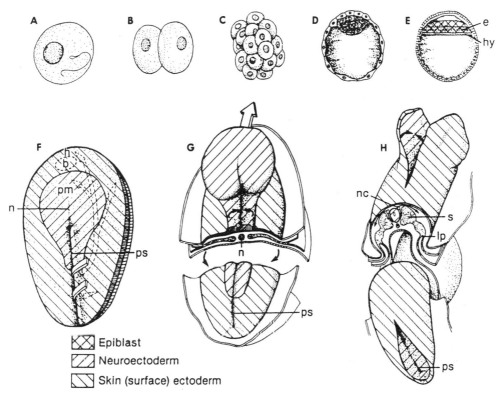

FIG V-1—Early stages of human embryonic development. *A–C,* Fertilization and earliest cell divisions to *morula* stage. *D,* Sectioned blastocyst. A fluid-filled cavity has formed, and cells that will form the embryo (darker area indicates inner cell mass) are distinct from other cells that will develop into support tissues (e.g., the placenta). *E,* Embryo-forming cells have now separated into two layers: the epiblast (*e*) and hypoblast (*hy*). *F,* Dorsal view of an embryo slightly more advanced than the sectioned embryo illustrated in *E.* Gastrulation movements (*arrows*) bring cells from the upper layer through the primitive streak (*ps*) into the potential space between the two layers to form the middle germ layer (*mesoderm*). Mesodermal cells fail to penetrate between the ectoderm and endoderm at the oral plate (*b,* buccopharyngeal membrane), which later forms the embryonic partition between the oral and pharyngeal cavities. At this stage, the heart primordium (*h*) lies anterior to the oral plate. The notochord (*n*) is formed from the anterior (cephalic) end of the primitive streak. The prochordal mesoderm (*pm*) is subjacent to the neural plate on the region between *n* and *b*. *G,* Early stages of neural tube folding and closure and folding of the lateral body walls (*solid arrows*). The anterior neural plate has begun to "overgrow" (*open arrow*) the heart primordium and future oral region, including the buccopharyngeal membrane. *H,* Embryo folding is nearing completion. Migration of cranial neural crest cells (*nc*) in the hindbrain region has been initiated. In contrast to the trunk crest cells, most of those forming in the head region migrate laterally under the surface ectoderm, but superficial to the somites (*s*) and the lateral plate (*lp*) of the mesoderm. (Reproduced by permission from Serafin D, Georgiade NG. *Pediatric Plastic Surgery.* St Louis: Mosby; 1984.)

133

into the embryo. The outer cell mass, or *trophoblast*, forms the placenta and support tissues. The formation of the *epiblast* and *hypoblast* from the inner cell mass precedes gastrulation, a process that results in the establishment of the three primary germ layers: ectoderm, mesoderm, and endoderm (Fig V-2).

Cells of the epiblast in the medial region of the embryonic disc begin to proliferate at the caudal end, which causes the development of a thickening known as the *primitive streak*. The cells of the primitive streak migrate both laterally and cephalad beneath the epiblast, where they give rise to the mesenchymal cells of the intraembryonic mesoderm. The cells that remain in the epiblast are now recognized as the embryonic ectoderm. Some cells of the primitive streak invade the hypoblast and displace laterally most of these cells to give rise to the embryonic endoderm. The primitive streak elongates by the addition of cells at the caudal end and thus establishes the axial orientation of the embryo. The cranial end of the primitive streak enlarges as the primitive node. Mesenchymal cells that migrate cranially from this site form the medial notochordal process, which develops into the primitive mesenchymal axial skeleton, or *notochord*, of the embryo. The development of the notochord induces the overlying ectoderm to differentiate as neuroectoderm that becomes identified as the *neural plate*. The brain and the eye develop from the anteriormost region of the neural plate.

Growth of the lateral part of the neural plate results in folds that grow upward and outward, parallel to the neural groove from the head to the caudal region. At this stage neuroectoderm lines the inner folds, and surface ectoderm covers the outer surface of the folds. The neuroectodermal cells at the apex of the folds proliferate and produce a population of neural crest cells, which contribute extensively to the tissues of the eye (Fig V-3). Growth and expansion of the cephalic neural folds is most marked. At the end of the third week after conception the neural folds begin to close to form the *neural tube*. This process starts in the midregion of the embryo and proceeds anteriorly and posteriorly at the same time. As the neural tube closes, three events important to the development of the eye and orbit occur simultaneously (Fig V-4):

□ Optic pits develop from the small depression, the optic sulcus, present in the cephalic neuroectoderm

□ Neural crest cells begin migration

□ As the anterior neural tube closes, it flexes ventrally

Organogenesis of the Eye

The chronology of ocular development is provided in Table V-2. The *optic sulci* are first recognizable as slight, curved indentations in the widest part of each neural fold just internal to the peak of the ridge (Fig V-5). The long axis of the depression is roughly parallel to that of the neural groove. The *optic pits*, formed of a single layer of neuroectoderm, develop from the continued evagination of the sulci. As the neural tube closes, the pits deepen and become optic vesicles, which appear as symmetrical, hollow hemispherical outgrowths on the lateral sides of what is now the forebrain vesicle. The *optic vesicles* remain attached to, and continuous with, the neural tube by *optic stalks* composed of neuroectodermal cells (Fig V-6). The expansion and ballooning that take place in the hollow optic vesicle do not occur in the stalk, which remains as a tubular link from the cavity of the vesicle to that of the diencephalon.

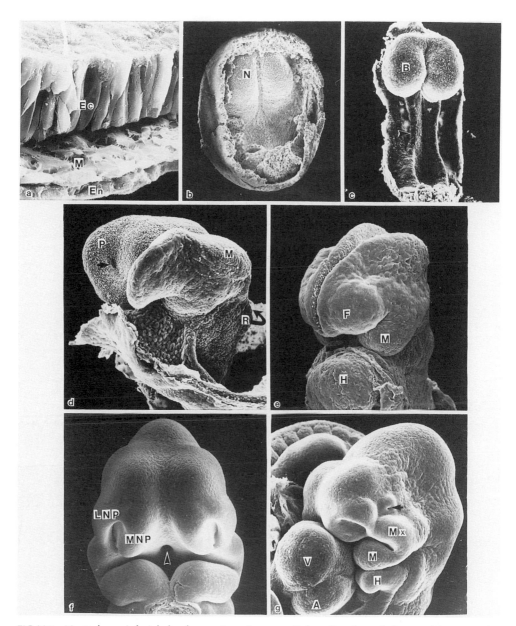

FIG V-2—Normal craniofacial development. *a,* A parasagittal section through the cranial aspect of a gastrulation-stage mouse embryo. The cells of the three germ layers, ectoderm (*Ec*), mesoderm (*M*), and endoderm (*En*), have distinct morphologies. *b,* The developing neural plate (*N*) is apparent in a dorsal view of this presomite mouse embryo. *c,* Neural folds (*arrow*) can be seen in the developing spinal cord region. The lateral aspects of the brain (*B*) region have not yet begun to elevate in this head fold–stage mouse embryo. *d,* Three regions of the brain can be distinguished at this 6-somite stage: prosencephalon (*P*), mesencephalon (*M*), and rhombencephalon (*R, curved arrow*). Optic sulci (*small arrow*) are seen as evaginations from the prosencephalon. *e,* The neural tube has not yet fused in this 12-somite embryo. The stomodeum (*arrow*), or primitive oral cavity, is bordered by the frontonasal prominence (*F*), the first visceral arch (mandibular arch, *M*), and the developing heart (*H*). *f,* Medial and lateral nasal prominences (*MNP, LNP*) surround olfactory pits in 36-somite mouse embryo. Rathke's pouch (*arrow*) can be distinguished in the roof of the stomodeum. *g,* In this lateral view of a 36-somite mouse embryo, the first and second (hyoid, *H*) visceral arches are apparent. The region of the first arch consists of maxillary (*Mx*) and mandibular (*M*) components. Note the presence of the eye with its invaginating lens (*arrow*). Atrial (*A*) and ventricular (*V*) heart chambers can be distinguished. (Reproduced with permission from Sulik KK. Embryonic origin of holoprosencephaly: Interrelationship of the developing brain and face. *Scan Electron Microsc.* 1982;1:311.)

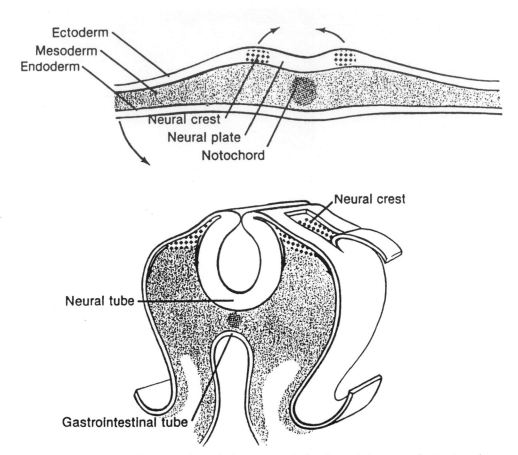

FIG V-3—Cross sections through embryos before (*top*) and after (*bottom*) the onset of migration of crest cells (*diamond pattern*). The ectoderm has been peeled back in the lower figure to show the underlying neural crest cells. (Reproduced with permission from Johnston MC, Sulik KK. Development of face and oral cavity. In: Bhaskar SN. *Orban's Oral Histology and Embryology.* 9th ed. St Louis: Mosby; 1980.)

As the optic vesicle approaches the outer wall of the embryo, a focal thickening of the cells, the *lens placode,* develops in the surface ectoderm, which has been primed by lens-bias signals during earlier embryogenesis. In the fourth week, invagination of the lens placode leads to formation of the *lens vesicle,* which initially remains attached to the surface ectoderm by the lens stalk. Simultaneously, differential growth and movement of the cells of the optic vesicle result in the invagination of its temporal and lower walls and the formation of the *optic cup.*

The outer layer of the optic cup will evolve as a monolayer of cells, the retinal pigment epithelium. The inner, invaginated layer will differentiate into the neurosensory retina. Initially, the cup is incomplete in its inferior portion (Fig V-7). The indentation, or fissure, between the folds or margins of the cup is called the *embryonic fissure,* previously the choroidal, or fetal, fissure. Invagination pushes the neuroectodermal cells originally near the surface to reside deep within the cup near the

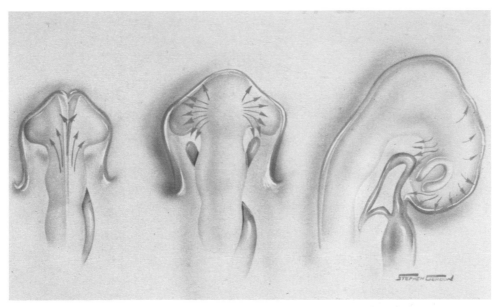

FIG V-4—Migration of cranial neural crest cells from dorsal diencephalic and mesencephalic regions. *Left,* Cells begin migration anteriorly as tube closes. *Center,* Crest cells move in waves around optic vesicle and lose continuity with the surface cells. *Right,* Neural tube flexes ventrally, carrying optic cup and crest cells ventrally (redrawn from M. Johnston, 1966).

outer layer. Invagination produces a fold in the neuroectoderm anteriorly, adjacent to the lens, called the *rim* of the optic cup. At first, the two layers of the developing cup have a small space between them, the optic ventricle, but as invagination proceeds and the inner layer becomes juxtaposed to the outer layer, the cavity of the optic ventricle progressively narrows. Basement membrane lines both the outer and inner layers of the cup. The apices of the cells in both layers meet end to end as the ventricle narrows. The ventricle cavity remains throughout life as a potential space, the subretinal space.

The embryonic fissure extends from the rim of the cup near the lens to the distal optic stalk. This fissure allows vessels of the hyaloid system to be incorporated within the eye (Fig V-8). To complete the entire wall of the globe, the two lips of the embryonic fissure meet and fuse. Closure begins in the midregion of the cup near the equator of the globe and proceeds anteriorly to the rim and posteriorly down the stalk, enclosing the hyaloid artery. In the course of this process a bridge coloboma with a posterior and peripheral component separated by a band of normal tissue occasionally occurs (see Figure VI-18D, p 173). The inner and outer layers of the cup meet end to end. Because the primitive cells are still labile, they seal the fissure without evidence of a seam or scar. Incomplete or inadequate closure produces a coloboma of the iris, ciliary body, choroid, or optic disc, depending on the extent of the failed closure and secondary attempts to close the defect (Fig V-9).

Table V-2

Chronology of Embryonic and Fetal Development of the Eye

22 days	Optic primordium appears in neural folds (1.5–3.0 mm).
25 days	Optic vesicle evaginates. Neural crest cells migrate to surround vesicle.
28 days	Vesicle induces lens placode.
Second month	Invagination of optic and lens vesicles. Hyaloid artery fills embryonic fissure. Closure of embryonic fissure begins. Pigment granules appear in retinal pigment epithelium. Primordia of lateral rectus and superior oblique muscles grow anteriorly. Eyelid folds appear. Retinal differentiation begins with nuclear and marginal zones. Migration of retinal cells begins. Neural crest cells of corneal endothelium migrate centrally. Corneal stroma follows. Cavity of lens vesicle is obliterated. Secondary vitreous surrounds hyaloid system. Choroidal vasculature develops. Axons from ganglion cells migrate to optic nerve. Glial lamina cribrosa forms. Bruch's membrane appears.
Third month	Precursors of rods and cones differentiate. Anterior rim of optic vesicle grows forward and ciliary body starts to develop. Sclera condenses. Vortex veins pierce sclera. Eyelid folds meet and fuse.
Fourth month	Retinal vessels grow into nerve fiber layer near optic disc. Folds of ciliary processes appear. Iris sphincter develops. Descemet's membrane forms. Schlemm's canal appears. Hyaloid system starts to regress. Glands and cilia develop.
Fifth month	Photoreceptors develop inner segments. Choroidal vessels form layers. Iris stroma is vascularized. Eyelids begin to separate.
Sixth month	Ganglion cells thicken in macula. Recurrent arterial branches join the choroidal vessels. Dilator muscle of iris forms.
Seventh month	Outer segments of photoreceptors differentiate. Central fovea starts to thin. Fibrous lamina cribrosa forms. Choroidal melanocytes produce pigment. Circular muscle forms in ciliary body.

TABLE V-2 (Continued)

CHRONOLOGY OF EMBRYONIC AND FETAL DEVELOPMENT OF THE EYE

Eighth month	Chamber angle completes formation. Hyaloid system disappears.
Ninth month	Retinal vessels reach the periphery. Myelination of fibers of optic nerve is complete to lamina cribrosa. Pupillary membrane disappears.

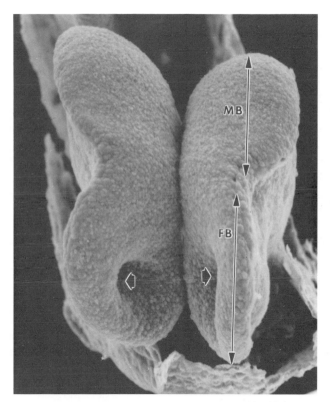

FIG V-5—Scanning electron microscopy of normal mouse embryo on day 8 of gestation; five somite pairs. The bilateral optic sulci (*short arrows*) form as evaginations of the forebrain (*FB*). *MB* = midbrain (×250). (Reproduced with permission from Cook CS, Sulik KK. Keratolenticular dysgenesis [Peters anomaly] as a result of acute embryonic insult during gastrulation. *J Pediatr Ophthalmol Strabismus.* 1988;25:60–66.)

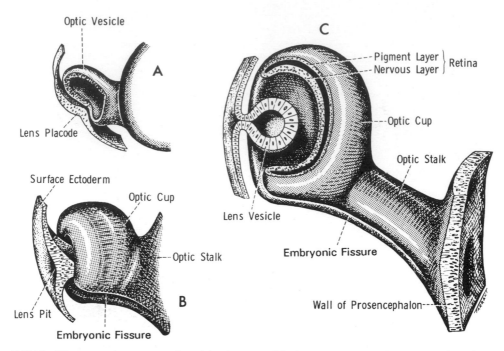

FIG V-6—Diagrammatic representation of development of the human optic cup. The optic vesicle and cup have been partly cut away in *A* and *C,* and the lens vesicle is sectioned for clarity. *A,* 4.5 mm embryo (27 days); *B,* 5.5 mm embryo; *C,* 7.5 mm embryo (28 days). (Reproduced from Tripathi RC, Tripathi BJ. Comparative physiology and anatomy of the aqueous outflow pathway. In: Davson H, ed. *The Eye.* 3rd ed. Orlando: Academic Press; 1984.)

Neurosensory Retina

The neurosensory, or neural, retina arises from the inner layer of neuroectodermal cells of the optic cup (Fig V-10). Differentiation of this cell layer commences early, and within 1 month of fertilization mitotic activity has produced three to four compact rows of cells that rapidly increase in numbers. The nuclei segregate at the outer two thirds of the primordial retina toward the outer layer of the optic cup. This region is recognized as the *primitive zone.* The ciliated apices of the cells are directed outward into the rapidly shrinking cavity of the optic ventricle. The inner one third of the developing retina is initially devoid of nuclei and is termed the *inner marginal zone;* it eventually differentiates as the nerve fiber layer. The primitive and marginal zones are recognizable only until the seventh week of gestation. Little is known about the stimuli that initiate and direct the complex migration and subsequent differentiation of the primitive neuroepithelial cells into the retina.

Differentiation of the retina begins in the center of the optic cup and gradually extends peripherally toward its rim. Neural and glial cells develop simultaneously. By 5 weeks of gestation, the putative ganglion and Müller cells have migrated from the outer neuroepithelial layers toward the vitreous cavity. As a result, the nuclei of

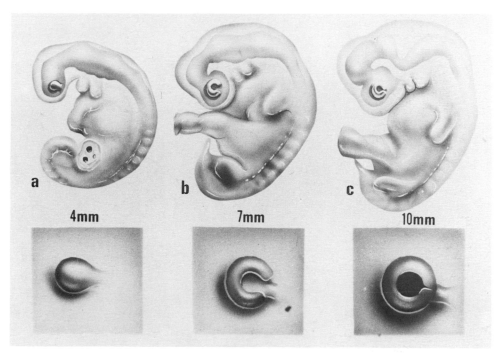

FIG V-7—Ocular and somatic development. *A,* Flexion of neural tube and ballooning of optic vesicle. *B,* Upper limb buds appear as optic cup and embryonic fissure emerge. *C,* Completion of optic cup with closure of fissure. Convolutions appear in the brain and leg buds appear. The size of the fetus is noted. *Lower sequence:* Optic vesicle; optic cup with open embryonic fissure; cup with fissure closing.

the neuroblastic cells become segregated as two distinct layers, the inner and outer neuroblastic layers. These two layers are separated by a region of tangled cell processes known as the *transient nerve fiber layer of Chievitz,* which becomes the definitive inner plexiform layer between weeks 9 and 12 of gestation, except in the macula where it persists until birth. At 9–12 weeks, the four major horizontal layers of the retina become distinguishable.

The *ganglion cells* are the first cells of the retina to become clearly differentiated. Their axonal processes and dendritic trees begin to develop at about the sixth week. Axons from ganglion cells nearest the posterior pole are the first to enter the optic stalk and induce formation of the optic nerve. The number of ganglion cells increases rapidly between weeks 15 and 17 of gestation, then decreases between weeks 18 and 30 as a result of apoptosis. The size of the ganglion cell somas increases with advancing gestational age.

The processes of the *Müller cells* extend from the inner basal lamina of the optic vesicle toward the optic ventricle. As soon as the photoreceptors enlarge and become distinct morphologically as cones, the development of junctional complexes on adjacent lateral surfaces of these cells and of the Müller cell processes gives rise to the *external limiting membrane.*

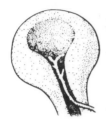

FIG V-8—Optic cup and stalk with open embryonic fissure below. Hyaloid artery from dorsal ophthalmic artery enters cavity through posterior aspect of the embryonic fissure. Rim of optic cup above. Lens is not pictured.

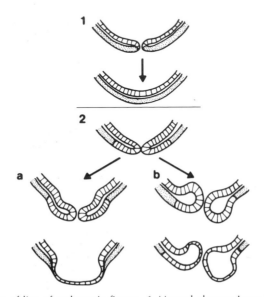

FIG V-9—Closure of lips of embryonic fissure. *1,* Normal closure: Inner layers (neurosensory retina) and outer layers (dotted area, retinal pigment epithelium) meet and merge. Basement membrane forms on both surfaces. *2,* Coloboma formation: Ectropion of the inner retina at the lips of the fissure results in imperfect fusion; pigment epithelium is displaced laterally by cells of neurosensory retina. *a,* A simple coloboma results in defective retina and retinal pigment epithelium. Uvea and sclera (not shown) are thin and dysgenic. *b,* In a cystic coloboma, the primary vesicular cavity enlarges adjacent to the point of defective closure.

Photoreceptors arise from the outermost layer of neuroblastic cells. Mitotic activity, abundant in the outer neuroblastic layers in weeks 4–12, ceases in the central retina by week 15 of gestation, and differentiation of the cones begins in the region of the putative fovea. The cilia on the apices of the cells that had invaginated the adjacent retinal pigment epithelium disappear, and precursors of outer segments gradually develop. Initially, cylindrical cytoplasmic processes extend toward the apical region of the retinal pigment epithelial cells.

Differentiation of cone outer segments begins at 5 months when multiple infoldings develop in the plasma membrane of the processes. The folds separate from the

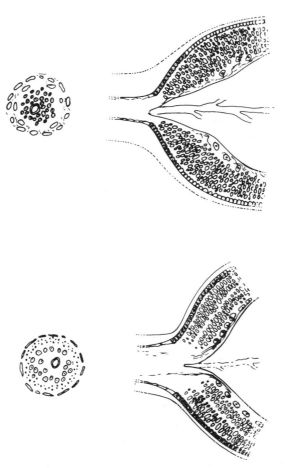

FIG V-10—Development of retina and optic nerve. *Top,* At right, fetal neurosensory retina develops from neuroectoderm as ganglion cells migrate from outer primitive zone of closely packed nuclei to inner marginal zone of fibrils. A few axons from ganglion cells grow toward the optic nerve. Retinal pigment epithelium begins melanization in posterior pole. At left, cross section shows fetal optic nerve with center of vacuolating primitive cells through which axons from ganglion cells will grow toward brain. Neural crest cells as mesenchyme loosely ring the nerve. Hyaloid artery enters vitreous (fifth week). *Bottom,* At right, migration of nuclei results in three nuclear layers and plexiform layers. Cross section of optic nerve on left shows axons of ganglion cells (black dots) migrating through vacuolating cells, first in periphery of the nerve. Neural crest cells condense to meningeal sheaths of optic nerve (seventh week).

plasma membrane, and their orientation as flattened, lamellar disks parallels the development of the horizontal cells. The cell bodies of the rods are dispersed among the cones and are first recognizable by their dark nuclei with condensed peripheral chromatin. Development of rod outer segments occurs during the seventh month of gestation.

Amacrine cells are identified by their large, round, pale-staining nuclei. They are first seen scattered at the inner border of the outer neuroblastic layer by week 14 of gestation. The differentiation of bipolar cells does not occur until week 23. The bipolar dendrites extend to the outer plexiform layer by the week 25, at which time the horizontal cells probably differentiate.

Fovea   The differentiation of the neurons, photoreceptors, and glial cells in the fovea occurs early because this region is the focal point for the centraperipheral development of the retina. The different cell types as well as many synapses and intercellular junctions are already established by 15 weeks of gestation. Thinning of the ganglion cell and inner nuclear layers begins at 24–26 weeks of gestation and gives rise to the earliest recognizable depression in the area of the macula.

The foveal pit becomes more prominent by the seventh month as a result of the marked thinning of the inner nuclear layer. An acellular fibrous zone is now present on both the nasal and temporal sides of the fovea. By this time major changes have occurred in the cones: the width of the inner segments is decreased, whereas their length is increased along with the length of the fibers of the fiber layer of Henle. Only two layers of ganglion cells remain at 8 months, and the inner nuclear layer at the foveola is reduced to three rows or fewer because of lateral displacement. At birth, axons of bipolar cells that pass to the inner plexiform layers constitute the prominent transient layer of Chievitz. Relocation of all layers to the periphery of the foveal slope, which leaves the nuclei of the cones uncovered in the foveola, occurs by 4 months after birth. However, remodeling of the elements of the fovea continues until nearly 4 years of age. At that time the transient layer of Chievitz is lost completely.

Hendrickson AE, Yuodelis C. The morphological development of the human fovea. *Ophthalmology.* 1984;91:603–612.

Rhodes RH. A light microscopic study of the developing human neural retina. *Am J Anat.* 1979;154:195–209.

Tripathi BJ, Tripathi RC. Development of the human eye. In: Bron AJ, Tripathi RC, Tripathi BJ, eds. *Wolff's Anatomy of the Eye and Orbit.* 8th ed. London: Chapman and Hall; 1997.

Yuodelis C, Hendrickson AE. A qualitative and quantitative analysis of the human fovea during development. *Vision Res.* 1986;26:847–855.

Retinal Pigment Epithelium (RPE)

Mitotic activity continues in the pseudostratified, columnar epithelial cells that constitute the outer wall of the optic cup up to the sixth week of gestation. The apical borders of adjacent cells are already joined by zonulae occludens and zonulae adherens junctional complexes. At week 6 melanogenesis begins, and, concurrently, the cilia that had been present on the inner cell surface (i.e., adjacent to the developing neurosensory retina) disappear. The RPE cells are the first in the body to produce melanin. Whether in the retina or the choroid, the stages of melanin production are the same: premelanosomes gradually become melanosomes.

Differentiation of the RPE begins at the posterior pole and proceeds anteriorly, so that by 8 weeks of gestation it is organized as a single layer of hexagonal columnar cells located posteriorly. The cells become tall and cuboidal in shape during the third and fourth months, and the terminal web becomes well established at the lateral apical borders. The RPE is believed to be fully functional at this stage. The increase in surface area of the RPE that takes place after birth to accommodate the subsequent growth of the globe is achieved by enlargement and expansion of individual cells.

The basement membrane of the RPE becomes the inner portion of *Bruch's membrane;* the outer layer of Bruch's membrane, also basement membrane, is laid down by the choriocapillaris layer. The embryonic pigment epithelial cells have a profound inductive influence on the development of the choroid, sclera, and neurosensory retina. In areas where pigment epithelium does not form, as sometimes happens along the line of closure of the embryonic fissure, the underlying choroid, sclera, and retina are hypoplastic (see Figure V-9). The nature of the inductive stimulus is not known.

Oguni M, Tanaka O, Shinohara H, et al. Ultrastructural study on the retinal pigment epithelium of human embryos, with special reference to quantitative study on the development of melanin granules. *Acta Anat* (Basel). 1991;140:335–342.

Optic Nerve

The optic nerve develops from the original connection between the optic vesicle and the forebrain, the *optic stalk.* Initially, the stalk is composed of an inner zone of closely packed neuroectodermal cells surrounded by a less compact layer of undifferentiated neural crest cells. Late in the sixth week of gestation, some cells of the inner region vacuolate and degenerate, and nerve fibers from the ganglion cells migrate through the spaces thus created. Other cells of the inner zone differentiate as glial cells. By the seventh week, the optic disc contains the hyaloid artery, which is surrounded by axons and covered by a mantle of glial cells, many of which disappear by the seventh month. The glial cells also give rise to the glial elements of the lamina cribrosa during the eighth week of gestation. Differentiation of the neural crest cells into the pia, arachnoid, and dura maters of the optic nerve begins in the seventh week, but only after the fourth month do the sheaths become well defined.

The number of axons increases rapidly: by 10–12 weeks of gestation some 1.9 million axons are present in the optic nerve, 3.7 million by 16 weeks. Attrition of axons causes the number of fibers to drop to approximately 1.1 million, which establishes the adult condition by 33 weeks. The loss of axons parallels the degeneration of ganglion cells in the fetal retina and may also be related to the segregation of terminals as discrete laminae in the dorsal lateral geniculate body.

As the axons grow toward the lateral geniculate body, partial crossover occurs at the optic chiasm. Cells located at the chiasm midline, probably radial glial cells, express certain repulsive or inhibitory molecules that provide a guidance cue by acting specifically on ipsilateral projecting axons.

Myelination starts in the chiasm at the seventh month of gestation, proceeds toward the eye, and ceases at the lamina cribrosa by about 1 month after birth. Occasionally, medullated fibers develop in the retina. They appear on ophthalmoscopic examination as a flat, serrated white patch on the inner surface of the retina. The medullation is usually interrupted at the lamina but it is occasionally continuous across the lamina from nerve to retina.

Some fetuses may demonstrate a response to light as soon as the eighth week of gestation, which indicates that at least some central nervous system pathways are established early. By 5 months 50% of the growth of the optic nerve and disc has occurred; by birth, 75%; and before one year, 95%.

Provis JM, van Driel D, Billson FA, et al. Human fetal optic nerve: overproduction and elimination of retinal axons during development. *J Comp Neurol.* 1985;238:92–100.

Rimmer S, Keating C, Chou T, et al. Growth of the human optic disk and nerve during gestation, childhood, and early adulthood. *Am J Ophthalmol.* 1993;116:748–753.

Wizenmann A, Thanos S, Boxberg Y, et al. Differential reaction of crossing and non-crossing rat retinal axons on cell membrane preparations from the chiasm midline: an in vitro study. *Development.* 1993;117:725–735.

Lens

One of the earliest events in embryogenesis is determination of lens development. The interaction that takes place between the surface ectoderm and the underlying chordamesoderm during midgastrulation imparts a lens-forming bias on an extensive region of head ectoderm. Next, the anlage of the eye conveys an inductive signal to the ectoderm, which determines the region of the presumptive lens. The mesoderm beneath the putative lens ectoderm transmits another signal late in gastrulation, but when the neural plate is still open, that potentiates the fate of this tissue. Finally, by invoking the final phase of determination and enhancing differentiation during neurulation, the optic vesicle designates the specific region of the head ectoderm that will become the lens. The surface ectoderm can respond to the influence of the optic vesicle only during a precise period of development.

The lens is first apparent at about 27 days gestation as a disk-shaped thickening of surface epithelial cells over the optic vesicle. This lens placode and its thin basal lamina are separated from the basal lamina of the optic vesicle by a narrow space containing fine filaments that have a role in the gradual invagination of the lens placode to form the lens vesicle. Initially, the vesicle, consisting of a single layer of cells with apices directed inward, is covered by a basal lamina that seals anteriorly to complete the formation of the lens capsule (Fig V-11). Ultimately, the lens vesicle separates from the surface epithelium at about 33 days gestation. The area of lens separation from the surface ectoderm heals without residuum. The epithelial cells deposit additional basal lamina material, which forms the lens capsule. Initially, the posterior capsule is more prominent than is the anterior capsule. The lens capsule isolates the lens constituents immunologically within the globe.

During closure of the lens vesicle, DNA synthesis decreases in the cells that form the posterior half of the lens, and, simultaneously, specific lens proteins (*crystallins*) are synthesized. By day 45 of gestation the posterior cells, or primary lens fibers, have lengthened to fill the cavity of the vesicle from posterior to anterior. The posterior cells of the vesicle account for most of the growth of the lens during the first 2 months of embryogenesis. The primary fibers form the compact core of the lens, known as the *embryonic nucleus.*

The preequatorial epithelial cells retain their mitotic activity throughout life, producing secondary lens fibers. These fibers are displaced inward between the capsule and the embryonic nucleus and meet on the vertical planes, the *lens sutures.* The first suture marking the fetal nucleus is shaped like a Y anteriorly and an inverted Y posteriorly. The basic anatomy of the lens is established after the first layer of secondary fibers has been laid down at the seventh week of gestation.

At first the lens is spherical, but it becomes ellipsoid with the addition of secondary fibers. As secondary fibers are added, the sutures become more complex and

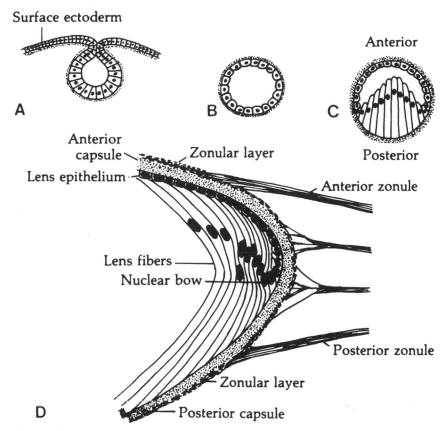

Surface ectoderm

A

B

Anterior

C

Posterior

Anterior capsule

Zonular layer

Lens epithelium

Anterior zonule

Lens fibers

Nuclear bow

Posterior zonule

Zonular layer

D

Posterior capsule

FIG V-11- Diagrammatic representation of stages in the development of the lens and its capsule. *A,* Formation of lens vesicle from invagination of surface ectoderm together with its basal lamina in an embryo corresponding to 32 days of gestation. *B,* Separation of the vesicle from the surface ectoderm and its surrounding basal lamina. *C,* Obliteration of lens vesicle cavity by elongation of posterior cells at about 35 days gestation. *D,* Equatorial region of the fully formed lens. Attachment of zonular fibers to the anterior, posterior, and equatorial regions of the lens periphery becomes apparent at approximately 5½ weeks gestation. Note the change in polarity of cells from anterior to posterior regions of the lens. (Reproduced from Tripathi RC, Tripathi BJ. Anatomy of the human eye. In: Davson H, ed. *The Eye.* 3rd ed. Orlando: Academic Press; 1984.)

dendriform. In the third month the innermost fibers mature; cytoplasmic fibrillar material increases and cellular organelles decrease. The nuclei of the deeper cells, at first homogeneous and dense, are lost; the chromatin and ribosomes disintegrate. The equatorial diameter of the unfixed human lens measures 2 mm at 12 weeks and 6 mm at 35 weeks. Both the growth and maturation of lenticular fibers continue throughout life. BCSC Section 11, *Lens and Cataract,* discusses the development of the lens in detail in its Chapter IV, Embryology.

The zonular apparatus begins to develop after the tertiary vitreous has formed. The ciliary epithelial cells then synthesize collagen fibrils of the zonular fibers. As they increase in number, strength, and coarseness, the fibers reach the lens and merge with the anterior and posterior capsule by the fifth month of gestation.

Grainger RM, Henry JJ, Saha MS, et al. Recent progress on the mechanisms of embryonic lens formation. *Eye.* 1992;6:117–122.

Saha MS, Spann CL, Grainger RM. Embryonic lens induction: more than meets the optic vesicle. *Cell Differ Dev.* 1989;28:153–171.

Vitreous (Fig V-12)

Between the fourth and fifth weeks of gestation, the space between the lens vesicle and the inner layer of the optic cup becomes filled with fibrils, mesenchymal cells, and vascular channels of the hyaloid system. Together these constitute the *primary vitreous.* Initially, the fibrillar content is of ectodermal origin, being derived from the fibrils already in place between the invaginating lens placode and the inner layer of the optic cup. The mesenchymal cells are mostly mesodermal in origin, having invaded the cavity of the optic cup with the hyaloid vessel through the patent optic fissure. However, some mesenchymal cells are derived from neural crest cells that migrated over the rim of the cup. The vascular primary vitreous attains its maximum development by 2 months of gestation.

The development of the *secondary vitreous* begins soon after the primary vitreous is established. The secondary vitreous is avascular and consists of Type II collagen fibrils and hyalocytes, which are presumed to be derived from mesenchymal cells of the primary vitreous that differentiated as monocytes. The content of hyaluronic acid in the vitreous is very low during the prenatal period but increases after birth. Initially, the secondary vitreous occupies only a narrow space between the retina and the posterior limit of the primary vitreous. The continued development of the secondary vitreous, until the end of the third month, is related to the regression of the hyaloid system and the simultaneous retraction of the primary vitreous. Remnants of the atrophied hyaloid system and primary vitreous remain throughout life as Cloquet's canal.

Between the third and fourth months of gestation, collagen fibrils of the secondary vitreous condense and become attached to the internal limiting membrane at the rim of the optic cup. The condensation of fibrils extends to the lens equator and constitutes the tertiary vitreous. The zonular apparatus of the lens ultimately develops anterior to these collagen fibrils.

Choroid

The development of the choroid begins at the anterior region of the optic cup and proceeds posteriorly toward the optic stalk. Choroidal development is associated with the condensation of neural crest cells around the cup that differentiate into cells of the choroidal stroma. Endothelium-lined blood spaces appear in this mesenchymal tissue and first coalesce as the embryonic annular vessel at the rim of the optic cup. During the fourth and fifth weeks of gestation, the *choriocapillaris* begins to differentiate. The choriocapillary network is formed by mesodermal cells that come in contact with the retinal pigment epithelium, which is differentiating simultaneously.

The embryonic eye is completely invested with a primitive layer of capillaries at the beginning of the sixth week of gestation. Adjacent endothelial cells are joined by punctate junctional complexes and zonulae occludens. Characteristic diaphragmed fenestrations develop in the endothelium between the seventh and ninth weeks. At the same time, the basal lamina becomes defined as a continuous layer of extra-

35 days

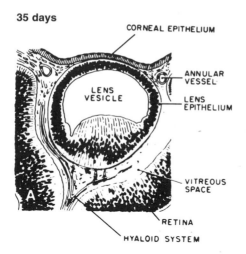

CORNEAL EPITHELIUM

ANNULAR VESSEL

LENS VESICLE

LENS EPITHELIUM

VITREOUS SPACE

RETINA

HYALOID SYSTEM

2 months

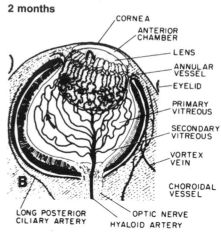

CORNEA

ANTERIOR CHAMBER

LENS

ANNULAR VESSEL

EYELID

PRIMARY VITREOUS

SECONDARY VITREOUS

VORTEX VEIN

CHOROIDAL VESSEL

LONG POSTERIOR CILIARY ARTERY

OPTIC NERVE

HYALOID ARTERY

FIG V-12—Main features in vitreous development and the regression of the hyaloid system shown in drawings of sagittal sections. *A,* At 35 days, hyaloid vessels and their branches, the vasa hyaloidea propria, occupy the space between the lens and the neural ectoderm. A capillary net joins the capsula perilenticularis fibrosa, which is composed of ectodermal fibrils associated with vasoformative mesenchyme from the periphery. The ground substance of the primary vitreous is finely fibrillar. *B,* By the second month, the vascular primary vitreous reaches its greatest extent. Arborization of the vasa hyaloidea propria (*curved arrow*) fills the retrolental area and is embedded in collagen fibrils. An avascular secondary vitreous of more finely fibrillar composition forms a narrow zone between the peripheral (outer) branches of the vasa hyaloidea propria and the retina. The *hooked arrow* points to the vessel of the pupillary membrane. The drawing is a composite of

3-4 months

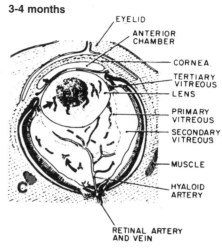

EYELID

ANTERIOR CHAMBER

CORNEA

TERTIARY VITREOUS

LENS

PRIMARY VITREOUS

SECONDARY VITREOUS

MUSCLE

HYALOID ARTERY

RETINAL ARTERY AND VEIN

embryos at 15–30 mm. *C,* During the fourth month, hyaloid vessels and the vasa hyaloidea propria, together with the tunica vasculosa lentis, atrophy progressively, with the smaller peripheral channels regressing first. The *large curved arrow* points to remnants of involuted vessels of the superficial portion of the vasa hyaloidea propria in the secondary vitreous. The *small curved arrow* indicates the pupillary membrane (not sketched). The *straight arrow* points to the remnants of the atrophied capsulopupillary vessels. Zonular fibers (tertiary vitreous) begin to stretch from the growing ciliary region toward the lens capsule. Vessels through the center of the optic nerve connect with the hyaloid artery and vein and send small loops into the retina (*open hollow arrow*). The drawing is a composite of fetuses at 75–110 mm. (Reproduced with permission from Cook CS, Ozanics V, Jakobiec FA. Prenatal development of the eye and its adnexa. In: Tasman W, Jaeger EA, eds. *Duane's Foundations of Clinical Ophthalmology.* Philadelphia: Lippincott; 1991.)

cellular material surrounding the capillaries. Toward the RPE, this basal lamina constitutes the fifth layer of Bruch's membrane.

The network of vascular channels is supplied by vessels from the internal carotid artery and, later, by the primitive ophthalmic arteries. The channels drain into two main blood spaces, the superior orbital and inferior orbital venous plexuses, and from there into what will become the cavernous sinuses. By the end of the second month of gestation, short ciliary arteries enter the capillary coat. Arteries can be distinguished by narrow lumina and walls two or more cells thick, while veins are larger and lined only by endothelium.

Definite layering of the choroidal vasculature begins in the third month, when the outer large-sized vessel layer develops. Mainly venous, this layer receives small efferent branches of the choriocapillaris and connects with the vortex veins that eventually perforate the neighboring sclera. During the fourth month of gestation, the anterior ciliary and long posterior ciliary arteries form the major arterial circle of the iris, and recurrent branches extend from this vessel into the ciliary body by the end of the fifth month. However, the final anastomosis with the arterial circulation of the choroid is not established until the eighth month. During the fifth month of gestation, the third layer of medium-sized arterioles develops between the choriocapillaris and the outer layer of large-sized vessels. This layer is initially confined to the level of the equator and only reaches the developing ciliary body at the sixth month.

The choroidal stroma is demarcated by the sclera at the end of the third month of gestation. Initially, the stroma consists of a loosely organized framework of collagen fibrils and abundant fibroblasts. Elastic tissue is laid down during the fourth month. Melanosomes appear between weeks 24 and 27 of gestation, most notably in the melanocytes of the outer choroid and suprachoroid. Melanocytes differentiate from neural crest cells. Melanogenesis proceeds anteriorly from the optic disc to the ora serrata. A few immature melanosomes can be found in the choroidal melanocytes at birth.

Heimann K. The development of the choroid in man. *Ophthalmic Res.* 1972;3:257–273.

Sellheyer K. Development of the choroid and related structures. *Eye.* 1990;4:255–261.

Cornea and Sclera

The separation of the lens vesicle from the surface ectoderm initiates the development of the cornea (Fig V-13). By the end of the fifth week of gestation, the ectoderm consists of two layers of epithelial cells that rest on a thin basal lamina (Fig V-14). Detachment of the lens vesicle induces the basal layer of epithelial cells to secrete collagen fibrils and glycosaminoglycans, which occupy the space between the lens and the corneal epithelium and constitute the primary stroma. Mesenchymal cells migrate from the margins of the rim of the optic cup along the posterior surface of the primary stroma. The first of three successive waves of ingrowth, these neural crest–derived cells form the corneal endothelium.

Between 5 to 6 weeks of gestation, the cornea consists of a superficial squamous and a basal cuboidal layer of epithelial cells, a primary stroma, and a double layer of endothelial cells posteriorly. Further development of the stroma is preceded by the ingrowth of another wave of mesenchymal cells from the rim of the optic cup, which proceeds in two directions. The cells of the posterior extension grow between the lens epithelium and the corneal endothelium and are destined to form the primary pupillary membrane. Concurrently, hydration of the hyaluronic acid component of the primary stroma causes swelling that seems to make space available for the next migratory wave of cells. At approximately 7 weeks gestation, the anterior extension of mesenchymal cells migrates into the corneal stroma. These cells differentiate as *keratocytes* that secrete Type I collagen fibrils and form the matrix of the mature (or secondary) corneal stroma.

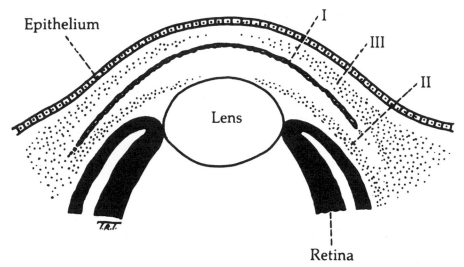

Epithelium

I

III

II

Lens

Retina

FIG V-13—Three successive waves of ingrowth of neural crest cells associated with differentiation of anterior chambers. *I,* First wave forms corneal endothelium. *II,* Second wave forms iris and part of the pupillary membrane. *III,* Third wave forms keratocytes.

The stroma attains its maximum width, which is approximately double the normal postembryonic width. Dehydration, especially of hyaluronic acid, and compression of the connective tissue cause the reduction in thickness. Morphogenesis of keratocytes begins in the posterior stroma and proceeds anteriorly. The cells synthesize proteoglycans and collagen fibrils, which are organized as lamellae. Each lamella continues to grow by the formation of additional fibrils (interstitial growth), and, simultaneously, successive layers of lamellae are added (appositional growth). As the lamellae increase in length and width, the diameter and thickness of the cornea enlarge.

The endothelium in the central region of the cornea becomes a single layer of flattened cells by the third month of gestation. The cells rest on an interrupted basal lamina, which is the future *Descemet's membrane.* At this stage in development, Descemet's membrane consists of two zones: the lamina densa toward the stroma and the lamina lucida adjacent to the endothelium. Subsequent growth of Descemet's membrane forms a unique organization which is recognized as the fetal banded zone that attains a maximum thickness of about 3 µm at birth. In postnatal life, the posterior nonbanded zone of Descemet's membrane is composed of a homogeneous, fibrillogranular material. This region continues to thicken with age.

By the middle of the fourth month of gestation, the apices of adjacent endothelial cells are joined by zonulae occludens. This development corresponds to the onset of production of aqueous humor by the ciliary processes. Late in the fourth month, the acellular *Bowman's zone* of the anterior stroma is formed (Fig V-15). It is thought that the most superficial keratocytes synthesize and lay down the collagen fibrils and ground substance as they migrate somewhat posteriorly in the stroma.

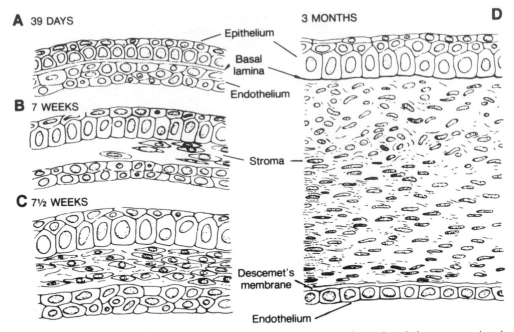

FIG V-14—Development of cornea in central region. *A,* At day 39, two-layered epithelium rests on basal lamina and is separated from endothelium (two to three layers) by narrow acellular space. *B,* At week 7, mesenchymal cells from periphery migrate into space between epithelium and endothelium. *C,* Mesenchymal cells (future keratocytes) are arranged in four to five incomplete layers by 7½ weeks, and a few collagen fibrils are present among cells. *D,* By 3 months, epithelium has two to three layers of cells, and stroma has about 25–30 layers of keratocytes that are arranged more regularly in the posterior half. Thin, uneven Descemet's membrane lies between the most posterior keratocytes and the now single layer of endothelium. (Reproduced with permission from Cook CS, Ozanics V, Jakobiec FA. Prenatal development of the eye and its adnexa. In: Tasman W, Jaeger EA, ed. *Duane's Foundations of Clinical Ophthalmology.* Philadelphia: Lippincott; 1991.)

The diameter of the unfixed cornea measures 2 mm at 12 weeks gestation, 4.5 mm at 17 weeks, and 9.3 mm at 35 weeks.

The *sclera* is formed by mesenchymal cells that condense around the optic cup. Most of these cells are derived from the neural crest. However, those in the caudal region of the sclera are probably derived from paraxial mesoderm that lies juxtaposed to the caudomedial surface of the optic cup throughout the period of crest cell migration. The sclera develops anteriorly before the seventh week of gestation and gradually extends posteriorly. The alignment of cells into parallel layers and the deposition of collagen fibrils are evidence of differentiation. Deposits of elastin and glycosaminoglycans are added to the extracellular matrix at a later stage. By the third month of gestation, some undifferentiated mesenchymal cells have migrated between the nerve fibers in the optic nerve. These cells become oriented transversely and synthesize extracellular matrix materials to form the lamina cribrosa.

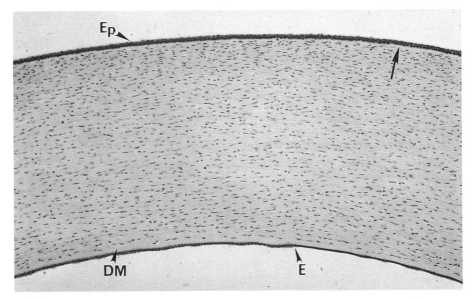

FG V-15—Light micrograph of central cornea in a 6-month fetus. Epithelium (*Ep*) consists of two to three cell layers. Stroma contains numerous keratocytes, and there is an indistinct Bowman's zone (*arrow*). Descemet's membrane (*DM*) is clearly demarcated. *E,* Endothelium. (Original magnification ×120.) (Reproduced with permission from Tripathi BJ, Tripathi RC, Wisdom J. Embryology of the anterior segment. In: Ritch R, Shields MB, Krupin T, eds. *The Glaucomas.* 2nd ed. St Louis: Mosby; 1996.)

Sellheyer K, Spitznas M. Development of the human sclera. A morphological study. *Graefes Arch Clin Exp Ophthalmol.* 1988;226:89–100.

Tripathi BJ, Tripathi RC, Wisdom JE. Embryology of the anterior segment of the human eye. In: Ritch R, Shields MB, Krupin T, eds. *The Glaucomas.* 2nd ed. St Louis: Mosby; 1996;1.

Tripathi BJ, Tripathi RC. Development of the human eye. In: Bron AJ, Tripathi RC, Tripathi BJ, eds. *Wolff's Anatomy of the Eye and Orbit.* 8th ed. London: Chapman and Hall; 1997.

Anterior Chamber, Angle, Iris, and Ciliary Body

The anterior chamber is first recognizable as the slitlike space that results after the ingrowth of the first wave of mesenchymal cells and the posterior extension of the second wave. By approximately 7 weeks gestation, the angle of the anterior chamber is occupied by a nest of loosely organized mesenchymal cells of neural crest origin. These cells will develop into the *trabecular meshwork.* At the posterior aspect of the angle, mesodermal cells are developing into the vascular channels of the pupillary membrane. Loosely organized mesenchymal cells and the pigment epithelium of the forward-growing optic cup are also present in this region.

Anteriorly, cells that resemble the corneal endothelium form a layer that extends to the angle recess; these cells meet the anterior surface of the developing iris, thus demarcating the angle of the anterior chamber by week 15 of gestation (Fig V-16). Beginning at the third month of gestation and continuing for a considerable time after birth (up to the age of 4 years), the angle recess progressively deepens. It also appears to be repositioned posteriorly because of the differential growth rate of adjacent tissues.

Initially, no demarcation exists between the mesenchymal cells that will form the trabecular meshwork and those that will differentiate into the ciliary muscle. The extracellular matrix of the trabecular beams is synthesized and deposited by the differentiating trabecular cells beginning at week 15 and continuing up to the eighth month of gestation. Already at 12–14 weeks gestation, the cellular layer that lines the trabecular meshwork on its anterior chamber aspect is perforated by gaps of 2–8 μm in diameter. As development proceeds, these gaps become larger, and eventually the open spaces of the meshwork come into direct communication with the anterior chamber.

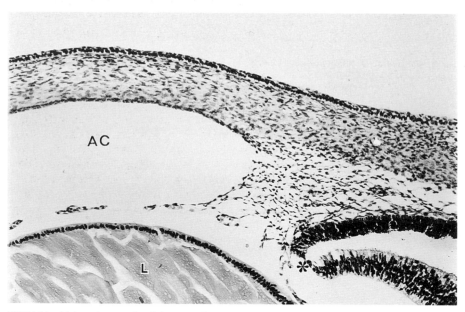

FIG V-16—Light micrograph of the eye of an 11-week fetus in meridional section. The angular region is poorly defined at this stage and is occupied by loosely arranged, spindle-shaped cells. Schlemm's canal is unrecognizable, and ciliary muscles and ciliary processes are not yet formed; the latter are derived from neural ectodermal fold (*asterisk*). Corneal endothelium appears continuous with cellular covering of primitive iris. *AC,* Anterior chamber. *L,* Lens. (Original magnification ×230.) (Reproduced by permission from Tripathi RC, Tripathi BC. Functional anatomy of the anterior chamber angle. In: Tasman W, Jaeger EA, eds. *Duane's Foundations of Clinical Ophthalmology.* Philadelphia: Lippincott; 1991.)

Schlemm's canal develops from a small plexus of venous canaliculi by the end of the third month of gestation. Derived from mesodermal mesenchyme, these channels function initially as blood vessels. Other mesenchymal cells surround the canal during the fourth month of gestation. These cells and their secreted extracellular matrix materials will form the juxtacanalicular tissue. Characteristic vacuolar configurations begin to appear in the endothelial cells that line Schlemm's canal at about the beginning of the fifth month. Their development corresponds to the onset of aqueous humor circulation. The canal begins to function as an aqueous sinus rather than as a blood vessel.

The differentiation of the ciliary epithelium occurs in the two layers of neuroectoderm just behind the advancing optic cup. Late in the third month, indentations that are oriented longitudinally appear in the outer pigmented layer. Between the third and fourth months the inner, nonpigmented layer starts to follow the contour and adhere to the pigmented layer. These radial folds, approximately 75 in number, are the beginning of the *ciliary processes.*

At week 10 of gestation, precursor *ciliary muscle* cells are identified as an accumulation of mesenchymal cells between the primitive ciliary epithelium and the anterior sclera condensation at the margin of the optic cup. Differentiation, which begins in the outermost (sclerad) cells during week 12, is evident from the myofilaments that surround plaques of dense bodies along the plasmalemma. The meridional portion of the muscle becomes organized during the fifth month, followed by the circular and radial components. The circular muscle continues to develop for at least 1 year after birth.

The development of the *iris* is associated with the formation of the anterior portion of the tunica vasculosa lentis. At about the sixth week of gestation, vascular channels of this embryonic structure are present as blind outgrowths from the annular vessel that encircles the rim of the optic cup. The developing vessels extend into the mesenchymal cells that cover the anterior lens surface and will ultimately be incorporated into the iris stroma. The most anterior region of the tunica vasculosa lentis is replaced subsequently by the pupillary membrane. At the end of the third month of gestation, after the future ciliary processes have formed, both walls of the optic cup at its margin grow forward beneath the pupillary membrane and mesenchymal cells. The mesenchymal tissue of the iris differentiates earlier than does the neuroectoderm. Cells in the developing stroma become fibroblast-like and secrete collagen fibrils and other components of the extracellular matrix.

The earliest differentiation of the *sphincter muscle* from the anterior layer of epithelium (the forward extension of the retinal pigment epithelium) occurs at 3 months of gestation. However, myofibrils are not synthesized until the fifth month, and the muscle does not come to lie free in the stroma until the eighth month of gestation. The dilator muscle is not apparent until the sixth month, and differentiation of the myoepithelial cells continues after birth.

Pigmentation of the posterior epithelial layer of the iris, which is a continuation of the nonpigmented layer of the ciliary body and hence of the neurosensory retina, commences at the pupillary margin at midterm and proceeds toward the periphery. It ceases at the iris root by the end of the seventh month.

The pupillary portion of the tunica vasculosa lentis is reabsorbed during the sixth month of gestation. The remains of an incomplete arteriovenous anastomose at the ciliary end of the sphincter muscle demarcates the collarette. The pupillary membrane atrophies near term.

The iris is still immature at birth. Much of the extracellular matrix is yet to be laid down in the stroma. The collarette is closer to the pupil in the newborn than it is in the adult eye.

McMenamin PG. A quantitative study of the prenatal development of the aqueous outflow system in the human eye. *Exp Eye Res.* 1991;53:507–517.

Reme C, d'Epinay SL. Periods of development of the normal human chamber angle. *Doc Ophthalmol.* 1981;51:241–268.

Sellheyer K, Spitznas M. Differentiation of the ciliary muscle in the human embryo and fetus. *Graefes Arch Clin Exp Ophthalmol.* 1988;226:281–287.

Strek W, Strek P, Nowogrodzka-Zagorska M, et al. Hyaloid vessels of the human fetal eye. A scanning electron microscopic study of corrosion casts. *Arch Ophthalmol.* 1993;111:1573–1577.

Tripathi BJ, Tripathi RC, Wisdom JE. Embryology of the anterior segment of the human eye. In: Ritch R, Shields MB, Krupin T, eds. *The Glaucomas.* 2nd ed. St Louis: Mosby; 1996;1.

Vascular System

The development of the vascular system of the eye and orbit is complex. Many vessels are transitory, arising and regressing in response to the changing needs of the embryonic eye. Vascular channels from the internal carotid artery develop in the mesenchyme around the optic vesicle late in the fourth week. Primitive dorsal and ventral ophthalmic arteries bud inward from the carotid and join a loose reticulum of capillaries around the optic vesicle. The system is drained into the future cavernous sinuses by way of plexuses. The early vessels are primarily ocular. A transient vessel, the stapedial artery, arises from the carotid to supply the expanding orbit. Later, the distal part of the stapedial artery is annexed to the ophthalmic artery.

The hyaloid artery is a branch of the primitive dorsal ophthalmic artery that arises at the juncture of the optic stalk and the optic cup at the time of closure of the embryonic fissure. The annular vessel that develops at the rim of the optic cup is supplied by the dorsal and ventral arteries. When incorporated in the optic cup, the hyaloid system extends toward and around the lens to join the annular vessel. Together with the tunica vasculosa lentis, the hyaloid system nourishes the interior of the developing eye.

The primitive dorsal ophthalmic artery becomes the definitive ophthalmic artery of the orbit at the sixth week of gestation. It supplies the temporal long posterior ciliary artery, the short posterior ciliary arteries, and the central retinal artery. The primitive ventral ophthalmic artery almost disappears; only a portion remains as the long posterior nasal ciliary artery.

The major arterial circle of the iris develops in the mesenchyme that surrounds the optic cup. It is located slightly lateral and anterior to the annular vessel and is formed by a coalescence of branches from the long ciliary arteries. Vascular twigs with little connective tissue grow from both the annular vessel and the major arterial circle to form the pupillary membrane, a system of radial vascular loops over the surface of the iris and lens. The pupillary arcades disappear centrally but remain peripherally as the minor circle of the iris. They provide vessels of the mature iris. Because the tissues that demarcate the anterior chamber angle are repositioned during development, the major arterial circle of the iris is ultimately located in the ciliary body.

At the fourth month of gestation, spindle-shaped mesenchymal cells arise from the hyaloid artery at the optic disc. These cells infiltrate the inner layers of the retina as solid cords of undifferentiated cells. Lumina develop, initially as slitlike openings behind the advancing edge of the invading mesenchymal cells. Retinal vascularization proceeds centripetally, and a boundary zone consisting of undifferentiated cells distinguishes the avascular and vascular retina. Endothelial cells differentiate first, and adjacent cells are joined by zonulae occludens and gap junctions.

Vascularization of the nasal retina is complete before that of the temporal retina, because of the shorter distance from the optic disc to the nasal ora serrata. By the fifth month, patent vessels have extended superiorly and inferiorly on the temporal aspect of the retina, sparing the region of the putative macula. Small blood vessels begin to develop in the ganglion cell layer of the foveal slope at the sixth month. The adult pattern of arterioles, veins, and capillaries is established through a process of remodeling and retraction of the primitive capillary network. Although capillaries reach the ora serrata by the eighth month, the mature pattern of vascularization is not achieved until 3 months after birth.

The hyaloid system and the tunica vasculosa lentis atrophy in the third trimester. Occasionally, either system may persist after birth (Fig V-17).

Penfold PL, Provis JM, Madigan MC, et al. Angiogenesis in normal human retinal development: the involvement of astrocytes and macrophages. *Graefes Arch Clin Exp Ophthalmol.* 1990;228:255–263.

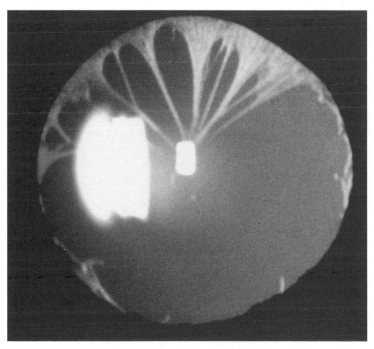

FIG V-17—Persistent pupillary membrane.

Periocular Tissues and Eyelids

The frontonasal and maxillary processes of neural crest cells occupy the space that surrounds the optic cups by the fourth week of gestation. The bones, cartilage, fat, and connective tissues of the orbit develop from these cells. All bones of the orbit are membranous except the sphenoid, which is initially cartilaginous. Ossification begins during the third month of gestation, and fusion occurs between the sixth and seventh months.

The extraocular muscles arise from myotomic cells of the preotic mesodermal somites that have shifted cranially. These cells become located within the neural crest mesenchyme that is situated on the dorsal and caudal aspects of the developing eye. Although the development of the extraocular muscles was thought to begin at the primitive muscle cone that surrounds the optic nerve in the fifth week of gestation, recent evidence suggests the muscles arise in situ. Myoblasts with myofibrils and immature Z bands are distinguishable by the fifth week of gestation. At about 7 weeks, the dorsomedial aspect of the superior rectus muscle gives rise to the levator muscle, which grows laterally and over the superior rectus toward the eyelid. The tendons of the extraocular muscles fuse with the sclera in the vicinity of the equator late in the third month.

The upper eyelid develops first as a proliferation of surface ectoderm in the region of the future outer canthus at 4–5 weeks gestation (Fig V-18). During the second month, both the upper and lower eyelids are discernible as undifferentiated skin folds that surround mesenchyme of neural crest origin. Later, mesodermal mesenchyme infiltrates the eyelids and differentiates into the palpebral musculature. The eyelid folds grow toward each other as well as laterally. Starting near the inner canthus, the margins of the folds fuse at approximately 10 weeks gestation. As the folds adhere to each other, evolution of cilia and glands continues. The orbicularis muscle condenses in the fold in week 12. The eyelid adhesions gradually break down late in the fifth month, coincident with the secretion of sebum from the sebaceous glands and cornification of the surface epithelium.

The lacrimal gland begins to develop between the sixth and seventh weeks of gestation. Solid cords of epithelial cells proliferate from the basal cell layer of the conjunctiva in the temporal region of the fornix. Neural crest–derived mesenchymal cells aggregate at the tips of the cords and differentiate into acini. Ducts of the gland are formed at approximately 3 months by vacuolation of the cord cells and the development of lumina. Lacrimal gland (reflex) tear production does not begin until 20 or more days after birth. Hence, newborn infants cry without tears.

Between the third and sixth months of gestation, eyelid appendages and pilosebaceous units develop from invaginations of epithelial cells into the underlying mesenchyme.

Oguni M, Setogawa T, Matsui H, et al. Timing and sequence of the events in the development of extraocular muscles in staged human embryos: ultrastructural and histochemical study. *Acta Anat* (Basel). 1992;143:195–198.

Sevel D. The origins and insertions of the extraocular muscles: development, histologic features, and clinical significance. *Trans Am Ophthalmol Soc.* 1986;84:488–526.

Tripathi BJ, Tripathi RC. Development of the human eye. In: Bron AJ, Tripathi RC, Tripathi BJ, eds. *Wolff's Anatomy of the Eye and Orbit.* 8th ed. London: Chapman and Hall; 1997.

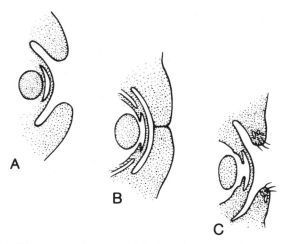

FIG V-18—Development of the eyelids. *A*, Seventh week: upper and lower eyelid folds grow over the eye. *B*, Eyelids fuse during the eighth week. Fusion starts along the nasal margin. *C*, As cilia and glandular structures develop, eyelids gradually open from the fifth to the seventh month.

Realignment of the Globe

Initially, the axes of the two optic cups and the optic stalks form an angle of 180°. At 3 months gestation, this angle has decreased to 105°. With continued enlargement, remodeling, and repositioning of the head, face, and brain throughout gestation, the eyes become oriented in their anterior position. At birth the axes form an angle of 71°. However, the adult orientation of 68° is not achieved until the age of 3 years.

CHAPTER VI

Congenital Anomalies

Introduction

Congenital anomalies are defects present at birth. They result both from genetic influences and from a variety of local and systemic environmental effects. A *teratogen* is an agent that produces or increases the incidence of congenital malformation. Nongenetic teratogens include the following:

- Toxins

- Maternal infections

- Nutritional deficiencies

- Radiation

- Drugs

- Developmental failures

Because exposure to a teratogenic influence can occur at any stage of embryonic development, its effects will differ according to the time, duration, and intensity of exposure. Conversely, during a critical period of development, different agents may cause the same type of anatomic defect.

A teratogen acting in the first trimester on primordial cells produces severe damage to the ocular primordium and its derivative tissues. Major ocular developmental disasters involve the entire globe and are often associated with defects in the orbital, cerebral, and facial tissues, although defects may be limited to one or more tissues in the eye (Fig VI-1). Cellular development continues after organogenesis, and genetic or environmental action at a later time may lead to dysfunction without gross structural abnormalities.

> Peiffer RL, McCullen R, Alles AJ, et al. Relationship of cell death to cyclophosphamide-induced ocular malformations. *Teratog Carcinog Mutagen.* 1991;11:203–212.

> Sulik KK, Cook CS, Webster WS. Teratogens and craniofacial malformations: relationships to cell death. *Development.* 1988;103(Suppl):213–231.

> Sulik KK, Dehart DB, Rogers JM, et al. Teratogenicity of low doses of all-trans retinoic acid in presomite mouse embryos. *Teratology.* 1995;51:398–403.

The mouse model of fetal alcohol syndrome (FAS) shows that injury results from an insult to the optic primordia during the gastrula stage. A small optic vesicle results in a deficient lens vesicle, which manifests as microphakia. Delay in lens detachment from surface ectoderm leads to myriad anterior segment anomalies, explicable by impaired migration of the neural crest cells that should have formed the corneal stroma, endothelium, and iris (Figs VI-2, VI-3). Together, they cause microphthalmos with a secondary persistence of primary vitreous. The embryonic fissure in this model often fails to close in the presence of microphthalmos.

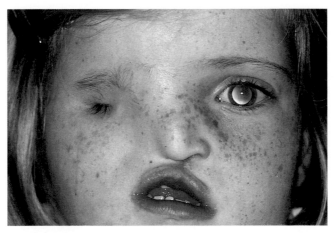

FIG VI-1—Microphthalmic eye with defects in eyelids, brow, nose, and mouth on same side as deformed eye.

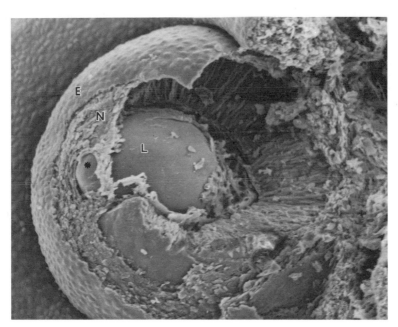

FIG VI-2—Eye of day 14 fetus exposed to ethanol on day 7 of gestation. Anterior lenticonus (*) as a result of delayed lens detachment prevents migration of neural crest (N) to form the axial corneal stroma and endothelium. E = surface ectoderm, L = lens. (Freeze fracture, scanning electron micrograph ×195.) (Reproduced with permission from Cook CS, Sulik KK. Keratolenticular dysgenesis [Peters anomaly] as a result of acute embryonic insult during gastrulation. *J Pediatr Ophthalmol Strabismus.* 1988;25:60–66.)

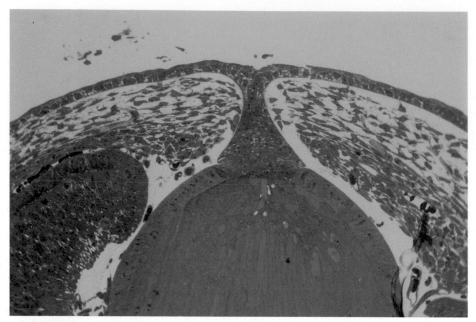

FIG VI-3—Histologic section of isotretinoin-exposed fetus. The lens stalk forms a barrier to neural crest migration (toluidine blue, ×100). (Reproduced by permission from Cook CS, Sulik KK. Keratolenticular dysgenesis [Peters anomaly] as a result of acute embryonic insult during gastrulation. *J Pediatr Ophthalmol Strabismus.* 1988;25:60–66.)

Persistence of the embryonic fissure, which leads to a failure in maintaining intraocular pressure, is one explanation for microphthalmos and coloboma formation. In the fetal alcohol mouse model these malformations appear to be primary events caused by faulty induction produced by the early insult of alcohol on the gastrula forebrain, which gives rise to the evaginating optic primordia. Defects of proliferation and of regression also occur in this model (Fig VI-4).

> Cook CS, Nowotny AZ, Sulik KK. Fetal alcohol syndrome. Eye malformations in a mouse model. *Arch Ophthalmol.* 1987;105:1576–1581.

> Cook CS, Sulik KK. Keratolenticular dysgenesis (Peters' anomaly) as a result of acute embryonic insult during gastrulation. *J Pediatr Ophthalmol Strabismus.* 1988; 25:60–66.

Microphthalmos and coloboma formation are associated with many different chromosomal anomalies, suggesting that the same morphologic defect can be caused by different genetic influences occurring at different stages in the process of neural crest cell evolution. Other examples of these relationships are discussed below.

> Warburg M, Friedrich U. Coloboma and microphthalmos in chromosomal aberrations. Chromosomal aberrations and neural crest cell developmental field. *Ophthalmic Pediatr Genet.* 1987;8:105–118.

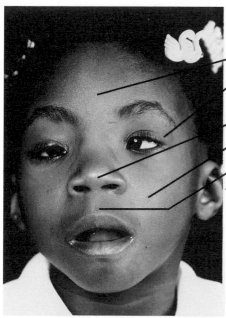
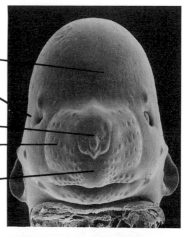
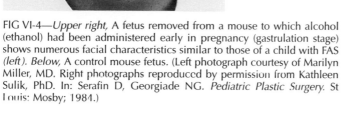
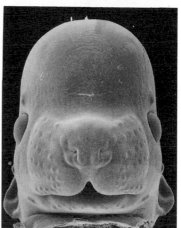

Narrow forehead

Short palpebral fissures

Small nose

Small midface

Long upper lip with deficient philtrum

FIG VI-4—*Upper right,* A fetus removed from a mouse to which alcohol (ethanol) had been administered early in pregnancy (gastrulation stage) shows numerous facial characteristics similar to those of a child with FAS *(left). Below,* A control mouse fetus. (Left photograph courtesy of Marilyn Miller, MD. Right photographs reproduced by permission from Kathleen Sulik, PhD. In: Serafin D, Georgiade NG. *Pediatric Plastic Surgery.* St Louis: Mosby; 1984.)

Anophthalmos, Microphthalmos, and Nanophthalmos

Anophthalmos is the total absence of ocular tissues (Figs VI-5 through VI-7). *Microphthalmos* is the presence of a small, often disorganized globe. True anophthalmos is extremely rare, and the diagnosis can be made with conviction only when the orbital contents are examined histologically and no evidence of ocular tissues can be identified. Most instances of clinical anophthalmos are actually severe microphthalmos (Fig VI-8).

Primary anophthalmos can occur in an otherwise normal child. It is usually bilateral and isolated, implying complete agenesis of the primitive ocular anlage. Secondary anophthalmos, a result of complete suppression of the development of the forebrain, is lethal. Consecutive anophthalmos implies the initial development of an ocular structure that undergoes secondary degeneration or destruction.

FIG VI-5—Bilateral clinical anophthalmos. Eyelids, brows, and orbits are well formed but small.

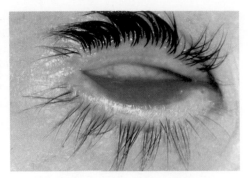

FIG VI-6—Partially opened small eyelids of anophthalmic orbit.

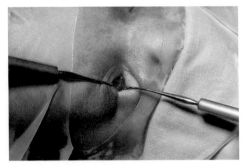

FIG VI-7—Anophthalmos. Palpebral fissure is fully opened, and no eye tissue is evident.

FIG VI-8—Severe microphthalmic eye is almost buried by redundant eyelid tissue.

Microphthalmos occurs as the result of a variety of conditions, notably trisomy 13. Defects in the microphthalmic eye include the following:

- Corneal leukomas
- Immature chamber angles
- Colobomas with or without cysts
- Cataract
- Keratolenticular adhesions
- Persistent hyperplastic primary vitreous
- Retinal dysplasia
- Bizarre migrations of the pigment epithelium
- Hypoplasia of the optic nerve

Other defects may also be associated with microphthalmos.

The *nanophthalmic* globe is a small eye without major internal disorganization. Associated anomalies may include narrow palpebral fissures, deep-set eyes, high hyperopia, thickened sclera, and, occasionally, glaucoma. Nanophthalmos can be inherited as either an autosomal dominant or an autosomal recessive trait.

Cyclopia and Synophthalmia

Cyclopia is a lethal condition in which a single eye or ocular structure appears in the upper, median portion of the face. It is associated with dramatic, symmetric deformities of the nose, skull, orbits, and brain (Fig VI-9). These include a holoprosencephalic (nonhemispheric) brain, a single median orbit, a proboscis (primitive dysplastic nose) above the eye, absence of nasal bones and upper nasal passages, hypoplastic oral cavity, and general midline hypoplasia. Although an optic nerve is not present, the eye may be reasonably well formed, or it may consist of various rudimentary dysplastic ocular tissues in the midline.

In cyclopia an inadequate amount of neuroectoderm was induced by mesoderm as ocular primordia, creating a shared zone of multipotential cells. Multipotency is the ability of embryonic cells to develop into many tissues, depending on local inductive and environmental factors. The primordial cells, once induced, produce a specific organ or tissue and lose their multipotency. The orderly structure of the cyclopean eye indicates that it was formed by abnormal anlagen that then faithfully completed a normal program of secondary inductions and anterior ocular histogenesis, including the retina. Optic nerve and chiasmal tissue is not midline and is relatively undifferentiated until later stages of ocular development, which accounts for the lack of an optic nerve and connection to the brain. Interference with migration around the central eye and subsequent abnormal interaction of neural crest cells with facial processes lead to the proboscis above the eye and the other associated facial anomalies.

Synophthalmia is a less severe condition, but it is also lethal. In this condition portions of two incomplete, usually symmetric, globes are joined in the midline as a single median ocular structure. Most infants born with cyclopia or synophthalmia do not show other somatic defects or chromosomal abnormalities.

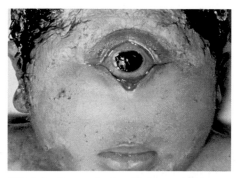

FIG VI-9—True cyclopia with large midline eye, hypoplastic philtrum. No proboscis. (Photograph courtesy of Ruiz and Biomedical Foundation.)

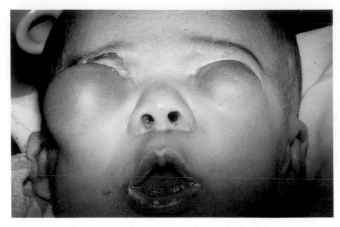

FIG VI-10—Orbital cysts replacing both globes.

Orbital Cyst and Cryptophthalmos

Several conditions may appear as a cystic bulge within the palpebral fissure when the eyelids are separated (Fig VI-10). They include congenital cystic eye, an eye with a cystic coloboma, a teratoma with cystic changes, orbital encephalocele, and congenital rhabdomyosarcoma. Rhabdomyosarcoma is discussed in BCSC Section 4, *Ophthalmic Pathology and Intraocular Tumors;* Section 6, *Pediatric Ophthalmology and Strabismus;* and Section 7, *Orbit, Eyelids, and Lacrimal System.*

In the true *cystic eye* the optic vesicles remain in an embryonic state. This extremely rare condition results from failure of invagination of the lens placode and optic vesicle. Differentiation of all ocular tissues is limited. Clinically smooth, undivided skin without eyelid differentiation may cover the bulging structure and appear as cryptophthalmos.

A *cystic coloboma* results from faulty closure of the fetal fissure. Ectropion of the inner layer of the optic cup occurs as the fissure closes. The two layers of the cup are not perfectly apposed to one another, leaving a remnant of the primary optic vesicle. With closure of the fissure, the remaining vesicular space expands, developing a cystlike structure external to the globe. The eye may be smaller than the cystic coloboma.

Orbital teratomas are rare and contain tissues representative of all primitive germ layers. The glandular tissues produce secretions in closed sacs, leading to the formation of either a single cyst or multiple cystic spaces.

Encephaloceles are soft and pulsatile. Anterior orbital encephaloceles occur at the inner angle of the orbit, with cerebral tissues bulging through any of the sutures involving the frontal, ethmoidal, lacrimal, or maxillary bones. The eye may be displaced laterally or downward. Anterior encephaloceles are usually evident at birth. Posterior encephaloceles are less obvious. Although the bony defect in the posterior orbit is present at birth, proptosis of the globe may evolve slowly over months or years, and this congenital defect may not be diagnosed until clinical symptoms present. Radiographs, CT, and MRI may be diagnostic. A defect in the sphenoidal bone may result in proptosis from a posterior encephalocele in neurofibromatosis.

Cryptophthalmos, the hidden or buried eye, represents a failure of normal eyelid formation in which folds do not form and the skin forms a single continuous layer over the anterior surface of the eye, extending from brow to cheek (Fig VI-11). A small linear dimpling may represent an aborted eyelid fold. Unlike cystic eyes, the lens in cryptophthalmos has usually formed and sits in a highly anomalous anterior chamber without iris or ciliary body. There is no cornea. The inward migration of the first, second, and third wave of neural crest cells did not take place. The retina and optic nerve are usually normal.

In limited cryptophthalmos bands of skin remain adherent to the eye, usually superiorly, and eyelid formation is incomplete. Other defects associated with cryptophthalmos include absence of the eyebrows, microphthalmos, cleft palate, cleft lip, facial fissure, malformed ears, malformations of the genitourinary tract, and syndactyly of the fingers and toes.

The cosmetic appearance in each of these conditions is usually unsatisfactory. Echographic and CT scanning provide useful information, not only about the orbit, but also about the intracranial variations. True diagnosis may be possible only with histologic examination of the excised structure. In some cases a multidisciplinary surgical team, including a neurosurgeon, is needed to extirpate or repair these defects, especially in the case of encephaloceles.

Developmental Anomalies of the Cornea

The corneas of infants appear large in relation to the rest of the face. At age 1 year, a cornea measuring less than 9 mm horizontally is too small (*microcornea*) and one more than 12 mm is too large (*megalocornea*). Microcornea (Fig VI-12) is frequently found with microphthalmos. In *sclerocornea* the scleral rim extends anteriorly to replace the peripheral cornea, leaving 3–8 mm of clear cornea centrally. Because of the opacity, the cornea appears small but may be of normal dimensions.

 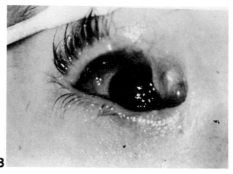

A **B**

FIG VI-11—*A,* Complete cryptophthalmos, both eyes. *B,* Incomplete cryptophthalmos of right eye with eyelid fused to cornea superonasally.

FIG VI-12—Severe microcornea and microph-thalmos OD. Both irides are colobomatous.

In megalocornea (Fig VI-13) the cornea may have a diameter of up to 18 mm. It must be differentiated from the enlarged cornea of congenital glaucoma.

Leukomas are discrete, white, opacified areas in the central or peripheral cornea. Opacification is variable and sometimes occurs only at the edge of a defect. The opacities may be round, oval, arcuate, or irregular. Congenital leukomas may be associated with other anomalies of anterior segment dysgenesis previously, but mistakenly, referred to as mesodermal dysgenesis. These anomalies, including congenital glaucoma, are now best called *neurocristopathies*. They are thought to result from defective terminal induction or migration of tissues derived from neural crest cells that form the chamber angle. Synonyms used clinically can be helpful, however, as they describe specific clinical entities. These other terms include posterior embryotoxon, posterior keratoconus, and the anomalies of Rieger, Axenfeld, and Peters.

Bahn CF, Falls HF, Varley GA, et al. Classification of corneal endothelial disorders based on neural crest origin. *Ophthalmology.* 1984;91:558–563.

The usual dermoid or dermolipoma is found at the limbus and only rarely is entirely corneal. Dermoids may also be found in the conjunctiva and orbit. *Dermoids* are choristomas that are thought to represent arrests or inclusions of epidermal and connective tissues during closure of fetal clefts. The dermoid is covered by squamous epithelium and may contain hair follicles, sebaceous glands, nerve bundles, fat, or glandular tissue. *Dermolipomas* are usually solid, consisting entirely of fatty and fibrous tissue, and are generally located between the lateral and superior rectus muscles. Dermoids that cover the entire eye usually herald a poorly formed globe. Epibulbar dermoids are found in Goldenhar syndrome (oculoauriculovertebral dysplasia), one of the neural crest cell–derived, first brachial arch, facial midline–clefting anomalies.

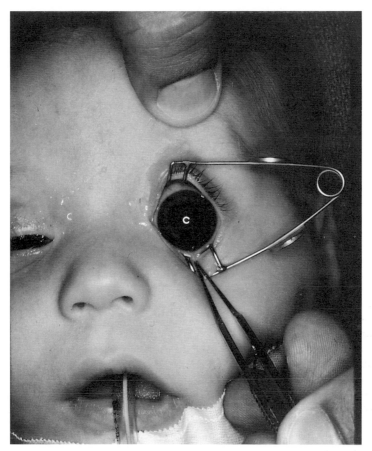

FIG VI-13—Megalocornea.

Congenital Anterior Chamber Anomalies

Anomalies of the normal anatomy of the anterior chamber result from inadequate regression of tissues or failure of cell differentiation. *Posterior embryotoxon,* the most common and benign of these anomalies, is an exaggerated, prominent, and centrally displaced Schwalbe's line (Fig VI-14) present in 3%–15% of normal eyes. Commonly inherited as an autosomal dominant trait, it may be noticed on biomicroscopic examination but is best seen gonioscopically.

    Axenfeld-Rieger syndrome has been chosen recently as the name for a spectrum of congenital anterior segment defects previously called by the term mesodermal dysgenesis and a variety of eponyms. All the conditions listed in the following paragraph are now subsumed under the single name Axenfeld-Rieger syndrome.

    Axenfeld anomaly includes both posterior embryotoxon and the insertion of iris processes crossing the angle on Schwalbe's line (Fig VI-15). *Rieger anomaly* includes posterior embryotoxon, iris strands, and hypoplasia of the iris stroma (Fig VI-16). In

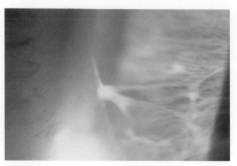

FIG VI-14—Posterior embryotoxon on biomicroscopic examination.

Rieger syndrome, anomalies of the face (maxillary hypoplasia, hypertelorism, hypodontia, oligodontia, or anodontia) and umbilicus are added to the anomalies of the anterior ocular segment. Strabismus, macrocornea, microcornea, cataracts, corectopia, and pseudopolycoria have been recorded. Rieger syndrome is inherited as an autosomal dominant trait with a high degree of penetrance.

Peters anomaly (Fig VI-17) includes a central defect in Descemet's membrane and absence of endothelium. Often iris strands are attached to the edges of the defect. Clinically, the defective central cornea is opacified. The lens may or may not be cataractous, and it may adhere to the defect in Descemet's membrane by a keratolenticular stalk. The condition may be bilateral or unilateral and can be dominantly inherited. An isolated presentation, often accompanied by chromosomal and other systemic anomalies, is common. Experimental studies have revealed that exposure of the embryo to ethanol or isotretinoin can cause structural abnormalities suggestive of Peters anomaly.

Cook CS, Sulik KK. Laminin and fibronectin in retinoid-induced keratolenticular dysgenesis. *Invest Ophthalmol Vis Sci.* 1990;31:751–757.

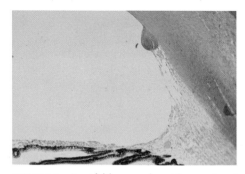

FIG VI-15—Axenfeld anomaly with prominent Schwalbe's line and iris strands.

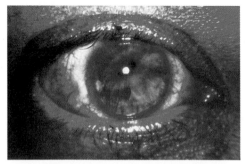

FIG VI-16—Rieger anomaly with stromal hypoplasia, visible sphincter muscle, oval pupil, and prominent Schwalbe's line.

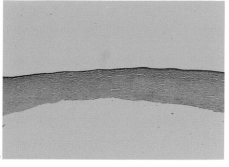

FIG VI-17—*A,* Clinical appearance of anterior segment in Peters anomaly. The lens is connected to the central posterior region of the cornea by a keratolenticular stalk. *B,* Histologic section of cornea in Peters anomaly. The central cornea is thinned and lacks Descemet's membrane and endothelium. Bowman's zone of the anterior stroma in this region is degenerate. (Original magnification ×10.)

Posterior keratoconus is a localized or diffuse, central or paracentral, craterlike depression in the posterior cornea associated with a deep stromal opacity. Unlike Peters anomaly, in posterior keratoconus both the endothelium and Descemet's membrane are present, and no other ocular abnormality is apparent. Because the anterior corneal curvature is unaffected, good vision is common. The term *internal ulcer of von Hippel* signifies a secondary infectious or inflammatory condition, but some cases may, in fact, fall within the spectrum of Peters anomaly and posterior keratoconus.

Iris

Anisocoria, a difference in size of 0.5–2.0 mm between the two pupils, occurs in 2% of the normal population. It may be transmitted as an autosomal dominant trait with variable expressivity. *Polycoria,* the presence of many openings in the iris, may result from local hypoplasia or hyperplasia of the stroma and pigment epithelium. *Ectopia,* or displaced pupil, and *corectopia,* or deformed pupil, may be caused by unequal growth in parts of the iris or by defective contributions of neural crest cells to the stroma. Both pigmented and nonpigmented congenital cysts of the iris may be present, sometimes in the pupillary area and sometimes buried beneath the peripheral iris.

Aniridia implies total absence of the iris, but some iris tissue usually remains. Rudimentary iris stumps occur around the entire circumference of the base of the iris. Dilator and sphincter muscles are usually absent. Retroillumination shows the pupil extending almost to the periphery of the cornea. Aniridic infants are highly photophobic. Aniridia can be inherited as an autosomal dominant or recessive trait. Nonfamilial aniridia occurs in association with Wilms tumor, ambiguous genitalia and other genitourinary anomalies, and mental retardation. A small but variable interstitial deletion of the short arm of chromosome 11 (11p–) is usually present. Aniridia has never been reported in families with autosomal dominant Wilms tumor.

Colobomas

The term *coloboma* implies the absence of part or all of a tissue. It may result from developmental aberrations, surgery, or injury. Congenital colobomas of the eye are classified as typical or atypical varieties (Fig VI-18). Typical colobomas are caused by the failure of the embryonic fissure to close in the fifth week. Atypical colobomas appear in locations outside the region of the embryonic fissure. Colobomas may be partial or complete. When they occur in the iris, they have the appearance of an obliquely placed, inverted teardrop; the ballooned area is uppermost and the tapered end of the drop is directed inferonasally. *Keyhole pupil* is a common lay term.

Closure of the embryonic fissure starts at the equator of the globe and proceeds anteriorly and posteriorly. Areas of normal fusion may alternate with areas of defective closure, resulting in partial or incomplete colobomas. The coloboma may extend completely from the optic disc through the pupillary margin, or it may be represented by one or more defects along the normal fusion line. Occasionally, only one tissue is involved. Thus, colobomas of the optic disc may or may not be associated with iridic colobomas and vice versa.

More than half of typical colobomas are bilateral, although often asymmetric. Typical colobomas may be inherited as an autosomal dominant trait with incomplete penetrance and expressivity. Although colobomas are caused by defective fusion of the lips of the embryonic fissure, the failure of retinal pigment epithelium to develop results in hypoplasia of the underlying choroid and sclera (and overlying retina) and in ectasia or staphyloma of the globe. A coloboma of the retina results in an absolute scotoma corresponding to the defect. In cases with a large posterior pole coloboma, visual acuity may be subnormal, with secondary strabismus and nystagmus. Lens colobomas usually result from lack of zonular pull in that region of the lens because of hypoplasia of the corresponding ciliary body and zonular fibers.

Lens

Spherophakia is a spherical lens that is occasionally associated with other defects, as in Marfan syndrome. In later life the lens often dislocates superiorly. In *microspherophakia,* which is associated with Weill-Marchesani syndrome, the lens is both small and spherical, and it may dislocate into the anterior chamber. The habitus of individuals with these two syndromes is profoundly different: the Marfan patient is tall and unusually lean with arachnodactyly; the Weill-Marchesani patient is short (usually less than 5 feet tall), muscular, and stocky.

In Lowe syndrome, developmental delay, neuromuscular hypotonia, and aberrations of amino acid metabolism are associated with congenital cataracts and, frequently, glaucoma. The lenses are small plaques reduced in both the anteroposterior and equatorial diameters. Lowe syndrome is found almost exclusively in males; the condition has a recessive X-linked pattern of inheritance and a characteristic lens opacity in carrier females.

A *cataract* is an opacity in the lens, whether or not visual impairment results. While congenital cataracts that impair vision are relatively uncommon, many types of opacities—including all manner of dots, clumps, lines, clefts, deposits, colors, membranes, and disks—have been described in the newborn lens. *Lenticonus* is a central outpouching of the anterior or posterior surface of the lens. High myopia is characteristic.

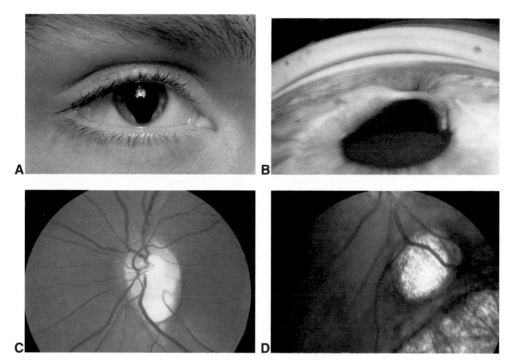

FIG VI-18—*A,* Iridic coloboma showing typical location with teardrop directed inferonasally. *B,* Gonioscopic view showing colobomatous dimple near iris root separated from main coloboma of iris by bridge of tissue. (Photograph courtesy of Alan R. Liss, Inc.) *C,* Small coloboma of optic disc inferonasally in left eye. *D,* Coloboma of fundus with skip areas. Note healthy tissue between optic disc and small colobomas and bridge of tissue above large inferior coloboma.

Scattered opacities and various embryonic sutural cataracts are compatible with good visual acuity, but total or nuclear cataracts often have a guarded prognosis for vision. The vision present and the potential for increased vision in an infant with congenital cataracts must be assessed carefully and weighed against the hazards of surgery and the problems of providing appropriate optical correction and orthoptic rehabilitation for the aphakic child. BCSC Section 11, *Lens and Cataract,* and Section 6, *Pediatric Ophthalmology and Strabismus,* discuss the management of cataract and aphakia in infants and children.

Cataracts resulting from congenital rubella are dense, white, pearly opacities in the nucleus. The virus invades the developing lens and damages it. The virus becomes sequestered in the lens and may remain there for months after birth. If maternal infection occurred in the first trimester, the infant is more likely to be severely damaged than if the infection occurred later. Many organs in the body can be damaged by rubella. The classic triad for an infant infected with rubella in the first trimester is ocular (cataracts), auditory (deafness), and systemic (cardiac). Glaucoma occasionally occurs in a child with rubella but is usually not concomitant with rubella cataracts. A diffuse, generalized, irregular pigmentation called *salt-and-*

pepper fundus may be the only residuum of a maternal rubella infection during the second trimester.

Retina

Folds, cysts, septa, and congenital nonattachment may be found in the retina. Dysplasia of the retina implies aberrant differentiation in any of the cellular layers and is often associated with the formation of *rosettes*, circular or oval groupings of dysplastic retinal cells that may be found in any retinal layer. In retinoblastoma the rosettes are uniform in size in a given specimen, whereas in dysplasia the rosettes are highly variable in size and shape. Rosettes may be an incidental finding in eyes enucleated for unrelated conditions later in life, or they may replace the entire retina. In such cases severe dysplasia is often associated with total retinal detachment. Profound retinal dysplasia, as in trisomy 13 and trisomy 18, may not be evident clinically, because the cornea and other ocular media may be too cloudy to allow ophthalmoscopic examination of the fundus. An abnormal electroretinogram can reveal the presence of retinal dysplasia not detectable by clinical inspection.

Retinal Pigment Epithelium

Variations in the RPE may be evident at birth. Localized hypertrophy of the RPE is the most common. These flat, heavily pigmented spots are sharply delineated from the surrounding normal pigment epithelium. They occur as an isolated lesion but may be clustered throughout the entire posterior pole and are uncommonly bilateral. When they are bilateral, Gardner syndrome, a familial cancer syndrome, must be considered. Patches are smaller proximal to the disc and generally increase in size toward the periphery. Several patches grouped together are called congenital grouped pigmentations, or *bear tracks.*

> Lewis RA, Crowder WE, Eierman LA, et al. The Gardner syndrome. Significance of ocular features. *Ophthalmology.* 1984;91:916–924.

The *macular coloboma* is so called because it appears as a punched-out macula lacking retina and choroid. Generally ascribed to congenital toxoplasmosis, it is bounded by dense irregular clumps of pigment, measuring 2–4 disc diopters and associated with temporal disc pallor. Such lesions are occasionally reported in siblings.

Optic Disc and Nerve

Aplasia of the optic nerve is extremely rare. Hypoplasia of the optic disc is more common (Fig VI-19). The condition may be associated with microphthalmos and malformations of the forebrain. Bilateral optic nerve hypoplasia and absent septum pellucidum indicate de Morsier syndrome. Unilateral hypoplasia is often found in normal individuals.

Colobomas and optic pits are found in the optic nerve. The coloboma may be limited to the nerve or may be continuous with a total uveal coloboma. A pit is a deep, circular depression in the nerve head, usually located temporally, inferotemporally, or inferiorly. During organogenesis, a small pouch of retinal tissue, including glia, nerve fibers, and RPE, pouches downward between the sclera and the nerve under the dural sheath. The lamina cribrosa is defective, but the adjacent choroid and sclera are normal. The abnormal saccular protrusion is thought to allow direct continuity of the subdural space with the subretinal space. In later life cerebrospinal fluid percolates through into the subretinal space as a serous detachment of the retina. Arcuate scotomata may be associated with optic pits.

Remnants of the hyaloid system may persist as white, fibrous, or glial strands, veils, or collarettes on the disc (Bergmeister's papilla). Remnants of hyaloid vessels may extend into the vitreous and are occasionally patent (persistent posterior hyaloid artery) (Figs VI-20, VI-21). Mittendorf's dot, a small white dot of tissue posterior to the lens on the nasal side, is a minute remnant of the anterior hyaloid artery (Fig VI-22).

Persistent Hyperplastic Primary Vitreous

Persistent hyperplastic primary vitreous (PHPV) is included in the differential diagnosis of leukocoria. Visual potential is limited. The condition is almost invariably unilateral and associated with microphthalmos. With growth of the child, the microphthalmos becomes accentuated, as the involved globe grows more slowly, if at all. The anterior chamber is shallow; the lens may be either clear or cataractous. A fibrovascular sheath forms behind the lens, contracts, and elongates the ciliary processes, which are seen as dark reflections when the pupil is dilated (Fig VI-23). Vessels may occasionally grow through a tear in the posterior capsule. As the retrolenticular membrane contracts, the retina may detach. Removal of the lens and vitreous through the pars plana often prevents the development of secondary glaucoma, but it may not improve the visual outcome because of retinal dysplasia and amblyopia.

Abnormalities of Pigmentation

The skin and the eye may be hyperpigmented or hypopigmented. Oculodermal melanocytosis (*nevus of Ota*) is a unilateral congenital condition with hyperpigmentation of the melanocytes in the periocular skin. The hyperpigmentation may also involve the uveal tract and the sclera. Open-angle glaucoma is occasionally associated.

Nevi that are pigmented at birth are sometimes found on the skin of the eyelids, conjunctiva, caruncle, iris, and choroid. Pigmentation developing at the time of puberty may cause concern. Malignant melanomas may arise from nevi, but usually only later in life. Malignant melanomas of ocular or periocular tissues are extremely rare in childhood.

Albinism is the result of a series of defects in the synthesis of melanin pigment. In *oculocutaneous albinism* all tissues of the body lack normal melanin (Fig VI-24). In so-called *ocular albinism* the globe is the most obvious clinical site of involvement, although recent histologic evaluations show that the skin is also a target of morphological changes in the X-linked form, in both affected males and carrier females. Visual acuity in tyrosinase-negative individuals is poor but stable throughout life. Nystagmus is almost invariably present. Visual acuity may be poor in the several tyrosinase-positive variants in the first decade of life, but it improves as some uveal pigmentation develops with age. Pigment deficiency in the pigment epithelium will be apparent as variable degrees of transillumination of the irides, but stromal iris pigmentation may occur in all forms of albinism. Foveal hypoplasia is characteristic.

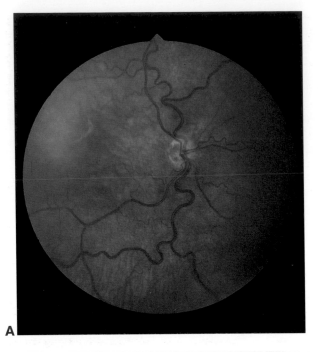

A

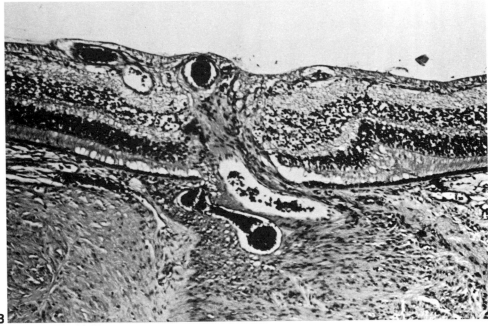

B

FIG VI-19—A, Optic nerve hypoplasia (ONH). A normal nerve of 1.5 mm diameter is 10–15 central retinal vessel widths across. This disc is far smaller. Part of what seems to be disc is a scleral rim (halo sign). B, Histologic section through a hypoplastic optic disc that shows a defect in retinal pigment epithelium with small central retinal artery (H&E ×125). C (facing page), CT scan of absent septum pellucidum with bilateral ONH (de Morsier syndrome).

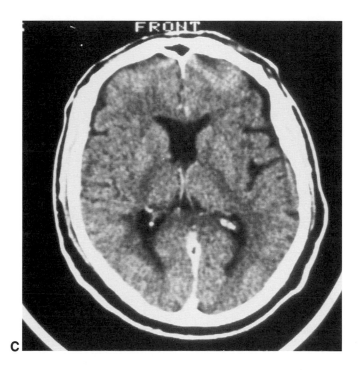

C

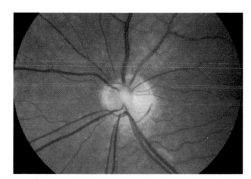

FIG VI-20—Remnant of glial tissue of hyaloid artery on optic disc.

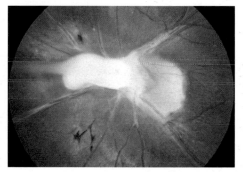

FIG VI-21—Atrophic stalk of hyaloid artery from optic disc into vitreous cavity.

Well-demarcated, highly pigmented spots may be found in one or more quadrants of the fundus. These areas, formed by hypertrophic RPE cells, are congenital and do not enlarge. The spots may be single (Fig VI-25) or multiple.

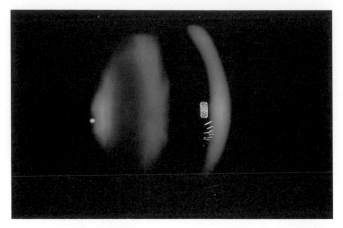

FIG VI-22—Clinical appearance of Mittendorf's dot, a retrolenticular remnant of anterior hyaloid.

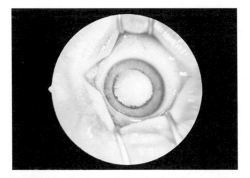

FIG VI-23—Persistent hypoplastic primary vitreous. Note ciliary processes visible in pupil.

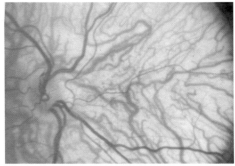

FIG VI-24—Fundus of albino. Optic disc is at left.

Orbital Dermoid Cyst

A dermoid cyst is a choristoma that may be found in several locations in the orbit, most frequently superior and temporal. An enlarging tumefaction displaces the globe. The tumors are congenital but may not be noted at birth because of their small size. Many become evident only in the second and third decades. Dermoid cysts produce a characteristic radiographic appearance of a well-circumscribed defect in the orbital bone with an increased bone density at the tumor margin. Disfiguring orbital dermoids may be removed.

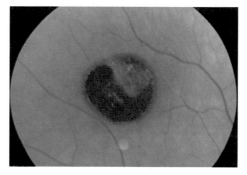

FIG VI-25—Congenital hypertrophy of retinal pigment epithelium.

Eyelid Colobomas

Colobomas of the eyelids occur infrequently. The upper eyelid is more commonly affected (Fig VI-26). Colobomas range in size from a small notch to the absence of most of the eyelid. Faulty fusion of the facial processes, which are the embryonic progenitors of much of the eyelid tissue, results in a coloboma.

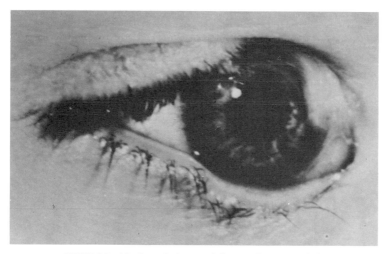

FIG VI-26—Moderately large coloboma of upper eyelid.

PART 3

GENETICS

CHAPTER VII

Introduction

Genetics is the study of human variability. Although a relatively new science compared to anatomy and physiology, for example, genetics carries a significance in the overall understanding of human life that cannot be overstated. Genetic knowledge can enhance our understanding of the processes of cellular function, embryology, and development and our concepts of what is and is not a genetic disease. Many researchers believe that as much as 90% of medical disease either has a major genetic component or involves genetic factors that influence the disease in a significant manner.

The discovery of unknown genes has opened new areas of understanding of physiology at the cellular or tissue level. One important example is the discovery of *homeotic selector genes* (e.g., the HOX and PAX gene families) that regulate, guide, and coordinate early embryologic development and differentiation. (These genes, also referred to as homeobox genes, are discussed as well in Part 2, Embryology.) Another example is the identification of the genes that appear to be transcribed as initiating events in the process of *apoptosis,* or programmed cell death, which itself appears critical for normal embryogenesis.

Genetic disorders affect about 5% of the liveborn infants in the United States. Approximately 50% of childhood blindness has a genetic cause. As of 1994 more than 6500 human gene loci were known by mendelian phenotypes and/or cellular and molecular genetic methods. More than 3000 human genes are presently assigned to specific chromosomes and more than 1600 human genes of known function have been cloned. About 10%–15% of known genetic disease has findings limited to the eye, while a similar percentage includes systemic disorders with ocular manifestations.

Terminology

Vocabulary is one of the greatest impediments to the understanding of genetics and molecular biology. Much of the knowledge is conveyed by terminology unfamiliar to the physician who has been in practice 10 years or more. The reader is urged to refer to the definitions of unfamiliar terms in the glossary before proceeding through the text. See also the glossary for Part 2, Embryology, on pp 125–127.

ACKNOWLEDGMENTS

The following individuals have made invaluable comments, suggestions, and critiques for this section: Albert O. Edwards, MD, PhD; Susan J. Hayflick, MD; Nancy G. Kennaway, DPhil; Robert D. Koler, MD; Robb E. Moses, MD; Martin Wand, MD; and Janey Wiggs, MD, PhD.

Glossary

Acceptor splice site   The junction between the 3′ or downstream end of an intron and the 5′ or upstream end of the next exon. The consensus sequence is $\frac{T}{G}N\frac{C}{T}AG/G$ for the intron-exon boundary, where N is a purine (G or A). See *donor splice site* and *splice junction site*.

Acrocentric   Type of chromosome in which the centromere is located near one end; for example, chromosomes 13, 14, 15, 21, and 22.

Allele   Alternative form of a gene or DNA sequence that may occupy a given locus on a pair of chromosomes. Clinical traits, gene products, or disorders are said to be *allelic* if they are determined to be at the same locus and *nonallelic* if they are determined to reside at different loci.

Allele-specific oligonucleotide (ASO)   A synthetic segment of DNA about 20 nucleotides in length. When hybridized to an unknown DNA sample, the ASO will bind to and thus identify the complementary sequence or specific string of base pairs. Used in disease mutation detection.

Allelic association   See *linkage disequilibrium*.

Allelic heterogeneity   The situation where different alleles at the same locus are capable of producing an abnormal phenotype.

Alu repeat sequence   A commonly occurring short interspersed element (SINE) of 300-base-pair length that occurs 500,000 times scattered throughout the genome. Often involved in errors of duplication or in mutational events. Unique to primates.

Amber codon   The primitive stop codon TAG, which is thought to become with loss of the thymine the consensus sequence for the exon-intron and intron-exon boundaries, or splice junction sites. See *stop codon*.

Aneuploidy   An abnormal number of chromosomes.

Anticipation   The occurrence of a dominantly inherited disease at an earlier age (often with greater severity) in subsequent generations. Now known to occur with expansion of a trinucleotide repeat sequence. Seen, for example, in fragile X syndrome, myotonic dystrophy, and Huntington disease.

Anti-oncogene   See *tumor-suppressor genes*.

Antisense strand of DNA   That strand of double-stranded DNA that serves as template for RNA transcription. Also called the *noncoding*, or *transcribed, strand*. See *sense strand*.

Apoptosis   The process by which internal or external messages trigger expression of specific genes and their products, resulting in the initiation of a series of cellular events that involve fragmentation of the cell nucleus, dissolution of cellular structure, and orderly cell death. Unlike traumatic cell death, apoptosis results in the death of individual cells rather than clusters of cells and does not lead to the release of inflammatory intracellular products. Also called *programmed cell death*, or *PCD*.

Ascertainment   The method of selecting families for inclusion in a genetic study.

Assortative mating   Mating between persons with preference for or against a specific genotype; that is, nonrandom mating.

Autosome   Any chromosome other than the sex (X or Y) chromosomes. The normal human has 22 pairs of autosomes.

Bacteriophage   A virus containing DNA or RNA whose host is bacteria. Bacteriophage can be used for the transduction or insertion of fragments of DNA into bacteria for cloning purposes.

Barr body   Inactive X chromosome seen in the nucleus of some female somatic cells.

Base pair (bp)   Two complementary nitrogen bases that are paired in double-stranded DNA. Used as a unit of physical distance or length of a sequence of nucleotides.

Carrier   An individual who has a pair of genes consisting of one normal and one abnormal, or mutant, gene. Usually, such persons are by definition phenotypically "normal," although in certain disorders biochemical evidence of a deficient or defective gene product may be present. Not infrequently, carriers of an X-linked disorder may show a partial expression of a genetic trait.

CCAAT box   A sequence of nucleotides about 75–80 bp upstream to the transcription initiation site of many genes that is believed to play a role in promoter function.

cDNA clone   A host cell that contains a vector containing a fragment of complementary DNA (cDNA) from another organism.

Centimorgan   A measure of the crossover frequency between linked genes. One centimorgan equals 1% recombination and represents a physical distance of about 1 million base pairs. Abbreviated cM.

Centromere   The constricted region of the chromosome that is associated with spindle fibers during mitosis and meiosis. It is important in the movement of chromosomes to the poles of the dividing cell.

Chorionic villus sampling (CVS)   Transcervical procedure in which chorionic villi are retrieved with a flexible suction catheter for use in studies to establish a prenatal diagnosis.

Chromatid   One of the duplicate arms (also called *sister chromatids*) of chromosomes that are created after DNA replication during mitosis or the first division of meiosis.

Chromatin   The complex of DNA and proteins that is present in chromosomes.

Clinical heterogeneity   Different mutations at the same locus producing different phenotypes. Examples include macular dystrophy and retinitis pigmentosa from differing mutations of peripherin/*RDS* and Crouzon, Pfeiffer, and Apert syndrome from mutations of *FGFR2*.

Cloning vector   Any DNA molecule capable of autonomous replication within a host cell into which DNA can be inserted for amplification. Cloning vectors can be derived from plasmids, bacteriophages, viruses, and yeast. Examples of cloning vectors include YAC (yeast artificial chromosome), BAC (bacterial artificial chromosome), and PAC (P1 artificial chromosome).

Codominance   Simultaneous expression of both alleles of a heterozygous locus (e.g., ABO blood groups).

Codon   The basic unit of the genetic code. The DNA molecule is a chain of nucleotide bases that is "read" in units of three bases (*triplets*), which will translate (through messenger RNA) to an amino acid. Thus, each triplet codon specifies a single amino acid.

Complementary DNA (cDNA)   DNA created by the action of reverse transcriptase from messenger RNA. Such DNA does not have introns as does genomic DNA.

Compound heterozygote   Gene locus having two different, abnormal alleles.

Congenital   Present at birth. The term has no implications about the origin of the feature.

Consanguinity   Mating between blood relatives, or a genetic relationship by descent from a common ancestor.

Consensus sequence   The most common or idealized sequence of base pairs (or encoded amino acids) for a given region of a gene. See *acceptor splice site* for an example.

Conservation   A genetic sequence or nucleotide position is said to be conserved or show conservation if a similar sequence is present among different species at one gene or related genes of similar sequence.

Contig   A set of overlapping clones, each containing a fragment of a specific region or DNA sequence, that collectively covers the region without an interruption.

Cosmid   A self-replicating vector (hybrid bacteriophage) used for cloning of DNA fragments into bacteria. Cosmids accommodate a DNA sequence of about 40 kilobase and are useful for creation of gene libraries.

Crossing over   A process in which homologous chromosomes (chromatids) exchange segments by breakage and the physical exchange of segments, followed by repair of the breaks. Crossing over is a regular event in meiosis but occurs only rarely in mitosis. Also termed *recombination*.

Degeneracy of the code   The genetic code is termed *degenerate* because most of the 20 amino acids are encoded by more than one of the 64 possible triplet codons.

Digenic inheritance   Simultaneous inheritance of two nonallelic mutant genes, giving rise to a genetic disorder where inheritance of only one of the two is insufficient to cause disease. An example is retinitis pigmentosa caused by simultaneous inheritance in the heterozygous state of otherwise tolerable mutations of both the *ROM1* and peripherin/*RDS* genes. The simplest form of polygenic inheritance.

Diploid   The number of chromosomes in most somatic cells, which in humans is 46. The diploid number is twice the haploid number, which is the number of chromosomes in gametes.

Dispersed repetitive DNA   Repeated sequences interspersed throughout the genome. These are either short interspersed elements (SINE) such as the Alu sequence family (about 300 bp in length), or long interspersed elements (LINE) up to 6000 bp in length such as the L1 family. These repetitive sequences can lead to mutational events through unequal recombination, causing disease or tumors.

DNA   Deoxyribonucleic acid, the nucleic acid of chromosomes.

Dominant   An allele that is expressed in the phenotype when inherited along with a normal allele. See *recessive*.

Dominant medical disorder   A distinctive disease state that occurs in a (dominant) heterozygous genotype. Classically, normal dominant traits give the same phenotype in both the heterozygous and homozygous states. Homozygotes for dominant disease-producing alleles are rare and usually more severely affected than heterozygotes.

Dominant negative   An autosomal dominant mutation that disrupts the function of the normal or wild-type allele in the heterozygous state, giving a phenotype approaching that of the homozygous mutant.

Donor splice site   The junction between the 3′ end of an exon and the 5′ end of the next intron. The consensus sequence is $\frac{C}{A}$AG/GT$\frac{A}{G}$AGT for the exon-intron boundary. See *acceptor splice site* and *splice junction site*.

Endonuclease   A phosphodiester-cleaving enzyme, usually derived from bacteria, that cuts nucleic acids at internal positions. Restriction endonucleases cut at specific recognition sites determined by the occurrence of a specific sequence of 4, 5, or 6 base pairs. Endonuclease specificity may also be confined to substrate conformation, nucleic acid species (DNA, RNA), and the presence of modified nucleotides.

Enhancer   Any sequence of DNA upstream or downstream of the coding region that acts in *cis* (i.e., on the same chromosome) to increase (or, as a negative enhancer, decrease) the rate of transcription of a nearby gene. Enhancers may display tissue specificity and act over considerable distances.

Eukaryote   Organisms with their DNA located within a nucleus (includes all multicellular and higher unicellular organisms). See *prokaryote*.

Exon   Any segment of a gene that is represented in the mature mRNA product. See *intron*.

Expressed-sequence tags (EST)   An oligonucleotide of a limited number of base pairs or a partial sequence of a gene that uniquely identifies its message. These tags are useful, through reverse-transcriptase polymerase chain reaction (PCR), for determining the expression of genes.

Expressivity   The variation in clinical manifestation among individuals with a particular genotype, usually a dominant medical disorder. The variability may be a difference in either age of onset (manifestation) or severity. See *penetrance*.

Fragile site   Reproducible sites of secondary constrictions, gaps, or breaks in chromatids. Fragile sites are transmitted as mendelian codominant traits and are usually not associated with abnormal phenotype. The most notable exceptions are the association of fragile X chromosomes and X-linked mental retardation and postpubertal macro-orchidism (fragile X syndrome). See *trinucleotide repeat expansion*.

Frame shift mutation   Any mutation, usually a deletion or insertion of a nucleotide or a number of nucleotides not divisible by three, that results in a loss of the normal sequences of triplets, causing the new sequence to code for entirely different amino acids from the original. It usually leads to the eventual formation by chance of a stop codon.

Galtonian inheritance   The form of inheritance whereby traits appear to be passed from one generation to the next in a particulate fashion rather than as segregating traits, as is the case with mendelian traits. Disorders of mitochondrial DNA (mtDNA) exhibit galtonian rather than mendelian inheritance characteristics.

Gene   The segment of DNA and its associated regulatory elements coding for a single trait, usually a single polypeptide or mRNA. Recently expanded to include any expressed sequence of nucleotides that has functional significance, including DNA sequences that govern the punctuation (promoter) or regulation (enhancer) of transcription.

Genetic   Related to or produced by a gene.

Genocopy   Different nonallelic genotypes that result in a similar phenotype (often a medical disorder).

Genome   The sum total of the genetic material of a cell or of an organism.

Genomic clone   A host cell that contains a vector containing a fragment of genomic DNA from another organism.

Genotype   The genetic constitution of an organism. Also used to denote the specific set of two alleles inherited at a locus.

Germinal mosaicism   The occurrence in an individual of two populations of gametes, one with a normal allele and the other with a disease-producing mutant gene. Of "new" cases of some autosomal dominant diseases (e.g., osteogenesis imperfecta), 5%–10% are believed to be a result of germinal mosaicism, and a significant risk exists for subsequent offspring of the affected parent.

Haploid   Half the number of chromosomes in most somatic cells, equal to the number of chromosomes in gametes. In humans the haploid number is 23. Also used to denote the state in which only one of a pair or set of chromosomes is present. See *diploid*.

Haploid insufficiency (haploinsufficiency)   The condition of dominant genetic disease caused by gene product insufficient to produce the desired function because of the absence of the mutant allele's contribution. For example, aniridia and Waardenburg syndrome result from insufficiency of the single functional copy of the PAX6 and PAX3 genes, respectively, to activate transcription of the genes that they normally control.

Haplotype   The combination of linked polymorphisms or marker alleles for a given region of DNA on a single chromosome.

Hemizygous (hemizygote)   Having only one allele at a locus; usually refers to X-linked loci in males, who normally have only one set of X-linked genes. An individual who is missing an entire chromosome or a segment of one chromosome is considered hemizygous for the genes on the homologous chromosome.

Hereditary   Genetically transmitted or capable of being genetically transmitted from parent to offspring. Not quite synonymous with *heritable,* which implies the ability to be transmitted to the next generation but does not intrinsically connote inheritance from the last generation. See *genetic.*

Heterogeneity (genetic heterogeneity)   The production of a phenotype (or apparently similar phenotypes) by different genetic entities. Refers to genetic disorders that are found to be two or more fundamentally distinct entities. See *genocopy.*

Heteronuclear RNA (hnRNA)   The messenger RNA from the initiator codon to the stop codon. About 25% of these represent immature RNAs prior to splicing out of the introns. The function of the other 75% is unknown. Also called *heterogeneous nuclear RNA.*

Heteroplasmy   The presence of two or more different populations of mitochondria within a cell, each carrying a different allele (or the presence or absence of a mutation) at a given locus.

Heterozygous (heterozygote)   Having two unlike alleles at a particular locus. See *hemizygous, homozygous.*

Holandric   Inheritance through genes on the Y chromosome.

Homeobox   A conserved 180-bp sequence of DNA, first detected within homeotic selector genes, that helps determine the cell's fate.

Homeotic selector genes   Genes that appear to regulate the activity or expression of other genes, eventually guiding the embryonic development of cells into body segments, body parts, and specialized organ systems. Examples are the HOX and PAX families of developmental genes. The HOX family represents 38 homeobox genes that are linearly arranged in four independent complexes termed HOX1, HOX2, HOX3, and HOX4. These gene clusters reside on chromosomes 7, 17, 12, and 2, respectively. Whereas HOX genes are involved in early body plan organization, PAX genes are involved in somewhat later organ and body part development. See *homeobox genes,* Embryology, p 129.

Homologous chromosomes   The two members of a matched pair of (sister) chromosomes, one derived from each parent, that have the same gene loci, but not necessarily the same alleles, in the same order.

Homoplasmy   The presence of a single population of mitochondria within a cell, each carrying the same allele (or the same presence or absence of a mutation) at a given locus.

Homozygous (homozygote)   Having two like or identical alleles at a particular locus in diploid genome. Sometimes misused to refer to compound heterozygote (see above).

Host cell   In the context of recombinant genetics, the organism, usually a bacterium such as *E coli,* into which is inserted the vector, usually a plasmid or bacteriophage, containing the foreign DNA. Hosts are used to propagate the vector and, hence, the cloned DNA segment.

Hybridization   The bonding by Watson-Crick base-pairing of single-stranded DNA or RNA into double-stranded DNA or RNA. The ability of stretches of DNA or RNA to hybridize with each other is highly dependent on the similarity or identity of the base-pair sequence.

Illegitimate transcripts   Rare transcripts isolated from white blood cells for genes that are not generally expressed in these cells. Reverse-transcriptase PCR (RT-PCR) can be used to generate cDNA from these transcripts for diagnostic purposes.

Imprinting   The reversible marking or inactivation of an allele by inheritance through either the maternal or paternal lineage, which may alter the expression of the gene in significant ways. The imprinting is reversed if the gene is passed through subsequent generations through the opposite parental line. This phenomenon occurs in Prader-Willi and Angelman syndromes and may also occur with mutations of the Wilms tumor gene. One mechanism of imprinting is thought to involve methylation of 5' elements of the gene.

Initiator codon   The triplet code that, when coded into messenger RNA, initiates translation of the mRNA by causing binding of a special type of transfer RNA called initiator tRNA. In prokaryotes (bacteria) either AUG or GUG can act as an initiator codon. In eukaryotes AUG is the only initiator codon and codes for methionine.

Intervening sequence   Intron.

Intron   A segment of DNA that is transcribed into RNA but is ultimately removed from the transcript by splicing together the sequences (exons) on either side of it.

Isochromosome   An abnormal chromosome created by deletion of one arm and duplication of the other arm, such that the chromosome has two equal length arms of the same loci sequence extending in opposite directions from the centromere.

Isolated   Occurring in a single member of a kindred, there being no other "affected" individuals in the family. The trait may or may not be heritable.

Karyotype   A photographic record or a computer printout of an individual's chromosome set arranged in a standard pattern in pairs by size, shape, band pattern, and other identifiable physical features.

Kilobase (kb)   1000 base pairs of DNA or 1000 bases of single-stranded RNA.

Kindred   An extended family group.

L1 repeat element   A repetitive long interspersed DNA element (LINE), of about 10,000 copies up to 6000 bp in length, dispersed throughout the genome. Believed to be involved in mutational events.

Liability   With reference to polygenic or multifactorial inheritance, the graded continuum of increasing susceptibility to a disease or trait.

Library   A complete set of clones presumably including all genetic material of interest from an organism, tissue, or specific cell type, at a specified stage of development. A *genomic library* contains cloned DNA fragments from the entire genome; a *cDNA library* contains fragments of cloned DNAs generated by reverse transcription from mRNA. Genomic libraries are useful sources to search or find genes, whereas cDNA libraries give information about expression within the source cell or tissue.

Linkage   A concept that refers to loci rather than to the alleles that reside on those loci. Exists when the loci of two genes or DNA sequences are physically close enough to each other on the same chromosome that alleles at the two loci do not assort independently at meiosis but tend to be inherited together.

Linkage disequilibrium   The state in which alleles that reside at loci close together in the genome remain inherited together through many generations because the close physical distance makes crossover between the loci extremely unlikely. Thus, alleles that are in linkage disequilibrium are present in subpopulations of individuals (e.g., those with a given disease) in frequencies greater than expected. Also called *allelic association.*

Locus   The physical site on a chromosome occupied by a particular gene; often colloquially used interchangeably with *gene.*

Locus heterogeneity   The situation when mutations at different loci produce a similar phenotype. An example would be X-linked retinitis pigmentosa from RP2 at Xp11 and RP3 at Xp21.

LOD score (log of the likelihood ratio)   A statistical method that tests whether a set of linkage data indicates two loci are linked or unlinked. The LOD score is the logarithm to the base 10 of the odds favoring linkage. By convention, a LOD score of 3 (1000:1 odds) is generally accepted as proof of linkage.

Lyonization   The term used for inactivation of genes on either the maternally or paternally derived X chromosome in somatic cells, occurring at about the time of implantation. First proposed by Mary Lyon.

Meiosis   The special form of cell division that occurs in germ cells by which gametes of haploid chromosomal number are created. Each of the chromatids, which are clearly visible by prophase, contains a long double helix of DNA associated with histones and other chromosomal proteins. At anaphase the chromatids separate at the centromere and migrate to each half of the dividing cell, so that each daughter cell receives an identical set of chromatids, which become the chromosomes for that cell. During the first, or *reduction,* division of meiosis, the chromatids of homologous chromosomes undergo crossover (during the diplotene phase), and the number of chromosomes is reduced to the haploid number by the separation of homologous chromosomes (with duplicate chromatids) to each daughter cell. During the second division of meiosis, the sister chromatids separate to form the haploid set of chromosomes of each gamete.

Mendelian disorder (single-gene disorder)   A trait or medical disorder that follows patterns of inheritance that suggest the state is determined by a gene at a single locus.

Microsatellite (e.g., dinucleotide or trinucleotide repeats)   Tandemly repeated segments scattered throughout the genome of varying numbers of two to four nucleotides in a row. For example, a stretch of consecutive CA combinations of bases (NNNCACACACACACACACACACANNN or $[CA]_{10}$, where N is any base) in a DNA strand. The highly variable nature of the number of repeats provides information useful as markers for establishing linkage to disease loci. See *satellite DNA* and *short tandem repeats.*

Minisatellite   Array of repeated, nested segments of the same sequence of multiple triplet codons, each segment (consensus repeat unit) varying between 14 and 100 base pairs. Minisatellites are extraordinarily polymorphic and extremely useful as markers for establishing linkage, because they are often situated upstream or downstream to genes. The repeats are inherently unstable and can undergo mutation at a rate of up to 10%. Defects of some minisatellites are associated with cancer and insulin-dependent diabetes mellitus. Other terms used are *variable number of tandem repeats (VNTRs)* or *variable tandem repeats (VTRs)*. See *satellite DNA.*

Missense mutation   A mutation, often the change of a single nucleotide, that results in the substitution of one amino acid for another in the final gene product.

Mitosis   The ordinary form of cell division that results in daughter cells identical in chromosomal number to the parent cell.

Mosaic   An individual or tissue with at least two cell lines of different genotype or distinctive chromosomal constitution that develop after the formation of the zygote.

Multifactorial inheritance   The combined operation of several unspecified genetic and environmental factors in the inheritance of a particular trait or disease. See *polygenic.*

Mutation   Any alteration of a gene or genetic material from its "natural" state, regardless of whether the change has a positive, neutral, or negative effect.

Nitrogen bases   Nitrogen-containing compounds, either the purines guanine and adenine or the pyrimidines cytosine, thymine, and uracil. These bases are abbreviated as G, A, C, T, and U, respectively.

Nondisjunction   Failure of two chromosomes to separate during meiosis or mitosis.

Nonpaternity   The situation in a family when the stated father is not the biological father.

Nonsense mutation   Any mutation that either results directly in formation of a stop codon or creates a stop codon down line in the sequence through creation of a frame shift.

Northern blot   Imprint of an electrophoretic gel that separates fragments of mRNA according to their size and mobility. The fragments are identified by hybridization to cDNA probes.

Nucleoside   The combination of a nitrogen-containing base and a five-carbon sugar. The five nucleosides are adenosine (A), guanosine (G), cytidine (C), uridine (U), and thymidine (T). Note that the abbreviations are the same as those for the nitrogen bases that characterize the nucleoside.

Nucleosome   The primary unit of chromatin, consisting of a 146-bp sequence of DNA wrapped twice around a core composed of eight histone molecules.

Nucleotide   The combination of a nitrogen-containing base, a five-carbon sugar, and one or more phosphate groups. The nucleotides are designated by three capital letters as follows: adenosine monophosphate (AMP), deoxyadenosine monophosphate (dAMP), uridine diphosphate (UDP), adenosine triphosphate (ATP), etc. Although nucleotides are linked together by phosphodiester linkage into long sequences known as *nucleic acids,* they also perform other important functions, such as carrying chemical energy (ATP), combining with other groups to form coenzymes (coenzyme A, or CoA), and acting as intracellular signaling molecules (cyclic AMP, or cAMP).

Oncogene   A defective gene that is capable of transforming cells to a neoplastic phenotype characterized by loss of growth control and/or tumorigenesis in a suitable host or site. In many cases cancer is caused by the growth-stimulating effects of increased expression, protein activation, or aberrant regulation of transcription factors required for normal growth. Certain oncogenes are produced by chromosomal translocations of normal transcription factor genes to other regions adjacent to more abundantly expressed genes, causing inappropriate excessive expression. See *tumor-suppressor genes.*

Open reading frame (ORF)   Any part of the genome that could be translated into a protein sequence because of the absence of stop codons. An exon is an example of an ORF. See *exon.*

Origin of replication   The site(s) on a chromosome where replication is initiated and proceeds bidirectionally. The site of binding of the origin replication complex (ORC). Also called the *replication origin.*

Origin replication complex (ORC)   A series of proteins involved in DNA synthesis and replication that bind to the origin of replication as one of the initiating events of DNA replication.

p arm   The short arm of a chromosome in relation to the centromere. From *petit.*

Penetrance   The proportion of individuals of a given genotype who show any evidence of an associated phenotype. Usually refers to the proportion of individuals heterozygous for a dominant disease who show any evidence of the disease. Non-penetrance is the lack of phenotypic evidence of the genotype. See *expressivity.*

Pharmacogenetics   The area of biochemical genetics concerned with genetically controlled variations in drug responses.

Phenocopy   The occurrence of a particular clinical phenotype (often a medical disorder) as a result of nonmutagenic environmental factors (e.g., exposure to a drug or virus), when the more usual basis for the phenotype is an altered genotype.

Phenotype   The total observable nature of an individual, resulting from interaction of the genotype with the environment (often, in medicine, a disease phenotype).

Plasmid   Circular extrachromosomal DNA molecules in bacteria that are capable of reproducing independently in a host. Plasmids were originally detected because of their ability to transfer antibiotic resistance genes to bacteria. They can be used as vectors in recombinant DNA research.

Pleiotropism   Multiple end effects (in different organ systems) arising from a single (mutant) gene or gene pair.

Polygenic   Determined by the operation of an unspecified number of genes with additive effects. See *multifactorial.*

Polymerase chain reaction (PCR)   A procedure whereby segments of DNA or RNA can be amplified without resorting to the conventional techniques of molecular cloning by use of flanking oligonucleotides called *primers* and repeated cycles of amplification with DNA polymerase. The steps involve heating to separate the molecules into single-stranded DNA; repeated annealing to the complementary target DNA sequences or primers specifically designed to delimit the beginning and ending of the target segment; extension of the primer sequences with the enzyme DNA polymerase, creating double-stranded DNA; and finally separation of the products into single-stranded DNA. In effect, the amount of DNA is doubled with each cycle. Often 30 or more cycles are used to obtain sufficient amplification for further testing.

Polymorphism   Two or more alleles with a frequency greater than 1% in a given population.

Posttranslational modification   Changes or modifications of gene products after translation, including removal of amino acids from the end of the peptide, addition or removal of sugars, and addition of lipid side chains or phosphate groups to specific sites in the protein. Often such changes are essential for proper protein localization or function.

Proband   The affected person whose disorder, or concern about a disorder, brings a family or pedigree to be genetically evaluated. Also called the *propositus* (male), *proposita* (female), or *index case.*

Prokaryote   Single-cellular organisms, such as bacteria, with their DNA located within the cytoplasm, with no nucleus. See *eukaryote.*

Promoter   That sequence of nucleotides upstream (5′) to the coding sequence of a gene that determines the site of binding of RNA polymerase and, hence, initiation of transcription. Different promoters for the same gene may exist and can result in alternately spliced gene products and tissue-specific expression. The promoter may contain the consensus DNA sequence TATA$\frac{A}{T}$A$\frac{A}{T}$ (the so-called TATA box) about 25–30 bp (5′) upstream to the transcription start site.

Proposita, propositus   Same as *proband,* above.

Proto-oncogene   A normal gene that is involved in cell division or proliferation. When abnormalities in expression or regulation occur, it may become activated to an oncogene that can lead to cancer. Several proto-oncogenes are involved in intracellular signal transduction, that process by which external messages influence the machinery that governs growth and differentiation.

Pseudodominance   The appearance of vertical transmission of a recessive genetic disorder from one generation to the next, usually through the mating of an affected homozygote with a heterozygote, which produces affected offspring.

Pseudogene   A defective copy of a gene. It often lacks introns and is rarely, if ever, expressed. Some pseudogenes are thought to have arisen by reverse transcription of mRNA that has had the introns spliced out. Others, for example globin pseudogenes, have arisen from silencing of a tandem duplicate. Since they are released from conservation (the maintenance of essential DNA sequences necessary for function) through selection, pseudogenes, compared to the original functional gene, often contain numerous base-pair changes and other mutational events.

Purine   Nitrogen-containing base: adenine (A) and guanine (G) in DNA or RNA.

Pyrimidine   Nitrogen-containing base: thymine (T) and cytosine (C) in DNA or uracil (U) in RNA.

q arm   The long arm of a chromosome. See *p arm.*

Recessive   Classically, a gene that results in a phenotype only in the homozygous state. See *dominant.*

Recessive medical disorder   A disease state whose occurrence requires a homozygous (or compound heterozygous) genotype, that is, a double dose of the mutant allele. Heterozygotes are essentially normal.

Recombinant   An individual who has a combination of genes on a single chromosome unlike that in either parent. Usually applied to linkage analysis where it refers to a haplotype, or set of alleles on a specific chromosome, that is not present in either parent from crossover.

Recombinant DNA   DNA that has been cut out of one organism, reinserted into the DNA of a vector (plasmid or phage), and then reimplanted into a host cell. Also, any act of altering DNA for further use.

Recombination   The formation of a new set of alleles on a single chromosome unlike that in either parent from crossing over during meiosis.

Relatives, first degree   Individuals who share one half of their genetic material with the proband: parents, siblings, offspring.

Relatives, second degree   Individuals who share one fourth of their genetic material with the proband: grandparents, aunts and uncles, nieces, and nephews, grandchildren.

Replication   Creation of a new linear DNA copy by the enzyme DNA polymerase, proceeding from the 5′ side of bound primer to the 3′ end of the DNA sequence. Replication of DNA occurs during chromosomal duplication.

Replication slippage   An error of DNA replication or copying. Because of the similarity of repeated base-pair sequences, one or more repeats are skipped over and not represented in the copied DNA sequence.

Replicative segregation   The process by which, through partitioning of copies of mtDNA to each daughter cell during division, some cells receive a preponderance of normal or mutant copies. Replicative segregation tends to result in conversion of heteroplasmy to homoplasmy with associated development of disease within the affected tissue, if the tissue becomes homoplasmic for the mutant mtDNA. This phenomenon explains the development of new organ system involvement in multisystem mitochondrial diseases.

Restriction fragment length polymorphisms (RFLPs)   RFLPs represent the variation in the length of genomic DNA fragments created by the loss or gain of an endonuclease restriction site. They can be used to map genes or link specific physical or genetic traits.

Retrotransposition   The insertion of a *retroposon,* a segment of DNA created by reverse transcription from an RNA template, into the genome. Because of the staggered cut made in the target DNA by the endonuclease involved in the recombination event, a short duplication (3–12 bp) of the target site sequence is created at the ends of the transposed element. Because the transposable element may contain transcriptional initiation and/or termination signals, this process is one mechanism by which fusion genes, such as those causing certain forms of leukemia or cancer formation, can arise.

Reverse transcription   The process, performed by the enzyme reverse transcriptase, whereby messenger RNA is converted back to DNA. If the introns have already been spliced out of the precursor mRNA, then the product of this process is complementary DNA (cDNA).

Satellite DNA   Nuclear DNA that migrates at separate positions or bands from the bulk of DNA during CsCl gradient centrifugation. Satellite DNAs are long segments of DNA that consist of short DNA sequences repeated hundreds or thousands of times at a stretch in the genome. Satellite DNAs form the ends and centers of chromosomes. Telomeric DNA is a form of satellite DNA.

Segregation   The separation of pairs of alleles at meiosis.

Sense strand of DNA   That strand of double-stranded DNA that corresponds in its 5′ to 3′ sequence to the expressed mRNA. Also called the *coding,* or *nontranslated, strand.*

Sequence-tagged sites (STS)   Short unique sequences of DNA, usually 200–500 bp, scattered throughout the genome that serve as landmarks for physical mapping of genes. The presence of a specific STS in any sample can be determined by PCR assay. If detected, the sample has genomic material from the known region of that STS. Currently, the average distance between STSs is 100 kb.

Sex linked   Genes on the X or Y (sex) chromosomes. Often used improperly to mean X linked.

Short tandem repeats (STRs)   Sequences of repeated copies of two to five base pairs that occur every 10 kb in the human genome. The variation in number of copies within a given STR is highly polymorphic and thus useful for gene mapping. See *microsatellites* and *minisatellites.*

Simplex   A term used to denote that only one individual is affected within a given family. For example, a single male or female with a genetic disease would be called a simplex case. This term makes no inference as to the inheritance type.

Smallest region of overlap (SRO)   The minimum chromosomal or nucleotide sequence that is deleted among all individuals who have a phenotype thought to be the result of a particular chromosomal deletion. This deleted region is presumed to contain the gene or genes that cause the phenotype.

Southern blot   Imprint of an electrophoretic gel that separates fragments of DNA according to their size.

Splice junction site   The DNA region that demarcates the boundaries between exons and introns. The specific sequence determines whether the site acts as a (5′) donor or a (3′) acceptor site during splicing. Single base-pair changes or mutations that involve splice junction sites may result in skipping of the following exon or incorporation of part of the adjacent intron into the mature mRNA. See *acceptor splice site* and *donor splice site* for the consensus sequences.

Spliceosome   Multicomponent ribosomal ribonuclear protein complex (40S to 60S) that is involved in the removal of introns from heteronuclear, or precursor messenger, RNAs.

Splicing   That process by which the introns are removed from the precursor messenger RNA and the exons are joined together as mature mRNA prior to translation. Takes place within spliceosomes.

Sporadic   A trait that occurs in a single member of a kindred with no other affected individuals in the family. The term has been used by some geneticists to imply that the trait is nongenetic.

Stop codon (termination codon)   The DNA triplet that causes translation to end when it is coded into messenger RNA. The DNA stop codons are TAG, TAA, and TGA. Expressed as mRNA these are UAG, UAA, and UGA.

Synteny   The presence of genes on the same chromosome, even if linkage cannot be demonstrated. Also used to denote homologous chromosomal locations between species.

TATA box   A promoter element about 25–30 bp (5′) upstream to the transcription start site that contains the consensus sequence TATA^A_TA^A_T. The TATA box is recognized by transcription factors that bind to the region, and it has a critical role in the initiation of transcription.

Telomeric DNA   A form of highly repetitive satellite DNA that forms the tips of chromosomes and prevents them from fraying or joining. It decreases in size as a concomitant of aging. Defects in the maintenance of telomeres may play a role in cancer formation.

Threshold   In polygenic or multifactorial inheritance, a relatively sharp qualitative difference beyond which individuals are considered to be affected. The threshold is presumed to have been reached by the cumulative effects of the polygenic and multifactorial influences.

Transcription   The synthesis as catalyzed by a DNA-dependent RNA polymerase of a single-stranded RNA molecule from the antisense strand of a double-stranded DNA template in the cell nucleus.

Translation   The process by which a polypeptide is synthesized from a sequence of specific messenger RNA.

Translocation   The transfer of a part of one chromosome to a nonhomologous chromosome.

Trinucleotide repeat expansion (contraction)   The process by which long sequences of multiple triplet codons (see *minisatellites*) are lengthened or shortened in the process of gene replication. The process of expansion of trinucleotide repeats over consecutive generations results in the genetic phenomenon of anticipation. The underlying mechanisms for expansion (or contraction) appear to be replication slippage and unequal crossing over in the region of the repeats. Most disorders involving trinucleotide repeats are dominant in inheritance (e.g., fragile X syndrome, myotonic dystrophy, Huntington disease, Kennedy disease), but one is autosomal recessive (Friedreich ataxia).

Tumor-suppressor genes   Genes that must be present in one fully functional copy in order to keep cells from uncontrolled proliferation. Two "hits" (inactivations) of the gene, one for each allele, must occur in a given cell for tumor formation to occur. Examples include the genes for retinoblastoma, Wilms tumor, tuberous sclerosis, p53, ataxia-telangiectasia, and von Hippel–Lindau disease. Also called *antioncogenes*. See *oncogenes*.

Unequal crossing over   An error in the events of chromosomal duplication and cell division occurring during meiosis and, rarely, during mitosis. Probably because of similar sequences or repeated segments, chromosomal exchange occurs between nonhomologous regions of the chromosome, resulting in duplication and deletion of genetic material in the daughter cells.

Uniparental disomy   The conveyance to a child of two copies of an abnormal gene or chromosome by only one parent, while the other parent makes no contribution. The child can be affected with autosomal recessive disease even if only one of the parents is a carrier for the abnormal gene. This occurrence has been reported in cystic fibrosis and Prader-Willi and Angelman syndromes.

Untranslated region (UTR)   The regions upstream (5′ UTR) and downstream (3′ UTR) of the open reading frame of a gene. The 5′ UTR contains the promoter and part or all of the regulatory regions of the gene. The 3′ UTR presumably also serves important functions in regulation and mRNA stability.

Vector   A viral, bacteriophage, or plasmid DNA molecule into which a stretch of either genomic DNA or cDNA or a specific gene can be inserted. The λ bacteriophage can accept segments of DNA up to 25 kb long. Cosmid vectors can accommodate a 40-kb length segment. BAC (bacterial artificial chromosomes) and YAC (yeast artificial chromosome) vectors can accept much larger fragments of DNA.

Western blot   Imprint of an electrophoretic gel that separates proteins according to their size and mobility. The proteins are usually identified by immunological methods.

Wild type   A normal phenotype of an organism. Also, a normal allele as compared to a mutant allele.

X linked   Term that refers to genes on the X chromosome.

Y linked   Term that refers to genes on the Y chromosome.

Yeast artificial chromosome (YAC)   Contig using the yeast artificial chromosome as the cloning vector. YACs can be used to clone very large segments of DNA or chromosomal material (up to 1000 kb).

CHAPTER VIII

Molecular Genetics

This chapter provides a review of molecular genetics with emphasis on basic concepts, an overview of the techniques for manipulating deoxyribonucleic acid (DNA) in the laboratory, and an appreciation of the power and implications of molecular investigations for the study of inherited diseases. Ophthalmic examples and applications are used whenever possible to illustrate concepts and techniques.

DNA, Genes, and Chromosomes

DNA

The genetic information encoded as DNA in each cell directs the development and function of complex organisms. All the information required to reproduce an organism from conception through the stages of embryonic development to adulthood is organized and stored in and retrievable from either nuclear or, to a limited but very important degree, mitochondrial DNA. Also contained in DNA is all the information necessary to establish normal physiologic cellular mechanisms to sustain life and function.

Structure of DNA *Chromosomes* are composed primarily of proteins and DNA. The helical structure of DNA, first defined in 1953 by James Watson and Francis Crick, consists of a chain of deoxyribose (pentose, or five-carbon, sugar) molecules, linked by phosphate, with each carrying a single nitrogenous base. Covalent phosphodiester bonds join the 5′ carbon of one deoxyribose sugar to the 3′ carbon of the next sugar in the sequence. The nitrogenous base is either a *purine* (adenine or guanine) or one of the *pyrimidines* (thymine or cytosine) (Fig VIII-1). A sugar-phosphate unit together with a nitrogen base is called a *nucleotide.* Each nitrogen base can form a hydrogen bond with only one of the other bases to form a *base pair.* Thus, within double-stranded DNA, two chains entwine into counterrotating helices. Adenine always pairs with thymine, while guanine always pairs with cytosine. Approximately 3.2 billion base pairs constitute human DNA.

> Rosenthal N. Molecular medicine: DNA and the genetic code. *N Engl J Med.* 1994; 331:39–41.

RNA Ribonucleic acid (RNA) differs from DNA in the following ways:

☐ It is usually a single, rather than a double, strand

☐ It contains the sugar ribose instead of the sugar deoxyribose

☐ It incorporates uracil instead of thymine as one of the four nitrogenous bases

Complementary nature of DNA The two strands of DNA are complementary. Each strand contains the information in the reverse sequence of the other strand. If the

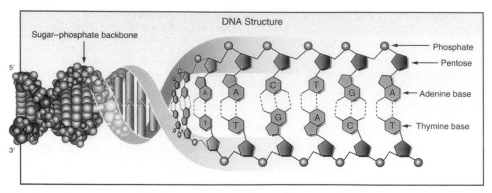

FIG VIII-1—The sequence of four bases (guanine, adenine, thymine, and cytosine, in orange) that determines the specificity of genetic information. The bases face inward from the sugar-phosphate backbone (green) and form pairs (dashed lines) with complementary bases on the opposing strand. (Reproduced with permission from Rosenthal N. Molecular medicine: DNA and the genetic code. *N Engl J Med.* 1994;331:40.)

sequence is known for one strand, the sequence for the other strand can always be inferred.

Double-stranded DNA dissociates with high pH or temperature and anneals with cooling or other appropriate conditions to re-form. The property of single-stranded DNA to reassociate only with sequences of complementary DNA is the basis for much of recombinant genetics and many of the modern techniques of DNA manipulation.

Genetic code Each base pair codes a "letter" and each triplet (*codon*) represents a word in a sort of biologic Morse code that passes on genetic information in the form of the two symbols, adenine-thymine (AT) and guanine-cytosine (GC), repeated with varying frequencies along the DNA molecule. Because of the pairing of adenine with thymine and guanine with cytosine in double-stranded DNA, the base pairs of each codon are made of differently oriented arrangements of AT and GC base pairs (Table VIII-1, Fig VIII-2).

The linear sequence of the four bases in RNA is a key factor in determining which of the 20 amino acids will make up a particular polypeptide chain. The four nucleotides (A, C, G, U) in RNA combine linearly in groups of three, or codons. Each codon represents a start, an amino acid, or a stop. Of the 64 possible codons, 61 code for amino acids, and 3 code for cessation of translation. Thus, the genetic code is redundant, with 18 amino acids coded by more than one triplet.

Four codons signal a start or stop of the construction of an amino acid chain. The AUG codon (which codes for methionine) initiates translation, whereas a UGA, UAA, or UAG codon stops translation. Translation is discussed on pp 213–215.

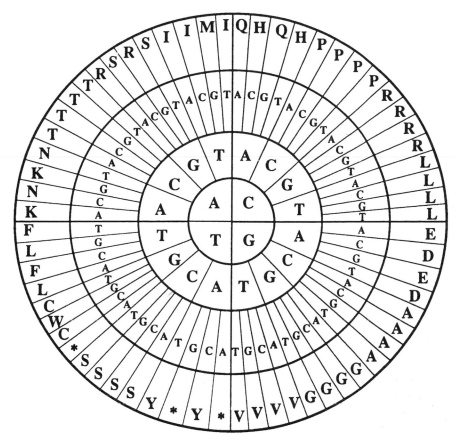

FIG VIII-2—The outermost circle represents the amino acid or termination code (*); the trinucleotide encoding the amino acid or "stop" signal is given on the radial, starting with the first base of the codon in the center. A = adenine; C = cytosine; G = guanine; T = thymine. See Table VIII-1 below for key to symbols. (Reproduced with permission from McKusick VA. *Mendelian Inheritance in Man: A Catalog of Human Genes and Genetic Disorders.* 11th ed. Baltimore: The Johns Hopkins University Press; 1994:xii.)

TABLE VIII-1

SYMBOLS FOR AMINO ACIDS

AMINO ACID	THREE-LETTER SYMBOL	ONE-LETTER SYMBOL	AMINO ACID	THREE-LETTER SYMBOL	ONE-LETTER SYMBOL
Alanine	Ala	A	Isoleucine	Ile	I
Arginine	Arg	R	Leucine	Leu	L
Asparagine	Asn	N	Lysine	Lys	K
Aspartic acid	Asp	D	Methionine	Met	M
Asn and/or Asp	Asx	B	Phenylalanine	Phe	F
Cysteine	Cys	C	Proline	Pro	P
Glutamine	Gln	Q	Serine	Ser	S
Glutamic acid	Glu	E	Threonine	Thr	T
Gln and/or Glu	Glx	Z	Tryptophan	Trp	W
Glycine	Gly	G	Tyrosine	Tyr	Y
Histidine	His	H	Valine	Val	V

Sense and antisense DNA Nuclear DNA in each chromosome exists in double-stranded helix conformation. Because of the complementary nature of DNA, all of the information is present on each strand. However, the information is read out as RNA by the transcription of only one of the single strands of DNA. The strand of DNA called the *sense,* or coding, strand is *not* translated by RNA polymerase, but it has the same 5′ to 3′ sequence as the messenger RNA (mRNA). The strand that actually is read is called the *antisense,* or translated, strand. This is the strand that is transcribed to mRNA, which, in turn, is processed and translated into the polypeptide.

Therefore, the genetic code for the strand of DNA that is untranslated must be considered in understanding the sequence of amino acids in a given peptide, because it is the coding sequence of this strand that is identical to the sequence of amino acids in the polypeptide finally released by the ribosomes.

One approach to treatment of autosomal dominant disease is to target the translated strand of the mutant allele by antisense DNA, a sequence of DNA designed to anneal to and block the processing or translation of the abnormal mRNA.

Gene structure A *gene* is the coding sequence for a protein, rRNA, or other gene product and its associated regulatory sequences. Genes contain several regulatory (enhancer, repressor) and structural (coding introns and exons) components to ensure accurate transcription and translation at the appropriate levels and times.

Genes are arranged linearly on chromosomes. The genomic structure can be divided into the so-called 5′ untranslated region, which contains the *promoter,* and regulatory regions (enhancer, inducer, and inhibitor) that serve as targets for *transcription factors,* which activate genes and regulate and help determine whether a gene is transcribed (Fig VIII-3). The promoter, which is under developmental and tissue-specific control, turns the gene on (i.e., allows transcription and translation).

Following the initiation codon is the open reading frame (ORF) composed of *exons,* sequences that code for amino acids that will be present in the final protein, and *introns,* sequences that are spliced out during the processing of mRNA. Several ORFs may follow. Following the last exon is the 3′ untranslated region (3′ UTR). The function of this region is known to be in part regulatory. Indeed, a mutation within the 3′ UTR region of the gene for the enzyme myotonin kinase is believed to cause myotonic dystrophy.

The development of introns in higher organisms may have had evolutionary benefits. Introns have allowed eukaryotes to evolve beyond the limits of genes seen in single-celled organisms, and they may have other roles as well. The compartmentalization of coding segments into exons may have allowed for more rapid evolution of proteins by allowing for alternative processing of precursor RNA (alternative splicing) and rearrangements of exons during gene duplication (exon shuffling). Encoded within some introns are so-called small nucleolar RNAs (snoRNAs), which are believed to play a role in ribosome assembly. Certain genes may be regulated by intron-encoded RNAs that bind either DNA or RNA. Introns may thus provide a previously unsuspected system for regulating gene expression and may also be involved in maintenance of genomic structure.

Some introns contain complete separate genes, and some of these may cause disease or influence expression of other genes. Expansion of unstable repeats within introns can cause abnormal splicing and result in genetic disease.

Gene Structure

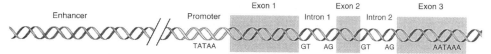

FIG VIII-3—The DNA sequences that are transcribed as RNA are collectively called the gene and include exons (expressed sequences) and introns (intervening sequences). Introns invariably begin with the nucleotide sequence GT and end with AG. An AT-rich sequence in the last exon forms a signal for processing the end of the RNA transcript. Regulatory sequences that make up the promoter and include the TATA box occur close to the site where transcription starts. Enhancer sequences are located at variable distances from the gene. (Reproduced with permission from Rosenthal N. Molecular medicine: regulation of gene expression. *N Engl J Med.* 1994;331:932.)

Untranslated and other "junk" genes   Approximately 97% of the base sequences in human DNA have been considered "biologically meaningless" in that they do not encode proteins or RNAs or have any other known function. This so-called junk DNA may play other important roles that will emerge when the structure and function of the genome, chromosomes, nucleus, and nuclear proteins are fully understood. It has been suggested that RNA transcribed from junk DNA may directly influence the transcription of other sequences and participate in normal genome repair and regulation. When defective, it may lead to cancer. Some of the repetitive sequences of nontranscribed DNA form *telomeric DNA,* which is essential for correct formation and maintenance of chromosomes. Indeed, loss of telomeric DNA correlates with cell senescence and carcinogenesis. Therefore, sequences within junk DNA may influence the transcription or otherwise regulate the expression of numerous other genes.

Much of this wasteland of DNA is composed of highly repetitive sequences. Some of these sequences include satellites, minisatellites, microsatellites, short interspersed elements (SINEs), and long interspersed elements (LINEs). The most frequent of the repetitive DNAs is the 300-bp *Alu* sequence, named for the restriction enzyme used to identify it. The Alu sequence is a SINE that occurs 500,000 times in the human genome. Alu sequences are distributed through retroposition (Alu → Alu RNA → Alu cDNA → Insertion) and may cause disease if one inserts within and disrupts a gene. This process accounts for one cause of type 1 neurofibromatosis. An important LINE is the L1 repeat sequence, composed of about 10,000 copies of 1–6 kb length each. The L1 repeat sequence has also been implicated as a cause of mutations.

Nucleus   *The nuclear envelope.* The nucleus matrix is separated from the cytoplasm by an envelope consisting of two membranes fenestrated with openings called *nuclear pores.*

The nucleolus. The structure within the nucleus called the nucleolus contains the nucleolar organizer, which directs the synthesis of ribosomal RNA needed for translation.

Nuclear matrix. Each nucleus contains an estimated 50,000–100,000 genes plus all the biochemical enzymes and products needed for gene duplication, chromosomal formation, mitosis, meiosis, gene regulation, transcription, imprinting, X chromosomal inactivation, and intron removal from mRNA. The nuclear matrix also contains numerous DNA-binding proteins that are involved in controlling expression and affecting regulation.

Histones. Histones are basic proteins that bind with DNA to form the stable structures called chromosomes. The five major types of histones are H1, H2A, H2B, H3, and H4. The amino acid composition of histones is highly conserved, even among distantly related species. The weight of histones in the chromosomes is approximately equal to that of the DNA itself. Probably because large amounts of histones are required during the S, or replication, phase of cell division and the half-life of histone mRNA is only minutes, 20–50 copies of histone genes exist in the human genome.

Proteins have been discovered that remodel histones, allowing access to the DNA. It is unclear whether such unfolding plays a role in gene regulation or is merely a consequence of transcription. Some histones appear to target the transcription of certain genes while suppressing the transcription of others, a process called *gene silencing.* Transcriptional regulators may make direct contact with specific domains of histones.

Grunstein M. Histones as regulators of genes. *Sci Am.* 1992;267(4):68–74B.

Wolffe AP. Histone deacetylase: a regulator of transcription. *Science.* 1996;272: 371–372.

Nonhistone proteins. Nonhistone proteins appear to be involved in organizing long regions or domains of DNA that match the units of replication in mammalian chromosomes.

Chromatin. Chromatin is the state of DNA in which it is tightly coiled up with histones, which keep it from being transcribed into mRNAs. The DNA is wound onto the histones like thread around a spool. Segments of 146 base pairs of DNA are wrapped almost twice around a core of eight histones to form units called *nucleosomes,* which resemble beads on a string. One of the primary purposes of the nucleosomes appears to be compacting DNA by supercoiling into 30-nm filaments that in turn can be arranged into thicker fibers composed of spirals or solenoid arrangements.

Enzymes in the nucleus control the process of chromatin formation. Acetyltransferase causes the DNA to unwind from the histones by catalyzing the addition of acetyl groups to certain histones. This process is apparently necessary to allow either replication or transcription. Another enzyme, deacetylase, removes these acetyl groups from the chromatin, allowing the DNA to again be tightly coiled around histones and thus incapable of being expressed.

On histological staining, chromatin within the nucleus appears as densely stained *heterochromatin,* which contains bound DNA not undergoing transcription, and more lightly stained *euchromatin,* which is the form of chromatin thought to be undergoing transcription for production of RNA. Centromeric and telomeric heterochromatin have been shown to be enriched for proteins that suppress gene transcription.

Some of the RNAs that never leave the nucleus and are not translated into protein may play important roles in the formation and maintenance of chromatin.

Transcript domains. Certain discrete regions of the nucleus appear to be involved in synthesis and splicing of messenger RNA. The centers of these regions contain high concentrations of splicing components, whereas the rims are crowded with newly synthesized RNAs.

Chromosomal Structure

Chromosomes are complex aggregations of DNA, histones, and nonhistone nucleoproteins that form prior to cell division. The DNA exists in the nucleus in the chromatin state at other times, but during cell division the chromatin is further packaged into the chromosome structure specifically to allow duplicated sets of genes to segregate to each daughter cell. The complement of human chromosomes can be pictured as a set of 23 heavily packed suitcases that are created to allow compartmentalization of duplicated chromosomal material prior to cell division (*meiosis* and *mitosis*).

Chromosomes also provide the platform for maintaining variation of the species through crossover and exchange during meiosis. Considering the 22 autosomes and the 2 sex chromosomes, the different combinations of sets of whole chromosomes possible from the formation of *gametes,* or reproductive cells, is 2^{23}, or 8,388,608. If recombination of whole chromosomes were the only determinant of variation, one out of every 8.4 million humans would be identical. However, with the added variation produced by meiotic crossover, the number becomes nearly infinite.

Chromatids The two individual strands of a duplicated chromosome as they exist during prophase and metaphase are often referred to as *sister chromatids.* During anaphase the chromatids separate, the long and short arm of each separating into the daughter cells.

Centromere The central constriction that divides the chromosome into two arms is called the centromere. Centromeric chromatin is a form of heterochromatin that encompasses many kb of DNA. The DNA that characterizes the centromere location on the chromosome is called *CEN.* Centromeres contain α-satellite DNA, a family of tandem arrays of different copies of about 171 base-pair units, along with intrinsic proteins that play multiple roles during the cell cycle. The centromere divides once during each cell cycle. This process of centromere duplication appears to be regulated in some way by the tumor-suppressor gene p53, because cells deficient in p53 accumulate multiple copies of functional centromeres.

The role of the centromeres during mitosis and meiosis is complex. Centromeres appear to have at least four functions:

☐ Centromeres are the sites of formation of the *kinetochore,* which binds the spindle microtubules that are essential for the direction of chromosomal segregation during cell division.

☐ The centromere is the final site of attachment of sister chromatid pairing, and thus it must play a role in the process of release of sister chromatids during the metaphase-anaphase transition.

☐ Centromeres are involved in cell cycle checkpoint regulation during mitosis and, as the site of the kinetochore, draw the chromosomes to separate daughter cells during anaphase.

☐ The centromere acts as a station for chromosomal passenger proteins (mitosis-specific cytoskeletal proteins) that pass from chromosomes to the mitotic spindle.

The actual process by which the *spindle plate* is formed is becoming better understood. When the nuclear membrane becomes disrupted as the cell enters mitosis, microtubules are elaborated from the ends of the centrosomes. These microtubules crisscross the cell, where they randomly encounter other chromosomes and attach to their kinetochores. Chromosome-microtubule attachments are not limited to the kinetochore but also occur along the chromosome arms, possibly to chromatin itself or to a new class of proteins called *chromokinesins,* which appear important for chromosome position and spindle assembly. (These nonkinetochore attachments may be particularly important during meiosis.)

Evidence suggests that spindle formation requires the proper pairing and alignment of chromosomes. Because the kinetochores of each pair of homologous centromeres are oriented in opposite directions, their attachments to microtubules tend to form a bipolar spindle. Kinetochore–spindle attachments are tension sensitive, and only bipolar attachments are stable. To some extent the plate formation is aided by the presence of chromokinesins or by the formation of chiasmata (crossover), both of which tend to keep the chromosome arms on the plate. They act as opposing forces to the microtubules, which tend to draw the chromosomes toward each spindle. Centromeres contain molecular motors that appear to actively adjust the tension of the microtubules. Through a balancing of forces, the chromosomes are eventually arranged in the midzone of the bipolar spindle where they form the typical metaphase plate configuration.

The centromeres appear to play an active role in signaling the end of the "wait anaphase" checkpoint, which must be released before cell division can proceed. When the kinetochore senses that the tensions are all uniform and other requirements are satisfied, the elaboration of an intrinsic protein that inhibits anaphase is decreased, signaling the release of the wait anaphase checkpoint. The importance of this function cannot be overstated. *Anaphase lag* and *chromosomal aneuploidy* can result from defective metaphase plate formation or premature transition into anaphase. These consequences are discussed in detail in the next chapter.

The role of the centromeres during interphase is unclear. Centromeres are detectable within the nucleus as condensed heterochromatin located in a nonrandom distribution, most often around nucleoli. Certain centromere proteins remain bound to the region throughout the cell cycle and may be needed to interact with other proteins that govern cell activity. Indeed, evidence suggests that centromeres may organize the nucleus to influence the expression of certain proteins during interphase. (A complex between centromeric proteins and the nucleolus appears to be an important autoantigen associated with development of scleroderma-like diseases.)

Pluta AF, Mackay AM, Ainsztein AM, et al. The centromere: hub of chromosomal activities. *Science.* 1995;270:1591–1594.

Short (p) and long (q) arms The centromere divides the chromosome into a short arm designated *p* for *petit* and a long arm designated *q.* The nomenclature of chromosomes is based on size and the position of the centromere.

Telomeres These structures at the ends of chromosomes are critical for the maintenance of chromosomal integrity. Telomeres protect chromosomes from DNA degradation, rearrangement, end-to-end fusion, and chromosomal loss. They are essential for avoidance of *end-replication problems,* or deletion during DNA duplication of terminal base pairs located at the ends of a linear chromosome. Telomeres in humans are composed of repetitive sequences of six nucleotides (TTAGGG) repeated from a few hundred to several thousands of times, occupying up to several kilobases.

The maintenance of telomeres is performed by the enzyme *telomerase,* a ribonucleoprotein enzyme (containing both RNA and protein) that synthesizes the sequences by reverse transcriptase of a portion of its own RNA sequence. Following synthesis, the new sequences are fused to the 3' terminus of the chromosomes to replace the telomeric DNA loss that occurs normally with each round of DNA duplication.

The length of telomeres is thus a function of the number of duplications a cell has undergone and the activity of telomerase in the cell line. Loss of telomeres is a sign of cellular senescence, and it occurs to a greater extent in premature aging syndromes, such as progeria.

This biological clock of progressive telomeric loss correlates with the normal life span of a cell and normally prevents unbridled cellular proliferation. Normal somatic cells produce low or undetectable amounts of telomerase activity, whereas germ-line cells produce significant telomerase activity that preserves telomere lengths. Activation of telomerase occurs as an early event in formation of cancers, possibly to overcome this normal limit to cellular division from telomere loss. Benign tumors are not associated with expression of telomerase.

Greider CW, Blackburn EH. Telomeres, telomerase and cancer. *Sci Am.* 1996; 274(2):92–97.

Zakian VA. Telomeres: beginning to understand the end. *Science.* 1995;270:1601–1607.

Gene Transcription (Expression)

Genes control cellular activity through two processes:

□ *Transcription,* in which DNA molecules give rise to RNA molecules, followed by translation in most cases

□ *Translation,* in which RNA directs the synthesis of proteins

Translation is discussed in the next section.

Transcription Factors and Regulation

Transcription factors contain DNA-binding domains that typically include a helical unit (α-helix) within or near positively charged amino acids. Four classes of structural protein motifs characterize 80% of transcription factors (Fig VIII-4):

□ Helix-turn-helix (HTH)

□ Zinc finger

□ Leucine zipper

□ Helix-loop-helix (HLH)

The *TATA box* is a highly conserved sequence of DNA in the 5' untranslated region of a gene that is involved in the turning on, or *expression,* of genes. The first

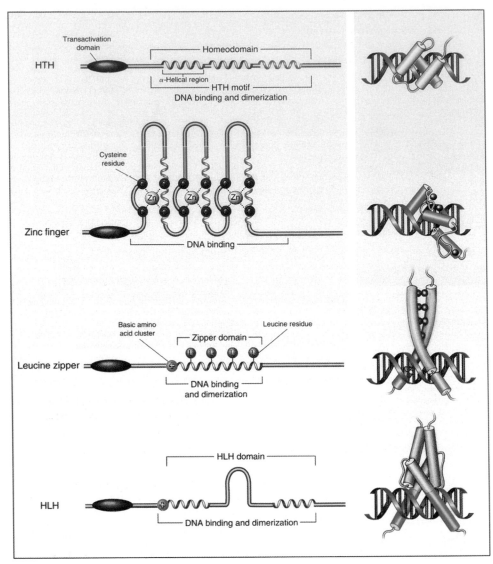

FIG VIII-4—The general protein structures of the four major classes of transcription factors are shown on the left. The structures include a transactivation domain linked to a DNA-binding domain and, in certain cases, a dimerization domain. The types of transcription factors take their names from the characteristic motifs involved in DNA binding and protein dimerization and are shown on the right interacting with DNA. The cylinders represent α-helical regions, and the areas that contact DNA directly are green. *Zn* denotes zinc, *C* cysteine, and *L* leucine. The plus sign indicates a positive charge. (Reproduced with permission from Papavassiliou AG. Molecular medicine: transcription factors. *N Engl J Med.* 1995;332:46.)

step in the assembly of the RNA polymerase transcription complex appears to be the binding of a transcription factor called the *TATA-box binding protein (TBP)* to the promoter region of DNA. Because of its importance in cellular function, the TBP is highly conserved over evolution, and its core domain of 180 amino acid residues is 80% identical between yeast and humans. An architectural protein, TBP induces a 70° bend in the DNA that exposes sites for other proteins to bind. Several other gene-regulating proteins, of which about 50 are known, are then able to bind to this region (Fig VIII-5).

One of the several basal transcription factors involved in assembly of RNA polymerase onto promoters is TFIIH, which is also necessary for nucleotide excision DNA repair. The TBP then directs the start of transcription to a site at the 5′ end of the DNA sequence about 25 bp downstream from the TATA box. The TBP is the target of several activators, enhancers, and repressors and therefore participates in regulation as well.

Many examples appear in ophthalmology of disease resulting from transcription-factor mutations, presumably by haploid insufficiency, the inadequacy of the single functional allele copy to activate transcription. PAX2 mutations cause colobomas of the optic nerve and renal hypoplasia. PAX3 mutations cause Waardenburg syndrome with dystopia canthorum (WS1 and WS3). PAX6 mutations are the basis of virtually all cases of aniridia, occasional cases of Peters anomaly, and several other rarer phenotypes, specifically autosomal dominant keratitis and dominant foveal hypoplasia.

Farrer LA, Arnos KS, Asher JH Jr, et al. Locus heterogeneity for Waardenburg syndrome is predictive of clinical subtypes. *Am J Hum Genet.* 1994;55:728–737.

Glaser T, Walton DS, Cai J, et al. PAX6 mutations in aniridia. In: Wiggs JL, ed. *Molecular Genetics of Ocular Disease.* New York: Wiley-Liss; 1995:51–82.

Hanson IM, Fletcher JM, Jordan T, et al. Mutations at the PAX6 locus are found in heterogeneous anterior segment malformations including Peters' anomaly. *Nat Genet.* 1994;6:168–173.

Latchman DS. Mechanisms of disease: Transcription-factor mutations and disease. *N Engl J Med.* 1996;334:28–33.

Mirzayans F, Pearce WG, MacDonald IM, et al. Mutation of the PAX6 gene in patients with autosomal dominant keratitis. *Am J Hum Genet.* 1995;57:539–548.

Papavassiliou AG. Molecular medicine: transcription factors. *N Engl J Med.* 1995; 332:45–47.

Rosenthal N. Molecular medicine: regulation of gene expression. *N Engl J Med.* 1994;331:931–933.

Sanyanusin P, Schimmenti LA, McNoe LA, et al. Mutation of the *PAX2* gene in a family with optic nerve colobomas, renal anomalies and vesicoureteral reflux. *Nat Genet.* 1995;9:358–363.

Tassabehji M, Read AP, Newton VE, et al. Waardenburg's syndrome patients have mutations in the human homologue of the Pax-3 paired box gene. *Nature.* 1992; 355:635–636.

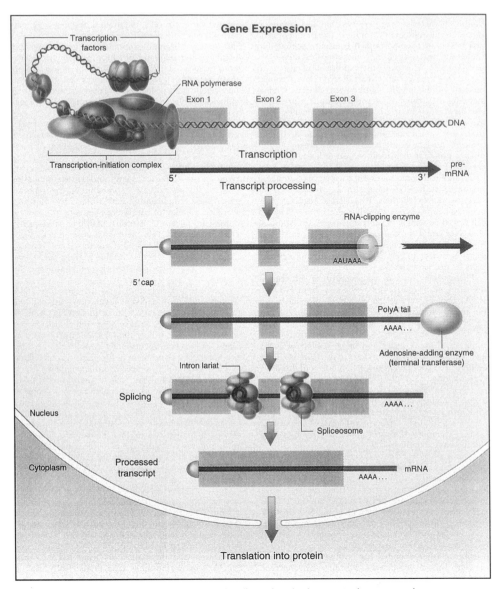

Gene Expression

FIG VIII-5—Gene expression begins with the binding of multiple protein factors to enhancer sequences and promoter sequences. These factors help form the transcription-initiation complex, which includes the enzyme RNA polymerase and multiple polymerase-associated proteins. The primary transcript (pre-mRNA) includes both exon and intron sequences. Posttranscriptional processing begins with changes at both ends of the RNA transcript. At the 5' end, enzymes add a special nucleotide cap; at the 3' end, an enzyme clips the pre-mRNA about 30 bp after the AAUAAA sequence in the last exon. Another enzyme adds a polyA tail, which consists of up to 200 adenine nucleotides. Next, spliceosomes remove the introns by cutting the RNA at the boundaries between exons and introns. The process of excision forms lariats of the intron sequences. The spliced mRNA is now mature and can leave the nucleus for protein translation in the cytoplasm. (Reproduced with permission from Rosenthal N. Molecular medicine: regulation of gene expression. *N Engl J Med.* 1994;331:932.)

Creation of RNA from DNA

The three major classes of RNA are

□ Transfer RNA (tRNA)

□ Ribosomal RNA (rRNA)

□ Messenger RNA (mRNA)

The RNA polymerase transcription complex creates a complete complementary copy of the antisense strand of DNA, including all exons and introns, called *heteronuclear RNA,* or *hnRNA.* About 25% of the hnRNA is eventually modified by RNA splicing that removes the introns, leaving a mature product. This modified hnRNA is the messenger RNA that leaves the nucleus to be translated into protein. DNA can also be transcribed into RNA that never leaves the nucleus and is involved in functions that take place exclusively within it, including regulation of transcription and X-inactivation. RNAs, either alone or combined with protein, may also have enzymatic activities that are very important for cellular function.

Processing of mRNA

After the DNA is transcribed to hnRNA, important modifications are made within the nucleus before the mature mRNA is transported to the cytoplasm. A cap that aids in the efficiency of ribosome binding is added to the 5′ end of the single-stranded RNA. Approximately 20 base pairs are removed from the 3′ untranslated end by a specific ribonuclease, and a stretch of adenine bases is attached, the *polyA* tail.

Intron Excision

The modified mRNA undergoes excision of the introns by a highly organized process called *splicing,* which leaves the mRNA composed of only exons, or coding segments. The exons can then undergo translation in the ribosomes. Splicing takes place in specialized structures composed of RNA and proteins called *spliceosomes.* The exact process of splicing is complex but involves intermediate steps that look like a lariat. Splicing must recognize precisely the beginning and end of each coding sequence, or exon, and errors of splicing can lead to genetic disease. Approximately 15% of point mutations that cause human disease do so by the generation of splicing errors that result in aberrations such as exon skipping, intron retention, or use of a cryptic splice site.

Alternate Splicing, Isoforms

Alternate splicing is the creation of multiple pre-mRNA sequences from the same gene by the action of different promoters. These promoters cause the transcription of the gene to skip certain exons. The protein products of alternate splicing are often called *isoforms.* The promoters are usually tissue specific, so different tissues express different isoforms. The gene for dystrophin is an example of alternate splicing: full-length dystrophin is the major isoform expressed in muscle, while shorter isoforms predominate in the retina, peripheral nerve, and central nervous system.

Methylation

Evidence suggests a close correlation of methylation with gene inactivation. Regions of DNA that are undergoing transcription lack 5-methyl cytidine residues, which normally account for 1%–5% of total DNA.

X-Inactivation (Lyonization)

A major occurrence in early development is the normally random inactivation of one of the two X chromosomes in the female, resulting in the lack of expression of the great majority of genes on that chromosome. The time of X-inactivation is not precisely known but is believed to occur with a variable onset over a period of several cell divisions during the blastocyst–gastrula transition. X-inactivation is also known as *Lyonization* after its discoverer Mary Lyon.

The XIST (X-inactivation–specific transcripts) gene is the only gene that is exclusively expressed from the inactive X chromosome. Its site is at the region designated the X-inactivation center (XIC), located at Xq13.2. In some way the XIC counts the number of X chromosomes in the cell and initiates the process of inactivation. An intact XIC is required in *cis* (on the same chromosome) for inactivation to occur. An X chromosome that is missing the XIC (through translocation or deletion) will not undergo inactivation. The XIST site on the active X chromosome is methylated and not expressed, whereas demethylation at the XIST site appears associated with expression of the gene and initiation of inactivation.

The XIST gene codes not for a protein but for an RNA 15–17 kb in length that remains intranuclear and directly binds to specific sites on the X chromosome that are to be inactivated. A dozen or more genes on the X chromosome, including the gene for choroideremia, can escape inactivation. Once established, X-inactivation is so stable that all daughter cells inactivate the same X chromosome. XIST RNA co-localizes with the Barr body during interphase. Certain DNA-binding nuclear proteins interact with the 5' end of the XIST gene and may influence its action.

The proportion of paternally and maternally derived X chromosomes that are inactivated in women approximates a normal distribution about a mean of 50:50. Thus, by chance alone, some women will preferentially inactivate a greater proportion of one of the two X chromosomes. However, nonrandom X-inactivation skewing sometimes occurs and results in the inactivation of a greater proportion of either the maternally or paternally derived X chromosome. X:autosome translocations are generally associated with preferential inactivation of the normal X chromosome, since the spreading of inactivation onto the autosome would result in monosomy for the genes on this segment.

Skewing of inactivation can also occur in single-gene mutations, for example, incontinentia pigmenti and focal dermal hypoplasia, where inactivating the abnormal gene-containing X chromosome carries a selective survival advantage. X-inactivation skewing favoring the X chromosome with the abnormal gene can occur when the abnormal gene product results in increased proliferation, or when the normal function of the XIC is somehow disrupted. Skewed inactivation of the X chromosome has also been reported in monozygous twins for X-linked disorders, resulting in apparent discordance for expected phenotype.

Belmont JW. Genetic control of X inactivation and processes leading to X-inactivation skewing. *Am J Hum Genet.* 1996;58:1101–1108.

Lyon MF. The William Allan Memorial Award Address: X-chromosome inactivation and the location and expression of X-linked genes. *Am J Hum Genet.* 1988;42:8–16.

Imprinting

Genetic imprinting, also called *allele-specific marking,* is a heritable yet reversible process by which a gene is modified depending on which parent provides it. The mechanism is unclear but appears to operate at the chromatin organization level and involves heterochromatization and CpG methylation. Examples of genes that can be imprinted include the Wilms tumor-suppressor gene and the human *SNRPN* (small nuclear ribonucleoprotein polypeptide N) gene.

Prader-Willi and Angelman syndromes are examples of diseases resulting from abnormalities of imprinting. About 70%–80% of patients with Prader-Willi syndrome harbor a deletion of the paternally derived chromosome 15q11–q13, resulting in loss of the normal contribution of this region from the paternal line. About 70%–80% of patients with Angelman syndrome also have a deletion of 15q11–q13 but from the maternally derived chromosome, resulting in loss of the maternal contribution. Uniparental disomy, where both 15 chromosomes are inherited from the same parent, can also cause each syndrome. Again, the two chromosomes 15 in uniparental disomy are maternal in Prader-Willi and paternal in Angelman syndrome. The *SNRPN* gene maps to 15q11–q13 but appears to be expressed only from the paternally inherited allele.

Gene Translation

Protein Synthesis

Protein synthesis occurs in the cell cytoplasm, mediated by messenger RNA that has migrated from the nucleus. Synthesis is facilitated by transfer RNAs that transport amino acids onto the sites of protein synthesis, the *ribosomes,* and by ribosomal RNAs that function in connection with the ribosomes during the final stages of protein synthesis (Fig VIII-6).

Transfer RNA   Specific transfer RNAs recognize each of the RNA triplets used in the genetic code. Because of the redundancy of the genetic code, more than one tRNA, as directed by its specific RNA triplet recognition site (or *anticodon*), may insert the same amino acid into the growing polypeptide. Some diseases, such as the mitochondrial DNA disorder MELAS (mitochondrial encephalomyopathy, lactic acidosis, and strokelike episodes), result from a genetic defect of a specific tRNA, in this case one for leucine. In this disorder a misreading of the genetic code is likely to occur whenever the mitochondrial translation machinery requires one of the specified leucine tRNAs.

Transfer RNAs are small molecules, having only 70–80 nucleotides. A three-dimensional cloverleaf structure is formed, predominately through G to C Watson-Crick base pairings of the RNA onto itself. One loop, the anticodon loop, contains the recognition site for the mRNA triplet for that specific tRNA.

Transfer RNAs must be charged by having their specific amino acid attached to a specific site in the molecule. This process is performed by 20 separate aminoacyl tRNA synthases; each attaches a specific amino acid onto the one or more tRNAs that code for that amino acid.

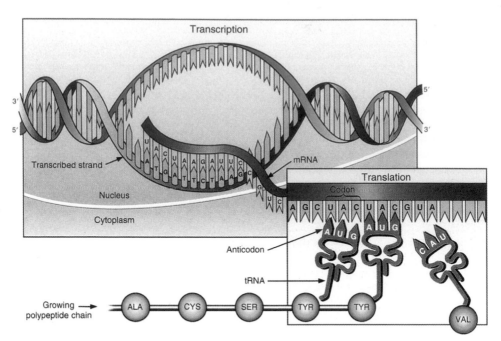

FIG VIII-6—Transcription in the nucleus creates a complementary nucleic acid copy (mRNA, in red) from one of the DNA strands in the double helix. The mRNA leaves the nucleus and associates with ribosomes in the cytoplasm, where it is translated into protein (inset). Special transfer RNAs (tRNA, in purple) align the corresponding amino acids (blue) along the mRNA, using the three-base genetic code to transform the nucleic acid sequence into a protein sequence. (Reproduced with permission from Rosenthal N. Molecular medicine: DNA and the genetic code. *N Engl J Med.* 1994;331:40.)

The tRNA–amino acid complex attaches to a site on the ribosome through the formation of hydrogen bonds between complementary base sequences on the tRNA and the ribosomal RNA. Protein synthesis begins at the N-terminal and proceeds through the carboxyl terminal. The N-terminal end of the final peptide therefore corresponds to the 5′ end of the open reading frame.

Ribosomal RNA   Ribosomal RNAs are coded by multiple copies of genes scattered throughout the genome. Human cells contain approximately 200 copies of the largest 45S component rRNA genes spread out in small clusters over five chromosomes. Each genome contains about 2000 copies of the genes for the smaller 5S rRNA, which is about 120 bp in length; these are located in a smaller cluster far away from the other rRNA genes. Such redundancy is essential to maintaining protein synthesis at the levels required for higher organisms.

Posttranslational Modification

Glycosylation   Following release from ribosomes, most newly synthesized proteins undergo glycosylation (glucosamine, mannose, and glucose) in the endoplasmic reticulum. This glycosylation occurs prior to transport through the Golgi apparatus, where further modifications occur, often with stripping of some of the sugars from the molecule.

Prenylation (protein lipidation)   Protein lipidation, also called prenylation, is the process of posttranslational insertion onto proteins of lipid side chains (e.g., farnysyl or geranylgeranyl) to facilitate attachment to membranes and to mediate protein-protein interactions. Prenylation for the farnysyl moiety is called *farnysylation,* and for the geranylgeranyl moiety it is called *geranylgeranylation.* This process of protein lipidation is essential for the very important cellular processes of endocytosis, vesicular trafficking, and vesicular fusion (docking) with membranes.

Farnysylation of rhodopsin kinase is required for its function in phosphorylation of activated rhodopsin. Choroideremia is a disorder of geranylgeranylation caused by a defect in the gene, CHM, for Rab Escort Protein-1, or REP-1, which is required for protein lipidation of a subset of G proteins essential for the retinal pigment epithelium and choriocapillaris.

Seabra MC, Ho YK, Anant JS. Deficient geranylgeranylation of Ram/Rab27 in choroideremia. *J Biol Chem.* 1995;270:24420–24427.

Gene Duplication (DNA Replication)

Gene replication occurs with surprising fidelity. The final error rate for DNA replication is about 1×10^{-10} mutations per base pair per cell generation. Approximately 1 individual in every 100,000 harbors a new disease-producing mutation. The incidence of neutral variations, including some that may even be beneficial, is probably slightly greater. If the error rate for DNA replication were zero, genetic diversity and evolution would be impossible. If the rate were much higher, the likelihood of receiving a faithful copy from one's parents would decrease and mutations would accumulate with each cell division, eventually resulting in cell dysfunction, cell death, or the formation of cancers. Evidence suggests that the aging process itself involves loss of fidelity or efficiency of DNA repair processes.

DNA replication begins at specific sites on the chromosomes, each called an *origin of replication* (or *replication origin*), where the double strands of DNA separate and replication proceeds bidirectionally. A simple concept of DNA replication suggests that the genetic information residing within the nucleus is merely duplicated during the S phase prior to cell division. However, the actual events that must take place are very complex. The logistics include copying the entire genome, which comprises billions of nucleotides; packaging the copies into duplicate chromosomes; and then directing the replicated chromosomes to segregate appropriately to the daughter cells through the intricate movements involved in the processes of mitosis and meiosis. Specific events must take place at the appropriate time over hundreds to thousands of sites. These events are coordinated by the joint actions of hundreds of gene products that govern the cell cycle, initiate replication, create chromosomes, and, in conjunction with the centromere, form the mitotic spindle. Many of these mechanisms are only now beginning to be understood.

Just as with transcription, where a complex must be assembled at the promoter region of the gene to initiate the process, for replication to occur a complex of proteins must be assembled to initiate the process of duplication. This *prereplication complex* is itself composed of several proteins, including the origin recognition complex (ORC), certain enzymes known as cyclin-dependent kinases (CDC6 and CDC7, and its partner DFB4), and the MCM proteins. The last are proteins that are believed to in some way license the cells to begin DNA replication. These proteins appear to gain access to the chromosomes only when the nuclear membrane is disrupted as the cell enters mitosis, then subsequently become inactivated or lost until the next round of mitosis. These prereplication complex proteins therefore not only allow initiation of replication to begin at the appropriate time in the cell cycle, but, once assembled, they also prevent re-formation of the initiation complex at that site until the cell has completed mitosis.

DNA Repair

DNA Damage

DNA is constantly sustaining damage from mutagens such as ultraviolet light, chemicals, and spontaneous deamination. Each cell loses 10,000 bases per day from spontaneous DNA breakdown related to normal body temperature alone. This process may involve hydrolytic loss of purine bases or deamination of cytosine to uracil and, less frequently, adenine to hypoxanthine. Oxidation, alkylation, generation of free radicals, and other common metabolic reactions can also injure DNA. In the absence of repair, these mutations would accumulate and result in tumor formation. Damaged DNA is estimated to cause about 80%–90% of cancers in humans.

Repair of damaged DNA sites is achieved chiefly by two mechanisms: *excision repair* and *mismatch repair.* The processes of replication, transcription, mismatch repair, excision repair, and gene expression are closely coordinated by crossacting systems. Enzymes that cut or patch segments of DNA during crossing over at meiosis are also involved in DNA repair. Molecules that unwind double-stranded DNA (called helicases) are involved in replication, transcription, and also DNA excision repair.

The anti-oncogene p53 appears to play an extremely important role as the "guardian of the genome" by preventing cells from proliferation if their DNA is irreparably damaged. Levels of p53 increase after ultraviolet or ionizing radiation. p53 inhibits DNA replication directly and binds with one of the RNA polymerase transcription factors, TFIIH. If the degree of damage is slight, increased production of p53 induces reversible cell arrest until DNA repair can take place. If DNA damage is too great or irreversible, then p53 production is massively increased and apoptosis occurs, probably through stimulation of the expression of the *BAX* gene, whose product promotes apoptosis. Loss of p53 causes cells to fail to arrest in response to DNA damage, and these cells do not enter apoptosis. Thus, mutations of p53 predispose to tumorigenesis.

The gene mutated in ataxia-telangiectasia, a protein kinase called *ATM,* also appears to be integrally involved in DNA repair, possibly by informing the cell of radiation damage. The ATM gene product associates with synaptonemal complexes, promotes chromosomal synapsis, and is required for meiosis. Individuals with ataxia-telangiectasia have a threefold greater risk of cancer, which can involve breast, lung, pancreas, stomach, or biliary tree.

Lane DP. Cancer. p53, guardian of the genome. *Nature.* 1992;262:15–16.

Latchman DS. Mechanisms of disease: transcription-factor mutations and disease. *N Engl J Med.* 1996;334:28–33.

Yu C-E, Oshima J, Fu Y-H, et al. Positional cloning of the Werner's syndrome gene. *Science.* 1996;272:258–262.

Excision Repair

Excision repair is essential for survival of the organism and indeed the species. Most DNA lesions block RNA transcription and DNA replication by interfering with normal polymerase function. Excision repair can operate on either single damaged bases (*base excision repair*) or larger, bulkier lesions in DNA (*nucleotide excision repair*). Base excision repair is the most important mechanism for repair of oxidative and spontaneous DNA damage, whereas nucleotide excision repair is the more versatile system for excising more complex, if less frequent, lesions. Excision repair is a complex process involving the coordinated action of up to 30 different gene products. Human nucleotide excision repair is ATP dependent and requires the cooperative action of at least 17 different polypeptides. The transcription factor TFIIH, which itself contains at least six subunits, is also integrally involved with nucleotide excision repair.

The complementary nature of DNA strands sets the stage for excision repair. In essence, the information from the intact strand is used to repair the damaged base or nucleotide. In base excision repair DNA glycosylase releases the damaged base and the enzyme AP(apurinic/apyrimidinic)-endonuclease excises the abasic sugar. (The nuclease repair process in excision repair is called *excinuclease* to distinguish it from activity usually associated with endonucleases.) The steps involved in nucleotide excision repair include recognition of DNA damage by the XPA protein in association with RPA followed by recruitment of TFIIH, whose helicases unwind the DNA. The process in humans excises a 27–29 nucleotide stretch of DNA encompassing the region of the damaged base(s) or nucleotide(s). In both base excision repair and nucleotide excision repair, the excised region is then filled in by the action of DNA polymerase (one of several) and the ends ligated by DNA ligase to close the break.

Unlike the mismatch repair system, which is discussed below, the excinuclease system is unable to differentiate which strand in a simple DNA mismatch is the correct one and which contains the mutation. Thus, if the excinuclease repairing a single mismatch chooses the normal strand to "repair," the effect will be fixation of the mutation. This may seem to be an excessive price to pay for a single damaged base or nucleotide, but excision repair appears to be the only system able to remove the nearly infinite spectrum of possible mutations in humans, especially the bulkier lesions. Fortunately, the mismatch repair system is much more efficient in making these smaller repairs, and such false repairs by the excinuclease system do not contribute significantly to the mutational load.

Three diseases in humans are associated with defects of genes involved in nucleotide excision repair: xeroderma pigmentosum (XP), Cockayne syndrome (CS), and trichothiodystrophy (TTD). All occur from defects of any of several excision repair genes. XP is characterized by defective replicational repair and associated with sun-induced photosensitivity, skin cancers, and neurologic abnormalities. CS is characterized by defective transcriptional repair and associated with mental retardation, retarded growth, cataracts, retinal degeneration, premature aging, and early death. Patients with TTD exhibit brittle hair, mental retardation, neurologic abnormalities, and skeletal abnormalities. Neither CS nor TTD patients are excessively susceptible to cancers during their life spans.

Mismatch Repair

Single base-pair mutations occur during DNA replication at the rate of 1 in 100,000 nucleotides copied. Such errors may occur because of insertion of the wrong base, for example an A opposite a C, or from the addition of extra nucleotides, creating a loop of up to five or more unpaired bases in the helix during DNA replication. Proofreading functions of the replication complex appear to be able to correct all but 1 in 1000 of the misincorporation errors, reducing the order of magnitude of remaining errors to 10^{-8}. The process of repair of these remaining mistakes involves the mismatch repair system, which corrects all but 1 in 100 of the errors, resulting in the final overall replication error rate of 10^{-10}.

The mismatch repair system appears to know which is the correct copy and which is the mutant copy. The actual process of mismatch repair is targeted to the newly created strand because of the transient unmethylated state of adenines at GATC sequences that occurs characteristically in newly replicated DNA strands. The actual process of mismatch correction involves a complex mechanism involving 10 separate activities. Four genes—MutH, MutL, MutS, and MutU—are required for mismatch repair in *E coli,* the system where the repair mechanism was first elucidated. Repair in *E coli* is initiated by binding of first MutS and then MutL and MutH to the mismatch, activation of a latent GATC-directed endonuclease that eventually incises the sequence that includes the mismatch, and finally restoration of the incised segment by resynthesis and ligation. Human mismatch repair appears to occur in a similar fashion.

Mismatch repair is highly conserved in nature, and defects of this system would be expected to be associated with disease or tumor formation. A particular form of genetic cancer, hereditary nonpolyposis colorectal cancer (HNPCC), is associated with severe deficiency of strand-specific mismatch repair from defects of any of four genes required for the strand-specific mismatch repair process (*hMSH2, hMLH1, hPMS1,* and *hPMS2*). HNPCC is an autosomal dominant trait, but the tumor cells are always defective for both copies of the gene in question, as in retinoblastoma. Normal somatic cells repair mutations normally because of the existence of one good copy of the gene, but cell lines derived from colorectal tumors collect mutations at a rate more than 100 times greater than that seen normally, suggesting that they have become homozygous for the mutant copy. The missing repair function leads to mutational events that defeat the normal control of cell proliferation and thereby result in cancer formation.

Mutations and Disease

Requirements for Identifying a Disease-Producing Mutation

The major characteristics required for a given DNA mutation to be verified as disease producing are the following:

□ It does not occur in the normal population (the variation cannot be more frequent than the disease)

□ It produces a DNA sequence that alters protein function or expression

□ The presence of the variation cosegregates with disease in family members according to the inheritance type (the significance of cosegregation in a given family depends on the number of possible chances for noncosegregation)

Mutations may be disease producing if they

□ Alter the final protein amino acid residue(s) from that which is normally conserved in nature among similar proteins or in the same gene product between different species

□ Have a greater frequency in patients than in the normal population

□ Produce a stop codon or absence of message

Mutations

Mutations can involve a change in a single base pair; simple deletion or insertion of DNA material; or more complex rearrangements such as inversions, duplications, or translocations. Deletion, insertion, or duplication of any number of base pairs in other than groups of three creates frame shifts of the entire DNA sequence downstream, resulting in the eventual formation of a stop codon and truncation of the message.

The great majority of mutations cause a loss of function of the gene product. Mutations that result in no active gene product being produced are called *null mutations.* Null mutations include missense or nonsense mutations that produce either a stop mutation directly or a frame shift with creation of a premature stop codon downstream or cause the loss or gain of a donor or acceptance splice junction site, resulting in the loss of exons or inappropriate incorporation of introns into the spliced mRNA.

Mutations can also lead to a gain of function that may be beneficial, leading to evolution, or detrimental, leading to disease. An example of a beneficial gain in function is the emergence of antibiotic resistance among bacteria. An example of a detrimental gain of function mutation is a receptor protein that binds too tightly with its target protein, creating loss of normal physiological function.

Single base-pair mutations may code for the same amino acid or a tolerable change in the amino acid sequence, leading to harmless polymorphisms or DNA variations that are in turn inherited. These are called *conserved base-pair mutations.*

Transitions and transversions   *Transitions* are replacements of a purine with another purine or a pyrimidine with another pyrimidine (C to T, G to A, T to C, A to G). *Transversions* are replacements of a purine with a pyrimidine, or vice versa (C to A, C to G, G to T, T to G).

Private sequence variations   The finding of a variation in the DNA sequence in association with a given disease does not by itself indicate that the variation causes the disease. The existence of tolerated mutations or mutations that do not significantly alter the gene product may, because of nonallelic disequilibrium, cosegregate with disease. This cosegregation is particularly a problem with mitochondrial DNA, where harmless DNA variation is routinely inherited along with disease-producing mutations elsewhere in the mitochondrial genome.

Polymorphisms   A polymorphism is any variation in DNA sequence that occurs frequently in the normal population. By convention, variations that are present at a frequency of 1% or greater are called polymorphisms.

Cancer Genes

Cancer can occur from any of a number of genetic mechanisms, including the activation of oncogenes and the loss of tumor-suppressor genes. The product of proto-oncogenes is often involved in signal transduction of external messages to the intracellular machinery that governs normal cell growth and differentiation (Fig VIII-7). As such, the DNA sequences of proto-oncogenes are highly conserved in nature between such different organisms as humans and yeast. Proto-oncogenes can be activated to oncogenes by loss or disruption of normal regulation, which often occurs because the structural portion of the proto-oncogene becomes translocated to the reading frame of another gene that is under different promoter control and regulation. This inappropriate, often excessive expression of the signal-transduction gene results in unbridled cell growth or tumor formation.

Oncogenes   Oncogenes were first detected in retroviruses that had acquired them from their host in order to take control over cell growth. Such oncogenes are often identified by names such as *ras* that refer to the viral source (*rat* sarcoma virus). They are found to be activated not only in virus-induced malignancies but also in common nonviral cancers in humans. Oncogenes behave as autosomal dominant traits, and only one mutant allele is needed for tumor formation, presumably by a dominant negative effect on regulation of signal transduction.

Some oncogenes result in congenital anomalies as well as tumor formation. The *RET* gene codes for a cell surface–membrane protein that appears to receive the messages from growth factors and relay the signal to intracellular pathways. When mutated at different nucleotide regions, *RET* can cause seemingly disparate phenotypes, including aganglionic megacolon (Hirschsprung disease), familial medullary thyroid carcinoma, and multiple endocrine neoplasia types IIA and IIB. *RET* is expressed in the developing CNS and peripheral nervous system (sensory, autonomic, and enteric ganglion) and the excretory system. This wide range of expression is probably the basis of the multiplicity of systems involved.

Tumor-suppressor genes   Tumor-suppressor genes, also called *anti-oncogenes,* are genes that must be present in one functional copy to prevent uncontrolled cell proliferation. Although some may represent genes whose products participate in checkpoints for the cell cycle, one characteristic of tumor-suppressor genes is the diversity of their normal functions. Examples of tumor-suppressor genes include the genes for retinoblastoma, Wilms tumor, neurofibromatosis types 1 and 2, tuberous sclerosis, ataxia-telangiectasia, von Hippel–Lindau disease, and hereditary nonpolyposis colorectal cancer. All of these examples except ataxia-telangiectasia behave as autosomal dominant traits, but the mechanism of tumor formation is very different for tumor-suppressor genes compared to oncogenes. If one allele is already defective

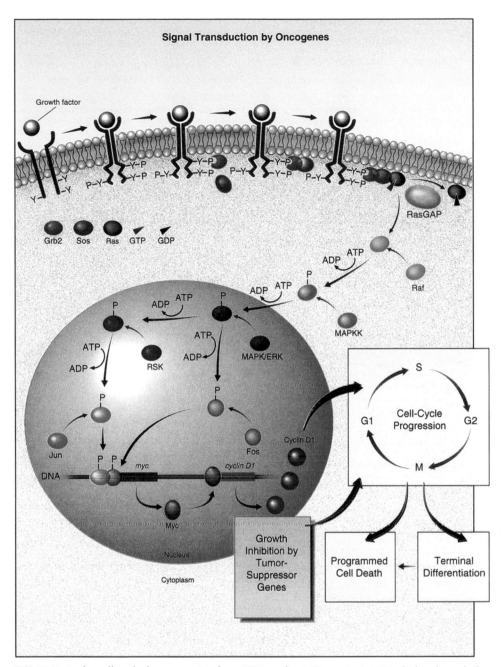

FIG VIII-7—In the cell cycle the progression from DNA synthesis (S) to mitosis (M) includes phases before (G1) and after (G2) the replication of DNA. On receiving signals to differentiate, cells leave the cycle and enter the pathway of terminal differentiation. Under certain circumstances cells may enter the pathway to programmed cell death, or apoptosis. Signal transduction begins with the binding of a growth factor to its transmembrane receptor (*upper left*). Usually, the next step is the dimerization of the receptor. The receptor subunits then phosphorylate one another on tyrosine residues (Y). The phospho-tyrosines (P) create docking sites on the receptor for many proteins, some of which undergo phosphorylation, whereas others recruit multicomponent complexes to the plasma membrane. One such interaction, shown here, is the activation of the Ras GTPase. In the cascade of phosphorylation initiated by the activation of Ras, the Raf kinase phosphorylates another kinase (mitogen-activated protein kinase kinase, or MAPKK), which in turn phosphorylates a third kinase, the mitogen-activated protein kinase, or MAPK. MAPK directly activates transcription factors and ribosomal S6 protein kinase (RSK), which also phosphorylates transcription factors. MAPK probably represents at least two related proteins. Two transcription proteins, Fos and Jun, are shown. They join to form a fully active transcription factor. The phosphorylation of Fos by MAPK and of Jun by RSK causes them to bind to specific DNA sequences near the myc gene, thereby initiating transcription of the gene. The Myc protein itself is a transcription factor with several binding partners (not shown). The binding of Myc to its specific recognition sites on DNA activates another set of genes. Cyclin D1 initiates the progression cells through G1 to the S phase. (Reproduced with permission from Krontiris TG. Molecular medicine: oncogenes. *N Engl J Med.* 1995;333:304.)

because of a hereditary mutation, the other allele must also be lost in order for tumor formation to occur. This loss of the second allele is termed *loss of heterozygosity,* and it can occur from a second mutation, gene deletion, chromosomal loss, or mitotic recombination.

Mutation-producing mutations Some mutations produce an increased frequency of chromosomal and locus-specific mutations, resulting in premature aging and, often, eventually cancers, lymphomas, or leukemias. Bloom syndrome, Werner syndrome, xeroderma pigmentosum, and Cockayne syndrome all result from genetic instability caused by mutations of DNA helicases involved in replication, transcription, or DNA repair. Hereditary nonpolyposis colorectal cancer is caused by a defect in DNA mismatch repair that increases the rate of mutation 100-fold, spawning mutations that finally lead to tumor formation.

Ellis NA. Mutation-causing mutations. *Nature.* 1996;381:110–111.

Krontiris TG. Oncogenes. *N Engl J Med.* 1995;333:303–306.

Mitochondrial Genome

Genetic Code

Mitochondrial DNA (mtDNA) constitutes 0.3% of the total DNA of a human cell but only 0.0005% of the human genome. The complete sequence, which in humans is 16,569 bp in length, is known for numerous species. Each small, circular chromosome contains 37 genes, including those for polypeptides of several respiratory complexes such as cytochrome oxidase as well as transfer RNAs and ribosomal RNAs. These extranuclear, or *cytoplasmic,* genes determine the production of 13 of the more than 69 peptides of the mitochondrial respiratory chain and ATP synthase. The remainder of the peptides of the mitochondrial respiratory chain are encoded by nuclear DNA.

The genetic code for the translation apparatus for mtDNA differs from the "universal" code in the following respects:

□ TGA, normally a stop codon, codes for tryptophan

□ AGA and AGG, which code for arginine in nuclear DNA, are stop codons

□ ATA and ATT, which code for isoleucine in nuclear DNA, code for methionine

Genetic transmission of mtDNA appears to be exclusively maternal. Each ovum contains about 100,000 copies of mtDNA, whereas somatic cells usually have 1000–10,000 copies. The midpiece of the mature sperm has about 50 copies and is degraded after the sperm enters the egg at conception.

Genomic Structure

Mitochondrial DNA exists as double-stranded circular DNA. Histones are not present. The DNA for its structural coding regions has no introns but is composed instead of an open reading frame similar to that of prokaryote DNA.

For DNA synthesis, mitochondria use a specific DNA polymerase (DNA polymerase γ), whereas the nucleus uses DNA polymerases α, β, δ, and ε. The mutation rate for mtDNA is 10–20 times higher than that for nuclear DNA. The absence of the protective histones; the absence of repair enzymes; and the high oxygen concentration in the mitochondria, leading to DNA damage by reactive oxygen species, all contribute to this increased mutation rate.

Mitochondrial DNA codes for the 2 rRNAs found in mitochondrial ribosomes, the 22 tRNAs used to translate the mitochondrial mRNAs, and structural genes for 13 polypeptides. Three of these polypeptides are subunits of the cytochrome-*c* oxidase complex, two are subunits of ATPase, seven are subunits of NADH-CoQ reductase complex (ND1, ND2, ND3, ND4L, ND4, ND5, ND6), and one is the cytochrome-*b* subunit of CoQ–cytochrome-*c* reductase.

Mitochondrial Disease

A significant number of disorders associated with the eye or visual system involve mitochondrial deletions and mutations. Mitochondrial diseases should be considered whenever the inheritance pattern of a trait suggests maternal transmission. The inheritance pattern might superficially resemble that of an X-linked trait. Maternal transmission differs from X-linked inheritance in that all of the offspring of affected females—both daughters and sons—can inherit the trait, but only the daughters can pass it on.

The phenotype and severity of mitochondrial disease appear to depend on the nature of the mutation, the presence or degree of heteroplasmy (coexistence of more than one species of mtDNA, i.e., wild type and mutant), and the oxidative needs of the tissues involved. Spontaneous deletions and mutations of mitochondrial DNA accumulate with age, and the effect of this accumulation is to decrease the efficiency and function of the electron-transport system, reducing the availability of ATP. When energy production becomes insufficient to maintain the function of cells or tissue, disease occurs. There appears to be an important interaction between age and tissue threshold of oxidative phosphorylation need and the expression of inherited mutations of mtDNA.

With each cell division the number of mutant mtDNA copies that are partitioned to a given daughter cell is random, obeying galtonian rather than mendelian inheritance characteristics. After a number of cell divisions, some cells, purely by chance, will receive more normal or more mutant copies of mtDNA, resulting in a drift toward homoplasmy in subsequent cell lines. This process is called *replicative segregation*. With mtDNA deletions preferential replication of the smaller deleted molecules causes an increase of deleted copy over time. The trend toward homoplasmy helps explain the worsening of disease with age and new involvement of organ systems not previously involved in multisystem mitochondrial disease.

Mitochondrial diseases can be subdivided into these categories (Fig VIII-8):

- Disorders resulting from large rearrangements of mtDNA (deletions and insertions), such as chronic progressive external ophthalmoplegia (CPEO), Kearns-Sayre syndrome, and Pearson marrow-pancreas syndrome

- Mutations of mtDNA-encoded ribosomal RNA, such as maternally inherited sensorineural deafness and aminoglycoside-induced deafness

- Mutations of mtDNA-encoded transfer RNA, such as the syndromes of mitochondrial encephalomyopathy, lactic acidosis, and strokelike episodes (MELAS); myoclonic epilepsy with ragged red fibers (MERRF); adult-onset diabetes and deafness; and, in about 30% of cases, CPEO

- Missense and nonsense mutations such as Leber hereditary optic neuropathy (LHON) and neuropathy, ataxia, and retinitis pigmentosa (NARP)

Chronic progressive external ophthalmoplegia   CPEO is a disorder involving progressive ptosis and paralysis of eye muscles associated with a ragged red myopathy, usually as a result of deletion of a portion of the mitochondrial genome. Patients with CPEO commonly have a pigmentary retinopathy that does not create significant visual disability. Infrequently, they may have more marked retinal or other system involvement, the so-called CPEO-plus syndromes. In Kearns-Sayre syndrome CPEO is associated with heart block and severe retinitis pigmentosa with marked visual impairment. Pearson marrow-pancreas syndrome results from a large deletion of mtDNA and presents in younger years with an entirely different phenotype involving sideroblastic anemia and pancreatic exocrine dysfunction. However, in later years, Pearson marrow-pancreas syndrome can evolve into a phenotype resembling Kearns-Sayre syndrome.

Although roughly 50% of patients with CPEO have demonstrable mtDNA deletions, virtually all patients with Kearns-Sayre have large deletions. As many as 30% of patients with CPEO who do not harbor demonstrable mtDNA deletions may have a point mutation at nucleotide position 3243, the same mutation in the tRNA for leucine that in other individuals is associated with MELAS syndrome. For all of the syndromes associated with deletions, such as Kearns-Sayre and CPEO, detection of the deletion usually requires study of muscle tissue.

Leber hereditary optic neuropathy   The most important ophthalmologic disease of mitochondria is Leber hereditary optic neuropathy (LHON), which has a higher prevalence in males than females but does not fit a classic X-linked pattern of transmission. Transmission of the trait does not occur for offspring of affected males, and virtually every daughter and son of a female patient with LHON inherits the trait. A single base change (G to A at nucleotide position 11778 in the ND-4 gene) in human mtDNA involved in the synthesis of NADH dehydrogenase is correlated with the development of LHON in about 50% of cases. In addition to optic atrophy, patients can exhibit peripapillary microangiopathy and cardiac abnormalities, especially Wolff-Parkinson-White syndrome. LHON can also occur from other so-called primary mutations at nucleotide positions 3460 of ND-1, 14484 of ND-6, 14459 of ND-6, and (more controversially) 15257 of Cyt-*b*. At least 12 secondary mutations have been associated with LHON, often when multiple mutations are present in a given individual's mitochondria. These secondary mutations are believed by some to cause disease by additive detrimental effects on the electron-transport system of oxidative phosphorylation. Most of these secondary mutations appear in the general population. Debate persists on whether each alone is truly pathogenic.

The likelihood of improvement with time in the recovery of visual acuity appears to differ among the separate mutations associated with LHON. Mutation at nucleotide position 11778 is associated with the least, and mutation at nt position 14484 is associated with the greatest likelihood of recovery. The mutation at 14459 of ND-6 appears to be associated with two very different clinical phenotypes, one LHON and the other a severe, early-onset progressive dystonia with pseudobulbar syndrome, short stature, and reduced intelligence. The two phenotypes may reflect different proportions or distribution of mutant mtDNA.

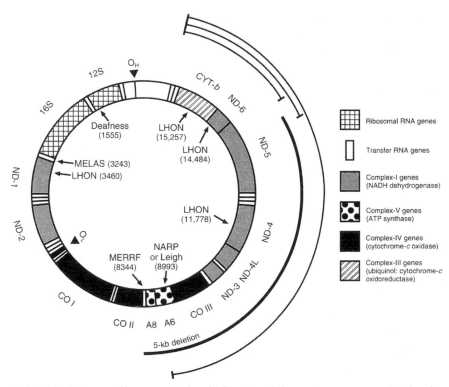

FIG VIII-8—Diagram of human mitochondrial DNA and the most common associated pathogenetic mutations. Point mutations in structural and protein-coding genes are shown inside the circle, with the clinical phenotype indicated and the nucleotide position of the mutation shown in parentheses. The position of the most common single deletion, which is 5 kb long, and the multiple deletions are indicated by the arcs outside the circle. MERRF denotes myoclonic epilepsy with ragged red fibers; NARP, neuropathy, ataxia, and retinitis pigmentosa; Leigh, maternally inherited Leigh disease; LHON, Leber hereditary optic neuropathy; and MELAS, the syndrome of mitochondrial encephalomyopathy, lactic acidosis, and strokelike episodes. O_H denotes the origin of heavy-stranded DNA replication, and O_L the origin of light-stranded DNA replication. CYT-*b* denotes the apocytochrome-*b* subunit; ND-1, ND-2, ND-3, ND-4L, ND-4, ND-5, and ND-6, NADH dehydrogenase subunits; CO I, CO II, and CO III, cytochrome-*c* oxidase subunits; 12S and 16S, ribosomal RNA subunits; and A6 and A8, ATPase subunits. The large open space at the top, which includes O_H, is the noncoding D (displacement) loop. (Reproduced with permission from Johns DR. Mitochondrial DNA and disease. *N Engl J Med.* 1995;333:641.)

Neuropathy, ataxia, and retinitis pigmentosa NARP is associated with a single base-pair mutation at nucleotide position 8993 in the ATPase-6 gene. The NARP phenotype occurs when the percentage of mutant mtDNA is lower than 80%, whereas the same mutation present at much higher proportions (greater than 95%) can cause Leigh syndrome, a severe neurodegenerative disease of infancy and early childhood. The 8993 mutation is demonstrable in fibroblasts and lymphoblasts.

Other mitochondrial diseases Aminoglycoside-induced deafness and streptomycin ototoxicity are instances where antibiotic administration, often only a modest dose, is associated with severe hearing loss. This susceptibility to ototoxicity is a maternally inherited trait. Aminoglycosides (kanamycin, gentamicin, tobramycin, and neomycin) "target" the evolutionarily related bacterial ribosome. The mechanism of action is believed to include interference with the production of ATP in the mitochondria of hair cells in the cochlea.

Finally, some mitochondrial diseases most assuredly involve defects of nuclear-encoded oxidative phosphorylation genes or interactions between products of mtDNA and nuclear DNA. Nuclear gene mutations may also be responsible for a phenotype similar to Leber hereditary optic neuropathy or may contribute to the expression of LHON in at least some families.

Brown MD, Wallace DC. Molecular basis of mitochondrial DNA disease. *J Bioenerg Biomembr.* 1994;26:273–289.

Johns DR. Mitochondrial DNA and disease. *N Engl J Med.* 1995;333:638–644.

Nikoskelainen EK, Savontaus ML, Wanne OP, et al. Leber's hereditary optic neuroretinopathy, a maternally inherited disease. A genealogic study in four pedigrees. *Arch Ophthalmol.* 1987;105:665–671.

Phillips CI, Gosden CM. Leber's hereditary optic neuropathy and Kearns-Sayre syndrome: mitochondrial DNA mutations. *Surv Ophthalmol.* 1991;35:463–472.

The Search for Genes in Specific Diseases

A variety of methods have been used to assign individual genes to specific chromosomes, to link individual genes to one another, and to link diseases to specific genes.

Synteny

The presence of genes on the same chromosome, even if the genes are too far apart to demonstrate linkage, is called *synteny*. Genes that are X linked, such as red-green color blindness, choroideremia, and hemophilia, are by definition syntenic. The term is also used to denote homologous chromosomal regions between species. For example, the mouse gene for rhodopsin is localized to the distal half of mouse chromosome 1, which is syntenic or homologous to human chromosome 3q.

Both the value and the limitations of the study of genetic disease in other animals can be seen in the following example: the use of the mouse in the discovery of the gene for one form of type I Usher syndrome (profound congenital deafness, vestibular dysfunction, and retinitis pigmentosa). A mouse mutant for deafness, *shaker1,* had been mapped to a conserved linkage region on mouse chromosome 7, and *USH1B* was linked to human chromosome 11q13, suggesting that the two might be the result of similar or homologous genes. The *shaker1* gene was isolated in 1995 by positional cloning and the mutated gene identified as *Myosin 7a*. The human counterpart to this gene, *MYO7A*, was quickly identified as the gene mutated also in *USH1B*. The subsequent twist to the story is that the mouse mutant has deafness and vestibular dysfunction but not retinitis pigmentosa because of differences in tissue-specific expression. Thus, animal models may help to find genes that cause human disease, but the expression of mutations in the homologous genes may have important species differences.

El-Amraoui A, Sahly I, Picaud S, et al. Human Usher IB/mouse shaker-1: the retinal phenotype discrepancy explained by the presence/absence of myosin VIIA in the photoreceptor cells. *Hum Mol Genet.* 1996;5:1171–1178.

Gibson F, Walsh J, Mburu P, et al. A type VII myosin encoded by the mouse deafness
gene *shaker-1. Nature.* 1995;374:62–64.

Meisler MH. The role of the laboratory mouse in the human genome project. *Am J Hum
Genet.* 1996;59:764–771.

Weil D, Blanchard S, Kaplan J, et al. Defective myosin VIIA gene responsible for Usher
syndrome type 1B. *Nature.* 1995;374:60–61.

Cytogenetic Markers (Morphologically Variant Chromosomes)

If a specific chromosomal structure is abnormal or even normally variant, its transmission through a family with a hereditary disease, as mapped by a pedigree, may
allow the assumption that the mutant gene and the variant chromosome are comi-
grating. Thus, the mutant gene is physically located on the variant chromosome.

Gene Dosage

If a portion of a chromosome containing a specific gene is physically deleted, the
amount of the gene product will only be determined by the remaining homologue.
For example, 50% of normal levels of esterase-D may be found in the serum of individuals with an interstitial deletion of part of the long arm of chromosome 13. When
several such individuals were also found to have retinoblastoma (RB), it was suggested that both the esterase and the RB genes are located in the missing segment.
By contrast, duplication mapping requires finding 150% of normal activity of a given
gene product, together with either a chromosomal trisomy or triplication of a specific chromosomal segment.

Segregation of Cellular Traits and Chromosomes in Clones
of Somatic Cell Hybrids

Occasionally, mutant enzymes can be assigned to specific chromosomes or chromosomal segments in laboratory studies of chromosomal rearrangements or hybrids
of human and animal cell lines. If an artificially created cell line incorporates only
a single human chromosome and the human variant of a particular enzyme or protein is expressed in that cell line, it is reasonable to conclude that the gene determining the cellular product is incorporated on the only human chromosome within
the cell line.

Association

Certain combinations of traits may occur among individuals for reasons other than
physical relationship of genes. For example, blood group O and peptic ulcer are
found together in the same person more often than would be expected from their
individual frequencies in the population. This finding occurs not because the ABO
gene and another gene for peptic ulcer are located on the same chromosome, but
rather because type O individuals have a physiological peculiarity that predisposes

them to peptic ulcerations. In another example, retinal detachment occurs more frequently in patients with Marfan syndrome and homocystinuria than in the general population. Rather than resulting from the concurrent action of two linked genes, this association is the result of *pleiotropism,* the multiple effects of a single gene.

> Goldberg MF, Renie WA, eds. *Genetic and Metabolic Eye Disease.* 2nd ed. Boston: Little, Brown & Co; 1986.

Linkage

Even if no information is known about the nature or function of a gene for a disease, linkage studies may be able to localize the gene to a given chromosome or specific marker.

The first linkage assignment   In 1937 Bell and Haldane recognized the first linkage between two diseases on a human chromosome: congenital color deficiency and hemophilia on the X chromosome. Subsequent investigations have led to the chromosomal mapping of over 100 different human ocular diseases.

Other gene assignments   As of January 1997 OMIM (*Online Mendelian Inheritance in Man**) listed 5372 established human gene loci with 3968 genes mapped to specific chromosomes. Every chromosome has numerous defined genes. Human gene mapping has two major applications. The first is identification of the gene for a specific genetic disease by its linkage to a known marker. For example, suppose gene A causes a hereditary disease and gene B is a known enzyme or polymorphic marker closely linked to A. Even though no biochemical test exists for A, a tight linkage to B would allow reasonable probability of identifying the disease for prenatal diagnosis and sometimes for carrier detection. The second impact of linkage is understanding the cause of the phenotypic malformations in specific chromosomal diseases. (For example, the phenotype of Down syndrome may result from triplication of only the distal long arm of chromosome 21 through a chromosome rearrangement rather than trisomy of the entire chromosome.)

> Mets MB, Maumenee IH. The eye and the chromosome. *Surv Ophthalmol.* 1983; 28:20–32.

Markers: RFLPs   Polymorphisms detectable by the presence or absence of a specific restriction endonuclease cleavage site are called *restriction fragment length polymorphisms (RFLPs).* The differences between two chromosomes in DNA genetic material fragment size between restriction endonuclease cleavage sites are inherited and become useful markers for following various genetically determined disorders.

Identification of RFLPs begins by isolating DNA from peripheral blood lymphocytes. The DNA fragments are then produced by cutting the DNA with restriction endonucleases. Each restriction endonuclease recognizes a highly specific sequence of four to nine bases and cuts double-stranded DNA wherever this sequence occurs. Change of a single base within the recognition sequence results in the loss of that

---

* *Online Mendelian Inheritance in Man (OMIM)* is the computer database upon which the last five editions of McKusick's *Mendelian Inheritance in Man* has been based. This catalog (http://www3.ncbi.nlm.gov/Omim/) is now maintained by the National Center for Biotechnology Information (NCBI) of NLM.

cleavage site and a change in the corresponding DNA fragment length. A single base-pair change elsewhere may create a new recognition cleavage site where before none existed. A variation in DNA sequence involving a single base pair occurs with a frequency of about 1 per 200–500 base pairs. The variable-length fragments, determined by the spacing of the restriction enzyme recognition sites, are then separated by agarose gel electrophoresis. The gel will contain millions of DNA fragments.

To identify a certain fragment that might be linked to a specific genetic locus (i.e., a defective gene), a radioactively labeled DNA probe is hybridized with the DNA fragments generated by the restriction endonucleases. The various probes represent cloned DNA sequences, which are complementary (homologous in base-pair sequence) to a part of the DNA fragment containing the RFLPs. Any fragments containing part or all of the radioactively labeled sequence can be identified by radioactive or nonradioactive detection methods (Fig VIII-9).

RFLPs have been used to map the gene locus implicated in numerous diseases. In many cases the gene in question has been identified by positional cloning or candidate screening, which are both discussed below.

It is possible to detect linkage by observing the frequency with which a polymorphic marker is inherited with a disease trait, provided that the disease locus is within 20–30 centimorgans (cM) of the *marker* site. The physical distance represented by 1 cM (.01 recombination fraction) is about 1 million base pairs (1000 kb) and corresponds to a 1% chance that recombination will result from a single meiosis. When a genetic probe is sufficiently close to a disease gene, they are rarely separated by meiotic recombination. The frequency of separation by chromosomal exchange at meiosis is their *recombination frequency.* Linked markers should be no more than 20 cM apart. For perspective, the average chromosome contains about 150 cM; there are about 3300 cM in the entire human genome, which corresponds to 3×10^9 base pairs.

Botstein D, White RL, Skolnick M, et al. Construction of a genetic linkage map using restriction fragment length polymorphisms. *Am J Hum Genet.* 1980;32:314–331.

When determining linkage between a diseased gene and a marker, geneticists compare different models by calculating likelihood ratios. When the likelihood ratio is 1000:1 that the odds of one model are greater than those of another, the first is accepted over the second. The log of the likelihood ratio, or *LOD score,* is usually reported. A LOD score of 1–2 is of potential interest in terms of linkage; 2–3 is suggestive, and greater than 3 is generally considered proof of linkage. Although a LOD score of 3 gives a probability ratio of 1000:1 in favor of linkage versus independent assortment, this score does not indicate a type 1 error as low as 0.001 but, in fact, is close to 0.05, the standard significance level used in statistics. (Part 6 of this volume, Statistics and Epidemiology, explains these concepts in depth.)

Markers: microsatellites, minisatellites, and satellites Within the genome exist variable lengths of repetitive DNA composed of multiple units that each may be 1–5 bp in length (microsatellites), 14–100 bp in length (minisatellites), or larger (satellites). One class of such repeats is also called *short tandem repeats* (STRs). These are tandemly repeated blocks of two to five nucleotides. The variability in the number of repeats produces polymorphisms that are useful for linkage studies (Fig VIII-10). STRs have moderate to high mutation rates. The instability of certain minisatellites can lead to cancer and acquired diseases, such as insulin-dependent diabetes mellitus.

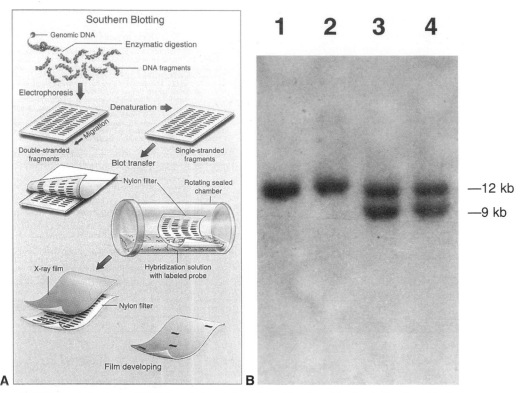

FIG VIII-9—*A*, Analysis of DNA by gel electrophoresis and Southern blotting. In Southern blotting, genomic DNA is cut with restriction enzymes into fragments before being separated according to size by gel electrophoresis. The four lanes on the gel represent the digestion of the DNA with four different restriction enzymes. After electrophoresis, the nucleic acids in the gel are transferred directly onto a charged nylon filter to which they are tightly bound. Thus, the filter contains a precise replica of the nucleic acid distribution in the gel. The filter is then hybridized in a rotating sealed chamber with a DNA or RNA probe specific for the target of interest (in this case, sequences in a microbial pathogen). Probes have traditionally been radioactively labeled with nucleotides containing phosphorus-32; however, use of nonradiolabeled probes is becoming more common. After the probe has hybridized to its target sequence, the nonhybridized probe is washed away and the filter is exposed to x-ray film. A DNA sequence complementary to the probe is seen as a dark band on the developed film. The position of the hybridized target sequence in each lane is unique to the restriction enzyme used to digest the DNA. (Reproduced with permission from Naber SP. Molecular pathology—diagnosis of infectious disease. *N Engl J Med.* 1994;331:1212.) *B,* Autoradiograph of a Southern blot with radiolabeled probe L1.28 after the DNA was cut with enzyme *Taq1,* separated by size on an agarose gel, and then transferred to a nylon filter. Four female carriers of X-linked retinitis pigmentosa are depicted. Note that two females, numbers 1 and 2, have only a 12-kb band, while carriers 3 and 4 have both 12-kb and 9-kb bands.

Housman D. Human DNA polymorphism. *N Engl J Med.* 1995;332:318–320.

Litt M, Luty JA. A hypervariable microsatellite revealed by in vitro amplification of a dinucleotide repeat within the cardiac muscle actin gene. *Am J Hum Genet.* 1989; 44:397–401.

Weber JL, May PE. Abundant class of human DNA polymorphisms which can be typed using the polymerase chain reaction. *Am J Hum Genet.* 1989;44:388–396.

Positional Cloning

After linkage studies suggest that a gene resides in a specific chromosomal region, the gene may be isolated and cloned by one of several molecular genetic techniques that eventually distinguish the gene from surrounding genes and noncoding DNA. The process involves successive refinements of the linkage mapping by use of probes or markers generated for regions close to the gene. The region of interest is successively narrowed to a segment small enough to be isolated and introduced into a cloning vector to produce large quantities of DNA for subsequent molecular analysis. In this manner, a group of cloned nucleotide sequences that are contiguous, called a *contig,* is created over the entire region that spans the locus.

Genes of interest from such clones can be identified by a number of strategies:

- Screening of human candidate genes known to be in the region
- Screening for homologous sequences of known animal genes that are syntenic to the region
- Searching for microdeletions (common in X-linked diseases) by determination of the presence or absence of expressed sequences (ESTs) in the region
- Competitive hybridization mapping techniques (cDNA library screening using total YAC or cosmids)

Genes or parts of genes can also be isolated by techniques that use the characteristic structure of a typical gene, for example, isolation of genes by identification of CpG-rich regions in the 5' UTR (*CpG island rescue*) and by identification of exons by their consensus splice site sequences (*exon trapping*). Finally, genes can be identified by direct sequencing of cosmid, BAC, or PAC DNA (*random shotgun sequencing*). Such physical mapping is aided greatly if any patient who is affected with the disease is found to have a chromosomal microdeletion involving the gene. The genes for choroideremia, aniridia, Treacher Collins syndrome, and one form of X-linked RP3 (*RPGR*) were all discovered by positional cloning.

Cremers FP, van de Pol DJ, van Kerkoff LP, et al. Cloning of a gene that is rearranged in patients with choroideraemia. *Nature.* 1990;347:674–677.

Glaser T, Walton DS, Cai J, et al. PAX6 mutations in aniridia. In: Wiggs JL, ed. *Molecular Genetics of Ocular Disease.* New York: Wiley-Liss; 1995:51–82.

Jordan T, Hanson I, Zaletayev D, et al. The human PAX6 gene is mutated in two patients with aniridia. *Nat Genet.* 1992;1:328–332.

Meindl A, Dry K, Herrmann K, et al. A gene (*RPGR*) with homology to the *RCC1* guanine nucleotide exchange factor is mutated in X-linked retinitis pigmentosa (RP3). *Nat Genet.* 1996;13:35–42.

Parimoo S, Patanjali SR, Kolluri R, et al. Review: cDNA selection and other approaches in positional cloning. *Anal Biochem.* 1995;228:1–17.

Ton CC, Hirvonen H, Miwa H, et al. Positional cloning and characterization of a paired box- and homeobox-containing gene from the aniridia region. *Cell.* 1991;67: 1059–1074.

Treacher Collins Syndrome Collaborative Group. Positional cloning of a gene involved in the pathogenesis of Treacher Collins syndrome. *Nat Genet.* 1996;12:130–136.

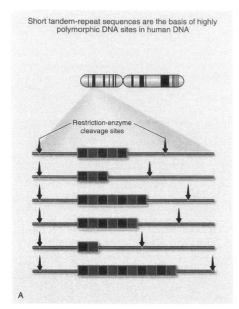

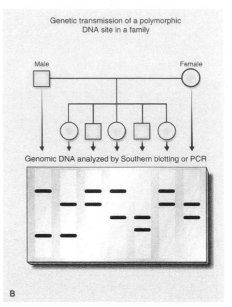

FIG VIII-10—*A,* Variable-length sequences in human DNA can be created by variations in the number of copies of a tandem-repeat DNA sequence. Each line in the figure represents a copy of a human DNA sequence. The copies are identical in sequence except for the tandemly repeated DNA sequence indicated by the boxes. The number of copies of the tandemly repeated DNA sequence is indicated by the number of boxes. The size of the DNA fragment that includes the tandem-repeat sequence is measured between two fixed points. In Southern blotting the sites of restriction-enzyme digestion are the fixed points that determine the ends of the DNA fragment. *B,* A family in which a highly polymorphic marker is used for genetic analysis. The two copies of the DNA fragment from the offspring can be distinguished from the two copies of the fragment from the father, making the inheritance pattern from each parent clear for this chromosomal site. Detection may be carried out by Southern blotting or PCR, depending on the size of the tandem-repeat sequence. (Reproduced with permission from Housman D. Human DNA polymorphism. *N Engl J Med.* 1995;332:319.)

Candidate Gene Approaches

Candidate gene screening This process involves the screening for mutations of genes that are abundantly expressed within a tissue and are either important for function or specifically expressed only in that tissue. Sometimes the candidate gene is one that causes an animal model similar to the human disease. Examples of candidate gene screening discoveries include the findings of mutations of peripherin/*RDS* in autosomal dominant retinitis pigmentosa and macular dystrophies and the finding of mutations of rod cGMP ß-PDE and the cGMP-gated cation channel in autosomal recessive retinitis pigmentosa.

Dryja TP, Finn JT, Peng Y-W, et al. Mutations in the gene encoding the α subunit of the rod cGMP-gated channel in autosomal recessive retinitis pigmentosa. *Proc Natl Acad Sci USA.* 1995;92:10177–10181.

Kajiwara K, Sandberg MA, Berson EL, et al. A null mutation in the human peripherin/RDS gene in a family with autosomal dominant retinitis punctata albescens. *Nat Genet.* 1993;3:208–212.

McLaughlin ME, Sandberg MA, Berson EL, et al. Recessive mutations in the gene encoding the ß-subunit of rod phosphodiesterase in patients with retinitis pigmentosa. *Nat Genet.* 1993;4:130–133.

Nichols BE, Sheffield VC, Vandenburgh K, et al. Butterfly-shaped pigment dystrophy of the fovea caused by a point mutation in codon 167 of the RDS gene. *Nat Genet.* 1993;3:202–207.

Positional candidate gene screening   Whenever linkage studies localize a gene to a given chromosomal region, genes already known to reside in the same region become candidate genes for that disease. Examples of instances where localization of a disease first by linkage to a given region led to finding the disease-causing gene by screening for mutations of genes in the region are autosomal dominant retinitis pigmentosa from rhodopsin mutations (3q), Sorsby fundus dystrophy from TIMP3 mutations (22q), and Oguchi disease from point deletions within the arrestin gene (2q).

Dryja TP, McGee TL, Reichel E, et al. A point mutation of the rhodopsin gene in one form of retinitis pigmentosa. *Nature.* 1990;343:364–366.

Fuchs S, Nakazawa M, Maw M, et al. A homozygous 1-base pair deletion in the arrestin gene is a frequent cause of Oguchi disease in Japanese. *Nat Genet.* 1995; 10:360–362.

Weber BH, Vogt G, Pruett RC, et al. Mutations in the tissue inhibitor of metalloproteinases-3 (TIMP3) in patients with Sorsby's fundus dystrophy. *Nat Genet.* 1994;8:352–356.

Molecular Manipulation and Analysis of DNA

Recombinant Genetics

DNA libraries   DNA libraries exist as a means of collecting and ordering genes of interest for future study. Libraries can be made from either genomic DNA or cDNA. *Genomic DNA libraries* are created by cleaving whole DNA from an organism, tissue, or cell type with restriction enzymes that produce fragments of DNA. These fragments can be cloned into vectors and plated onto media. The specific clones are identified with probes derived from the original sequence or gene of interest and then isolated and grown as needed (Fig VIII-11). *cDNA libraries* are created by using reverse transcriptase to generate complementary DNA from mRNA expressed by the cell or tissue to be studied.

Rosenthal N. Stalking the gene—DNA libraries. *N Engl J Med.* 1994;331:599–600.

Recombinant DNA   DNA that is coupled from different sources within a single DNA molecule is called recombinant DNA. One of the most important techniques of molecular genetics has been the creation of recombinant DNA by bacterial cloning. DNA is cleaved with a restriction enzyme to create fragments that can be inserted into vectors such as plasmids, cosmids, BACs, or YACs. These vectors can then be used to produce nearly unlimited quantities of the inserted genetic sequences (Fig VIII-12, top).

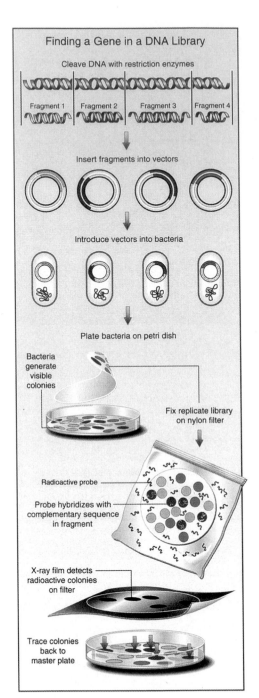

Finding a Gene in a DNA Library

Cleave DNA with restriction enzymes

Fragment 1 Fragment 2 Fragment 3 Fragment 4

Insert fragments into vectors

Introduce vectors into bacteria

Plate bacteria on petri dish

Bacteria generate visible colonies

Fix replicate library on nylon filter

Radioactive probe

Probe hybridizes with complementary sequence in fragment

X-ray film detects radioactive colonies on filter

Trace colonies back to master plate

FIG VIII-11—The first step in making a library of DNA sequences is to cut DNA into fragments with restriction enzymes. These DNA fragments, when inserted into vectors, form recombinant molecules with the DNA of the vector (a plasmid vector is shown, but viral vectors are also used). Bacteria carrying the vectors can replicate on an agar-coated petri dish, where they grow to form colonies. Each colony originates from a single bacterial cell and thus contains a single type of recombinant DNA fragment. A nylon filter put on the surface of the petri dish picks up a portion of each colony. Chemical treatment of the filter lyses the bacterial cells, denaturing the DNA and fixing it in place. A radioactive probe for a known sequence of nucleotides can reveal the desired fragment on the filter. The filter, with the replicate library of the colonies on its surface, is incubated with a solution containing the radioactive DNA probe in a plastic bag (or glass dish), and after the unbound probe is washed away, an x-ray film can locate the radioactive colonies (black ovals). The position of the signals on the film serves as a map with which to locate the corresponding colonies on the original master plate. Once identified, these colonies can then be amplified in culture to produce large quantities of the desired recombinant DNA molecule. (Reproduced with permission from Rosenthal N. Molecular medicine: stalking the gene—DNA libraries. *N Engl J Med.* 1994;331:599.)

Polymerase Chain Reaction (PCR)

The polymerase chain reaction is an in vitro method for the enzymatic synthesis of specific DNA sequences from a small amount of template DNA. An exponential increase in the quantity of specific fragments of DNA can be obtained by repetitive synthesis, starting with a minuscule amount of DNA as a template (Fig VIII-12, bottom). Automated PCR was made possible by the isolation of a thermostable DNA polymerase from the bacteria *Thermus aquaticus.*

PCR has transformed the means by which molecular biologists approach biological problems. The results of two experiments recently demonstrated the power of PCR. Pittler and Baehr amplified DNA recovered from a formalin-fixed, paraffin-embedded section of rd mouse retina and showed that the defective gene was identical to the one they were studying. Remarkably, the slides had been prepared almost 70 years ago.

An even more remarkable feat was the recent demonstration by Hunt and colleagues of the molecular basis of the color vision defect for John Dalton (1766–1844). John Dalton had written elegantly in 1794 about how his own color perceptions were different from those of others. Thinking that his color vision defect must have been caused by an alteration of the color of the media of his eyes, he left his physician instructions to remove his eyes after death for examination. Dalton's physician sectioned one eye and, finding the media clear, preserved the other eye by air drying without fixation. Hunt and coworkers used DNA extracted by PCR from this eye to show that John Dalton was a deuteranope with a hybrid green pigment gene with predicted altered spectral sensitivity, rather than a protanope as many had assumed.

PCR requires the creation of two primers, one for the sense strand (the *sense primer*) and the other for the antisense strand (the *antisense primer*). For amplification of genomic DNA the coding sequence of the flanking intronic sequences must be known so that each exon and adjacent splice sites can be selectively amplified. A 40-bp sequence rich in GC base pairs (the so-called GC clamp) is often attached at the 5' end of the sense primer to increase the sensitivity of the products for mutational detection by denaturing gradient gel electrophoresis (DGGE) (see below).

Some large exons require overlapping subregions for amplification. Often a stretch of the 5' UTR and the 3' UTR will also be amplified to search for defects in the promoter or presumed regulatory regions of the gene.

Hunt DM, Dulai KS, Bowmaker JK, et al. The chemistry of John Dalton's color blindness. *Science.* 1995;267:984–988.

Pittler SJ, Keeler CE, Sidman RL, et al. PCR analysis of DNA from 70-year-old sections of *rodless* retina demonstrates identity with the *rd* defect. *Proc Natl Acad Sci USA.* 1993;90:9616–9619.

Rosenthal N. Tools of the trade—recombinant DNA. *N Engl J Med.* 1994;331:315–317.

Southern, Northern, and Western blotting   Genomic or complementary DNA that is partially digested by endonucleases can be separated on an electrophoretic gel. This process is called *Southern blotting,* named after the developer of the technique. *Northern blotting* is the analogous application of gel electrophoresis to separate sequences or fragments of messenger RNA. The nucleotide of interest for either Southern or Northern blotting can be identified by hybridization to cDNA probes. The separation of proteins on gel electrophoresis for identification by immunological techniques is called *Western blotting.*

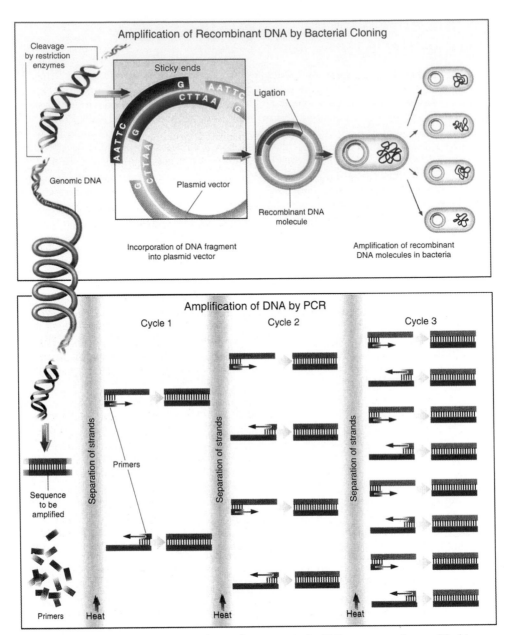

FIG VIII-12—*Top,* In the amplification of recombinant DNA, the DNA segment to be amplified is separated from surrounding genomic DNA by cleavage with a restriction enzyme. The enzymatic cuts often produce staggered or "sticky" ends. In the example shown here, the restriction enzyme *Eco*R1 recognizes the sequence GAATTC and cuts each strand between G (guanine) and A (adenine); the two strands of the genomic DNA are shown as blue and purple (C denotes cytosine and T thymine). The same restriction enzyme cuts the circular plasmid DNA (tan) at a single site, generating sticky ends that are complementary to the sticky ends of genomic DNA fragment. The cut genomic DNA and the remainder of the plasmid, when mixed together in the presence of a ligase enzyme, form smooth joints on each side of the plasmid-genomic DNA junction. This new molecule—recombinant DNA—is carried into bacteria, which replicate the plasmid as they grow in culture. *Bottom,* In the amplification of DNA by PCR, the DNA sequence to be amplified is selected by primers, which are short, synthetic oligonucleotides that correspond to sequences flanking the DNA to be amplified. After an excess of primers is added to the DNA, together with a heat-stable DNA polymerase, the strands of both the genomic DNA and the primers are separated by heating and allowed to cool. A heat-stable polymerase elongates the primers on either strand, thus generating two new, identical double-stranded DNA molecules and doubling the number of DNA fragments. Each cycle takes just a few minutes and doubles the number of copies of the original DNA fragment. (Reproduced with permission from Rosenthal N. Tools of the trade—recombinant DNA. *N Engl J Med.* 1994;331:316.)

Mutation Screening

Single-stranded conformational polymorphism (SSCP) With this technique for mutation detection, single-stranded DNA is electrophoresed under nondenaturing conditions, allowing the molecules to fold on themselves according to their inherent similarity of sequences. Molecules of differing size and sequences fold differently and migrate at different rates of speed on the gel. Mutations that alter amino acid residues very often change the way in which single-stranded DNA will fold upon itself, creating different tertiary configurations that can be separated from the normal sequence by differences in mobility on gel electrophoresis.

Denaturing gradient gel electrophoresis (DGGE) With DGGE, double-stranded DNA samples are electrophoresed against a gradient of denaturing agent such as urea. Molecules of differing size and composition reach differing points on the gel before they become denatured. Mutations affect the point in the gel for which a given DNA molecule will denature and hence alter the migration patterns. The sensitivity of DGGE in detecting mutations is improved if the PCR process includes a GC clamp. Identification of a polymorphism detected by DGGE can be determined by direct DNA sequencing of the PCR-amplified exonic product.

Direct sequencing One of the most important advances in molecular genetics has been the development of techniques for rapid sequencing of DNA. Currently, it is far cheaper to sequence a stretch of DNA than to sequence and characterize the amino acid peptide that it produces.

Although other mutation screening techniques exist, sequencing of DNA is the surest and most direct. Sequencing of cDNA derived from mRNA provides a quick look at the reading frames (exons) of the gene. Sequencing of genomic DNA is more time consuming because of the presence of introns between the exons. The intron-exon boundaries must be known and multiple PCR assays set up to screen not only the exons and their splice-site junctions but also upstream and downstream regions that may play important roles in gene activation and regulation.

The two DNA sequencing techniques used today are the *enzymatic,* or *Sanger, method,* which can be implemented manually or semiautomated; and *automated sequencing,* which for high-volume laboratories is faster and less prone to errors of reading. Figure VIII-13 illustrates how these procedures are performed.

> Rosenthal N. Molecular medicine: fine structure of a gene—DNA sequencing. *N Engl J Med.* 1995;332:589–591.

Use of restriction endonucleases for mutation screening If a point mutation destroys or creates a restriction site, screening for this mutation can be quickly accomplished through the use of the particular enzyme that recognizes the changed restriction site. Figure VIII-14 illustrates the detection of mutations using restriction enzymes, oligonucleotide hybridization, PCR, and Southern blot analysis.

Allele-specific oligonucleotides (ASO) An allele-specific oligonucleotide is a synthetic probe made of a sequence of nucleotides. It is constructed to recognize by hybridization a specific DNA sequence in order to detect a specific point mutation. Often diagnostic testing is done with two separate ASOs, one that recognizes the

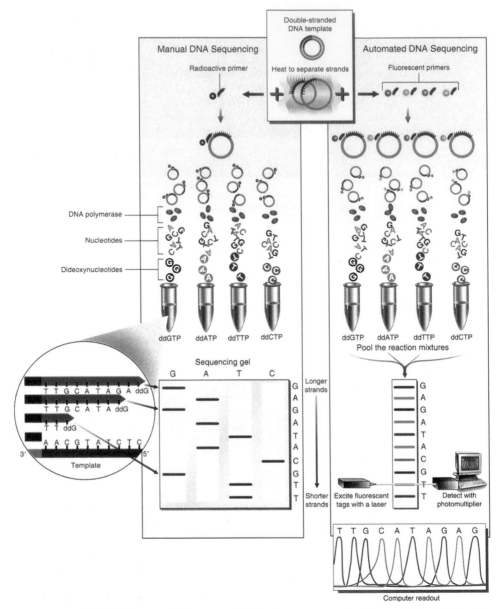

FIG VIII-13—*Left,* A double-stranded fragment of DNA whose sequence is unknown is cloned into a plasmid, which is then heated to separate the two strands. A primer with a sequence complementary to a short plasmid sequence near the junctional site is added and hybridizes to one of the two template strands. In manual sequencing the DNA primer has a radioactive tag (alternatively, one of the nucleotide precursors is radioactive). The plasmid-primer hybrid is added to four tubes, each containing DNA polymerase, all four nucleotides, and a single dideoxynucleotide—dideoxyguanosine triphosphate (ddGTP), dideoxyadenosine triphosphate (ddATP), dideoxythymidine triphosphate (ddTTP), or dideoxycytidine triphosphate (ddCTP). DNA polymerase extends the DNA primer, which incorporates nucleotides (and occasionally dideoxynucleotides) into the growing DNA chains. The incorporation of dideoxynucleotides prevents further elongation of the chain (the circular inset shows the elongation products in the ddGTP sample). Electrophoresis of the four reactions on a very thin gel separates the radioactive fragments according to size. Autoradiography reveals these fragments as bands. Each band corresponds to a nucleotide in the DNA sequence. *Right,* Automated sequencing uses a DNA primer labeled with four different fluorescent tags. Each fluorescent primer hybridizes to the template DNA and undergoes the same synthesis reactions as in manual sequencing. After elongation of the primer, samples containing the four kinds of newly synthesized fragments are pooled and undergo electrophoresis in a single lane of a gel. A laser beam directed near the bottom of the gel excites each fragment, which emits a specific fluorescent signal as it passes through the beam. A photomultiplier senses the specific wavelength of each signal, which corresponds to the dideoxynucleotide incorporated in the elongation reaction. A computer stores and translates the signals as a nucleotide sequence. (Reproduced with permission from Rosenthal N. Molecular medicine: fine structure of a gene—DNA sequencing. *N Engl J Med.* 1995;332:590.)

specific base-pair change that occurs with a given genetic mutation and the other that recognizes the normal allelic sequence. ASOs are commonly used for diagnosing point mutations that occur frequently or for testing multiple members of a large family with a previously identified genetic disorder.

Transgenic and Knockout Animals

The fertilized egg of a *transgenic animal* has had new genetic material introduced that becomes incorporated into the genome and is duplicated and transmitted to subsequent generations along with the normal genes (Fig VIII-15). The entire genetic material needed for transcription must be included in the transgene, including the following:

- Promoter
- 5′ transcription-initiation site
- 5′ untranslated region
- Translation-initiation codon
- Coding section
- Stop codon
- 3′ untranslated region
- Polyadenylation site (in most instances)

The promoter is chosen to assure expression within the tissue of interest.

Exactly where the transgene becomes inserted within the genome of the animal is usually unknown. Transgenic animals have been rescued or cured of autosomal recessive disease by insertion of a copy of the normal gene. Transgenic animals that carry copies of specific mutations of human genes (e.g., mutant rhodopsins) that appear to cause dominant disease (retinitis pigmentosa) have been successfully created.

Shuldiner AR. Transgenic animals. *N Engl J Med.* 1996;334:653–655.

A *knockout mutation* in an animal strain is created by targeting a known gene to disrupt its function, usually by replacement in embryonic stem cells of a portion of the coding region with a sequence of DNA that destroys the original function. The incorporation of the desired gene into the stem cell is accomplished through homologous recombination with a specially constructed vector that contains the bacterial neomycin resistance gene sandwiched between two sequences that are homologous, or identical, to the wild strain (Fig VIII-16). The homologous regions undergo recombination, and, rarely, a double recombination will occur, resulting in the swapping of the new sequence for the targeted sequence.

Since such double homologous recombinations occur at a very low rate, the selection of the rare cells where the desired events have occurred is the next essential step. The knockout vector contains a bacterial neomycin resistance gene, which is used to help provide positive selection (resistance to neomycin, which is added to the culture). The vector also contains a gene that encodes viral thymidine kinase and produces ganciclovir sensitivity, but in this instance the gene lies outside the segment of DNA to be incorporated into the genome of the stem cells. Adding ganciclovir to the culture kills cells that have incorporated the thymidine kinase gene into the genome of the stem cells in a nonspecific fashion. Thus, through a combination of positive and negative selection, only the desired recombinant events are favored.

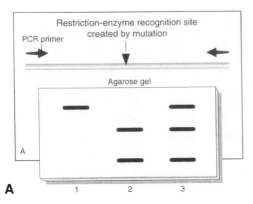

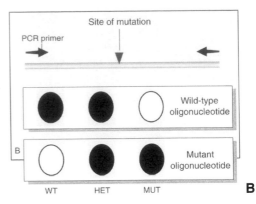

FIG VIII-14—*A,* The detection of a point mutation by digestion of DNA with a restriction enzyme. The mutation creates a new recognition site. The region surrounding the mutation is amplified by PCR, and the resulting PCR product is incubated with the restriction enzyme and then analyzed by agarose-gel electrophoresis. Lane 1 shows DNA from a person without the mutation; only one band appears because the enzyme does not cut the DNA. Lane 2 shows DNA from a person homozygous for the mutation; two bands represent the two fragments obtained after enzyme digestion. Lane 3 shows DNA from a heterozygote; there is one uncut fragment and two cut fragments. *B,* A mutation detected by oligonucleotide hybridization. The segment of DNA is amplified by PCR, divided into aliquots, and spotted onto separate filter membranes, which are hybridized with a labeled oligonucleotide corresponding to the wild-type or mutant sequence. The amplified segment of DNA from a person with the wild-type sequence (WT) hybridizes only with the wild-type oligonucleotide, whereas the DNA from a person homozygous for the mutant sequence (MUT) hybridizes only with the mutant oligonucleotide. DNA from a heterozygote (HET) hybridizes with both oligonucleotides. *C,* The detection of a mutation by PCR. The mutant sequence differs from the wild-type sequence by the substitution of an A for a C. To search for the two kinds of sequences by PCR, two primers are necessary. A separate reaction is carried out with each, together with a common downstream primer. With a wild-type gene, the primer corresponding to the wild-type sequence yields a PCR product. Similarly, the mutant primer produces a product with the mutant sequence. However, with the wild-type primer and the mutant sequence, or the mutant primer and the wild-type sequence, there is no PCR product. The agarose-gel pattern shows that DNA from a person homozygous for the wild-type allele (WT) reacts only with the wild-type primer; DNA from a person homozygous for the mutant sequence (MUT) reacts only with the mutant primer; and DNA from a heterozygote (HET) yields PCR products with both primers. *D,* Detection of a triplet-repeat mutation by Southern blot analysis or PCR. In the fragile X syndrome, a CGG repeat occurs near the 5' end of the gene. The number of repeats ranges from 5 to 50 in the general population and from approximately 50 to 200 in those with the fragile X syndrome. To detect the abnormality, DNA is treated with a restriction enzyme that cuts at recognition sites flanking the CGG repeat. Hybridization on a Southern blot with labeled DNA from the region of the gene reveals a single band in a normal male subject (wild type). An asymptomatic male carrier will have a band of higher molecular weight, and a subject with a full mutation will have a very large, diffuse band because of the instability of the full-mutation allele. The normal and asymptomatic-carrier alleles can also be detected by PCR (right). The full-mutation allele cannot be amplified by PCR because it is too large. (Reproduced with permission from Korf B. Molecular diagnosis. *N Engl J Med.* 1995;332:1500–1501.)

The clone of mutant embryonic stem cells with the disrupted gene is then introduced into a host embryo at the blastocyst stage, resulting in a chimeric animal. Some of the mutant cells are incorporated into the germ line, allowing for breeding of animals that are homozygous for the defective gene. The creation of knockout animals is useful for determining the phenotype of the absence of a normal gene product in those instances where a natural-occurring recessive animal model does

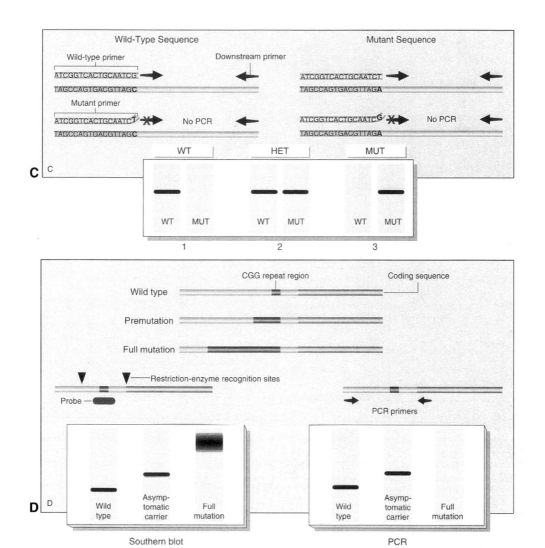

not exist. The knockout technique is used to generate animal models for autosomal recessive disease in humans.

Capecchi MR. Targeted gene replacement. *Sci Am.* 1994;270(3):52–59.

Majzoub JA, Muglia LJ. Knockout mice. *N Engl J Med.* 1996;334:904–907.

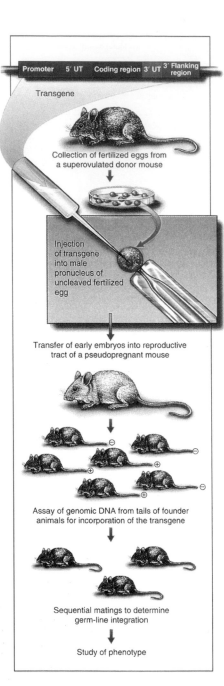

Promoter 5′ UT Coding region 3′ UT 3′ Flanking region

Transgene

Collection of fertilized eggs from a superovulated donor mouse

Injection of transgene into male pronucleus of uncleaved fertilized egg

Transfer of early embryos into reproductive tract of a pseudopregnant mouse

Assay of genomic DNA from tails of founder animals for incorporation of the transgene

Sequential matings to determine germ-line integration

Study of phenotype

FIG VIII-15—The transgene containing the DNA sequences necessary for the expression of a functional protein is injected into the male (larger) pronucleus of uncleaved fertilized eggs through a micropipette. The early embryos are then transferred into the reproductive tract of a mouse rendered "pseudopregnant" by hormonal therapy. The resulting pups (founders) are tested for incorporation of the transgene by assaying genomic DNA from their tails. Founder animals that have incorporated the transgene (+) are mated with nontransgenic mice and their offspring are mated with each other to confirm germ-line integration and to establish a line of homozygous transgenic mice. Several transgenic lines that have incorporated different numbers of transgenes at different integration sites (and thus express various amounts of the protein of interest) are usually studied. (Reproduced with permission from Shuldiner AR. Transgenic animals. *N Engl J Med.* 1996;334:654.)

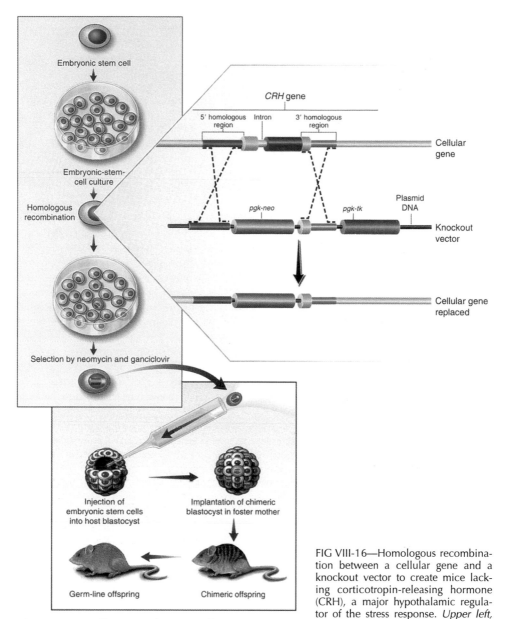

Embryonic stem cell

Embryonic-stem-cell culture

Homologous recombination

Selection by neomycin and ganciclovir

CRH gene

5' homologous region | Intron | 3' homologous region

Cellular gene

pgk-neo | pgk-tk | Plasmid DNA

Knockout vector

Cellular gene replaced

Injection of embryonic stem cells into host blastocyst

Implantation of chimeric blastocyst in foster mother

Germ-line offspring

Chimeric offspring

FIG VIII-16—Homologous recombination between a cellular gene and a knockout vector to create mice lacking corticotropin-releasing hormone (CRH), a major hypothalamic regulator of the stress response. *Upper left,* Embryonic stem cells contain the *CRH* cellular gene (*right*), which consists of exon 1 (olive green, a 5' noncoding region), an intron, and exon 2 (red, a protein-coding region, and yellow, a 3' noncoding region). A knockout vector, consisting of a collinear assembly of a DNA flanking segment 5' to the cellular gene (blue), the phosphoglycerate kinase-bacterial neomycin gene (*pgk-neo,* violet), a 3' segment of the cellular gene (yellow), a DNA flanking segment 3' to the cellular gene (green), and the phosphoglycerate kinase–viral thymidine kinase gene (*pgk-tk,* orange), is created and introduced into the embryonic stem cell culture. Double recombination occurs between the cellular gene and the knockout vector in the 5' homologous regions and the 3' homologous regions (dashed lines), resulting in the incorporation of the inactive knockout vector, including *pgk-neo* but not *pgk-tk,* into the cellular genomic locus of the embryonic stem cell. The presence of *pgk-neo* and the absence of *pgk-tk* in these replaced genes will allow survival of these embryonic stem cells after positive-negative selection with neomycin and ganciclovir. *Bottom,* The clone of mutant embryonic stem cells is injected into a host blastocyst, which is implanted into a pseudopregnant foster mother and subsequently develops into chimeric offspring. The contribution of the embryonic stem cells to the germ cells of the chimeric mouse results in germ-line transmission of the embryonic stem cell genome to offspring that are heterozygous for the mutated *CRH* allele. The heterozygotes are mated to produce mutant mice homozygous for CRH deficiency, with impaired hormal responses to multiple stressors. (Reproduced with permission from Majzoub JA, Muglia LJ. Molecular medicine: knockout mice. *N Engl J Med.* 1996;334:905.)

Gene Therapy

Replacement of Absent Gene Product in X-Linked and Recessive Disease

For genetic diseases where the mutant allele produces either no message or an ineffective gene product (a so-called null allele), correction of the disorder may be possible simply by replacing the gene in the deficient cells or tissues. It is theoretically possible to transfer normal genes into human cells that harbor either null or mutant genes that do not produce a stable, translated product. Vectors used to carry the genetic material into the cells include retroviruses, adenoviruses, and plasmid-liposome complexes. Early attempts have met with limited success because of problems with delivery, specificity of targeting, stability, and regulation.

Retroviral vectors carry the risk of inducing toxicity from overexpression or insertional mutagenesis if the inserted sequence disrupts a tumor-suppressor gene or activates an oncogene. The target cell cannot be a terminally differentiated cell, and it must proliferate in order to integrate the inserted DNA into its genome (Fig VIII-17). Transfer of adenosine deaminase (ADA) with expression has been accomplished in T cells, cord blood, and placental cells from children with ADA deficiency and has resulted in partial immune function. Low-density lipoprotein (LDL) receptor cDNA has been transferred to autologous hepatocytes of patients with familial hypercholesterolemia. Cytokine cDNAs and p53 antisense DNA have been transferred to individuals and cells from patients with tumors.

Current *adenoviruses* in usage excite nonspecific inflammation or cellular immunity directed against the vector, limiting the longevity of new gene expression (Fig VIII-18). However, limited, short-term expression of the normal human cystic fibrosis transmembrane conductive regulator (CFTR) has been achieved in patients with cystic fibrosis.

Plasmid-liposome complexes may have advantages as vectors, because they can be used for nondividing cells and may be less likely to incite inflammation or immune responses (Fig VIII-19). However, as vectors they are inefficient and may not produce sufficient expression of the wanted product. Strategies are being developed to direct the new genetic material into the nucleus, with the possibility of subsequent incorporation into the genome, perpetuating expression of the new gene.

Blau HM, Springer ML. Molecular medicine: gene therapy—a novel form of drug delivery. *N Engl J Med.* 1995;333:1204–1207.

Crystal RG. Transfer of genes to humans: early lessons and obstacles to success. *Science.* 1995;270:404–410.

Hangai M, Kaneda Y, Tanihara H, et al. In vivo gene transfer into the retina mediated by a novel liposome system. *Invest Ophthalmol Vis Sci.* 1996;37:2678–2685.

Strategies for Dominant Diseases

Dominant diseases are caused by production of a gene product that is either insufficient (*haploid insufficiency*) or conducive to disease (*dominant-negative effect*). Haploid insufficiency theoretically should be treatable by gene replacement as outlined above for recessive or X-linked disease. (For dominant disorders produced by defective developmental genes this correction would have to occur in early uterine development.)

Disorders resulting from a dominant-negative effect require a different approach. Thus, strategies for treatment of dominant disease differ depending upon whether a functional gene product is produced. Some genes code for RNA that can

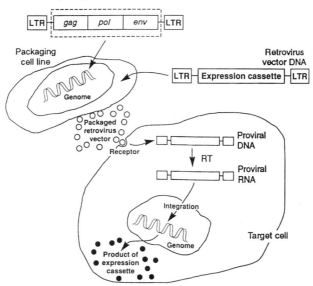

Retrovirus (wild-type) DNA

FIG VIII-17—Retrovirus vector design, production, and gene transfer. Retroviruses are RNA viruses that replicate through DNA intermediates. The vectors are rendered incapable of causing disease by deletion of the sequences (*gag, pol,* and *env*) that are required for replication. The gene that is to be transferred to the cell, including the sequences that control expression, is placed within the expression cassette. Special cell lines produce the packaged retrovirus vectors, which are then used to carry the expression cassette into the target cell, using specific cell surface receptors. Within the cytoplasm reverse transcriptase converts the vector RNA into DNA that is randomly inserted into the genome. (Figures 17–19 are reproduced with permission from Crystal RG. Transfer of genes to humans: early lessons and obstacles to success. *Science.* 1995;270:404–405. © 1995 American Association for the Advancement of Science.)

bind to mRNA from another gene and block its ability to make a protein. Greater understanding of these genes may allow for creation of either drugs or new gene-encoded RNAs that can block the translation of mRNA for defective alleles, thus allowing only the normal allele to be expressed.

Another approach is the use of oligonucleotides that are designed to bind with mRNA from mutant alleles, stopping the mRNA from being translated by ribosomes (Fig VIII-20). Although many problems need to be worked out for such a therapy to work effectively, this approach holds promise for autosomal dominant disorders where disease is caused by the expression of the mutant gene product.

Askari FK, McDonnell WM. Molecular medicine: antisense-oligonucleotide therapy. *N Engl J Med.* 1996;334:316–318.

Della NG. Molecular biology in ophthalmology. A review of principles and recent advances. *Arch Ophthalmol.* 1996;114:457–463.

Musarella MA. Gene mapping of ocular diseases. *Surv Ophthalmol.* 1992;36:285–312.

Petrash JM. Applications of molecular biological techniques to the understanding of visual sytem disorders. *Am J Ophthalmol.* 1992;113:573–582.

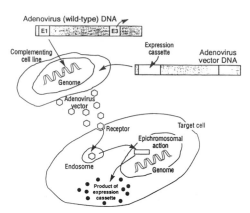

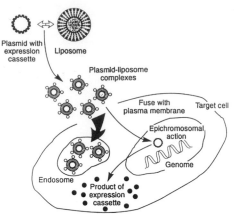

FIG VIII-18—Adenovirus vector design, production, and gene transfer. The expression cassette is inserted into the adenoviral genome in place of early genes that are needed for viral replication (E1 and, if needed, E3). The replication-disabled vector is transfected into a complementary cell line for production of large numbers of the new gene-containing vector. The vector binds to the target cell through viral-specific receptors and enters the cytoplasm within endosomes. It then enters the nucleus and in an epichromosomal fashion directs the expression of the desired gene product.

FIG VIII-19—Plasmid-liposome complex design and gene transfer. Liposomes used for gene transfer use positively charged synthetic cationic lipids that are complexed with a plasmid containing the expression cassette. These fuse with the plasma membrane of the target cell, discharging their genetic material into the cytoplasm. By chance, some sequences are taken up by the nucleus and in an epichromosomal fashion expressed, but the overall efficiency of this process is low.

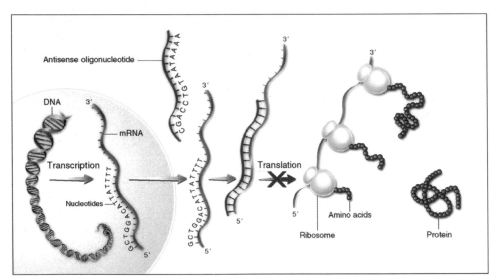

FIG VIII-20—Blockade of translation by antisense oligonucleotides. Normal gene transcription of DNA into mRNA is followed by translation of mRNA into protein. Antisense oligonucleotides complementary to a portion of mRNA bind mRNA, preventing translation, either by the steric effect of the binding process itself or, possibly, by inducing degradation of the mRNA by RNase. (Reproduced with permission from Askari FK, McDonnell WM. Molecular medicine: antisense-oligonucteotide therapy. *N Engl J Med.* 1996;334:316.)

CHAPTER IX

Clinical Genetics

Introduction

Ophthalmology as a science of human medicine has played an important historical role in human genetics, providing the following breakthroughs:

- First modern description of a familial disease (daltonism, or dichromatic red-green color blindness, 1798)
- First textbook of human genetics (Waardenburg, 1932)
- Establishment of the first linkage of one human disease to another trait (color vision deficiency and hemophilia, 1937)
- First human disease linkage to an autosome (cataracta nucleus pulverulenta to the Duffy blood group on chromosome 1, 1963)
- First clear demonstration of mitotic recombination in human cell lines (in retinoblastoma, 1983)

It is important for a clinician not only to diagnose a disease state accurately and minimize its effects in the patient but also to ensure that the siblings and parents are evaluated for milder or earlier forms of the disease. Any family with a genetic disorder should receive genetic counseling as a primary care responsibility. However, only the ophthalmologist will be sensitive to the wide variability of traits affecting the visual system and to the subtleties of carrier state detection both by direct evaluation and with indirect diagnostic technology. Furthermore, only the ophthalmologist can appropriately counsel the patient and family about the ocular effects of a given genetic disorder, its attendant risks and burdens.

Terminology: *Hereditary, Genetic, Familial, Congenital*

Not infrequently, uncertainty surrounds the accurate use of the terms hereditary, genetic, familial, and congenital. *Hereditary* indicates that a disease or trait under consideration results directly from an individual's particular genetic composition, or genome, and that it can be passed from one generation to another. *Genetic* denotes that the disorder is caused by a defect of genes, whether acquired or inherited. In some instances, for example with large deletions of mtDNA associated with chronic progressive ophthalmoplegia, the disease is clearly genetic but is not passed to subsequent generations and is therefore not hereditary. These deletions associated with ocular myopathies presumably arise in the oocyte or during early embryologic development. Thus, the terms *hereditary* and *genetic* are not exactly synonymous but are sometimes used to convey similar concepts. A hereditary or a genetic disorder may or may not be congenital.

A condition is *familial* if it occurs in more than one member of a family. It may, of course, be hereditary but need not be. A familial disorder can be caused by common exposure to infectious agents (e.g., tuberculosis), traumatizing materials (e.g., radiation), deficient or excess food intake (e.g., vitamin deficiencies or obesity), or environmental agents such as asbestos or coal dust.

The term *congenital* refers to characteristics that are present at birth; these may be hereditary or familial, or they may occur as an isolated event, often as the result of an infection (e.g., rubella, toxoplasmosis, or cytomegalic inclusion disease). The occurrence at birth is the defining factor. Findings suggesting but not establishing that a congenital anomaly may be genetic include a phenotype similar to that from known genetic disorders (e.g., aniridia) or a tendency toward bilaterality (e.g., bilateral colobomas) and symmetry. However, some nongenetic congenital disorders, such as cataracts from rubella, can be bilateral. Moreover, not all hereditary disorders are bilateral or symmetric; for example, optic nerve coloboma that was present in only one eye has been observed in multiple generations and presumably in this case is an autosomal dominant trait.

Although numerous hereditary disorders are expressed at the time of birth, the complex interrelationships between genomic expression and factors such as the environment may alter the time of onset and the extent to which a disorder is manifest. For example, the overt clinical onset of signs for diabetes mellitus, a condition with a heritable tendency mediated by multiple genes, in individual monozygotic twins can differ appreciably depending on each twin's level of carbohydrate intake or other factors. In addition, although the enzyme deficiency responsible for galactosemia is clearly inherited, the expression of systemic disease as well as the cataract formation can be avoided by the removal of galactose from the diet. Von Hippel–Lindau disease and lattice dystrophy of the cornea are additional examples of genetic disorders in which signs of ocular disease may not be apparent at birth.

A condition known to be genetic and hereditary may appear in only one individual of a family (e.g., retinitis pigmentosa). Such an individual is said to have a *simplex* presentation of a genetic disease. Some authors apply the confusing term *sporadic* to describe the occurrence of a trait in a single member of a kindred, often erroneously implying that this case is not genetic. A genetically determined trait may be isolated in the pedigree for several reasons:

- The pedigree is small
- The full expression of the disease has not been sought or has not manifested in other relatives
- The disorder represents a new genetic mutation
- The disorder is recessive and the investigation to determine whether the parents are carriers has been inadequate
- The disorder is caused by chromosomal changes

Clinically similar disorders may be inherited in several different manners; for example, retinitis pigmentosa can occur as an autosomal dominant, autosomal recessive, or X-linked trait or as the result of a mitochondrial mutation. These various genetic forms represent distinct gene defects with different alterations in gene structure and different biochemical pathogeneses, each of which has similar clinical phenotypic expressions. Clarification of genetic heterogeneity is important, since only with the proper diagnosis and inheritance pattern can appropriate genetic counseling and prognosis be offered.

Some genetic disorders originally thought to be single and unique are found on close scrutiny to be two or more fundamentally distinct entities. Further clarification of the inheritance pattern or biochemical analysis will permit separation of initially similar disorders. Such has been the case for Marfan syndrome and homocystinuria.

Although both disorders have unusual body habitus and ectopia lentis, the presence of dominant inheritance, aortic aneurysms, and valvular heart disease in Marfan syndrome distinguishes it from the recessive pattern and thromboembolic disease of homocystinuria.

Recently, the term *heterogeneity* has been expanded and modified. *Genetic heterogeneity* is a general term that applies to the phenotypic similarity that may be produced by two or more fundamentally distinct genetic entities; this term implies that the genes are nonallelic. The term *locus heterogeneity* has been used when linkage studies have shown that different families have a similar phenotype map at different loci and, hence, caused by mutations of different genes. *Allelic heterogeneity* describes the situation in which different alleles at the same locus are capable of producing an abnormal phenotype. With *clinical heterogeneity* different mutations at the same locus can produce different phenotypes.

Once the location on a chromosome is determined for a particular disease gene and the gene's molecular structure is identified, most examples of genetic heterogeneity cease to be a problem for diagnosis or classification. However, clinical, allelic, and locus heterogeneity can remain perplexing issues. For example, mutations of the same gene, *FGFR2,* which codes for fibroblast growth factor receptor–2, can cause Pfeiffer syndrome, Crouzon disease, and Apert syndrome. Identical mutations in the *FGFR2* gene cause both Pfeiffer syndrome and Crouzon disease phenotypes. Mutation of the Norrie disease gene, *NDP,* usually results in the typical phenotype of pseudoglioma from exudative retinal detachments, but some mutations of *NDP* have been associated with X-linked exudative vitreoretinopathy. Mutations of the proto-oncogene *RET* can give rise to medullary thyroid carcinoma, multiple endocrine neoplasia IIA and IIB, and Hirschsprung disease. Such examples give added meaning to the term heterogeneity. Ultimately, greater understanding of these and other disorders at the molecular and cellular level will result in more reliable patient management and improved classification of genetic disease. However, considerably more information is needed about how seemingly similar mutations can produce such differing phenotypes.

McKusick VA. *Mendelian Inheritance in Man: A Catalog of Human Genes and Genetic Disorders.* 11th ed. Baltimore: Johns Hopkins University Press; 1994.

Mulvihill JJ. Craniofacial syndromes: no such thing as a single gene disease. *Nat Genet.* 1995;9:101–103.

Rutland P, Pulleyn LJ, Reardon W, et al. Identical mutations in the *FGFR2* gene cause both Pfeiffer and Crouzon syndrome phenotypes. *Nat Genet.* 1995;9:173–176.

Thompson MW, McInnes RR, Willard HF. *Genetics in Medicine.* 5th ed. Philadelphia: Saunders; 1991:427, 429, 432, 435.

van Heyningen V. Genetics. One gene—four syndromes. *Nature.* 1994;367:319–320.

Wilkie AO, Slaney SF, Oldridge M, et al. Apert syndrome results from localized mutations of *FGFR2* and is allelic with Crouzon syndrome. *Nat Genet.* 1995;9:165–172.

Genes and Chromosomes

In 1909 the Danish biologist Wilhelm Johannsen coined the word *genes,* from the Greek for "giving birth to," as a name for segments of the DNA molecule containing individual units of hereditary information. Genes are the basic units of inheritance, and they include the length of nucleotides that codes for a single trait or a single polypeptide chain and its associated regulatory regions. Human genes vary greatly in size from approximately 500 to more than 2 million bp. However, more than 98% range from <10 kb to 500 kb in size. Many are considerably larger than 50,000 bp. Whereas a single human cell contains enough DNA for 6 million genes, about 50,000–100,000 genes are found among the 23 pairs of known chromosomes. The function of the remaining 95% of the genetic material is unknown.

The relative sequence of the genes, which are arranged in a linear fashion along the chromosome, is referred to as the *genetic map*. The physical position or region on the chromosome occupied by a single gene is known as a *locus*. The physical contiguity of various gene loci becomes the vehicle for close association of genes with one another (*linkage*) and their clustering in groups that characteristically move together or separately (*segregation*) from one generation to the next.

It was not until 1956 that Tjio and Levan in Lund, Sweden, determined that each normal human somatic cell has 46 chromosomes composed of 23 homologous pairs, not 48 chromosomes as previously believed. Each member of a homologous pair carries matched, although not necessarily identical, genes in the same sequence. One member of each chromosome pair is inherited from the father and the other from the mother. Each normal sperm or ovum contains 23 chromosomes, one representative from each pair; thus, each parent transmits half of his or her genetic information to each child. Of the 46 chromosomes, 44 are called *autosomes* because they provide information on somatic characteristics. (The X and Y chromosomes provide such information as well; e.g., genes on the Y chromosome influence teeth and height.) At metaphase the longest human autosome measures approximately 8.0–10.0 μm and the smallest is 1.2–1.5 μm.

The pair of chromosomes that is not identical in the two sexes consists in females of two similar sex-determining chromosomes, *X chromosomes,* with a length of 4.0–5.0 μm each. Males have one X chromosome and another smaller sex chromosome, about 1.5 μm in size, called a *Y chromosome.* The Y chromosome is unique to phenotypic normal males. It determines development of the testes and other male secondary sexual characteristics.

The two female X chromosomes, although similar in length and position of the centromere, show differences during cell division with one being more condensed, darker staining, and replicating its DNA later. This mechanism of inactivation avoids an "overdose" of information from the two X chromosomes in females. Not all genes are unexpressed on the inactivated X chromosome. Certain genes, including that for steroid sulfatase (STS) and that for choroideremia (CHM), can escape inactivation. One gene that always escapes inactivation is the X inactivation center on band q13. Expression of this gene from one X chromosome is directly involved in inactivation of the remainder of the genetic material for this chromosome.

In some female somatic cells a mass of chromatin in the nucleus appears to represent the inactive X chromosome. This so-called Barr body, first identified by Barr and Bertram in cat nerve cells, is easiest to demonstrate in the epithelium of the buccal mucosa. However, the presence of the Barr body is highly variable and dependent on multiple factors, including the stage of the cell cycle and orientation of the nucleus on a microscopic slide; therefore, evaluation of smears of mucosal epithelium for Barr bodies has little usefulness in modern clinical genetics.

Bishop JE, Waldholz M. *Genome.* New York: Simon & Schuster; 1990.

Emery AEH, Rimoin DL, Connor JM, et al, eds. *Principles and Practice of Medical Genetics.* 3rd ed. New York: Churchill Livingstone; 1996.

Goldberg MF, Renie WA, eds. *Genetic and Metabolic Eye Disease.* 2nd ed. Boston: Little, Brown & Co; 1986.

Schmickel RD. The genetic basis of ophthalmological disease. *Surv Ophthalmol.* 1980;25:37–46.

Thompson MW, McInnes RR, Willard HF. *Genetics in Medicine.* 5th ed. Philadelphia: Saunders; 1991:31–51.

Alleles

Alternative forms of a particular gene at the same locus on each of an identical pair of chromosomes are called *alleles* (Greek for "reciprocals"). If both members of a pair of alleles for a given autosomal locus are identical (i.e., the DNA sequence is the same), the individual is *homozygous* (a homozygote); if the allelic genes are distinct from each other (i.e., the DNA sequence differs), the individual is *heterozygous* (a heterozygote). Different gene defects can cause dramatically different phenotypes and still be allelic. For example, sickle cell disease (SS hemoglobinopathy) caused by homozygosity of one mutant gene is significantly different from the phenotypic expression of SC hemoglobinopathy, yet the Hb S gene and the Hb C gene are allelic. The term *polyallelism* refers to the many possible variants or mutations of a single gene.

As more sophisticated biochemical analysis has become available, different alleles frequently can be shown to have slightly different biochemical properties. Among the mucopolysaccharidoses, for example, the enzyme alpha-L-iduronidase is defective in both Hurler disease and Scheie syndrome. Since these are mutations of the same gene, they are abnormalities of the same enzyme and thus allelic. However, the clinical severity of these two disorders (age of onset, age of detection, and severity of affliction of skeleton, liver, spleen, and cornea) is entirely different, presumably because the function of the mutant enzyme is less altered by the Scheie syndrome mutation. Since the enzyme is a protein composed of hundreds of amino acids, a mutation resulting in a base substitution within a certain codon might cause a change in one or more amino acids in a portion of the enzyme remote from its active site, reducing the effect on the enzyme's function. On the other hand, the substitution of one amino acid at a critical location in the active site of the enzyme might abolish most or all of its enzymatic activity. Several examples of allelic disorders appear among the mucopolysaccharidoses.

The phenotype of the usual heterozygote is determined by one mutant allele and one "normal" allele. However, the genotype of a compound heterozygote comprises two different mutant alleles, each at the same locus. The genetic Hurler-Scheie compound is biochemically proven and clinically manifests features intermediate between the homozygotes of the two alleles. Whenever detailed biochemical analysis is possible, the products of the two alleles will manifest slightly different properties such as rates of enzyme activity or electrophoretic migration. Among other autosomal recessive diseases a spectrum of phenotypes can be caused by a diversity of mutant alleles occurring in various paired combinations. Current knowledge about most recessive diseases (as well as dominant disorders) does not permit more than the speculative consideration of this alternative in the clinical setting.

By contrast, some genetic disorders originally thought to be single and unique may be found upon close scrutiny to be two or more fundamentally distinct entities. Occasionally, this genetic heterogeneity is seen with diseases that are inherited in the same manner, such as tyrosinase-negative and tyrosinase-positive oculocutaneous albinism. Since these two conditions are phenotypically similar, and each is inherited as an autosomal recessive trait, it was assumed for some time that they were allelic. When a tyrosinase-negative individual bears children with a tyrosinase-positive individual, the offspring appear clinically normal. This observation excludes the possibility that these two conditions are allelic, since every offspring must be heterozygous for the gene for each condition. Separate gene loci (the tyrosinase gene and the *P* gene) are now appreciated to cause oculocutaneous albinism. The offspring of such matings of individuals with phenotypically similar but genotypically different disorders are called *double heterozygotes* since they are heterozygous for each of the two loci.

Because a female has two X chromosomes, she may be either homozygous or heterozygous with respect to X-linked genes. A male is said to be *hemizygous* for X-linked genes since he has only a single X chromosome, and the Y chromosome has little comparable material. A person is also termed hemizygous for a given genetic locus when the second allele is missing, either through loss of an entire chromosome or through rearrangements resulting in deletion of any segment of one of a pair of chromosomes.

Mitosis

A cell may undergo two types of cell division, mitosis and meiosis. Mitosis gives rise to the multiple generations of genetically identical cells needed for the growth and maintenance of the organism. When mitosis is about to occur, the cell accurately duplicates all of its chromosomes. The replicated chromosomes then separate into two identical groups that migrate apart and eventually reach opposite sides of the cell. The cell and its contents then divide, forming two genetically identical daughter cells, each with the same diploid chromosome number and genetic information as the parent cell.

Meiosis, Segregation, Independent Assortment, Linkage

Meiosis

In contrast to mitosis, meiosis leads to the production of cells that have only one member of each chromosome pair (Fig IX-1). The specialized cells that arise from meiosis and participate in sexual reproduction are called *gametes*. The male gamete is a sperm, and the female gamete an ovum. During meiosis, a modified sequence of divisions systematically reduces the number of chromosomes in each cell by one half to the haploid number. Consequently, each gamete contains 23 chromosomes, one representative of each pair. This assortment occurs in a random fashion, except that one representative of each pair of chromosomes is incorporated into each sperm or egg.

At conception a sperm and an ovum unite, forming a single cell called a *zygote* that contains 46 chromosomes. Since both parents contribute equally to the genetic makeup of their offspring, new and often advantageous gene combinations may emerge. Meiosis also provides the essential mechanism for sex determination. Since females possess two X chromosomes, they always produce ova that contain 22 autosomes and one X chromosome. Males, in contrast, have one X and one Y chromosome. Half of their sperm carry 22 autosomes and one X chromosome; the other half carry 22 autosomes and one Y chromosome. When a sperm bearing an X chromo-

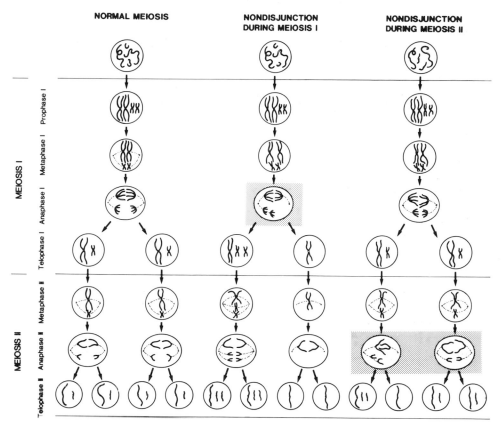

NORMAL MEIOSIS NONDISJUNCTION DURING MEIOSIS I NONDISJUNCTION DURING MEIOSIS II

MEIOSIS I

Prophase I Metaphase I Anaphase I Telophase I

MEIOSIS II

Metaphase II Anaphase II Telophase II

FIG IX-1—Normal meiosis and chromosomal nondisjunction occurring at different phases of meiosis. Nondisjunction is discussed in the text on pp 259-264.

some fuses with an ovum, the result is a female. If, instead, the sperm contains a Y chromosome, a male is conceived.

Segregation

Two allelic genes, which occupy the same gene locus on two homologous chromosomes, separate with the division of the two chromosomes during meiosis, and each goes to a different gamete. Thus, the genes are said to *segregate*, a property limited to allelic genes, which cannot occur together in a single offspring of the bearer. For example, if a parent is a compound heterozygote for both hemoglobin S and hemoglobin C, which occupy the same genetic locus on homologous chromosomes, none of the offspring will inherit both hemoglobins from that parent; each will inherit either one or the other.

Independent Assortment

Genes on different (nonhomologous) chromosomes may or may not separate together during meiotic cell division. This random process is called *independent assortment,* based on Mendel's law of independent assortment, which states that nonallelic genes assort independently of one another. Since *crossing over,* or exchange of chromosomal material between the members of a pair of homologous chromosomes, can occur in meiosis, two nonallelic genes originally on opposite members of the chromosomal pair may end up together on either of the two or remain separated, depending on their original positions and on the sites of genetic interchange. Thus, the gametes of an individual with two nonallelic dominant traits, or *syntenic traits,* located on the same chromosome could produce four possible offspring. A child may inherit

□ Both traits if the separate alleles remain on the same chromosome and the child inherits this chromosome

□ Neither trait if the genes remain on one chromosome, but the child inherits the opposite chromosome with neither allele

□ Only one of the two alleles if crossing over occurred between the loci and the child received the chromosome with that particular allele

This scheme for nonallelic traits depends on the independent assortment of chromosomes in the first division of meiosis. About 50 crossovers (1–3 per chromosome) occur during an average meiotic division.

Linkage

Linkage is the major exception or modification to the law of independent assortment. Nonallelic genes located reasonably close together on the same chromosome tend to be transmitted together from generation to generation at a frequency greater than would be expected on the basis of chance alone; thus, they are said to be linked. The closer together the two loci, the less likely they are to be affected by crossovers. Linear physical proximity along a chromosome cannot be considered an automatic guarantor of linkage, however. In fact, there may be sites on each chromosome that are more vulnerable to homologous crossing over than others.

Musarella MA. Gene mapping of ocular diseases, *Surv Ophthalmol.* 1992;36:285–312.

Chromosomal Analysis

Cytogenetics is a branch of genetics concerned with the study of chromosomes and their properties. Chromosomal defects are changes in the chromosome number or structure that damage sensitive genetic functions and lead to developmental or reproductive disorders. These defects usually result from a disruption of the mechanisms controlling chromosome movement during cell division or alterations of chromosome structure that lead to changes in the number or arrangement of genes or to abnormal chromosomal behavior.

Chromosomal abnormalities occur in about 1 of 200 term pregnancies and in 1%–2% of all pregnancies involving parents over the age of 35 years. About 7% of perinatal deaths and some 40%–50% of retrievable spontaneous abortuses have significant chromosomal aberrations. Virtually any change in chromosome number during early development has a profound effect upon the formation of tissues and organs and the viability of the entire organism. Most major chromosomal disorders are characterized by both developmental and mental retardation as well as a variety of somatic abnormalities.

Indications for Chromosome Analysis

The usual indications for chromosome analysis are listed below in Table IX-1. Ophthalmologists should be aware of the value of constitutional and tumor karyotypes in infants with retinoblastoma, especially if the tumor represents a new genetic mutation. Chromosome analysis is also suggested in patients with isolated (nonfamilial) aniridia, which is often associated with Wilms tumor, and other systemic malformations and in patients who survive a neoplasia syndrome and develop a second neoplasm.

The occurrence of a chromosomally abnormal state in a child or in an adult of reproductive age warrants consideration of amniocentesis or chorionic villus sampling for prenatal diagnosis in subsequent pregnancies to avoid the risk of recurrence. Amniocentesis can be undertaken at about the 16th week of pregnancy.

TABLE IX-1

SOME INDICATIONS FOR CHROMOSOME ANALYSIS

Clinical diagnosis in newborns: multiple malformations, especially involving more than one organ system, with or without intrauterine growth retardation; perinatal death

Clinical diagnosis at any age: mental retardation with or without congenital malformations, in the absence of unequivocal identifiable cause; gonadal ambiguity; infertility, amenorrhea, or reproductive dysfunction; ocular malformations associated with any malformations of other organ systems with no known cause

Multiple miscarriages: spontaneous abortions or stillbirths without apparent cause, even in clinically normal parents

Studies of malignancy: constitutional and tumor karyotypes, especially leukemia, retinoblastoma, aniridia–Wilms tumor, and other embryonal malignancies; specific syndromes with high risks of malignancy–ataxia-telangiectasia, Bloom syndrome, Fanconi anemia; tumor karyotypes on all second tumors in neoplasia syndromes

Prenatal diagnosis: in advanced maternal age, known translocation carrier state, X-linked carrier state for sexing; previous child with chromosomal abnormalities; and as part of either amniocentesis or chorionic villus sampling

Preparation for Chromosomal Analysis

Karyotype The systematic display of chromosomes from a single somatic cell is called a karyotype. Chromosome preparations can be made from any tissue whose cells will divide in culture. The tissue most commonly used is peripheral venous blood, although bone marrow, skin fibroblasts, and cells from amniotic fluid or chorionic villi are useful under specific circumstances. In special situations chromosome analyses can be obtained directly from rapidly dividing neoplastic tissues, as has been done with fresh cells from retinoblastoma and Wilms tumor.

The blood of healthy, nonleukemic individuals contains no dividing cells. Therefore, T lymphocytes in a small sample (often less than 5 ml) of fresh heparinized blood are stimulated to divide by adding phytohemagglutinin to a culture medium. After about 72 hours, as the dividing cells approach metaphase, a drug that has colchicine-like effects is added to prevent formation of the mitotic spindle apparatus.

Chromosomal banding After the cells are spread on slides, ruptured, and fixed, they can be stained directly with modified Giemsa techniques (G-banding) or with quinacrine (Q-banding) or prepared with a variety of other materials (Fig IX-2). Faint horizontal differences in staining density called *bands* are enhanced by these procedures. Before the era of chromosomal banding the chromosomes were arranged in the karyotype into seven groups according to size. Within each group the specific chromosomes were often impossible to differentiate. The development of chromosomal banding has allowed all 24 chromosomes (22 autosomes plus the X and Y chromosomes) to be uniquely identified, permitting each specific autosome to be identified with the chromosome number alone. Arabic numerals written after the letters *p* or *q* designate a specific band region on the short or long arm of a chromosome (Fig IX-3).

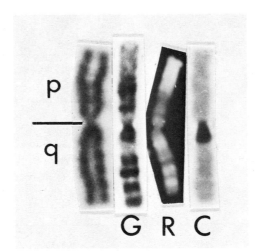

FIG IX-2—Human chromosome 1 prepared by different banding techniques. The unbanded chromosome of the far left was stained with Giemsa stain without any pretreatment. The line indicates the location of the primary constriction, or *centromere,* which divides the chromosome into a short (*p*) and a long (*q*) arm. The second chromosome was prepared by trypsin G-banding, the current standard technique in most clinical cytogenetics laboratories. The third chromosome was prepared with a fluorescent R-banding (reverse banding) technique, which produces a pattern essentially opposite that of G-banding. The chromosome on the far right was prepared by C-banding, which selectively stains regions containing constitutive heterochromatin (genetically inert regions of highly repeated DNA sequences).

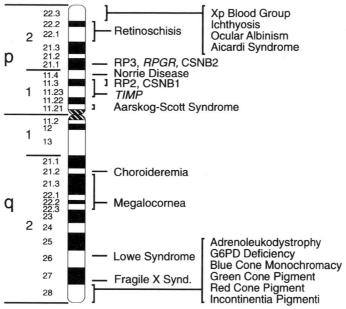

FIG IX-3—Approximate location on the X chromosome of genes for various X-linked disorders.

The smallest human chromosome bands that can be recognized under the microscope contain from 1 to 5 million base pairs of DNA and are, therefore, likely to contain many genes. Members of each of the autosomes plus the sex chromosomes can be distinguished on the basis of overall size, their morphology with respect to the position of their centromere, and the pattern of banding as determined by their staining properties. The longest chromosome is about 7.0–8.0 μm in length, and the shortest is about 1.5 μm.

The introduction of prophase rather than metaphase banding has provided even more detailed understanding of individual chromosomes and microscopic structural aberrations. Currently used banding techniques on prophase cells can distinguish up to 850 bands. Figure IX-4 shows the karyotype of a human male conventionally stained and arranged. Chromosome morphology is determined by the position of the centromere, or central constriction, that divides the chromosome into a short arm designated *p* (*petit*) and a long arm designated *q*. Chromosomes are termed *metacentric* if the centromere lies in the center of the chromosome, *submetacentric* if the centromere is somewhat distant from the center, and *acrocentric* if the centromere lies near the end of the chromosome.

A karyotype is prepared from a photomicrograph of the chromosomes in one cell that are cut out, paired, ordered, and numbered according to their structural and banding features. Recently, equipment has been developed to handle and process digital images of the chromosomes that promises greater sensitivity for detection of small chromosomal abnormalities and better understanding of complex chromosomal rearrangements in conjunction with the newer techniques for labeling of specific regions of a chromosome discussed on the following pages.

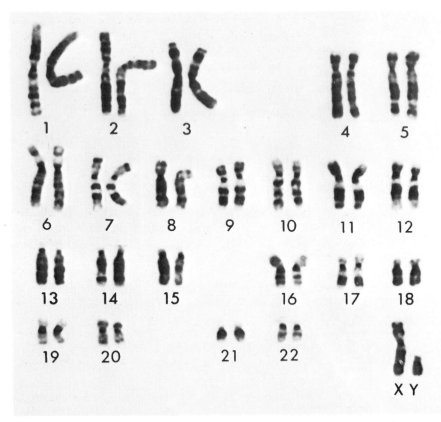

FIG IX-4—Photomicrograph of chromosomes arranged by size, shape, and banding pattern, according to the Paris classification. Note the two dissimilar chromosomes in the last row, called X and Y, which identify this subject as a male.

Fluorescence In Situ Hybridization (FISH) and Chromosome Arm Painting (CAP)

With the *fluoresence in situ hybridization (FISH)* technique, DNA fragments from genes of interest are first tagged with a fluorescent compound and then annealed or hybridized to chromosomes. The regions of interest are stained to determine whether duplication, deletion, or rearrangement has occurred. Such molecular probes can detect and often quantify the presence of specific DNA sequences on a chromosome and can find microscopic abnormalities that would be indiscernible by conventional cytogenetic methods.

Probes have been developed from microdissections of chromosomal regions and FISH that label entire arms of chromosomes, a process called *chromosome arm painting (CAP)*, and each of the individual chromosomes, termed *multicolor spectral karyotyping* and *combinatorial multi-fluor FISH*. With two-color FISH both arms of each chromosome can be simultaneously labeled (Fig IX-5). These probes are valuable for detecting and understanding the mechanisms of formation of complex chromosomal rearrangements (Fig IX-6), such as can occur in cancer. Chromosome painting is also being used to generate information on the three-dimensional organization of chromatin domains within the nucleus in interphase.

Guan X-Y, Zhang H, Bittner M, et al. Chromosomal arm painting probes. *Nat Genet.* 1996;12:10–11.

Schröck E, du Manoir S, Veldman T, et al. Multicolor spectral karyotyping of human chromosomes. *Science.* 1996;273:494–497.

Speicher MR, Ballard SG, Ward DC. Karyotyping human chromosomes by combinatorial multi-fluor FISH. *Nat Genet.* 1996;12:368–375.

Aneuploidy of Autosomes

Aneuploidy denotes an abnormal number of chromosomes in nongametic cells. The presence of three homologous chromosomes in a cell rather than the normal pair is termed *trisomy. Monosomy* is the presence of only one member of any pair of autosomes or only one sex chromosome. The absence of a single autosome is almost always lethal to the embryo, while the presence of an extra autosome is often catastrophic to surviving embryos. Aneuploidy of sex chromosomes such as X, XXX, XXY, and XYY is less disastrous. Monosomies and trisomies are generally caused by mechanical accidents that increase or decrease the number of chromosomes in the gametes. The most common type of accident, meiotic *nondisjunction,* results from a disruption of chromosome movement during meiosis, as shown in Figure IX-1, p 253. *Polyploidy* describes a cell that contains an exact multiple of the normal diploid number: 3n(69), 4n(92), etc.

de Grouchy J, Turleau C. *Clinical Atlas of Human Chromosomes.* 2nd ed. New York: Wiley; 1984.

Thompson MW, McInnes RR, Willard HF. *Genetics in Medicine.* 5th ed. Philadelphia: Saunders; 1991:201–229.

Trisomy 13 syndrome (Patau syndrome)   Trisomy for chromosome 13 occurs with a frequency of about 1:25,000 live births. About 50% of affected infants die within the first month, 75% die by the sixth month, and fewer than 5% survive more than 3 years. As in all trisomies, the risk of this syndrome increases with advancing maternal age. About 20% of cases are caused by unbalanced translocations.

The phenotype includes severe central nervous system anomalies. The most characteristic CNS anomaly involves varying degrees of aberration in formation of the forebrain (holoprosencephaly). Anomalies of the olfactory system (arrhinencephalia) and microcephaly are found, and 80% of patients have bilateral cleft lip and palate. Other manifestations may include

□ Binaural deafness

□ Polydactyly (more frequently in the hands than the feet)

□ A characteristic clenched fist

□ Rocker-bottom feet

□ Severe congenital heart defects including atrial and ventricular septal defects, patent ductus arteriosus, and dextrocardia (80%)

□ Polycystic kidney disease (30%)

□ Hydronephrosis

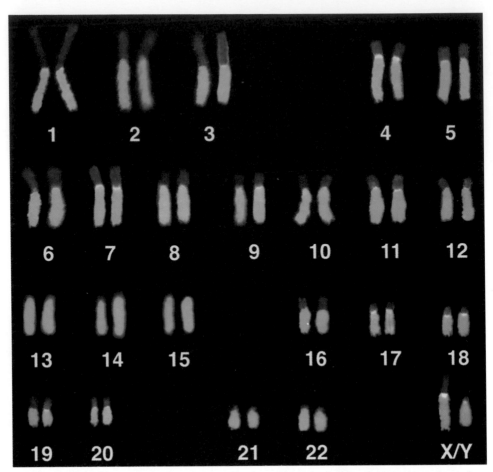

FIG IX-5—Composite karyotype of all human chromosomes hybridized with CAPs. Metaphase chromosomes were hybridized with a corresponding short arm (red) and long arm (green) painting probes simultaneously, and a composite karyotype was generated. Short arm probes were not generated for the acrocentric chromosomes 13, 14, 15, 21, and 22. Minimal regions of overlap (yellow) between long and short arm probes were identified for chromosomes 2, 3, 11, 18, and X. The size distribution of PCR-amplified microdissected DNA fragments of each individual arm were analyzed by running PCR products on 1% agarose gels. All PCR products showed a smear ranging from 200 to 600 base pairs with no apparent dominant bands. After PCR amplification, microdissected DNA fragments from all 19 short arms were labeled with SpectrumOrange. To avoid cross-hybridization between repetitive sequences localized on the short arms of the acrocentric chromosomes, the short arms of the acrocentrics were not dissected. Microdissected DNA fragments from all long arms were labeled with biotin and detected with FITC-conjugated avidin. (Reproduced with permission from Guan X-Y, Zhang H, Bittner M, et al. Chromosomal arm painting probes. *Nat Genet.* 1996;12:10.)

In 1960 Klaus Patau and coworkers correlated this complex of abnormalities with a specific chromosomal abnormality based on a trisomy of the 13–15 (D) chromosome group.

Many of the clinical features of this syndrome require trisomy not of the entire chromosome 13 but only of the portion from 13q14 to q terminus. The features of

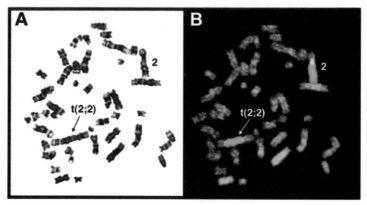

FIG IX-6—Application of CAPs to detect complex chromosome rearrangements. A cell line with complex defined chromosome rearrangements was identified for hybridization [human lymphoma cell line SU-DHL-4]8. *A*, G-banded metaphase from SU-DHL-4. *B*, The identical metaphase hybridized with CAPs 2p (red) and 2q (green). A normal 2 and a rearranged chromosome 2[t(2;2)(q37;p13)] (arrow) was observed. (Reproduced with permission from Guan X-Y, Zhang H, Bittner M, et al. Chromosomal arm painting probes. *Nat Genet.* 1996;12:11.)

the full clinical syndrome considerably overlap Meckel syndrome, an autosomal recessive entity with a recurrence risk of 25%. If the clinical signs suggest Patau syndrome, chromosome analysis is imperative to establish the diagnosis of trisomy and to identify translocations or other rearrangements. This chromosomal aberration is closely associated with severe intraocular abnormalities (Table IX-2).

de Grouchy J, Turleau C. *Clinical Atlas of Human Chromosomes.* 2nd ed. New York: Wiley; 1984:226–237.

TABLE IX-2

OCULAR FINDINGS IN TRISOMY 13 (PATAU) SYNDROME

Hypotelorism (sometimes hypertelorism)
Shallow supraorbital ridges
Absent eyebrows
Epicanthal folds
Cyclopia, rarely
Microphthalmos, sometimes clinical anophthalmos
Corneal "clouding"
Cataracts
Uveal colobomas, iridoschisis
Intraocular connective tissue, including cartilage
Persistent hyperplastic primary vitreous
Retinal dysplasia
Optic nerve hypoplasia, atrophy, or occasionally colobomas
Anterior "cleavage" syndrome

Trisomy 18 syndrome (Edwards syndrome) Trisomy 18 is the second most common chromosomal syndrome with multiple malformations in humans, having an incidence of about 1:8000 live newborns. The incidence at conception is much higher, but early spontaneous abortion occurs in approximately 95% of cases. Half of the affected live newborns die in the nursery before 4 months of age, and 90% die before 1 year, although a few have lived as long as 15 years. There is a 3:1 preponderance of females affected, perhaps because of preferential survival. The outstanding features of trisomy 18 include the following:

- Low birth weight and growth failure
- Mental retardation
- A skull with a narrow bifrontal diameter and protruding occiput
- Micrognathia
- Misshapen ears
- Flexion deformities of the fingers with the second finger overlapping the third, and the fifth finger overlapping the fourth
- Nail hypoplasia
- A low arch dermal ridge pattern
- Atrial and ventricular septal defects
- Inguinal or umbilical hernias (and frequently a single umbilical artery)
- Cryptorchidism
- Rocker-bottom feet
- Myelomeningocele (occasionally)

A maternal age effect has been demonstrated in this trisomy also. The critical region for many of the phenotypic features appears to be near 18q12.2. The most frequent ocular abnormalities are listed in Table IX-3.

> de Grouchy J, Turleau C. *Clinical Atlas of Human Chromosomes.* 2nd ed. New York: Wiley; 1984:290–302.

TABLE IX-3

OCULAR FINDINGS IN TRISOMY 18 (EDWARDS) SYNDROME

Prominent epicathal folds, ptosis
Blepharophimosis with unusually small or oblique palpebral fissures
Unusually thick lower eyelid
Hypertelorism (sometimes hypotelorism)
Hypoplastic supraorbital ridges
Congenital glaucoma
Corneal opacities
Microphthalmos
Optic disc anomalies
Iris and uveal colobomas

Trisomy 21 syndrome (Down syndrome)   Down syndrome is the most common chromosomal syndrome in humans with an overall incidence of 1:800 live births. It was the first chromosomal disease defined in humans. Clinical features of this syndrome have been well known since the British physician John Langdon Down made the original description in 1866.

The frequency of Down syndrome clearly increases with age of the mother, from about 1:1400 live births to mothers aged 20–24 years to about 1:40 live births to mothers aged 44 years. Yet the frequency of Down syndrome is greater (1:1250) for mothers between 15 and 19 years than it is in the next higher age range. Above age 50 the frequency is 1:11 live births. The eponym *Down syndrome* summarizes a clinical description of certain distinctive if variable phenotypic features, whereas the karyotype provides chromosomal constitution of the cells and tissue studied.

The chromosomal basis of this disorder was first demonstrated by French geneticist Jerome Lejeune and coworkers in 1959. Approximately 95% of children with this disorder have an extra chromosome 21 as a result of meiotic nondisjunction. Either parent may contribute the third chromosome 21, but the most important factor that influences the risk of having a child with Down syndrome is maternal age. In instances when it has been possible to determine where the meiotic error took place, more than 80% occurred in the first meiosis, and more than 95% occurred with maternal rather than paternal meiosis.

Approximately 5% of patients with Down syndrome have a *translocation* resulting from the attachment of the long arm of chromosome 21 with the long arm of one of the other acrocentric chromosomes, usually 14 or 22. These translocations cause pairing problems during meiosis, and the translocated fragment of chromosome 21 appears in one of the daughter cells along with a normal 21. As in nondisjunction, the fragment becomes trisomic on fertilization. Trisomy of only the distal third of chromosome 21q is sufficient to cause the disorder. Genes that lie within the q22 band of chromosome 21 appear to be specifically responsible for the pathogenesis of Down syndrome.

The increased incidence of this disorder with maternal age is principally the result of a greater likelihood of nondisjunction, since translocation errors are not related to maternal age. The extra chromosome is of paternal origin in fewer than 5% of affected individuals. A major positive correlation between advanced paternal age and an increased incidence of Down syndrome has not been established. The empirical recurrence risks to parents who have had one child with trisomy 21 are approximately 1%, although this number is higher among older women. Patients with Down syndrome exhibit the following features:

□ Mental retardation

□ Short stature

□ Poor muscular control (hypotonia)

□ Brachycephaly with a broad flat occiput

□ Hypoplasia of the middle phalanx of the fifth finger

□ Wide space between the first and second toes

□ Small ears

□ Various forms of congenital heart disease including ventricular and atrial septal defects (40%) and, occasionally, duodenal atresia and tracheoesophageal fistulas

□ Infertility

□ Dental hypoplasia

□ Characteristic dermatoglyphic findings

A single palmar crease occurs in about 50% of those with Down syndrome, but in only 1% of the general population. About half of the infants and young children with this disorder have hearing loss of an unspecified nature. The most common ocular findings of Down syndrome are presented in Table IX-4.

Additional medical complications in Down syndrome patients include an increased susceptibility to infection and a 20- to 50-fold increase in the risk of developing leukemia. The shortened life span in patients affected by Down syndrome is secondary, in part, to these related medical problems. Studies of autopsy material from affected patients show that virtually all individuals with Down syndrome over the age of 35 years develop abnormal microscopic senile plaques and neurofibrillary tangles in the brain similar to those seen in Alzheimer disease. Down syndrome patients also appear to be at a significantly increased risk of developing the cognitive symptoms of Alzheimer disease. Glenner and colleagues demonstrated that the amyloid beta precursor protein, a major component of the neurofibrillary plaques that accumulate in the brain of individuals with Alzheimer disease, is identical to the protein that accumulates in apparently identical lesions in individuals with Down syndrome who are more than 35 years old. However, the APP gene, which is apparently responsible for a familial form of Alzheimer disease, resides at q21 on chromosome 21, outside the critical region (21q22.3) for Down syndrome. The relationship of the gene for amyloid precursor protein and the form of Alzheimer disease in Down patients is unknown.

Catalano RA. Down syndrome. *Surv Ophthalmol.* 1990;34:385–398.

de Grouchy J, Turleau C. *Clinical Atlas of Human Chromosomes.* 2nd ed. New York: Wiley; 1984:338–349.

TABLE IX-4

OCULAR FINDINGS IN DOWN SYNDROME (TRISOMY 21)

Almond-shaped palpebral fissures
Upslanting (mongoloid) palpebral fissures
Prominent epicanthal folds
Blepharitis, usually chronic, with cicatricial ectropion
Strabismus, usually esotropic
Nystagmus (typically horizontal)
Aberrant retinal vessels (at disc)
Iris stromal hypoplasia
Brushfield's spots
Keratoconus
Cataract
Myopia
Optic atrophy

Patterson D. The causes of Down syndrome. *Sci Am.* 1987;257:52–60.

Thompson MW, McInnes RR, Willard HF. *Genetics in Medicine.* 5th ed. Philadelphia: Saunders; 1991:215, 219–225.

Aneuploidy of Sex Chromosomes

Recognized characteristic eye findings do not appear in most sex chromosomal abnormalities, except possibly *Turner syndrome.* About 55%–60% of patients with Turner syndrome have a complete absence of one X chromosome in all cells (45,X), usually as a result of paternal X or Y chromosomal nondisjunction. The rest have a variety of structural changes of the X chromosome such as isochromosomes for the long arm of X, deletions from the long or short arms, or a ring-X chromosome, or they exhibit mosaicism (see below). Affected individuals always develop as females except in X/XY mosaicism. They tend toward short stature, do not develop secondary sexual characteristics, and often have webbing of the neck with low-set nuchal hair, cubitus valgus, nonpitting edema of the hands and feet (at birth), and coarctation of the aorta. Their ovaries fail to develop properly (gonadal dysgenesis), resulting in sterility and amenorrhea.

Turner syndrome occurs in about 1 out of every 5000 live female births. The incidence of X-linked color deficiency is the same in monosomy-X Turner syndrome as in normal males. Complete expression of other X-linked disorders in monosomy Turner syndrome, such as choroideremia, X-linked retinitis pigmentosa, or X-linked ocular albinism could also be anticipated. Other ocular findings are summarized in Table IX-5.

Thompson MW, McInnes RR, Willard HF. *Genetics in Medicine.* 5th ed. Philadelphia: Saunders; 1991:231–245.

Mosaicism

Occasionally, an individual or a tissue will contain two or more cell lines with distinctly different chromosomal constitutions. These individuals are termed *mosaics.* Sometimes the peripheral blood, which is the usual source for chromosome analysis, will contain populations of cells with completely different chromosomal constitutions. One population of cells may be so infrequent that a second tissue, such as skin fibroblasts, must be analyzed to demonstrate the mosaicism. The incidence of mosaicism in all tissues in humans is unknown.

Cytogenetic defects arise because of abnormal chromosomal distribution during the early stages of embryonic development. These embryos possess two or more chromosomally different cell populations. Mosaicism usually results from either *mitotic nondisjunction,* in which one replicated chromosome fails to separate in the dividing cell; or from *anaphase lag,* in which normal separation occurs, but one member of the replicated pair fails to migrate and is lost.

TABLE IX-5

OCULAR FINDINGS IN TURNER SYNDROME

Pigmented areas on eyelids

Prominent epicanthal folds

Accentuated downslanting of palpebral fissures

Ptosis

Strabismus

Nystagmus

Blue sclera

Cornea with short horizontal axis

Pupillary heterotopia

Anterior axial embryonic cataract

Incidence of color deficiency same in 45,X as in normal male population

The clinical effects of mosaicism are difficult to predict because the distribution of abnormal cells in the embryo is determined by the timing of the error and other variables. If mitotic nondisjunction occurs immediately after conception, the zygote divides into two abnormal cells, one trisomic and one monosomic. The monosomic cells rarely survive and may decrease in number or even disappear entirely over time. Mitotic nondisjunction may occur when the embryo is composed of a small population of cells. Thus, three populations of cells are established, one normal and two abnormal, although some abnormal cell lines may be "discarded" or lost during development. If mitotic nondisjunction occurs at a more advanced stage of development, resulting abnormal populations constitute a minority of the embryo's cells, and mosaicism may have little or no measurable effect upon development.

A small population of aneuploid mosaic cells may not have a direct effect on development. However, when cells of this type occur in the reproductive tissues of otherwise normal individuals, some of the gametes may carry extra or missing chromosomes. Consequently, mosaic parents tend to have a high risk for chromosomally abnormal children.

The most common example of autosomal mosaicism is *trisomy 21 mosaicism.* Some patients with trisomy 21 mosaicism have the typical features of Down syndrome, while others show no abnormalities in appearance or intelligence. The critical variable seems to be the frequency and the embryologic distribution of the trisomic cells during early development, which does not necessarily correlate with the percentage of trisomic cells seen in any one tissue, such as peripheral blood.

Several types of sex chromosome mosaicism may occur. Again, the physical effects tend to be variable, probably reflecting the quantity and distribution of the abnormal cells during development. For example, the cell population that lacks one of the X chromosomes can arise in a female embryo, leading to 45,X/46,XX mosaicism. In some cases these individuals develop normally, but in others some or all of the features of Turner syndrome appear. Similarly, the Y chromosome may be lost in some cells of a developing male embryo. This produces 45,X/46,XY mosaicism. X/XY mosaics may develop as normal males, as females with the features of Turner syndrome, or as individuals with physical characteristics intermediate between the sexes (intersexes or pseudohermaphrodites).

Mechanisms of Chromosomal Abnormalities

Several well-defined and common chromosomal syndromes result from the structural abnormality of a specific autosome. They present with major developmental aberrations of the visual system, which bring the patient to an ophthalmologist for recognition or management. These *structural aberrations* may be divided into several groups.

Fragility and breakage on specific chromosomes   A break is a fracture in a segment of a chromosome when the fractured segment is retained. Breaks are found under normal physiologic conditions, but certain stresses, such as exposure to x-rays, various drugs, and viral infections, increase the number of breaks.

Deletion   Loss of chromosomal material may arise in two fashions: as a *terminal deletion,* with one break resulting in loss of the extremity of a chromosome; or as an *interstitial deletion,* with two breaks along an arm, resulting in the loss of the portion between the breaks. A *ring chromosome* is a type of deletion in which both ends have been lost and the two broken ends have united to form a ring-shaped configuration. Sizable deletions of genetic material are often lethal.

Duplication   The addition of genetic material along a chromosome results from unequal crossing over between two homologous chromosomes or between two sister chromatids.

Translocations   The transfer of part of one chromosome to a nonhomologous chromosome is called translocation. *Robertsonian translocations* occur with breaks at the centromere when entire arms of the chromosomes are exchanged. A fragment without a centromere that has broken off a chromosome is not retained unless it becomes attached to another chromosome that has a raw end from having also been broken. *Reciprocal translocations* occur when genetic material is exchanged between chromosomes without either addition or loss of chromosomal material. *Insertional translocations,* in which a broken piece of chromosome is inserted into a nonhomologous chromosome, require at least three chromosomal breaks to occur. *Isochromosomes* form when a duplicated chromosome divides through its centromere into two separate arms rather than into two sister chromatids. Thus, a duplicated chromosome will divide through the centromere to form both an iso–short-arm chromosome and an iso–long-arm chromosome.

de Grouchy J, Turleau C. *Clinical Atlas of Human Chromosomes.* 2nd ed. New York: Wiley; 1984.

Thompson MW, McInnes RR, Willard HF. *Genetics in Medicine.* 5th ed. Philadelphia: Saunders; 1991:201–219.

Etiology of Chromosomal Aberrations

Parental age The way in which maternal age is associated with nondisjunction is unknown. The significance of this mechanism has been discussed in the section on Down syndrome, p 263. Increased paternal age has been associated with de novo mutations of several autosomal dominant diseases, including the following:

- The craniosynostoses (Apert and Pfeiffer syndromes and Crouzon disease)
- Achondroplasia
- Oculodentodigital dysplasia
- Treacher Collins syndrome
- Marfan syndrome
- Waardenburg syndrome type I
- Multiple endocrine neoplasia type IIB (MEN2B)
- von Recklinghausen disease (neurofibromatosis type 1)

In some disorders, such as Apert syndrome and MEN2B, virtually all of the new mutations appear to have a paternal origin. The presumed reason for the paternal age effect is that spermatogenesis occurs over many years and the much larger number of cell divisions increases the likelihood of replication errors.

Carlson KM, Bracamontes J, Jackson CE, et al. Parent-of-origin effects in multiple endocrine neoplasia type 2B. *Am J Hum Genet.* 1994;55:1076–1082.

Moloney DM, Slaney SF, Oldridge M, et al. Exclusive paternal origin of new mutations in Apert syndrome. *Nat Genet.* 1996;13:48–53.

Thompson MW, McInnes RR, Willard HF. *Genetics in Medicine.* 5th ed. Philadelphia: Saunders; 1991:215.

Chromosomal instability A high prevalence of chromosomal breaks and rearrangements appears in both cultured cells and in vivo preparations derived from individuals with ataxia-telangiectasia, Fanconi syndrome, Bloom syndrome, and xeroderma pigmentosum. Patients with these conditions have a markedly increased risk of developing malignant neoplasias. It is likely that the increased likelihood of tumor formation is related to the chromosomal instability.

Environmental agents In some laboratory models radiation, certain chemicals, and some viruses are responsible for a moderate frequency of chromosomal breaks and rearrangements. The specific mechanism by which each or any of these environmental agents induces genetic abnormalities is no more apparent than their roles in spontaneous birth defects or mutations.

Specific Chromosomal Abnormalities

The phenotypic features of three specific deletion syndromes are sufficiently characteristic and important to warrant summarizing here.

Long arm 13 deletion (13q14) syndrome Retinoblastoma is one of several heritable childhood malignancies. Ocular tumors, which are usually noted before the age of 4 years, affect between 1 in 15,000 and 1 in 34,000 live births in the United States. The disease exhibits both hereditary occurrence (approximately 30%–40%), in which tumors tend to be bilateral and multicentric; and sporadic occurrence, in which unilateral and solitary tumors are the rule. Only about 10% of patients with hereditary retinoblastoma have a family history of the disease; the remaining 90% have a new mutation in their germ cells.

Retinoblastoma does not develop in approximately 10% of all obligate carriers of a germ-line mutation. In addition, 3%–7% of all cases of retinoblastoma have a karyotypically visible deletion of part of the long arm of chromosome 13. The larger this deletion, the more severe is the phenotypic syndrome, which includes mental and developmental retardation, microcephaly, hand and foot anomalies, and ambiguous genitalia (Table IX-6).

Although the hereditary pattern in familial retinoblastoma is that of an autosomal dominant mutation, the defect is recessive at the cellular level. The predisposition to retinoblastoma is caused by hemizygosity of the Rb locus within human chromosome band 13q14. The Rb locus is a member of a class of genes called *recessive tumor-suppressor genes.* The alleles normally present at these loci have a role in preventing tumor formation. At least one active normal allele is needed to prevent the cell from losing control of proliferation. Patients who inherit a defective allele from one parent are at greater risk to lose the other allele through a number of mechanisms. Thus, tumor formation in retinoblastoma is caused by the loss of function of both normal alleles. Homozygous deletions within the 13q14 region have been noted in retinoblastomas derived from enucleated eyes.

The first step in tumorigenesis is the occurrence of a recessive mutation of one of the homologous alleles at the retinoblastoma locus by inheritance, germinal mutation, or somatic mutation. Hereditary retinoblastomas arise from a single additional somatic event in a cell that carries an inherited mutation, while sporadic cases require two somatic events. In approximately 50% of tumors homozygosity for such a recessive mutation results from the mitotic loss of a portion of chromosome 13 including the 13q14 band. The resulting homozygosity for recessive mutant alleles at this locus allows the genesis of the tumor. Retinoblastoma, therefore, seemingly represents a malignancy caused by defective gene regulation rather than the presence of a dominant mutant oncogene. Those who inherit a mutant allele at this locus have a high incidence of nonocular, second tumors believed to be caused by the same mutation. Almost half of these tumors are osteosarcomas.

The retinoblastoma gene was identified and cloned in 1986. Haplotype testing can determine the alleles for polymorphic marker loci immediately adjacent to and within the retinoblastoma gene in various family members and in the tumor. This testing allows the identification of the segment of DNA containing the mutant allele that has become homozygous or hemizygous (i.e., underwent loss of heterozygosity) in the tumor. This information can be used to predict the risk for developing retinoblastoma in siblings or other family members. For optimal success, such testing requires availability of tumor tissue and the testing of parents, siblings, and others in the family who might carry the mutation. Even without the information gained from studying the tumor itself, haplotype testing can occasionally determine that a particular sibling did not inherit either of the haplotypes that are present in DNA from peripheral blood from the affected child. BCSC Section 4, *Ophthalmic Pathology and Intraocular Tumors,* discusses retinoblastoma in greater detail.

TABLE IX-6

SYSTEMIC FINDINGS IN THE LONG ARM (13q14) DELETION SYNDROME

"Failure to thrive" growth retardation
Mental retardation
Microcephaly
Trigonencephaly; scalp defect
Micrognathia
Large, malformed, low-set ears
Cleft of highly arched palate
Facial asymmetry
Congenital heart disease
Pelvic girdle anomalies
Anal atresia
Cryptorchidism, bifid scrotum
Hypospadias or epispadias, underdeveloped labia
Hypoplastic thumbs
Short incurved fourth and/or fifth finger
Foot anomalies (clubfoot, short great toe, syndactyly of the fourth and fifth toes)
Associated esterase D deficiency

Cavenee WK, Dryja TP, Phillips RA, et al. Expression of recessive alleles by chromosomal mechanisms in retinoblastoma. *Nature.* 1983;305:779–784.

Dryja TP, Rapaport JM, Joyce JM, et al. Molecular detection of deletions involving band q14 of chromosome 13 in retinoblastomas. *Proc Natl Acad Sci USA.* 1986;83:7391–7394.

Friend SH, Bernards R, Rogelj S, et al. A human DNA segment with properties of the gene that predisposes to retinoblastoma and osteosarcoma. *Nature.* 1986;323:643–646.

Friend SH, Dryja TP, Weinberg RA. Oncogenes and tumor-suppressing genes. *N Engl J Med.* 1988;318:618–622.

Godbout R, Dryja TP, Squire J, et al. Somatic inactivation of genes on chromosome 13 is a common event in retinoblastoma. *Nature.* 1983;304:451–453.

Lohmann DR, Brandt B, Oehlschläger U, et al. Molecular analysis and predictive testing in retinoblastoma. *Ophthalmic Genet.* 1995;16:135–142.

Wiggs J, Nordenskjold M, Yandell D, et al. Prediction of the risk of hereditary retinoblastoma, using DNA polymorphisms within the retinoblastoma gene. *N Engl J Med.* 1988;318:151–157.

Short arm 11 deletion (11p13) syndrome *Aniridia* (AN2) occurs from a defect of a gene that encodes a transcription factor needed for development of the eye. This developmental gene, PAX6, is located at 11p13. Aniridia is a panophthalmic disorder characterized by the following:

□ Subnormal visual acuity

□ Congenital nystagmus

□ Strabismus

□ Corneal pannus

□ Cataracts

□ Ectopia lentis

□ Glaucoma

□ Optic nerve hypoplasia

□ Foveal or macular hypoplasia

□ Iris absence or severe hypoplasia

Although almost all cases of aniridia result from PAX6 mutations, a rare autosomal recessive disorder called *Gillespie syndrome* (MIM 206700) also demonstrates partial aniridia, cerebellar ataxia, mental deficiency, and congenital cataracts.

Aniridia (often with cataract and glaucoma) can also occur sporadically in association with Wilms tumor, other genitourinary anomalies, and mental retardation, the so-called WAGR syndrome. This complex of findings is called a *contiguous gene deletion syndrome* because it results from a deletion involving nearby genes in the region. Most of the affected patients have a karyotypically visible interstitial deletion of a segment of chromosome 11p13. This region also includes the gene for the enzyme catalase, and an adjacent locus (11p12) contains the gene LDH-A for lactic dehydrogenase. Patients with aniridia that is not clearly part of an autosomal dominant trait and those with coincident systemic malformations should undergo chromosomal analysis and observation for possible Wilms tumor.

The ophthalmologist confronted with a new aniridia patient should conduct a careful biomicroscopic examination of both parents for the variable expression of autosomal dominant aniridia. For female infants with isolated aniridia, a high-resolution banded chromosomal analysis is essential, as the genital variation caused by 11p deletion can be extraordinarily subtle. If a male infant with isolated aniridia has no genital aberrations, the chromosome analysis is desirable although probably not mandatory, because of the more severe expression of 11p deletions in males. In older children without other anomalies or developmental delay, a baseline intravenous pyelogram and periodic urinalysis (for microscopic hematuria) are recommended. Intravenous pyelography is probably a more sensitive procedure than either echography or computed tomography for the embryonal malignancy associated with this chromosomal deletion.

The PAX6 gene product is a transcription factor that is required for the normal development of the eye. Mutations of PAX6 have also been reported in Peters anomaly, autosomal dominant keratitis, and dominant foveal hypoplasia. The mechanism for disruption of normal embryology and the degenerative disease in aniridia and other PAX6 disorders appears to be *haploinsufficiency,* the inability of a single active allele to activate transduction of the developmental genes that are regulated by the PAX6 gene product. In this way aniridia is different from retinoblastoma and Wilms tumor, which result from an absence of both functional alleles at each of homologous gene loci.

de Grouchy J, Turleau C. *Clinical Atlas of Human Chromosomes.* 2nd ed. New York: Wiley; 1984:208–209.

Fearon ER, Vogelstein B, Feinberg AP. Somatic deletion and duplication of genes on chromosome 11 in Wilms' tumours. *Nature.* 1984;309:176–178.

Littlefield JW. Genes, chromosomes, and cancer. *J Pediatr.* 1984;104:489–494.

Solomon E. Recessive mutation in aetiology of Wilms' tumor. *Nature.* 1984;309: 111–112.

Short arm 5 deletion   A short-arm deletion in chromosome 5 is found in the so-called cat's cry, or *cri du chat,* syndrome. The critical region for this syndrome is 5p15. Infants with cri du chat have a typical cry, which is present only in the first few months of life, that resembles the mewing of a cat. The abnormal cry is the result of hypoplasia of the larynx. Other systemic findings include

□ Severe mental retardation

□ Microcephaly

□ Hypotonia

□ Micrognathia

□ Low-set or poorly formed ears

□ Low birth weight

□ Slow growth

□ Congenital heart disease

Ocular findings involve

□ Hypertelorism

□ Downward slanting palpebral fissures

□ Epicanthal folds

□ Myopia

□ Exotropia

□ Iris coloboma

□ Optic atrophy

Mutations

Change in the structure or sequence of a gene is called a *mutation.* A mutation can occur more or less randomly anywhere along the DNA sequence of a gene and may result when one nucleotide is substituted for another (sometimes called a *point mutation*). A mutation that occurs in a noncoding portion of the gene may or may not be of any clinical consequence. Similarly, a mutation may structurally alter a protein but in a manner that does not notably compromise its function. A new mutation that compromises function appears in a given gene as the gene is transmitted from parent to offspring at a frequency of about 1 in a million. Mutations are more likely to occur within certain genes than in others. Aniridia has a mutation rate (mutations/locus/generation) of $2.5–5.0 \times 10^{-6}$ and retinoblastoma, $5.0–12.0 \times 10^{-6}$. Two examples of disorders with even higher mutation rates are von Recklinghausen neurofibromatosis type 1 and Duchenne muscular dystrophy, each with an estimated mutation rate of approximately $0.4–1.0 \times 10^{-4}$.

A classic example of a simple point mutation is sickle cell anemia, which affects about 1 in 600 African Americans. This disorder results from a mutant gene that defines the sequence of amino acids in the ß-polypeptide chain of adult hemoglobin. In sickle cell hemoglobin, the valine is substituted for glutamic acid at the sixth position in the ß-polypeptide chain. This substitution is caused by an abnormal specific base, where adenine is substituted for thymine. This seemingly small alteration causes a profound reduction of solubility when hemoglobin is deoxygenated: red blood cells tend to become deformed into a characteristic sickle shape when the partial pressure of oxygen is low.

More gross mutations may involve deletion, translocation, insertion, or internal duplication of a portion of the DNA. Some mutations cause either destruction of the offspring or sterility. Others are less harmful or may be potentially beneficial and become established in subsequent generations. Mutations can occur spontaneously, for reasons not understood. They may also be produced by a variety of environmental agents called *mutagens,* such as radiation, viruses, and certain chemicals.

Mutations may arise in somatic as well as germinal cells, but these are not transmitted to subsequent generations. Somatic mutations in humans are difficult to identify, but some account for the inception of certain forms of neoplasia, for example, retinoblastoma.

Nichols EK. *Human Gene Therapy.* Cambridge, MA: Harvard University Press; 1988: 17–39.

Thompson MW, McInnes RR, Willard HF. *Genetics in Medicine.* 5th ed. Philadelphia: Saunders; 1991:118–119, 253–257.

Polymorphisms

Many mutations have either little or no deleterious effect on the organism. A polymorphism is defined as the occurrence of two or more alleles at a specific locus with a frequency greater than 1% each. At least one third of all structural genes may exist in polymorphic forms. For example, at least 400 variants of hemoglobin are known, many with essentially no detectable phenotypic abnormalities. Similarly, several dozen functional and electrophoretic variants of glucose-6-phosphate dehydrogenase exist; again, many have no significant effect on the biochemical function of the affected individual. Finding additional polymorphisms will be important for completion of gene mapping and for linkage to human diseases.

Genome, Genotype, Phenotype

The *genome* is the sum total of the genetic material within a cell or of an organism—thus, the total genetic endowment. By contrast, the *genotype* defines the genetic constitution, and thus biological capacity, with regard to a specific locus (e.g., individual blood groups or a specific single enzyme). *Phenotype* indicates the total observable or manifest physical, physiologic, biochemical, or molecular characteristics of an individual, which are determined by the genotype but can be modified by the environment.

The phenotype of a disease is often known before its specific metabolic, genetic, or chromosomal basis. For example, several chromosomal aberrations lead to the phenotype of Down syndrome, and several different enzyme deficiencies may manifest themselves as a "Morquio syndrome phenotype." In these instances only a tentative molecular diagnosis can be made from the clinical information. Specific information from a chromosomal analysis or an enzyme assay then establishes the genetic mechanism unique for the physical features: trisomy 21 or a chromosome 14 to 21 translocation in the example of Down syndrome, or β-glucuronidase deficiency that causes a disease state often confused clinically with true Morquio syndrome.

A clinical picture produced entirely by environmental factors that nevertheless closely resembles, or is even identical with, a phenotype is known as a *phenocopy.* Thus, for example, the pigmentary retinopathy of congenital rubella has occasionally been confused with a hereditary dystrophic disorder of the retinal pigment epithelium. Similarly, chloroquine-induced changes in the corneal epithelium resemble those seen as cornea verticillata in the X-linked dystrophic disorder Fabry disease.

Single-Gene Disorders

About 4500 different diseases are known to be caused by a defect in a single gene. As a group, these disorders are called *monogenic,* or *mendelian, diseases.* They most often show one of three patterns of inheritance: autosomal dominant, autosomal recessive, or X linked. Disorders of mtDNA are inherited in a fourth manner termed maternal inheritance. These mtDNA disorders obey galtonian rather than mendelian inheritance characteristics.

Variability, Penetrance, and Expressivity

Variability   Variability is an intrinsic property of human genetic disease that reflects the quantitative and qualitative differences in phenotype among individuals with the "same" mutant allele. Even within the homogeneous population of a single family with a genetic disease, every affected individual may not manifest the disease to the same degree, with the same features, or at the same age. Steinert myotonic dystrophy, for example, presents its features of motor myotonia, characteristic cataracts, gonadal atrophy, and presenile baldness with a wide variation in severity and age of detection. Even within a single family, the cataracts may begin to affect vision any time from the second decade to the seventh.

Such variability of clinical manifestation led to the concept of *anticipation,* the phenomenon of apparently earlier and more severe onset of a disease in successive generations within a family. As recently as 5–10 years ago, most geneticists believed that anticipation was not a biological phenomenon but an artifact of ascertainment. With the relatively recent discovery of triplet or trinucleotide tandem repeat expansion diseases, anticipation has been shown to reflect the increased length of trinucleotide tandem repeats from one generation to the next. Myotonic dystrophy, fragile-X syndrome, Huntington disease, and one form of spinal and bulbar muscular atrophy called Kennedy disease are some of the diseases whose discovery contributed to the rejuvenation of the concept of anticipation.

Some human variability may result from the intrinsic differences in genetic background of every human being. Other recognizable or presumptive influences on the variable intra- or interfamilial phenotype of the same gene include the following:

- Sex influences or limitations
- Maternal factors such as intrauterine environment and even cytoplasmic (e.g., mitochondrial) inheritance factors
- Modifying loci
- Genetic heterogeneity, including both isoalleles and genocopies
- Gene alterations induced either by position effects with other genes or by somatic mutations

Obviously, nongenetic factors extrinsic to a cell, tissue, or organism such as diet, temperature, and drugs may effect major changes in gene expression, either as phenocopies or through ecologic parameters.

Thompson JS, Thompson MW. *Genetics in Medicine*. 3rd ed. Philadelphia: Saunders; 1980:76–79, 88–92.

Penetrance   The presence or absence of any effect of a gene is referred to as *penetrance*. If a gene generates any evidence of phenotypic features, no matter how minimal, it is termed *penetrant;* if it is not expressed at any level of detection, it is *nonpenetrant*. Thus, penetrance is an all-or-nothing concept, statistically representing the fraction of individuals carrying a given gene that manifests any evidence of the specific trait. In families with an autosomal dominant mutant gene that has 100% penetrance of the phenotype, on average 50% of the offspring will inherit the gene and show evidence of the disease.

Even though penetrance has an exact statistical definition, its clinical application is affected by the diagnostic sophistication and methodology applied for the examination. For example, many mild cases of Marfan syndrome are missed unless careful biomicroscopy of the fully dilated pupil and echocardiography of the heart valves and great vessels are performed. Similarly, if the criteria for identification of the retinoblastoma gene include indirect ophthalmoscopy and scleral depression, some "nonpenetrant" parents or siblings in families with "dominantly inherited" retinoblastoma may be found to have a spontaneously involuted tumor, which clearly identifies them as bearers of the gene. In another example, some family members who have a gene for Best macular dystrophy will be identified not by clinical ophthalmoscopic examination but only by electro-oculographic testing. Therefore, the examiner must carefully search for any manifestations of the gene's effects in all susceptible tissues among its potential bearers before dismissing someone as a "skipped generation."

Lack of penetrance does not prevent molecular diagnosis. Whenever the gene product or the presence of the gene defect at the molecular level can be examined directly, there is complete correlation with the expected genotype.

Expressivity   The presence of a defective gene does not necessarily imply a complete expression of every potential manifestation. The variety of ways and levels of severity in which a particular genetic trait manifests its presence between different affected individuals is called *expressivity*. In von Recklinghausen disease, for example, an affected child may have only café-au-lait spots. The affected parent may have Lisch nodules of the iris, extensive punctiform and pedunculated neurofibromas of the skin, a huge plexiform neurofibroma of one lower extremity, and a glioma of the anterior visual pathway. It is extremely rare that all affected members in the same family have uniform textbook presentations of the disorder.

Variation in the time or age of onset of manifestations is one characteristic of difference in expressivity commonly seen in dominant disorders. Using the von Recklinghausen example, the affected child may have only café-au-lait spots at birth, develop iris Lisch nodules that gradually increase in number and size at around age 5–10 years, develop punctiform neurofibromas of the skin in early adolescence, evolve subareolar neurofibromas (in a postpubertal female), and experience visual impairment from the effect of an optic glioma in the late teens. While all of these features are phenotypic components of the mutant gene, each has a characteristic age of onset and a natural history of growth and effect within the umbrella of the total disease.

Pleiotropism

Alteration within a single mutant gene may have consequences in various tissues in a given individual. The presentation of multiple phenotypic abnormalities produced by a single mutant gene is termed *pleiotropism.* For example, in Marfan syndrome, ectopia lentis is coupled with arachnodactyly, aortic aneurysms, and long extremities. Optic atrophy is found in association with juvenile diabetes mellitus, diabetes insipidus, and moderate perceptive hearing impairment in an autosomal recessive syndrome known as the DIDMOAD syndrome. Neurosensory hearing loss can also be found in association with hereditary hematuric nephritis, lenticular changes (anterior lenticonus, spherophakia, cataracts), arcus juvenilis, and whitish yellow retinal lesions in the dominantly inherited Alport syndrome. Similarly, the Bardet-Biedl syndrome comprises pigmentary retinopathy, obesity, genital hypoplasia, mental debility, and polydactyly. In each of these disorders, a single mutant gene is responsible for dysfunction in multiple systems.

Frequently, however, a disease is mistakenly termed pleiotropic when several different disorders with the same inheritance pattern and similar clinical manifestations are actually present. Thus, Leber congenital amaurosis has been attributed to a single pleiotropic gene. Based on the symmetry of the phenotype of affected siblings in individual families, it seems more likely that the clinical disease is heterogeneous and can be caused by several genes (not necessarily allelic), each of which is autosomal recessive.

Heterogeneity

Because of limited diagnostic discriminators, similar or apparently identical phenotypes may be caused by different genotypes. When multiple gene mutations can independently produce a single trait or traits that are difficult to resolve clinically, that trait is said to be genetically heterogeneous. Allelic heterogeneity refers to different mutations at the same genetic locus, while locus heterogeneity refers to mutations at different loci. Some disorders, such as Ehlers-Danlos syndrome, show evidence of both allelic and locus heterogeneity among the different genotypes. An example of allelic heterogeneity is found in the human major histocompatibility complex (HMC) genes located on the short arm of chromosome 6.

The division of large groups of patients into smaller but more uniform subgroups by more careful analysis of phenotypes and investigations of the hereditary pattern has been essential for accurate clinical diagnosis and genetic counseling. For example, the phenotypes for Marfan syndrome and homocystinuria were formerly confused but can now be distinguished by biochemical testing, differences in ocular and cardiovascular involvement, and different inheritance patterns. Albinos also represent a heterogeneous group of genetic disorders. Some are tyrosinase positive and others tyrosinase negative. Differences in pigmentation may be helpful as well in distinguishing different subgroups of albinos. Genetic heterogeneity clearly also exists in the group of disorders classified under the rubric of retinitis pigmentosa in which the symptom of night blindness is coupled with a characteristic pigmentary retinopathy and abnormalities on psychophysical and electrophysiologic testing. These similar clinical manifestations of various genetically distinct disorders represent *genocopies.*

Racial and Ethnic Concentration of Genetic Disorders

Most genetic diseases occur without regard to the affected individual's racial or ethnic background. Some, however, are concentrated in certain population groups.

Tay-Sachs disease, with its characteristic macular cherry-red spot, occurs predominantly in individuals of eastern European Jewish (Ashkenazi) ancestry, especially those whose ancestors lived in northeastern Poland and southern Lithuania. An estimated rate of 1 in 30 for carriers of this disorder in the Jewish population of New York City compares with an estimated carrier rate of 1 in 300 in non-Jewish Americans. Although the reported incidence of this disorder among Ashkenazi Jewish newborns is 1 in 6000, the actual incidence among this population may be closer to 1 in 3600 births. About 50 new cases occur each year in the United States. In addition, familial dysautonomia (*Riley-Day syndrome*) with hypolacrima, corneal hypoesthesia, exodeviation, and methacholine-induced miosis also occurs more frequently in individuals of Ashkenazi ancestry, as do *Gaucher disease* and *Niemann-Pick disease.*

An X-linked recessive gene that causes a *deficiency in the enzyme glucose-6-phosphate dehydrogenase (G6PD)* is found predominantly in people from southern Italy and surrounding areas on the Mediterranean and south into the interior of Africa. Somewhat less than 10% of African Americans show a reduced activity of the G6PD enzyme. Males with this trait develop a hemolytic anemia after eating fava beans or ingesting antimalarial drugs such as primaquine or sulfanilamide. A variety of *achromatopsia with myopia* is common on the South Pacific island of Pingelap, affecting 5% of the Pingelapese population in the Caroline Islands of Micronesia. *Oguchi disease* is seen primarily, although not exclusively, in Japanese individuals. Similarly, *sickle cell hemoglobinopathies* are inherited largely among blacks.

A high prevalence of *oculocutaneous albinism* can be found among the Cuna Indians in Panama. *Hermansky-Pudlak syndrome* is known to occur with a higher frequency in individuals of Puerto Rican ancestry, especially those from the northwestern towns of Aguadilla and Arecibo. In this tyrosinase-positive phenotype of autosomal recessively inherited oculocutaneous albinism, findings include a history of easy bruisability and bleeding tendency, associated with a prolonged bleeding time and abnormal platelet aggregation.

Some specific human malformations have been observed to occur with greater frequency in certain races than in others. For example, polydactyly is about 10 times more frequent in blacks than in whites, and preauricular sinus may be equally more frequent in blacks.

Goldberg MF. An introduction to basic genetic principles applied to ophthalmology. *Trans Am Acad of Ophthalmol Otolaryngol.* 1972;76:1137–1159.

Palmer DJ, Miller MT, Rao S. Hermansky-Pudlak oculocutaneous albinism: Clinical and genetic observations in six patients. *Ophthalmic Paediatr Genet.* 1983;3:147–156.

Patterns of Inheritance

Recessivity versus Dominance

The terms *dominant* and *recessive* were first used by Gregor Mendel, an Austrian monk who formulated the fundamental laws of heredity in 1865 while cultivating peas in a monastery garden in Brno. In classic genetics a dominant gene is one that is always expressed with similar phenotype, whether the mutant gene is present in a homozygous or heterozygous state. Stated simply, a dominant gene is one that is expressed when present in only a single copy. A gene is called recessive when its expression is masked by a normal allele or, more precisely, when it is expressed only in the homozygote (or compound heterozygote), when both alleles at a specific locus are mutant.

A *trait* is the consequence of the gene's action. It is the trait, or phenotypic expression of the gene at a clinical level, rather than the gene itself that is dominant or recessive. A trait is recessive if its expression is suppressed by the presence of a normal gene (as in galactosemia), and dominant if it is apparently unaffected by a single copy of the normal allele (as in Marfan syndrome). If the alleles are different and yet they are both manifested in the phenotype, they are said to be *codominant*. Examples of codominant inheritance include the ABO and MN blood types, leukocyte antigens, and the hemoglobins.

As a result of transcription, a gene may have a greater or lesser effect on the individual or an organ, and therefore the trait may be more or less apparent. Thus, the designation of a trait as either dominant or recessive depends upon the testing method used. For example, sickle cell hemoglobinopathy is recessive if the clinical disease is considered, dominant if the sickle preparation test is positive, and codominant if hemoglobin electrophoresis is used to look for the specific product of each allele. Similarly, retinoblastoma may occur in some families as a dominant trait. However, it is now well established that at a genetic level, two independent mutations inactivating both alleles must occur in the same retinoblast for a retinoblastoma to form. In familial retinoblastoma one mutation is inherited (germinal) and the second is acquired (somatic).

Although, classically, a dominant gene is one that has the same phenotype when the mutant allele is present in either the heterozygous or homozygous state, most dominant medical diseases stray from this strict definition. For many dominant disorders, individuals who are homozygous for a mutant allele or who harbor two mutant alleles (one on each homologous chromosome) will have more severe expression.

Benedict WF, Murphree AL, Banerjee A, et al. Patient with 13 chromosome deletion: evidence that the retinoblastoma gene is a recessive cancer gene. *Science.* 1983; 219:973–975.

Schmickel RD. The genetic basis of ophthalmological disease. *Surv Ophthalmol.* 1980;25:37–46.

Experimentally, the biochemical mechanisms of "dominant" hereditary diseases appear different from those of "recessive" disorders. Recessive traits usually result from enzyme deficiency caused by structural mutations of the gene specifying the affected enzyme. The altered enzyme often can be shown to be structurally abnormal or unstable. Heterozygotes usually have approximately 50% of normal enzyme activity but are clinically unaffected, implying that half of the normal enzyme activity is compatible with near-normal function. If adequate biochemical testing can be performed and the specific enzyme isolated, the reduced enzyme activity can be quantified and the heterozygous genetic state inferred. Thus, clinically unaffected heterozygotes can be detected for such disorders as homocystinuria (decrease in cystathionine β-synthase), galactokinase deficiency (low blood galactokinase activity), classic galactosemia (galactose 1-phosphate uridyl transferase deficiency), gyrate atrophy of the choroid and retina (decreased ornithine-δ-aminotransferase), and Tay-Sachs disease (decreased hexosaminidase A). Table IX-7 outlines several disorders with ocular manifestations for which an enzyme defect is known.

Autosomal Recessive Inheritance

An autosomal recessive disease is expressed fully only in the presence of a mutant gene at the same locus on both homologous chromosomes (i.e., homozygosity for a mutant gene) or two different mutant alleles at the same locus (compound heterozygosity). A single mutant allele is sufficient to cause a recessive disorder if the

TABLE IX-7

KNOWN ENZYME DISORDERS AND CORRESPONDING OCULAR SIGNS

DISORDER	DEFECTIVE ENZYME	OCULAR SIGN
Storage diseases		
Fabry disease	Ceramide trihexosidase (alpha-galactosidase)	Corneal epithelial verticillate changes; aneurysmal dilation and tortuosity of retinal and conjunctival vessels
Krabbe leukodystrophy	Cerebroside beta galactosidase	Macular cherry-red spot; optic atrophy
Mannosidosis	Alpha-mannosidase	Lenticular opacities
Metachromatic leukodystrophy	Arylsulfatase A	Retinal discoloration, degeneration
Hurler IH	Alpha-L-iduronidase	Corneal opacity; pigmentary retinal degeneration
Hunter II	Sulfoiduronate sulfatase	Corneal opacity (mild type); older age patients
Scheie IS	Alpha-L-iduronidase	Corneal opacity; pigmentary retinal degeneration
Sanfilippo III	Heparan sulfate sulfatase	Pigmentary retinal degeneration; optic atrophy
Tay-Sachs disease (GM$_2$ gangliosidosis, type I)	Hexosaminidase A	Macular cherry-red spot; optic atrophy
Sandhoff disease (GM$_2$ gangliosidosis, type II)	Hexosidase A and B	Macular cherry-red spot
GM$_1$ gangliosidosis, type I (generalized gangliosidosis)	Beta-galactosidase	Macular cherry-red spot; optic atrophy; corneal clouding (mild)

TABLE IX-7 (continued)

KNOWN ENZYME DISORDERS AND CORRESPONDING OCULAR SIGNS

DISORDER	DEFECTIVE ENZYME	OCULAR SIGN
Metabolic disorders		
Alkaptonuria	Homogentisic acid oxidase	Dark sclera
Albinism	Tyrosinase	Foveal hypoplasia; nystagmus; iris transillumination
Intermittent ataxia	Pyruvate dicarboxylase	Nystagmus
Crigler-Najjar syndrome	Glucuronide transferase	Extraocular movement
Ehlers-Danlos syndrome	VI lysyl hydroxylase	Microcornea; retinal detachment; ectopia lentis; blue scleras
Familial dysautonomia	Dopamine-beta-hydroxylase	Alacrima; corneal hypoesthesia; exodeviation; methacholine-induced miosis
Galactokinase deficiency	Galactokinase	Cataracts
Galactosemia	Galactose 1-phosphate uridyl transferase	Cataracts
Gyrate atrophy of the choroid and retina	Ornithine aminotransferase	Degeneration of the choroid and retina; cataracts; myopia
Homocystinuria	Cystathionine synthase	Dislocated lens
Hyperglycinemia	Glycine cell transport	Optic atrophy
Leigh necrotizing encephalopathy	Pyruvate carboxylase	Optic atrophy
Maple syrup urine disease	Branch chain decarboxylase	Ophthalmoplegia; nystagmus
Niemann-Pick disease	Sphingomyelinase	Macular cherry-red spot
Refsum syndrome	Phytanic acid oxidase	Retinal degeneration
Tyrosinosis	Tyrosine aminotransferase	Corneal dystrophy
Sulfite oxidase deficiency	Sulfite oxidase	Ectopia lentis
Tyrosinemia	Tyrosine aminotransferase	Lens opacity

normal allele on the homologous chromosome is deleted. A recessive trait can remain latent through several generations until the chance mating of two heterozygotes for a mutant allele gives rise to an affected individual. The frequency of heterozygotes for a given disorder will always be considerably greater than that of homozygotes. It is estimated that all human beings inherit about six or seven mutations for different recessive disorders for which they are heterozygotes.

For example, if the frequency of a mutant gene for a recessive disorder in a given population is 1 in 100, the chance that a given individual at random will carry the gene is 1 in 50 since there are two copies of each gene at a given locus in all cells. The likelihood of a carrier parent giving the abnormal gene to each child is $1/2 \times 1/50$ or 1/100. The chance that an individual at random will receive the gene from both parents is 1 in 10,000 (1/100 × 1/100). Therefore, the likelihood of being a heterozygote is 200 times greater than that of being a homozygote (10,000/50).

The frequency of a mutant allele for a recessive gene in a population and the chance of an individual's being a carrier can therefore be determined by calculating the square root of the frequency of homozygous or affected individuals. In the above example, if a recessive defect is observed in 1 out of every 10,000 persons, the gene frequency is 1 in 100 and the chance of an individual's being a carrier is 1 in 50.

Enzymatic defects   Autosomal recessive diseases often result from defects in enzymatic proteins. Most of the so-called inborn errors of metabolism that result from enzymatic defects are autosomal recessive traits, although a few are X-linked recessive disorders, for example, Lesch-Nyhan syndrome. The defect in *alkaptonuria* involves homogentisic acid oxidase, an enzyme involved in the metabolism of homogentisic acid. Large amounts of homogentisic acid are excreted in the urine, which turns black when mixed with alkali or exposed to light or air. The black urine causes diaper stains, calling attention to the condition. In addition, aggregates of homogentisic acid accumulate in the body, becoming attached to the collagen of cartilage and other connective tissues. The cartilage of the ears and nose and the collagenous sclera are stained black or brownish blue. These manifestations are called *ochronosis.* The coloration in the sclera assumes a more or less triangular form, with a limbic base in the region of the palpebral tissue. In the joints, such as those of the spine, the accumulations lead to arthritis. Alkaptonuria is an example of a genetic enzyme block in which the phenotypic features are caused by the accumulation of excess substances just proximal to the block.

In some other disorders with genetic blocks in metabolism, the phenotypic consequences are related to the lack of a normal product distal to the block. An example is *albinism,* in which the metabolic block involves a step between the amino acid tyrosine and the formation of melanin. In still other inborn errors of metabolism the phenotypic expression results from excessive production of a product through a normally alternative and minor metabolic pathway. *Phenylketonuria,* like alkaptonuria and albinism, is a genetic defect in aromatic amino acid metabolism. The defect is in the enzyme involved in the conversion of phenylalanine to tyrosine. An affected individual has a reduction of hair and skin pigmentation. Severe mental retardation is one of the most prominent symptoms. Alternative metabolites of phenylalanine, especially phenylpyruvic acid, are excreted in the urine, providing one basis for diagnosis of the disorder.

The difference in phenotype of these three diseases—alkaptonuria, albinism, and phenylketonuria—is noteworthy, although they involve closely related metabolic pathways.

Carrier heterozygotes   The heterozygous carrier of a mutant gene may show minimal evidence of the gene defect, particularly at a biochemical level. Thus, carrier heterozygotes have been detected by a variety of methods:

☐ Identification of abnormal metabolites by electrophoresis (e.g., galactokinase deficiency)

☐ Liver biopsy (e.g., phenylketonuria)

☐ Hair bulb assay (e.g., oculocutaneous albinism and Fabry disease)

☐ Monitoring of enzyme activity in leukocytes (e.g., galactose 1-phosphate uridyl transferase in galactosemia), fibroblasts from skin culture (e.g., ornithine-δ-aminotransferase deficiency in gyrate atrophy of the retina and choroid), serum and tears (e.g., hexosaminidase A in Tay-Sachs disease)

In contrast to the transmission of dominant traits, most matings resulting in recessive disorders involve phenotypically normal heterozygous parents. Out of four offspring produced by carrier parents with the same gene for an autosomal recessive disease, usually one will be affected (homozygote), two will be carriers (heterozygotes), and one will be genetically and phenotypically normal. Thus, clinically normal heterozygous parents will produce offspring with a ratio of one clinically affected to three clinically normal. There is no predilection for either sex. In two-child families the patient with a recessive disease is frequently the only affected family member. For instance, about 40%–50% of patients with retinitis pigmentosa have no family history of the disorder. However, their age of onset, rate of progression, and other phenotypic characteristics are similar to those with defined recessive inheritance patterns.

Once one child is born with a recessive disorder, the genetic risk for each subsequent child of the same parents is 25%. This concept has specific implications for genetic counseling. All offspring of an affected individual will be carriers; they are unlikely to be affected with the disorder unless their clinically unaffected parent is also by chance a carrier of the gene. However, since a specific method for identifying a carrier rarely exists for many recessive diseases, the normal-appearing sibling of a child with a recessive disorder has a statistical risk of two chances out of three of being a genetic carrier. This liability must be accounted in any equation to predict the small risk that a normal-appearing sibling may have an affected child.

Consanguinity The mating of close relatives can increase the probability that their children will inherit a homozygous genotype for recessive traits, particularly for those that are relatively rare. For example, the probability that the same allele is present in first cousins is 1 in 8. In the offspring of a first-cousin marriage 1 of every 16 of the genes is commonly present in a homozygous state. It follows that each offspring from a first-cousin marriage has a 1 in 16 chance of manifesting an autosomal recessive trait within a given family. About 1% of all marriages may be consanguineous. A vigorous search for consanguinity between the parents should be made in any case of a rare recessive disease. Incest is one form of consanguinity that is not infrequent and often not acknowledged.

The expression of common recessive genes, by contrast, is less influenced by inbreeding, because most homozygous offspring are the progeny of unrelated parents. This is usually the case with such frequent disorders as sickle cell disease and cystic fibrosis. The characteristics of autosomal recessive inheritance are summarized in Table IX-8.

Francois J. *Heredity in Ophthalmology.* St Louis: Mosby; 1961:86–92.

Pseudodominance Occasionally, an affected homozygote will mate with a heterozygote. Of their offspring 50% will be carriers and 50% will be affected homozygotes. Because this segregation pattern mimics that of dominant inheritance, it is called *pseudodominance.* Fortunately, such matings are usually rare and are unlikely to affect more than two vertical generations.

Familial penetrance Penetrance of recessive disorders within families is rarely if ever incomplete. Expressivity of recessive disorders is characteristically more uniform among affected siblings within families, as each affected individual apparently has a double dose of the same gene. However, appreciable variability in age of onset, severity, and rate of progression may occur between families with the same

TABLE IX-8

The mutant gene usually does not cause clinical disease (recessive) in the heterozygote.

Individuals inheriting both the genes (homozygote) of the defective type express the disorder.

Typically, the trait appears only in siblings, not in their parents or offspring or in other relatives.

The ratio of normal to affected in a sibship is 3:1. The larger the sibship, the more often will more than one child be affected.

The sexes are affected in equal proportions.

Parents of the affected person may be genetically related (consanguinity); this is increasingly likely, the rarer the trait.

Affected individuals have children who, although phenotypically normal, are carriers (heterozygotes) of the gene.

---

apparent genetic disease. These variations may reflect intrinsic constitutional differences between families or the modifying effects of unrelated, unknown genes in different families. Alternative (even nonallelic) genes, which cause distantly similar phenotypic diseases, may cause dissimilar expression, as might environmental modifiers.

If the homozygote is defined as a specific base (pair) substitution in a codon, many "autosomal recessive" diseases result from genetically compound heterozygotes, that is, individuals who have two different (but both "defective") alleles at a given locus. Whenever detailed biochemical or molecular testing becomes possible, the products of different alleles will have slightly different properties or behaviors. Hemoglobin sickle cell disease and Hurler-Scheie syndrome are well-established compound heterozygote disorders.

Autosomal Dominant Inheritance

When an autosomal allele leads to a regular, clearly definable abnormality in the heterozygote, the trait is termed *dominant.* The first pedigree to be interpreted in terms of mendelian dominant inheritance was a family with brachydactyly (short fingers) reported by Farabee in 1903. Autosomal dominant traits often represent defects in structural nonenzymatic proteins, such as in fibrillin in Marfan syndrome or collagen in Stickler syndrome. In addition, a dominant mode of inheritance has been observed for some malignant neoplasia syndromes, such as retinoblastoma, von Hippel–Lindau disease, tuberous sclerosis, and Gardner syndrome. Although the neoplasias in these diseases are inherited as autosomal dominant traits, the tumors themselves result from loss of function of both alleles of autosomal recessive tumor-suppressor genes.

Almost all bearers of dominant disorders in the human population are heterozygotes. In dominant inheritance the heterozygote is clinically affected and a single dose of the mutant gene interferes with normal function. Occasionally, depending on the frequency of the abnormal gene in the population and the phenotype, two bearers of the same abnormality may marry and produce children. Any offspring of two heterozygous parents has a 25% risk of being an affected homozygote. This circumstance has been recorded in achondroplastic dwarfism. The homozygous achondroplastic dwarf has severe cranial and thoracic skeletal disorders and dies at an early age. Since the heterozygote has one normal allele and the homozygote has none, it is not surprising that the phenotype of the homozygote is more severely abnormal. Homozygotes (or double heterozygotes) for autosomal dominant retinitis pigmentosa also appear to have a much more severe form of retinal degeneration.

It has been suggested that dominant diseases are caused by mutations affecting structural proteins, such as cell receptor growth factors (e.g., FGFR-2 in Crouzon disease), or by functional deficits generated by abnormal polypeptide subunits (e.g., unstable hemoglobins). The dominant disorders aniridia and Waardenburg syndrome result from loss of one of the two alleles for the developmental transcription factors Pax-6 and Pax-3, respectively. However, it is not at all clear exactly how a single gene abnormality can produce the pleiotropic manifestations of such dominant diseases as von Recklinghausen neurofibromatosis or tuberous sclerosis.

In some instances dominantly inherited traits may not be clinically expressed. In other instances, such as some families with autosomal dominant retinitis pigmentosa, individuals who do not manifest any discernible clinical or functional impairment are infrequently determined by pedigree analysis to have a defective gene. This situation is called incomplete penetrance, or *skipped generation.*

Conclusive evidence of autosomal dominant inheritance requires the demonstration of the disease in at least three successive generations. Transmission of the disorder from male to male with both sexes showing the typical disease must also occur. The criteria for autosomal dominant inheritance with complete (100%) penetrance are summarized in Table IX-9. In the usual clinical situation any offspring of an affected heterozygote with a dominant disorder has one chance in two of inheriting the mutant gene and thereby demonstrating some effect, regardless of sex. The degree of variability in the expression of certain traits is usually more pronounced in the case of autosomal dominantly inherited disorders than in other types of genetic disorders. Moreover, when a clinical disorder is inherited in more than one mendelian pattern, the dominantly inherited disorder is, in general, clinically less severe than the recessively inherited one.

Counseling for recurrence risk of autosomal dominant traits must involve thorough examination of not only the affected person, who may have the full syndrome, but also the parents. If one parent is even mildly affected, the risk for additional genetically affected siblings rises to 50%. It is unacceptable to miss variable expressivity when parents and other family members can be examined. In some ocular disorders family members can inherit a gene for a dominant trait and not show clinically apparent manifestations; electrophysiologic testing must be used to detect the impairment. An example is Best vitelliform macular dystrophy, in which clinically normal family members can be diagnosed as having the gene for this disorder only by the presence of an abnormal electro-oculographic light–dark (peak–trough) ratio.

X-Linked Inheritance

A trait determined by genes on either of the sex chromosomes is properly termed *sex linked.* This genetic pattern became widely known with the occurrence of hemophilia in European and Russian royal families. The earliest known record of a correct analysis in an X-linked pattern of inheritance for a human trait appears to be in the Talmud, which decreed that if two boys in a family died from bleeding following cir-

TABLE IX-9

CHARACTERISTICS OF AUTOSOMAL DOMINANT INHERITANCE WITH COMPLETE PENETRANCE

Trait appears in multiple generations (vertical transmission).

Affected males and females are equally likely to transmit the trait to male and female offspring. Thus, male-to-male transmission occurs.

Each affected individual has an affected parent, unless the condition arose by new mutation in the given individual.

Males and females are affected in equal proportions.

Unaffected persons do not transmit the trait to their children.

The trait is expressed in the heterozygote but is more severe in the homozygote.

The age of fathers of isolated (new mutation) cases is usually advanced.

The more severely the trait interferes with survival and reproduction, the greater the proportion of isolated (new mutation) cases.

Variability in expression of the trait from generation to generation and between individuals in the same generation is expected.

Affected persons transmit the trait to 50% of their offspring on average.

---

cumcision, the later-born sons from the same mother or from her sisters need not be circumcised. Thus, even in antiquity, it was recognized that this trait—subsequently identified as hemophilia—affecting only males was transmitted through unaffected females. As of January 1997, 277 established X-linked gene loci were known, of which at least 50 involved disorders affecting the eye or visual system.

The rules governing all modes of sex-linked inheritance can be derived logically by considering the chromosomal basis. Females have two X chromosomes, and one of these will go to each ovum. Males have both an X and a Y chromosome. The male parent contributes his only X chromosome to all his daughters and his only Y chromosome to all his sons. Traits determined by genes carried on the Y chromosome are called *holandric* and are transmitted from a father to 100% of his sons. As of January 1997, 20 genes were assigned to the Y chromosome, none known to affect the human eye. Among these Y-chromosomal genes is the testis-determining factor (TDF), also called sex-determining region-Y (SRY). Genes controlling tooth size, stature, and spermatogenesis are also on the Y chromosome. Finally, a gene determining hairy pinnae (i.e., hair on the outer rim of the ear) may also be located on the Y chromosome. All other sex-linked traits or diseases are thought to result from genes on the X chromosome and are properly termed *X linked*. Some X-linked conditions have considerable frequencies in human populations; the various protan and deutan color vision defects were also among the first human traits assigned to a specific chromosome.

The distinctive feature of X-linked inheritance, both dominant and recessive, is the absence of father-to-son transmission. Since the male X chromosome passes only to daughters, all daughters of an affected male will inherit the mutant gene.

X-linked recessive inheritance A male has only one representative of any X-linked gene and therefore is said to be hemizygous for the gene, rather than homozygous or heterozygous. Since there is no normal gene to balance a mutant X-linked gene in the male, its resulting phenotype, whether dominant or recessive, will always be expressed. A female may be heterozygous or homozygous for a mutant X-linked gene. X-linked traits are commonly called recessive if they are caused by genes located on the X chromosome, which express themselves fully only in the absence of the normal allele. Thus, males with their single X chromosome are predominantly affected. All their phenotypically healthy but heterozygous daughters are carriers. By contrast, each son of a heterozygous woman has an equal chance of being normal or hemizygously affected.

A female will be affected with an X-linked recessive trait under a limited number of circumstances:

□ She is homozygous for the mutant gene by inheritance, i.e., from an affected father and a heterozygous mother

□ Her mother is heterozygous and her father contributes a new mutation

□ She has Turner syndrome with only one X chromosome and therefore is effectively hemizygous

□ She has a partial deletion of one X chromosome either by rearrangement or by formation of an isochromosome and is thereby effectively hemizygous

□ She has a highly unusual skewing of inactivation of her normal X chromosome, as explained by the Lyon hypothesis (see p 288)

□ Her disorder is actually an autosomal genocopy of the X-linked condition

Table IX-10 summarizes the criteria for X-linked recessive inheritance, which should be considered if all affected individuals in a family are males, especially if they are related through historically unaffected women (e.g., uncle and nephew, or multiple affected half brothers with different fathers).

X-linked dominant inheritance X-linked dominant traits are caused by mutant genes expressed in a single dose and carried on the X chromosome. Thus, both heterozygous women and hemizygous men are clinically affected. Females are affected nearly twice as frequently as males. All daughters of affected males are affected. However, all sons of affected males are free of the trait unless their mothers are also affected. Since only children of affected males provide information in discriminating X-linked dominant from autosomal dominant disease, it may be impossible to distinguish these modes on genetic grounds when the pedigree is small or the available data are scarce. Some X-linked dominant disorders such as incontinentia pigmenti (Bloch-Sulzberger syndrome) may prove lethal to the hemizygous male. X-linked hypophosphatemic rickets (vitamin D–resistant rickets) is an example of an X-linked dominant disease. The characteristics of X-linked dominant inheritance are summarized in Table IX-11.

Thompson MW, McInnes RR, Willard HF. *Genetics in Medicine*. 5th ed. Philadelphia: Saunders; 1991:72–82.

TABLE IX-10

CHARACTERISTICS OF X-LINKED RECESSIVE INHERITANCE

Usually only males are affected.

An affected male transmits the gene to all of his daughters (obligate carriers) and none of his sons.

All daughters, even phenotypically normal, of affected males are carriers.

Affected males in a family are either brothers or are related to one another through carrier females, e.g., maternal uncles.

If an affected male has children with a carrier female, 50% of their daughters will be homozygous and affected and 50% will be heterozygous and carriers.

Heterozygous females may rarely be affected (manifesting heterozygotes) because of Lyonization.

Female carriers transmit the gene on average to 50% of their sons, who are affected, and to 50% of their daughters, who will in turn be carriers.

TABLE IX-11

CHARACTERISTICS OF X-LINKED DOMINANT INHERITANCE

Both males and females are affected, but the incidence of the trait is approximately twice as great in females as in males (unless the trait is lethal in the male).

An affected male transmits the trait to all of his daughters and to none of his sons.

Heterozygous affected females transmit the trait to both sexes with equal frequency.

The heterozygous female tends to be less severely affected than the hemizygous male.

X-linked disorders   Females with X-linked diseases have milder symptoms than males. Occasionally, males may be affected severely enough that they die before the reproductive period, thus preventing transmission of the gene. Such is the case with Duchenne muscular dystrophy, in which most affected males die before their mid-teens. In other disorders males are so severely affected that they die before birth, and only females survive. Families with such disorders would include only affected daughters, unaffected daughters, and normal sons at a ratio of 1:1:1. Incontinentia pigmenti is such a genetic lethal disorder. Perinatally, affected females develop an erythematous, vesicular skin eruption, which progresses to marbled, curvilinear pigmentation. The syndrome includes dental abnormalities, congenital or second-ary cataracts, proliferative retinopathy and pseudogliomas, and tractional retinal detachment.

Among the most severe X-linked dominant disorders with lethality for the hemizygous males is Aicardi syndrome. No verified birth of males with this entity has ever been reported, although several XXY pseudomales have occurred. Females have profound mental and developmental retardation; muscular hypotonia; blindness associated with a characteristic lacunar juxtapapillary chorioretinal dysplasia and optic disc anomalies; and central nervous system abnormalities, most characteristically agenesis of the corpus callosum. No recurrences have been reported among siblings, and parents can be reassured that the risk for subsequent children is minimal. All instances of the disease appear to arise from a new X-dominant lethal mutation, and females do not survive long enough to reproduce. The critical area appears to be on the distal end of the short arm of the X chromosome, since some patients with a deletion in this region have also been shown to have features of Aicardi syndrome.

Maternal Inheritance

When nearly all offspring of an affected woman appear to be at risk to inherit and express the trait and the daughters are at risk to pass the trait on to the next generation, the pattern of inheritance is called *maternal inheritance*. The disease stops with all male offspring, whether affected or not. This form of inheritance is highly suggestive of a mitochondrial disorder. The structure and molecular aspects of the mitochondrial genome and a general discussion of mitochondrial disease are covered in chapter VIII.

Lyonization (X Chromosome Inactivation)

In classic human genetics females with a gene for a recessive disease or trait on only one X chromosome should show no manifestations of the defect. However, ophthalmic examples of structural and functional abnormalities in females heterozygous for supposedly recessive X-linked traits abound. Such *carrier states,* usually mild but occasionally severe, have been described in carriers of choroideremia, X-linked Nettleship-Falls ocular albinism, X-linked retinitis pigmentosa, X-linked sutural cataracts, Lowe syndrome, Fabry disease, and color vision defects of the protan and deutan types, among others (Table IX-12; Fig IX-7).

Detection of these carrier states of the X-linked traits has become clinically relevant, especially for sisters and maternal aunts of affected males. In 1961 Mary Lyon, a British geneticist, advanced an explanation for the unanticipated or partial expression of a trait by a heterozygous female. Briefly, the Lyon hypothesis stated that in every somatic cell of a female, only one X chromosome is actively functioning. The second X chromosome is inactive and forms a densely staining marginal nuclear structure demonstrated as a Barr body in a buccal smear or in "drumsticks," pedunculated lobules of the nucleus identified in about 5% of the leukocytes of the normal female. Warburg (1971) reasoned that X chromosome inactivation occurs between approximately 6 and 11 days after fertilization, before the process of embryonic lateralization at 11–16 days of embryogenesis. The "decision" to inactivate one X chromosome is random, but, once it is made, every daughter of each of these "committed" primordial cells will have the same X chromosome irreversibly inactive. With only one X chromosome "functioning," the active gene is dominant at a cellular level. Thus, a heterozygous female for an X-linked disease will have two clonal cell populations (mosaic phenotype), one with normal activity for the gene in question and the other with mutant activity.

TABLE IX-12

OCULAR FINDINGS IN CARRIERS OF X-LINKED DISORDERS

DISORDER	OCULAR FINDINGS
X-linked retinitis pigmentosa	Regional fundus pigmentary changes, "gold-dust" tapetal-like reflex; ERG amplitude and implicit time abnormalities
Choroideremia	"Moth-eaten" fundus pigmentary changes with areas of hypopigmentation, mottling, and pigment clumping in a striated pattern near the equator
Ocular albinism	Chocolate brown clusters of pigment prominent in the midperipheral retina; mottling of macular pigment; iris transillumination
Congenital stationary night blindness with myopia	Reductions in ERG oscillatory potentials
Blue-cone monochromatism	Abnormalities in cone function on ERG, psychophysical thresholds, and color vision testing
Red-green color vision deficiencies (protan and deutan)	Abnormally wide or displaced color match on a Nagel anomaloscope; decrease in sensitivity to red light in protan carriers (Schmidt's sign)
Lowe syndrome	Scattered punctate lens opacities on slit-lamp examination
Fabry disease	Fingerprint or whorl-like (verticillate) changes within the corneal epithelium

The proportion of mutant to normal X chromosomes inactivated usually follows a normal distribution, since presumably the inactivations in various cells are random events. Thus, an average of 50% of the paternal X chromosomes and 50% of maternal X chromosomes are inactivated. It is conceivable, however, that in some cases almost all the cells may have the mutant X active; in others nearly all the cells have the mutant X inactivated. By this mechanism a female may express an X-linked disorder, and rare cases are known of women who have a classic color deficiency or X-linked ocular albinism, X-linked retinitis pigmentosa, or choroideremia.

Some possible clinical implications of X inactivation are the following:

□ The abnormalities in carrier females from different families and even within the same family may vary greatly in degree because of random inactivation and the resultant tissue derivatives containing differing proportions of the active X cells.

□ A large population sample should have as many severely affected as mildly affected heterozygous carriers.

□ In some tissues both normal and abnormal areas could be found if a known biochemical defect could be mapped in a carrier, especially if the gene product is nondiffusible. For example, each hair bulb is ultimately derived from a single primordial cell. Therefore, biochemical analysis of hair roots may demonstrate the mutant phenotype directly: in Fabry disease, X-linked Nettleship-Falls ocular albinism, and Lesch-Nyhan syndrome, the scalp is a mosaic of hairs that have either normal or defective enzyme activity but not an intermediate activity.

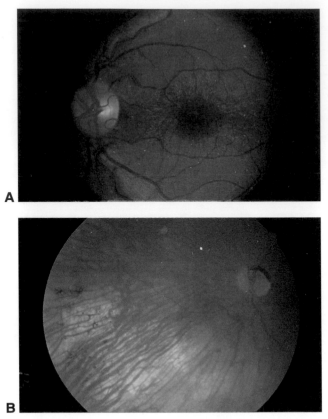

FIG IX-7—*A*, Yellow, "gold-dust" tapetal-like reflex in the left retina of a carrier for X-linked retinitis pigmentosa. *B*, Nasal midperipheral retina in the left eye of a carrier for X-linked retinitis pigmentosa, showing patchy bone spicule–like pigment clumping. *C*, Peripheral retina from the left eye of a carrier of choroideremia showing a "moth-eaten" fundus appearance from areas of hypopigmentation and hyperpigmentation. *D*, Characteristic iris transillumination from a carrier of X-linked ocular albinism. *E*, Midperipheral retina from the left eye of a carrier for ocular albinism showing a chocolate brown pigmentation from areas of apparently enhanced pigmentation and clusters of hypopigmentation.

□ In certain diseases interactions between cells with the normal X active alter the ability of cells with the mutant X active to survive. The enzyme hypoxanthine phosphoribosyltransferase travels from "normal" skin fibroblasts through gap junctions to mutant cells, allowing them to survive. Under other situations, normal cells survive by favorable growth characteristics. In bone marrow and white blood cells a progressive elimination of the abnormal X active cells in the heterozygote and protective survival of cells with a normal X active occurs.

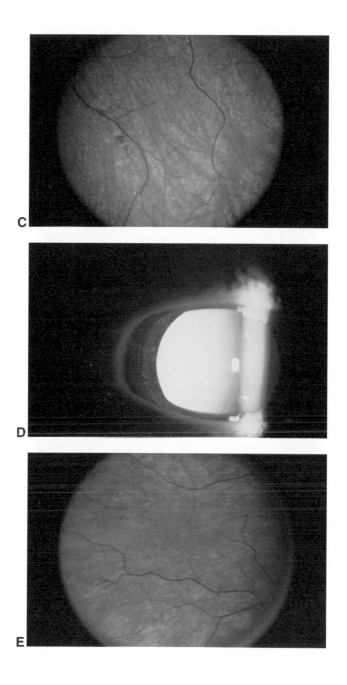

Carriers of the X-linked variety of Nettleship-Falls ocular albinism may have a mottled mosaic fundus; the pigmented retinal epithelial cells have the normal X chromosome active, whereas the nonpigmented have the mutant X active. However, these distinguishing features of the carrier state are not always present. The possibility that the patient is a carrier cannot be entirely eliminated if a given sign is not present, since a female might have inactivated by chance the mutant X chromosome in most of her primordial cells, which evolved into the specific tissue observed and may appear phenotypically normal. This subtlety is even more important in evaluating family members with X-linked disease if the phenotypic carrier state is age dependent; thus, even in obligate carrier females for Lowe syndrome, lenticular cortical opacities are not necessarily seen before the third decade of life.

Krill AE. X-chromosome-linked diseases affecting the eye: status of the heterozygote female. *Trans Am Ophthalmol Soc.* 1969;67:535–608.

Warburg M. Random inactivation of the X chromosome in intermediate X-linked retinitis pigmentosa. Two hypotheses. *Trans Ophthalmol Soc UK.* 1971;91:553–560.

Polygenic and Multifactorial Inheritance

In chromosomal and mendelian (single-gene) disorders, genetic analysis of either phenotypic, biochemical, or molecular parameters is imperative. However, a simple mode of inheritance cannot be assigned and a recurrence risk cannot be predicted for many common normal characteristics or disorders for which genetic variability clearly exists. Such traits as stature, facial features, refractive error, intraocular pressure, iris color, and intelligence are usually distributed as a continuous variation over a wide range without sharp distinction between normal and abnormal phenotypes. This distribution contrasts with the bimodal curve noted in conditions transmitted by a single gene. Common diseases are often superimposed on this substrate of normal variation, perhaps with a threshold level beyond which individuals may be regarded as abnormal. Consequently, the level of blood sugar in diabetes mellitus, the level of intraocular pressure for glaucoma, or the intermedial canthal distance for telecanthus is somewhat arbitrary. Such conditions are often termed *polygenic,* implying that they result from the operation of multiple collaborating genes, each with rather minor additive but individually indeterminate effects.

The term *multifactorial* denotes a combination of genetic and environmental factors in the etiology of disease without specifying the nature of the genetic influence. Examples in humans include intelligence, stature, blood pressure, atherosclerosis, and refractive index of the eye, among many others. The distinction between polygenic and multifactorial inheritance is not one of exclusion but rather of emphasis: most diseases can be thought of as constituting a spectrum of varying degrees of relative importance of genetic and nongenetic factors in their causation.

Counseling for recurrence may be difficult in this type of inheritance. Ideally, empiric data is summarized from exhaustive analyses of similarly affected families in the population. Regrettably, such empiric data are rarely available for ophthalmologic disorders. However, several general guidelines can be offered. If one offspring has the defect, such as cleft lip/palate, and the parents are normal, the chance that a subsequent child will inherit a similar set of genes and thus manifest the same type of malformation is considerably higher than the frequency of the defect in the general population but much lower than the risk of a mendelian defect. The usual estimate for such recurrence is 5% or less for common polygenic diseases. In addition, the more severe the abnormality in the index case, the higher the risk of recurrence of the trait in relatives, presumably because either a greater number of deleterious genes are at work or a fixed population of more harmful genes exists. The risk that an affected individual will have an affected offspring is also about 5%, similar to the recurrence risk for siblings. The risk of recurrence in future children is increased when more than one member of the family is affected, which is not true for mendelian disorders. Such observations have been offered for various forms of strabismus, glaucoma, and significant refractive errors.

Polygenic traits with a threshold (either present or absent) may be much more frequent in one sex if the threshold is sex-influenced. For example, isolated cleft lip is more common in males and isolated cleft palate is more common in females. The risk of recurrence should be higher among relatives of index cases of the less susceptible sex, who are genetically more highly predisposed or who carry more deleterious genes. For example, perinatal pyloric stenosis is much more common in males than females. Thus, if a female infant is affected, she presumably has either more deleterious genes or a higher personal liability to manifest the trait and, accordingly, a greater likelihood of having an affected sibling or relative.

Finally, if the malformation or disorder has occurred in both paternal and maternal relatives, the recurrence risk is distinctly higher because of the consanguineous sharing of multiple unspecifiable but potentially harmful genes in their offspring. Such empiric risks clearly increase the likelihood of diabetes mellitus in the offspring of two affected parents, even if neither parent has an antecedent family history of the disease.

Table IX-13 lists common polygenic disorders, and Table IX-14 summarizes the principles of recurrence risks for these disorders.

Thompson MW, McInnes RR, Willard HF. *Genetics in Medicine.* 5th ed. Philadelphia: Saunders; 1991:349–363.

Pedigree Analysis

Recording a family history for general medical and eye disease is an essential part of an ophthalmic consultation. Family data can be summarized in a pedigree chart, a shorthand method for recording data for visual reference. While cumbersome for the novice, it should be incorporated into every medical record. The word *pedigree* is derived from the French expression *pied de grue,* or crane's foot, from the branching pattern of the diagram.

The affected individual who brings a family to the attention of the physician is the *proband* (propositus or proposita). The person seeking counseling is most frequently identified as the *consultand.* The most commonly used symbols for drawing a pedigree are shown in Fig IX-8. In human pedigree charts the usual practice is to place the male symbol first on the left, while breeding records of other species generally list the female symbol first.

Accurate completion of the pedigree drawing is essential to its interpretation. The health history of family members may be as important as the ocular history. The interviewer must always inquire specifically about abortions, stillbirths, and deceased family members. Often information on these individuals is erroneously omitted, and prenatal or postnatal lethal disorders or relevant medical and genetic causes of death are overlooked. Ages at death may be useful in specific situations and can be recorded directly near the appropriate symbols. For example, a clinician evaluating a child with ectopia lentis and no family history of similar ocular disease

TABLE IX-13

COMMON POLYGENIC/MULTIFACTORIAL TRAITS

Anencephaly/spina bifida
Cleft lip/palate
Cleft palate
Clubfoot (pes equinovarus)
Common psychoses (schizophrenia, affective disorder)
Congenital heart disease (some forms)
Congenital scoliosis
Coronary heart disease (some forms)
Diabetes mellitus (some forms)
Hirschsprung disease
Hydrocephalus, nonspecific neural tube defects
Hypertension
Mental retardation
Open-angle glaucoma (some forms)
Pyloric stenosis
Refractive errors
Strabismus (some forms)
Urinary tract malformations

TABLE IX-14

RECURRENCE RISK FOR POLYGENIC DISORDERS

Increased risk above the general population for recurrence of the disorder among first-, second-, and third-degree relatives of the affected person

Baseline 3%–5% risk of recurrence for first-degree relatives of proband; about half that risk for second-degree relatives

Increasing risk with increasing numbers of affected genetic relatives, especially first- and second-degree

Increased risk of recurrence if affected person is of the sex usually less affected

Increased risk of recurrence with increased severity of the trait

Risk of recurrence greater for siblings in families with two affected than for families with one affected

PEDIGREE SYMBOLS

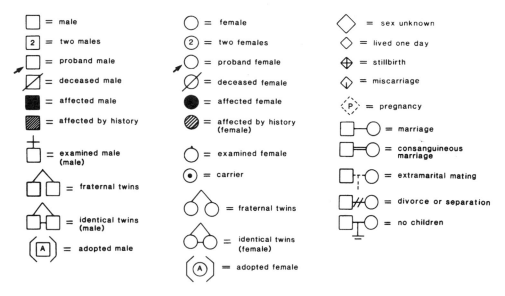

FIG IX-8—Symbols commonly used for pedigree analysis.

can find the identification of a relative deceased from a dissecting thoracic aortic aneurysm in his fourth decade very informative, leading to a tentative consideration of Marfan syndrome in the differential diagnosis. The casual observation in a young adult of multiple patches of congenital hypertrophy of the retinal pigment epithelium in each eye may stimulate the recognition of a parent deceased at age 50 from metastatic adenocarcinoma of the colon and a sibling deceased from a brain tumor at 10 years of age, thus leading to a diagnosis of Gardner syndrome and referral to a gastroenterologist for further diagnostic evaluation.

The interviewer should always clarify whether brothers and sisters are half siblings or full siblings. This procedure may not only limit the possible patterns of inheritance but may also identify other individuals at risk for the disorders under consideration. Occasionally, information about parentage must be pursued aggressively but always privately and confidentially. In the United States in 1990 28% of babies, 3 out of every 11, were born to parents who were not legally married. The frequency of offspring born to teenage mothers outside of conventional marriages ranges from 30% to 80%. Both incest and nonpaternity are sensitive issues, but clearly neither is rare in our society. The national nonpaternity rate is presently estimated at 5%, but in some urban societies it may be as high as 15%. In considering rare autosomal recessive diseases, the interviewer must ask specifically about consanguinity, either by searching for common last names in the families of both parents, by finding identical birthplaces for the parents, or by identifying similar parental backgrounds from known ethnic or religious isolates.

Thompson JS, Thompson MW. *Genetics in Medicine*. 3rd ed. Philadelphia: Saunders; 1980.53–94.

Genetic Counseling

The ophthalmologist who understands the principles of human genetics has a foundation for counseling patients about their diseases. Genetic counseling imparts knowledge of human disease, including a genetic diagnosis and its ocular and systemic implications; information about the risk of occurrence or recurrence of the disorder within the family; and an open discussion of the options for reproduction. All genetic counseling is predicated on certain essential requirements.

Accurate diagnosis The physician must be sufficiently aware of the range of human ocular pathology to derive an accurate and specific diagnosis. It is impossible to counsel or refer patients on the basis of "congenital nystagmus" or "color blindness" or "macular degeneration"; these are signs, not diagnoses.

Complete family history A family history will narrow the choices of possible inheritance patterns, but it may not necessarily exclude new mutational events, isolated occurrences of recessive diseases, and chromosomal rearrangements in individual circumstances. The ophthalmologist must examine or arrange to have examined the parents, siblings, and other family members for mild manifestations of dominant diseases or characteristic carrier states in X-linked disorders. Identification of one young adult with the findings of Usher syndrome—prelingual deafness, night blindness, visual field constriction, and ultimately deterioration of central vision—obligates the ophthalmologist to evaluate a younger sibling who is congenitally deaf but "historically" has no eye problems. There is an overwhelming probability that the sibling has the same disease. Only an ophthalmologist will be cognizant of and attentive to the atypical findings of hereditary ocular disorders.

Understanding the genetic and clinical aspects of the disorder The ophthalmologist should appreciate, perhaps more intimately than any other physician, how some clinically similar diseases inherited in the same pattern may be the result of different and even nonallelic defects. For example, the visual implications and prognosis of the tyrosinase-positive and tyrosinase-negative oculocutaneous albinism are considerably different. Some entities that are clinically similar may be inherited differently and thus have differential impact on other family members. Pseudoxanthoma elasticum is often a late-onset disease in both its autosomal dominant and autosomal recessive modes that has serious implications for cardiovascular disease, stroke, and gastrointestinal bleeding. Informed counseling falls short if the ophthalmologist advises only about visual disability associated with angioid streaks without attention to the complete disease and risks to other family members.

Obstacles to Genetic Counseling

The ophthalmologist must be aware of the possibility that an isolated individual affected by a condition that can be inherited may represent a homozygous recessive trait and should search for parental consanguinity or ambiguous parentage (nonpaternity, incest, and even occult adoption) or for a new mutation and should inquire about advanced paternal (or maternal grandparental) age. Heterogeneity may confuse the diagnosis. Somatic mutations also occur, as with segmental neurofibromatosis or unilateral unifocal retinoblastoma. Nonpenetrance or mild expressivity in other family members should be excluded by diligent examination. Chromosomal abnormalities and phenocopies caused by infections or drugs may account for the isolated affected person. Nonetheless, the obligation of the ophthalmologist to explain the disorder begins with accurate diagnosis and establishment of the mode of heritability.

Counseling can be considered successful if the patient or family, having acquired the facts, makes a reproductive decision that is reasonable and appropriate. The counselor is an informer, not an advisor. Properly done, genetic counseling is nondirective. It is inappropriate, if not unethical, to tell the patient what to do (for instance, not to have any children).

In any circumstance, the counseling ophthalmologist should outline the options for family planning when it is necessary. The responsibility of the ophthalmic practitioner is to suspect and establish the diagnosis of inherited disease, to inform the patient of the findings and their implications for health, and to provide accurate answers to direct and implied questions about risks for recurrence and burden of disease.

Some individuals may accept a high statistical risk and have children. This decision must be based on how they perceive the social and psychological burdens of the disorder. The attitude toward reproduction may be considerably different for a female carrier of protanopia than of X-linked retinitis pigmentosa or choroideremia, even though the statistical risk for an affected son is the same for each of them.

Some individuals may elect to delay childbearing in hopes of medical advances in prenatal diagnosis or postnatal treatment of a disorder. Others may choose for a variety of personal and ethical considerations not to have natural offspring and may proceed with contraception, termination of pregnancy, sterilization, or adoption.

Artificial insemination by donor is a useful option in family planning if the father has a dominant disease or if both parents are carriers of a biochemically detectable recessive disorder. However, it is clearly not applicable if the mother is the carrier of an X-linked disorder or the individual affected by an autosomal dominant mutation. Finally, although its acceptance and legal implications may lag behind, embryo adoption (transplantation) and surrogate motherhood may soon become useful alternatives for some families.

Prenatal Diagnosis

Prenatal diagnosis with amniocentesis or chorionic villus sampling for biochemically identifiable disorders (e.g., Tay-Sachs disease, many mucopolysaccharidoses, and about 100 other diseases) is also useful in the proper genetic settings. However, since most genes are expressed in a tissue-specific manner, biochemical diagnostic techniques are limited to those diseases for which the gene products are expressed in amniocytes.

Other possible indications for amniocentesis include advanced maternal age, with its increased risk for chromosomal abnormalities, elevated maternal serum alpha-fetoprotein suggesting a neural tube defect, and the presence of a familial disease detectable by DNA analysis.

Amniocentesis is usually performed at 15–16 weeks of gestation when enough fluid and cells can be obtained for culture and the maternal risk of abortion is relatively low. The risk of spontaneous abortion or fetal morbidity from the procedure is about 0.5%. Earlier prenatal diagnosis of chromosome abnormalities, at about 10 weeks of gestation, is available through the use of chorionic villus sampling. In this procedure tissue from the placenta is obtained under ultrasound visualization. It is then cultured and karyotyped in a manner similar to that used for amniocentesis. As a first trimester procedure, chorionic villus sampling allows for an earlier diagnosis and a safer means of pregnancy termination. The rate of spontaneous abortion associated with this procedure is estimated at 1%–2%. Since the yield of DNA is greater than that from 20 ml of amniotic fluid withdrawn in amniocentesis, a direct DNA analysis of cells can often be done without first culturing the cells. Thus, information can be obtained in a considerably shorter time than with amniocentesis.

New Developments

In the future it is likely that certain aspects of genetic counseling will have a more precise basis as the consequence of a coordinated international effort to study the entire human genome. A number of agencies around the world are orchestrating *the human genome project,* whose ultimate goal is to determine the precise nucleotide sequences not only of the human genome but also of several model organisms including yeast, nematodes, and fruit flies. In the United States, the National Center for Human Genome Research at the National Institutes of Health and the Department of Energy serve as coordinating agencies. It is anticipated that information obtained from this Herculean effort will eventually aid in the identification and characterization of numerous additional genes that lead to human disease.

Pharmacogenetics

The study of heritable factors that determine how drugs are chemically metabolized in the body is called *pharmacogenetics.* The field addresses genetic differences among population segments that are responsible for variations in both the therapeutic and adverse effects of drugs. Investigations in pharmacogenetics are important not only for more rational approaches to therapy, but also because they facilitate a deeper understanding of drug pharmacology. Part 5 of this volume, Ocular Pharmacology, offers more detail.

Isoniazid is a drug that provides an example of pharmacogenetics. This antituberculosis drug is normally inactivated by the liver enzyme acetyltransferase. A large segment of the population, which varies by geographic distribution, has a reduced amount of this enzyme; these individuals are termed *slow inactivators.* When they take isoniazid, the drug reaches higher-than-normal concentrations, thus causing a greater incidence of adverse effects. Family studies have shown this reduced level of acetyltransferase to be inherited as an autosomal recessive trait.

Several other well-documented examples of pharmacogenetics exist. One example occurs in 10% of the male African American population, a high percentage of male Sephardic Jews, and males from a number of other ethnic groups. They have an X-linked recessive trait that causes affected males to have glucose-6-phosphate dehydrogenase (G6PD) enzyme deficiency in their erythrocytes. As a consequence, a number of drugs, including sulfacetamide, vitamin K, acetylsalicylic acid, quinine, chloroquine, and probenecid, may produce acute hemolytic anemia in these individuals. Pharmacogenetic causes have also been ascribed to variations in response to ophthalmic drugs, such as the increased intraocular pressure seen in a segment of the population after prolonged use of topical corticosteroids.

Children with Down syndrome have been shown to be more reactive than normal children to several drugs. Some children with Down syndrome have died after systemic administration of atropine as a result of supersensitivity. This supersensitivity is also seen with the topical use of atropine by its greater-than-normal effect on pupillary dilation in these patients. A hyperactivity secondary to the use of echo-thiophate iodide has been noted in several children with Down syndrome being treated for strabismus several hours after local instillation of a 0.125% concentration of this drug.

One of the earliest examples noted of an inherited deficit in drug metabolism involved succinylcholine, a strong muscle relaxant that interferes with acetyl-cholinesterase, the enzyme that catabolizes acetylcholine at neuromuscular junctions. Normally, succinylcholine is rapidly destroyed by plasma cholinesteras (sometimes called pseudocholinesterase) so that its effect is short-lived, usually no more than a few minutes. Some individuals are homozygous for a recessive gene that codes for a form of cholinesterase with a considerably lower substrate affinity. Consequently, at therapeutic doses of succinylcholine, almost no destruction occurs, and the drug continues to exert its inhibitory effect on acetylcholinesterase, resulting in prolonged periods of apnea.

Goldberg MF, Renie WA, eds. *Genetic and Metabolic Eye Disease*. 2nd ed. Boston: Little, Brown & Co; 1986:579–584.

Sutton HE. *An Introduction to Human Genetics*. 2nd ed. New York: Holt, Rinehart & Winston; 1975:211–214.

Clinical Management of Genetic Disease

Genetic disease may not be curable, but in most cases the patient can obtain considerable benefit through the appropriate management of medical care by the physician. Such care should include all of the steps discussed below.

Accurate Diagnosis

Unfortunately, because health care providers may not be as knowledgeable about genetic diagnoses as they are about other areas of medicine, many patients may not have a precise diagnosis or, worse yet, an incorrect diagnosis. A patient with deafness and pigmentary retinopathy may be called rubella syndrome when he or she really has Usher syndrome. Patients with retinitis pigmentosa may go unrecognized for a syndrome associated with their disease. For example, patients with retinitis pigmentosa and congenital hexadactyly (surgically corrected in infancy) may be not recognized as having Bardet-Biedl syndrome. The correct diagnosis in the above cases is important to assure that the patient's educational, career planning, and lifetime support needs are truly met.

Complete Explanation of the Disease

Patients are often very disturbed when they do not understand the nature of their disease. A careful explanation of the disorder, as currently understood, will often dispel myths that patients may have about how they became the way they are.

Virtually all genetic disorders carry burdens to the individual that may interfere with certain activities later in life. The appropriate time to discuss these with patients and family members is often when the questions are first asked about the consequences of a disease. Such explanations need to be tempered with compassion and sympathetic appreciation of the possible emotional and psychological effects of this information.

Treatment of the Disease Process

Although definitive cures—that is, reversing or correcting of underlying genetic defects—are yet to emerge for various heritable disorders, some conditions in which metabolic defects have been identified can often be managed through five fundamental approaches:

□ Dietary control

□ Chelation of excessive metabolites

□ Enzyme or gene product replacements

□ Vitamin and cofactor therapy

□ Drug therapy to reduce accumulation of harmful products

Some genetic disorders affecting the eye that arise from an inborn error of metabolism can effectively be managed by dietary therapy. These include familial hyperlipoproteinemia, tyrosinosis, homocystinuria, Refsum disease, phenylketonuria, fructose or lactose intolerance, galactokinase deficiency, and galactosemia. Implementing a galactose-free diet can reverse such main features of galactosemia as hepatosplenomegaly, jaundice, and weight loss. Progression of cortical cataracts can be avoided, and less extensive lens opacities may even regress with a galactose-free diet. With time, galactosemic patients are able to metabolize galactose through alternate pathways, obviating the need for life-long dietary restriction. In phenylketonuria mental retardation can be prevented by early phenylalanine restriction.

In disorders that result from enzyme or transport protein deficiencies, a metabolite or metal may accumulate that has deleterious effects on various tissues. For example, in Wilson disease decreased levels of serum ceruloplasmin result in poor transport of free copper (Cu^{2+}) ions and storage of copper in tissues such as the brain, liver, and cornea. Resultant clinical signs can be reversed at least partially after the administration of D-penicillamine, a chelator of Cu^{2+} ions. Other copper chelators such as BAL (British antilewisite) can be employed in addition to copper-deficient diets to reverse clinical signs of Wilson disease.

In theory, replacement of deficient enzymes in disorders resulting from metabolic dysfunction by either plasma or leukocyte infusions could be beneficial in preventing the accumulation of toxic metabolites. Both in vitro and in vivo investigations on the transfusion of plasma or leukocytes in patients with Hunter or Hurler syndrome showed some preliminary promise for lessening the musculoskeletal signs of these disorders. Plasma infusions in patients with Fabry disease have succeeded temporarily in decreasing plasma levels of the accumulated substrate ceramide trihexoside, although clinical improvement was not detected. Further in-depth investigations are necessary before intervention with this type of therapy is meaningful, for circulating enzymes from infusions are rapidly degraded or excreted by the kidneys. Nevertheless, a slow-release depot preparation administered intramuscularly is at least feasible in providing short-term improvement in some metabolic disorders.

Organ transplantation can be considered as a form of regionalized enzyme replacement. In patients with cystinosis, cystine crystals accumulate in the kidney. If a normal kidney, with its rich source of enzymes, is transplanted into a patient with cystinosis, cystine does not accumulate in the cells of the renal tubules, and renal function tends to remain normal.

In addition to enzyme replacement, synthetic or recombinant gene product replacement can effectively manage a gene defect. Hemophilia, for example, can be treated through the administration of a missing clotting factor (VIII). The value of gene product replacement is demonstrated in the use of thyroid hormone for hypothyroidism, insulin for diabetes, erythropoietin for anemia, and growth hormone for pituitary dwarfism. However, caution should be given to the possible spread of acquired immunodeficiency syndrome (AIDS) caused by the human immunodeficiency virus (HIV) if the gene product is extracted from pooled human tissues.

Vitamin therapy appears to be of benefit in two autosomal recessive disorders. In at least some patients with homocystinuria, vitamin B_6 (pyridoxine) administration has been shown to decrease homocystine accumulation in plasma and to reduce the severity of the disorder. Vitamin A and vitamin E therapy have been noted to benefit some patients with abetalipoproteinemia with regard to neurologic impairment; such therapy is also likely to slow or lessen the development and progression of retinal degeneration. More long-term therapeutic trials are necessary to better define the efficacy of vitamin therapy for these and perhaps other metabolic disorders.

Berson and colleagues have recommended that most patients with retinitis pigmentosa take 15,000 IU/day of the palmitate form of vitamin A and avoid vitamin E. This recommendation was based on data from a single study that was interpreted by the authors as showing a very modest reduction in the rate of loss of certain ERG parameters with vitamin A and a similar modest increase with vitamin E. However, no significant change was demonstrated in the rates of visual field loss, which were not significantly different from controls for the vitamin A or vitamin E supplementation groups. This study and its interpretation are highly controversial. Questions remain concerning the appropriateness of small changes in very low amplitude ERGs as an endpoint, and the recommendations to take supplemental vitamin A or avoid vitamin E are not universally accepted. If patients decide to take vitamin A at the recommended dosage, they should have yearly liver function tests to monitor for hepatic toxicity. Women of child-bearing status should be firmly warned of the risks of congenital malformations if the supplementation is taken just prior to conception or during early pregnancy. In addition, systemic toxicity could occur to newborn infants who are breast-fed if the mother takes vitamin A at this dosage.

Berson EL, Rosner B, Sandberg MA, et al. A randomized trial of supplemental vitamin A and vitamin E supplementation for retinitis pigmentosa. *Arch Ophthalmol.* 1993; 111:761–772.

Berson EL, Rosner B, Sandberg MA, et al. Vitamin A supplementation for retinitis pigmentosa [letter]. *Arch Ophthalmol.* 1993;111:1456–1457.

Massof RW, Finkelstein D. Editorial: Supplemental vitamin A retards loss of ERG amplitude in retinitis pigmentosa. *Arch Ophthalmol.* 1993;111:751–754.

Massof RW, Finkelstein D. Vitamin A supplementation for retinitis pigmentosa [letter]. *Arch Ophthalmol.* 1993;111:1458–1459.

Norton EW, Marmor MF, Clowes DD, et al. Felix JS, Laties AM. A randomized trial of vitamin A and vitamin E supplementation for retinitis pigmentosa [letters]. *Arch Ophthalmol.* 1993;111:1460–1465.

Various genetically determined disorders can be managed by use of an appropriate drug. For example, excess accumulation of uric acid in primary gout can be prevented or reduced by blocking the activity of the enzyme xanthine oxidase with the drug allopurinol or by increasing its excretion by the kidneys with the use of probenecid. In addition, a reduction in serum cholesterol found with familial hypercholesterolemia can often be achieved with the use of various cholesterol-lowering drugs or substances that bind bile acids in the gastrointestinal tract.

Goldberg MF, Renie WA, eds. *Genetic and Metabolic Eye Disease*. 2nd ed. Boston: Little, Brown & Co; 1986:569–578.

Sutton HE. *An Introduction to Human Genetics*. 2nd ed. New York: Holt, Rinehart & Winston; 1975:477–496.

Appropriate management of sequelae and complications   Some of the sequelae of genetic diseases, such as glaucoma in Rieger syndrome or cataracts in patients with retinitis pigmentosa, can be successfully managed to preserve or partially restore vision. However, patients need to understand how the treatment of the sequelae or complication may differ in their situation, especially if it has an impact on the expected outcome.

Genetic Counseling

The responsibility of the physician is to either provide genetic counseling or arrange for this service through referral to a geneticist. However, unless the genetic consultant is also an ophthalmologist, the referring ophthalmologist will almost always have to provide the explanations of the ocular aspects of the disease and their ramifications for treatment and management. It must be emphasized that all genetic counseling should be nondirective. Physicians have no right to tell couples whether or not to have children but should instead strive to provide information about risks, burdens, and options so that the individuals can make informed decisions.

Referral to providers of support for disabilities   Individuals and families often receive considerable benefit from referral to local, regional, or national agencies, support groups, or foundations that provide services for those with their particular disease. These organizations include local and state agencies for the blind or visually impaired, special school education programs, and appropriate consumer groups. Particularly when disability is chronic and progressive, these agencies or support groups can often be of great help to the individual or family in the adjustment to the changing disabilities.

A Directory of National Genetic Voluntary Organizations (list of support groups) is available from:
The Alliance of Genetic Support Groups
Toll-free telephone: 1-800-336-4363
Internet: http://medhlp.netusa.net/www/agsg.htm
or through the *Online Mendelian Inheritance in Man* home page website (under OMIM Allied Resources): http://www3.ncbi.nlm.nih.gov/Omim/

PART 4

BIOCHEMISTRY AND METABOLISM

Robert E. Anderson, MD, PhD (Dean A McGee Eye Institute, Oklahoma City) direct-ed the initial version of this Part. The following authors have contributed material for the revision: James L. Lewis, PhD (UC, Santa Cruz); Katherine Ochsner, MD (UTMB, Galveston); Brian Wong, MD (UTMB, Galveston); Martin Wand, MD (POACE, Hartford); Randolph Glickman, PhD (UTHSC, San Antonio); Ata Abdel-Latif, PhD (Medical College of Georgia, Augusta); Satish Srivastava, PhD (UTMB, Galveston); Naseem Ansari, PhD (UTMB, Galveston). Diane Edwards (Big Sandy, MT) is grate-fully acknowledged for editing the manuscript.

CHAPTER X

Tear Film

The primary functions of the tear film are to provide a smooth optical surface at the air–eye interface, to serve as a medium for removal of debris, and to supply oxygen to the corneal epithelium. The tear film carries tear constituents and debris to the puncta. In addition, it contains a number of antimicrobial systems, lubricates the cornea–eyelid interface, and prevents desiccation of the anterior eye surface. The human tear film is composed of the following:

- The marginal strip
- The film covering the palpebral and tarsal conjunctival surfaces
- The film covering the cornea

The marginal tear strip forms the *tear meniscus,* which is confluent with the *preocular tear film* covering the conjunctival surface and the *precorneal tear film* covering the corneal surface.

The precorneal tear film is a trilaminar structure consisting of an anterior lipid layer, a middle aqueous phase, and a posterior glycoprotein mucin layer. The average thickness of the precorneal tear film is about 7 μm with the aqueous phase constituting nearly all the thickness (Fig X-1). The volume of the tear film is 7.4 μl for the unanesthetized eye and 2.6 μl for the anesthetized eye, and it decreases with age. Some properties of tears are given in Table X-1.

Lipid Layer

The anterior layer of the tear film contains polar and nonpolar lipids (approximately 100 molecules thick) secreted primarily by the *meibomian (tarsal) glands* (see Figures I-30, I-31, p 35). These glands are located in the tarsal plate of the upper and lower eyelids and are surrounded by cholinesterase-positive nerves. There are approximately 30–40 meibomian glands in the upper eyelid and 20–30 smaller glands in the lower. Each gland has an orifice that opens on the eyelid margin between the tarsal *gray line* and the mucocutaneous junction. The sebaceous glands of Zeis, located at the palpebral margin of the tarsus, also secrete lipid, which is incorporated into the tear film.

The four functions of the lipid layer are to

- Contribute to the optical properties of the tear film
- Maintain a hydrophobic barrier (*lipid strip*) that prevents tear overflow by increasing surface tension
- Retard evaporation
- Provide lubrication for the eyelids as they pass over the globe

Because the polar lipids are charged compounds (*phospholipids*), they are located at the aqueous–lipid interface. The fatty acids of the phospholipids interact

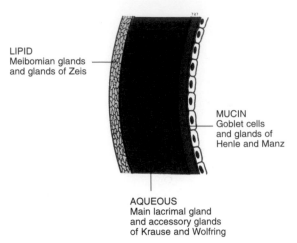

LIPID
Meibomian glands
and glands of Zeis

MUCIN
Goblet cells
and glands of
Henle and Manz

AQUEOUS
Main lacrimal gland
and accessory glands
of Krause and Wolfring

FIG X-1—Three layers of the precorneal tear film. (Reproduced with permission from Kanski JJ. *Clinical Ophthalmology: A Systematic Approach*. 3rd ed. Oxford: Butterworth-Heinemann; 1994:92.)

through noncovalent, noncharged bonds with the other hydrophobic lipids that make up the bulk of the lipid layer. The tear lipids are not susceptible to lipid peroxidation because they contain extremely low levels of polyunsaturated fatty acids.

Aqueous Phase

The middle aqueous layer, secreted by the main lacrimal glands and by the accessory glands of Krause and Wolfring, consists of electrolytes and proteins.

Electrolytes and small molecules regulate the osmotic flow of fluids between the corneal epithelial cells and the tear film, buffer tear pH, and serve as enzyme cofactors in controlling membrane permeability. The Na^+ concentration of tears parallels that of serum, while the concentration of K^+ is 5–7 times greater than that in serum. Na^+, K^+, and Cl^- regulate the osmotic flow of fluids from the cornea to the tear film. Bicarbonate regulates tear pH. Other tear electrolytes (Fe^{++}, Cu^{++}, Mg^{++}, Ca^{++}, PO_4^{3-}) are enzyme cofactors.

Tear film solutes include urea, glucose, lactate, citrate, ascorbate, and amino acids. All enter the tear film via the systemic circulation, and their concentrations parallel serum levels. Fasting tear glucose levels are 3.6–4.1 mg% in diabetic and nondiabetic individuals. However, after a 100 mg oral glucose load, tear glucose levels are >11 mg% in 96% of diabetic individuals tested.

Proteins in the tear film include immunoglobulin A (IgA) and secretory IgA (S-IgA). IgA is formed by plasma cells in interstitial tissues of the main and accessory lacrimal glands and the substantia propria of the conjunctiva. The secretory component is produced within lacrimal gland acini, with S-IgA being secreted into the lumen of the main and accessory lacrimal glands. IgA plays a role in local host defense mechanisms of the external eye, as shown by increased levels of IgA and

TABLE X-1

PROPERTIES OF HUMAN TEAR FILM

Composition	Water	98.2%
	Solid	1.8%
Thickness	Total	6.5–7.5 μm
	Lipid layer	0.1–0.2 μm
Volume	Unanesthetized	7.4 μl
	Anesthetized	2.6 μl
Secretory rate	Unanesthetized	
	Schirmer	3.8 μl/min
	Fluorophotometry	0.9 μl/min
	Anesthetized	
	Schirmer	1.8 μl/min
	Fluorophotometry	0.3 μl/min
Turnover rate	Normal	12–16%/min
	Stimulated	300%/min
Evaporation rate		0.06 μl/cm²/min
Osmolarity		296–308 mOsm
pH		6.5–7.6
Electrolytes (mmol/l)	Na^+	134–170
	K^+	26–42
	Ca^{2+}	0.5
	Mg^{2+}	0.3–0.6
	Cl^-	120–135
	HCO_3^-	26

IgG in human tears associated with ocular inflammation. Other immunoglobulins in tears are IgM, IgD, and IgE. Individuals manifesting vernal conjunctivitis demonstrate elevated tear and serum levels of IgE, IgE-producing plasma cells in the giant papillae of the superior tarsal conjunctiva, and histamine. Increased levels of tear histamine support the concept of conjunctival mast-cell degranulation triggered by IgE–antigen interaction.

Lysozyme, β-lysin, and lactoferrin are important tear antimicrobial constituents. Also present in tears is interferon, which inhibits viral replication and may be efficacious in limiting the severity of ulcerative herpetic keratitis.

The aqueous layer has the following four functions:

□ Supplying oxygen to the avascular corneal epithelium

□ Serving as an antibacterial agent

□ Smoothing minute irregularities of the anterior corneal surface

□ Washing away debris

Mucoid Layer

The posterior tear film mucins coat the microplicae of the superficial corneal epithelial cells and form a fine network over the conjunctival surface. Functions of the mucin layer include the following:

☐ The mucins convert the corneal epithelium from a hydrophobic to a hydrophilic layer, which is essential for the even and spontaneous distribution of the tear film.

☐ The mucins also interact with the tear lipid layer to lower surface tension, thereby stabilizing the tear film.

☐ The loose mucous network covering the bulbar conjunctiva traps exfoliated surface cells, foreign particles, and bacteria.

Tear mucins are secreted principally by the conjunctival goblet cells and minimally by lacrimal glands of Henle and Manz. Goblet cell mucin production is 2–3 μl/day, which contrasts with aqueous tear production of 2–3 ml/day. Both conjunctival and tear mucins are negatively charged glycoproteins. Tear dysfunction may result when the quantity of tear mucins is deficient (avitaminosis A, conjunctival destruction), excessive (hyperthyroidism, foreign-body stimulation), or biochemically altered from acidic to neutral mucopolysaccharides (keratitis sicca).

Tear Secretion

Functionally, the lacrimal secretory system has two components: *basic secretors* and *reflex secretors*. No stimulus for basic tear secretion is known. In the past basic secretion was ascribed to the accessory lacrimal glands of Krause and Wolfring, and reflex secretion to the main lacrimal gland. However, it is now thought that all lacrimal glands respond as a unit. The glands of Krause, which constitute two thirds of the accessory lacrimal glands, are located in the lateral part of the upper fornix, proximal to the main lacrimal gland. A number of Krause glands are also present in the lower fornix. The glands of Wolfring are variably located along the orbital margin of each tarsus (see Figure I-26, p 31).

The main lacrimal gland is divided into two anatomical parts, the *orbital* and the *palpebral* portions, by the levator aponeurosis. Reflex secretion is induced in response to physical irritation (superficial corneal and conjunctival sensory stimulation), by psychogenic factors, and by bright light.

Eyelid movement is important in tear film renewal and distribution. As the eyelids close in a complete blink, the superior and inferior fornices are compressed by the force of the preseptal muscles, and the eyelids move toward each other, with the upper eyelid moving over the longer distance and exerting force on the globe. This force clears the anterior surface of debris and any insoluble mucin and expresses secretions from meibomian glands. The lower eyelid moves horizontally in a nasal direction and pushes tear fluid and debris toward the superior and inferior puncta. When the eyelids are opened, the tear film is redistributed by a two-step process. Initially, the upper eyelid pulls the aqueous phase of the tear film by capillary action. Secondarily, the lipid layer spreads slowly upward over the aqueous phase. It increases tear layer thickness and stabilizes the tear film. Polar lipids, present in the meibomian secretions, concentrate at the lipid–water interface and enhance the stability of the lipid layer.

Tear Dysfunction

A qualitative or quantitative abnormality of the tear film may occur as a result of

◻ Imbalance of tear film constituents

◻ Uneven dispersion of the tear film as a result of corneal surface irregularities

◻ Ineffective distribution caused by eyelid–globe incongruity

An imbalance of tear film constituents most often results from aqueous deficiency, mucin deficiency (Fig X-2) or excess (with or without associated aqueous deficiency), and/or lipid abnormality (meibomian gland dysfunction). An uneven dispersion of the preocular tear film results from an irregular corneal or limbal surface (inflammation, scarring, dystrophic changes) or poor contact lens fit. Eyelid–globe incongruity occurs as a result of congenital, traumatic, or neurogenic eyelid dysfunction or absent or dysfunctional blink mechanism. Diagnostic tests for tear dysfunction include the tear breakup time, lissamine green staining, and Schirmer tests (see also BCSC Section 8, *External Disease and Cornea*).

The tear dysfunction state is managed by creating a more regular corneal or conjunctival contour or by facilitating eyelid–globe congruity. The tear constituent imbalance can be corrected by decreasing evaporation of tears through reduced room temperature or increased humidity and changing contact lenses for regular glasses. Tear film instability secondary to aqueous and/or mucous deficiency can be improved by the use of topical tear substitutes. Reduction of tear drainage by punctal occlusion prolongs the effect of artificial tears and preserves the natural tears.

BCSC Section 7, *Orbit, Eyelids, and Lacrimal System*, discusses the lacrimal system in depth with numerous illustrations.

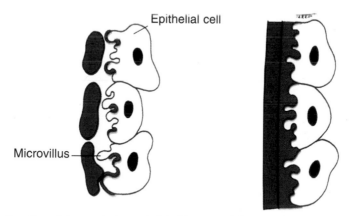

FIG X-2—Function of the mucin layer. *Left,* With mucin deficiency the aqueous layer (blue) does not wet the corneal epithelium. *Right,* A normal amount of mucin (red) allows proper wetting of the corneal epithelium by the aqueous layer. (Reproduced with permission from Kanski JJ. *Clinical Ophthalmology: A Systematic Approach.* 3rd ed. Oxford: Butterworth-Heinemann; 1994:93.)

CHAPTER XI

Cornea

The cornea is a remarkable optic structure, possessing a high degree of order and transparency with excellent self-protective and reparative properties. The cornea is made up of the following histological layers (Fig XI-1):

□ Epithelium with basement membrane

□ Bowman's layer

□ Stroma, or substantia propria

□ Descemet's membrane

□ Endothelium

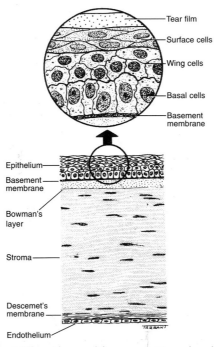

FIG XI-1—Diagram of different layers of the cornea. (Reproduced with permission from Kanski JJ. *Clinical Ophthalmology: A Systematic Approach.* 3rd ed. Oxford: Butterworth-Heinemann; 1994:100.)

The human cornea has a rich afferent innervation. The long posterior ciliary nerves (branches of the ophthalmic division of cranial nerve V_1) penetrate the cornea in three planes: scleral, episcleral, and conjunctival. Peripherally, approximately 70–80 branches of the long posterior ciliary nerves enter the cornea and lose their myelin sheath 1–2 mm from the limbus. A plexus posterior to Bowman's layer sends branches anteriorly into the epithelium.

Oxygen is provided to the epithelium by the preocular tear film and to the stroma and endothelium from the aqueous humor. The primary metabolic substrate for the epithelial cells, keratocytes, and endothelium is glucose. Glucose is provided to the stroma primarily from the aqueous humor by carrier-mediated transport through the endothelium and to the epithelium by passive diffusion through the stroma. The preocular tear film and limbal vessels supply approximately 10% of the glucose used by the cornea; however, this pathway is not adequate to maintain normal physiologic function of epithelial and stromal cells. Glucose is metabolized through glycolysis and the hexose monophosphate shunt (Fig XI-2). Approximately 85% of glucose is metabolized to lactate through glycolysis, and 15% becomes pyruvate and enters the Krebs cycle.

Glycogen stored in basal epithelial cells is converted to glucose-1-phosphate for catabolism when the corneal epithelium is traumatized or deprived of oxygen. The cornea consumes O_2 and produces CO_2 at rates commensurate with free diffusion of gases.

Epithelium

The epithelium is about 35 μm thick, and its hydrophobic character is a result of the lipid content of the plasma membranes of the epithelial cells. Hydrophilic molecules penetrate the epithelium poorly, but they may pass through intercellular tight junctions if the polar molecule is <500 daltons in apparent molecular mass. Knowing the ionic dissociation constant of a molecule is important for determining its permeability across the cornea. In order to diffuse across the epithelium, organic molecules should exist in an uncharged state. However, penetration of the stroma is more readily achieved by a charged molecule. Therefore, to penetrate the cornea and enter the anterior chamber, an organic molecule should be able to dissociate at physiologic pH and temperature, i.e., within the stroma.

When the epithelium is abraded, necrosis of the injured cells at the wound margin occurs. A shift to anaerobic metabolism causes glycogen depletion from the adjacent epithelial cells. If most of the corneal epithelium is destroyed (approximately 95%), the conjunctival epithelium becomes the source of new epithelium and healing is prolonged. An intact basal lamina is essential for wound healing. When the basal lamina is interrupted, wound healing is prolonged (>6 weeks).

Bowman's Layer

Bowman's layer is immediately posterior to the epithelial basal lamina. This layer is 12 μm thick and is composed of randomly packed Type I collagen fibers of 25 nm diameter. These fibers are enmeshed in a glycosaminoglycan (GAG) matrix, which provides plasticity and structural support. Immunochemical studies demonstrate the presence of fibronectin, which is enriched at the transition zone between Bowman's layer and the stroma. Bowman's layer is secreted during embryogenesis by the anterior stromal keratocytes. It is acellular, and anterior keratocytes do not repair damage to this layer after initial formation. Thus, it does not regenerate when damaged.

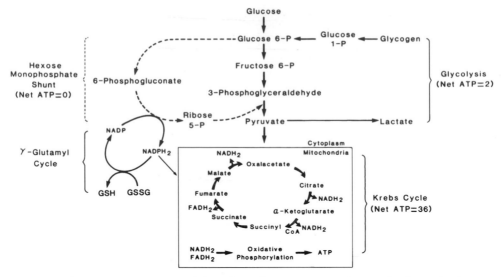

FIG XI-2—Schematic representation of the relationship among cytoplasmic glycolysis, the hexose monophosphate shunt, the γ-glutamyl cycle, and the mitochondrial Krebs cycle. GSH is reduced glutathione; GSSG is oxidized glutathione. (Reproduced with permission from Anderson RE, ed. *Biochemistry of the Eye.* San Francisco: American Academy of Ophthalmology; 1983:25.)

During photorefractive keratectomy (PRK) with the excimer laser, small amounts of tissue are removed from the anterior corneal surface so that the anterior dome of the cornea becomes flatter. Removal of about 10 μm of tissues corrects 1.0 D of myopia (Fig XI-3). Persistent blurring may occur after PRK, and its cause is not well understood at this time. See also BCSC Section 8, *External Disease and Cornea.*

Stroma

The stroma (500 μm) makes up 90% of the corneal thickness and is primarily composed of collagen fibers that measure 24–30 nm in diameter. The collagen fibers, which are enmeshed in a mucopolysaccharide matrix, form lamellar sheets that lie parallel to the corneal surface. Parallel fibers in one lamella are at oblique angles to those in an adjacent lamella. Each lamella is continuous across the cornea and is 1.5–2.5 μm thick and 9–260 μm wide. The regular packing and equal spacing of the collagen fibers allows the cornea to transmit 98% of the incoming light.

Four types of collagen are present in the stroma. Normal stromal fibers are Type I collagen, which was originally thought to be identical to Type I skin collagen. Recent evidence indicates that corneal Type I collagen is more extensively glycosylated (52%), and different genes have been identified for these two Type I collagens. Type I represents 50%–55% of the total in corneal stroma.

Types III, V, and VI are also present in the stroma. Type III collagen production is associated uniquely with stromal wound healing, and it represents less than 1%

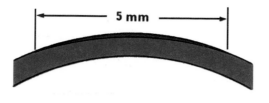

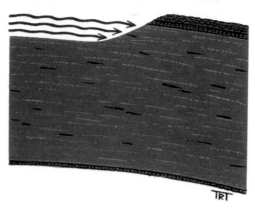

FIG XI-3—Part of the cornea removed with photorefractive keratectomy. (Reproduced with permission from Kanski JJ. *Clinical Ophthalmology: A Systematic Approach*. 3rd ed. Oxford: Butterworth-Heinemann; 1994:144.)

of the total. Type V represents 8%–10%. Type VI, which represents 25%–30% of the total, is unusual since it contains extensive interchain disulfide linkages and large globular domains, one of which is a 140-kD glycoprotein. It may be involved in the development of transparency in neonatal cornea. Types I–III and V are the classical types, but there are also eight, more recently described collagens (see Table XV-1, p 339).

The remainder of the stroma consists of proteoglycans, which are made of glycosaminoglycans (GAGs) that are covalently linked to a core protein. Corneal GAGs consist of keratan sulfate (KS) (65% of total) and dermatan sulfate/chondroitin sulfate (DS/CS) (35% of total). Two types of each of the GAGs have been identified. KS is a heteropolysaccharide that contains N-acetylglucosamine, galactose, and sulfate KS I is unique to the cornea, having aspartate as its principal amino acid, and it differs from cartilaginous KS II. If GAG catabolism is altered, corneal opacification is seen clinically, as is the case with the mucopolysaccharidoses and the mucolipidoses.

When the stroma is injured, the epithelium and keratocytes secrete collagenase, which disrupts the collagen fibers. Stromal collagen degradation is mediated by the interplay of these collagenases and collagenase inhibitor substances also secreted by the corneal epithelium. The keratocytes become fibroblastic, phagocytize the necrotic debris, and undergo shifts in GAG and collagen synthesis. Injured keratocytes secrete Type III collagen, with the peak synthesis occurring at about 2 weeks post-injury. Reversion to synthesis of Type I collagen occurs at about 2 months. In stromal scar formation, increased amino acid glycosylation and a shift of the major biosynthetic cross-linking pathways alter fiber diameter and interfiber spacing, resulting in decreased stromal transparency. See also BCSC Section 4, *Ophthalmic Pathology and Intraocular Tumors,* chapter III, Ophthalmic Wound Healing, Surgical Complications, and Trauma.

Descemet's Membrane

Descemet's membrane is a basal lamina secreted by the endothelium. The most anterior layer is secreted during fetal development. This layer is differentiated from the adult layers by its banding pattern, as observed by electron microscopy. At birth Descemet's membrane is a banded region, 3–4 μm thick (anterior banded zone), that progressively increases in thickness by addition to its posterior surface throughout life (posterior nonbanded zone). The adult membrane is 10–12 μm thick. Descemet's membrane is composed of Type IV collagen in various self-assembly patterns in numerous strata. Traumatized endothelial cells that are undergoing fibroblastic changes secrete bursts of Type IV collagen with concomitant thickening of Descemet's membrane.

Endothelium

At birth the endothelium is a single layer, 5 μm thick, of approximately 1 million postmitotic, hexagonally packed cells. With aging the number of endothelial cells decreases, with a concomitant spreading and thinning of the remaining cells. The endothelial cytoplasm contains rough endoplasmic reticulum, a well-developed Golgi apparatus, and numerous mitochondria and pinocytotic vesicles. A band of tight junctions forms the apical junctional complex between cells, which occludes the lateral extracellular spaces from the aqueous humor. Approximately 20–30 short microvilli per cell extend from the apical plasma membrane into the aqueous humor.

The endothelium functions as a permeability barrier between the aqueous humor and the corneal stroma and as a pump to maintain the cornea in a partially dehydrated state. Water is pumped across the endothelial apical plasma membrane into the aqueous humor in an energy-dependent process. The endothelium derives oxygen from the aqueous humor, which has a low oxygen tension. Elevating the aqueous humor pO_2 increases pO_2 tensions in the stroma and basal epithelial cells but not at the corneal surface. Therefore, the aqueous humor cannot supply the corneal epithelium with oxygen. In vivo, the endothelium derives sufficient oxygen from the aqueous humor to maintain normal pump function.

All human cells possess a pump in which Na^+/K^+-ATPase transfers sodium (and water) to the extracellular space and potassium to the intracellular space. However, the corneal pump is more complicated (Fig XI-4). It has seven major components, which are listed in the caption of Figure XI-4. Through these mechanisms, fluid is pumped from the stroma (S) across the endothelium (E) and into the aqueous humor (*). A thorough description of the corneal pump is given on page 38 of the Academy manual *Biochemistry of the Eye.*

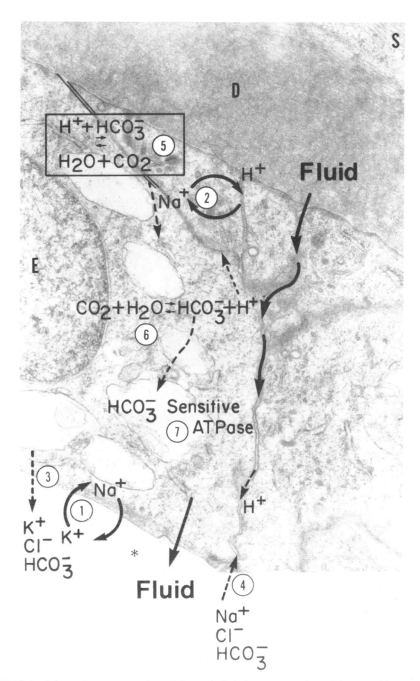

FIG XI-4—Schematic representation of the endothelial pump, as adapted from Fischbarg and Lim and superimposed on an electron micrograph (×25,000) of the corneal endothelium of a proband with Smith-Lemli-Opitz syndrome, in which mitochondrial atrophy and bloating occur at sites of active transport. S, stroma; D, Descemet's membrane; E, endothelium; (*), anterior chamber. Seven components of the endothelial pump are diagrammed: (1) Na^+/K^+ ionic pump at the aqueous surface; (2) Na^+/H^+ ionic pump at the lateral plasma membrane; (3) passive diffusion of K^+, Cl^-, and HCO_3^- into the aqueous humor; (4) passive diffusion of Na^+, Cl^-, HCO_3^- from the aqueous humor across the apical junctional complex into the extracellular space; (5) reactions in the extracellular space between H^+ and HCO_3^-, producing CO_2 which passively diffuses into the endothelial cytoplasm; (6) cytoplasmic carbonic anhydrase reactions that produce HCO_3^- (which diffuses into the mitochondria) and H^+ (which diffuses into the extracellular space); and (7) a mitochondrial HCO_3^- sensitive ATPase. (Reproduced with permission from Anderson RE, ed. *Biochemistry of the Eye*. San Francisco: American Academy of Ophthalmology; 1983:39.)

CHAPTER XII

Iris–Ciliary Body

The iris and the ciliary body are two highly specialized separate tissues that are difficult to separate mechanically in the majority of experimental animals used for models. The *ciliary body* overlaps the iris and is tightly bound to it. The *iris* is a highly pigmented tissue that functions as a delicate and movable diaphragm between the anterior and posterior chambers of the eye, regulating the amount of light reaching the retina. It is a dynamic structure, capable of precise and rapid changes in pupillary diameter in response to both light and specific pharmacologic stimuli. The ciliary body regulates the composition and production of aqueous humor and affects the ionic environment and metabolism of the lens, cornea, and trabecular meshwork. These functional activities require morphobiochemical changes within the ciliary body to accommodate for both the rapid changes in surface area from constriction to dilation and for the movement of ions.

The following section describes biochemical aspects of the iris–ciliary body such as aqueous humor formation, eicosanoids, and membrane signal transduction and second messenger systems. Chapter III of Part 1 of this volume, Anatomy, discusses and illustrates all of the various structures mentioned in this chapter.

Aqueous Humor Dynamics

Ocular fluids are separated from blood by barriers formed by tight junctions between epithelial and endothelial cells. These barriers are called either *blood–aqueous* or *blood–retina*, depending on their location in the eye. Because of these barriers, the composition and amounts of all materials entering and leaving the eye can be carefully controlled, except for exit through Schlemm's canal. Perturbations in these blood–ocular barriers result in mixing of blood constituents with the ocular fluids and may be the cause of plasmoid aqueous, retinal exudates, retinal edema, and other conditions.

Aqueous humor enters the posterior chamber from the ciliary processes by means of four physiological mechanisms:

□ Diffusion

□ Ultrafiltration

□ Carbonic anhydrase II (CA II) activity

□ Active secretion

Diffusion and ultrafiltration are passive, whereas both CA II and secretion are active energy-requiring processes. *Diffusion* involves movement of ions like sodium across a membrane toward the side with the most negative potential. *Ultrafiltration* is that nonenzymatic component of aqueous formation that is dependent on intraocular pressure (IOP), on the blood pressure, and on the blood osmotic pressure in the ciliary body. *CA II* in humans is present in pigmented and nonpigmented epithelium, and its inhibitors cause a reduction in the rate of entry of sodium and bicarbonate in the posterior aqueous, leading to a reduction in aqueous flow. The formation of aqueous humor is largely a product of *active secretion* by the inner, nonpigmented ciliary epithelium involving membrane-associated Na^+,K^+-ATPase.

The following observations support the involvement of active-transport mechanisms in secretion:

- Aqueous concentrations of Na^+, K^+, Cl^-, *myo*-inositol, certain amino acids, and glucose are maintained by specific active-transport systems located in the ciliary epithelium.

- The high level of ascorbic acid in the aqueous humor suggests that there is an active pump mechanism for its secretion into the aqueous.

- Both the iris and ciliary body accumulate p-aminohippuric acid from the aqueous against a concentration gradient (the accumulation shows saturation kinetics; is inhibited at 0°C; and is depressed by cyanide, dinitrophenol, ouabain, iodopyracet, and probenecid).

- The low protein concentration of aqueous humor relative to serum results from exclusion of large molecules by the blood–aqueous barrier. The presence of such a barrier requires active-transport systems either for moving substances across the cellular layer into the eye or for their removal from the aqueous humor.

- The rate of aqueous humor formation differs between species, being about 2 μl/min in humans and 3–4 μl/min in rabbits. IOP is maintained by steady aqueous formation and drainage, which allows the surrounding tissues to remove waste products of metabolism. Inhibitors of enzymatic processes decrease aqueous humor inflow by different amounts and thus provide additional evidence for active secretory processes. Carbonic anhydrase inhibitors and beta blockers (discussed below) are used systemically and topically in the treatment of glaucoma to reduce the rate of aqueous humor formation. See Part 5, chapter XXI, of this volume, Ocular Pharmacology, and BCSC Section 10, *Glaucoma,* for more detail.

Eicosanoids

Eicosanoids, which include prostaglandins (PGs), prostacyclin, thromboxanes, and leukotrienes, are an important family of compounds with hormonal activity. They are synthesized as a result of phospholipase A_2 stimulation that causes the release of arachidonic acid (20:4ω-6) from membrane glycerolipids (Fig XII-1). These agents affect both the male and female reproductive systems, the gastrointestinal system, the cardiovascular and renal systems, the nervous system, and the eye. Prostacyclin (PGI_2) and thromboxane A_2 (TXA_2) are natural biological antagonists. PGI_2, which is synthesized mainly in endothelial cells of vascular tissues, is a potent vasodilator, a potent platelet-antiaggregating agent, and a stimulator of adenylate cyclase. In contrast, TXA_2, which is synthesized mainly by platelets, is a potent vasoconstrictor and a platelet-aggregating agent.

PGs have profound effects on inflammation in the eye, aqueous humor dynamics, and blood–ocular barrier functions. PGs of the E and F types and arachidonic acid, when administered intracamerally or topically at high concentrations, cause miosis, an elevation of IOP, an increase in aqueous protein content, and the entry of white cells into the aqueous and tear fluid. Evidence indicates that some antiglau-

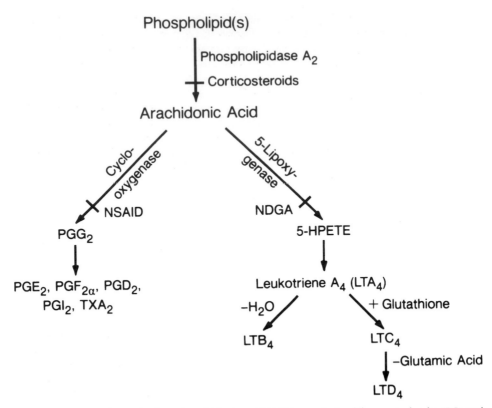

FIG XII-1—Enzymatic conversion of arachidonic acid (AA) to products of the prostaglandin (PG) and leukotriene (LT) pathways. Hydrolysis of esterified AA from cellular phospholipids (phosphoinositides and other phospholipids) by phospholipidase A_2 is the first rate-limiting step in the eicosanoid pathway. It can be inhibited by corticosteroids such as dexamethasone. The cyclo-oxygenase pathway (inhibited by nonsteroidal anti-inflammatory drugs such as indomethacin and aspirin) results in the formation of the endoperoxides (PGG_2 and PGH_2). Further conversion of endoperoxides to other metabolites is cell- and tissue-specific. TXA_2 and PGI_2 are measured as their end products, TXB_2 and 6-keto-$PGF_{2\alpha}$, respectively. The 5-lipoxygenase pathway (inhibited by nordihydroguairetic acid [NDGA]) results in the formation of the leukotrienes.

coma drugs such as epinephrine may affect IOP by influencing the production of PGs. More recently, PGs, other eicosanoids, and their derivatives have been found to be potentially useful as antiglaucoma agents. Several reports indicate that moderate and low doses of PGE_2 and $PGF_{2\alpha}$ reduce IOP in several species, including rabbits, cats, and monkeys. $PGF_{2\alpha}$ has also been shown to reduce IOP in humans. For example, latanaprost, a $PGF_{2\alpha}$ receptor agonist currently available, has been shown to decrease IOP by 30%.

The release of arachidonic acid can be brought about by a wide variety of stimuli: inflammatory, immunologic, neural, chemical, or simple mechanical agitation.

The free arachidonic acid reacts either with cyclo-oxygenase (also known as PG synthetase), the first enzyme of the PG biosynthetic sequence, or with lipoxygenase to generate hydroperoxy fatty acids. In the cyclo-oxygenase reaction the released arachidonate is converted into endoperoxides (PGG_2 and PGH_2) by the membrane-bound cyclo-oxygenase. The endoperoxides are then converted to thromboxane A_2 by thromboxane synthetase or to various PGs by isomerase or reductase enzymes.

PG biosynthesis from arachidonic acid can be blocked by most nonsteroidal anti-inflammatory drugs (NSAIDs) such as indomethacin and aspirin. The NSAIDs bind irreversibly to the cyclo-oxygenase enzyme. Topical NSAIDs have been used in the treatment of anterior segment inflammation, aphakic and pseudophakic cystoid macular edema, allergic conjunctivitis, and pain after refractive surgery. Flurbiprofen 0.03% (Ocufen) does not dilate the pupil on its own, and suprofen 1% (Profenal) drops are used preoperatively for the prevention of prostaglandin-mediated pupillary miosis during ocular surgery. Diclofenac 0.1% (Voltaren) has been approved for the treatment of postoperative inflammation following cataract extraction. Ketorolac tromethamine 0.05% (Acular) is indicated for the relief of itching from allergic conjunctivitis.

Jampol LM. Nonsteroidal anti-inflammatory drugs: 1997 update. In: *Focal Points: Clinical Modules for Ophthalmologists*. San Francisco: American Academy of Ophthalmology; 1997;15:6.

The leukotrienes are another group of compounds that are formed from arachidonic acid by a variety of tissues. Their formation in ocular tissues through the lipoxygenase pathway has not yet been thoroughly investigated. Leukotrienes C_4 and D_4 have recently been identified as the major active constituents of the slow-reacting substance of anaphylaxis (SRS-A). These compounds are powerful smooth muscle contractors that alter muscle permeability. They are much more active than histamine. NSAIDs do not inhibit lipoxygenase, but nordihydroguairetic acid (NDGA) does. BCSC Section 9, *Intraocular Inflammation and Uveitis*, discusses these processes in detail in Part I, Immunology.

Neurotransmitters and Receptors

In the iris–ciliary body the sphincter muscle and the ciliary muscles are innervated by the third cranial (oculomotor) nerve (parasympathetic), and cholinergic impulses are transmitted to the muscle by acetylcholine (ACh). In the ciliary processes non-medulated nerve fibers, many of them adrenergic, can be found surrounding the blood vessels. The dilator muscle fibers of the iris are innervated by the sympathetic nerves from the superior cervical ganglion, and the adrenergic nerve impulses are transmitted to the muscle cells by norepinephrine (NE). The neurons that synthesize, store, and release ACh are called *cholinergic neurons;* and those that synthesize, store, and release NE are called *adrenergic neurons.*

There are also two major types of autonomic receptors: *cholinergic receptors* receive input from cholinergic neurons, and *adrenergic receptors* from adrenergic neurons. These receptors are further divided as shown in Table XII-1. In the iris–ciliary body both the iris sphincter and the ciliary muscle are of the cholinergic muscarinic receptor type, and the iris dilator is mainly of the alpha-adrenergic receptor type.

Table XII-1

Cholinergic and Adrenergic Receptors

RECEPTORS	AGONISTS	BLOCKING AGENTS
Cholinergic (sphincter)	Acetylcholine	
Muscarinic	Muscarine	Atropine
Nicotinic	Nicotine	d-Tubocurarine
Adrenergic (dilator)	Norepinephrine	
Alpha*	Phenylephrine	Phentolamine and phenoxybenzamine
Alpha$_1$	Phenylephrine	Prazosin, thymoxamine, dapiprazole
Alpha$_2$	Apraclonidine	Yohimbine
Beta	Isoproterenol	Propranolol and timolol
Beta$_1$	Tazolol	Betaxolol
Beta$_2$	Albuterol	Butoxamine

The cholinergic agonists and the adrenergic blockers listed cause miosis; the adrenergic agonists and the cholinergic blockers listed cause dilation.

*The prefixes α_1 and α_2 have been proposed for post- and presynaptic α-adrenoceptors, respectively. According to the present view, the classification into α_1 and α_2 subtypes is based exclusively upon the relative potencies and affinities of agonists and antagonists, regardless of their function and localization.

Miotics

Miotics act either by stimulating the sphincter (cholinergic agonists) or by blocking the dilator (adrenergic blockers).

Stimulators   Sphincter stimulators produce responses similar to ACh. They contract the sphincter, resulting in an increase in pupillary contraction, and the ciliary muscles, resulting in accommodation. Sphincter activity can be affected by two mechanisms:

▫ Direct action on the muscles through ACh, carbachol, and pilocarpine

▫ Inhibition of acetylcholinesterase (AChE) either reversibly with physostigmine (Eserine) or neostigmine (Prostigmin), or irreversibly with diisopropyl fluorophosphate (DFP) or echothiophate iodide (Phospholine)

The AChE inhibitors allow ACh to accumulate at the parasympathetic third nerve endings and to produce accommodative spasm.

Blockers   Two mechanisms for the action of dilator blockers are available:

▫ Inhibition of the release of norepinephrine at the myoneural junction by guanethidine (Ismelin), which acts by depleting NE stores at the nerve terminals (once these stores are depleted, miosis ensues)

▫ Blockage of the alpha-adrenergic receptors of the dilator muscle by thymoxamine, dapiprazole, phenoxybenzamine, dibenamine, or phentolamine, which prevent contraction and produce miosis

The pupillary dilator muscle has predominantly alpha-adrenergic receptors, whereas the ciliary muscle is under parasympathetic control. Thymoxamine and dapiprazole are selective alpha₁-adrenergic blocking agents and can cause miosis through dilator muscle paralysis without affecting the ciliary muscle–controlled facility of outflow, IOP, or amplitude of accommodation. Thymoxamine has been advocated for many uses but is not commercially available in the United States. Dapiprazole is commercially available for reversal of pupillary dilation after pharmacologic mydriasis. With thymoxamine and dapiprazole the pupil returns to its predilated state in 30 min versus 3–4 hours without these agents. Angle-closure glaucoma will not be prevented with these agents, but they move the pupil through the more dangerous mid-dilated state more quickly.

Mydriatics

Mydriatics act by stimulating the dilator (adrenergic agonists) or by blocking the sphincter (cholinergic blockers).

Stimulators   Dilator stimulators increase dilator activity in three ways:

◻ By increasing NE release, as with hydroxyamphetamine, which causes NE to be released rapidly, thus resulting in mydriasis

◻ By interfering with NE reuptake, as with cocaine, which in addition to acting as a local anesthetic prevents NE reuptake (inactivation) and thus prolongs or potentiates the action of released NE

◻ By directly stimulating the alpha receptors of the dilator, as with phenylephrine (Neo-Synephrine)

Blockers   An adrenergic agent is only mydriatic, but an anticholinergic is mydriatic and cycloplegic. An effective anticholinergic (sphincter-blocking) agent that produces both mydriasis and cycloplegia is atropine, which blocks the action of ACh and pilocarpine at the muscle. Its effects are long lasting. A drug that produces rapid cycloplegia but has a relatively short action is tropicamide. Cyclopentolate is a blocker of intermediate duration.

Calcium Channels and Channel Blockers

Calcium channels are membrane-bound receptors that contain multiple subunits, one of which is the active site for binding of calcium channel blockers. Calcium plays a major role in influencing cellular function, and the most common pathway for entry in cells is through the calcium channels. Six subclasses of calcium channel blockers have been identified: L, T, N, P, Q, and R. The L-type blocker is predominant in skeletal, cardiac, and vascular smooth muscle. Calcium channel blockers bind to membrane-bound calcium channels and inhibit the influx of extracellular calcium in vascular smooth muscle, thereby causing direct arteriolar vasodilation and depression of myocardial contractility. They are widely used for treatment of hypertension, and they do not affect glucose tolerance, lipoproteins, uric acid, or serum electrolytes in therapeutic doses. Topically applied calcium channel blockers lower IOP. Since normal-tension glaucoma may be associated with vasospastic disease, calcium channel blockers may play a role in the treatment of this poorly understood condition. See also BCSC Section 10, *Glaucoma*.

Netland PA, Erickson KA. Calcium channel blockers in glaucoma management. *Ophthalmol Clin North Am.* 1995;8:327–334.

Varadi G, Mori Y, Mikala G, et al. Molecular determinants of Ca^{2+} channel function and drug action. *Trends Pharmacol Sci.* 1995;16:43–49.

Signal Transduction in the Iris–Ciliary Body

The concept that most drugs, hormones, and neurotransmitters produce their biological effects by interacting with receptors has been substantiated in the past few years by the isolation and identification of various receptors and their subtypes. Receptors for neurotransmitters and peptide hormones are located on the surface of the cell, whereas receptors for steroid hormones are intracellular. The iris–ciliary body contains adrenergic, muscarinic, cholinergic, peptidergic, prostaglandin, serotonin, and purinergic receptors. Membrane receptors have several characteristics:

☐ They are responsible for transmitting the signal across the membrane by recognizing molecules such as hormones, peptides, drugs, and neurotransmitters, which are the first messengers, or *ligands*

☐ They are specific for agonists or hormones that can cause positive and negative responses (different cells can have different responses to the same messenger)

☐ The number of receptors occupied by ligands determines the response of the cell

Receptor–Effector Coupling

Signal transduction across the plasma membrane occurs by several basic mechanisms. They include

☐ Ligand-gated ion channels: A ligand (e.g., neurotransmitters such as glycine, glutamate, γ-aminobutyric acid) binds to a receptor that functions as an ion channel and causes it to open, allowing cations in the cells

☐ Receptors that have integral enzyme activity such as tyrosine-kinase

☐ G protein–coupled receptors activate effector proteins, which include ion channels and enzymes (Fig XII-2).

G protein–coupled receptors involve a cascade of three steps: A stimulus excites a receptor protein to activate a G protein, which in turns activates an effector protein (E). The effector proteins shown in Figure XII-2 are usually second enzymes such as adenylyl cyclase (AC), phospholipase C, phospholipase A_2, or phosphodiesterase (PDE). They produce second messengers like cyclic nucleotides (cAMP, cGMP) and lipid-derived molecules (prostaglandins, discussed above, and IP_3 and DAG, discussed below). Rhodopsin, one of the most studied G protein–coupled receptors, is discussed in detail on pp 346–353.

Cyclic AMP and Polyphosphoinositide Turnover

In the past decade the concept has emerged that the primary control for many intracellular events is the concentration of free Ca^{2+} in the cytosol. Many Ca^{2+}-mobilizing hormones and neurotransmitters, such as ACh, NE, and $PGF_{2\alpha}$, act by changing the intracellular Ca^{2+} concentration $[Ca^{2+}]_i$. Recently, much attention has been focused on phosphatidyl-inositol-4,5-bisphosphate (PIP_2) turnover and its role in the regulation of $[Ca^{2+}]_i$. PIP_2 is hydrolyzed by phospholipase C into inositol 1,4,5-triphosphate (IP_3) and diacylglycerol (DAG) (Fig XII-3), which have a physiological

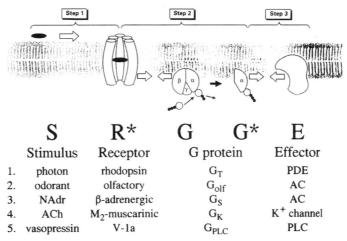

S	R*	G	G*	E
Stimulus	**Receptor**	**G protein**		**Effector**
1. photon	rhodopsin	G_T		PDE
2. odorant	olfactory	G_{olf}		AC
3. NAdr	β-adrenergic	G_S		AC
4. ACh	M_2-muscarinic	G_K		K^+ channel
5. vasopressin	V-1a	G_{PLC}		PLC

FIG XII-2—Receptor/G protein cascades typically involve three steps. *Step 1*, Stimulus S excites receptor protein R, *step 2*, which enzymatically activates a G protein G, *step 3*, which in turn activates an effector protein E. Examples of stimulus, receptor, G protein, and effector are given for five typical cascades: 1, photoreceptor; 2, olfactory receptor; 3, β-adrenergic receptor; 4, muscarinic receptor; 5, vasopressin receptor. (From *Biochemistry 3/E* by Stryer. ©1988 by Lubert Stryer. Used with permission of W.H. Freeman and Company.)

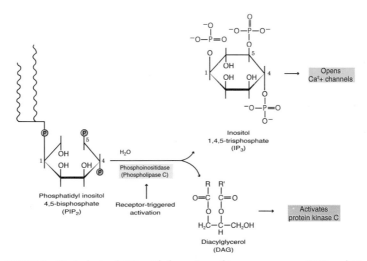

FIG XII-3—Hydrolysis of PIP_2 with formation of two messengers, DAG and IP_3.

role as second messengers. IP_3 opens Ca^{2+} channels, triggering smooth muscle contraction, glycogen breakdown, and exocytosis. DAG activates protein kinase C, which phosphorylates serine and threonine residues in many proteins. For example, phosphorylation of glycogen synthetase by protein kinase C inhibits synthesis of glycogen. Thus protein kinase C complements IP_3-induced glycogen breakdown mediated by increase in cytosolic Ca^{2+}.

In the iris sphincter, as well as in other types of smooth muscle, activation of Ca^{2+}-mobilizing (e.g., muscarinic) receptors leads to IP_3 production, Ca^{2+} mobilization, and muscle contraction. In contrast, activation of β-adrenergic receptors leads to cAMP formation, reduction in intracellular Ca^{2+} concentration, and muscle relaxation.

The IP_3-DAG-Ca^{2+} signaling system contains a number of potential target sites for the regulation of smooth muscle tension responses. Sites of interaction between the two second messenger systems are possible, leading to the formation of IP_3 and DAG and the subsequent increase in intracellular Ca^{2+} concentrations, which results in contraction of the muscle. Contraction-relaxation responses are regulated by increases in the level of cAMP. In the iris sphincter PGs can trigger either IP_3 production and muscle contraction or cAMP formation and muscle relaxation, depending on the species, cell types, and different tissues.

It is possible that these two transduction systems are coupled to different PG receptor subtypes or different G proteins, or that one of them is deficient or masked in certain species. Short-term desensitization of $PGF_{2\alpha}$ receptors in the bovine iris sphincter, in a species that produces very few PGs, increases cAMP formation and reduces IP_3 production and muscle contraction. These effects of PGs demonstrate functional and biochemical interactions between the IP_3-DAG-Ca^{2+} and cAMP messenger systems in the iris of the mammalian eye. Such interactions between the two signaling systems could constitute the biochemical basis for the multiple functions observed for PGs in a wide variety of systems. Ample evidence now suggests that the sympathetic nervous system can regulate or inhibit, through alterations in cAMP concentrations, the cholinergic stimulation of IP_3 production and muscle contraction. In spite of the large amount of effort made in this area of research, information about the exact loci and the molecular mechanisms underlying the antagonistic and synergistic interactions between the two signaling pathways remains scanty.

Abdel-Latif AA. Minireview: Cross talk between cAMP and the polyphosphoinositide signalling cascade in iris sphincter and other nonvascular smooth muscle. *Proc Soc Exp Biol Med.* 1996;211:163–177.

CHAPTER XIII

Aqueous Humor

The aqueous humor may be considered a substitute blood supply for the avascular lens, cornea, and trabecular meshwork. It contains all the nutrients essential to these tissues and removes all their waste products. It is devoid of all blood cells and of more than 99% of the plasma proteins and, hence, provides an optically clear medium for transmission of light along the visual path. Aqueous humor is derived by secretion, ultrafiltration, and diffusion of components of the ciliary blood supply. The ciliary epithelium is the filtering mechanism that forms the blood–aqueous barrier and is the site of the selective active-transport systems. Aqueous humor composition is in a dynamic equilibrium determined by its rate of production and outflow and by continuous exchanges with the tissues of the anterior segment. It contains

- Inorganic ions and organic anions
- Carbohydrates
- Glutathione and urea
- Proteins
- Growth modulatory factors
- Oxygen and carbon dioxide

Inorganic Ions

The concentrations of sodium, potassium, and magnesium in the aqueous are similar to those in plasma, but the level of calcium is only half that of plasma. The two major anions are chloride and bicarbonate. In some species their concentrations in the aqueous are as much as 20%–30% above and below (in inverse ratios) those in the plasma. Phosphate is also present in the aqueous at an aqueous:plasma ratio of about 0.5 or less, but its concentration is too low to have any significant buffering capacity. Iron, copper, and zinc are all found in the aqueous humor at concentrations of approximately 1 mg/ml, essentially the same as the levels in plasma.

Organic Anions

Lactate is the most abundant of organic anions in the aqueous, and its concentration is always higher than that in plasma. A direct relationship between plasma and aqueous levels of lactate is apparent, and the contribution resulting from the glycolytic metabolism of intraocular tissues is significant. Ascorbic acid (vitamin C) is perhaps the most unique constituent of the aqueous humor. In most mammalian species its concentration ranges from 0.6 to 1.5 mM, levels that are some 10–50 times higher than in the plasma. Ascorbic acid is an important antioxidant both for the aqueous humor and for the tissues of the anterior segment.

Carbohydrates

Glucose concentration in the aqueous is roughly 70% of that in plasma. The rate of entry of glucose into the posterior chamber is much more rapid than would be expected by its size and lipid solubility, suggesting that its passage across the ciliary epithelium occurs by facilitated diffusion. Saturation studies have demonstrated that a specific carrier is involved, but no evidence of active transport has been detected, nor has insulin been found to affect the entry of glucose into the aqueous. Aqueous glucose levels are increased in diabetic individuals, leading to higher concentrations in the lens. Inositol, important for phospholipid synthesis in the anterior segment, occurs at a concentration about 10 times that in plasma.

Glutathione and Urea

Glutathione, an important tripeptide with a reactive sulfhydryl group, is found in the aqueous humor. Its concentration in primates ranges from 1 to 10 μM. Blood contains a high concentration of glutathione, but virtually all resides within the erythrocytes, and plasma has only a low concentration of 5 μM or less. While aqueous glutathione may be derived by diffusion from the blood or by an active-transport system in the ciliary epithelium analogous to that of the lens, it probably also arises by loss from the lens and cornea. Glutathione acts as a stabilizer of the redox state of the aqueous by reconverting ascorbate to its functional form following oxidation as well as by removing excess hydrogen peroxide.

The concentration of urea in the aqueous is between 80% and 90% of that in the plasma. This compound is distributed passively across nearly all biological membrane systems, and its high aqueous:plasma ratio indicates that this small molecule (molecular weight of 60) crosses the epithelial barrier quite readily. Urea is effective in the hyperosmotic infusion treatment for glaucoma. However, mannitol is preferred to urea, as it crosses the barrier even more rapidly despite its higher molecular weight of 182.

Proteins

The aqueous differs from plasma chiefly in its almost complete absence of protein. In humans the normal aqueous contains about 0.02 g of protein per 100 ml, as compared to the typical plasma level of 7 g/100 ml. The vast majority of the aqueous protein is accounted for by the albumins and globulins from plasma with a higher proportion of the former because of their smaller size. Other blood proteins penetrate the blood–aqueous barrier to a very limited extent, and it should be noted that primary aqueous humor does not clot. However, activators, proenzymes, and fibrinolytic enzymes are present in the aqueous, and these may play a role in the regulation of outflow resistance. Plasminogen and plasminogen activator are both found in human and monkey aqueous, but only traces of plasmin have been reported.

In addition to the proteins mentioned above, other enzymes have been reported in the aqueous humor. Several of these are of interest chiefly because of their increased levels in certain pathological conditions, such as retinoblastoma, where tissue damage results in the release of intracellular enzymes. The frequent absence of coenzymes or substrates of such enzymes from the aqueous, as in the case of NAD for lactic dehydrogenase or of oxaloacetate for glutamic-oxaloacetic transaminase, leads to the conclusion that these enzymes have no significant catalytic role in the normal aqueous.

Three enzymes in the aqueous appear to be exceptions to this nonreactive role.

□ *Hyaluronidase* may be important in the normal regulation of the resistance to outflow through the trabecular meshwork, since injection of this enzyme into the anterior chamber has been shown to increase outflow facility in some species.

□ *Carbonic anhydrase* is present in trace amounts. Because it is an enzyme with an extremely high turnover number, even a low concentration may be significant in the catalysis of the equilibrium between bicarbonate and CO_2 plus water.

□ *Lysozyme* is found in the aqueous of the rabbit at 1 µg/ml, about 25% of the plasma level, which is a high aqueous:plasma ratio for a protein, even though its molecular mass is only 15 kD. It provides significant antibacterial protection. Most probably, the origin of lysozyme is only in part from the blood; in cases of ocular inflammation the intraocular level may be raised 10-fold or more, reaching concentrations well above those in plasma.

Growth Modulatory Factors

The physical and chemical properties of the aqueous humor have a substantial role in modulating the proliferation, differentiation, functional viability, and wound healing of ocular tissues in health and disease. These properties are largely influenced by a number of growth-promoting and differentiation factors that have been identified or quantified in aqueous humor. They include

□ Transforming growth factor–β1 and –β2 (TGF–β1 and –β2)

□ Acidic and basic fibroblast growth factor (aFGF and bFGF)

□ Insulin-like growth factor–1 (IGF–1)

□ Insulin-like growth factor binding proteins (IGFBPs)

□ Vascular endothelial growth factor (VEGF)

□ Transferrin

The growth factors in the aqueous humor perform diverse, synergistic, or sometimes opposite biological activities. Normally, the lack of significant mitosis of the corneal endothelium and trabecular meshwork in vivo is probably controlled by the complex coordination of effects and interactions among the different growth modulatory substances present in the aqueous humor (see Part 5, Ocular Pharmacology). Disruption in the balance between various growth factors that occurs with the production of plasmoid aqueous humor may explain the abnormal hyperplastic response of the lens epithelium and corneal endothelium observed in chronic inflammatory conditions and traumatic insults to the eye. Ultimately, however, the effect of a given growth factor in the aqueous humor is determined primarily by its bioavailability. Bioavailability depends on many factors, including the expression of receptors on target tissues, interactive effects with components of the extracellular matrix, and the levels of circulating and matrix-bound proteases.

The role of several growth factors has been studied in diabetic patients. IGFBPs are elevated fivefold in human diabetic patients without retinopathy, and IGF–1 levels are elevated in patients with diabetic retinopathy. This elevation suggests that the increase in vitreal IGFBPs is not the result of a preexisting endstage retinopathy but is rather an early ocular event in the diabetic process.

VEGF levels are increased not only in patients with active ocular neovascularization from proliferative diabetic retinopathy, but also after central retinal vein occlusion and with iris neovascularization. Actually, VEGF mediates the retinal vasoproliferative response to hypoxic stimuli observed in a variety of ocular ischemic diseases. Its expression is increased by hypoxia in retinal endothelial cells, retinal pericytes, Müller cells, and retinal pigment epithelium cells.

Takagi H, King GL, Ferrara N, et al. Hypoxia regulates vascular endothelial growth factor receptor *KDR/Flk* gene expression through adenosine A$_2$ receptors in retinal capillary endothelial cells. *Invest Ophthalmol Vis Sci.* 1996;37:1311–1321.

Tripathi RC, Borisuth NSC, Tripathi BJ, et al. Growth factors in the aqueous humor and their therapeutic implications in glaucoma and anterior segment disorders of the eye. *Drug Dev Res.* 1991;22:1–23.

Waldbillig RJ, Jones BE, Schoen TJ, et al. Vitreal insulin-like growth factor binding proteins (IGFBPs) are increased in human and animal diabetes. *Curr Eye Res.* 1994; 13:539–546.

Oxygen and Carbon Dioxide

Oxygen is present in the aqueous humor at a partial pressure of about 55 mm Hg, roughly one third of its concentration in the atmosphere. It is derived from the blood supply to the ciliary body and iris, for there is no net flux of oxygen from the atmosphere across the cornea. Indeed, the corneal endothelium is critically dependent upon the aqueous oxygen supply for the active fluid transport mechanism that maintains corneal transparency. The lens and the endothelial lining of the trabecular meshwork also derive their oxygen supply from the aqueous humor.

Carbon dioxide content of the aqueous humor is in the range of 40–60 mm Hg, contributing approximately 3% of the total bicarbonate. The relative proportions of CO_2 and HCO_3^- determine the pH of the aqueous, which in most species has been found to be in the range of 7.5–7.6. CO_2 is continuously lost from the aqueous by diffusion across the cornea into the tear film and atmosphere. The Na^+-K^+-Cl^- cotransporter (see Figure XI-4, p 315) is also important in the trabecular meshwork and for control of aqueous outflow.

Gong H, Tripathi RC, Tripathi BJ, et al. Morphology of the aqueous outflow pathway. *Microsc Res Tech.* 1996;33:336–367.

Clinical Implications of Breakdown of the Blood–Aqueous Barrier

With compromise of the blood–aqueous barrier in conditions such as ocular insult (trauma or intraocular surgery), uveitis, and other inflammatory disorders, the protein content of aqueous humor may increase 10–100 times, especially in the high-molecular-weight polypeptides. The levels of inflammatory mediators, immunoglobulins, fibrin, and proteases rise, and the balance among the various growth factors is disrupted (see Part 5, Ocular Pharmacology, chapter XXI). The clinical sequelae include fibrinous exudate and clot, with or without a macrophage reaction and formation of cyclitic membranes, and synechiae formation (peripheral and posterior), as well as an abnormal neovascular response, which further exacerbates breakdown of the barrier. Chronic disruption of the blood–aqueous barrier is implicated in the abnormal hyperplastic response of the lens epithelium, corneal endothelium, trabecular meshwork, and iris and in the formation of complicated cataract. Degenerative and proliferative changes may occur in various ocular structures as well. The use of anti-inflammatory steroidal and nonsteroidal drugs, cycloplegics, protease activators or inhibitors, growth and antigrowth factor agents, and even surgical intervention may be necessary in response to these events.

CHAPTER XIV

Lens

The crystalline lens forms the second refracting unit of the human eye, adding 15–20 D of plus power to the 43 D created by the cornea. As such, it must remain perfectly clear, or light will not reach the retinal sensory elements in an undisturbed state. The lens must also remain flexible to produce the accommodative changes necessary for the eye to focus at different distances. BCSC Section 11, *Lens and Cataract,* provides additional detail on the lens. This chapter discusses

□ Structural features (capsule, epithelium, cortex, and nucleus)

□ Chemical composition (fibers, various proteins)

□ Transport function (maintenance of ionic balance)

□ Metabolism (carbohydrates)

Structure of the Lens

Capsule

The lens is surrounded by a typical basement membrane known as the lens capsule. The capsule is created anteriorly by the epithelial cells and posteriorly by the cortical fibers. The capsule itself is noncellular, having a structure composed largely of glycoprotein-associated Type IV collagen. Glycosaminoglycans are also present and may play a role in organization of collagen and glycoproteins (matrix). The mucopolysaccharide heparan sulfate makes up less than 1% of the lens capsule but is considered very important in determining the structure of the matrix, which in turn is probably critical to maintaining capsule clarity. When the capsule is separated carefully from the underlying cells, it is found to be inert metabolically. Its structure is somewhat amorphous, showing a lamellar arrangement only during development.

The lens capsule acts as a barrier in keeping back the vitreous, helping to prevent postsurgical secondary open-angle glaucoma. It also acts as a barrier against fluorescein, bacteria, and growth factors. For example, the incidence of endophthalmitis following cataract surgery is decreased when the capsule remains intact. Incidence of clinical and experimental anterior segment neovascularization is also decreased. The lens capsule has been shown to be a source of antiangiogenesis factors.

Epithelium

Lens epithelial cells have the metabolic capacity to carry out all normal cell activities, including DNA, RNA, protein, and lipid biosynthesis, and to generate sufficient ATP to meet the energy needs of the lens. The epithelial cells are mitotic. The highest activity of premitotic (replicative, or S phase) DNA synthesis occurs in a ring

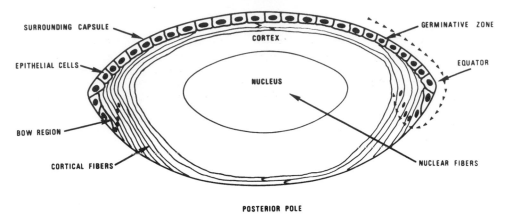

FIG XIV-1—Schematic representation of the mammalian lens in cross section. Arrowheads indicate direction of cell migration from the epithelium to the cortex. (Reproduced with permission from Anderson RE, ed. *Biochemistry of the Eye*. San Francisco: American Academy of Ophthalmology; 1983;112.)

around the anterior lens known as the *germinative zone*. These newly formed cells migrate equatorially (see the arrowheads in Figure XIV-1), where they differentiate into fibers.

Cortex and Nucleus

As the epithelial cells progress to the bow region, they change in both morphology and macromolecular synthetic activity. These cells have begun the process of terminal differentiation into *lens fibers*. Certain morphologic features become apparent immediately, the most striking of which is the increase in cell size, which is associated with a tremendous increase in the mass of cellular proteins and in the membranes of each individual fiber cell. As these two constituents increase, most other cell organelles diminish and ultimately disappear.

As the epithelial cells move to the equator and differentiate into fibers, each new fiber is laid down upon an increasing bundle of previously formed fibers. The oldest of these fibers were produced in embryonic life and persist in the very center of the lens to form the lens *nucleus.* The fibers in the outermost portion are the most recently formed and make up the *cortex* of the lens. No distinct morphological division differentiates the cortex of the lens from its nucleus; the transition from one region to the other is gradual. The overall structure resembles an onion with the oldest layers forming the center.

Chemical Composition of the Lens

Lens Fibers

The chemical composition of the lens fiber plasma membranes suggests that they are both very stable and rigid. A high content of saturated fatty acids, high cholesterol: phospholipid ratio, and high concentration of sphingomyelin all contribute to the tight packing and low fluidity of the membrane. Although lipids make up roughly only 1% of the total lens mass, they constitute about 55% of the plasma membrane dry weight, with cholesterol being the major neutral lipid. As the lens ages, the protein:lipid and cholesterol:phospholipid ratios increase, especially in the nucleus, as a result of loss of phospholipid.

Lens Proteins

The lens has a protein concentration of about 35% of its wet weight, twice that of most other tissues. The majority of these proteins are present in the lens fibers, which make up the bulk of the lens. These fiber proteins exist in two major groups: water soluble and water insoluble. The water-soluble proteins are mostly the crystallins. The water-insoluble proteins have been referred to as the *albuminoid* fraction, although this is no longer considered a meaningful term. It is now preferable to refer to these proteins as the water-insoluble fraction.

Crystallins and other water-soluble proteins   Most of the water-soluble proteins fall into one of three major groups (the α, β, and γ crystallins) that were originally defined on the basis of their chromatographic properties (Table XIV-1). More recently, the crystallins have been classified by size, electrophoretic mobility, and immunochemical properties. Gel filtration, which separates by size, yields four fractions. They have been labeled α, β_H, β_L, and γ crystallins in the mammalian lens. The avian lens contains yet another crystallin that has been designated δ crystallin.

The largest crystallin, with a molecular mass greater than 500 kD, is α crystallin. Representing about 35% of the lens proteins, the α crystallin fraction is not one discrete protein but is composed of a mixture of different-sized macromolecular aggregates of four distinct but closely related protein subunits. Studies on the primary structure of α crystallin show a marked conservation of the sequence of the polypeptide chains during evolution. Each of these subunit polypeptides has a molecular weight (MW) of about 20 kD, and the chains are held together by hydrogen bonds and hydrophobic interactions. Whereas it was always believed that crystallins are strictly lens specific, recent sequence data have led to the startling discovery that α crystallin is closely related to a ubiquitous, small, heat-shock protein first sequenced in *Drosophila*. At present, the functional relationship, if any, between α crystallin and this small, heat-shock protein is not understood. It is conceivable that the sequence homology represents a highly stable common structural unit that is necessary for protection of a protein in a stressful environment.

The most abundant (slightly less than 55% by weight) water-soluble proteins in the lens are the β crystallins. They are the most heterogeneous of the crystallins. The human β crystallin fraction separates into three fractions of different molecular weights, all of which appear to be composed of largely identical subunits. Human β crystallin has no α-helical coils, being structured instead as β-pleated sheets and random coils. Immunofluorescence has shown that β crystallins appear at about the time the cortical fibers begin to form.

TABLE XIV-1

SUMMARY OF GENERALIZED CHARACTERISTICS OF MAJOR LENS PROTEINS FROM ADULT MAMMALS

	AVERAGE MOLECULAR MASS (DALTONS)	FRACTION OF LENS PROTEINS	SUBUNITS	SITE OF FIRST APPEARANCE IN LENS
Water soluble				
α crystallin	80×10^4	35%	Multiple with MW of 20 kD (α-A_1, α-A_2, αB_1, αB_2)	In epithelium
β crystallin		55%		As cortical fibers begin to differentiate
β_H	10–55×10^4		Multiple with subunits of MW 25.0–27.5 kD	
β_L	5–8×10^4		Multiple with subunits of MW 23.5–30.5 kD	
γ crystallin	21×10^3	1.5%	Monomeric	As cortical fibers begin to differentiate
HM cystallin	$>50 \times 10^6$	Variable	α and β crystallins	Increases from cortex to nucleus
Water insoluble				
Main intrinsic polypeptide (MIP)	26×10^3 or 20×10^3	55% of membrane protein		As cortical fibers begin to differentiate

The γ crystallins are the smallest of the crystallins, having a molecular weight in the range of 21 kD. The γ crystallins make up about 1.5% of the lens proteins of the adult mammal but constitute as much as 60% of the soluble protein in weanling animals. Perhaps some of the most important advances in our understanding of the structure of the lens crystallins come from the x-ray crystallographic studies on γ crystallin. The three-dimensional structure of γ crystallin has been reported at a resolution of 1.9 Å. The structural knowledge gained from these studies provides us with important information about the stability of this structural protein.

In recent years, with advances in molecular biology, much has been learned about the various crystallins and their genes. At present, sequence data for most of the β and γ crystallins are available, and this knowledge has led to the discovery that β and γ crystallins are essentially highly homologous and related proteins. Thus, at present, both β and γ crystallins are considered to be in one large superfamily designated the βγ crystallins.

Water-insoluble proteins   The water-insoluble fraction of the lens proteins received little attention from the time of its discovery by Moerner in 1894 until Dische determined that it could be further separated into two fractions, one soluble and one insoluble in 8M urea. The *urea-insoluble fraction* contains the fiber plasma membranes with which several proteins are associated. One of these makes up nearly 50% of the membrane proteins and has come to be known as the *main intrinsic polypeptide (MIP)*. This protein, with a molecular mass of 28 kD, is cleaved to a 22-kD protein, and the relative proportions of the two proteins become about equal at 20–30 years of age. The 22-kD protein predominates in the nucleus. The MIP first appears in the lens just as the fibers begin to elongate, and it can be detected in membranes throughout the mass of the lens. It is not found in the epithelial cell at all, however, and thus seems to be associated with differentiation of the fiber cell from the epithelial cell. The MIP is concentrated in the gap junctions and is the predominant protein of junction-enriched membrane proteins. It is certainly an inherent part of the membrane, in which it has been localized by immunofluorescence.

It has been hypothesized that when lens proteins become water insoluble and aggregate, they form very large particles that scatter light, producing lens opacities. Many researchers have attempted to correlate increases in the percentage of water-insoluble proteins with increases in lens opacification, but controversy continues over this hypothesis. The water-insoluble protein fraction increases with age even if the lens remains clear. Conversion of the soluble proteins into water-insoluble proteins seems to be a natural process in lens fiber maturation. The process may, however, be accelerated or occur to excess in certain cataractous lenses.

In cataracts with marked browning of the lens nucleus (*brunescent cataracts*), the increase in the amount of insoluble protein does correlate with the degree of opacification. In severe brunescent nuclear cataracts as much as 90% of the nuclear proteins are insoluble in water. Increased protein glycation and formation of high-molecular-weight aggregates also occurs. In addition, there are associated oxidative changes, including protein-to-protein and protein–to–glutathione disulfide bond formation, decreased reduced glutathione, and increased glutathione disulfide. Membrane-associated methionine and cysteine also become oxidized.

In the young lens most of the water-insoluble proteins of the lens can be solubilized in urea. With age and especially with brunescent nuclear cataract formation, the nuclear proteins become increasingly insoluble in urea. In addition to the increases in disulfide linkages, these nuclear proteins are highly cross-linked by nondisulfide bonds. This insoluble protein fraction contains a yellow to brown protein that is found in high concentration in nuclear cataracts. Fluorescence not produced from tryptophan increases in the lens and is associated with the nondisulfide cross-links that increase in brunescent nuclear cataracts.

Transport Functions in the Lens

A specific internal ionic osmotic milieu appears to be critically important in normal lens metabolism. Maintenance of ionic balance depends on the communication between the epithelial cells and the fibers. By means of energy-requiring (active-transport) processes, internal sodium is maintained at about 20 mM and potassium at about 120 mM, whereas their respective concentrations in the aqueous humor are 150 mM and 5 mM. Because this balance is readily disrupted by the specific ATPase inhibitor ouabain, a significant portion of the gradient must be maintained by Na^+/K^+-dependent ATPases that are found at highest concentration in the epithelium. The active-transport mechanisms are lost if the capsule and attached epithelium are removed from the lens, but not if the capsule alone is removed enzymatically by collagenase. These findings support the hypothesis that the primary site for active transport in the lens lies in the epithelium.

According to the *pump-leak hypothesis,* potassium and various other molecules such as amino acids are actively transported into the anterior lens through the epithelium, and they then diffuse out with the concentration gradient through the back of the lens, where no active-transport mechanisms exist. Conversely, sodium is postulated to flow in through the back of the lens with the concentration gradient and then to be actively exchanged for potassium by the epithelium (Fig XIV-2). In support of this theory, an anteroposterior gradient was found for both ions, with potassium being most concentrated in the anterior lens and sodium being concentrated in the posterior lens. These gradients are nullified by manipulations such as refrigeration that inactivate the energy-dependent enzyme pumps.

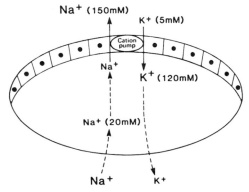

FIG XIV-2—Schematic representation of the pump-leak mechanism. Potassium is actively transported into the lens in exchange for sodium. Potassium then leaks out the back of the lens where sodium leaks in, each in accordance with the concentration gradient. (Reproduced with permission from Anderson RE, ed. *Biochemistry of the Eye.* San Francisco: American Academy of Ophthalmology; 1983:129.)

Carbohydrate Metabolism

Glucose Metabolism and Energy Production

Lens carbohydrate metabolism has become a very active area of research. Overwhelming evidence from animal studies suggests that alterations in carbohydrate utilization can lead to lens opacification. This finding raises hope that pharmaceuticals can be developed to control pathways of sugar metabolism and thus prevent the cataracts associated with diabetes and galactosemia in humans.

Most of the glucose that is transported into the lens is phosphorylated into glucose-6-phosphate (G6P) by the enzyme hexokinase (see Figure XI-2, p 312). This rate-limiting reaction is 70–1000 times slower than that of the other enzymes involved in lens glycolysis. Once formed, G6P enters two possible metabolic pathways: anaerobic glycolysis or the pentose phosphate pathway.

Anaerobic glycolysis The more active pathway is anaerobic glycolysis, which provides most of the high-energy phosphate bonds required for lens metabolism. Substrate-linked phosphorylation of ADP to ATP occurs at two steps along the way to lactate. The rate-limiting step in the glycolytic pathway itself is at the level of the enzyme phosphofructokinase, which is regulated through feedback control by metabolic products of the glycolytic pathway. This pathway is much less efficient than *aerobic glycolysis*. Anaerobic glycolysis produces only two net molecules of ATP for each glucose molecule used, whereas aerobic glycolysis produces an additional 36 molecules of ATP from each glucose molecule metabolized in the tricarboxylic acid (TCA, or Krebs) cycle (oxidative metabolism, see Figure XI-2, p 312).

Because of the low oxygen tension in the lens, only about 3% of the lens glucose passes through the TCA cycle to produce ATP. However, even this low level of aerobic metabolism still produces about 25% of the lens ATP. The ability of the lens to sustain normal metabolism in a nitrogen environment shows that it is not dependent on oxygen. Provided with ample glucose, the anoxic in vitro lens remains completely transparent, has normal levels of ATP, and maintains its ion and amino acid pump activities. In contrast, if glucose is not provided, the lens cannot maintain these functions and becomes hazy after several hours even in the presence of oxygen.

Pentose phosphate pathway, or hexose monophosphate shunt A less active pathway for utilization of G6P in the lens is the pentose phosphate pathway, or hexose monophosphate (HMP) shunt. About 5% of lens glucose is metabolized by this route, although the pathway is stimulated under oxidative stress. The activity of the HMP shunt is higher in the lens than in most tissues, but its role is far from established. As in other tissues, it may provide NADPH for fatty acid biosynthesis and ribose for nucleotide biosynthesis. It also provides NADPH necessary for glutathione reductase and aldose reductase activities in the lens. The carbohydrate products of the HMP shunt enter the glycolytic pathway and are metabolized to lactate.

Sorbitol pathway Aldose reductase is the key enzyme in yet another pathway for lens sugar metabolism, the sorbitol pathway. This enzyme has been found to play a pivotal role in the development of "sugar" cataracts. Because the $K_{m\text{-glucose}}$ (affinity constant) of this enzyme is about 700 times that of hexokinase (700×10^{-4} M versus 1×10^{-4} M), less than 5% of lens glucose is normally converted to sorbitol. As pointed out above, the phosphofructokinase reaction is rate limiting in phosphorylating glucose in the lens and is inhibited by feedback mechanisms by the products of glycolysis. Therefore, when glucose increases in the lens, the sorbitol pathway is activated relatively more than glycolysis, and sorbitol accumulates. Sorbitol is metabolized to fructose by the enzyme polyol dehydrogenase. Unfortunately, this enzyme has a relatively high $K_{m\text{-sorbitol}}$ (low affinity, 1×10^{-2} M), which means that considerable sorbitol will accumulate before it is further metabolized. This accumulation combined with poor permeability of the lens to sorbitol results in retention of sorbitol in the lens. The sorbitol pathway is shown in Figure XIV-3.

A high NADPH/NADH ratio drives the reactions in the forward direction. The accumulation of NADP that occurs as a consequence of activation of the sorbitol pathway may be the cause of the stimulation of the HMP shunt that is observed in

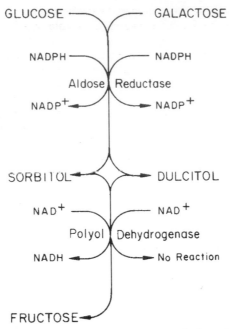

FIG XIV-3—Sorbitol pathway for glucose and galactose metabolism. The reduction of glucose and galactose to sorbitol and dulcitol, respectively, is catalyzed by aldose reductase using NADPH as cofactor. The second step is the oxidation of sorbitol only to fructose, catalyzed by polyol dehydrogenase using NAD^+ as cofactor. This step is reversible in the human lens, as indicated by the arrows. (Reproduced with permission from Berman ER. *Biochemistry of the Eye*. New York: Plenum Press; 1991:249.)

the presence of elevated lens glucose (see Figure XI-2, p 312). Along with sorbitol, fructose also builds up when a lens is incubated in high glucose. Together, these two sugars increase the osmotic pressure within the lens, drawing in water. At first the energy-dependent pumps of the lens are able to compensate, but ultimately they are overwhelmed. Swelling of the fibers, disruption of the normal architecture, and lens opacification result.

Like glucose, galactose is a substrate for aldose reductase, producing the alcohol galactitol (dulcitol). Galactitol, however, is not a substrate for polyol dehydrogenase and thus accumulates rapidly, producing the same osmotic effects as sorbitol and the same consequences. Excess production of galactitol occurs in patients who have inborn errors of metabolism of galactose, of which two disorders are known: galactose-1-phosphate uridyl transferase deficiency (*galactosemia*) and galactokinase deficiency. These disorders feature an inability to utilize galactose properly, with an accumulation of galactitol and other galactose metabolites. Galactose cataracts can also be induced experimentally by maintaining animals on diets extremely rich in galactose.

The pivotal role of aldose reductase in cataractogenesis in animals is apparent from studies on the development of sugar-induced cataracts in various species of animals. Those species that have high aldose reductase activities develop lens opacities, whereas those lacking in aldose reductase do not. In addition, specific inhibitors of this enzymatic activity, applied either systemically or topically to the eye, decrease the rate of onset and severity of sugar cataracts in experimental animals. Aldose reductase inhibitors also have potentially beneficial and harmful systemic effects. Sorbinil, an aldose reductase inhibitor that prevents retinal changes in galactosemic dogs, has proven to be too toxic for human use. Tolrestat has been shown to decrease peripheral neuropathy in diabetic patients. However, neither sorbinil nor tolrestat has improved or inhibited the progression of diabetic retinopathy in humans.

Although the role of the sorbitol pathway has been firmly established in animal models, its role in the etiology of human diabetic cataracts is still an open question. Controversy remains as to whether sorbitol and fructose levels are altered in the diabetic patient. Also, aldose reductase levels are low and polyol dehydrogenase levels are high in humans, which is opposite to animals. Studies of the kinetics of these two enzymes in humans show that their activities would not support polyol accumulation in the lens of the adult diabetic patient. In young diabetic patients, however, aldose reductase levels were found to be sufficiently high to produce an osmotic stress by retention of sorbitol that might account for the early onset of cataracts in diabetic patients. Besides polyol dehydrogenase accumulation, oxidative stress has also been implicated in the etiology of diabetic cataractogenesis (see chapter XVIII of this volume and BCSC Section 11, *Lens and Cataract,* chapter V).

Kahn CR, Weir GC, eds. *Joslin's Diabetus Mellitus.* 13th ed. Philadelphia: Lea & Febiger; 1994:682.

CHAPTER XV

Vitreous

The vitreous body is a specialized connective tissue that has two basic functions:

☐ To serve as a transparent medium occupying the major volume of the globe

☐ To absorb and redistribute forces applied to surrounding ocular tissues

The basic physical structure of the vitreous is a gel composed of a collagen framework interspersed with hydrated hyaluronic acid molecules. The hyaluronic acid contributes to the viscosity of the vitreous humor and is believed to have a stabilizing influence on the collagen network.

Composition

The vitreous contains about 98% water and 0.1% colloids. The remainder of the solid matter consists of ions and low-molecular-weight solutes. The two major structural components are collagen and hyaluronic acid (HA). A number of noncollagenous proteins and glycoproteins have also been isolated.

Collagen

The origin of vitreous collagen is not completely established. It has been shown that the cells of the vitreous body secrete a collagen precursor and glycosaminoglycans (GAGs). However, electron microscopic examination of retinal glial cells has shown that these cells produce a collagen similar to vitreal collagen throughout life, thus lending support to the theory that the vitreous is of neuroectodermal origin. Vitreous collagen was formerly classified as Type II collagen, similar to cartilage collagen. This collagen differs from the more abundant Type I collagen found in dermis, scar tissue, cornea, and sclera. Type I fibrils measure an average diameter of 67 nm with axial periodicity of 64 nm. In general, vitreous collagen fibrils are found to measure between 8 and 16 nm, with poorly visible banding periodicity. More recent biochemical studies of pepsin-solubilized vitreous collagen have not revealed patterns identical to classic Types I, II, III, or IV collagen. These studies support the view that vitreous collagen is very specific and may be the product of the neuroectoderm. The vitreous collagen fibrils are firmly anchored at the vitreous base to peripheral retina, at the pars plana of the ciliary body, and around the optic disc. The 12 types of collagen (Table XV-1) fall into three groups (Table XV-2).

Hyaluronic Acid

Hyaluronic acid is a polysaccharide (glycosaminoglycan) that has a repeating unit of glucuronic acid and N-acetyl-glucosamine linked with a β 1–3 glycosidic bond (Fig XV-1). The repeating units are linked with β 1–4 glycosidic bonds to a long, linear (unbranched) molecular chain. It is a polyanion, since the chain has a negative

TABLE XV-1

STRUCTURALLY AND GENETICALLY DISTINCT COLLAGENS

TYPE	CHAIN COMPOSITION	LOCALIZATION
I	two α1, one α2	Cornea, bone, skin
II	three α1	Vitreous, cartilage
III	three α1	Cornea, blood vessels, skin
IV	three α1, three α2	Lens capsule, cornea, all basement membranes
V	one α1, one α2, one α3	Cornea, retina, interstitial tissues
VI	one α1, one α2, one α3	Cornea, interstitial tissues
VII	three α1	Cornea, anchoring fibrils
VIII	one α1	Descemet's membrane, some endothelial cells
IX	one α1, one α2, one α3	Vitreous, cartilage
X	one α1	Cartilage
XI	not yet defined	Cartilage
XII	one α1	Tendon

TABLE XV-2

CLASSES OF COLLAGEN MOLECULES

Group 1	Chain M, $\geq$ 95,000 Continuous helical domain of $\approx$ 300 nm	Type I Type II Type III Type V Type K (1α, 2α, 3α)
Group 2	Chain M, $\geq$ 95,000 Helical domains separated by nonhelical segments	Type IV Type VI Type VII Type VIII
Group 3	Chain M, < 95,000	Type IX Type X

charge when the carboxyl group of the glucuronic acid is dissociated. At physiologic pH, hyaluronic acid occurs in the vitreous gel as the salt sodium hyaluronate. It is spheroidal and can hold an extremely large volume of water relative to its weight. Hyaluronic acid is present in nearly all vertebral connective tissue and is nontoxic, noninflammatory, and nonimmunogenic.

Both the concentration and the molecular weight of hyaluronic acid in the vitreous are variable, depending on species, location in the vitreous body, and type

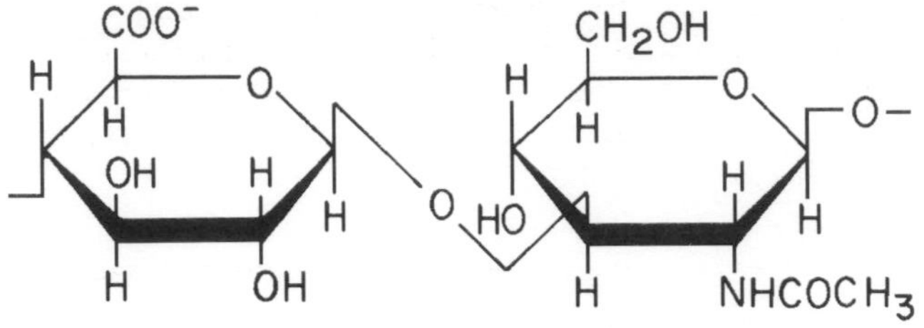

FIG XV-1—Hyaluronic acid consists of a repeating disaccharide (glucuronic acid and N-acetylglucosamine). It is a polyanion at physiologic pH with a net negative charge resulting from ionization of the carboxyl groups of the glucuronic acid residues. (Reproduced with permission from Berman ER. *Biochemistry of the Eye.* New York: Plenum Press; 1991:296.)

of analysis. With hydration the hyaluronic acid molecule in vitreous can achieve lengths of up to 400 nm and a molecular weight of greater than 1 million.

Hyalocytes are thought to synthesize a low-molecular-weight precursor of hyaluronic acid that is polymerized into a large molecule in the extracellular space of the cortical vitreous gel. The regeneration of hyaluronic acid removed from the normal vitreous occurs very slowly if at all. In all species of animals hyaluronic acid concentration is highest in the posterior cortical layer near the retina and lowest in the anterior portion behind the lens. The composition of the vitreous is governed by the presence of collagen and hyaluronic acid, with the relative amounts of these two components determining the existence of a vitreous liquid or a gel. When only a low concentration of collagen fibers is present, as in the owl monkey (25 µg/ml), a liquid vitreous predominates; in humans, where the concentration is much greater (286 µg/ml), the vitreous is a gel. The rigidity of the gel is greatest in the regions of highest collagen concentration. The collagen is responsible for forming the bulk of the gel network with hyaluronic acid interacting at the junctions. The collagen fibrils supply a resistance to tensile forces and give plasticity to the vitreous, while the hyaluronic acid resists compression and confers viscoelastic properties.

Proteins

Soluble vitreous proteins remain in solution after the insoluble elements present in the vitreous gel have been removed by filtration or centrifugation. The concentration of soluble proteins of a number of species ranges from 1.0 to 1.2 mg/ml. Both albumin and globulin are present in the vitreous gel, but albumin is the major vitreous protein. Vitreous albumin resembles serum albumin, and the electrophoretic mobility of vitreous globulin is similar to that of γ globulin. The quantity of serum proteins in the vitreous gel is dependent on the integrity of the retinal vasculature and the degree of inflammation.

The vitreous also contains iron-binding proteins such as transferrin, which serves an important protective role in cases of vitreous hemorrhage or iron foreign-body toxicity. Glycoproteins make up 20% of the total vitreous protein and are thought to originate from surrounding tissues and not from blood. Glycoproteins isolated from vitreous include interphotoreceptor retinol-binding protein and a small peptide of 5.7 kD that inhibits angiogenesis and collagenase activity. Two other proteins include neutrophil elastase inhibitor, which may play a role in resisting neovascularization; and tissue plasminogen activator, which may have a fibrinolytic role in the event of vitreous hemorrhage.

Zonular Fibers, Lipids, and Low-Molecular-Weight Solutes

Zonular fibers are present in the anterior vitreous and differ chemically from collagenous fibers. They are composed of a acidic glycoprotein and have an unusually high cysteine content, but further data are needed for precise characterization.

Lipids account for about 7% w/w of the pellet obtained after centrifugation of the vitreous. The major fatty acids in human vitreous include palmitate (25%), stearate (18%), oleate (23%), and arachidonate (17%). Little variation occurs with age.

Ions and organic solutes originate from adjacent ocular tissues and blood plasma. The barriers that control entry into the vitreous include the vascular endothelium of retinal vessels, the retinal pigment epithelium, and the inner layer of the ciliary epithelium. The concentrations of Na^+ and Cl^- are similar to those in plasma, but K^+ is 9.5 mM, which is the concentration measured in anterior aqueous.

Biochemical Changes with Aging and Disease

Syneresis

With aging the vitreous collagen fibers collapse or contract, resulting in a decreased volume of the gel vitreous, and pockets of fluid form within the vitreous. This reorganization of the vitreous is often considered to be one of the major causes of posterior vitreous detachment (PVD). The coalesced collagen fibrils and other debris are frequently noticed by patients as "floaters." Females have a much lower concentration of hyaluronic acid than males, and a considerable variation in hyaluronic acid concentration between different aging individuals has been described, but this finding has not yet been correlated with the degree of syneresis or PVD. Except for the collagen concentration, which has been found to be very low in the liquid pockets, the gel and liquid components show no significant differences.

Myopia

When the globe's axial length is greater than 26 mm, both collagen and hyaluronic acid concentration are approximately 50% lower than in emmetropic eyes. This finding suggests a correlation between the macromolecular composition and the physical state of the vitreous.

Aphakia

Intracapsular cataract extraction (ICCE) causes a significant decrease in hyaluronic acid concentration as compared with the fellow unoperated eye. In specimens collected postmortem from individuals who had undergone uneventful ICCE in one eye only, a consistently lower hyaluronic acid concentration was found in the aphakic eyes. No correlation appeared between the duration of aphakia and the concentration of hyaluronic acid in the operated eyes, but no eyes were available for examination until at least 2 years after surgery.

Diabetes Mellitus

The collagen content of the vitreous of diabetic patients has been reported to be lower than in unaffected individuals. Hexosamine concentration in diabetic patients has been found to be higher than that in nondiabetic eyes. This finding does not appear to be related in any way to the severity of the diabetes or to the presence or absence of diabetic retinopathy.

Injury with Hemorrhage and Inflammation

The vitreous becomes liquefied in the area of a hemorrhage. The catabolic products of red blood cells, hemosiderin and iron, cause depolymerization of hyaluronic acid. If blood remains in liquid vitreous, clot formation is avoided and the blood is slowly absorbed. If the blood penetrates the vitreous cortex, platelets come in contact with vitreous collagen, aggregate, and initiate clot formation. The clot in turn stimulates a phagocytic inflammatory reaction. Hemoglobin-laden macrophages may cause secondary glaucoma by blocking the trabecular outflow channels. Erythroclasts (rigid degenerated blood cells) can also cause secondary glaucoma (see BCSC Section 10, *Glaucoma*).

If the vitreous is largely fluid, as in myopic, aphakic, or senile eyes, then the clot that is formed is loosely aggregated and early removal is likely. Hemorrhage into vitreous gel is less freely dispersed and a more compact clot is formed. The subsequent inflammatory reaction is variable for unknown reasons.

Inflammation is beneficial in the sense that it increases the rate of hemolysis of the clotted red blood cells and lysis of the fibrin clot itself. Besides the beneficial effects of the inflammatory response after vitreous hemorrhage, fibroblastic scar tissue formation may also be stimulated by the inflammation. Two types of collagen are found in this fibroblastic tissue. Some areas contain fine unbanded fibers of an average diameter of 14 nm that are similar to normal vitreous fibers but occur in excess concentration. More prevalent are thick banded fibers with a periodicity of 64 nm and an average diameter of 66 nm.

Profound biochemical changes occur after simulated vitreous hemorrhage in rabbits. Intravitreal blood results in an elevated protein concentration in the vitreous for a prolonged period. Hyaluronic acid concentration, which is low in normal rabbit vitreous (10–50 µg/ml), falls to almost zero. As the vitreous hemorrhage clears over 6 weeks to 3 months, hyaluronic acid concentration increases again up to five times the normal vitreous levels in those eyes in which significant amounts of fibroblastic scar tissue are present. If the scar tissue contracts and causes localized or total retinal detachment, the vitreous protein concentration remains at a very high level. If the vitreous clears and retinal detachment is not present, the protein concentration decreases to the low level present in normal eyes. It is likely that the reformation of hyaluronic acid is a result of the proliferating scar tissue rather than a restoration of native vitreous hyaluronic acid.

Hyaluronic Acid (Sodium Hyaluronate) and Ophthalmic Surgery

Hyaluronic acid, because of its high viscosity, has become a useful aid in many types of surgical procedures. Four physical properties make hyaluronic acid extremely useful in ophthalmic surgery:

□ Viscosity

□ Viscoelasticity

□ Pseudoplasticity

□ Surface tension, or cohesiveness

Viscosity provides tissue lubrication and maintains space within the ocular structure. It permits wider and clearer space for surgical manipulation. *Viscoelasticity* provides protection against mechanical insults such as vibrations associated with phacoemulsification or turbulence induced by an irrigation system. It resists the compressive forces inside the eye during surgery and cushions endothelial cells, lessening their loss and reducing postoperative corneal edema. *Pseudoplasticity* influences the ability to maintain space and allows hyaluronic acid to be easily injected into the eye even with a 30-gauge cannula. *Surface tension* allows hyaluronic acid to leave the eye as a single mass that can therefore be easily aspirated.

Purified hyaluronic acid is used intraocularly in situations that require separating tissue surfaces and minimizing adhesion. In the anterior segment and in intraocular lens (IOL) implantation surgery, hyaluronic acid protects the corneal endothelium, maintains a deep anterior chamber during the operative procedure, and helps push back the iris and vitreous when necessary. BCSC Section 11, *Lens and Cataract,* discusses viscoelastic materials, including hyaluronic acid, in detail.

Hyaluronic acid may have some undesirable qualities. It may not spread evenly and may remain at the site of injection. Fibrin and blood may be trapped within the molecule, hindering clearance and increasing postoperative inflammation. Sometimes, it may be difficult to remove in certain areas such as beneath the iris. Occasionally, it causes postoperative elevation in IOP that is maximal at 4–7 hours and usually resolves spontaneously within 72 hours.

Liesegang TJ. Viscoelastic substances in ophthalmology. *Surv Ophthalmol.* 1990;34: 268–293.

Partamian LG. Prospective study of intraocular pressure after using Viscoat versus Healon in phacoemulsification and P/C IOL insertion. *Ophthalmology.* 1995;102(Suppl):159.

Vitreous Collagen Cross-Linking

Recognition of the importance of vitreous collagen concentration in the pathogenesis of both retinal detachment and posttraumatic vitreous proliferation is growing. Most investigations into the cause and prevention of posttraumatic retinal detachment (and related conditions such as massive periretinal proliferation and vitreous fibrous proliferation) have so far focused on the identification and control of contractile cellular elements. However, it has been demonstrated in rabbits that inhibition of collagen cross-linking by penicillamine and β-aminopropionitrile causes a clinically significant decrease in vitreous proliferation after perforating injury.

CHAPTER XVI

Retina

The retina is a peripheral extension of the forebrain, which shares common embryologic origins. It consists of six neuronal cell types:

- Photoreceptors (rods and cones)
- Bipolar cells
- Horizontal cells
- Amacrine cells
- Interplexiform cells
- Ganglion cells

The photoreceptors are the light-detecting cells in the outer layer, which receive their blood supply from the choroidal circulation. The other cells make up the signal-processing inner layer and receive their blood supply from the retinal circulation. The emphasis of this section will be on the biochemistry of the photoreceptors, their synthesis and turnover, and vitamin A metabolism with effects of light.

Chemistry of the Photoreceptor Outer Segments

The outer segment membranes of rods and cones contain certain proteins, also known as *visual pigments,* that absorb light and initiate visual excitation. These protein molecules are embedded in a lipid bilayer, and the function of the retina depends partly on the photochemical and biochemical reactions that take place within this hydrophobic lipid domain. Knowledge of the chemistry of the constituents of the outer segments is essential to understand photoreceptor function.

Lipids of Photoreceptor Membranes

The photoreceptor membranes of both rods and cones contain a lipid bilayer as part of their basic structure. This bilayer creates a passive permeability barrier to ions, allowing for their subcellular compartmentalization, and provides a stable matrix in which integral membrane proteins such as rhodopsin may be firmly embedded.

In the *rod outer segments (ROS)* from human retinas, lipids make up about 50 wt % and proteins 50 wt % of the bilayer. Most of the lipids are phospholipids. These lipids contain a glycerol "backbone" to which two long-chain fatty acids are esterified at positions –1 and –2. Position –3 contains a phosphate group in phosphodiester linkage to glycerol and a small organic molecule, which in ROS is most commonly choline, ethanolamine, serine, or inositol.

In the lipid bilayer (shaded area of Figure XVI-1) the fatty acid chains abut to form the hydrophobic region of the membrane, while the glycerol/phosphate/small-molecule groups are aligned on either side of the bilayer at the aqueous interface. ROS membranes are very fluid, having the viscosity of olive oil. This property is

C-terminus

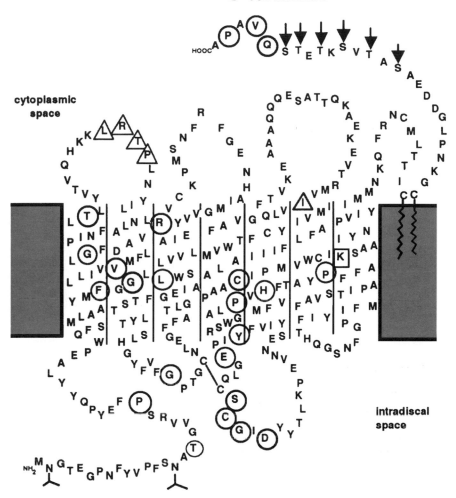

N-terminus

FIG XVI-1—Proposed model for the orientation of human opsin in the lipid bilayer of rod outer segments. The shaded area is the lipid bilayer, which is traversed by seven α-helical loops of opsin. Each letter represents a particular amino acid. Two asparagines (*N*) near the N-terminus are glycosylated, as indicated by the crow's feet. 11-*cis*-retinaldehyde is attached to opsin at lysine-296 (boxed *K* in transmembrane segment on the far right). The circles identify point mutations that have been found in autosomal dominant retinitis pigmentosa; the triangles represent deletions. The arrows point to serine (*S*) and threonine (*T*) residues on the cytoplasmic surface near the C-terminus, which are sites of phosphorylation of bleached rhodopsin. Two palmitoylated cysteine molecules are near the C-terminus; the fatty acid chains can be seen embedded in the lipid bilayer. (Figure courtesy of Wolfgang Baehr, MD.)

undoubtedly important to outer segment function, since the intermolecular associations of integral and peripheral proteins that follow photon capture by rhodopsin—for example the reaction rate of activated rhodopsin with transducin molecules—proceed more readily in a fluid membrane.

The very high levels of long-chain polyunsaturated fatty acids found in all phospholipid classes are a unique feature of retinal lipids. In all vertebrate species that have been examined, including humans, the major polyunsaturated fatty acid is *docosahexaenoic acid* (abbreviated 22:6ω3 or DHA), a 22-carbon acid with 6 double bonds. The only other tissues where relatively large amounts of this fatty acid occur are the brain and reproductive organs. DHA is an essential fatty acid; it or its short-chain precursor (18:3ω3) must be obtained from the diet. The retina is quite specific in its preference for DHA, since attempts to lower its content by diets devoid of ω3 fatty acids produce only modest changes in retinal levels. However, the amplitudes of the a- and b-waves of the rat electroretinogram (ERG) are significantly reduced in rats denied precursors of DHA. Monkeys deprived from birth of ω3 fatty acids show decreased visual acuity and a prolonged recovery time of the dark-adapted ERG measured after a saturating flash of light. Also, peak latencies of both cone and rod ERGs are delayed in ω3-deprived monkeys, compared to controls.

The importance of DHA in human retinal development was recently demonstrated. Preterm infants fed standard formulas containing no DHA had significantly lower rod amplitudes and higher rod thresholds than infants receiving mother's milk, which does contain DHA. Cone function was not affected in these infants.

The cone-rich macular region in the human retina contains less DHA than the rod-rich peripheral region. DHA is an important component of retinal membranes, although its precise function is not known. A molecular spring model has been proposed in which DHA functions as a spring that helps to expand the membrane to facilitate opening of the active state of rhodopsin, as illustrated in Figure XVI-2.

Dratz EA, Holte LL. The molecular spring model for the function of docosahexaenoic acid in biological membranes. In: Sinclair A, Gibson R, eds. *Essential Fatty Acids and Eicosanoids.* Champaign, IL: American Oil Chemists' Society; 1992:122–127.

van Kuijk FJGM, Buck P. Fatty acid composition of the human macula and peripheral retina. *Invest Ophthalmol Vis Sci.* 1992;33:3493–3496.

Proteins of Photoreceptor Outer Segments

Rod outer segments contain a number of integral, peripheral, and soluble proteins. Those involved in some aspect of visual transduction are listed in Table XVI-1. Mutations have been demonstrated in three of these proteins in humans and animals with inherited retinal degenerations. The major protein in isolated ROS is the integral protein *rhodopsin,* the visual pigment of the rod photoreceptors. Mutations in rhodopsin are associated with retinitis pigmentosa. The molecular mass of rhodopsin is about 40 kD, and each molecule contains two carbohydrate chains composed of N-acetylglucosamine and mannose linked to the protein through asparagine residues near the N-terminus. The chromophore of rhodopsin is 11-*cis*-retinaldehyde (vitamin A aldehyde), which is linked to the protein through a Schiff's base with the ε-amino group of one of the lysine residues of the protein (boxed K in Figure XVI-1).

Rhodopsin is a transmembrane protein, with its N-terminus exposed to the intradiscal space and its C-terminus exposed to the interdiscal (cytoplasmic) space. Rhodopsin has enough amino acids and sufficient hydrophobic character to span the

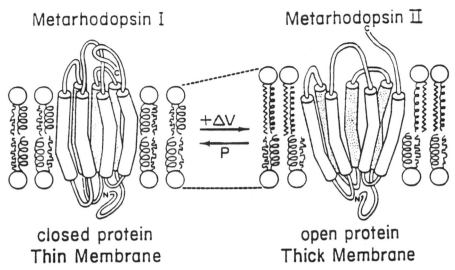

Metarhodopsin I   Metarhodopsin II

+ΔV →
← P

closed protein   open protein
Thin Membrane   Thick Membrane

FIG XVI-2—Schematic of the molecular spring model, which proposes that a coupling exists between light-mediated (+ΔV) functional and conformational changes in excited rhodopsin and the conformation of DHA chains in the lipid bilayer of the membranes. The DHA is proposed to act as a molecular spring, which prefers a compact formation and a thin membrane during dark adaptation (P), but which can expand and facilitate opening of the active state of rhodopsin following light exposure.

bilayer seven times. Since the carbohydrate residues are attached to the N-terminus, they are exposed to the intradiscal space. The covalently bound retinaldehyde is sequestered in a hydrophobic region of rhodopsin that is embedded in the lipid bilayer. The chromophore is aligned parallel to the plane of the bilayer and is thus perpendicular to the path of incident photons, an arrangement that provides the greatest probability for photon capture. Rhodopsin can be phosphorylated under certain conditions (see p 357), and the sites are located near the C-terminus.

Visual Pigments

Four classes of visual pigments occur in the human retina: rhodopsin in the rods, and three color-sensitive visual pigments in the cones. Outer segments of rods and cones contain only one type of visual pigment molecule per cell. Based on their spectral absorption characteristics, the cone pigments are labeled *long-wavelength sensitive* (570 nm), *mid-wavelength sensitive* (540 nm), and *short-wavelength sensitive* (440 nm). In the past they were called red-, green-, and blue-sensitive cones, respectively. The chromophore is 11-*cis*-retinaldehyde for all four classes of the human visual pigments.

Recent studies have revealed extensive sequence homologies (areas of like amino acid sequence) between rhodopsin and the color vision proteins. Thus, the four visual pigments used by humans probably arose from some common ancestral gene. Since they each absorb different wavelengths of light, the unique spectral char-

TABLE XVI-1

PROTEINS IN ROD OUTER SEGMENTS

PROTEIN	SUB-UNIT	MASS (kDa)	ESTIMATED NUMBER OF COPIES/ROS	LOCATION	FUNCTION
Rhodopsin (R)		40	3×10^8	Disc and plasma membrane	Converts light into chemical signals
Transducin (T)	T_α T_β T_γ	40 37 8	4×10^7	Disc surface	Mediates signal coupling between rhodopsin and phosphodiesterase
Phosducin (Pdc)		28	4×10^7	Cytosol	Binds $T_{\beta,\gamma}$ and blocks T recycling
Phosphodiesterase (PDE)	α β γ	88 86 13	1×10^7	Disc surface	Hydrolyzes cGMP to 5'-GMP
cGMP-regulated channel		79	1×10^6	Disc and plasma membranes	Regulates cation permeability
Rhodopsin kinase (RK)		68	1×10^6	Cytosol	Phosphorylates photolyzed rhodopsin (R*)
Arrestin (48K protein, S antigen)		48	4×10^7	Cytosol	Binds to phosphorylated R* and blocks R*-T interaction
Guanylate cyclase		110	—	Cytosol and axoneme	Converts GTP to cGMP
Recoverin		26	—	Cytosol	Controls cGMP synthesis
Peripherin		39	—	Disc margins	Unknown
Phospholipase C (PLC)		70, 140	—	Cytosol and disc membranes	Hydrolyzes PIP_2
Protein kinase C (PKC)		85	—	Cytosol	Phosphorylates ROS proteins
Phosphoprotein phosphatase		—	—	Cytosol	Dephosphorylates ROS proteins
Protein kinase (cGMP-dependent)		—	—	Cytosol	Phosphorylates ROS proteins

acteristics of each pigment are dictated by the interaction of the chromophore with the protein. This interaction is achieved either at the hydrophobic cleft in which the retinaldehyde molecule resides or at the Schiff's base linkage between retinaldehyde and the protein.

Color deficiency is caused by the absence of one or more functional visual pigments from mutations that result in the synthesis of visual pigment apoproteins that do not combine with 11-*cis*-retinaldehyde. Another possibility is anomalous color deficiency, which is manifested by a functional pigment that does not match the spectral response of the unaffected population. Anomalous pigments result from the substitution of amino acid(s) in the primary structure of the protein. 11-*cis*-retinaldehyde is not prevented from combining with the protein to form a light-sensitive pigment, but it forms a pigment with spectral properties different from those of the "normal" pigment.

Synthesis and Turnover of Photoreceptor Outer Segments

Rod and cone visual cells in the mature retina do not undergo cell division. In order to ensure their long-term viability and structural integrity, they have developed an alternative means of replenishing old, damaged, or defective parts. Rod and cone outer segments are dynamic structures whose molecular constituents are constantly being renewed. New membrane material is added at the inner–outer segment junction, and old membranes are shed from the apical tips of both rods and cones and phagocytized by the retinal pigment epithelium.

Renewal of Rod Outer Segments

The renewal rate of mammalian rods is 9–13 days. The renewal of ROS including their lipids and proteins is depicted in Figure XVI-3. Once opsin is incorporated into a lipid membrane, 11-*cis*-retinaldehyde is added to form the light-sensitive photopigment. Rhodopsin remains in its original disc throughout its lifetime in the outer segment. No interdiscal transfer of integral membrane proteins in the outer segments takes place.

Lipids are synthesized on the smooth endoplasmic reticulum of the inner segment and transported to the outer segment by at least two mechanisms. Some lipids accompany newly synthesized opsin in vesicles (as described above) and others are delivered independently of vesicles, presumably by exchange proteins. Once incorporated into the ROS, lipids, unlike integral proteins, diffuse throughout the entire outer segment. An active lipid metabolism takes place in the outer segments, with breakdown through phospholipase A_2 and C activities and phospholipid "retailoring" through acyl exchange reactions. Rhodopsin is acylated with two molecules of palmitic acid on adjacent cysteines near the C-terminus (see Figure XVI-1). However, no de novo lipid synthesis occurs in outer segments.

Renewal of Cone Outer Segments

The renewal of cone outer segments has not received as much attention as the renewal of rods, primarily because of the difficulty in obtaining enough cone material to carry out biochemical analyses. The early autoradiographic studies showed a diffuse labeling of the cone outer segments following the injection of radioactive precursors of protein, indicating that the integral membrane proteins of cone outer segments were free to diffuse throughout the entire outer segment. This is to be expected, since the plasma membrane is continuous with the cone discs throughout the entire expanse of the outer segment.

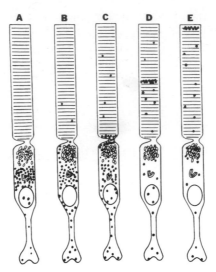

FIG XVI-3—Schematic depicting the renewal of rod outer sements. *A*, Radioactive amino acids (black dots) are injected. *B*, Radioactive proteins are observed over the Golgi apparatus of the inner segments, a secondary site of addition of some of the carbohydrate molecules of opsin. *C*, Vesicles containing opsin migrate to the base of the outer segment and fuse with the plasma membrane in the region of the connecting cilium. *D*, Within a few hours, a band of radioactivity can be observed in the basal part of the ROS. At this time, biochemical studies reveal the presence of radioactivity in the visual pigment rhodopsin. *E*, The band of radioactivity is displaced apically until it reaches the tips of the outer segments. (Reproduced with permission from Anderson RE, ed. *Biochemistry of the Eye.* San Francisco: American Academy of Ophthalmology; 1983:172.)

Shedding of Rod and Cone Outer Segments

Numerous studies have established that the tips of the ROS are shed and phagocytized by the retinal pigment epithelium (RPE). The shedding process was assumed to be a random event until LaVail observed in 1976 that the number of phagosomes in the RPE of rats depended on the period of the light cycle. The smallest number of phagosomes was observed in the early morning hours just prior to the onset of light, and the largest number appeared within the 1–3 hour period following light onset. It was soon learned that the shedding of rat ROS was cued but not driven by light. Failure of light onset in the morning did not prevent shedding; indeed, shedding events were observed at predicted times for several days in animals maintained in constant darkness. However, as is true of circadian events cued by light, maintenance of rats in constant light, depriving them of a dark period, resulted in obliteration of the rhythmic shedding.

The orderly shedding of cone tips was not appreciated until some time later. A burst of cone shedding occurs just after the onset of darkness, the opposite of what is observed with rods. Thus, rods shed early in the light cycle, during the period of time when they are functionally less active, while cones shed in the early darkness hours, also at a time when they are functionally less active. This orderly shedding of photoreceptor tips provides the rods and the cones with a mechanism for renewing the components of their visual membrane apparatus. It is thought that cones do not "shed" in the same manner as the rods, possibly because of their different structures. Cone outer segment discs are formed by infoldings of the plasma membrane, whereas rod outer segment discs are separate from the plasma membrane (see Figure III-29, p 78).

LaVail MM. Rod outer segment disk shedding in rat retina: relationship to cyclic lighting. *Science.* 1976;194:1071–1074.

Visual Pigment (Rhodopsin) Dynamics and the Vitamin A Cycle

Absorption of a photon by a visual pigment molecule is the initial event in visual excitation. A variety of reactions follow, some of which are involved in the transmission of the visual message to the brain. In general terms, the light-evoked reactions in photoreceptor cells are associated with changes in

☐ The chemistry of the visual pigments

☐ Vitamin A metabolism

☐ Cyclic nucleotide (cGMP) metabolism

Light-Evoked Changes in Rhodopsin

As described earlier, rhodopsin and the cone pigments are integral membrane proteins that are firmly embedded in the hydrophobic lipid bilayer. The single known action of light in initiating visual excitation is to isomerize 11-*cis*-retinaldehyde to all-*trans*-retinaldehyde (Fig XVI-4). The straightening out of the retinaldehyde molecule disrupts its snug fit with the visual pigments, resulting in the unfolding of the proteins. Several *bleaching intermediates* of rhodopsin have been identified by their spectrophotometric properties (Fig XVI-5). These intermediates, originally captured at very low temperatures, have now been characterized at physiologic temperatures in optical experiments with high time resolution.

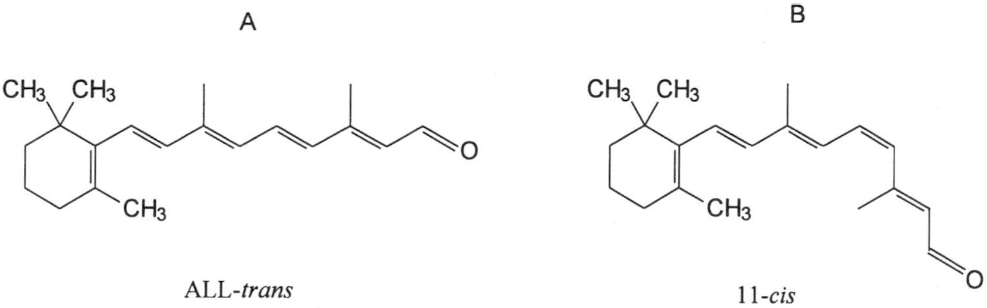

FIG XVI-4—Chemical structures of (A) all-*trans*-retinaldehyde and (B) 11-*cis*-retinaldehyde.

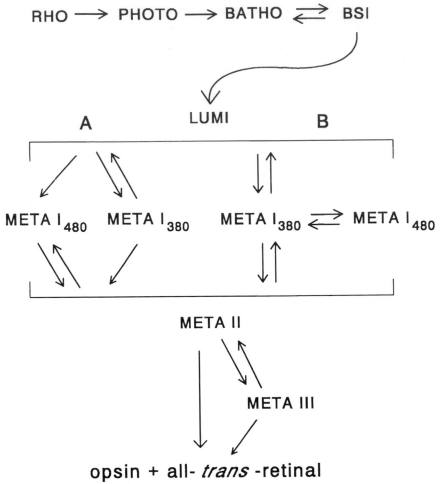

FIG XVI-5—Bleaching sequence of rhodopsin (*RHO*). (*PHOTO* = photorhodopsin; *BATHO* = bathorhodopsin; *BSI* = blue-shifted intermediate.) Rhodopsin decays to lumirhodopsin (LUMI) on the nanosecond time scale. There are two possible mechanisms for further decay to metarhodopsin II (*META II*). Mechanism A involves lumirhodopsin decay through both meta I_{480} and meta I_{380}, and both these intermediates can form metarhodopsin II. In mechanism B lumirhodopsin is only in equilibrium with meta I_{380}, which can form meta I_{480} and vice versa, but only meta I_{380} decays to metarhodopsin II.

The intermediates represent metastable conformational states that result from the perturbation of the native photopigment following *cis–trans* isomerization. The first intermediate, photorhodopsin, forms within 200 femtosec (10^{-15}) and then relaxes on the picosecond time scale to the vibrationally relaxed, less red-shifted bathorhodopsin, which absorbs at 530 nm. Bathorhodopsin then relaxes to a blue-shifted intermediate (BSI) in which the all-*trans*-retinaldehyde has torsionally relaxed, triggering a protein change that produces lumirhodopsin. Subsequent events become more dependent on the type of pigment, rod or cone, but as shown in Figure XVI-5 for the better understood case of rhodopsin, lumirhodopsin decays to a 380-nm absorbing pigment, metarhodopsin I_{380}. Mechanistic details of this reaction are still unresolved, but metarhodopsin I_{380} decays in approximately 1 msec to a final equilibrium mixture of two other intermediates, metarhodopsin I_{480} and metarhodopsin II (also absorbing at 380 nm).

Formation of metarhodopsin II involves extensive rearrangement of the loops of rhodopsin in the cytoplasm (requiring more space in the membrane, which is provided by changes in DHA, as discussed above). This rearrangement allows transducin, the G protein carrying the excitation signal, to recognize stimulation of rhodopsin by light. Metarhodopsin II slowly decays to metarhodopsin III, which in turn progresses to a simple Schiff base between retinaldehyde and opsin. The Schiff base can be hydrolyzed to free all-*trans*-retinaldehyde plus opsin. Alternatively, metarhodopsin II can decay directly to these products. In the human retina about 25% of the retinaldehyde is produced by direct hydrolysis. All-*trans*-retinaldehyde is rapidly reduced to all-*trans*-retinol by retinol dehydrogenase present in the photoreceptor outer segments. NADPH is the preferred cofactor, although NADH is also active. The fate of the all-*trans*-retinol is covered below in the discussion of vitamin A metabolism.

Without its light-sensitive chromophore, opsin is unresponsive to light. However, a functional rhodopsin molecule can be regenerated by the condensation of 11-*cis*-retinaldehyde with opsin. The factors that govern regenerability are the availability of 11-*cis*-retinaldehyde and the ability of the opsin to condense with the chromophore to form a functional pigment. During photoreceptor renewal, new opsin molecules are constantly being added to outer segments to replace those that may have become nonfunctional. This process is also true for vitamin A, the precursor of retinaldehyde. However, during the normal course of light and dark adaptation, an efficient recycling of the liberated chromophore within the eye also takes place. This recycling process, which occurs primarily between the photoreceptor cells and the RPE, is referred to as the *visual cycle* (Fig XVI-6).

Lewis JW, Kliger DS. Photointermediates of visual pigments. *J Bioenerg Biomembr.* 1992;24:201–210.

Lewis JW, van Kuijk FJGM, Thorgeirsson TE, et al. Photolysis intermediates of human rhodopsin. *Biochemistry.* 1991;30:11372–11376.

Vitamin A Metabolism

Vitamin A compounds occur primarily in four forms:

- Vitamin A *acid* (retinoic acid)
- Vitamin A *aldehyde* (retinaldehyde)
- Vitamin A *alcohol* (retinol)
- Vitamin A *ester* (retinyl ester)

The principal geometric isomers in the eye are 11-*cis* and all-*trans*. The fatty acids that are esterified to retinol to form the retinyl esters are primarily palmitic (16:0), stearic (18:0), and oleic acids (18:1). The largest amounts of vitamin A compounds in the eye are found in the outer segments of the retina and the RPE.

Because of the large species variation in the amounts of vitamin A compounds in the retina and the RPE, only generalizations can be made about their relative

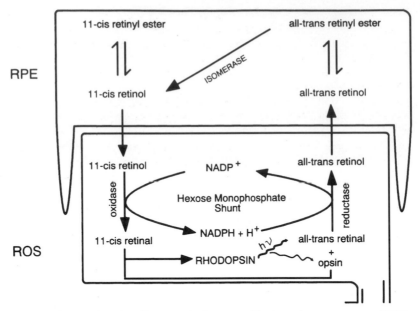

FIG XVI-6—The visual cycle. All-*trans*-retinol generated in the rod outer segments (*ROS*) goes to the retinal pigment epithelium (*RPE*), where it is converted to a retinyl ester and isomerized to 11-*cis*-retinol. 11-*cis*-retinol returns to the ROS, where it is oxidized to 11-*cis*-retinaldehyde. (Reproduced with permission from Anderson RE. Metabolism and photochemistry of the retina. In: Tasman W, Jaeger EA, eds. *Duane's Foundations of Clinical Ophthalmology.* Philadelphia: Lippincott; 1991; vol 2; chap 12:7.)

distributions. Almost all of the vitamin A compounds in the ROS exist as 11-*cis*-retinaldehyde present in the visual pigment. In frog ROS small amounts of 11-*cis*-retinol and retinyl ester appear. In contrast, virtually all of the vitamin A compounds in the oil droplets of the RPE of frogs exist as retinyl ester. In dark-adapted animals about equal proportions of the all-*trans* and 11-*cis* isomers are present in the oil droplets. Most mammals do not have oil droplets but nevertheless store vitamin A in their RPE, also in the ester form.

Vitamin A is stored in the liver as retinyl ester, and it may be hydrolyzed to retinol and free fatty acid. The retinol combines with a serum retinol binding protein (SRBP) with a molecular mass of about 21 kD. The binding is noncovalent and the stoichiometry is one molecule of retinol per molecule of SRBP. This small complex is bound in the serum to a larger protein, prealbumin. Because the capillaries in the choroid are fenestrated, this RBP–prealbumin complex (76 kD) penetrates Bruch's membrane and interacts with specific receptors on the basal side of the RPE. The protein itself does not enter the cell but delivers the vitamin A to the membrane for transport inside the cell. Once separated from vitamin A, the receptor for RBP shows reduced affinity, leading to its replacement by another RBP containing a molecule of vitamin A. Although the RBP will bind several forms of vitamin A, RBP isolated from human plasma contains exclusively all-*trans*-retinol.

The total amount of all vitamin A compounds in the eye remains relatively constant during light and dark adaptation. However, there is a net movement of vitamin A derivatives from the outer segments to the RPE during light adaptation and a reversal of this flow in the dark.

During the bleaching process, all-*trans*-retinaldehyde is released from the visual pigment and converted to all-*trans*-retinol, which is transported from the outer segments to the RPE. Proteins that bind retinol have been recovered from the interphotoreceptor matrix (discussed below), and these presumably aid in the transport of vitamin A compounds between the outer segments and the RPE. Once inside the RPE, all-*trans*-retinol is esterified to an all-*trans*-retinyl ester and then isomerized to 11-*cis*-retinol by a retinoid isomerase. It is now clear that the RPE plays two important roles in vitamin A metabolism: storage of retinyl esters and isomerization of all-*trans*-retinyl esters.

Following its return to the outer segments, 11-*cis*-retinol is oxidized to 11-*cis*-retinaldehyde, which is then incorporated into opsin. Evidence suggests that the photoreceptor oxidase and the reductase are separate entities linked through a common NADPH cofactor recycling system. The newly generated rhodopsin can absorb another photon and initiate the visual cycle once again. The same opsin molecule may be used many times in visual excitation. However, after each isomerization, all-*trans*-retinol must go to the RPE for reisomerization to 11-*cis*-retinol.

Rando RR. Molecular mechanisms of visual pigment regeneration. *Photochem Photobiol.* 1992;56:1145–1156.

Signal Transduction in the Retina

Dark-adapted photoreceptor cells are depolarized because sodium channels in the outer segment plasma membranes are open in the dark and allow the passive influx of sodium from the extracellular space into the cytoplasm of the outer segment (Fig XVI-7). An ouabain-sensitive Na^+,K^+-ATPase located in the plasma membrane of the mitochondria-rich ellipsoid region pumps sodium out of the inner segment in light and dark. The diffusion of sodium from the outer segment into the inner segment in the dark completes a current loop known as the *dark current*. The sodium channels are kept open by cGMP, which is present in high concentrations in outer segments in the dark. In the depolarized state (dark), neurotransmitters are released from the photoreceptor synaptic terminal. The photoreceptor transmitter, which has not been positively identified in the human retina (but is glutamate or a glutamate-like substance in other vertebrate species), interacts with postsynaptic sites on bipolar and horizontal cells. Depending on the nature of the interaction, the bipolar cells may be either depolarized or hyperpolarized in the resting (dark) state. Horizontal cells, like photoreceptor cells, are depolarized in the dark.

Almost all of the cGMP in the retina is localized in rod photoreceptors, and most of it is concentrated in the outer segment. Since the electrical events in photoreceptors that initiate visual excitation are controlled by cGMP, it is important to understand the metabolism of cGMP in darkness and in light. A mutation in one of the enzymes involved in cGMP catabolism is responsible for the retinal degeneration in the *rd* mouse. cGMP is synthesized from GTP by the enzyme guanylate cyclase, which is present in outer segments.

The hydrolysis of cGMP is triggered by the bleaching of rhodopsin (Fig XVI-8). The proteins involved in this process are listed in Table XVI-1. The high levels of

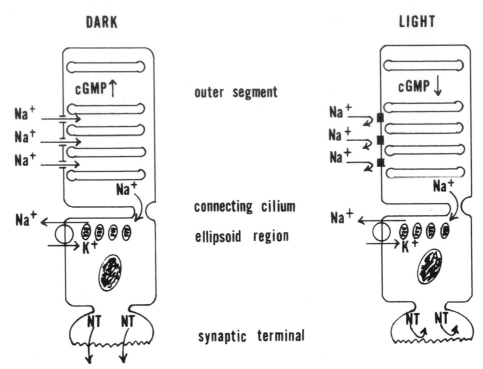

FIG XVI-7—The effect of light on plasma membrane activities in rod photoreceptor cells. In the dark the high levels of cGMP in the outer segments keep the sodium channels open, allowing for passive entry of sodium into the outer segment. Sodium ions diffuse through the connecting cilium into the inner segment and are actively extruded to the interphotoreceptor matrix by a Na^+,K^+-ATPase located in the ellipsoid region. This movement of sodium is the *dark current* described for rod cells. In the dark the cell is depolarized and neurotransmitter is released from the synaptic terminal. In the light decreased levels of cGMP lead to the closure of the sodium channels in the rod outer segments, which leads to hyperpolarization of the cell and reduction in neurotransmitter (*NT*) release.

cGMP that are characteristic of dark-adapted outer segments are reduced rapidly in light by a series of metabolic reactions that are now fairly well understood. Bleached rhodopsin (Rho*) interacts with transducin (a G protein: $T_{\alpha\beta\gamma}$ • GDP) that is bound to the surface of discs in the dark. Transducin is composed of three polypeptides (α, β, and γ) that act as a cooperative unit in the dark and display no enzymatic activity. However, $T_{\alpha\beta\gamma}$ • GDP interacts with bleached rhodopsin (Rho*) and exchanges GTP for GDP (GDP is bound to $T_{\alpha\beta\gamma}$ in the dark). Binding of GTP leads to dissociation into active T_{α} • GTP and inactive $T_{\beta\gamma}$ components. T_{α} • GTP then binds to inactive phosphodiesterase (PDE_i) and releases an inhibitory subunit, resulting in the activation of the enzyme (PDE_a). The activated PDE_a hydrolyzes cGMP to 5'-GMP. Decreased levels of cGMP lead to closing of the sodium channels. For this reaction to be of physiologic significance in visual transduction, the rapid reduction of cGMP levels must take place within the time frame of visual excitation (approximately 100 msec), which has indeed been shown to be the case.

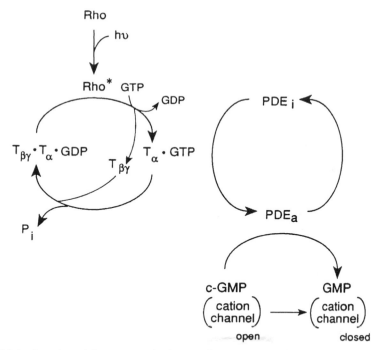

FIG XVI-8—Function of the receptor rhodopsin (Rho) as an example of a general mechanism for G protein–coupled receptors. Rho in rod cells of the retina is activated (Rho*) by light (hυ). Rho* activates the G protein transducin ($T_{\alpha\beta\gamma}$), causing the subunit T_α to exchange its bound GDP for GTP, which causes it to dissociate from the subunits $T_{\beta\gamma}$. The $T_\alpha \bullet$ GTP complex causes inactive cGMP–phosphodiesterase (PDE_i) to become activated (PDE_a). PDE hydrolyzes cGMP, which in high concentrations keeps the plasma membrane cation channel open. The channel closes, however, at the lowered concentrations of cGMP.

During two steps in the cGMP cascade, significant amplification of the response takes place. The first is at the level of interaction between transducin ($T_{\alpha\beta\gamma} \bullet$ GDP) and activated rhodopsin (Rho*). One Rho* can produce 100 or more molecules of $T_\alpha \bullet$ GTP. The second amplification occurs through the high activity of activated PDE_a, which can hydrolyze thousands of cGMP molecules per second. Thus, during the time course of visual transduction, one molecule of bleached rhodopsin can lead to the hydrolysis of 100,000 molecules of cGMP.

Given that the rapid hydrolysis of cGMP is an integral part of visual transduction, it is also important that the hydrolysis be controlled. Reestablishment of cGMP levels is necessary for further visual activity of the photoreceptor cell. Control of cGMP levels is exerted at several points in the cascade. T_α is a GTPase, and hydrolysis of GTP to GDP leads to reassociation of T_α and $T_{\beta\gamma}$ to form $T_{\alpha\beta\gamma} \bullet$ GDP, which does not activate PDE_i. Also, phosphorylation of opsin by rhodopsin kinase and binding by arrestin (also called S antigen and 48K protein) inhibit the ability of Rho* to bind $T_{\alpha\beta\gamma} \bullet$ GDP. Rhodopsin kinase is active at all times in ROS but reacts with bleached rhodopsin only when serine and threonine residues on the C-terminus of opsin become exposed following photobleaching. Arrestin combines with rhodopsin only after it has been phosphorylated. This intricate metabolic system allows the levels of cGMP in ROS to be precisely controlled and rapidly altered by changes in levels of illuminance.

Hargrave PA, McDowell JH. Rhodopsin and phototransduction: a model system for G protein–linked receptors. *FASEB J.* 1992;6:2323–2331.

The Interphotoreceptor Matrix

The interphotoreceptor matrix (IPM), referred to clinically as the *subretinal space,* lies between the outer sensory retina (photoreceptors) and the retinal pigment epithelium. The photoreceptor inner and outer segments, projecting from the outer sensory retinal surface into this compartment, are surrounded by constituents of the IPM (Fig XVI-9). Proteins, glycoproteins, and proteoglycans make up the major groups of macromolecules present in the IPM. Some components of the IPM, such as the glycoprotein called *interphotoreceptor retinoid binding protein,* are readily soluble and can easily be removed from the IPM by rinses in physiologic salt solutions. Other components, such as *chondroitin sulfate proteoglycan (CSPG),* are relatively insoluble and resist such removal. CSPGs are the predominant class of proteoglycans detected in normal, mature mammalian IPM. Proteoglycan metabolism has been shown to change with retinal development and in certain types of retinal degeneration.

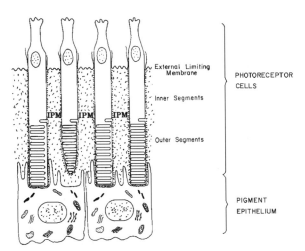

FIG XVI-9—Schematic diagram showing the interphotoreceptor matrix (IPM) lying between the apical surface of the retinal pigment epithelium and the external limiting membrane. Soluble proteoglycans and glycoproteins are dispersed throughout the IPM, and insoluble glycoconjugates are concentrated in specialized domains that form sheaths surrounding the photoreceptor cells. (Reproduced with permission from Berman ER. *Biochemistry of the Eye.* New York: Plenum Press; 1991:371.)

For many years the IPM was considered to be an unstructured, amorphous entity. More recently, studies employing wheat germ agglutinin (WGA), peanut lectin (PNA), antibodies to CSPG, and anionic dyes (cuprolinic blue) selective for sulfated proteoglycans have documented the presence of highly organized, relatively insoluble domains that are present as matrix sheaths surrounding rod and cone photoreceptors. These rod- and cone-associated IPM domains are tubular structures that surround the outer segments and extend from the external limiting membrane of the retina beyond the distal tip of the outer segment to terminate at the apical surface of the RPE. Figure XVI-10 includes micrographs of rhodamine-labeled WGA that show rod photoreceptors (small dark holes) surrounded by insoluble IPM components. In sections stained with PNA (not shown) the IPM sheath can be seen surrounding cones. The following activities are thought to be mediated through the IPM:

□ Retinal attachment by promotion of adhesion between the photoreceptor cells and the pigment epithelium

□ Visual pigment chromophore exchange

□ Creation of a route for passage of nutrients and metabolites between the RPE and photoreceptors

□ Establishment of specialized photoreceptor microenvironments, photoreceptor alignment, and factors for cell-to-cell recognition before phagocytosis

Defects or alterations in the IPM could underlie or contribute to a variety of clinical conditions that are manifest at this interface and are as diverse as retinal detachment, some forms of macular degeneration, central serous retinopathy, and some forms of retinitis pigmentosa.

Bridges CD, Adler AJ, eds. *The Interphotoreceptor Matrix in Health and Disease.* New York: Liss; 1985.

Molecular Biology of the Retina

A variety of molecular biology techniques have been adopted in recent years to enhance our understanding of the visual process and of some genetic disorders at the molecular level. This research has focused either on direct isolation of genes that code for proteins involved in the phototransduction cascade and expressed abundantly in the retina or on specific genetic disorders in the hope of identifying the responsible gene(s). See also Part 3, Genetics, of this volume.

Bovine rhodopsin was the first retinal protein to be purified and sequenced. The sequencing of this protein paved the way for the isolation of the bovine opsin gene, which led to the isolation of the human opsin gene as well as the human cone pigments (blue, red, and green). The isolation of both bovine and human opsin genes was followed by the isolation of genes for other protein members of the phototransduction cascade, such as phosphodiesterase (PDE), transducin, S antigen, and recoverin. Two other photoreceptor-specific proteins not known to be involved in transduction have also been cloned and sequenced: interphotoreceptor retinoid binding protein (IRBP) and peripherin.

These advances in molecular biology of the visual system were greatly enhanced by the development of polymerase chain reaction (PCR) and transgenic mice technology, both discussed and illustrated in chapter VIII. PCR was used by several groups to determine the genetic lesions associated with forms of retinitis pigmentosa. By amplifying specific DNA fragments with PCR and directly sequencing regions of

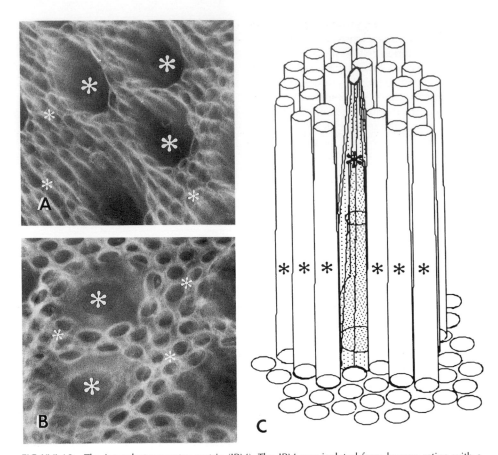

FIG XVI-10—The interphotoreceptor matrix (IPM). The IPM was isolated from human retina with a distilled water treatment. Following staining with WGA conjugated to rhodamine, the IPM was viewed with epifluorescence microscopy from the distal side adjacent to the pigment epithelial surface (A) or from the retinal side at the level of the outer limiting membrane (B). The unstained small holes are occupied by rods and the large holes by cones. The regions of intense staining surround rod photoreceptors as they course through the IPM. The matrix material surrounding the cone domains is only weakly stained with WGA-rhodamine. C, The three-dimensional diagram of the rod and cone matrix compartment. The large asterisk in the center identifies the cone matrix, and the small asterisks identify the rod matrix. (Figure courtesy of Joe G. Hollyfield, MD.)

the human opsin gene, a point mutation in 17 of 148 unrelated patients with autosomal dominant retinitis pigmentosa (ADRP) was found that was not detected in unaffected family members. The point mutation caused the conversion of proline to histidine at codon 23 (see Figure XVI-1). Following this important discovery, several laboratories reported a number of point mutations and a microdeletion in different regions of the human opsin gene in ADRP (circles and triangles in Figure XVI-1). The occurrence in ADRP of a large number of point mutations, each presumably responsible for the degeneration, gives genotypic evidence for the phenotypic differences that ophthalmologists have argued over for many years.

Attempts to identify mutations in other genes such as IRBP and PDE that segregate with different forms of ADRP have failed. However, a form of ADRP was recently identified that was associated with a mutation in the peripherin gene, the gene identified as being responsible for the *rds* mouse degeneration. Thus, at least one inherited retinal degeneration has the same genetic lesion in animals and humans.

Berson EL, Rosner B, Sandberg MA, et al. Ocular findings in patients with autosomal dominant retinitis pigmentosa and a rhodopsin gene defect (Pro-23-His) *Arch Ophthalmol.* 1991;109:92–101.

Dryja TP, Li T. Molecular genetics of retinitis pigmentosa. *Human Mol Gen.* 1995; 4:1739–1743.

Signal Processing in the Retina

Neurons of the retina share two special properties with other neurons in both the central and peripheral nervous systems:

□ They generate and conduct bioelectrical signals along their membrane surfaces

□ They excite and/or inhibit specific sets of associated neurons by means of a chemical signal

These two types of transmission, electrical and chemical, involve different mechanisms and, as such, have different properties.

In general, *electrical transmission* is usually initiated in response to chemical stimulation, except in some primary sensory neurons such as photoreceptors. It is mediated by a change in membrane potential caused by a flow of ions across the plasma membrane of the cell. Subsequently, an electrotonic spread of the potential change occurs along the entire expanse of plasma membrane in the cell and, in some cases, through low-impedance connections called *gap junctions* to adjoining cells. *Chemical transmission* is triggered by electrical stimulation. It involves release of a chemical agent, the neurotransmitter, from the presynaptic cell and diffusion of the transmitter across the extracellular space called the *synaptic cleft* to the target or postsynaptic cell, which is excited or inhibited by the neurotransmitter.

The transfer of visual information along cellular elements of the visual pathways results from a chain of electrical and chemical stimulation reactions, each triggered by the previous event. The initial trigger in the retina is the electrical response (hyperpolarization) of the photoreceptor cells to light; the final output from the retina is the train of electrical discharges or spikes generated by ganglion cells that travel along ganglion cell axons to the brain. Between the initial trigger and the final output, many cycles of electrical and chemical transmission occur within and among retinal neurons, and these intermediate steps are responsible for processing the visual information within the retina.

The mechanism that couples electrical stimulation to the process of neurotransmitter secretion is commonly called *stimulus-secretion coupling* (Fig XVI-11). In the first step of the process, the membrane potential of the secreting or presynaptic neuron becomes depolarized by the invasion of an action potential or a graded potential (electrical transmission). This step leads to an increase in intracellular calcium, which results in the release of transmitter agents from membrane-enclosed, intra-

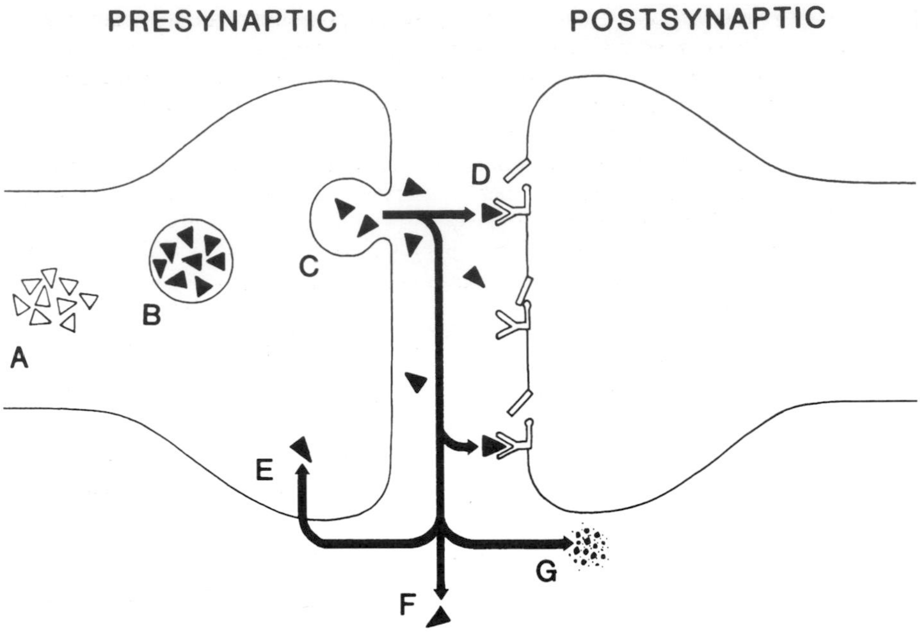

PRESYNAPTIC   POSTSYNAPTIC

FIG XVI-11—A simplified schematic representation of the cellular events associated with chemical transmission. Molecules of neurotransmitter (triangles) are synthesized (A) by enzymes located in the presynaptic terminal and subsequently concentrated (B) within vesicular storage sites. Depolarization of the plasma membrane of the presynaptic terminal (C) causes an increase in intracellular calcium, which triggers the fusion of the synaptic vesicle with the plasma membrane and the exocytosis of neurotransmitter. The released transmitter (D) diffuses across the synaptic cleft and binds to receptor sites located on the postsynaptic cell. Occupation of receptor sites by the transmitter molecules causes ion-specific channels to open in the postsynaptic membrane, thus producing hyperpolarization (inhibition) or depolarization (excitation) in the postsynaptic cell. The neurotransmitter is removed from the cleft by uptake systems (E), diffusion (F), and/or enzymatic degradation (G). (Reproduced with permission from Anderson RE, ed. *Biochemistry of the Eye*. San Francisco: American Academy of Ophthalmology; 1983:197.)

cellular storage sites called *synaptic vesicles.* The transmitter then interacts with receptor sites on the postsynaptic cell. The final step in chemical transmission is the removal of the transmitter from the synaptic cleft and the resetting of the system for subsequent stimulation. This step is achieved by one of the following:

□ Active uptake of the transmitter by specific transport systems located on the presynaptic neuron

□ Catabolism of the transmitter by enzymes located in the synaptic cleft

□ Simple diffusion of the neurotransmitter from the synaptic cleft

Most intrinsic neurons of the retina do not generate action potentials and therefore demonstrate significantly different and, in some cases, rather unique release properties. As discussed earlier, the photoreceptors in the vertebrate retina are depolarized in the dark, so neurotransmitter is continually released at a relatively high rate. An increase in light levels causes a graded hyperpolarization that causes less synaptic release of transmitter; a decrease in light intensity leads to release of more transmitter. This arrangement allows the photoreceptor–bipolar (and horizontal) cell synapses to operate in the region of maximum synaptic gain; i.e., neither is completely turned off nor completely saturated.

It is the transient change in the concentration of neurotransmitter in the cleft that influences the membrane properties of the second-order neurons (the bipolar cell) and the related interneuron (the horizontal cell). Horizontal and bipolar cells, like photoreceptors, do not generate action potentials and thus respond to the light-evoked decrease in release of photoreceptor transmitter with graded potentials. The third-order neuron (the ganglion cell) generates action potentials, while the associated interneuron (the amacrine cell) generates partial action potentials or, in some cases, sustained (graded) potentials.

A variety of experimental techniques have been developed for the specialized study of neurotransmitter agents within a specific neuronal tissue such as the retina. Most of these techniques were designed to address one or more of the specific criteria that must be met in order to establish that a given substance is used as a transmitter. These criteria are as follows:

□ The substance must be synthesized and stored in the presynaptic terminal

□ The substance must be released by the presynaptic neuron upon the appropriate stimulation

□ The substance, when exogenously applied, must evoke the appropriate response in the postsynaptic neuron

□ A mechanism must exist for removing the substance from the cleft in order to terminate transmitter action

Neurotransmitters in the retina include acetylcholine, catecholamines, γ-aminobutyric acid (GABA), glycine, glutamate, and a dozen peptides.

Intermediary Metabolism of the Retina

The unique function of the retina is visual excitation. This function requires energy in the form of adenosine triphosphate (ATP) derived from metabolism. The metabolic processes subserve cellular homeostatic mechanisms that are supportive of and essential for cell life. They include the constant renewal of vital cell constituents and the maintenance of intracellular concentrations of specific ions and amino acids at functionally required levels. The ATP produced in the retina comes largely from the metabolism of glucose. Glucose from the retinal capillaries and choroidal circulation diffuses into the retinal cells and is rapidly metabolized through three main pathways, as shown in Figure XI-2 (p 312):

□ Glycolytic pathway

□ Tricarboxylic acid (TCA, or Krebs) cycle

□ Hexose monophosphate pathway (HMP)

Carbohydrate Metabolism

Studies of retinal metabolism over many years have demonstrated that the retina has unusually high rates of glycolysis and respiration. One of the striking metabolic features of the retina is that it produces lactic acid from glucose at a rapid rate even in the presence of oxygen; this process is referred to as *aerobic glycolysis.* Despite the high rate of oxygen uptake by this tissue, the oxidation of pyruvate by the TCA cycle fails to keep up with the production of pyruvate from glucose. The extra pyruvate is converted to lactic acid, which accumulates in the retina. Excess lactate is lost by diffusion, but the mechanisms that govern its removal across limiting cellular membranes, such as the capillary endothelium and RPE, are not understood.

Although glycolysis is an inefficient method of producing energy, it has the advantage of being functional in the absence of oxygen. Under anaerobic conditions, lactate production increases by about 22 times because of the Pasteur effect (inhibition of glycolysis by oxygen), resulting in an increased utilization of glucose. Of various sugars tested as glucose substitutes, mannose, but not galactose or fructose, is a substrate of glycolysis. Retinal glycogen is very low in several species, including humans. What little glycogen is present seems to be localized primarily within the Müller (glial) cells.

Total glucose consumption in the presence of oxygen is about 0.7 µM/mg dry wt/hr, and about 90% of the total glucose utilized aerobically is converted to lactate (1.12 µM/mg dry wt/hr). In comparison, 80%–85% of the glucose consumed by the cornea and ciliary processes is converted to lactate, while in the RPE and the lens, lactate production accounts for more than 95% of the glucose utilized. These results demonstrate that lactic acid production accounts for the predominant utilization of glucose in many ocular tissues. Oxygen uptake of the retina is 2–5 times higher (on a mg dry wt basis) than that of the corneal endothelium, the ciliary processes, and the RPE, and the difference is much greater between the retina and the lens. The major substrate for respiration in the retina is glucose, since approximately 70% of oxygen uptake is a result of the oxidation of glucose to CO_2. Glucose, therefore, is the primary source of metabolic energy (ATP) in the retina. Glucose oxidation and oxygen consumption are considerably higher in the photoreceptor layer than in the other layers of the retina.

Metabolism and ERG Potentials

In vivo studies designed to clarify the dependence of the electroretinogram (ERG) potentials of the mammalian retina on metabolism began with Granit, who showed that the b-wave of the cat retina was highly sensitive to oxygen supply. Following compression of the carotids, this potential showed a selective decline. Within minutes after the intravenous injection of iodoacetate in the rabbit, the amplitudes of the a- and b-waves declined to low levels and visual cell function was lost. Moreover, within 12–14 hours the photoreceptors began to show signs of cellular death, and ultimately this cell layer disappeared with little or no change in any other retinal cell layer. More recently, an in vitro retinal preparation has been used to study the effects of glucose or oxygen deprivation as well as the effects of metabolic poisons on ERG potentials. Changes in these potentials are measured during the period of deprivation and during the period of recovery when the control incubation medium is restored. BCSC Section 12, *Retina and Vitreous,* shows examples of normal and abnormal ERG patterns.

When the retina is incubated in oxygenated medium containing 5 mM glucose, ERG potentials remain stable over several hours. In fact, they are also relatively unchanged when the glucose concentration is reduced to 1 mM. The amplitudes of the a- and b-waves, however, are not maintained in the presence of a glucose concentration of less than 1 mM. Thus, in the absence of glucose, endogenous energy stores are insufficient to support electrical activity in the retina. The rates of loss of these ERG potentials are much faster when both glucose and oxygen are withdrawn.

The dependence of the ERG potentials on glucose metabolism is also demonstrated by the effects of iodoacetate. Iodoacetate at a concentration that blocks glycolysis abolishes these potentials irreversibly within 5–10 minutes. This poison appears to cause a nearly simultaneous decrease in the amplitudes of the a- and b-waves. Iodoacetate clearly accelerates their rates of decline in comparison to the rates observed in the absence of glucose alone, suggesting that the oxidative production of ATP that supports the generation of light-induced electrical activity in the absence of substrate depends very much on endogenous stores derived from glucose metabolism.

After a 5-minute period of anoxia, a selective decrease in b-wave amplitude occurs. Concomitant with the reduction in amplitude of the b-wave is the disappearance of the oscillatory potentials. Thus, in the absence of oxygen, these two ERG potentials do not survive in the superfused retina. It has been reported that the amplitude of the a-wave decreases only 20% during periods of anoxia lasting more than 30 minutes, suggesting that anaerobic metabolism is capable of maintaining the electrical activity of the photoreceptor cell. In the presence of 5 mM glucose, the replacement of oxygen by nitrogen for 30 minutes leads to a 60% decrease in the amplitude of the a-wave of the isolated retina. This decrease shows that glycolysis alone is not able to support the a-wave at a high level in vitro when a concentration of glucose similar to that found in the blood is used. The electrical activity of the mammalian retina is very dependent on glucose as a substrate for glycolysis and oxidative metabolism, and an oxygen supply and glucose oxidation are of prime importance in providing the necessary energy for optimal function. Diabetic retinopathy and central retinal vein occlusion are conditions that contribute to anoxia of the retina.

Winkler BS. Glycolytic and oxidative metabolism in relation to retinal function. *J Gen Physiol.* 1981;77:667–692.

CHAPTER XVII

Retinal Pigment Epithelium

The pigment epithelium, more properly called the *retinal pigment epithelium (RPE)*, is one of the most important cell layers in the eye. Located between the rich vasculature of the choriocapillaris and the photoreceptor cells of the outer retina, the RPF performs a number of functions crucial for preserving the integrity of the visual system. The major functions of the RPE are shown in Table XVII-1.

Anatomically, the RPE is a single layer of cuboidal epithelial cells. It has extensive basal infoldings adjacent to Bruch's membrane, a layer of extracellular matrix between the RPE and the choriocapillaris, and an extensive array of apical microvilli ensheathing and interdigitating between the rod and cone photoreceptor outer segments. Numerous gap junctions exist between RPE cells. Although their function is not yet clear, their presence results in extensive electrical coupling between RPE cells. More important, tight junctions between the RPE cells constitute half of the blood–ocular barrier, the other half lying at the level of the retinal capillaries in the neurosensory retina.

TABLE XVII-1

THE MAJOR FUNCTIONS OF THE RPE

Biochemical

Development of photoreceptors during embryogenesis

Uptake, transport, storage, metabolism, and isomerization of vitamin A

Recognition, ingestion, and phagocytosis of shedded photoreceptor outer segment tips

Detoxification of drugs

Synthesis of melanin and extracellular matrixes

Physiologic

Maintenance of the photoreceptor environment

Selective transport of metabolites to and from the retina to contribute to adhesion between the retina and RPE

Physical and optical

Promotion of retinal adhesion

Maintenance of the outer blood–retinal barrier

Stray light absorption by melanin to control light scatter

Its unique anatomic arrangement means that the RPE is in a position to control the exchange of materials between choriocapillaris and neurosensory retina, thus placing considerable metabolic demands on this important cell layer. Without question, maintenance of a healthy RPE is critical for normal retinal function, and little doubt remains that the etiologies of many retinal disorders may have their primary origin in the RPE. Indeed, gyrate atrophy of the choroid and retina is now known to involve primary damage to the RPE, because of the RPE's unique susceptibility to the high levels of ornithine that result from this inherited disease.

Biochemically, the RPE has a metabolism typical of neuroepithelial tissue. All the basic metabolic pathways are present, as are the major cellular organelles for anabolic and catabolic metabolism. In addition, however, the RPE has a number of unique biochemical systems required by its numerous physiological functions, and many components of the RPE are in a constant state of turnover through autophago-cytosis and resynthesis. Thus, the biochemistry of the RPE is particularly dynamic and complex in order to meet demands for its own active metabolism, its function as a biological filter for the neurosensory retina, and the metabolic load required by its constant phagocytic function.

Interposed as it is between the rich blood supply of the choriocapillaris and the neurosensory retina, the RPE controls the entry and exit of many compounds and metabolites to and from the neurosensory retina. Many of these transport processes are energy dependent, and the requirement for energy by the RPE is quite high. The RPE contains all the enzymes of the three major biochemical pathways: glycolysis, Krebs cycle, and the pentose phosphate pathway. Glucose is the primary carbon source used for energy metabolism and conversion to protein. Although the RPE does make a minor contribution to the glycosaminoglycan- and proteoglycan-containing interphotoreceptor matrix, glucose is not converted to glycogen in the RPE. Glucosamine, fucose, galactose, and mannose are all metabolized to some extent in the RPE, although mannose seems to be passed on almost directly to the photoreceptors.

Composition

Lipids and *phospholipids* represent about 3% of the wet weight of the RPE. Phosphatidylcholine and phosphatidylethanolamine make up more than 80% of the total phospholipid content. In general, levels of saturated fatty acids in the RPE are higher than in the adjacent outer segments. The saturated fatty acids palmitic acid and stearic acid are used to esterify retinol and for energy metabolism by the RPE mitochondria. The level of the polyunsaturated fatty acids, particularly docosahexaenoic acid ($22:6\omega3$), is mostly much lower in the RPE than in the outer segments, although the level of arachidonic acid is relatively high. A number of studies have suggested that the retina may be spared the effects of essential fatty acid deficiency because the RPE efficiently sequesters fatty acids from the blood. It also actively conserves and efficiently reuses them, preventing their loss as waste products.

RNA is continually synthesized by the active nuclei of the RPE, which is not surprising considering the large variety of enzymes needed for cell metabolism and phagocytosis. In addition, a portion of the apical plasma membrane must be continuously replaced, since the membrane surrounding the ingested outer segment tips is internalized as well.

Proteins consisting of cytoskeletal proteins, receptors in plasma membranes, and hydrolytic enzymes make up 8% of the weight of RPE. Protein turnover in the RPE is quite active, although protein synthesis is thought to occur exclusively in the cell body and not in the villous processes, which must receive cellular components by cytoplasmic flow, diffusion, or transport. Taurine, which is present in very high concentration in the photoreceptor layer of the retina, is efficiently transported actively both into and out of the retina by the RPE.

Nearly 850 proteins have been identified in RPE. Up to 200 acidic proteins are present, and two-dimensional gel electrophoresis has revealed that actin, a prominent cytoskeletal protein, is one of them. Receptors in plasma membranes play key roles in many essential cellular functions. Plasma membrane–enriched fractions contain about 180 different proteins. Hydrolytic enzymes (Table XVII-2) are proteins that also include detoxifying enzymes present in the RPE such as glutathione peroxidase, catalase, and superoxide dismutase. The RPE is particularly rich in microperoxisomes, suggesting that it is quite active in detoxifying the large number of free radicals and oxidized lipids that are generated in this highly oxidative and light-rich environment (see chapter XVIII).

Cellular Biochemistry of the RPE

Vitamin A Metabolism

Perhaps the best-known biochemical function of the RPE is its role in visual pigment regeneration. As discussed in chapter XVI, vitamin A (as 11-*cis*-retinaldehyde) is an essential constituent of all visual pigments. Upon bleaching, the retinaldehyde (in the all-*trans* form) is released from the visual pigment protein opsin and thus must be reisomerized and recombined with the protein to form a regenerated visual pig-

TABLE XVII-2

HYDROLYTIC ENZYMES OF THE RETINAL PIGMENT EPITHELIUM

LYSOSOMAL FRACTION	NONLYSOSOMAL FRACTION
Acid lipase	Acid phosphatase
Acid phosphatase	Arylsulfatase
Arylsulfatase	Cathepsin D
β-galactosidase	5′-nucleotidase
β-glucuronidase	N-acetylglucosaminidase
Cathepsin D	
N-acetylglucosaminidase	
Phospholipase A_1	
Phospholipase A_2	

ment. Reisomerization is performed by enzymes in the RPE. Metabolic transformation of retinoids in RPE includes the following steps:

- Esterification of all-*trans*- and 11-*cis*-retinol
- Hydrolysis of retinyl esters
- Oxidoreduction of 11-*cis*-retinal and 11-*cis*-retinol
- Isomerization of all-*trans*-retinol to 11-*cis*-retinol

Vitamin A present in the RPE is derived from three sources: the circulatory system, ingested outer segment material (phagosomes), and releases that occur during the bleaching of visual pigment in the photoreceptors. Since both the aldehyde and alcohol forms of vitamin A are membrane-lytic compounds, it is likely that a series of retinoid-binding proteins mediate both vitamin A metabolism within the RPE and its exchange with adjacent outer segments. A number of retinoid-binding proteins have been isolated and characterized in the RPE, in the subretinal space, and in photoreceptors. In addition, the RPE esterifies retinol with available fatty acids (predominantly palmitic acid and, to a lesser extent, stearic and oleic acids) and stores retinol as a retinyl ester, a form no longer lytic to cell membranes. In conditions of hypervitaminosis A, toxicity to the RPE is minimal because of vitamin A storage as the ester.

The RPE as a Biological Filter

Because the RPE constitutes half of the blood–retina barrier (through tight junctions surrounding each cell), it plays an essential role in the metabolism of the underlying retina, particularly the photoreceptors. Metabolites and waste products entering and leaving the neurosensory retina must be transported and processed by the RPE. For example, glucose, the major carbon source for the retina, and vitamin A, essential for visual function, are both efficiently passed to the retina by the RPE. Other metabolites, such as taurine and choline, seem to first be concentrated in the RPE before passage to the retina. Finally, molecules degraded by the active lysosomal system of the RPE are mostly conserved for reuse by the underlying retina.

Maintenance of the Subretinal Space

The RPE–photoreceptor interface must be intact for normal visual function; a separation at this interface quickly spells dire consequences for the photoreceptors. Proper adhesion between these two cell layers is achieved and maintained through processes not yet well understood. However, the interdigitation of the apical processes of the RPE that surround and ensheathe the outer segments no doubt plays an essential role in this process, as do the complex molecules that make up the interphotoreceptor matrix. Some of the proteoglycans and GAGs found in the subretinal space are synthesized in and secreted by the RPE, although most are probably secreted by the photoreceptors. In addition, maintenance of the proper ionic and fluid environment at this complex interface is to a great extent the responsibility of the RPE.

The aqueous environment of the subretinal space is actively maintained by the ion transport systems of the RPE. The active transport of a variety of ions (K^+, Ca^{2+}, Na^+, Cl^-, and HCO_3^-) across the RPE has been well documented. This transport is vectorial in most cases; for example, sodium is actively transported from the choriocapillaris toward the subretinal space, while potassium is transported in the opposite direction. The apical membrane of the RPE appears to be the major locus of this transport. For example, an active ouabain-sensitive Na^+,K^+-ATPase is present on the apical, but not the basal, side. Similarly, an active bicarbonate transport system appears to be located in this portion of the RPE membrane. High carbonic anhydrase activity seems to be associated with both the apical and basal sides of the cell.

The net ionic fluxes are responsible for the transepithelial electrical potential that can be measured across the RPE apical membrane, a potential rapidly modified in the presence of a variety of metabolic inhibitors (e.g., ouabain, dinitrophenol) or other conditions that affect the various ionic gradients. In addition, the RPE apical membrane must be responsive to the changing conditions that occur during transduction. For example, light evokes a decrease in potassium ion concentration in the subretinal space, hyperpolarizing the RPE. Since the activity of Na^+,K^+-ATPase is controlled in part by potassium ion concentration, light can affect the ionic composition of the subretinal space and the transport functions of the RPE. Active vectorial transport systems for other retinal metabolites, such as taurine and methionine, have also been demonstrated. Thus, it appears that the RPE, particularly its apical membrane, plays an important role in maintaining the ionic environment of the subretinal space, which in turn is responsible for maintaining the integrity of the RPE–photoreceptor interface. The trans–RPE potential is the basis for the electrooculogram, which is the most common electrophysiologic test for evaluating the RPE. (See also BCSC Section 12, *Retina and Vitreous*.)

Pigment Granules

The RPE contains a large number of ellipsoidal and spherical pigment granules that contain the melanoprotein pigment melanin. The granules are located principally in the apical portion of the RPE and in the microvillous processes that interdigitate among the photoreceptor outer segments. Some granules are located more basally and are generally more spherical in shape. These melanin granules play a significant role in absorbing stray light and may provide a binding site for free radicals generated by photochemical events occurring in the RPE. In addition, peroxides produced in similar reactions are detoxified by a peroxidase found associated with melano-lysosome complexes (see chapter XVIII).

Melanin is synthesized from the amino acid tyrosine, which is first converted to dihydroxyphenylalanine (DOPA) through the action of the copper-containing enzyme tyrosinase. An absence of tyrosinase results in one form of albinism. Following conversion of DOPA to a series of indole and quinone intermediates, the black pigment melanin is formed. Melanin has not been fully characterized chemically, but it is an insoluble high-molecular-weight polymer or group of polymers composed of oxidized derivatives of tyrosine. Melanin granules are made up of melanin complexed with protein and constitute approximately 20% of the melanosome (organelles containing melanin). Melanin synthesis has been described as occurring only during embryogenesis and for a brief time postnatally. However, structures definitely resolvable as premelanosomes are observed in the adult RPE, and numerous melanolysosomes as well are always seen in RPE cells. The latter represent fusion products of melanosomes with lysosomes and may signify degeneration of the melanin granules themselves. These findings suggest that there may be a slow but steady renewal of melanin in the RPE throughout life.

Autophagy

Like other neuroepithelial tissues, the RPE under physiological conditions is a non-mitotic tissue, although RPE cells under certain pathological conditions and in tissue culture are observed to undergo mitosis. In order to replace and repair its various constituents and organelles, the postmitotic RPE relies upon a constant process of autophagocytosis (autophagy) and resynthesis of its components. Biosynthesis of new membranes, ribosomes, lysosomes, peroxisomes, mitochondria, and melanosomes occurs in response to the destruction of old organelles by autophagy. Autophagic vacuoles form from the fusion of lysosomes with organelles. Phagocytosis contributes to this turnover as well because a small amount of the RPE plasma membrane is lost each time the tip of an outer segment is internalized.

Phagocytosis

Perhaps one of the most important roles played by the RPE is the phagocytosis of the tips shed from the constantly renewing photoreceptor outer segments. Phagocytosis can be divided into four steps:

- Shed photoreceptor tips, both rod and cone, are enveloped by the pseudopodial processes of the pigment epithelial cell
- The shed tip is internalized into the RPE cell
- Lysosomes containing digestive enzymes fuse with the ingested tip to form a phagolysosome
- The phagolysosome is digested, finally forming a residual body

Actin filaments and microtubules in the RPE are known to be involved in the phagocytic process. Since each photoreceptor completely renews its outer segments every 10 days, the amount of material ingested and disposed of by the RPE is indeed awesome. Each RPE cell must phagocytize 10% of each rod outer segment each day. Since some RPE cells overlay 100–200 photoreceptors and may need to ingest 100 or more tips each day, each RPE cell is digesting the equivalent of 10 or more entire rod outer segments each day. An imbalance in this process, or a lack of recognition of material to be ingested, has been demonstrated in rats with a defect at the *rds* locus and leads to retinal degeneration in these animals. Human analogues for this defect have been discovered (see chapter VIII, Molecular Genetics).

In order to digest its phagocytic load, the RPE synthesizes proteolytic and lipolytic enzymes, many of which are packaged into lysosomes. These migrate to and fuse with the newly ingested outer segment tips (phagosomes) to form phagolysosomes. The phagolysosomes then begin a basal migration while digestion occurs. As the contents of the phagolysosomes are digested and liberated into the RPE cell, much of the material is then reused by both the RPE and the photoreceptor. Residual undigested material apparently accumulates throughout life and fuses to form the lipofuscin granules so noticeable along the basal margin in older eyes.

CHAPTER XVIII

Free Radicals and Antioxidants

Adverse effects of reactive forms of oxygen have been repeatedly proposed as causal factors in many types of tissue pathology, including cataract and age-related macular degeneration. Lipid peroxides are formed when oxyradicals or singlet oxygen molecules react with unsaturated fatty acids, which are largely present in cells as glycerylesters in phospholipids or triglycerides. The oxidation of membrane phospholipids has been hypothesized to increase permeability of cell membranes and/or to inhibit membrane ion pumps. This loss in barrier function is thought to lead to edema, disturbances in electrolyte balance, and elevation of intracellular calcium, all of which contribute to malfunctioning of the cell.

Cellular Sources of Oxygen Radicals

Free radicals are molecules or atoms that possess an unpaired electron. This property makes them highly reactive toward other molecular species. For example, free radical reactions with polyunsaturated fatty acids in the presence of oxygen lead to the rapid formation of fatty acid hydroperoxides, which increases permeability of membranes, causing electrolyte disturbances. Some free radical reactions are involved in normal cell function, while others are thought to be important mediators of tissue damage. Oxygen-derived free radicals and their metabolites are generated within aerobic organisms in several ways.

Oxygen necessary for normal metabolism usually undergoes tetravalent (four-electron) reduction by intracellular systems, such as cytochrome oxidase in mitochondria (Fig XVIII-1), and is finally discarded as water (H_2O) without leakage of reactive intermediates. However, a small percentage of the oxygen metabolized undergoes univalent reduction in four one-electron steps. Oxygen accepts an electron from a reducing agent in each of these steps, and several highly reactive intermediates are formed: the superoxide free radical (O_2^-), hydrogen peroxide (H_2O_2), and the hydroxyl radical (OH·). Some of the reactive species leak out of their enzyme-binding sites and may damage other components of tissues such as proteins, membrane lipids, and DNA if not captured by detoxifying enzymes. Superoxide is not only produced in mitochondrial electron transport systems but is also formed in some enzymatic reactions, such as the xanthine and xanthine oxidase system. Hydrogen peroxide is produced directly in peroxisomes, as well as by enzyme-catalyzed dismutation of superoxide. Hydroxyl radicals can be formed through the mechanism shown in Figure XVIII-1. In addition, any free iron (Fe^{2+}) present may catalyze formation of the hydroxyl radical from superoxide and hydrogen peroxide. Iron may also be involved in generation of these species by accelerating nonenzymatic oxidation of several molecules, such as glutathione.

Other sources of activated oxygen species include products from the enzymatic synthesis of prostaglandins, leukotrienes, and thromboxanes (see Figure XI-2). The synthesis of these compounds starts with formation of arachidonic acid hydroperox-

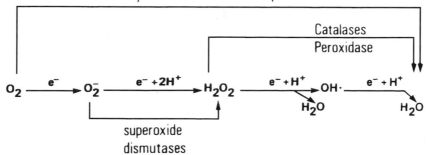

FIG XVIII-1- Enzymes involved in the metabolism of oxygen and in the detoxification of oxygen radicals generated by the univalent reduction of molecular oxygen. The univalent pathway involves a series of single electron transfers, producing the superoxide free radical (O_2^-), hydrogen peroxide (H_2O_2), water and the hydroxyl radical (OH·), and water. Superoxide dismutase catalyzes the conversion of superoxide to hydrogen peroxide without oxidizing other molecules. Catalase and peroxidase catalyze the reduction of hydrogen peroxide to water without formation of the toxic hydroxyl radical. These enzyme systems are capable of preventing the buildup of toxic species produced from the univalent reduction of oxygen. The cytochrome oxidase complex appears to catalyze the tetravalent reduction of oxygen to water without leakage of reactive intermediates.

ide by the enzyme lipoxygenase or cyclic peroxide by the enzyme cyclo-oxygenase. The NADPH oxidase system of phagocytes yields activated oxygen species especially during inflammation reactions. Oxygen radical production is also associated with ionizing radiation, and metabolism of many chemicals and drugs, including carcinogenic compounds. Formation of reactive oxygen species such as singlet oxygen by a light-mediated mechanism is considered below.

Superoxide and hydrogen peroxide are relatively stable in biological systems, whereas the hydroxyl radical is extremely reactive and capable of producing broad, nonspecific oxidative damage. However, free radicals also play important roles in many biological reactions that maintain normal cell functions, such as mitochondrial and microsomal electron transport systems.

Mechanisms of Lipid Peroxidation

The mechanism by which random oxidation of lipids takes place is called *auto-oxidation*. This oxidation is a free radical chain reaction usually described as a series of three processes: initiation, propagation, and termination. The reaction sequence during the auto-oxidation of the fatty acid linoleate (18:2ω6) is shown in Figure XVIII-2. During the initiation step, the fatty acid is converted to an intermediate radical after removal of an allylic hydrogen. Immediately, the propagation step follows, and the fatty acid radical intermediate reacts with oxygen at either end to produce fatty acid peroxy radicals, removing hydrogens from other fatty acids to form the 9 and 13 conjugated hydroperoxides. Thus a new fatty acid radical is formed, which again can react with oxygen. As long as oxygen is available, one free radical can lead to oxidation of thousands of fatty acids. A termination reaction, in which two radicals form a nonradical product, can interrupt the chain reaction. Auto-oxidation

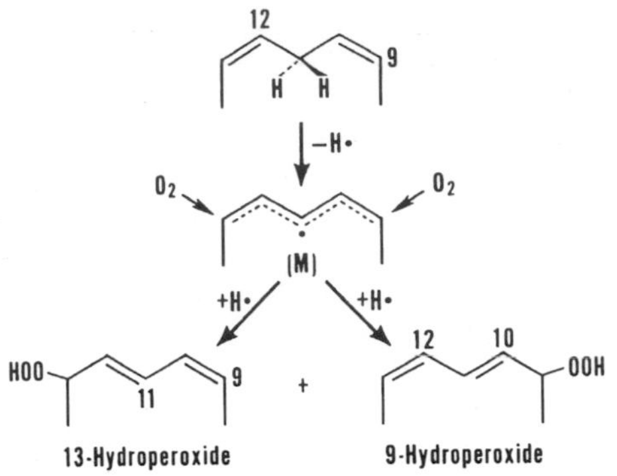

FIG XVIII-2—Mechanism of linoleate auto-oxidation. Formation of two conjugated isomers: 9-hydroperoxide and 13-hydroperoxide.

is also inhibited by free radical scavengers such as vitamin E, which cause termination reactions. Auto-oxidation of arachidonic acid and docosahexaenoic acid yields 6 and 10 conjugated isomers, respectively.

Polyunsaturated fatty acids are susceptible to auto-oxidation because their allylic hydrogens are easily removed by several types of initiating radicals. The primary products of auto-oxidation formed during the propagation step are hydroperoxides (ROOH), which may decompose, especially in the presence of trace amounts of transition metal ions (e.g., free iron or copper), to create peroxy radicals (ROO·), hydroxy radicals (HO·), and oxy radicals (RO·).

Photo-oxidation is a process by which oxygen is activated electronically by light to form singlet oxygen, which in turn reacts at a diffusion-controlled rate with unsaturated fatty acids or other cellular constituents. The mechanism of singlet oxygen generation most often discussed involves exposure of a photosensitizer to light in the presence of normal triplet oxygen ($^3O_2$). A photosensitizer is excited by absorption of light energy to an excited singlet state, which rapidly relaxes to an excited triplet state. In this state the sensitizer may react with triplet oxygen ($^3O_2$) to form singlet

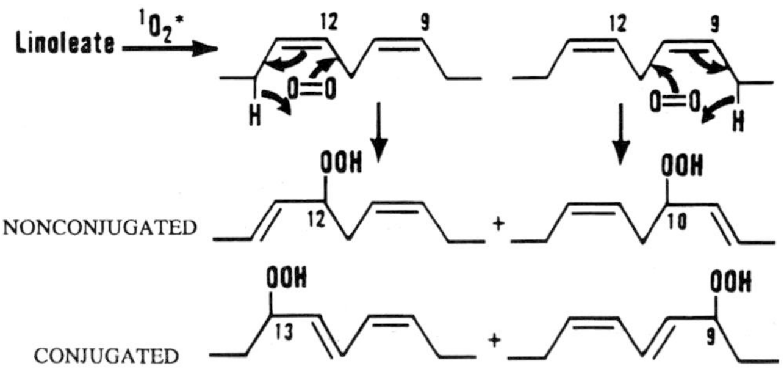

FIG XVIII-3—Mechanism of linoleate photo-oxidation. Formation of two conjugated and two nonconjugated isomers (10-hydroperoxide and 12-hydroperoxide).

oxygen ($^1O_2$). Compared with auto-oxidation, for example, the photo-oxidation of linoleate yields not only the conjugated 9 and 13 hydroperoxides, but the nonconjugated 10 and 12 hydroperoxides as well (Fig XVIII-3). Therefore the occurrence of the nonconjugated hydroperoxide isomers indicates singlet oxygen–induced damage to the polyunsaturated fatty acids. Photo-oxidation can be inhibited by singlet oxygen quenchers such as carotenoids, which are discussed later in this chapter.

Lipid peroxidation not only causes direct damage to the cell membrane but also causes secondary damage in cells through its aldehydic breakdown products. Lipid hydroperoxides are unstable, and they break down to form many aldehydes such as malondialdehyde and 4-hydroxyalkenals. These aldehydes can react quickly with proteins, inhibiting their normal functions. For example, Na^+,K^+-ATPase is easily inhibited by low concentrations of 4-hydroxyalkenals, causing severe electrolyte imbalances. Both the lens and the retina are susceptible to such oxidative damage.

Oxidative Damage to the Lens

Because oxygen tension in the lens is low, free radical reactions in this tissue need not involve molecular oxygen. Once produced, the radicals may react directly with any molecule. DNA, for example, is readily damaged by free radicals. Some of this damage may be repaired, and some may become permanent. Free radicals can also attack the proteins or membrane lipids in the cortex. Repair mechanisms are known to exist for such damage, but they may not be able to keep up, and aldehydic products may accumulate with time. Considerable damage can also be incurred by direct attack of free radicals on proteins. In the lens fibers, where protein synthesis has ceased, the result is thought to be polymerization and cross-linking of proteins, resulting in an increase in water-insoluble material (see chapter XIV).

The lens has several enzymes that function to protect against free radical or oxidative damage, including glutathione peroxidase, catalase, and superoxide dismutase (Fig XVIII-4). Glutathione disulfide (GSSG) is reconverted to glutathione (GSH) by glutathione reductase, using the pyridine nucleotide NADPH provided by the hexose monophosphate shunt as the reducing agent. Thus, glutathione acts indirectly as a major free radical scavenger in the lens. Oxidizing conditions are minimized through effective scavenging of free radicals and enzymatic reduction of compounds capable of initiating or perpetuating lipid peroxidation.

The lens, like all other tissues, must be maintained in a reduced state to remain viable. As discussed above, this state is maintained by a series of chemical and biochemical reactions. The continuous production of small molecules such as reduced glutathione is essential. These molecules react enzymatically and nonenzymatically with a multitude of macromolecules in the cell to keep their sulfhydryl groups reduced.

Ascorbic acid and, to a smaller extent, vitamin E are also present in the lens, and they can protect against oxidative damage, since each has the capacity to act as a free radical scavenger. Carotenoids that can quench singlet oxygen are also present in the lens. Epidemiologic (observational) studies have shown that people with higher levels of plasma antioxidants have a reduced risk of developing cataract. However, this observation does not automatically mean that antioxidant supplements would prevent cataract formation. The effectiveness of antioxidants remains to be established through double-blind controlled trials.

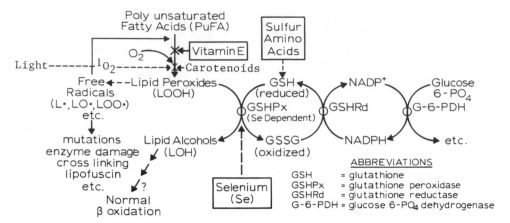

FIG XVIII-4—Diagram illustrating mechanisms by which several antioxidants protect against oxidative damage. *Upper left*, Free radicals lead to the formation of lipid peroxides. Vitamin E inhibits this auto-oxidation process by scavenging free radical intermediates. Carotenoids inhibit photo-oxidation by quenching singlet oxygen ($^1O_2$). *Center*, If lipid hydroperoxides are formed, they can be reduced by glutathione peroxidase (GSHPx), which requires selenium as a cofactor. If these protective enzymes are not fully active, more free radicals are formed by breakdown of lipid peroxides, which in turn leads to additional oxidation of polyunsaturated fatty acids.

Synthetic antioxidants such as butylated hydroxytoluene have been shown to prevent hyperglycemic cataractogenesis in experimental animals despite high polyol levels. It has been proposed that the oxidative mechanism of cataractogenesis involves lipid peroxidation and formation of α-β-unsaturated aldehydes that modifiy proteins. Lipid peroxidation also causes a loss of membrane fluidity with changes in ionic composition of the lens epithelium and fibers, leading to cataract formation.

Ansari NH, Wang L, Srivastava SK, et al. Role of lipid aldehydes in cataractogenesis: 4-hydroxynonenal induced cataract. *Biochem Mol Med*. 1996;58:25–30.

Taylor A, Jacques PF, Epstein EM, et al. Relations among aging, antioxidant status, and cataract. *Am J Clin Nutr*. 1995;62:1439S–1447S.

Vulnerability of the Retina to Free Radicals

Experimental data have shown that retinal photoreceptors degenerate when they are exposed to oxidative challenges such as hyperbaric oxygen, iron overload, or injection of lipid hydroperoxides into the vitreous humor. The retina also degenerates when antioxidative defenses are reduced, which presumably elevates levels of lipid peroxidation in the absence of unusual oxidative stress. The retina is made vulnerable to damage from lipid peroxidation by several distinctive characteristics, four of which are considered here:

□ Vertebrate retinal rod outer segments are susceptible to damage by oxygen because of their high content of polyunsaturated fatty acids. Their phospholipids typically contain about 50 mol% docosahexaenoic acid, the most highly polyunsaturated fatty acid that occurs in nature. It is well established that polyunsaturated fatty acids are sensitive to peroxidation in proportion to their number of double bonds.

□ The rod inner segment is very rich in mitochondria, which may leak activated oxygen species.

□ The excellent oxygen supply through the choroid and the retinal vessels elevates the risk of oxidative damage. Vertebrate retinas maintained in vitro showed at least a sevenfold higher rate of oxygen consumption per mg protein as compared to all other tissues tested, with exception of the adrenal gland. The oxygen tension is highest at the choroid, and drops toward the inner segments as a result of the high metabolic demand for oxygen by their mitochondria. Oxygen consumption has been reported to decrease when the retina is illuminated.

□ Light exposure may trigger singlet oxygen–mediated photooxidative processes, and the RPE may play a key role.

The RPE is tightly packed with endoplasmic reticulum and appears to be rich in antioxidant enzymes in most species tested. The RPE of pigmented animals contains melanin granules, which function as a light trap. Although melanin is commonly assumed to be photoprotective, its role in prevention of light damage to ocular tissues is not clearly understood. Evidence suggests that the RPE is quite sensitive to dietary antioxidant deficiency, in which light-activated melanin may contribute to phototoxicity. If an RPE cell dies, then the numerous photoreceptors supported by that RPE cell may suffer severe damage or death.

Intense light at levels that may be encountered in daily life is phototoxic to the retina. Even though the cornea absorbs some UV light, the retina of young people is exposed to a substantial amount of light in the 350–400 nm range, since young lenses transmit these wavelengths. The lens yellows with age, and the cutoff wavelength in the elderly moves up to about 430 nm. Because the adult lens absorbs nearly 100% of light below 400 nm, little or no UV light reaches the retina in older people. In addition to UV light, blue light (400–500 nm) can be harmful to the retina (blue light hazard). Carotenoids present in the retina act as a blue light filter, shielding the photoreceptors in the retina from this radiation.

Young, RW. Solar radiation and age-related macular degeneration. *Surv Ophthalmol.* 1988;32:252–269.

Antioxidants in the Retina and RPE

Several antioxidant mechanisms have been established in biological systems, including free radical scavenging, quenching of singlet oxygen, and enzymatic reduction of hydroperoxides. Antioxidants characterized in vertebrates include vitamin E, carotenoids, selenium, glutathione (GSH), selenium-dependent glutathione peroxidase, and non-selenium-dependent glutathione peroxidase (glutathione-S-transferase). Antioxidants in vertebrates also include catalase and superoxide dismutase, and antioxidant roles for ascorbate and melanin have also been reported. The relation between some of these antioxidants and the protective mechanisms is shown in Figure XVIII-4.

Yu BP. Cellular defenses against damage from reactive oxygen species. *Physiol Rev.* 1994;74:139–162.

Selenium, Glutathione, Glutathione Peroxidase, and Glutathione-S-Transferase

A number of enzymes have been identified that can provide antioxidant protection by a peroxide-decomposing mechanism. For example, selenium-dependent glutathione peroxidase (GSH-Px) and several enzymes of the glutathione-S-transferase (GSH S Ts) group can reduce organic hydroperoxides. The GSH-Px is also active with H_2O_2 as a substrate, although the GSH-S-Ts group cannot act on H_2O_2. All of these enzymes require GSH, which is converted to oxidized glutathione (GSSG) during the enzymatic reaction. The hexose monophosphate shunt enzymes produce NADPH, which is needed for reduction of GSSG by GSH-reductase. Both GSH-Px and GSH-S-Ts activities have been measured in human and animal retinas. It was found that the human retina also has GSH-S-Ts activities that specifically utilize 4-hydroxyalkenals as substrate and thus may constitute another defense mechanism. The highest concentration of selenium in the human eye is present in the RPE: 100–400 ng in RPE cells of a single human eye, up to 10 times more than in the retina (40 ng). The selenium level in the human retina is constant with age, whereas in the human RPE, selenium increases with age. The two eyes of the same subject show no differences.

Superoxide Dismutase (SOD) and Catalase

Superoxide dismutase catalyzes the dismutation of superoxide to hydrogen peroxide, which is further reduced to water by catalase or peroxidase. Two types of SOD are usually isolated from mammalian tissues: Cu-Zn SOD, the cytoplasmic enzyme, which is inhibited by cyanide; and Mn SOD, the mitochondrial enzyme, which is not inhibited by cyanide.

Catalase catalyzes the reduction of hydrogen peroxide to water. Information on catalase activity in the retina is currently rather limited. Total retinal catalase activity was found to be very low but detectable in the rabbit. A protective role for catalase has been reported in rats in experimental allergic uveitis.

Vitamin E

Vitamin E acts by scavenging free radicals, thus terminating the propagation steps and leading to interruption of the auto-oxidation reaction. Reports on the vitamin E content of the retina of the adult rat raised on normal chow diets show values ranging from 215 to 325 ng. A detailed study on vitamin E content of microdissected parts of vertebrate eyes showed that the RPE is enriched in vitamin E relative to the photoreceptors, and that photoreceptors are enriched relative to most other tissues in the rat. An analysis of the effects of varying dietary vitamin E intake on the vitamin E content of the isolated rod outer segments and other retinal components showed that these tissues are depleted of vitamin E more slowly than most other tissues during dietary vitamin E deficiency. Studies on vitamin E in postmortem human eyes found that vitamin E is higher in the RPE than in the retina. Furthermore, the vitamin E levels in human retinal tissues increase with age until the sixth decade and then decrease. This decrease begins at the age that also marks an increase in the incidence of age-related macular degeneration (ARMD). Epidemiological studies on the relation between antioxidants and ARMD have yielded different results, and currently the AREDS (Age-Related Eye Disease Study) is under way to help understand the role of antioxidants in ARMD.

Friedrichson T, Kalbach HL, Buck P, et al. Vitamin E in macular and peripheral tissues of the human eye. *Curr Eye Res.* 1995;14:693–701.

Ascorbate

Ascorbate (vitamin C) is thought to function synergistically with vitamin E to terminate free radical reactions. It has been proposed that vitamin C can react with the vitamin E radicals formed when vitamin E scavenges free radicals. Vitamin E radicals are then regenerated to native vitamin E. The vitamin C radicals thus produced can be reduced by NADH reductase with NADH as electron acceptor. Ascorbic acid is found throughout the eye of many species in concentrations that are high relative to other tissues.

Garland, DL. Ascorbic acid and the eye. *Am J Clin Nutr.* 1991;54:1198S–1202S.

Carotenoids

Various roles have been proposed for carotenoids (xanthophylls) in biological systems, including limiting chromatic aberration at the fovea of the retina and the quenching of singlet oxygen. β-carotene is the precursor for vitamin A and can act as a free radical trap at low oxygen tension. In postmortem human retinas, carotenoids have been shown to make up the yellow pigment in the macula. A mixture of the two carotenoids *lutein* and *zeaxanthin* is present in the macula and located in the fibers of Henle. Recently, it was demonstrated that in humans zeaxanthin is primarily concentrated in the fovea, whereas lutein is dispersed throughout the retina. Interestingly, there is no β-carotene present in the human eye. Furthermore, carotenoids are only present in the retina and not at all in the RPE. In the peripheral retina, lutein and zeaxanthin are also enriched in the photoreceptor outer segments (Sommerburg et al, unpublished results). It is not yet known if carotenoids are also present in cone outer segments, because a good purification method for cones is not available (note that there is no yellow color in the cones in Figure XVIII-6B). Figure XVIII-5 shows the structure of vitamin E and the carotenoids. Figure XVIII-6A shows their localization in the human macula and peripheral retina, whereas Figure XVIII-6B shows their localization in a cross section of the peripheral retina.

Bone RA, Landrum JT, Tarsis SL, et al. Preliminary identification of the human macular pigment. *Vision Res.* 1985;25:1531–1535.

Handelman GJ, Dratz EA, Reay CC, et al. Carotenoids in the human macula and whole retina. *Invest Ophthalmol Vis Sci.* 1988;29:850–855.

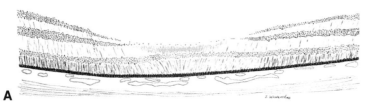

Vitamin E

Lutein

Zeaxanthin

FIG XVIII-5—Structure of vitamin E and the carotenoids lutein and zeaxanthin.

A

FIG XVIII-6—*A,* The localization of antioxidants in the human macula and peripheral retina. Yellow represents carotenoids, blue represents vitamin E, and red represents selenium. Vitamin E and selenium are primarily concentrated in the RPE. In the macula carotenoids are present in the fibers of Henle, but in the peripheral retina carotenoids are also present in the rods. *B,* The localization in a cross section of the peripheral retina. Vitamin E and selenium remain primarily concentrated in the RPE but are also enriched in the rod outer segments. Carotenoids have been found in rod outer segments in the peripheral retina, but it is not yet known if they are also present in outer segments of cones. (Illustrations by J. Woodward, MD.)

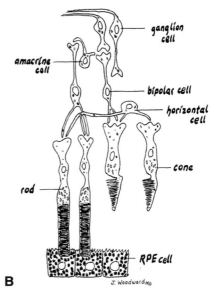

B

PART 5

OCULAR PHARMACOLOGY

Contributors to this revised section include Vipul Dutta, MD, and Mark Pophal, MD, from University of South Carolina School of Medicine.

CHAPTER XIX

Introduction

The majority of drugs used to treat ocular conditions either mimic or block the actions of neural or humoral transmitters. Pharmacologic interventions generally work by manipulation of physiologic processes, yet they differ from these processes in many ways. For example, the pharmacologic agents in dilating drops are applied in a location remote from their intended sites of action but in relatively enormous quantities that swamp homeostatic mechanisms, while the neurotransmitters that control the pupil are released in precise locations in minute quantities and participate in a delicately balanced system.

Chronic pharmacologic interventions, as in the treatment of glaucoma, depend upon a frequently unreliable mechanism—the patient—to deliver agents. These interventions use bolus administration and require empirical adjustment of doses. Physiologic processes in healthy patients are, by contrast, reliable mechanisms that deliver appropriate quantities of agents on a continuous basis through the use of well-controlled avenues of feedback.

Pharmacologic agents often produce unwanted side effects by acting at sites other than the intended ones, often induce counteracting mechanisms (induction of drug-metabolizing enzymes, down-regulation of receptors) that alter their effectiveness, and occasionally induce allergic reactions. Physiologic agents are generally highly specific, work in concert with feedback mechanisms, and usually have immune privilege.

All of these differences between pharmacologic interventions and physiologic processes have practical implications for both the present and future practice of ophthalmology. Even in situations in which underlying pathophysiologic lesions are unknown and current therapies merely create counteracting lesions, modeling therapies to mimic features of physiologic processes can often create an advantage. Attempts to deliver agents preferentially to the desired site of action and continuously from sustained-release devices or depots have been and will be rewarded by improved efficacy and compliance and reduction of side effects. Future advances in therapy might come from mimicking or harnessing physiologic processes, as in the following examples:

- Coupling drug release to feedback-control mechanisms (e.g., glaucoma therapy regulated by a pressure-sensing strain gauge)
- Achieving higher specificity of action by designing drugs to complement the geometry of receptor sites
- Manipulating the genome to effect repair or regeneration through direction of physiologic processes

CHAPTER XX

Pharmacologic Principles

The study of ocular pharmacology begins with a review of some general principles of pharmacology with particular attention to special features of the eye that facilitate or impede certain therapeutic approaches.

Pharmacokinetics

To achieve a therapeutic effect, a drug must reach its site of action in sufficient concentration. The concentration at the site of action is a function of the following:

□ Amount administered

□ Extent and rate of absorption at the administration site

□ Distribution and binding in tissues

□ Movement by bulk flow in circulating fluids

□ Transport between compartments

□ Biotransformation

□ Excretion

Eyedrops

Most ocular medications are administered as eyedrops. With this route of administration adequate concentrations can be achieved in the anterior segment without incurring unwanted effects in other body systems, an advantage over systemic therapy for most drugs.

Some features of topical ocular therapy limit its effectiveness, however. Very little of an administered drop is retained by the eye. When a 50-μl eyedrop is delivered from the usual commercial dispenser, the volume of lacrimal fluid held by the eyelids and cul-de-sac rises from 7 μl to only 10 μl in the blinking eye of an upright patient. Thus, at most 20% of the administered drug is retained (10 μl/50 μl). A rapid turnover of fluid in the tear reservoir also occurs, 16% per minute in the undisturbed eye and much more if the drop elicits reflex tearing. Consequently, for slowly absorbed drugs, only 50% of the drug that reached the tear reservoir remains 4 minutes after instillation ($0.84^4 = 0.50$), and only 17% after 10 minutes.

Some simple measures have been shown to improve ocular absorption of materials that do not traverse the cornea rapidly. Patients taking more than one eyedrop medication should be instructed to wait 5 minutes between drops; otherwise, the second drop may simply wash out the first. Patients can also be instructed to compress the nasolacrimal duct with digital pressure at the medial canthus, both to prevent egress of tear fluid by that route and to reduce systemic absorption through the nasal mucosa. The lacrimal pumping mechanism can also be halted by the simpler measure of instructing patients to keep their eyes closed for 5 minutes after taking drops. This step increases the ocular absorption of topically applied materials (Fig XX-1) and decreases systemic absorption (Fig XX-2).

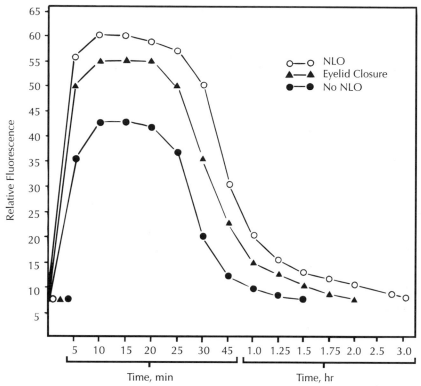

FIG XX-1—Fluorescein concentration in the anterior chamber at various times after application: with nasolacrimal occlusion (NLO), with 5 minutes of eyelid closure, or with no intervention (no NLO).

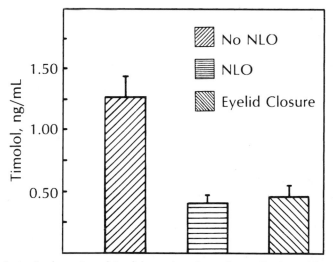

FIG XX-2—Systemic absorption of timolol at various times after application: with nasolacrimal obstruction (NLO), with 5 minutes of eyelid closure, or with no intervention (no NLO).

Because the contact time of eyedrop medications is short, the rate of transfer from the tear fluid into the cornea is critical. The cornea lacks fenestrated barriers such as the vascular endothelium and mucosa of the stomach, which allow rapid diffusion of all but large molecules through extracellular passages. Instead, the corneal epithelium and endothelium have tight intercellular junctions that limit passage in the extracellular space; therefore, drugs must pass through cell membranes. Breakdown of these barriers in clinical situations such as corneal abrasion multiplies the rates of intraocular drug penetration.

Among the other factors that determine the amount of medication to penetrate the cornea are drug concentration and solubility, viscosity, lipid solubility, surfactants, and reflex tearing.

Drug concentration and solubility In order to get a sufficient amount of a drug through the corneal barriers, it is often necessary to load the small tear reservoir with concentrated solutions (e.g., 1%–4% pilocarpine). A practical limit to exploiting these high concentrations is reached when the high tonicity of the resulting solutions elicits reflex tearing or when drugs that are poorly water soluble reach their solubility limits.

Viscosity The addition of high-viscosity substances such as methylcellulose and polyvinyl alcohol increases drug penetration. However, because there is little correlation between effectiveness and solution viscosity, such substances may act by altering the barrier function of the corneal epithelium as well as by increasing drug contact time with the cornea.

Lipid solubility To traverse the cornea, a drug must pass in turn through the lipid-rich environment of the epithelial cell membranes, the water-rich environment of the stroma, and another lipid barrier at the endothelium. Studies of the permeability of isolated corneas to families of chemical compounds show that lipid solubility is more important than water solubility in promoting penetration.

First, the ratio of lipid solubility to water solubility is ascertained for each compound in the series. This ratio is determined by adding the drug to a phase separation, such as octanol floating on water, and then calculating the ratio of concentrations (partition coefficient) in the two compartments. The greater the relative lipid solubility, the higher the partition coefficient.

For substituted ethoxzolamides, a 70-fold higher permeability coefficient is observed for compounds of high lipid solubility compared to those of low lipid solubility (Fig XX-3). However, compounds with excessively high partition coefficients are often poorly soluble in tears. To develop the most effective drugs, studies of systematically substituted compounds need to take into account the effects of substituents on potency and solubility as well as on the permeability coefficient.

Many eye medications are alkaloids, or weak bases. Such drugs as tropicamide, cyclopentolate, atropine, and epinephrine exist in both charged and uncharged forms at the slightly alkaline pH of tears. The partition coefficients of these drugs can be increased by raising the pH of the water phase, thereby increasing the proportion of drug molecules in the more lipid-soluble, uncharged form.

Surfactants Many preservative agents used in eyedrops to prevent bacterial contamination are surface-active agents that alter cell membranes in the cornea as well as in bacteria. They reduce the barrier effect of the corneal epithelium and increase

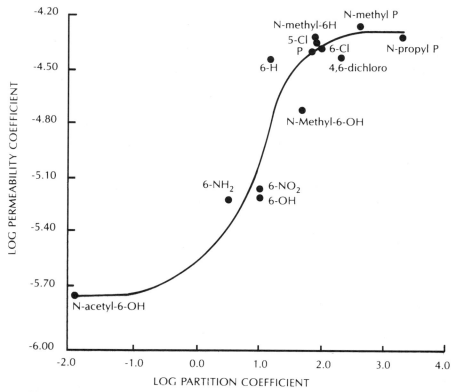

FIG XX-3—The log-log relationship of permeability coefficient (rabbit cornea) and partition coefficient (octanol/buffer). The more lipid-soluble compounds in the series (toward the right in the plot) are also the best able to penetrate the cornea (toward the top of the plot).

drug permeabilities. For example, a 0.1% carbachol solution containing 0.03% benzalkonium chloride can elicit the same miotic response as a 2% solution without it.

Reflex tearing   Such tearing reduces the contact time of the drug with the cornea. It can occur when eyedrops have a pH value much different from the physiologic 7.4, are not isotonic, or contain irritants.

Ointments

Another strategy for increasing the contact time of ocular medications is the use of ointments. Commercial oil-based ointments usually consist of petrolatum and mineral oil. The mineral oil allows the ointment to melt at body temperature. Both ingredients are also effective lipid solvents. However, most water-soluble medications are insoluble in the ointment and are present as microcrystals. Only those microcrystals on the surface of the ointment dissolve in the tears, while the rest are trapped until the ointment melts. Such protracted but slow release may prevent the drug from reaching a therapeutic level in the tears. Only if the drug has a high lipid solubility, which allows it to diffuse through the ointment, and some water solubility will it escape from the ointment into both the corneal epithelium and the tears. Fluorometholone, chloramphenicol, and tetracycline are examples of drugs that achieve higher aqueous levels when administered as ointment than as drops.

Periocular Injections

Injection of medication beneath the conjunctiva or Tenon's capsule allows drugs to bypass the conjunctival and corneal epithelial barriers. Injections into these sites and retrobulbar injections can allow medications to reach therapeutic levels behind the lens–iris diaphragm. This approach is especially useful for drugs with low lipid solubilities (such as penicillin), which do not penetrate the eye adequately if they are given topically.

Intraocular Injections

Intraocular injection of drugs delivers effective concentrations at the target site instantly. However, the dangers inherent in intraocular injections far outweigh possible benefits in almost all circumstances. The only clear indication for this route is the administration of antibiotics during surgery for endophthalmitis associated with an infected laceration. Only minute amounts of antibiotic are tolerated within the eye. For example, the maximum safe anterior chamber dose of polymyxin B is 0.1 mg.

Sustained-Release Oral Preparations

The practical value of sustained-release preparations is significant. For example, a single dose of acetazolamide will reduce IOP for up to 10 hours, whereas a single dose of sustained-release acetazolamide will produce a comparable effect lasting 20 hours. Sustained-release medications offer a more steady blood level of the drug, avoid marked peaks and valleys, and reduce the frequency of administration.

Systemic Therapy

Just as the intercellular tight junctions of the corneal epithelium and endothelium limit anterior access to the interior of the eye, similar barriers limit access through vascular channels. The vascular endothelium of the retina, like that of the brain, is nonfenestrated and knitted together by tight junctions. While both the choroid and the ciliary body have fenestrated vascular endothelia, the choroid is effectively bound by the retinal pigment epithelium and the ciliary body by its nonpigmented epithelium.

The blood–ocular barrier, like the cornea, is more readily penetrated by drugs with higher lipid solubilities. Thus, chloramphenicol, which is highly lipid soluble, penetrates 20 times better than penicillin, which has poor lipid solubility.

The ability of systemically administered drugs to gain access to the eye is also influenced by the degree to which they are bound to plasma proteins. Only the unbound form can cross the blood–ocular barriers. Sulfonamides are lipid soluble but penetrate poorly, because at therapeutic levels more than 90% of the medication is bound to plasma proteins. Similarly, the greater protein binding of oxacillin reduces its penetration, compared with methicillin. Bolus administration of a drug exceeds the binding capacity of plasma proteins and leads to higher intraocular drug levels than can be achieved by a slow intravenous drip. This approach is used for the administration of antibiotics, which must reach high peak intraocular levels.

Intravenous Injections

Continuous intravenous administration of an antibiotic is assumed to be an effective way of maintaining intraocular levels. Because of the barriers and possible reservoir effects of the eye, however, antibiotics such as ampicillin, chloramphenicol, and erythromycin penetrate the eye at higher initial levels and maintain at least comparable intraocular levels for 4 hours when given as a single intravenous bolus rather than by continuous infusion.

Inflammation may affect the barrier properties of the eye to permit better penetration of substances from the circulation. This effect is demonstrated by the appearance of fluorescein in the vitreous as a result of leakage from the retinal vessels in the presence of inflammation.

The distribution of ampicillin, tetracycline, and dexamethasone in rabbit eye tissues after intravenous administration has been studied. The highest levels were found in the sclera and conjunctiva, followed by the iris and ciliary body, cornea, aqueous humor, choroid, and retina. Very low levels appeared in the lens and vitreous. The drugs showed no marked differences in their distribution. The distribution pattern is determined by the vascularity of the tissue and the barriers that exist between the blood and the tissue.

Methods of Ocular Drug Design and Delivery

Ocular drugs are being designed with a focus on specificity and safety, and new delivery systems hold promise for improving convenience and compliance. Each of the approaches that are discussed below responds to a specific problem in ocular pharmacokinetics.

Pro-drugs Pro-drugs are compounds that are inactive until enzymatically activated. *Dipivefrin HCl* (DPE, Propine) is a pro-drug of epinephrine. The presence of two pivalyl residues increases 17-fold the parent compound's ability to penetrate the cornea (Fig XX-4). Thus, a 0.1% solution of DPE can be used in place of epinephrine 1%–2%. The pivalyl groups are cleaved by corneal esterases, releasing epinephrine into the anterior chamber. Because DPE has low intrinsic activity and is used in a lower concentration, it is virtually free of the systemic side effects of epinephrine. It is therefore a better-targeted drug.

Sustained-release devices and gels Drop therapy involves periodic delivery of relatively large quantities of a drug. Enough of the drug must reach receptors to achieve a therapeutic effect, while more remains in the surrounding tissues to act as a local reservoir between applications. This application of greater quantities of the drug than would be needed to achieve short-term effects leads in many cases to unwanted side effects (e.g., miosis and induced accommodation with the use of pilocarpine).

Devices have been developed that deliver an adequate supply of medication at a steady-state level, thus achieving beneficial effects with fewer side effects. The

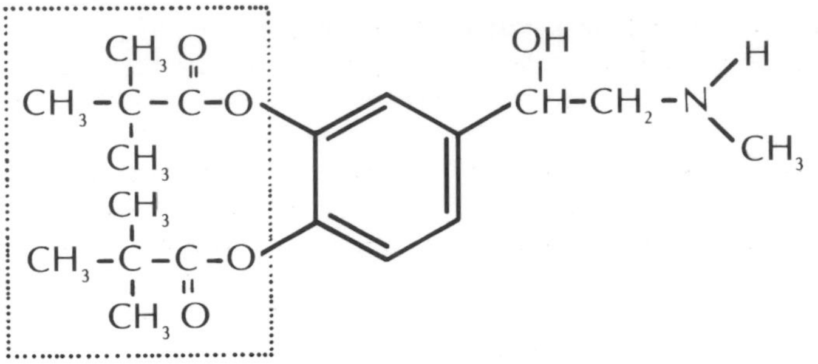

FIG XX-4—The structure of dipevefrin (DPE).

Ocusert Delivery System (Fig XX-5) delivers pilocarpine at a steady rate of 40 µg/hr, and its therapeutic effect in lowering intraocular pressure is equivalent to 2% pilocarpine used 4 times a day. Yet because the total daily dose of pilocarpine is only 960 µg (24 hours × 40 µg/hr) when delivered with the device as compared to 4000 µg (4 doses × 2000 mg/100 cc × 0.05 cc/dose) with drops, miosis is less marked and the induced accommodation is reduced.

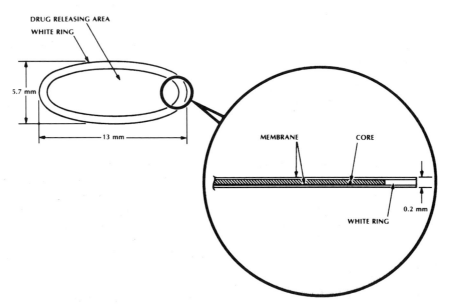

FIG XX-5—The Ocusert Delivery System.

A newer form of timolol maleate, *Timoptic-XE,* is a novel example of sustained release. It contains a heteropolysaccharide that becomes a gel on contact with tear film and acts as a local reservoir, delivering therapeutic levels of the drug between applications.

Another example is the *gancyclovir sustained-release intraocular device (GIOD).* Gancyclovir, an antiviral agent, is incorporated in a polyvinyl alcohol coating and suspended from the sclera into the intravitreal cavity. An ethylvinyl acetate disc with polyvinyl alcohol coating serves as a reservoir. The thickness of the polyvinyl alcohol lid regulates the delivery of gancyclovir to target tissue. Typically, the implant is effective for 8 months. It was recently approved by the Food and Drug Administration for intraocular use.

Collagen cornea shields   Porcine scleral tissue is extracted and molded into these contact lens–like shields, which are useful as a delivery system to prolong the contact between a drug and the cornea. Drugs can be incorporated into the collagen matrix during the manufacturing process, absorbed into the shield during rehydration, or applied topically over the shield in the eye. Because the shield dissolves in 12, 24, or 72 hours, depending on the manufacturing process for collagen cross-linking, the drug is released gradually into the tear film, and high concentrations are maintained on the corneal surface and conjunctival cul-de-sac.

The results of experimental investigations suggest that drug delivery by collagen shields may be more helpful in the early management of bacterial keratitis than other conventional modes. Clinical studies indicate that collagen shield drug delivery may be useful in providing antibiotic prophylaxis against possible infection while promoting epithelial healing after ocular surgery, trauma, or spontaneous erosion. Despite these therapeutic benefits, the collagen shields are poorly tolerated as they are very uncomfortable.

Liposomes   Liposomes are synthetic lipid microspheres that serve as multipurpose vehicles for the topical delivery of drugs, genetic material, and cosmetics. They are produced when certain phospholipid molecules interact to form a bilayer lipid membrane in an aqueous environment. The interior of the bilayer consists of the hydrophobic fatty acid tails of the phospholipid molecule, whereas the outer layer is composed of hydrophilic polar-head groups of the molecule. The lipid membranes close up to produce a spherical envelope with the formation of either unilamellar or multilamellar liposomes.

Depending on their chemical properties, drugs can be incorporated into liposomes in several ways. A water-soluble drug is dissolved in the aqueous phase of the interior compartment, whereas a hydrophobic drug can be intercalated into the lipid bilayer itself. Liposome encapsulation of drugs for topical application and injection permits sustained levels of drug release over prolonged periods of time, and it may also permit the use of high concentrations of drugs by substantially reducing toxicity to surrounding tissues. Gels that release pilocarpine and ocular lubricant slowly have also been developed.

Iontophoresis   The physical process of moving charged molecules by an electrical current is called *iontophoresis.* This mechanism is based on the physical principle that ions are repelled by poles of the same charge and attracted by poles of opposite charge. A major advantage of using iontophoresis for drug delivery is the elimination of systemic toxicity. This procedure places a relatively high concentration of the drug locally, where it can achieve maximum benefit with little wastage or systemic absorption. Animal studies have demonstrated that iontophoresis increases penetration of various antibiotics and antiviral drugs across ocular surfaces into the cornea and the interior of the eye. However, the disadvantages associated with the procedure, such as patient discomfort, ocular tissue damage, and necrosis, restrict the popularity of this mode of drug delivery.

Pharmacodynamics

Most drugs act by binding to and altering the function of regulatory macromolecules, usually neurotransmitter or hormone receptors or enzymes. Binding may be a reversible association mediated by electrostatic and/or van der Waals forces, or it may involve formation of a covalent intermediate. If the drug-receptor interaction stimulates the receptor's natural function, the drug is termed an *agonist*. Stimulation of an opposing effect characterizes an *antagonist*. Corresponding effectors of enzymes are termed *activators* and *inhibitors*. This terminology is crucial to understanding the next chapter.

The relationship between the initial drug-receptor interaction and the clinical drug's dose-response may be simple or complex. In some cases the drug's clinical effect closely reflects the degree of receptor occupancy on a moment-to-moment basis. Such is usually the case for drugs that affect neural transmission or that are enzyme inhibitors. In contrast, some drug effects lag hours behind receptor occupancy or persist long after the drug is gone. Such is the case with many drugs acting on hormone receptors, because their effects are often mediated through a series of biochemical events. In addition to differences in timing of receptor occupancy and drug effects, considerable differences can be seen between the degree of receptor occupancy and corresponding drug effect. For example, because the amount of carbonic anhydrase present in the ciliary processes is 100 times that required to support aqueous secretion, more than 99% of the enzyme must be inhibited before a reduction in secretion is observed. On the other hand, some maximal hormone responses occur at concentrations well below that required for receptor saturation, indicating the presence of "inbound receptors."

Eller MG, Schoenwald RD, Dixson JA, et al. Topical carbonic anhydrase inhibitors. III: Optimization model for corneal penetration of ethoxzolamide analogues. *J Pharm Sci.* 1985;74:155–160.

Mandell AI, Stentz F, Kitabchi AE. Dipivalyl epinephrine: a new pro-drug in the treatment of glaucoma. *Ophthalmology.* 1978;85:268–275.

Poland DE, Kaufman HE. Clinical uses of collagen shields. *J Cataract Refract Surg.* 1988;14:489–491.

Schaeffer HE, Krohn DL. Liposomes in topical drug delivery. *Invest Ophthalmol Vis Sci.* 1982;22:220–227.

Zimmerman TJ, Kooner KS, Kandarakis AS, et al. Improving the therapeutic index of topically applied ocular drugs. *Arch Ophthalmol.* 1984;102:551–553.

CHAPTER XXI

Ocular Pharmacotherapeutics

Cholinergic Agents

A number of commonly used ophthalmic medications affect the activity of acetylcholine receptors in synapses of the peripheral nervous system (Fig XXI-1). Such receptors are found in

☐ The motor end plates of the extraocular muscles and levator palpebrae superioris (supplied by *somatic motor nerves*)

☐ The cells of the superior cervical ganglion (sympathetic) and the ciliary and sphenopalatine (parasympathetic) ganglia (supplied by *preganglionic autonomic nerves*)

☐ Parasympathetic effector sites in the iris sphincter and ciliary body and in the lacrimal, accessory lacrimal, and meibomian glands (supplied by *postganglionic parasympathetic nerves*)

Although all cholinergic receptors are by definition responsive to acetylcholine, they are not homogeneous in their responsiveness to other agents. Such agents fall into two categories:

☐ *Nicotinic agents* are supplied by somatic motor and preganglionic autonomic nerves and are responsive to nicotine

☐ *Muscarinic agents* are supplied by postganglionic parasympathetic nerves and are responsive to muscarine

Cholinergic agents are further divided into the following groups (Fig XXI-2):

☐ *Direct-acting agonists* act on the receptor to elicit an excitatory postsynaptic potential

☐ *Indirect-acting agonists* inhibit the acetylcholinesterase of the synaptic cleft, preventing deactivation of endogenous acetylcholine

☐ *Antagonists* block the action of acetylcholine on the receptor

Muscarinic Drugs

Direct-acting agonists Topically applied direct-acting agonists have three actions. First, they cause contraction of the iris sphincter, which not only constricts the pupil (miosis) but also changes the anatomical relationship of the iris to the lens and the chamber angle. Second, they cause contraction of the circular fibers of the ciliary muscle, relaxing the zonular tension on the lens equator and allowing the lens to assume a more spherical shape (accommodation). The lens also undergoes a small forward displacement. Third, they cause contraction of the longitudinal fibers of the ciliary muscle, producing tension on the scleral spur and on the trabecular meshwork lamellae, which spreads the trabecular lamellae and increases aqueous out-

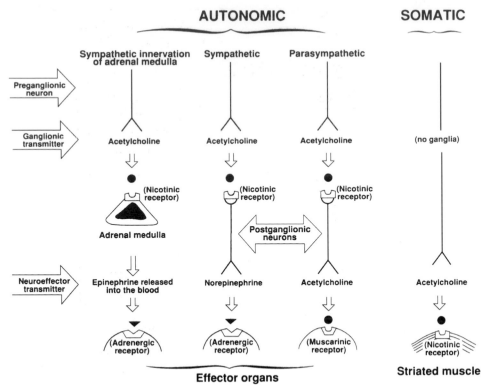

FIG XXI-1—Summary of the neurotransmitters released and the types of receptors found within the autonomic and somatic nervous systems. (Reproduced with permission from Mycek MJ, Harvey RA, Champe PC, eds. *Lippincott's Illustrated Reviews: Pharmacology.* 2nd ed. Philadelphia: Lippincott-Raven; 1997:32.)

flow facility. Contraction of the ciliary musculature also produces tension on the peripheral retina, occasionally resulting in a retinal tear or even rhegmatogenous detachment.

Acetylcholine does not penetrate the corneal epithelium well, and it is rapidly degraded by acetylcholinesterase (Fig XXI-3). Thus, it is not used topically. Acetylcholine 1% (Miochol) and *carbachol* 0.01% (Miostat) are, however, available for intracameral use in anterior segment surgery. These drugs produce prompt and marked miosis, which helps avoid iris capture by the optic of posterior chamber lenses and may prevent iris incarceration in surgical wounds. However, the drugs may also increase the risk of pupillary-block angle closure in the absence of a patent peripheral iridectomy.

Acetyl-beta-methylcholine, also known as *methacholine* (Mecholyl) 2.5%, and *pilocarpine* 0.12% are used to confirm Adie's tonic pupil, a condition in which the parasympathetic innervation of the iris sphincter and ciliary muscle is defective as a result of the loss of postganglionic fibers. Denervated muscarinic smooth muscle

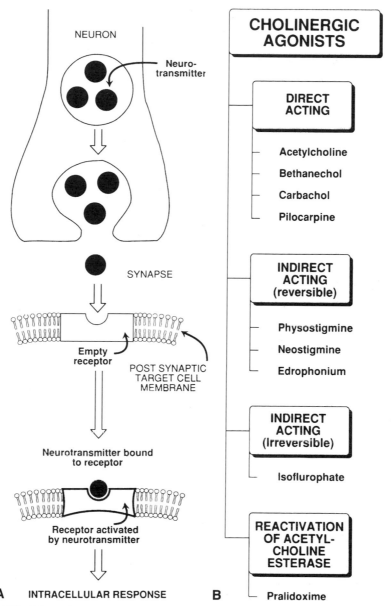

A   INTRACELLULAR RESPONSE   **B**

FIG XXI-2—*A,* Neurotransmitter binding triggers an intracellular response. (Reproduced with permission from Harvey RA, Champe PC, eds. *Lippincott's Illustrated Reviews: Pharmacology.* Philadelphia: Lippincott; 1992:30.) *B,* Summary of cholinergic agonists. (Reproduced with permission from Mycek MJ, Harvey RA, Champe PC, *Lippincott's Illustrated Reviews: Pharmacology.* 2nd ed. Philadelphia: Lippincott-Raven; 1997:35.)

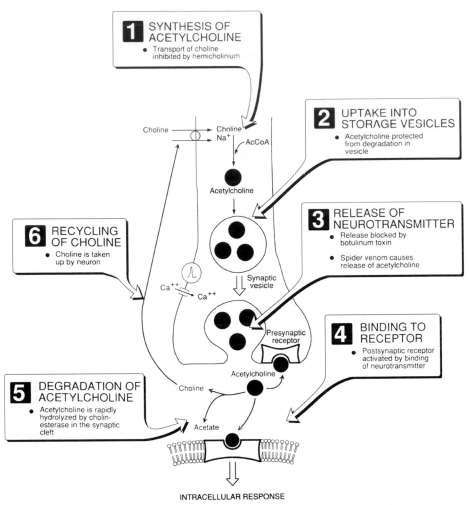

FIG XXI-3—Synthesis and release of acetylcholine from the cholinergic neuron. (Reproduced with permission from Mycek MJ, Harvey RA, Champe PC, eds. *Lippincott's Illustrated Reviews: Pharmacology.* 2nd ed. Philadelphia: Lippincott-Raven; 1997:37.)

fibers in the affected segments of the iris exhibit supersensitivity and respond well to these weak miotics, while normal iris does not.

Pilocarpine 1%–6% and carbachol 0.75%–3.00% (qid) are used in the treatment of primary open-angle glaucoma because they lower IOP by increasing outflow facility (Table XXI-1). Usage of 4% pilocarpine is contraindicated in acute attacks, which may induce intense anterior movement of the lens–iris diaphragm, closing the angle completely. Miotic therapy is not an adequate substitute for laser iridotomy and should not be relied upon for chronic control or prophylaxis of

TABLE XXI-1

MIOTICS

GENERIC NAME	TRADE NAME	STRENGTHS (%)
Cholinergic Agents		
Carbachol	Isopto Carbachol	0.75%–3%
Pilocarpine hydrochloride	Akarpine	1%–4%
	Isopto Carpine	0.25%–10%
	Ocusert Pilo	20, 40 µg/hr
	Pilocar	0.5%–0.6%
	Pilopine HS gel	4%
	Piloptic	0.5%–0.6%
	Pilostat	1%–4%
	Storzine	1%–4%
	Available generically	0.5%–0.6%
Pilocarpine nitrate	Pilagan	1%–4%
Cholinesterase Inhibitors		
Physostigmine	Isopto Eserine	0.25%, 0.5%
	Available generically as	
	Eserine Oph Oint	0.25%
Demecarium	Humorsol	0.25%, 0.5%
Echothiophate iodide	Phospholine iodide	0.03%–0.25%

pupillary-block angle-closure glaucoma. (See also BCSC Section 10, *Glaucoma,* chapter XI.)

Miosis, cataractogenesis, and induced myopia are generally unwelcome side effects of muscarinic therapy. While the broad range of retinal dark adaptation usually compensates sufficiently for the effect of miosis upon vision during daylight hours, patients may be visually incapacitated in dim illumination. In addition, miosis often compounds the effect of axial lenticular opacities; many cataract patients are unable to tolerate miotics. The myopia induced by ciliary muscle contraction may be disabling in individuals below the age of 50, who show substantial induced accommodation. Miotic cysts and increased incidence of retinal detachment are some of the other complications. Systemic side effects after ocular use of pilocarpine are rare. They include salivation, diarrhea, vomiting, bronchial spasm, and diaphoresis (Fig XXI-4).

Ciliary muscle stimulation can be desirable in the management of accommodative esotropia. The near response is a synkinesis of accommodation, miosis, and convergence. Muscarinic agonists reduce the need to accommodate; thus, accommodative esotropia is also reduced because the patient not only accommodates less but also converges less.

Side effects may be reduced by using a device (Ocusert) that delivers the drug continuously at a low rate. Alternatively, a sufficient amount of the drug for a day's therapy can be delivered in a slowly dissolving gel (Pilopine HS gel) administered at bedtime so that the unwanted effects occur primarily during sleep.

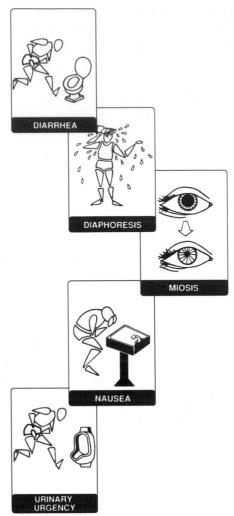

FIG XXI-4—Some adverse effects observed with cholinergic drugs. (Reproduced with permission from Mycek MJ, Harvey RA, Champe PC, eds. *Lippincott's Illustrated Reviews: Pharmacology.* 2nd ed. Philadelphia: Lippincott-Raven; 1997:40.)

Aceclidine is a synthetic cholinergic drug that acts directly on muscarinic end plates in a manner similar to pilocarpine. In human eyes with open angles the pressure-lowering effect of 4% aceclidine was found comparable with that of 2% pilocarpine. Aceclidine produces far less accommodative spasm than does pilocarpine and could become the drug of choice for glaucoma patients young enough to retain considerable accommodation. In a recent study the induced myopia 45 minutes after administration of 2% aceclidine was 0.34 D, compared with 2.96 D from instillation of 2% pilocarpine. This drug is currently available only in Europe.

Indirect-acting agonists Topically applied indirect-acting muscarinic agonists (cholinesterase inhibitors) have the same actions as direct-acting muscarinic agonists, although they have a longer duration of action and are frequently more potent. Treatment twice a day is sufficient. They work by reacting with the active serine hydroxyl site of cholinesterases, creating the formation of a slowly hydrolyzed intermediate (Fig XXI-5). Thus, they render the enzyme unavailable for hydrolyzing spontaneously released acetylcholine. There are two classes of cholinesterase inhibitors:

□ *Reversible inhibitors*, such as *physostigmine* (Eserine), which carbamylate acetylcholinesterase

□ *Irreversible inhibitors,* such as echothiophate (Phospholine Iodide) and *diisopropyl phosphorofluoridate* (DFP), which phosphorylate both the acetylcholinesterase of the synaptic cleft and the butyrylcholinesterase (pseudocholinesterase) of plasma

One carbamylating agent, *demecarium bromide* (Humorsol) is also irreversible; it contains two carbamyl groups and cross-links units of the enzyme.

Carbamylenzyme is regenerated by hydrolysis of the carbamyl-ester linkage over a 3–4 hour period. Regeneration of dialkylphosphorylated enzyme is so slow, however, that recovery of activity depends primarily upon new enzyme synthesis.

The action of phosphorylating cholinesterase inhibitors can be reversed acutely by treatment with oxime-containing compounds that remove the dialkylphosphate moiety from the enzyme. This treatment must take place rapidly, before the spontaneous elimination of one of the alkyl residues ($T\frac{1}{2}$ = 20 minutes for butyrylcholinesterase, 270 minutes for acetylcholinesterase), which makes the monoalkylphosphate intermediate no longer susceptible to regeneration by oxime. Thus, the oxime *pralidoxime* (2-PAM), although useful in the treatment of acute organophosphate poisoning (e.g., insecticide exposure), is of little value in reversing the marked reduction of plasma butyrylcholinesterase activity that occurs with chronic irreversible cholinesterase-inhibitor therapy.

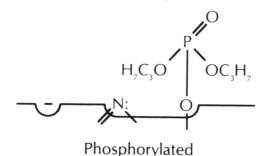

Phosphorylated Enzyme

FIG XXI-5—The enzyme-inhibitor intermediate.

Patients on such therapy may experience toxic reactions from systemic absorption of local anesthetics containing ester groups (e.g., procaine) that are normally inactivated by plasma cholinesterase. Administration of the muscle relaxant succinylcholine during induction of general anesthesia is also hazardous in such patients, because the drug would not be metabolized and would result in prolonged respiratory paralysis.

Phosphorylating cholinesterase inhibitors also have local ocular toxicities. Children may develop cystlike proliferations of the iris pigment epithelium at the pupil margin that can block the pupil. For unknown reasons, cyst development can be minimized by concomitant use of phenylephrine (2.5%) drops. Adults may develop cataracts or have progression of preexisting opacities. Interestingly, children rarely if ever develop such cataracts, and adults rarely if ever develop significant epithelial cysts.

Therapy with cholinesterase inhibitors should not be combined with direct-acting cholinergic agonists, because the combination is less effective than either drug given alone.

Pilocarpine has less intrinsic muscarinic activity than acetylcholine. If cholinesterase inhibitors are given first, then pilocarpine acts as a partial antagonist because it competes with acetylcholine. Thus, the miosis from physostigmine decreases slightly after administration of pilocarpine, and a similar reduction in pressure-lowering effect probably occurs as well.

Because cholinesterase inhibitors are potent insecticides, they have been used in the treatment of lice infestations of the eyelashes. The adult form of the crab louse appears susceptible, while the nits are more resistant and must be removed mechanically. *Demodex folliculorum,* or hair follicle mite, is less sensitive and can survive 3 or more days of treatment with echothiophate or DFP.

Antagonists   Topically applied muscarinic antagonists, such as *atropine,* react with postsynaptic muscarinic receptors and block the action of acetylcholine. The resultant paralysis of the iris sphincter, coupled with the unopposed action of the dilator muscle, causes pupillary dilation, or *mydriasis* (Table XXI-2). Mydriasis facilitates examination of the peripheral lens, ciliary body, and retina and is used therapeutically in the treatment of iritis, because it reduces contact between the posterior iris surface and the anterior lens capsule, thereby preventing the formation of iris–lens adhesions, or posterior synechiae.

Muscarinic antagonists also paralyze the ciliary muscles, which is beneficial in relieving pain associated with iridocyclitis, in inhibiting accommodation for accurate refraction in children, and in treating ciliary-block (malignant) glaucoma. However, use of cycloplegic agents to dilate the pupils of patients with primary open-angle glaucoma frequently elevates the IOP dramatically, especially in patients requiring miotics for pressure control. It is advisable to use short-acting agents and to monitor the pressure in patients with severe optic nerve damage.

In situations requiring complete cycloplegia, such as the treatment of iridocyclitis or the full refractive correction of accommodative esotropia, the more potent agents *atropine* and *scopolamine* are preferred. Although some cycloplegic effect of a single drop of atropine lasts for days, two or three instillations a day may be required for maintenance of full cycloplegia to relieve pain in iritis. It may become necessary to change medications if atropine elicits a characteristic local irritation with swelling and maceration of the eyelids and conjunctival hyperemia. When

TABLE XXI-2

MYDRIATRICS AND CYCLOPLEGICS

GENERIC NAME	TRADE NAME	CONCENTRATION (%)	ONSET	DURATION OF ACTION
Phenylephrine hydrochloride	AK-Dilate Mydfrin Neo-Synephrine Available generically	Soln, 2.5%, 10% Soln, 2.5% Soln, 2.5%, 10% Soln, 2.5%, 10%	30–60 min	3–5 h
Hydroxyamphetamine hydrobromide*	Paremyd	Soln, 1%	15–60 min	3–4 h
Atropine sulfate	Atropisol Atropine-Care Isopto Atropine Available generically	Soln, 0.5%–2% Soln, 1% Soln, 0.5%–3% Soln, 1% Ointment, 0.5%, 1%	45–120 min	7–14 days
Cyclopentolate hydrochloride	AK–Pentolate Cyclogyl Available generically	Soln, 1% Soln, 0.5%–2% Soln, 1%	30–60 min	2 days
Homatropine hydrobromide	Isopto Homatropine Available generically	Soln, 2%, 5% Soln, 2%, 5%	30–60 min	3 days
Scopolamine hydrobromide	Isopto Hyoscine	Soln, 0.25%	30–60 min	4–7 days
Tropicamide	Mydriacyl Tropicacyl Available generically	Soln, 0.5%, 1% Soln, 0.5%, 1% Soln, 0.5%, 1%	20–40 min	4–6 h

*In combination with tropicamide

mydriasis alone is necessary to facilitate examination or refraction, agents with shorter residual effect are preferred, because they allow quicker return of pupil response and reading ability.

Systemic absorption of topically administered muscarinic antagonists can produce a dose-related toxicity, especially in children, whose dose is distributed in a smaller body mass. Flushing, fever, tachycardia, and even delirium can result from a combination of central and peripheral effects (Fig XXI-6). Mild cases may require only discontinuation of the drug, but severe cases can be treated with subcutaneous physostigmine 0.25 mg every 15 minutes until the symptoms subside. Physostigmine is used because it is a tertiary amine (uncharged) and can cross the blood–brain barrier.

Systemic administration of atropine blocks the oculocardiac reflex, a reflex bradycardia sometimes elicited during ocular surgery by manipulation of the conjunctiva, the globe, or the extraocular muscles. The reflex can also be prevented at the afferent end by retrobulbar anesthesia.

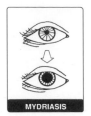

A **BLURRED VISION** **CONFUSION** **MYDRIASIS** **CONSTIPATION** **URINARY RETENTION**

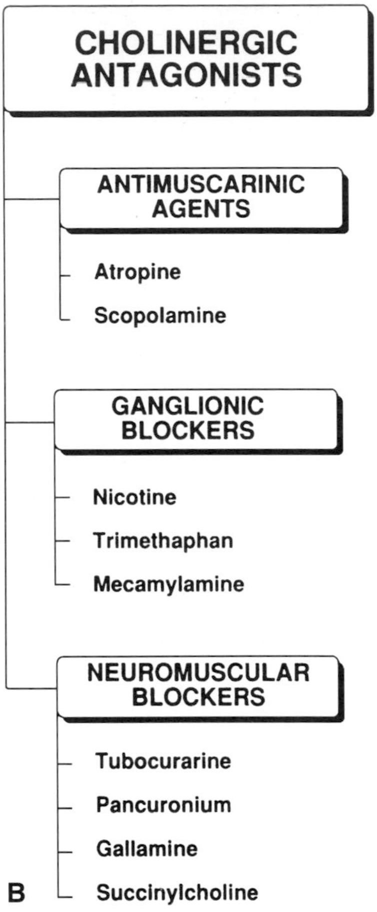

FIG XXI-6—*A,* Adverse effects commonly observed with cholinergic antagonists. *B,* Summary of cholinergic antagonists. (Reproduced with permission from Mycek MJ, Harvey RA, Champe PC, eds. *Lippincott's Illustrated Reviews: Pharmacology.* 2nd ed. Philadelphia: Lippincott-Raven; 1997:45, 49.)

CHOLINERGIC ANTAGONISTS

ANTIMUSCARINIC AGENTS

- Atropine
- Scopolamine

GANGLIONIC BLOCKERS

- Nicotine
- Trimethaphan
- Mecamylamine

NEUROMUSCULAR BLOCKERS

- Tubocurarine
- Pancuronium
- Gallamine

B - Succinylcholine

Nicotinic Drugs

Indirect-acting agonists The only cholinesterase inhibitor administered by oph-thalmologists in a sufficient dose to act as an indirect-acting nicotinic agonist is *edrophonium* (Tensilon). It is a competitive inhibitor of acetylcholinesterase that binds to the enzyme's active site but does not form a covalent linkage with it.

Edrophonium is used in the diagnosis of myasthenia gravis, a neuromuscular disease characterized by muscle weakness and marked fatigability of skeletal mus-cles. Occasionally, this disease is manifested primarily by ptosis and diplopia. Myasthenia gravis is caused by an autoimmune mechanism in which antibodies deplete acetylcholine receptors in the neuromuscular junction with a resultant sub-sensitivity of synaptic transmission. To determine the diagnosis a 2 mg dose is rapid-ly injected intravenously, followed 60 seconds later by an additional 8 mg if the first dose has no effect, and the patient is examined for improvement in muscle function. BCSC Section 5, *Neuro-Ophthalmology,* discusses myasthenia gravis and the use of edrophonium in detail, chapter VIII.

In myasthenic patients the inhibition of acetylcholinesterase by edrophonium allows acetylcholine released into the synaptic cleft to accumulate to levels ade-quate to act through the reduced number of acetylcholine receptors. Because edro-phonium also augments muscarinic transmission, muscarinic side effects (vomiting, diarrhea, urination, bradycardia) may occur unless atropine 0.4–0.6 mg is coadmin-istered intravenously.

Antagonists Nicotinic antagonists are administered as neuromuscular blocking agents to facilitate intubation for general anesthesia. They are of two types:

□ *Nondepolarizing agents* including curare-like drugs such as *gallamine* and *pan-curonium,* which bind competitively to nicotinic receptors on striated muscle but do not cause contraction

□ *Depolarizing agents* such as *succinylcholine* and *decamethonium,* which bind competitively to nicotinic receptors and cause an initial receptor depolarization and muscle contraction

In singly innervated (en plaque) muscle fibers, this depolarization-contraction is followed by a prolonged unresponsiveness and flaccidity. However, these drugs pro-duce sustained contractions of multiply innervated fibers, which make up one fifth of the muscle fibers of extraocular muscles. Such contractions of extraocular mus-cles (a nicotinic agonist action) exert force on the globe, an undesirable effect in cases in which the IOP is to be measured. The use of these agents in the induction of general anesthesia should be avoided in operations upon lacerated eyes, because the force of the muscles upon the globe could expel intraocular contents.

Adrenergic Agents

Several ophthalmic medications affect the activity of adrenergic receptors in syn-apses of the peripheral nervous system. Such receptors are found in the following locations:

□ The cell membranes of the iris dilator muscle, the superior palpebral smooth mus-cle of Müller, the ciliary epithelium and processes, the trabecular meshwork, and the smooth muscle of ocular blood vessels (supplied by postganglionic autonom-ic fibers from the superior cervical ganglion)

□ The presynaptic terminals of some sympathetic and parasympathetic nerves, where they have feedback inhibitory actions

Though adrenergic receptors were originally defined by their response to epinephrine (adrenaline), the transmitter of most sympathetic postganglionic fibers is actually norepinephrine. Adrenergic receptors have been subclassified into four categories, alpha$_1$, alpha$_2$, beta$_1$, and beta$_2$, based on their profile of responses to natural and synthetic catecholamines (Fig XXI-7). The *alpha$_1$ receptors* generally mediate smooth muscle contraction, while *alpha$_2$ receptors* mediate feedback inhibition of presynaptic sympathetic (and sometimes parasympathetic) nerve terminals. The *beta$_1$ receptors* are found predominantly in the heart, where they mediate stimulatory effects, while *beta$_2$ receptors* mediate relaxation of smooth muscle in most blood vessels and in the bronchi.

Systemic absorption of ocular adrenergic agents is frequently sufficient to cause systemic effects, which are manifested in the cardiovascular system, the bronchial airways, and the brain. Much remains to be determined regarding the ocular pharmacologic mechanisms of adrenergic agents currently in use, let alone those under investigation. Adrenergic agents may be direct-acting agonists, indirect-acting agonists, or antagonists at one or more of the four types of receptor.

Alpha-Adrenergic Agents

Direct-acting alpha$_1$-adrenergic agonists The primary clinical use of direct-acting alpha$_1$-adrenergic agonists, such as *phenylephrine,* is stimulation of the iris dilator muscle to produce mydriasis. However, the parasympathetically innervated iris sphincter muscle is much stronger than the dilator muscle, and therefore dilation achieved with phenylephrine alone is overcome to a large extent by the pupillary light reflex during ophthalmoscopy. Coadministration of a cycloplegic agent allows sustained dilation.

Systemic absorption of phenylephrine may elevate systemic blood pressure. This effect is of clinical significance only if the patient is an infant or has an abnormally increased sensitivity to alpha agonists, which occurs with orthostatic hypotension and in association with the use of drugs that accentuate adrenergic effects (e.g., reserpine, tricyclic antidepressants, cocaine, monoamine oxidase inhibitors—discussed below). Even with lower doses of phenylephrine (2.5%) infants may exhibit transient rise in blood pressure, because the dose received in an eyedrop is large for them on a per weight basis.

Indirect-acting adrenergic agonists These agents are used to test for and localize defects in sympathetic innervation to the iris dilator muscle. Normally, nerve fibers from a hypothalamic nucleus for pupil response pass down the spinal cord to synapse with cells in the intermediolateral columns. In turn, preganglionic fibers exit the cord through the anterior spinal roots in the upper thorax to synapse in the superior cervical ganglion in the neck. Finally, postganglionic adrenergic fibers terminate in a neuroeffector junction with the iris dilator muscle. The norepinephrine released is inactivated primarily by reuptake into secretory granules in the nerve terminal (Fig XXI-8). Approximately 70% of released norepinephrine is recaptured.

If a defect occurs anywhere in the pathway, the baseline release of norepinephrine to the iris dilator will be lower on the side of the injury, resulting in a relatively miotic pupil. The presence of a lesion can be confirmed by applying 4% cocaine to each eye and comparing the pupil sizes at one hour. Cocaine blocks reuptake of norepinephrine into the presynaptic vesicles, causing it to accumulate and resulting in pupillary dilation. The injured side will have less accumulation and show less dilation.

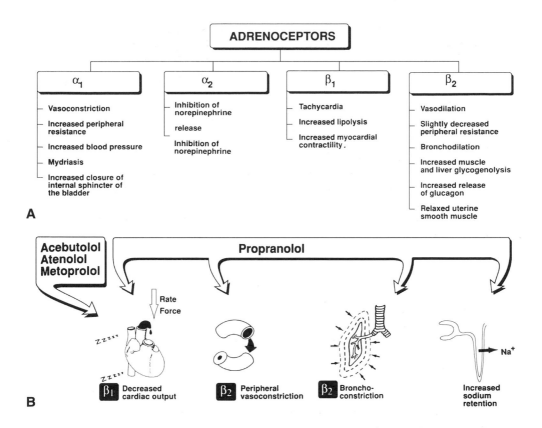

FIG XXI-7—A, Major effects mediated by α- and β-adrenoceptors. B, Actions of propranolol and β1 blockers. (Reproduced with permission from Mycek MJ, Harvey RA, Champe PC, eds. *Lippincott's Illustrated Reviews: Pharmacology.* 2nd ed. Philadelphia: Lippincott-Raven; 1997:60, 75.)

The site of the lesion can be determined to be either preganglionic or postganglionic by a Paredrine test: a drop of 1% *hydroxyamphetamine* (Paredrine) is applied to each eye and the pupil responses are compared. Hydroxyamphetamine acts by penetrating the sympathetic nerve terminals adjacent to the dilator muscle and releasing stored norepinephrine, resulting in pupillary dilation. On the side of a postganglionic injury fewer fibers will be intact, less norepinephrine will be released, and less dilation will ensue. In the case of a preganglionic lesion, however, the postganglionic fibers synthesize and store norepinephrine normally but are not neurally stimulated to release it. A Paredrine test will therefore dilate the pupil normally. If the dilator muscle has developed supersensitivity by a compensatory increase in receptor number or responsiveness, the dilation may be greater than that in the normal eye. (See also BCSC Section 5, *Neuro-Ophthalmology,* chapter IV.)

Apraclonidine (Iopidine), an alpha$_2$-agonist, reduces IOP by inhibiting aqueous secretion. The drug has been approved for use in reducing the IOP rise that may

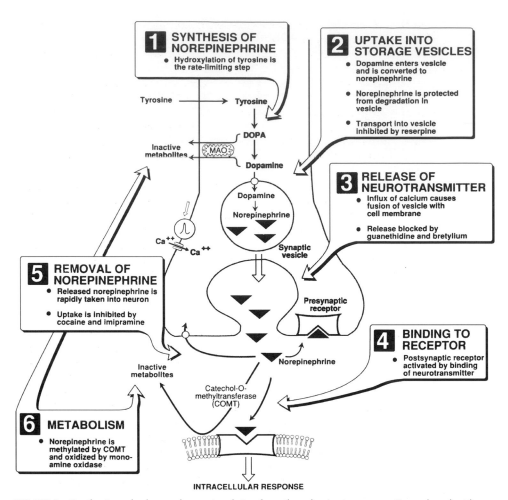

FIG XXI-8—Synthesis and release of norepinephrine from the adrenergic neuron. (Reproduced with permission from Mycek MJ, Harvey RA, Champe PC, eds. *Lippincott's Illustrated Reviews: Pharmacology.* 2nd ed. Philadelphia: Lippincott-Raven; 1997:57.)

occur after anterior segment laser procedures. Apraclonidine is also useful in preventing the similar elevation of IOP that occurs shortly after cataract surgery as well as in controlling IOP in chronic glaucoma. Reported side effects include conjunctival blanching, eyelid retraction, dry mouth, lethargy, and local allergy; no important cardiovascular or respiratory effects have been reported. Apraclonidine is contraindicated in patients using monoamine oxidase (MAO) inhibitors.

Ligand binding to alpha$_2$ receptors in other systems has been shown to mediate inhibition of the enzyme adenylate cyclase. Adenylate cyclase is present in the ciliary epithelium and is thought to have a role in aqueous production.

Antagonists *Thymoxamine,* an alpha$_1$-adrenergic blocking agent, acts by competitive inhibition of norepinephrine at the receptor site. As pupillary muscle, unlike ciliary muscle, has predominantly alpha-adrenergic receptors, use of thymoxamine inhibits alpha-adrenergic tone to the dilator muscle of the iris and results in pupil constriction. Thymoxamine does not have any significant activity on ciliary muscle contraction and therefore does not induce a significant change in anterior chamber depth, facility of outflow, IOP, or accommodation. It is useful for differentiating angle-closure glaucoma from POAG with closed angles and can also be used to reverse the pupil dilation caused by phenylephrine. Thymoxamine is not available commercially in the United States even though it has been used widely in Europe for several years.

Dapiprazole hydrochloride (Rev-Eyes), an alpha-adrenergic blocking agent, produces miosis through its effect on the dilator muscle of the iris. Like thymoxamine, it does not have significant activity on ciliary muscle contraction and therefore does not induce a significant change in anterior chamber depth, facility of outflow, or accommodation. Topical application of dapiprazole 0.5% solution reverses the mydriasis produced by phenylephrine and tropicamide in 30 minutes, but it is not effective in reversing the mydriasis produced by cycloplegics.

Beta-Adrenergic Agents

Beta$_2$-adrenergic agonists These agents lower IOP by increasing uveoscleral outflow and perhaps also by increasing outflow through the trabecular meshwork. The beneficial effect on outflow more than compensates for a small increase in aqueous inflow as detected by fluorophotometry.

Beta$_2$ receptors linked to adenylate cyclase are present in the ciliary epithelium and processes and also in the trabecular meshwork. Treatment with *L-epinephrine,* an alpha and beta agonist, increases intracellular levels of cyclic AMP (cAMP) in these tissues and in the aqueous humor. In other tissues, beta receptor–mediated generation of cAMP in turn activates cAMP-dependent enzymes that result in responses such as glycogenolysis and gluconeogenesis in the liver and lipolysis in adipose tissue. However, the biochemical mechanisms responsible for the lowering of IOP remain to be determined.

L-epinephrine is commercially available as a borate, a hydrochloride, and a bitartrate (Table XXI-3). The molecular weight of L-epinephrine bitartrate is approximately twice that of the borate and hydrochloride. Therefore, L-epinephrine bitartrate 2% contains as much free base as a 1% solution of either of the other forms. Borate form is more comfortable than other forms, whose low pH induces burning on application. Local allergic and irritative manifestations and systemic side effects (headache, palpitations, and cardiac arrhythmias) are common causes of intolerance of long-term epinephrine therapy. Oxidation products of epinephrine may produce black deposits in the conjunctiva. While such deposits are harmless, they have been mistaken for foreign bodies or even melanomas. Epinephrine therapy has also been associated with a reversible cystoid maculopathy that occurs in approximately 25% of chronically treated aphakic eyes that lack a posterior lens capsule. While epinephrine maculopathy does not occur in phakic eyes, it has not yet been established whether or not an intact posterior lens capsule, hyaloid membrane, and/or the presence of an intraocular lens retards the development of the condition.

The pro-drug dipivefrin HCl (DPE, Propine) 0.1% is therapeutically equivalent to epinephrine compounds of 1%–2%, because the presence of two pivalyl residues

TABLE XXI-3

BETA-ADRENERGIC AGONISTS

GENERIC NAME	TRADE NAME	CONCENTRATION (%)
Dipivefrin hydrochloride	Propine	0.1%
Epinephrine bitartrate	Epitrate	2.0%
Epinephrine borate	Epinal	0.5%, 1%
	Eppy/N	1%, 2%
Epinephrine hydrochloride	Epifrin	0.5%–2%
	Glaucon	1%, 2%

(see Figure XX-4, p 390) increases its lipid solubility and corneal penetration by a factor of 17. The drug has little adrenergic activity until the pivalyl groups are cleaved by corneal esterases. Together, the reductions in both intrinsic activity and concentration employed virtually eliminate the systemic side effects of epinephrine. Extraocular irritation is also reduced, because of either the lower concentration or the reduction in auto-oxidation of the phenolic hydroxyls. However, because epinephrine is liberated from the pro-drug inside the eye, the risk of epinephrine maculopathy should be unchanged.

Chronic therapy with epinephrine has been shown in an animal model to result in a down-regulation of the number of beta receptors. This phenomenon may underlie the loss of some of its therapeutic effectiveness over time (tachyphylaxis).

Beta-adrenergic antagonists   (Table XXI-4) These agents, also known as *beta blockers,* lower IOP by reducing aqueous humor production as much as 50%. While it is likely that the site of action resides in the ciliary body, it is not known whether the vasculature of the ciliary processes or the pumping mechanism of the ciliary epithelium is primarily affected. One possible mechanism may be an effect on the beta-adrenergic–receptor–coupled adenylate cyclase of the ciliary epithelium. Although systemic administration of beta blockers has been reported to elevate blood lipid, such elevation has not been demonstrated with topical beta blockers such as timolol.

Timolol maleate 0.25%–0.50% (Timoptic) and *levobunolol* (Betagan) 0.5% are mixed $beta_1$/$beta_2$ antagonists. Tests of more specific beta blockers suggest that $beta_2$ antagonists have a greater effect on aqueous secretion than do $beta_1$ antagonists. For example, comparative studies have shown that the specific $beta_1$ antagonist *betaxolol* 0.5% (Betoptic) is about 85% as effective in lowering IOP as timolol. However, preliminary evidence indicates that some or all of the deficit in betaxolol's ability to lower IOP can be made up by its greater additive effect in combined therapy with epinephrine or dipivefrin. Mixed beta and $beta_2$ agonists show little or no additive effect on the lowering of IOP with the use of an alpha-adrenergic agonist.

Betaxolol, as a $beta_1$ antagonist, has the advantage of being cardioselective and pulmonary sparing, making it the drug of choice to treat glaucoma in most patients with coexisting bronchoconstrictive disease. Nonselective beta blockers are contraindicated in patients with this condition. Even though betaxolol is cardioselective, it has less effect upon exercise tachycardia than the two nonselective agents, appar-

TABLE XXI-4

β–Adrenergic Blocking Agents (Beta Blockers)

GENERIC NAME	TRADE NAME	CONCENTRATION (%)
Betaxolol hydrochloride	Betoptic-S	0.25%
	Betoptic	0.5%
Carteolol hydrochloride	Ocupress	1.0%
Levobunolol hydrochloride	Betagan	0.25%, 0.5%
	Available generically	0.25%, 0.5%
Metipranolol	OptiPranolol	0.3%
Timolol maleate	Timoptic	0.25%, 0.5%
	Timoptic-XE	0.25%, 0.5%
	Available generically	
Timolol hemihydrate	Betimol	5.12 mg/mL
Timolol maleate (preservative free)	Timoptic in OCUDOSE	0.25%, 0.5%

ently because it is more tightly bound to plasma proteins and thus less available to cardiac receptors.

Pro-drugs of nonselective beta blockers are being developed, and they may offer the benefit of the higher potency of beta$_1$/beta$_2$ blocking agents while reducing their potential systemic side effects.

Metipranolol hydrochloride (OptiPranolol) is a nonselective beta$_1$- and beta$_2$-adrenergic receptor blocking agent. As a 0.3% topical solution, it is similar in effect to other topical nonselective beta blockers and is efficacious in reducing IOP.

Carteolol is another potent nonselective beta-adrenergic receptor antagonist with partial agonist activity. Twice-daily ocular administration of carteolol 1% or 2% lowered IOP by an average of 32% in patients with glaucoma or ocular hypertension, an efficacy equivalent to that of timolol 0.25% or 0.5%. Carteolol eyedrops lack local anesthetic activity, appear to cause less local irritation than timolol, and produce less pronounced decrease in heart rate or dyspnea.

It is curious that both beta-agonist and beta-antagonist drugs can lower IOP. This paradox is compounded by the observation that beta-agonist and -antagonist drugs have slightly additive effects in lowering IOP.

Carbonic Anhydrase Inhibitors (CAIs) (Table XXI-5)

Aqueous humor is secreted into the posterior chamber by the nonpigmented epithelium of the ciliary processes. While the physiologic mechanisms of secretion are not fully understood, secretion is known to depend in large measure upon active transport of sodium by Na$^+$,K$^+$-ATPase on the surface of nonpigmented epithelial cells. Inhibition of that enzyme by *ouabain* injected into the vitreous cavity of experimental animals reduces secretion markedly. Unfortunately, ouabain and other cardiac glycosides cannot be used clinically to treat glaucoma because effective doses for the eye would require systemic doses toxic to the heart.

Table XXI-5

Carbonic Anhydrase Inhibitors

GENERIC NAME	TRADE NAME	DOSAGE	ONSET	DURATION OF ACTION
Systemic				
Acetazolamide	Diamox Available generically	125, 250, 500 mg	2 h	4–6 h
Acetazolamide sodium	Diamox Parenteral	500 mg, 5–10 mg/kg[3]	5–10 min	2 h
Dichlorphenamide	Daranide	50 mg	30 min	6 h
Methazolamide	Glauctabs MZM	2 h	4–6 h	
	Neptazane Available generically	20, 50 mg		
Topical				
Dorzolamide HCl	Trusopt	2% solution	5 min	8 h

However, Na$^+$ transport and coupled aqueous secretion can be inhibited indirectly. Na$^+$ transport and fluid flow seem to be partially linked to HCO$_3^-$ formation in the ciliary epithelium, and HCO$_3^-$ formation can be substantially reduced by inhibition of the enzyme carbonic anhydrase. The linkage between HCO$_3^-$ and Na$^+$ transport is demonstrated by the fact that the effect on aqueous flow is no greater when ouabain and a carbonic anhydrase inhibitor are given together than when each drug is given alone.

Carbonic anhydrase catalyzes the hydration of dissolved CO$_2$ to HC$_2$CO$_3$, which ionizes into HCO$_3^-$ and H$^+$. The HCO$_3^-$ is then available to accompany secreted Na$^+$. When the enzyme is inhibited, the transport of radiolabeled HCO$_3^-$ into the posterior chamber is reduced by up to 60%. That portion (60%) of Na$^+$ transport accompanied by Cl$^-$ is unaffected by inhibition of carbonic anhydrase and, curiously, is unaffected by coadministration of ouabain. The mechanism(s) of the residual secretion and means of inhibiting it are yet to be determined. Carbonic anhydrase inhibitors such as acetazolamide are also effective in treating certain cases of cystoid macular edema.

The concentration of carbonic anhydrase in the ciliary epithelium of rabbits is 0.3 μm, and it is 10 times more concentrated in the kidney and in the choroid plexus of the brain. Carbonic anhydrase is present in considerable excess of what is needed to supply the amount of HCO$_3^-$ transported. Calculations based upon the K_{cat} (catalysis constant) and K_m (apparent affinity constant) of the enzyme and the concentrations of substrates and product indicate that 100 times as much enzyme is present as is needed in the ciliary body. Correspondingly, in clinical use the enzyme must in fact be more than 99% inhibited in order to reduce aqueous flow significantly. The enzyme in the kidney, present in 1000-fold excess, must be more than 99.9% inhibited to affect the usual pathway for HCO$_3^-$ reabsorption. With the inhibitor *methazolamide* the difference in concentration of carbonic anhydrase in the ciliary body and the kidney can be exploited to lower IOP without incurring renal HCO_3^- loss, and an unpleasant metabolic acidosis can be avoided. Even though renal stone formation has been reported with use of methazolamide, it is significantly less than with other agents because of this specific property. In contrast, *acetazolamide* is actively secreted into the renal tubules, and renal effects are unavoidable.

The necessity to inhibit more than 99% of the enzyme has made it difficult to achieve a clinical effect with topically applied agents until recently. *Dorzolamide* (*Trusopt*) (4-ethylamino-5,6-dihydro-4-(2methylpropyl)amino-4*H* thieno (2,3b) thiopyran-2-sulfonamide 7,7-dioxide), a topical CAI hydrochloride, was approved by the FDA in 1994. It is water soluble, penetrates the cornea easily, and is specially formulated for topical ophthalmic use. When administered as 2% solution 3 times a day, it effectively inhibits carbonic anhydrase–II, reduces IOP, and avoids the systemic side effects of oral administration. The IOP-lowering effect of dorzolamide was approximately 5 mm Hg throughout the day. This measurement was consistent in clinical studies lasting up to 1 year. The concomitant administration of dorzolamide and oral CAIs is not recommended at the present time because of potentially additive side effects.

The four compounds other than dorzolamide that are used clinically are all administered orally and/or parenterally. The longer half-life of methazolamide allows it to be used twice daily, and acetazolamide is also available in a 500 mg sustained-release form used twice a day. The others must be used 4 times a day. None of the compounds has the ideal combination of features:

□ High potency (low K_i)

□ Good ocular penetration (high percentage in the non-ionized form and high lipid solubility to facilitate passage through the blood–ocular barrier)

□ High proportion of the drug present in the blood in the unbound form

□ Long plasma half-life

In addition to lowering IOP by inhibiting ciliary body carbonic anhydrase, each of the agents at high doses further lowers IOP by causing a renal metabolic acidosis. The mechanism by which acidosis lowers secretion is uncertain, but it plausibly involves reduction in HCO_3^- formation.

At the onset of acidosis, the renal effects cause an alkaline diuresis, with loss of Na^+, K^+, and HCO_3^-. Severe hypokalemia can result in patients concurrently receiving diuretics, steroids, or ACTH. This situation may be dangerous for patients using digitalis, in whom hypokalemia may elicit arrhythmias. Patients on chronic CAI therapy should have potassium levels checked at regular intervals, preferably by their primary care physician.

The acidosis sets into action a renal mechanism for HCO_3^- reabsorption unrelated to carbonic anhydrase, and this mechanism limits the degree of acidosis and halts both the diuresis and K^+ loss after the first few days of treatment. However, *dichlorphenamide* also acts as a chloruretic agent and may cause continued K^+ loss.

CAI therapy may interact unfavorably with certain systemic conditions. The alkalinization of the urine present during initial CAI treatment prevents excretion of NH_4^+, a factor to consider in patients with cirrhosis of the liver. Metabolic acidosis may exacerbate diabetic ketoacidosis. In patients with severe chronic obstructive pulmonary disease, respiratory acidosis may be caused by impairment of CO_2 transfer from the pulmonary vasculature to the alveoli.

The use of acetazolamide has been linked to the formation of stones in the urinary tract. In a retrospective case-control series the incidence of stones was 11 times higher in the patients using this drug. The increased risk occurred primarily during the first year of therapy. Continued use after occurrence of a stone was associated with a high risk of recurrent stone formation. However, a history of spontaneous stone formation more than 5 years prior to acetazolamide therapy did not appear to be associated with a special risk. The mechanisms responsible for such stone formation may be related to metabolic acidosis and the associated pH changes as well as decreased excretion of citrate.

Nearly 50% of patients are intolerant of carbonic anhydrase inhibitors because of distressing central nervous system and gastrointestinal side effects including

- Numbness and tingling of the hands, feet, and lips

- Malaise

- Metallic taste of carbonated beverages

- Anorexia and weight loss

- Nausea

- Somnolence

- Impotence and loss of libido

- Depression

Whenever the clinical situation allows, it is wise to begin therapy at low doses (for example, 25–50 mg methazolamide bid or 125 mg acetazolamide qid), because side effects will be less severe, and weaning may actually reduce their incidence. Patients should be informed of the potential side effects of these agents; otherwise, many may fail to associate their systemic symptoms with the use of a medicine given by the ophthalmologist.

Rare side effects from this class of drugs include those common to other members of the sulfonamide family such as transient myopia, hypersensitive nephropathy, skin rash, thrombocytopenia, and aplastic anemia. The latter effect is idiosyncratic and dose related; white blood counts will not detect susceptible patients. Carbonic anhydrase inhibitors have been associated with teratogenic effects (forelimb deformity) in rodents, and their use is not advised during pregnancy.

Osmotic Agents

Actions and Uses

Increased serum osmolarity reduces IOP and vitreous volume by drawing fluid out of the eye across vascular barriers. The osmotic activity of an agent depends on the number of particles in solution and the maintenance of an osmotic gradient between the plasma and the intraocular fluids. It is independent of the molecular weight. Low-molecular-weight agents such as urea that penetrate the blood–ocular barriers produce a small rebound in IOP after an initial lowering because of a reversal of the osmotic gradient when the kidneys clear the blood of excess urea. Osmotic agents are used in the short-term management of acute glaucomas and in reducing vitreous volume prior to cataract surgery.

TABLE XXI-6

HYPEROSMOTIC AGENTS

GENERIC NAME	TRADE NAME	PREPARATION	DOSE	ROUTE
Glycerin	Osmoglyn	50%	1–1.5 g/kg	Oral
Isosorbide	Ismotic	45%	1.5 g/kg	Oral
Mannitol	Osmitrol	5%–20%	0.5–2 g/kg	IV
Urea	Ureaphil	Powder or 30% soln	0.5–2 g/kg	IV

Agents

Osmotic agents should be used with care in patients in whom cardiovascular overload might occur with moderate vascular volume expansion, such as patients with a history of congestive heart failure, angina, systemic hypertension, or recent myocardial infarct. The osmotic agents that have been used clinically are mannitol, urea, glycerol (glycerin), sodium ascorbate, and isosorbide (Table XXI-6).

Intravenous agents   *Mannitol* must be given intravenously because it is not absorbed from the gastrointestinal tract. *Urea* is unpalatable and thus is used intravenously. Use of urea is out of favor because of the rebound mentioned above and its tendency to cause tissue necrosis if it extravasates during administration. IV administration produces a rapid onset of action, which is usually desirable, but both mannitol and urea have been associated with subarachnoid hemorrhage attributed to rapid volume overload of the blood vessels and/or rapid shrinkage of the brain with traction of the subarachnoid vessels.

These agents are cleared by the kidneys and produce a marked osmotic diuresis that may be troublesome in the operating room. The conscious patient should void shortly before surgery, and a urinal should be available. If general anesthesia is employed, an indwelling urethral catheter may be required to prevent bladder distension.

Oral agents   *Glycerol* (Osmoglyn) is the most frequently used oral osmotic agent. Its nauseating sweet taste can be minimized by giving it with cracked ice. In diabetic patients, the nonmetabolized sugar *isosorbide* (Ismotic) is often preferred.

Sodium ascorbate is metabolized, and thus its osmotic diuretic effects are less marked. *Ethanol* has the disadvantages of producing inebriation and suppressing antidiuretic hormone release, causing additional diuresis. *Ascorbate* is unstable in solution and crosses the blood–ocular barriers.

Abrams DA, Robin AL, Pollack IP, et al. The safety and efficacy of topical 1% ALO 2145 (p-aminoclonidine hydrochloride) in normal volunteers. *Arch Ophthalmol.* 1987; 105:1206–1207.

Allen RC, Epstein DL. Additive effect of betaxolol and epinephrine in primary open-angle glaucoma. *Arch Ophthalmol.* 1986;104:1178–1184.

Berry DP Jr, Van Buskirk EM, Shields MB. Betaxolol and timolol. A comparison of efficacy and side effects. *Arch Ophthalmol.* 1984;102:42–45.

Chrisp P, Sorkin EM. Ocular carteolol: A review of its pharmacological properties, and therapeutic use in glaucoma and ocular hypertension. *Drugs Aging.* 1992;2:58–77.

Friedland BR, Maren TH. Carbonic anhydrase: the pharmacology of inhibitors related to the treatment of glaucoma. In: Chader G, Sears ML, eds. *Pharmacology of the Eye: Handbook of Experimental Pharmacology.* New York: Springer-Verlag; 1983: 279–309.

Kass MA, Kolker AE, Gordon M, et al. Acetazolamide and urolithiasis. *Ophthalmology.* 1981;88:261–265.

Kolker AE, Becker B. Epinephrine maculopathy. *Arch Ophthalmol.* 1968;79:552–562.

Lees BJ, Cabal LA. Increased blood pressure following pupillary dilation with 2.5% phenylephrine hydrochloride in preterm infants. *Pediatrics.* 1981;68:231–234.

Maren TH, Bar-Ilan A. Ocular pharmacology and hypotensive activity of a topically active carbonic anhydrase (CA) inhibitor, 4-alkylaminothienothiopyran-2-sulfonamide, MK-927. *Invest Ophthalmol Vis Sci.* 1988;29(suppl):16.

Potter DE, Shumate D, Bundgaard H, et al. Prodrugs can enhance the duration of action and oculoselectivity of timolol. *Invest Ophthalmol Vis Sci.* 1988;29(suppl):89.

Schenker HI, Yablonski ME, Podos SM, et al. Fluorophotometric study of epinephrine and timolol in human subjects. *Arch Ophthalmol.* 1981;99:1212–1216.

Schoene RB, Abuan T, Ward RL, et al. Effects of topical betaxolol, timolol and placebo on pulmonary function in asthmatic bronchitis. *Am J Ophthalmol.* 1984;97:86–92.

Shaw BR, Lewis RA. Intraocular pressure elevation after pupillary dilation in open-angle glaucoma. *Arch Ophthalmol.* 1986;104:1185–1188.

Stewart RH, Kimbrough RL, Ward RL. Betaxolol vs timolol. A six-month double-blind comparison. *Arch Ophthalmol.* 1986;104:46–48.

Thomas JV, Epstein DL. Timolol and epinephrine in primary open-angle glaucoma. Transient additive effect. *Arch Ophthalmol.* 1981;99:91–95.

Tripathi RC, Fekrat S, Tripathi BJ, et al. A direct correlation of the resolution of pseudophakic cystoid macular edema with acetazolamide therapy. *Ann Ophthalmol.* 1991; 23:127–129.

Anti-Inflammatory Agents

Ocular inflammation can be treated with drugs administered topically, by local injection, or systemically. These drugs may be classified as glucocorticoids (a form of corticosteroid), nonsteroidal anti-inflammatory agents (NSAIDs), antihistamines, histamine release blockers, or antifibrotics (Table XXI-7).

TABLE XXI-7

TOPICAL ANTI-INFLAMMATORY AGENTS

NAME	DOSAGE FORM	TRADE NAME
Dexamethasone	Ophthalmic suspension 0.1%	Maxidex
Dexamethasone sodium phosphate	Ophthalmic ointment 0.05%	AK-Dex Decadron Maxidex Available generically
Dexamethasone sodium phosphate	Ophthalmic solution 0.1%	AK-Dex Decadron Available generically
Fluorometholone	Ophthalmic ointment 0.1% Ophthalmic suspension 0.1% Ophthalmic suspension 0.1% Ophthalmic suspension 0.25%	FML S.O.P. Fluor-Op FML FML Forte
Fluorometholone acetate	Ophthalmic suspension 0.1%	Flarex
Medrysone	Ophthalmic suspension 1%	HMS
Prednisolone acetate	Ophthalmic suspension 0.12% Ophthalmic suspension 0.125% Ophthalmic suspension 1% Ophthalmic suspension 1%	Pred Mild Econopred Econopred Plus Pred Forte
Prednisolone sodium phosphate	Ophthalmic solution 0.125% Ophthalmic solution 0.125% Ophthalmic solution 0.125% Ophthalmic solution 1% Ophthalmic solution 1%	AK-Pred Inflamase Mild Available generically AK-Pred Inflamase Forte
Rimexolone	Ophthalmic solution 1%	Vexol
Nonsteroidal Anti-Inflammatory Drugs		
Diclofenac	Ophthalmic solution 0.1%	Voltaren
Flurbiprofen	Ophthalmic solution* 0.03%	Ocufen
Ketorolac	Ophthalmic solution 0.5%	Acular
Suprofen	Ophthalmic solution* 1%	Profenal

*Indicated for intraoperative miosis only

Glucocorticoids

Steroids are applied topically to prevent or suppress corneal graft rejection, anterior chamber reaction after anterior segment surgery, filtering bleb scarring, and immune or traumatic iritis and uveitis. Subconjunctival and retrobulbar injections of steroids are used to treat severe ocular inflammations. Systemic steroid therapy is used to treat giant cell arteritis and severe ocular inflammations. Treatment of acute inflammatory ischemic optic neuritis with steroids is a subject of controversy and ongoing research. BCSC Section 5, *Neuro-Ophthalmology,* discusses these issues in depth.

The ocular anti-inflammatory action of glucocorticoids is achieved by separate cell-specific effects on lymphocytes, macrophages, polymorphonuclear leukocytes, vascular endothelial cells, fibroblasts, and other cells. In each of these types of cells glucocorticoids must

□ Penetrate the cell membrane

□ Bind to soluble receptors in the cytosol

□ Bring about a conformational shift that allows translocation of the glucocorticoid-receptor complex to nuclear binding sites

□ Induce or suppress the transcription of specific messenger ribonucleic acids

The proteins produced in the eye under the control of these mRNAs are not known, and only resultant effects have been described.

At the tissue level glucocorticoids prevent or suppress the local hyperthermia, vascular congestion, edema, and pain of initial inflammatory responses, whether the cause is traumatic (radiant, mechanical, or chemical), infectious, or immunologic. They also suppress the late inflammatory responses of capillary proliferation, fibroblast proliferation, collagen deposition, and scarring.

At the biochemical level the most important effect of anti-inflammatories may be the inhibition of arachidonic acid release from phospholipids (see Part 4, Biochemistry). Liberated arachidonic acid is otherwise converted into prostaglandins, prostaglandin endoperoxides, leukotriene, and thromboxane, which are potent mediators of inflammation. Glucocorticoids also suppress the liberation of lytic enzymes from lysozymes.

The effects of glucocorticoids upon immune-mediated inflammation are complicated. Glucocorticoids do not affect the titers of either IgE, which mediates allergic mechanisms, or IgG, which mediates autoimmune mechanisms. Nor do glucocorticoids appear to interfere with the normal processes in the afferent limb of cell-mediated immunity, as in graft rejection. Apparently, they interfere instead with the efferent limb of the immune response. For example, glucocorticoids prevent macrophages from being attracted to sites of inflammation by interfering with their response to lymphocyte-released migration inhibiting factor (MIF). Systemically administered glucocorticoids cause sequestration of lymphocytes, especially the T lymphocytes that mediate cellular immunity. However, the posttranscriptional molecular mechanisms of these responses are as yet unknown. BCSC Section 9, *Intraocular Inflammation and Uveitis,* discusses immune responses in detail.

Adverse effects   Glucocorticoids may cause several adverse effects in the eye and elsewhere in the body. Complications in the eye include the following:

□ Glaucoma

□ Posterior subcapsular cataracts

□ Exacerbation of bacterial and viral (especially herpetic) infections through suppression of protective immune mechanisms

□ Ptosis

□ Mydriasis

□ Scleral melting

□ Eyelid skin atrophy

In the body oral doses can cause the following:

- Suppression of the pituitary-adrenal axis
- Gluconeogenesis resulting from hyperglycemia, muscle wasting, osteoporosis
- Redistribution of fat from the periphery to the trunk
- Central nervous system effects such as euphoria
- Insomnia
- Aseptic necrosis of hip
- Peptic ulcer
- Diabetes
- Occasionally psychosis

The systemic side effects of steroids and the benefits and limitations of alternate-day therapy are discussed in BCSC Section 1, *Update on General Medicine.*

Steroid-induced elevation in IOP may occur with topical, periocular, nasal, and systemic glucocorticoid therapy. Individuals differ in their responsiveness: approximately 31% develop ocular hypertension higher than 20 mm Hg, and 4% develop pressures higher than 31 mm Hg after 6 weeks of therapy with topical dexamethasone. High levels of response are generally reproducible. The mechanism by which steroids decrease the facility of aqueous outflow through the trabecular meshwork remains unknown. Studies in vitro have shown an endoreplication of DNA in the trabecular cells, as well as the production of aberrant sialated polypeptides.

Individual response to steroids is highly dependent upon the duration, strength, and frequency of therapy and the potency of the agent used. Steroid-induced IOP elevation almost never occurs in less than 5 days and rarely in less than 2 weeks. It is not generally appreciated that late responses to therapy are common and that failure of the IOP to rise after 6 weeks of therapy is no assurance that the patient will not develop a marked elevation in pressure after several months of therapy. For this reason *intraocular pressure monitoring is required at periodic intervals during the entire course of chronic steroid therapy* to prevent the occurrence of iatrogenic glaucomatous nerve damage.

Steroid-induced IOP rises are usually reversible by discontinuance of therapy if the drug has not been used for more than 1 year, but permanent elevations of pressure are common if therapy has continued for 18 months or more. Return to baseline pressure usually occurs within 2 weeks in reversible cases.

The anti-inflammatory and pressure-elevating potencies of six steroids used in ophthalmic therapy are given in Table XXI-8. The anti-inflammatory potency was determined by an in vitro assay of inhibition of lymphocyte transformation, and the IOP effects were determined by testing in persons already known to be highly responsive to topical dexamethasone. Some dissociation of effects was observed. However, until all these agents are compared in a model of ocular inflammation relevant to human disease, no conclusion can be reached about the dissociation of effects. The lower-than-expected effect on pressure of some of these agents may be explained by more rapid metabolism of fluorometholone in the eye compared to dexamethasone and by the relatively poor penetration of medrysone. The efficacy of these agents for intraocular inflammation may be similarly reduced.

TABLE XXI-8

COMPARISON OF ANTI-INFLAMMATORY AND IOP-ELEVATING POTENCIES

GLUCOCORTICOID	RELATIVE POTENCY	RISE IN IOP (mm Hg)
Dexamethasone 0.1%	24	22
Fluorometholone 0.1%	21	6
Prednisolone 1%	2.3	10
Medrysone 1%	1.7	1
Tetrahydrotriamcinolone 0.25%	1.4	2
Hydrocortisone 0.5%	1.0	3

When a steroid-induced pressure rise is suspected but continued steroid therapy is warranted, the physician faces the following choices:

□ Continue the same treatment and closely monitor the status of the optic nerve

□ Attempt to offset the pressure rise with other agents

□ Reduce the potency, concentration, or frequency of the steroid used, while monitoring both pressure and inflammation

When alternative classes of anti-inflammatory agents could be employed, a change may be advisable.

Agents and regimens   Choice of available corticosteroid agents and dosage regimens remains somewhat empirical (Table XXI-9). Steroids can be used topically (iritis), intravenously (optic neuritis), intravitreally (endophthalmitis), or in a periocular fashion (uveitis).

Rimexolone (Vexol) is a newly designed steroid for topical use. It is available as multidose topical ophthalmic suspension (1%), and its mechanism of action is very similar to that of other steroids. Clinical studies have demonstrated that rimexolone 1% ophthalmic suspension is efficacious for treatment of anterior chamber inflammation following cataract surgery. After 5–7 hourly doses, the mean serum concentrations were approximately 130 pg/mL with a half-life of approximately 1–2 hours.

Rimexolone is indicated for the treatment of postoperative inflammation following ocular surgery and of anterior uveitis. The main advantage of rimexolone is that it offers a low steroid response similar to that of fluorinated steroids while still exerting full anti-inflammatory activity equal to that of glucocorticoids. Common side effects include visual acuity and field defects and posterior subcapsular cataracts. Elevated IOP has been reported, even though it is rare. Systemic side effects including headache, hypotension, rhinitis, pharyngitis, and taste perversion occur in fewer than 2% of patients.

Application of 1–2 drops of rimexolone into the conjunctival sac of the affected eye every hour during waking hours effectively controls anterior uveitis initially. Dosage can be modified according to the intensity of uveitis later.

TABLE XXI-9

CONDITION	ROUTE
Blepharitis	Topical
Conjunctivitis	Topical
Episcleritis	Topical
Scleritis	Topical and/or systemic
Keratitis	Topical
Anterior uveitis	Topical and/or periocular
Posterior uveitis	Systemic and/or periocular, intravitreal
Endophthalmitis	Systemic/periocular, intravitreal
Optic neuritis	Systemic or periocular
Cranial arteritis	Systemic
Sympathetic ophthalmia	Systemic and topical

Nonsteroidal Anti-Inflammatory Drugs (NSAIDs)

Derivation   Derivatives of the 20-carbon essential fatty acid arachidonic acid have been shown to be mediators of a wide variety of biological functions, including regulation of smooth muscle tone (in blood vessels, bronchi, uterus, and gut), platelet aggregation, hormone release (growth hormone, ACTH, insulin, renin, and progesterone), and inflammation.

The synthetic cascade that results in the production of a wide variety of derivatives (depending upon the stimulus and tissue) begins with stimulation of phospholipase A_2, the enzyme that liberates arachidonic acid from phospholipids of the cell membrane. (Phospholipase A_2 is inhibited by corticosteroids.) Arachidonic acid is then converted into either cyclic endoperoxides by *cyclo-oxygenase* (prostaglandin synthase) or into hydroperoxides by *lipoxygenase*. Among the subsequent products of the endoperoxides are the prostaglandins, which mediate inflammation and other responses; prostacyclin, a vasodilator and platelet anti-aggregant; and thromboxane, a vasoconstrictor and platelet aggregant. The hydroperoxides form a chemotactic agent and the leukotrienes C_4, D_4, and E_4, previously known as the slow-reacting substance of anaphylaxis.

Classification   The currently available NSAIDs inhibit the production and, thus, the inflammation-inducing effects of prostaglandins through the cyclo-oxygenase pathway. On the basis of chemical structures, NSAIDs can be classified as

- *Salicylates:* aspirin, etofenamic acid, flufenamic acid, meclofenamate, mefenamic acid, tolfenamic acid

- *Indoles:* indomethacin, sulindac, tolmetin

- *Phenylalkanoic acids:* diclofenac, fenoprofen, flurbiprofen, ibuprofen, ketoprofen, ketorolac, naproxen, piroxicam, sutoprofen

- *Pyrazolones:* oxyphenbutazone, phenylbutazone

Table XXI-10

Nonsteroidal Anti-inflammatory Drugs

DRUG	STARTING DOSE
Aspirin	650 mg qid
Indomethacin (Indocin)	25 mg tid
Fenoprofen (Nalfon)	600 mg qid
Ibuprofen (Motrin)	400 mg qid
Ketoprofen (Orudis)	75 mg tid
Naproxen (Naprosyn)	250 mg bid
Piroxicam (Feldene)	20 mg qid
Sulindac (Clinoril)	150 mg bid
Tolmetin (Tolectin)	400 mg tid

Agents Table XXI-10 lists a number of these agents with their starting dosages. *Aspirin* and a number of other compounds have been found to inactivate cyclo-oxygenase in circulating platelets and megakaryocytes. They inhibit a host of biological functions, including the local signs of inflammation (local heat, vasodilation, edema, swelling) as well as pain and fever, and they have complex effects on clotting. At low doses (300 mg every other day) aspirin inhibits the cyclo-oxygenase in platelets that is essential for conversion of arachidonic acid to PGG_2 and thromboxane. Inhibition of thromboxane production prevents coagulation. Platelets have a life span of 7–10 days, and, as anucleate platelets cannot produce new cyclo-oxygenase in their lifetime, this anticoagulant effect lasts for 7–10 days even after the discontinuation of aspirin administration.

In contrast, production of prostacyclin by the vascular endothelium is only briefly suppressed, because cyclo-oxygenase can be replenished by these nucleated cells. As a consequence, aspirin therapy for postoperative pain or for pain associated with traumatic hyphema may increase the risk of hemorrhage. However, low-dose aspirin therapy may benefit patients having platelet emboli (as in some cases of amaurosis fugax). Diversion of arachidonic acid to the lipoxygenase pathway by inhibition of cyclo-oxygenase may explain why aspirin use can be associated with asthma attacks and hypersensitivity reactions (mediated by leukotrienes C_4, D_4, and E_4) in susceptible persons.

High doses of aspirin, such as those employed in the treatment of arthritis, may occasionally have toxic effects such as headache, dizziness, tinnitus, dimmed vision, mental confusion, drowsiness, hyperventilation, nausea, and vomiting. These effects may be potentiated by the concomitant use of carbonic anhydrase inhibitors at doses sufficient to cause systemic acidosis. During metabolic acidosis, a higher proportion of aspirin molecules are shifted into the more lipid-soluble un-ionized form, which more readily penetrates the blood–brain barrier.

Systemic therapy with aspirin and other cyclo-oxygenase inhibitors is occasionally effective in the treatment of scleritis and uveitis but is generally disappointing. These agents do not appear to be as effective as steroids.

Flurbiprofen (Ocufen) was the first commercially available topical ocular non-steroidal anti-inflammatory agent. When applied preoperatively, it helps to retard the prostaglandin-mediated pupillary constriction that can otherwise interfere with extracapsular cataract surgery.

Diclofenac (Voltaren) is another topical NSAID. It has an FDA-approved indication for the postoperative prophylaxis and treatment of ocular inflammation and has also been used successfully to prevent and treat cystoid macular edema (CME).

Suprofen (Profenal), available in 1% ophthalmic solution, is indicated for inhibition of intraoperative miosis only.

The role of topical NSAIDs in the treatment of ocular inflammation and in the prevention of aphakic CME is under investigation. NSAIDs such as *indomethacin* can be effective in treating orbital inflammatory diseases with minimal side effects. The prophylactic use of indomethacin in cataract patients has been reported to reduce the incidence of angiographically detected CME, but its effect upon visually significant CME has yet to be reported.

Latanoprost (Xalatan) is a newly approved antiglaucoma agent that belongs to the class of $F_{2\alpha}$ prostaglandins. It is highly selective for PGF receptors, with a distribution limited to the anterior segment on topical application. Latanoprost has a half-life of 17 minutes and is eliminated through kidneys. It reduces IOP by increasing the uveoscleral outflow. A single topical application of 0.005% solution results in 22%–31% reduction of IOP and the effect lasts for 24 hours. It is especially effective in low-tension glaucoma patients, who show 20% reduction in IOP from baseline levels. Because of its mode of action, latanoprost has additive effect with both beta blockers and carbonic anhydrase inhibitors. Conjunctival hyperemia (13%–36%) and increased iris pigmentation (3%–10%) are the most commonly noted topical side effects. Latanoprost (0.005%) is recommended to be used once a day.

Antihistamines and Cromolyn Sodium

Allergic conjunctivitis is an immediate hypersensitivity reaction in which triggering antigens couple to reaginic antibodies (IgE) on the cell surface of mast cells and basophils, leading to release of histamine from secretory granules. The released histamine causes capillary dilatation and increased permeability and thus conjunctival injection and swelling. It also stimulates nerve endings, causing pain and itching. Table XXI-11 lists agents for the relief of allergic conjunctivitis by class.

Short-term relief for mild allergic symptoms may be achieved with topical antihistamines such as *antazoline*. More recalcitrant cases often require short-term use of topical steroids.

Hydroxymethyl progesterone (HMS) is well suited for this use, since it has a low potential for elevating IOP. Unfortunately, more potent steroids are often used and abused for this relief, because of either limited response to other agents or chronic disease.

Cromolyn sodium 4% (Crolom), a blocker of histamine release, is currently the therapy of choice for severe vernal and atopic conjunctivitis. However, it has no direct antihistamine effect and must be used prophylactically for several weeks to be effective. It has few, if any, side effects and is thus much preferred to potent steroids.

Lodoxamide (Alomide) is a mast-cell stabilizer that has been used for the treatment of allergic conjunctivitis. The human eye has approximately 50 million mast cells. Each contains several hundred granules that in turn contain preformed chemical mediators. Chronic exposure to antigen results in an antigen–IgE antibody bound to the mast-cell membrane. The release of a cascade of mediators such as his-

TABLE XXI-11

AGENTS FOR RELIEF OF ALLERGIC CONJUNCTIVITIS

GENERIC NAME	TRADE NAME	CLASS
Cromolyn sodium	Crolom	Mast-cell inhibitor
Lodoxamide	Alomide	Mast-cell inhibitor
Ketorolac tromethamine	Acular	NSAID
Levocabastin	Livostin	H_1- antagonist
Naphazoline/antazoline	Vasocon-A	Antihistamine/ decongestant
Naphazoline/pheniramine	Naphcon-A Opcon-A	Antihistamine/ decongestant

tamine, prostaglandin, leukotrienes, and chemotactic factors follows. These mediators cause the itching and hyperemia associated with allergic conjunctivitis. Mast-cell stabilizers have traditionally been viewed as preventing calcium influx across mast-cell membranes, thereby preventing mast-cell degranulation and mediator release. Recent studies, however, demonstrate that cromolyn sodium inhibits neutrophil, eosinophil, and monocyte activation in vitro.

Lodoxamide has beneficial effects in both allergic conjunctivitis and vernal keratoconjunctivitis. It has been shown to produce stabilization of the mast-cell membrane 2500 times greater than cromolyn sodium. Clinically, lodoxamide onset is quicker with less stinging than cromolyn sodium in treating allergic conjunctivitis. One recent multicenter, double-masked study has shown lodoxamide superior to cromolyn sodium in treating vernal keratoconjunctivitis. However, as with all mast-cell stabilizers, it takes several weeks to become clinically effective. For patients who are very uncomfortable it may be necessary to use topical steroids concurrently with mast-cell stabilizers for the first weeks until these agents are fully effective.

The usual dose of Alomide 0.1% for adults and children older than 2 years of age is 1–2 drops in the affected eye 4 times daily for up to 3 months. The most frequently reported adverse reactions are burning, stinging, and discomfort upon instillation (15%).

Levocabastin (Livostin) is a newly synthesized H_1 receptor antagonist. It has been shown to be significantly effective in reducing the signs and symptoms of allergen-induced allergic conjunctivitis. Its onset of action occurs within minutes and lasts for at least 4 hours. Levocabastin has been shown to be more effective than placebo or vasoconstrictor-antihistamine combinations. It appears to have equal effectiveness as cromolyn sodium in some studies, and has the advantage of a quicker onset compared to mast-cell stabilizing medications.

The usual dose of Livostin 0.05% is 1 drop 4 times per day for up to 2 weeks. The most frequent side effects reported were mild, transient stinging and burning (15%) and headache (5%).

Keratolac (Acular) is an NSAID that blocks the metabolism of arachidonic acid by cyclo-oxygenose. Arachidonic acid metabolites are present in higher quantities in the tears of ocular allergic disease patients. Two recent double-masked studies revealed that ocular allergic patients treated with ketorolac tromethamine had significantly less conjunctival inflammation, ocular itching, and tearing when compared to placebo. Even though ketorolac is effective in allergic disease, it does not have a decongestant effect and does not relieve redness.

The recommended dose of ketorolac is 1 drop (0.25 mg) 4 times per day. The most common side effects are stinging and burning on instillation (40%).

Antagonists of leukotriene, platelet-activating factor, and bradykinin are some of the other promising drugs currently under investigation. Manipulation of T-cell activity with cyclosporine or immunosuppressives such as azathioprine may also prove to be useful.

Bito LZ. Prostaglandins: Old concepts and new perspectives. *Arch Ophthalmol.* 1987; 105:1036–1039.

Flach AJ. Nonsteroidal anti-inflammatory drugs. In: Zimmerman TJ, Kooner KS, eds. *Ophthalmol Clin North Am.* Philadelphia: Saunders; 1989:151–161.

Foster CS, Forstot SL, Wilson LA. Mortality rate in rheumatoid arthritis patients developing necrotizing scleritis or peripheral ulcerative keratitis. Effects of systemic immunosuppression. *Ophthalmology.* 1984;91:1253–1263.

Leibowitz HM, Bartlett JD, Rich R, et al. Intraocular pressure–raising potential of 1.0% rimexolone in patients responding to corticosteroids. *Arch Ophthalmol.* 1996; 114:933–937.

Mishima HK, Masuda K, Kitazawa Y, et al. A comparison of latanoprost and timolol in primary open-angle glaucoma and ocular hypertension. *Arch Ophthalmol.* 1996; 114:929–932.

Noble AG, Tripathi RC, Levine RA. Indomethacin for the treatment of idiopathic orbital myositis. *Am J Ophthalmol.* 1989;108:336–338.

Tripathi BJ, Millard CB, Tripathi RC. Corticosteroids induce a sialated glycoprotein (Cort-GP) in trabecular cells in vitro. *Exp Eye Res.* 1990;51:735–737.

Antifibrotic Agents

Antiproliferative agents, also known as *antimetabolites,* are occasionally required in the treatment of severe ocular inflammatory diseases, such as Behçet syndrome and sympathetic ophthalmia, or when the ocular disease is part of a systemic vasculitis. Systemic therapy with such agents is best carried out in consultation with a chemotherapist. The uses and side effects of these agents are discussed in BCSC Section 9, *Intraocular Inflammation and Uveitis.*

Intravitreal injection of *5-fluorouracil* has been reported to be beneficial in preventing recurrent proliferative vitreoretinopathy after surgery for complex retinal detachments in an experimental model, although a suitable delivery system for use in patients has yet to be developed. Subconjunctival injection improves the success of filtering surgery in difficult glaucoma cases. Studies are also under way to evaluate the beneficial effect of intraoperative topical use during filtering surgery. The drug is thought to inhibit the cellular proliferation that could otherwise occur in response to inflammation. In high-risk eyes including young glaucoma patients (40 years of age or younger), the initial trabeculectomy with adjunctive *5-fluorouracil* had a higher success rate than surgery without the adjunct.

Mitomycin-C is a compound isolated from the fungus *Streptomyces caespitosus.* The parent compound becomes a bifunctional alkylating agent after enzymatic alteration within the cell, and it then inhibits DNA synthesis and cross-links DNA. Mitomycin's immunosuppressive properties are fairly weak; however, it is a potent inhibitor of fibroblast proliferation.

Topical mitomycin-C has also been used in filtering surgery. It has the advantage of functioning with a single intraoperative application and not requiring the repeated postoperative injections of 5-fluorouracil. Randomized comparative studies of mitomycin-C with 5-fluorouracil in high-risk patients show lower average pressures with fewer corneal surface and hypotony-related complications in the groups treated with mitomycin-C. It is used as a single topical application during glaucoma filtering operations to impede scarring and prevent surgical failure. Complications of therapy are wound leakage, hypotony, and localized scleral melting. Severe toxicity has been reported in an animal model with intraocular instillation of mitomycin-C, resulting in irreversible progressive bullous keratopathy in three of four rabbits.

Topical mitomycin-C has also been recommended for use in the prevention of recurrence after pterygium excision. Recommended dosage is 0.02%–0.04% 4 times daily for 1–2 weeks after surgery. The recurrence rate with such therapy has been reported as low as 0%–11%. Unfortunately, several side effects such as corneal edema, corneal perforation, corectopia, iritis, cataract, and intractable pain have been reported. A primary conjunctival graft after pterygium removal may offer similar low recurrence rates without these serious complications.

Blumenkranz MS, Ophir A, Claflin AJ, et al. Fluorouracil for the treatment of massive periretinal proliferation. *Am J Ophthalmol.* 1982;94:458–467.

Whiteside-Michel J, Liebmann JM, Ritch R. Initial 5-fluorouracil trabeculectomy in young patients. *Ophthalmology.* 1992;99:7–13.

Antibiotics (Table XXI-12)

Penicillins and Cephalosporins

The penicillins and cephalosporins are beta-lactam–containing antibacterial agents that react with and inactivate a particular bacterial transpeptidase essential for bacterial cell-wall synthesis (Fig XXI-9). The amide bond of the beta-lactam group is surrounded by structural features in the antibiotic molecule that resemble the portion of the natural substrate with which the transpeptidase reacts. The peptidase reacts with the antibiotic, forming an inactive acyl intermediate.

Some bacteria are resistant to the action of penicillins and cephalosporins. The lipopolysaccharide outer coat of many gram-negative bacteria may prevent certain hydrophilic antibiotics from reaching their cytoplasmic membrane site of action. Furthermore, some bacteria produce *beta-lactamases* (penicillinase), enzymes capable of cleaving the critical amide bond within these antibiotics. The different penicillins and cephalosporins vary in susceptibility to the beta-lactamases produced by different bacterial species.

The penicillins and cephalosporins penetrate the blood–ocular and blood–brain barriers poorly and are actively transported out of the eye by the organic acid transport system of the ciliary body. However, their penetration into the eye increases with inflammation, and coadministration of probenecid inhibits ciliary body outward transport.

TABLE XXI-12

PRINCIPAL ANTIBIOTIC AGENTS

DRUG NAME	TOPICAL	SUBCONJUNCTIVAL	INTRAVITREAL	INTRAVENOUS (ADULT)
Amikacin sulfate	10 mg/ml	25 mg	400 µg	15 mg/kg daily in 2–3 doses
Ampicillin sodium	50 mg/ml	50–150 mg	500 µg	4–12 g daily in 4 doses
Bacitracin zinc	10,000 units/ml	5,000 units		
Carbenicillin disodium	4–6 mg/ml	100 mg	250–2000 µg	8–24 g daily in 4–6 doses
Cefazolin sodium	50 mg/ml	100 mg	2250 µg	2–4 daily in 3–4 doses
Ceftazidime		200 mg	2200 µg	1 g daily in 2–3 doses
Clindamycin	50 mg/ml	15–50 mg	1000 µg	900–1800 mg daily in 2 doses
Colistimethate sodium	10 mg/ml	15–25 mg	100 µg	2.5–5.0 mg/kg daily in 2–4 doses
Erythromycin	50 mg/ml	100 mg	500 µg	
Gentamicin sulfate	8–15 mg/ml	10–20 mg	100–200 µg	3–5 mg/kg daily in 2–3 doses
Imipenem/ Cilastatin sodium	5 mg/ml			2 g daily in 3–4 doses
Kanamycin sulfate	30–50 mg/ml	30 mg		
Methicillin sodium	50 mg/ml	50–100 mg	1000–2000 µg	6–10 g daily in 4 doses
Neomycin sulfate	5–8 mg/ml	125–250 mg		
Penicillin G	100,000 units/ml	0.5–1.0 million units		12–24 million units daily in 4 doses
Polymyxin B sulfate	10,000 units/ml	100,000 units		
Ticarcillin disodium	6 mg/ml	100 mg		200–300 mg/kg daily
Tobramycin sulfate	8–15 mg/ml	10–20 mg	100–200 µg	3–5 mg/kg daily in 2–3 doses
Vancomycin hydrochloride	20–50 mg/ml	25 mg	1000 µg	15–30 mg/kg daily in 1–2 doses

Serious and occasionally fatal hypersensitivity (anaphylactoid) reactions can occur in association with penicillin and cephalosporin therapy. Although anaphylaxis is more frequent following parenteral administration, it can occur with oral therapy. Such reactions are more likely to occur in individuals who have a history of sensitivity to multiple allergens. A history of immediate allergic response (anaphy-

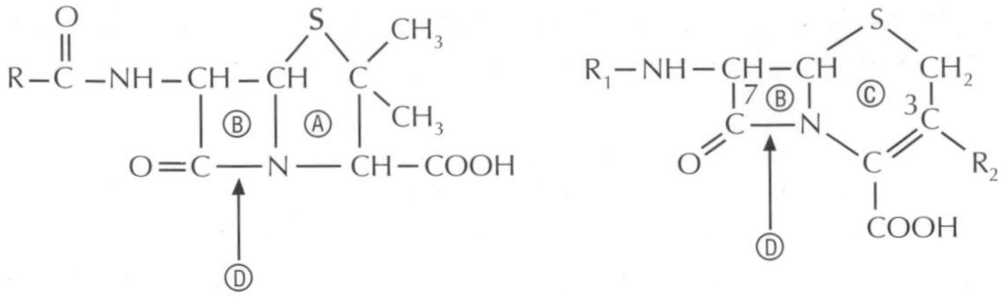

FIG XXI-9—Structure of the penicillins and cephalosporins. *A* = Thiazole ring; *B* = Beta-lactam ring; *C* = Dihydrothizine ring; *D* = Site of action of beta-lactam. (From Mandell GL, Sande MA. Penicillins and cephalosporins. In: Gilman AG, Goodman LS, Gilman A, et al, eds. *The Pharmacological Basis of Therapeutics.* 6th ed. New York: Macmillan; 1980:1126–1161.)

laxis or rapid onset of hives) to any penicillin is a strong contraindication to the use of any other penicillin. Approximately 10% of persons allergic to a penicillin will have a cross-reactivity to cephalosporins.

Penicillins There are five classes of penicillins, which differ in their spectrum of antibiotic activity and in their resistance to penicillinase:

□ *Penicillin G, penicillin V,* and *phenethicillin* are highly effective against most gram-positive and gram-negative cocci, anaerobes, *Actinomyces, Leptospira,* and *Treponema.* However, most strains of *Staphylococcus aureus* and many strains of *S epidermidis* and *Neisseria gonorrhoeae* are now resistant, often through production of penicillinase. Penicillin V and phenethicillin are absorbed well orally, while penicillin G is better given intravenously because it is inactivated by stomach acid. These penicillins are excreted rapidly by the kidneys and have short half-lives unless given in depot forms (i.e., procaine penicillin G) or administered with probenecid, which competitively inhibits excretion by the kidneys.

□ The *penicillinase-resistant penicillins* include *methicillin, nafcillin, oxacillin, cloxacillin, dicloxacillin,* and *floxacillin.* They are less potent than penicillin G against susceptible organisms but are the drugs of choice for infections caused by penicillinase-producing *S aureus.* Methicillin and nafcillin are acid labile and are therefore given either parenterally or by subconjunctival injection. The other agents in this group have reasonable oral absorption. When they are given systemically, coadministration of probenecid reduces renal excretion and outward transport from the eye.

□ The broad-spectrum penicillins such as *ampicillin* and *amoxicillin* have antibacterial activity that extends to such gram-negative organisms as *Haemophilus influenzae* and *Proteus mirabilis.* Resistant strains of *H influenzae* are becoming more common. These drugs are stable in acid and may be given orally. They are not resistant to penicillinase.

□ *Carbenicillin, ticarcillin,* and *azlocillin* have antimicrobial activity extended to include *Pseudomonas, Enterobacter,* and indole-positive strains of *Proteus.* These drugs are given parenterally or subconjunctivally, though the indanyl ester of carbenicillin may be given orally. They are not resistant to penicillinase.

□ *Piperacillin* and *mezlocillin* are particularly potent against *Pseudomonas.* They are administered parenterally or subconjunctivally, and they are not resistant to penicillinase.

Cephalosporins Bacterial susceptibility patterns and resistance to beta-lactamases have determined the classification of the cephalosporins as first, second, or third generation:

▫ First generation: *Cephalothin, cefazolin, cephalexin,* and *cephradine* have antimicrobial activity against gram-positive and gram-negative organisms, especially group-A *Streptococcus pyogenes, viridans,* and *pneumoniae; S aureus* and *epidermidis; Clostridium perfringens; Bacillus subtilis;* and *Corynebacterium diphtheriae.* They are also active against *Proteus mirabilis, Salmonella, Shigella, Klebsiella,* and *Escherichia coli* but only half of the isolates of *H influenzae.* They are not active against *Enterobacter,* other *Proteus* species, *P aeruginosa, Bacteroides, Serratia,* and enterococci. Cephalothin is the most resistant of these agents to staphylococcal beta-lactamase. Cefazolin has somewhat greater activity against *Klebsiella.* Cephalexin and cephradine are stable in acid and available in oral forms.

▫ Second-generation: *Cefamandole* and *cefoxitin* display greater activity against three additional gram-negative organisms: *H influenzae, Enterobacter aerogenes,* and *Neisseria* species. *Cefuroxime* has a similar spectrum of activity. Cefamandole has increased activity against *Enterobacter* species, indole-positive *Proteus, H influenzae,* and *Bacteroides.* Cefoxitin is active against indole-positive *Proteus* and *Serratia.* Cefuroxime is valuable in the treatment of penicillinase-producing *N gonorrhoeae* and ampicillin-resistant *H influenzae,* and its penetration of the blood–brain barrier is adequate for initial treatment of suspected pneumococcal, meningococcal, or *H influenzae* meningitis.

▫ Third-generation: *Cefotaxime* and *moxalactam* have enhanced activity against gram-negative bacilli, but they are inferior to first-generation cephalosporins in regard to their activity against gram-positive cocci. *Cefoperazone* and *ceftizoxime* have a similar spectrum of activity against gram-positive and -negative organisms, anaerobes, *Serratia, Proteus,* and some *Pseudomonas* isolates. Cefoperazone is particularly effective against *Pseudomonas.* Cefotaxime is able to penetrate the blood–brain barrier better than the other cephalosporins, and it presumably also penetrates the blood–ocular barrier.

Other Antibacterial Agents (Table XXI-13)

Sulfonamides Sulfonamides are derivatives of para-aminobenzenesulfonamide. They are structural analogues and competitive antagonists of para-aminobenzoic acid (PABA) for the bacterial synthesis of folic acid. Only bacteria that must synthesize their own folic acid are affected by these drugs. Mammalian cells are not affected, because they are unable to synthesize folic acid. Sulfonamides are only bacteriostatic. They are more effective when administered with *trimethoprim,* a potent inhibitor of bacterial dihydrofolate reductase; together, they block successive steps in the synthesis of tetrahydrofolic acid.

Sulfacetamide ophthalmic solution (10%–30%) penetrates the cornea well. Susceptible organisms include *Streptococcus pneumoniae, Corynebacterium diphtheriae, H influenzae, Actinomyces,* and *Chlamydia trachomatis.* However, a 3-week course of systemic sulfonamide therapy is required to eradicate *Chlamydia.* Local irritation, itching, periorbital edema and transient stinging are some of the common side effects from topical administration. As with all sulfonamide preparations, severe sensitivity reactions such as toxic epidermal necrolysis and Stevens-Johnson syndrome have been reported.

Tetracyclines Tetracyclines enter bacteria by an active transport across the cytoplasmic membrane. They inhibit protein synthesis by binding to the 30 S ribosomal subunit, thus preventing access of aminoacyl tRNA to the acceptor site on the mRNA–ribosome complex. Host cells are less affected because they lack an active-transport system.

Tetracyclines are broad-spectrum bacteriostatic antibiotics, active against many gram-positive and -negative bacteria and also against *Rickettsiae, Mycoplasma pneumoniae,* and *Chlamydiae.* However, many strains of *Klebsiella* and *H influenzae* and nearly all strains of *Proteus vulgaris* and *P aeruginosa* are resistant. Tetracycline is poorly water soluble but is soluble in eyedrops containing mineral oil; it penetrates the corneal epithelium readily.

Systemic therapy with tetracycline is used for chlamydial infections and, because the drug is excreted into oil glands, also for staphylococcal infections of the meibomian glands. It chelates to calcium in milk and antacids and is best taken on an empty stomach. Tetracycline should not be given to children or pregnant women, because it can be deposited in growing teeth, discoloring them. Tetracycline depresses plasma prothrombin activity and thereby potentiates coumadin.

Chloramphenicol This broad-spectrum bacteriostatic agent inhibits bacterial protein synthesis by binding reversibly to the 50 S ribosomal subunit, preventing aminoacyl tRNA from binding to the ribosome. Chloramphenicol is effective against most *H influenzae* and *N meningitidis* and *gonorrhoeae* and all anaerobic bacteria. It has some activity against *Streptococcus pneumoniae, S aureus, Klebsiella pneumoniae, Enterobacter, Serratia,* and *Proteus mirabilis. P aeruginosa* is resistant.

Chloramphenicol penetrates the corneal epithelium well during topical therapy and penetrates the blood–ocular barriers readily when given systemically. However, the use of this agent is limited because it has been implicated in an idiosyncratic and potentially lethal aplastic anemia. While most cases of this anemia have occurred after oral administration, some have been reported in association with parenteral and even topical ocular therapy.

Aminoglycosides The aminoglycosides consist of amino sugars in glycosidic linkage. They are bacteriocidal agents that are transported across the cell membrane into bacteria and bind to the 30 S and 50 S ribosomal subunits, interfering with initiation of protein synthesis. The antibacterial spectrum of these agents is determined primarily by the efficiency of their transport into bacterial cells. Such transport is energy dependent and may be reduced in the anaerobic environment of an abscess. Resistance to aminoglycosides may be caused by failure of transport, low affinity for the ribosome, or plasmid-transmitted ability to enzymatically inactivate the drug. The coadministration of drugs such as penicillin that alter bacterial cell-wall structure can markedly increase aminoglycoside penetration, resulting in a synergism of antibiotic activity against gram-positive cocci, especially enterococci. Amikacin is remarkably resistant to enzymatic inactivation.

Gentamicin, tobramycin, kanamycin, and *amikacin* have antibacterial activity against aerobic, gram-negative bacilli such as *Proteus mirabilis, P aeruginosa,*

TABLE XXI-13

OPHTHALMIC ANTIBACTERIAL AGENTS

GENERIC NAME	TRADE NAME	CONCENTRATION OPHTHALMIC SOLUTION (%)
Individual Agents		
Bacitracin zinc	AK-Tracin	Not available
Chloramphenicol	AK-Chlor	0.5%
	Chloromycetin	0.5%
	Chloroptic	0.5%
	Ocu-Chlor	0.5%
	Available generically	0.5%
Chlortetracycline hydrochloride	Aureomycin	Not available
Ciprofloxacin hydrochloride	Ciloxan	0.3%
Erythromycin	AK-Mycin	Not available
	Ilotycin	Not available
	Available generically	Not available
Gentamicin sulfate	Garamycin	0.3%
	Genoptic	0.3%
	Gentacidin	0.3%
	Gentak	0.3%
	Available generically	0.3%
Norfloxacin	Chibroxin	0.3%
Ofloxacin	Ocuflox	0.3%
Sulfacetamide sodium	AK-Sulf	10%
	Bleph-10	10%
	Cetamide	Not available
	Isopto Cetamide	15%
	Ophthacet	10%
	Sulamyd sodium	10%, 30%
	Sulf-10	10%
	Available generically	10%–30%
Sulfisoxazole diolamine	Gantrisin	4%
Tetracycline hydrochloride	Achromycin	1%
Tobramycin sulfate	Defy	0.3%
	Tobrex	0.3%
	Available generically	0.3%
Mixtures		
Polymyxin B/Bacitracin	AK-Poly-Bac	Not available
	Polysporin	
Polymyxin B/Neomycin	Statrol	16,250 units 3.5 mg/ml
Polymyxin B/Neomycin/Bacitracin	Neotal	Not available
	AK-Spore	Not available
	Neosporin	
	Available generically	
Polymyxin B/Neomycin/Gramicidin	AK-Spore	10,000 units
	Neosporin	1.75 mg
	Available generically	0.025 mg/ml
Polymyxin B/Oxytetracycline	Terramycin	Not available
Polymyxin B/Trimethoprim	Polytrim	10,000 units 1 mg/ml

Klebsiella, Enterobacter, and *Serratia.* Gentamicin and tobramycin are active against *S aureus* and *epidermidis.* Kanamycin is generally less effective than the others against gram-negative bacilli. Resistance to gentamicin and tobramycin has gradually increased as a result of a plasmid-transmitted ability to synthesize inactivating enzymes. Thus, amikacin, which is generally impervious to these enzymes, is particularly valuable in treating such resistant organisms.

Aminoglycosides are not absorbed well orally but are given systemically by intramuscular or intravenous routes. They do not readily penetrate the blood–ocular barrier but may be administered as eyedrops, ointments, or periocular injections. Gentamicin and carbenicillin should not be mixed for IV administration because the carbenicillin inactivates the gentamicin over several hours. Similar incompatibilities exist in vitro between gentamicin and other penicillins and cephalosporins.

Use of *streptomycin* is now limited to *Streptococcus viridans* bacterial endocarditis, tularemia, plague, and brucellosis. *Neomycin* is a broad-spectrum antibiotic, effective against *Enterobacter, Klebsiella pneumoniae, H influenzae, N meningitidis, Corynebacterium diphtheriae,* and *S aureus.* It is given topically in ophthalmology and orally as a bowel preparation for surgery. Neomycin is too toxic to be used intravenously but can be given orally because it is not absorbed from the gut. Topical allergy to ocular use of neomycin occurs in about 8% of cases. It can cause punctate epitheliopathy and retard reepithelialization of abrasions.

All aminoglycosides can cause dose-related vestibular and auditory dysfunction and nephrotoxicity when they are given systemically. Systemic use of aminoglycosides should be limited to serious infections, and the plasma concentration of drug and blood urea nitrogen should be monitored to avoid overdosing.

Fluoroquinolones   These fluorinated derivatives of nalidixic acid are available in a variety of chemical structures that include *norfloxacin, ofloxacin, perfloxacin, ciprofloxacin, enoxacin, lomefloxacin, temafloxacin, fleroxacin,* and *tosufloxacin.* These agents are highly effective broad-spectrum antimicrobials with potent activity against common gram-positive and -negative ocular pathogens. Their mechanism of action targets bacterial DNA supercoiling through the inhibition of DNA gyrase, which is one of the enzymes responsible for replication, genetic recombination, and DNA repair.

Studies in vitro have demonstrated that the fluoroquinolones, especially ciprofloxacin and temafloxacin, inhibit 90% of common bacterial corneal pathogens and have a lower minimum inhibitory concentration than gentamicin, tobramycin, and cefazolin. They are also less toxic to the corneal epithelium than are the aminoglycosides. Initial clinical studies have shown that a 0.3% ciprofloxacin ophthalmic solution is highly effective against corneal and conjunctival bacterial pathogens without serious side effects and is potentially useful in treating bacterial conjunctivitis and keratitis, although information regarding larger clinical trials and bacterial resistance is needed.

Miscellaneous antibiotics   *Vancomycin* is a tricyclic glycopeptide derived from cultures of *Nocardia orientalis.* It is bactericidal for most gram-positive organisms through the inhibition of glycopeptide polymerization in the cell wall. It is useful in the treatment of staphylococcal infections in patients who are allergic to or have failed to the respond to the penicillins and cephalosporins as well as in the treatment of methicillin-resistant streptococci. It can also be used in combination with amino-glycosides to treat *S viridans* or *bovis* endocarditis. Vancomycin is especially indicated in the treatment of pseudomembranous colitis caused by *Clostridium difficile.*

Vancomycin may be used topically or intraocularly to treat sight-threatening infections of the eye, including infectious keratitis and endophthalmitis caused by methicillin-resistant staphylococci or streptococci. It is a preferred substitute for a cephalosporin used in combination with an aminoglycoside in the empiric treatment of endophthalmitis. See BCSC Section 8, *External Disease and Cornea,* for further discussion.

The intravenous dosage of vancomycin in adults with normal renal function is 500 mg every 6 hours or 1 g every 12 hours. Dosing must be adjusted in subjects who have renal impairment. Topical vancomycin may be given in a concentration of 50 mg/ml in the treatment of infectious keratitis. Lower concentrations (5 mg/ml) have been used successfully in the treatment of susceptible staphylococcal blepharo-conjunctivitis. Intravitreal vancomycin with an aminoglycoside is recommended for initial empiric therapy for exogenous bacterial endophthalmitis. A dose of 1 mg in 0.1 ml establishes intraocular levels significantly higher than the minimum inhibitory concentration for most gram-positive organisms.

Unlike systemic treatment, topical and intraocular vancomycin have not been associated with ototoxicity or nephrotoxicity. Hourly use of 50 mg of vancomycin/ml delivers a dose of 36 mg/day, which is well below the recommended systemic dose.

Erythromycin is a macrolide (many-membered lactone ring attached to deoxy sugars) antibiotic that binds to the 50 S subunit of bacterial ribosomes and interferes with protein synthesis. It is effective against gram-positive cocci such as *Strepto-coccus pyogenes* and *pneumoniae,* gram-positive bacilli such as *Corynebacterium diphtheriae* and *Listeria monocytogenes,* and a few gram-negative organisms such as *N gonorrhoeae.* It is the treatment of choice for *Legionella pneumophila,* the agent of legionnaires' disease, as well as for *Mycoplasma pneumoniae.* Erythromycin is administered orally as enteric-coated tablets or in esterified forms to avoid inactivation by stomach acid. It can also be administered parenterally or topically as an ophthalmic ointment. The drug penetrates the blood–ocular and blood–brain barriers poorly.

Polymyxin B is a mixture of basic peptides that function as cationic detergents to dissolve phospholipids of bacterial cell membranes, thus disrupting the cells. It is used topically or by local injection to treat corneal ulcers. Gram-negative bacteria are susceptible, including *Enterobacter, Klebsiella,* and *P aeruginosa.*

Bacitracin is a mixture of polypeptides that inhibit bacterial cell-wall synthesis. It is active against *Neisseria, H influenzae, Actinomyces,* and most gram-positive bacilli and cocci. It is available as an ophthalmic ointment either alone or in combination with polymyxin and neomycin.

Antifungal Agents (Table XXI-14)

Polyenes The polyene antibiotics are named for a component sequence of four to seven conjugated double bonds. That lipophilic region allows them to bind to sterols in the cell membrane of susceptible fungi, an interaction that results in damage to the membrane and leakage of essential nutrients. Other antifungals such as flucyto-sine and the imidazoles and even other antibiotics such as tetracycline and rifampin can enter through the damaged membrane, yielding synergistic effects.

TABLE XXI-14

ANTIFUNGAL AGENTS

GENERIC (TRADE) NAME	ROUTE	DOSAGE	SPECTRUM
Amphotericin B	Topical	0.1–0.5% solution; dilute with water for injection or dextrose 5% in water	*Blastomyces* *Candida* *Coccidioides* *Histoplasma*
	Subconjunctival	0.8–1.0 mg	
	Intravitreal	5 µg	
	Intravenous	Because of side effects and toxicity, dose needs to be cautiously adjusted	
Fluconazole (Diflucan)	Oral	800 mg on day 1, then 400 mg daily in divided doses	*Candida*
Flucytosine (Ancobon)	Oral	50–150 mg/kg daily in 4 divided doses	*Candida* *Cryptococcus*
	Topical	1% solution	
Natamycin (Natacyn)	Topical	5% suspension	*Candida* *Aspergillus* *Cephalosporium* *Fusarium* *Penicillium*
Miconazole nitrate (Monistat)	Topical	1% solution	*Candida* *Cryptococcus* *Aspergillus*
	Subconjunctival	5–10 mg	
	Intravitreal	10 µg	
Ketoconazole (Nizoral)	Oral	200–400 mg daily	*Candida* *Cryptococcus* *Histoplasma*

Natamycin is available as a 5% suspension for topical ophthalmic use (once an hour). Local hypersensitivity reactions of the conjunctiva and eyelid and corneal epithelial toxicity may occur. *Amphotericin B* may be reconstituted at 0.25%–0.50% in sterile water (with deoxycholate to improve solubility) for topical use (every 30 minutes). It may also be administered systemically for disseminated disease, although careful monitoring for renal and other toxicities is required. These agents penetrate the cornea poorly. They are active topically against a variety of filamentous fungi, including *Aspergillus, Cephalosporium, Curvularia, Fusarium,* and *Penicillium,* and the yeast *Candida albicans.* Systemic amphotericin B is used in the treatment of systemic *Blastomyces, Coccidioides, Histoplasma, Cryptococcus, Candida, Mucorales,* and *Aspergillus.*

Imidazoles The imidazole-derived antifungal agents also increase fungal cell-membrane permeability. *Miconazole* is available in a 1% solution that may be injected subconjunctivally (5 mg in 0.5 ml, once or twice daily) or applied topically. Miconazole penetrates the cornea poorly. *Ketoconazole* is available in 200 mg tablets for oral therapy (every 6–8 hours). Ketoconazole normally penetrates the blood–brain barrier and, presumably, the blood–ocular barrier poorly, but therapeutic levels can be achieved in inflamed eyes. The imidazole antifungals act against various species of *Aspergillus, Coccidioides, Cryptococcus,* and *Candida.*

Flucytosine Flucytosine (5-fluorocytosine) is converted by some species of fungal cells to 5-fluorouracil by cytosine deaminase, and then to 5-fluorodeoxyuridylate. The latter compound inhibits thymidylate synthase, an important enzyme in DNA synthesis. Host cells lack cytosine deaminase activity and are less affected. Only fungi that have both a permease to facilitate flucytosine penetration and cytosine deaminase are sensitive to flucytosine. It is taken orally at 50–150 mg/kg daily, divided into four doses (one every 6 hours). While the drug is well absorbed and penetrates the blood–ocular barrier well, the majority of *Aspergillus* and half of *Candida* isolates are resistant. Flucytosine is used primarily as an adjunct to systemic amphotericin B therapy.

Abrams SM, Degnan TJ, Vinciguerra V. Marrow aplasia following topical application, of chloramphenicol eye ointment. *Arch Intern Med.* 1980;140:576–577.

Leibowitz HM. Antibacterial effectiveness of ciprofloxacin 0.3% ophthalmic solution in the treatment of bacterial conjunctivitis. *Am J Ophthalmol.* 1991;112:29S–33S.

Leibowitz HM. Clinical evaluation of ciprofloxacin 0.3% ophthalmic solution for treatment of bacterial keratitis. *Am J Ophthalmol.* 1991;112:34S–47S.

Mandell GL, Sande MA. Antimicrobial agents: Sulfonamides, trimethoprim-sulfamethoxazole, and urinary tract antiseptics and Mandell GL, Sande MA. Antimicrobial agents: The aminoglycosides. In: Gilman AG, Goodman LS, Gilman A, et al, eds. *The Pharmacological Basis of Therapeutics.* 6th ed. New York: Macmillan; 1980:1106–1125, 1162–1180.

Antiviral Agents (Table XXI-15)

Topical Antiviral Agents

Three agents that compete with natural nucleotides for incorporation into viral and mammalian DNA are available for treatment of herpes simplex keratitis. *Idoxuridine* (5-iodo-2'-deoxyuridine) and *trifluridine* (Viroptic) are structural analogues of thymidine, and *vidarabine* (adenine arabinoside, ara-A) is an analogue of adenine.

Trifluridine (1% drops, every 2–4 hours) has the advantage of being more soluble than the other agents. As a result, it can be used in drop form and can penetrate diseased corneas to treat herpetic iritis. It also has a greater efficacy (95% versus 75% of cases healed in 2 weeks) than idoxuridine (0.5% ointment, every 4 hours) and equivalent or greater efficacy than vidarabine (3% ointment, every 3 hours). Cross-resistance does not seem to occur among the three agents.

Synthetic oligonucleotide analogues complementary to specific mRNAs of herpes simplex virus are emerging as promising agents in the treatment of herpes simplex keratitis.

TABLE XXI-15

ANTIVIRAL AGENTS

GENERIC NAME	TRADE NAME	TOPICAL CONCENTRATION/ OPHTHALMIC SOLUTION (%)	SYSTEMIC DOSAGE
Idoxuridine	Herplex	0.1%	
Trifluridine	Viroptic	1.0%	
Vidarabine monohydrate	Vira-A	3.0%	
Acyclovir sodium	Zovirax		Oral: Herpes simplex keratitis 200 mg 5 times daily for 7–10 days Oral: Herpes zoster ophthalmicus 600–800 mg 5 times daily for 10 days IV if patient is immunocompromised
Famciclovir	Famvir		Oral: Herpes simplex keratitis 500 mg tid for 7 days
Foscarnet sodium	Foscavir		IV: by controlled infusion only, either by central vein or by peripheral vein induction: 60 mg/kg (adjusted for renal function) given over 1 h every 8 h for 14–21 days Maintenance: 90–120 mg/kg given over 2 h once daily
Ganciclovir sodium	Cytovene		IV induction: 5 mg/kg every 12 h for 14–21 days Maintenance: 5 mg/kg daily for 7 days

Because of potential side and toxic effects with systemic dosage, the possible dosage adjustments and warnings should be followed properly.

Systemic Antiviral Agents

Acyclovir is a synthetic guanosine analogue that requires phosphorylation to become active. It undergoes monophosphorylation by viral thymidine kinase. Because the viral thymidine kinase in herpes simplex types 1 and 2 has many times more affinity to acyclovir than does host thymidine kinase, high concentrations of acyclovir monophosphate accumulate in infected cells. Acyclovir monophosphate is then further phosphorylated to the active compound acyclovir triphosphate. The triphosphate cannot cross cell membranes and accumulates further. This increased concentration of acyclovir triphosphate is 50–100 times greater in infected cells than in uninfected cells.

Acyclovir triphosphate inhibits virus growth in three ways:

☐ It can function as a competitive inhibitor of DNA polymerases, with viral DNA polymerases being significantly more susceptible to acyclovir triphosphate than human DNA polymerases

☐ It can be a DNA chain terminator

☐ It can produce irreversible binding between viral DNA polymerase and the interrupted chain, causing permanent inactivation

The result is a several hundred–fold inhibition of herpes simplex virus growth with minimal toxicity to uninfected cells.

Acyclovir-resistant thymidine kinase herpes simplex viruses have evolved. They occur primarily in patients receiving multiple courses of therapy or in patients with AIDS. Thymidine kinase mutants are susceptible to vidarabine and foscarnet. Changes in viral DNA polymerase structures can also mediate resistance to acyclovir.

Acyclovir can be used topically, orally, or intravenously. Usual oral dosage is 600 mg 5 times a day. Oral acyclovir is only 15%–30% bioavailable, and food does not affect absorption. For unknown reasons, bioavailability is lower in patients with transplants. Acyclovir is minimally protein bound (10%–30%), and drug interactions through binding displacement have not been reported. The drug is well distributed, with CSF and brain concentrations equaling approximately 50% of serum values. Concentrations of acyclovir in zoster vesicle fluid are equivalent to those in plasma. Aqueous humor concentrations are 35% and salivary concentrations 15% that of plasma. Vaginal concentrations are equivalent to those of plasma, and breast milk concentrations exceed them.

The percutaneous absorption of topical acyclovir is low and occurs primarily when large areas are treated. Plasma concentrations of 0.3 µg/ml were noted in patients treated topically with this drug for herpes zoster. Peak serum concentrations after oral ingestion of acyclovir average 0.6 mg/ml and occur 90 minutes after dosing, but peak serum concentrations after intravenous administration reach approximately 10 mg/ml.

The plasma half-life for normal adults and neonates is 3.3 and 3.8 hours, respectively. It increases to 20 hours in anuric patients. In the urine 60%–90% of acyclovir is excreted unchanged through both glomerular filtration and tubular secretion. As a result, acyclovir may interfere with the renal excretion of drugs such as methotrexate that are eliminated through the renal tubules; probenecid significantly decreases the renal excretion of acyclovir. A major metabolite of acyclovir, 9-carboxymethoxymethylguanine, accounts for 10%–20% of the total administered dose and is also excreted in urine. Acyclovir is effectively removed by hemodialysis (60%) but only minimally by peritoneal dialysis. Commonly used intravenous dosage for acyclovir is 1500 mg/m^2/day.

Famciclovir is currently indicated for the management of uncomplicated acute herpes zoster. It has demonstrated efficacy in relieving acute zoster signs and symptoms and reducing the duration of postherpetic neuralgia when administered during acute zoster. The recommended dosage for the management of acute herpes zoster is 500 mg three times a day for 7 days. The efficacy of famciclovir in herpes zoster ophthalmicus as well as herpes simplex keratitis is currently being evaluated in an ongoing multicenter multinational study.

Ganciclovir (9-2-hydroxypropoxymethylguanine) is a synthetic guanosine analogue active against many herpes viruses. As with acyclovir, it must be phosphorylated to become active. Infection-induced kinases, viral thymidine kinase, or deoxyguanosine kinase of various herpes viruses can catalyze this reaction. After monophosphorylation, cellular enzymes convert ganciclovir to the triphosphorylated form, and the triphosphate inhibits viral DNA polymerase rather than cellular DNA polymerase. Ganciclovir triphosphate competitively inhibits the incorporation of guanosine triphosphate into DNA. Because of its toxicity and the availability of acyclovir for treatment of many herpes virus infections, its use is currently restricted to treatment of cytomegalovirus (CMV) retinitis.

Ganciclovir is used only IV, since less than 5% of an oral dose is absorbed. Intravenous induction dose is 5mg/kg every 12 hours for 14–21 days. Once the infection is under control, daily dose of 6 mg/kg is required for maintainance of the virus-free state. CSF concentrations are approximately 50% of plasma with peak plasma concentrations reaching 4–6 sLg/ml. The plasma half-life is 3–4 hours in persons with normal renal function, increasing to over 24 hours in patients with severe renal insufficiency. Over 90% of systemic ganciclovir is eliminated unchanged in urine, and dose modifications are necessary for persons with compromised renal function. Ganciclovir is approximately 50% removed by hemodialysis. It can be administered intravitreally with a half-life of 50 hours.

Foscarnet (phosphonoformic acid) inhibits DNA polymerases, RNA polymerases, and reverse transcriptases. In vitro it is active against herpes viruses, influenza virus, and HIV. Foscarnet is used primarily in the treatment of AIDS patients with CMV retinitis, and it acts by blocking the pyrophosphate receptor site of CMV DNA polymerase. Viral resistance is attributable to structural alterations in this enzyme. Foscarnet inhibits herpes viruses and cytomegaloviruses that are resistant to acyclovir and ganciclovir. It is administered IV in doses of 20 mg/kg as bolus followed by 0.16 mg/kg/min infusion for maintainance.

Foscarnet bioavailability is approximately 20%. Because it can bind with calcium and other divalent cations, foscarnet becomes deposited in bone and may be detectable for many months. Distribution follows a three-compartment model and produces peak serum concentrations of approximately 30 pg/ml. It is eliminated by both glomerular filtration and tubular secretion with 80%–90% of the administered dose appearing unchanged in the urine. Dosage adjustment is required in persons with impaired renal function.

Ribavirin is a synthetic purine nucleoside analogue active in vitro against many viruses, including some that cause viral pneumonia, Lassa fever, and influenza. Ribavirin appears to undergo phosphorylation in host cells by host adenosine kinase. The 5′-monophosphate subsequently inhibits cellular inosine monophosphate formation, resulting in depletion of intracellular guanosine triphosphate. In some viruses ribavirin triphosphate suppresses guanosine triphosphate–dependent capping of messenger RNA, thereby inhibiting viral protein synthesis. It also acts by suppressing viral mRNA initiation or elongation. Exogenous guanosine can reverse the antiviral effects of ribavirin in some viruses. Resistance to ribavirin has not been found.

Ribavirin's bioavailability is about 45%, and peak concentrations after IV administration are 10-fold greater than those after oral administration. It accumulates with prolonged oral use. After drug distribution the half-life is 2 hours with a subsequent delayed half-life of 36 hours. Ribavirin is administered by aerosol in the treatment of severe respiratory syncytial virus infections. Some ribavirin is absorbed during aerosol treatments, and after 20 hours of aerosol therapy, plasma concentrations in treated infants range from 0.8 to 3.3 pg/ml. Ribavirin concentrations in respiratory secretions are approximately a thousandfold greater.

Zidovudine (azidodeoxythymidine [AZT]) is a thymidine nucleoside analogue with activity against HIV. Zidovudine becomes phosphorylated to monophosphate, diphosphate, and triphosphate forms by cellular kinases in infected and uninfected cells. It has two primary methods of action:

□ The triphosphate acts as a competitive inhibitor of viral reverse transcriptase

□ The azido group prevents further chain elongation and acts as a DNA chain terminator

Zidovudine inhibits HIV reverse transcriptase at much lower concentrations than those needed to inhibit cellular DNA polymerases. Zidovudine is currently indicated as treatment for some stages of HIV infection.

Zidovudine is administered orally in doses of 1500 mg/day and is about 60% bioavailable with 40% metabolized by first pass. Peak concentrations occur within 30–90 minutes to give steady-state peak concentrations of 0.05–1.5 fg/ml. Zidovudine is about 40% protein bound. CSF concentrations vary widely and range from 25% to 100% of serum values. Zidovudine enters the brain, phagocytic cells, liver, muscle, and placenta. Plasma half-life is about 1 hour. IV dosage used is 1–2 mg/kg 4 times a day.

Didanosine (dideoxyinosine) is an adenosine derivative with activity against HIV. The exact mechanism of action is unclear; however, after administration it must be aminated to dideoxyadenosine and phosphorylated to the triphosphate derivative ddATP. The ddATP subsequently inhibits the reverse transcriptase of HIV and can function as a DNA chain terminator. Since didanosine has little affinity for human DNA polymerase, cellular DNA synthesis is not significantly affected. Didanosine is active against most zidovudine-resistant HIV strains. HIV resistance to didanosine also occurs, associated with changes in reverse transcriptase.

Zalcitabine (dideoxycytidine) is an analogue of deoxycytidine. Zalcitabine becomes triphosphorylated by cellular kinases and serves as a competitive inhibitor of HIV reverse transcriptase and as a DNA chain terminator. Resistance to zalcitabine by HIV has been reported through changes in reverse transcriptase. In combination with zidovudine, zalcitabine has shown additive or synergistic effects against HIV. It can inhibit zidovudine-resistant HIV isolates.

Cidofovir (HPMPC) is another effective antiviral drug that was shown to inhibit CMV replication when administered intravitreally in a small series of patients. Dosage administered was 20 µg/0.1 ml. Long-lasting suppression of CMV retinitis was noted with average time to progression in 55 days. Ocular side effects included mild uveitis and a small drop in IOP.

Fluorouracil is a fluorinated pyrimidine nucleoside analogue that blocks production of thymidylate and interrupts normal cellular DNA and RNA synthesis. Its primary action may be to cause cellular thymine deficiency and resultant cell death. The effect of fluorouracil is most pronounced on rapidly growing cells, and its use as an antiviral agent is primarily related to destruction of infected cells (warts) by topical application.

Medications for Acanthamoeba *Infections*

Acanthamoeba is a ubiquitous, free-living amoeba that inhabits soil, water, and air. Its appearance as a corneal pathogen is no longer infrequent as a result of a number of factors, including the increased use of contact lenses. The species responsible for corneal infections, which include *A polyphaga, A castellanii, A hatchetti,* and *A culbertsoni,* exist as both trophozoites and double-walled cysts. Because of the variations among species of *Acanthamoeba,* no single drug is effective in treating all *Acanthamoeba* keratitis. Medications that appear most useful include neomycin, neomycin–polymyxin B–gramicidin mixtures, natamycin 5% topical suspension, imidazoles such as miconazole 1% topical solution, propamidine isothionate 0.1% drops (Brolene), and topical dibromopropamidine 0.15% ointment (the last two agents are not yet available in the United States).

Kaufman HE, Centifanto-Fitzgerald YM, Varnell ED. Herpes simplex keratitis. *Ophthalmology.* 1983;90:700–706.

Metcalf JF, Cosper CS, Rich LS. A synthetic antisense oligonucleotide analogue prevents herpetic stromal keratitis in CF-1 mice. *Invest Ophthalmol Vis Sci.* 1991;32:806.

Moore MB. Management of *Acanthamoeba* keratitis. In: Cavanagh HD, ed. *The Cornea: Transactions of the World Congress on the Cornea, III.* New York: Raven Press; 1988:517–521.

Local Anesthetics

Local anesthetic agents are used extensively in ophthalmology. Topical preparations yield corneal and conjunctival anesthesia for comfortable performance of examination techniques such as tonometry, gonioscopy, removal of superficial foreign bodies, corneal scraping for bacteriologic studies, and paracentesis and for use of contact lenses associated with fundus examination and laser procedures. Local retrobulbar and eyelid blocks yield excellent anesthesia and akinesia for intraocular and orbital surgery (Tables XXI-16, XXI-17).

The local anesthetic agents used in ophthalmology are tertiary amines linked by either *ester* or *amide* bonds to an aromatic residue. Because the protonated form is far more soluble and these compounds undergo hydrolysis more slowly in acidic solutions, they are supplied in the form of their hydrochloride salts. When exposed to tissue fluids at pH 7.4, about 5%–20% of the anesthetic agent molecules will be in the unprotonated form, as determined by the pKa (8.0–9.0) of the individual agent. The more lipid-soluble unprotonated form penetrates the lipid-rich myelin sheath and cell membrane of axons. Once inside, most of the molecules are again protonated. The protonated form gains access to and blocks the sodium channels on the inner wall of the cell membrane and increases the threshold for electrical excitability. As increasing numbers of sodium channels are blocked, nerve conduction is impeded and finally blocked.

After administration of a local anesthetic, nerve fibers that are small or unmyelinated are blocked most quickly because their higher discharge rates open sodium channel gates more frequently and also because conduction can be prevented by the disruption of a shorter length of axon. The action potential in unmyelinated fibers spreads continuously along the axon, while in myelinated fibers it spreads by saltation. Therefore, only a short length of an unmyelinated fiber need be functionally interrupted, while one or more nodes must be blocked in a myelinated fiber. In larger myelinated fibers the nodes are farther apart.

Table XXI-16

Regional Anesthetics

GENERIC	CONCENTRATION (%) MAXIMUM DOSE	ONSET OF ACTION	DURATION OF ACTION	MAJOR ADVANTAGES/ DISADVANTAGES
Procaine*	1%–4%/500 mg	7–8 min	30–45 min 60 min (with epinephrine)	Short duration; poor absorption from mucous membranes
Tetracaine*	0.25%	5–9 min	120–140 min (with epinephrine)	
Hexylcaine*	1%–2%	5–10 min	60 min	
Bupivacaine[†]	0.25%–0.75%	5–11 min	480–720 min (with epinephrine)	Long duration of action
Lidocaine[†]	1%–2%/500 mg	4–6 min	40–60 min 120 min (with epinephrine)	Spreads readily without hyaluronidase
Mepivacaine[†]	1%–2%/500 mg	3–5 min	120 min	Duration of action greater without epinephrine
Prilocaine[†]	1%–2%/600 mg	3–4 min	90–120 min (with epinephrine)	As effective as lidocaine
Etidocaine[†]	1%	3 min	300–600 min	

*Ester type compound
[†]Amide type compound

Table XXI-17

Topical Anesthetic Agents

GENERIC	TRADE NAME	CONCENTRATION (%)
Cocaine hydrochloride		1%–4%
Proparacaine hydrochloride	AK-Tain Alcain Ophthaine Ophthetic	0.5% 0.5% 0.5% 0.5%
Tetracaine hydrochloride	AK-T-Caine Pontocaine hydrochloride	0.5% 0.5%

Clinically, local anesthetics first block the poorly myelinated and narrow parasympathetic fibers (as evidenced by pupil dilation) and sympathetic fibers (vasodilation), followed by sensory fibers (pain and temperature), and finally the larger and more myelinated motor fibers (akinesia). The optic nerve, enclosed in a meningeal lining, is often not blocked by retrobulbar injections.

Amide local anesthetics are preferred to ester agents for retrobulbar blocks because the amides have a longer duration of action and less systemic toxicity. However, this duration of action is limited by diffusion from the site of injection because amide agents are not metabolized locally but are metabolized and inactivated in the liver, primarily by dealkylation.

Ester agents are susceptible to hydrolysis by serum cholinesterases in ocular vessels as well as by metabolism in the liver. Toxicity of ester anesthetics may occur at lower doses when serum cholinesterase levels are low as a result of echothiophate eyedrop treatment or a hereditary serum cholinesterase deficiency.

The toxic manifestations of local anesthetics are generally related to dose. However, patients with severe hepatic insufficiency may have symptoms of toxicity with either amide or ester local anesthetics even at lower doses. These manifestations include restlessness and tremor that may proceed to convulsions, and respiratory and myocardial depression. CNS stimulation can be counteracted by IV diazepam, while respiratory depression calls for ventilatory support.

Because local anesthetics block sympathetic vascular tone and dilate vessels, a 1:200,000 concentration of epinephrine is frequently added to shorter-acting agents to retard vascular absorption. Such use of epinephrine raises circulating catecholamine levels and may result in systemic hypertension and cardiac arrhythmias.

Topically applied anesthetics disrupt intercellular tight junctions, resulting in increased corneal epithelial permeability to subsequently administered agents (i.e., dilating drops). They also interfere with corneal epithelial metabolism and repair and thus cannot be used on a chronic basis for pain relief.

Lidocaine (Xylocaine) is an amide local anesthetic used in strengths of 1%–4% (with or without epinephrine) for injection and 2%–4% for topical mucosal anesthesia. It yields a rapid (5 minute) retrobulbar or eyelid block that lasts 1–2 hours. The topical solution, applied to the conjunctiva with a cotton swab for 1–2 minutes, reduces the discomfort of subconjunctival injections. Topical lidocaine is preferable to cocaine or proparacaine as anesthesia for conjunctival biopsy because it has less effect upon epithelial morphology. Lidocaine is also extremely useful for suppressing cough during ocular surgery. The maximum safe dose of the 2% solution for local injection is 15 ml in adults. A common side effect is drowsiness.

Mepivacaine (Carbocaine) is an amide agent used in strengths of 1%–3% (with or without a vasoconstrictor). It has a rapid onset and lasts about 2–3 hours. The maximum safe dose is 25 ml of a 2% solution.

Bupivacaine (Marcaine) is an amide agent that has a slower onset of action than lidocaine. It may yield a relatively poor akinesia but has the advantage of long duration of action, up to 8 hours. It is available in 0.25%–0.75% solutions (with or without epinephrine) and is frequently administered in a mixture with lidocaine or mepivacaine to achieve a rapid, complete, and long-lasting effect. The maximum safe dose is 25 ml of a 0.75% solution.

Etidocaine (Duranest) is a rapid-onset (5 minutes), long-acting (over 5 hours) derivative of lidocaine, used in 0.5%–1.5% solutions (with or without epinephrine). It usually blocks motor fibers before sensory fibers. The maximum safe dose is 30 ml of a 1% solution.

The following agents are commonly used for topical anesthesia. They have higher lipid solubilities and therefore more rapid onset than other agents. Thus, the period of initial discomfort caused by the drops is shortened.

Proparacaine (e.g., Ophthaine, Ophthetic) is an ester topical anesthetic available as a 0.5% solution. It is the least irritating topical anesthetic, has a rapid onset of about 15 seconds, and lasts about 20 minutes. It has been reported that proparacaine used without a preservative does not inhibit the growth of *Staphylococcus,*

Candida, or *Pseudomonas* and thus might be preferred to other agents for corneal anesthesia prior to obtaining a scraping for culture from a corneal ulcer. Its structure is sufficiently different from the other local anesthetics that cross-sensitization apparently does not occur.

Benoxinate is an ester topical anesthetic available in a 0.4% solution with fluorescein (Fluress) for use in tonometry. It has an onset and duration similar to proparacaine.

Tetracaine is an ester topical anesthetic available in 0.5% solution. It has a longer onset of action and duration of action than proparacaine and causes more extensive corneal epithelial toxicity.

Crandall DC. Pharmacology of ocular anesthetics. In: Duane JD, Jaeger EA, eds. *Biomedical Foundations of Ophthalmology.* Philadelphia: Harper & Row; 1983; vol 3; chap 25:1–22.

Ritchie JM, Greene NM. Local anesthetics. In: Gilman AG, Goodman LS, Gilman A, et al, eds. *The Pharmacological Basis of Therapeutics.* 6th ed. New York: Macmillan; 1980:300–302.

Purified Neurotoxin Complex

Botulinum toxin type A (Botox, formerly called Oculinum) is produced from cultures of the Hall strain of *Clostridium botulinum.* It blocks neuromuscular conduction by binding to receptor sites on motor nerve terminals, entering the nerve terminals, and inhibiting the release of acetylcholine. Botulinum toxin type A injections provide effective relief of the excessive, abnormal contractions associated with blepharospasm. Typically, 5 units are placed subcutaneously at each of the two sites over the brow, on the upper eyelid, and on the lower eyelid of one side, for a total of six injections per side. Botulinum can also be used to treat strabismus, possibly by inducing an atrophic lengthening of the injected muscle and a corresponding shortening of the muscle's antagonist.

Jordan DR, Anderson RL. Essential blepharospasm. In: *Focal Points: Clinical Modules for Ophthalmologists.* San Francisco: American Academy of Ophthalmology; 1988:6.

Scott AB. Botulinum toxin treatment of strabismus. In: *Focal Points: Clinical Modules for Ophthalmologists.* San Francisco: American Academy of Ophthalmology; 1989:12.

Medications for the Dry Eye

Artificial tear preparations (demulcents) and emollients form an occlusive film over the corneal surface to lubricate and protect the eye from drying. The active ingredients in demulcent preparations are polyvinyl alcohol, cellulose, and methylcellulose and their derivatives: hydroxypropyl cellulose, hydroxyethylcellulose, hydroxypropyl methylcellulose, and carboxymethylcellulose. Multidose preparations contain preservatives, including benzalkonium chloride, chlorobutanol, thimerosal, and sorbic acid. However, the new generation of ophthalmic preservatives is virtually nontoxic. Unit-dose preparations are unpreserved drops that eliminate the cytotoxic effects of preservatives.

Ocular emollients are ointments prepared with sterile petrolatum, liquid lanolin, mineral oil, methylparaben, and polyparaben. Future development of medications for dry eye should be aimed at providing nourishment for the keratoconjunctival surface as well as revitalizing the tear-secreting system. (See also BCSC Section 8, *External Disease and Cornea.*)

Ocular Decongestants

Common agents such as naphazoline, tetrahydrozoline, and phenylephrine hydrochloride are used as topical drops to cause temporary vasoconstriction of conjunctival vessels. Side effects include rebound vasodilation and conjunctival hyperemia.

Irrigating Solutions

Sterile isotonic solutions are for general ophthalmic use, and sterile, physiologically balanced salt solutions that are isotonic to eye tissues are used for intraocular irrigation during surgical procedures. Irrigating solutions contain sodium chloride, potassium chloride, calcium chloride, magnesium chloride, sodium acetate, dextrose, glutathione disulfidehydrochloric acid, and sodium hydroxide. Intraocular irrigating solutions contain no preservatives.

Diagnostic Agents

Fluorescein 2%, lissamine green 1%, and rose bengal 1% are some of the most commonly used solutions in the examination and diagnosis of external ocular diseases. The first two stains outline the defects of the conjunctival and corneal epithelium, while the rose bengal indicates abnormal devitalized epithelial cells. For the study of retinal and choroidal circulation as well as abnormal changes of retinal pigment epithelium, sodium fluorescein solution in concentrations of 5%, 10%, or 25% is injected intravenously. Fundus fluorescein angiography is helpful in diagnosing various vascular diseases and neoplastic disorders.

Viscoelastic Agents

Viscoelastic agents possess certain chemical and physical properties that include the capacity to resist flow and deformation. Viscoelastics for ophthalmic use must also be inert, isosmotic, sterile, nonpyrogenic, nonantigenic, and optically clear. In addition, they must be sufficiently hydrophilic to allow easy dilution and irrigation from the eye. Naturally occurring and synthetic compounds include *sodium hyaluronate, chondroitin sulfate, hydroxypropyl methylcellulose,* and *polyacrylamide.* Combined chondroitin sulfate/sodium hyaluronate materials are also available. Viscoelastic agents protect ocular tissues such as the corneal endothelium and epithelium, help to maintain intraocular space, and facilitate tissue manipulation; thus, they are indispensable tools in cataract or glaucoma surgery, penetrating keratoplasty, anterior segment reconstruction surgery, and retinal surgery. (See also page 343 in this book and BCSC Section 11, *Lens and Cataract.*)

Fibrinolytic Agents

Tissue plasminogen activator (tPA), *urokinase,* and *streptokinase* are all fibrinolytic agents. tPA is a naturally occurring serine protease with a molecular mass of 68 kD. Because tPA is normally present at a higher concentration in the aqueous humor of the human eye than it is in blood, it is less toxic to ocular tissues and is specific for dissolution of fibrin clots. tPA has been used successfully in the resolution of fibrin clots after vitrectomy, keratoplasty, and glaucoma filtering procedures. These drugs are not approved by the FDA for ocular use.

Thrombin

Thrombin, a sterile protein substance, is a useful adjunct for maintaining hemostasis during complicated intraocular surgery. Intravitreal thrombin may be used to control intraocular hemorrhage during vitrectomy. The addition of thrombin (100 units/ml) to the vitrectomy infusate significantly shortens intraocular bleeding time. Thrombin produced by DNA recombinant techniques minimizes the degree of postoperative inflammation. Thrombin causes significant ultrastructural corneal endothelial changes when human corneas are perfused with 1000 units/ml.

Antifibrinolytic Agents

Antifibrinolytic agents, such as *ε-aminocaproic acid* and *tranexamic acid,* inhibit the activation of plasminogen. The action of plasminogen activators and plasmin is inhibited. These agents may be used systemically to treat cases of hemorrhage secondary to excessive fibrinolysis and to prevent recurrent hyphema. They are contraindicated in the presence of active intravascular clotting. Recurrent hyphema most commonly occurs 2–6 days after the original hemorrhage.

ε-aminocaproic acid is used in a dosage of 50–100 mg/kg every 4 hours up to 30 g daily. Adverse reactions include nausea, vomiting, muscle cramps, conjunctival suffusion, nasal stuffiness, headache, rash, pruritus, dyspnea, tonic toxic confusional states, cardiac arrhythmias, and systemic hypotension. Gastrointestinal side effects are similar with either 50 or 100 mg/kg dosing. The drug should be continued for a full 5–6 days to achieve maximal clinical effectiveness. Topical ε-aminocaproic acid may be an attractive alternative to systemic delivery in the treatment of traumatic hyphema. Optimal topical concentration to maximize aqueous levels and minimize corneal epithelial toxicity is 30% ε-aminocaproic acid in 2% carboxypolymethylene.

Tranexamic acid is another antifibrinolytic agent that reduces the incidence of rebleeding after traumatic hyphema. It is 10 times more potent in vitro than ε-aminocaproic acid. Usual dosage is 25 mg of tranexamic acid/kg 3 times daily for 3–5 days. Gastrointestinal side effects are rare.

Corneal Storage Medium

Corneal storage medium helps to prolong the viability of donor corneas to be used for transplantation. The main components of the various kinds of media include a bicarbonate-buffered minimum essential medium (MEM) or a hybrid medium of MEM/TC 199, chondroitin sulfate, and dextran (to retard proteoglycan loss during storage and reduce intraoperative and postoperative rebound swelling), as well as gentamicin sulfate or other antibiotics as prophylactic agents. Corneal tissue storage can be prolonged with the addition of recombinant growth factors such as epidermal growth factor, antioxidants, insulin, adenosine triphosphate precursors, anticollagenases, and antiproteases.

Drugs on the Horizon

Interferon

A naturally occurring species-specific defense against viruses, interferon is synthesized intracellularly and increases resistance to virus infection. Synthetic analogues such as polyinosinic acid–polycytidylic acid have been used to induce patients to form their own interferon.

Topically administered interferon has been found to be ineffective in the treatment of epidemic keratoconjunctivitis caused by adenovirus. Interferon used in conjunction with acyclovir showed significantly quicker healing time in herpes simplex keratitis patients than treatment with acyclovir alone (5.8 versus 9.0 days). Interferon has also been found to speed healing of an epithelial defect when used in combination with trifluridine. The dosage of interferon used with 30 million IU/ml was 2 drops per day for the first 3 days of treatment. Interferon alone has little effect on the treatment of herpes simplex keratitis. In combination, it seems to act as a topical adjuvant to traditional antiviral therapy in resistant herpes simplex keratitis.

Interferon has also been shown to inhibit vascular endothelial cell proliferation and differentiation. It is particularly effective in the treatment of juvenile pulmonary hemangiomatosis, which used to be a fatal condition before the invention of interferon. Intralesional administration of interferon has been reported to be especially effective in ocular kaposi sarcoma. Currently, a multicenter clinical trial is under way to test interferon's efficacy in treatment of choroidal neovascular membranes secondary to exudative macular degeneration. A multicenter clinical trial is also under way to evaluate the role of recombinant interferon-β-1a in the prevention of multiple sclerosis.

Growth Factors

Growth factors are a diverse group of proteins that act at autocrine and paracrine levels to affect various cellular processes including

- Metabolic regulation
- Tissue differentiation
- Cell growth and proliferation
- Maintenance of viability
- Changes in cell morphology

They are synthesized in a variety of cells and have a spectrum of target cells and tissues. The presence of various growth factors in retina, vitreous humor, aqueous humor, and corneal tissues has been demonstrated. These include

- Epidermal growth factor
- Fibroblast growth factors
- Transforming growth factors
- Vascular endothelial growth factor
- Insulin-like growth factors

These growth factors are capable of diverse, synergistic, and sometimes antagonistic biological activities.

Under normal physiological conditions, the complex and delicate coordination of the effects of and the interactions among growth factors maintains the homeostasis of intraocular tissues. The net effect of a growth factor depends on its bioavailability, which is determined by its concentration, its binding to carrier proteins, the level of its receptor in the target tissue, and the presence of other complementary or antagonistic regulatory factors.

Pathologically, the breakdown of blood–ocular barriers disrupts the balance among growth factors in the ocular media and tissues and may result in various abnormalities. The disruption in the balance among transforming growth factor–βs, basic fibroblast growth factor, vascular endothelial growth factor, and insulin-like growth factors is suspected to cause ocular neovascularization. Transforming growth factor–βs and platelet-derived growth factor are implicated in the pathogenesis of proliferative vitreoretinopathy and excessive proliferation of Tenon's capsule fibroblasts that can result in the scarring of the glaucoma filtration bleb. Increased concentrations of insulin-like growth factors in plasmoid aqueous humor may be responsible for the abnormal hyperplastic response of the lens epithelium and corneal endothelium seen in inflammatory conditions and in traumatic insults to the eye.

Identifying growth factors and understanding their mechanisms of action in the eye offers great potential for providing the ophthalmologist with new methods for manipulation of and intervention in ocular disorders. Epidermal growth factor and fibroblast growth factor can accelerate corneal wound repair after surgery, chemical burns, or ulcers and can increase the number of corneal endothelial cells. Fibroblast growth factor has also been shown to delay the process of retinal dystrophy in Royal College of Surgeons rats.

Vascular endothelial growth factor (VEGF), also known as *vasculotropin*, deserves special mention. It is a dimeric, heparin-binding polypeptide mitogen and has four isoforms that are generated from alternative splicing of mRNA. VEGF gene is widely expressed in actively proliferating vascular tissue and is implicated in the pathogenesis of various neovascular retinopathies such as diabetes and age-related choroidal neovascularization. Currently, the role of monoclonal antibodies specifically targeted against VEGF as a therapeutic modality in angiogenic eye disease is being evaluated, and this approach holds great promise.

The development of a "cocktail" of growth factors and the use of growth factor antagonists will provide an effective therapeutic modality for the treatment of various ocular disorders. With the advance of genetic engineering and innovations in drug delivery systems, growth factors will probably make up the next generation of ophthalmic pharmaceuticals for the physiologic regulation of tissue maintenance, restoration, and repair.

Calcium Channel Blockers

Calcium channel blockers like *verapamil* have several ocular effects that may be beneficial in glaucoma patients. These drugs generally lower IOP, in particular following topical administration. The mechanism of action appears to be a result of increased outflow facility. In addition, the use of calcium channel antagonists is associated with slowed rate of progression of low-tension glaucoma, possibly by increasing optic nerve blood flow, reducing vasospasm, or creating a neuroprotective effect. Blood pressure should be monitored in patients treated with these drugs because of their hypotensive effect. Systemic calcium channel blockers are probably the antihypertensive drug of choice in patients with hypertension and low-tension glaucoma. A 15% decrease in IOP was noted after topical application of calcium channel blocker in a recently concluded phase III trial. (See also BCSC Section 10, *Glaucoma*.)

Compounds for Lowering Intraocular Pressure

In addition to prostaglandin $F_{2\alpha}$ and its derivatives and topically active carbonic anhydrase inhibitor, the following compounds are also under further investigation for their ocular hypotensive effects. Topical application of selective alpha$_2$-adrenergic agonists *BHT-920, BHT-933, UK-14303,* and *para-aminoclonidine* reduces IOP in rabbits, monkeys, and normal volunteers. The mechanism by which these alpha$_2$-adrenergic agonists act appears to be by reducing formation of aqueous humor. Topical application of *vanadate* (a Na^+,K^+-ATPase inhibitor) 1% drops in normotensive and laser-induced glaucomatous monkey eyes reduces IOP by decreasing the rate of aqueous humor flow. However, clinical studies have failed to demonstrate a therapeutic effect in treating ocular hypertensive patients. *Forskolin,* a novel compound that stimulates the cyclic AMP secondary messenger system at the site of the catalytic subunit, has received conflicting reports regarding its IOP-lowering effects.

Bioadhesives

The use of bioadhesives is in an experimental stage. *Cyanoacrylates* are used to seal penetrating corneal wounds and leaking filtering blebs, with or without bandage contact lens, as well as to seal leaks during lamellar or penetrating keratoplasty so the globe remains firm enough for the surgical maneuver. BCSC Section 8, *External Disease and Cornea,* discusses these procedures in greater depth. Other adhesives such as *collagen* and *fibrin* are under investigation. The use of bioadhesives for the precise delivery of growth factors is also being explored.

Gene Therapy

Instead of delivering a drug to the circulation aimed to affect a specific condition, gene therapy involves the treatment of disease by the delivery of a human gene to a target organ. The subsequent production of a *gene product,* or protein, then acts as the "drug." The phases of gene delivery, expression, and action of the gene product are analogous to conventional drug therapy, and each gene therapy system has its own specific pharmacologic characteristics.

Gene therapy currently follows two basic approaches. The more obvious is *gene replacement therapy* to correct hereditary conditions in which defective production of an essential enzyme or protein is attributable to the gene. Here, the goal is to insert the normal gene into a cell so that a sufficient amount of product becomes available. The second approach, called *gene addition therapy,* attempts to treat acquired diseases. An example is the use of *cytokine gene transfer* into tumor cells to stimulate the immune response against these cells.

Genes that are transferred to cells must contain all components necessary to direct the production of RNA that will result in functional protein production. The transferred DNA must therefore contain promoter elements necessary for transcription and the entire protein coding region of the gene. Other elements to enhance RNA stability, such as a polyadenylation sequence, are often included. (See Part 3, Genetics, for illustrations and more detail.)

Several methods can be used to introduce DNA into mammalian cells. DNA can be introduced in vitro, into cells by microinjection, by coprecipitation with calcium phosphate, or by increasing cell permeability by electrical shock (electroporation). These techniques allow insertion of DNA into only a small number of cells and therefore have limited use for therapeutic application. Instead, more efficient vehicles have been developed for gene transfer that make possible in vivo gene delivery.

Vehicles for DNA delivery include a variety of plasmid- and virus-based vectors (Table XXI-18). Examples include recombinant plasmids; plasmid mixed with lipid micelles called *liposomes;* and genetically engineered, recombinant DNA or RNA viruses that can carry exogenous genes, infect mammalian cells, and transfer the functional genetic material to that cell. The most widely investigated vehicles for gene transfer are genetically engineered retrovirus vectors derived from the Moloney murine leukemia retrovirus. Additionally, gene-transfer vectors have been developed from adenovirus and herpes simplex virus. Virus-based vectors are engineered to maximize the safety of gene transfer by modification of the viral genome so that normal virus replication does not occur.

Regardless of the vector used, the introduction of foreign genes into cells begins with the identification and cloning of a gene. That gene then can be inserted into a plasmid or grown in bacteria. Then, alone or combined with one of the many vehicles for gene transfer it can be delivered to target cells. The vehicle carrying the DNA enters the cell by passing through the host cell membrane or by active transport through a specific receptor site. The DNA is then taken up into the nucleus where it can function.

If a retrovirus vector is used, DNA can be permanently, though randomly, integrated into the host cell genome. In most systems the host cell machinery supplies enzymes necessary for the transcription of the DNA into messenger RNA, which can then be translated by the host cell into protein. This protein can function intracellularly or extracellularly either to replace a hereditary deficient or defective protein or to provide an additional therapeutic function. It can be one of the following:

□ A protein that functions intracellularly, such as the enzyme adenosine deaminase used to correct the mutation in lymphocytes responsible for the severe combined immunodeficiency syndrome

□ A cell membrane protein, such as the chloride channel cystic fibrosis transmembrane conductance regulator that is mutant in cystic fibrosis

□ A secreted protein, such as the cytokine interleukin-2 used for anticancer therapy

TABLE XXI-18

GENE THERAPY VECTORS

PLASMID-BASED VECTORS	VIRUS-BASED VECTORS
Plasmid	Retrovirus
Plasmid with liposome	Adenovirus
Plasmid linked to ligand	Adeno-associated virus
	Herpes simplex virus

Two basic experimental approaches have been used for gene therapy. The first is to remove the target cells from the affected individual, add the normal gene to the cells in vitro, and return these modified cells to the donor. If a target cell expressing a mutation can be removed from an organ, modified in vitro, and then returned to that organ to function correctly, then the disease may be ameliorated. This strategy has been widely used in animal models for the transfer of new genes to bone marrow cells and was also used in the first approved human gene therapy protocol for the correction of adenosine deaminase deficiency. In these studies T lymphocytes, which are known to be the critical functional site of the deficient enzyme, were removed from the blood and infected in vitro with a retrovirus vector containing the normal adenosine deaminase gene. The genetically modified lymphocytes were reinfused, where they functioned normally and improved the clinical status of the treated individuals.

This strategy cannot be applied to all diseases because it is virtually impossible to remove and then replant a large number of cells from organs such as the heart, lung, or brain. Therefore, a second approach is needed: genes must be delivered to the target organ or organs in vivo in a highly efficient manner. This method, called *in vivo gene transfer,* has been successful in several experimental models, such as the transfer of the chloride channel transmembrane regulator gene to lung cells by aerosolization into the airway to treat cystic fibrosis, and the injection of a "healthy" dystrophin gene for the treatment of muscular dystrophy into skeletal muscle.

Although gene therapy is in its infancy, several clinical trials involving a variety of creative approaches for the treatment of hereditary and acquired diseases are under way. For example, gene therapy is being used for the treatment of hereditary hypercholesterolemia caused by low-density lipoprotein receptor deficiency: the normal gene for the low-density lipoprotein receptor is added into resected defective hepatocytes, which are then injected into the liver. In addition, cancer therapies that attempt to enhance the immune response to tumors are in progress. These therapies involve the use of a retrovirus for the transfer of genes for interleukin-2 and tumor necrosis factor to tumor cells, or the use of liposomes for the transfer of human leukocyte–associated antigens by direct injection into tumors. Using analysis identical to that employed in the assessment of other kinds of pharmacotherapy, a major research effort is under way to determine the utility of gene therapy for the treatment of many other diseases, including AIDS, leukemia, and hemophilia.

Fraunfelder FT. *Drug-Induced Ocular Side Effects and Drug Interactions.* 4th ed. Baltimore: Williams & Wilkins; 1996.

Lee PP, Yang JC. The nonapproved use of medications. *Ophthalmology.* 1991;99: 1071–1074.

Netland PA, Erickson KA. Calcium channel blockers in glaucoma management. *Ophthalmol Clin North Am.* 1995;8:327–334.

Podos SM, Camras CB, Serle JB. Experimental compounds to lower intraocular pressure. *Aust N Z J Ophthalmol.* 1989;17:129–135.

Samples JR. Benign essential blepharospasm. In: Fraunfelder FT, Roy FH, eds. *Current Ocular Therapy.* 4th ed. Philadelphia: Saunders; 1995.

Tripathi BJ, Kwait PS, Tripathi RC. Corneal growth factors: A new generation of ophthalmic pharmaceuticals. *Cornea.* 1990;9:2–9.

Tripathi RC, Borisuth NSC, Tripathi BJ. Growth factors in the aqueous humor and their therapeutic implications in glaucoma and anterior segment disorders of the human eye. *Drug Dev Res.* 1991;22:1–23.

Tripathi RC, Raja SC, Tripathi BJ. Prospects for epidermal growth factor in the management of corneal disorders. *Surv Ophthalmol.* 1990;34:457–462.

Tripathi RC, Tripathi BJ, Park JK, et al. Intracameral tissue plasminogen activator for resolution of fibrin clots after glaucoma filtering procedures. *Am J Ophthalmol.* 1991;111:247–248.

Tripathi RC, Tripathi BJ. The eye. In: Riddell RH, ed. *Pathology of Drug-Induced and Toxic Diseases.* New York: Churchill Livingstone; 1982:377–456.

US Food and Drug Administration. Adverse effects with isotretinoin. *FDA Drug Bulletin.* 1983:13(4).

CHAPTER XXII

Legal Aspects of Medical Therapy

The United States Food and Drug Administration (FDA) has statutory authority both to approve the marketing of prescription drugs and to specify the uses of these drugs. The FDA has created a three-step process regulating human testing of new drugs before they are approved for marketing. After animal and in vitro studies, *phase I* testing begins. This testing varies with the drug but generally involves 10–80 individuals and collects toxicology and pharmacokinetic data concerning dosage range, absorption, metabolism, and toxicity. *Phase II* testing involves randomized, controlled clinical trials on a minimum of 50–100 affected individuals to determine safety and effectiveness. A drug then enters *phase III* testing, which involves expanded controlled and uncontrolled trials, to evaluate the overall benefit-risk relationship and to provide an adequate basis for physician labeling. The data gathered from these tests are then submitted as part of a new drug application for marketing. The FDA's approval of each drug and its specific uses is based on documentation submitted by manufacturers that supports the safety and efficacy of specific drug applications.

Once approved for any use, a drug may be prescribed by individual physicians for any indication in all age groups without violating federal law. However, physicians remain liable to malpractice actions. In particular, a nonapproved use that does not adhere to an applicable standard of care places a practitioner in a difficult legal position. If a respectable minority of similarly situated physicians prescribe in the same manner, a standard of care could be met in most jurisdictions. In addition, informed consent in equivocal cases would be helpful.

The FDA has established clear guidelines on investigational drugs, and their use must meet specified commercial and investigative requirements.

BASIC TEXTS

Anatomy

Beard C, Quickert MH. *Anatomy of the Orbit: A Dissection Manual.* 3rd ed. Birmingham, AL: Aesculapius; 1988.

Duke-Elder S, ed. *System of Ophthalmology.* Vol II, *The Anatomy of the Visual System.* St Louis: Mosby; 1961.

Dutton JJ. *Atlas of Clinical and Surgical Orbital Anatomy.* Philadelphia: Saunders; 1994.

Fine BS, Yanoff M. *Ocular Histology: A Text and Atlas.* 2nd ed. Hagerstown, MD: Harper & Row; 1979.

Hogan MJ, Alvarado JA, Weddell JE. *Histology of the Human Eye.* Philadelphia: Saunders; 1971.

Mausolf FA. *The Anatomy of the Ocular Adnexa.* Springfield, IL: Thomas; 1975.

Miller NR, Newman NJ, eds. *Walsh and Hoyt's Clinical Neuro-Ophthalmology.* 5th ed. Baltimore: Williams & Wilkins; 1997.

Tasman W, Jaeger FA, eds. *Duane's Clinical Ophthalmology.* Philadelphia: Lippincott; 1994.

Zide BM, Jelks GW, eds. *Surgical Anatomy of the Orbit.* New York: Raven Press; 1985.

Embryology

Jakobiec FA, ed. *Ocular Anatomy, Embryology, and Teratology.* Philadelphia: Harper & Row; 1982.

Genetics

Emery AEH, Rimoin DL, Connor JM, et al, eds. *Principles and Practice of Medical Genetics.* 3rd ed. New York: Churchill Livingstone; 1996.

McKusick VA. *Mendelian Inheritance in Man: A Catalog of Human Genes and Genetic Disorders.* 11th ed. Baltimore: Johns Hopkins University Press; 1994.

Renie WA, ed. *Goldberg's Genetic and Metabolic Eye Disease.* 2nd ed. Boston: Little, Brown; 1986.

Thompson MW, McInnes RR, Willard HF. *Genetics in Medicine.* 5th ed. Philadelphia: Saunders; 1991.

Biochemistry and Metabolism

Anderson RE, Hollyfield JG, LaVail MM, eds. *Retinal Degenerations.* Boca Raton, FL: CRC Press; 1991.

Berman ER. *Biochemistry of the Eye.* New York: Plenum Press; 1991.

LaVail MM, Anderson RE, Hollyfield JG, eds. *Inherited and Environmentally Induced Retinal Degenerations.* New York: Liss; 1989.

Shichi H. *Biochemistry of Vision.* New York: Academic Press; 1983.

Sies H, ed. *Antioxidants in Disease Mechanisms and Therapy.* Orlando, FL: Academic Press; 1996.

Ocular Pharmacology

Gilman AG, Goodman LS, Gilman A, eds. *Goodman and Gilman's The Pharmacological Basis of Therapeutics.* 8th ed. New York: Pergamon Press; 1990.

Sears ML, ed. *Handbook of Experimental Pharmacology: Pharmacology of the Eye.* New York: Springer-Verlag; 1984.

RELATED ACADEMY MATERIALS

Focal Points: Clinical Modules for Ophthalmologists

Brazis PW, Lee AG. Neuro-ophthalmic problems caused by medications (Module 11, 1998).

Hodge WG, Hwang DG. Antibiotic use in corneal and external eye infections (Module 10, 1997).

Jampol LM. Nonsteroidal anti-inflammatory drugs: 1997 update (Module 6, 1997).

Mieler WF. Systemic therapeutic agents and retinal toxicity (Module 12, 1997).

Publications

Anderson RE, ed. *Biochemistry of the Eye* (Ophthalmology Manual, 1983).

Bradford CA, ed. *Basic Ophthalmology for Medical Students and Primary Care Residents* (1999).

Jordan DR, Anderson RA. *Surgical Anatomy of the Ocular Adnexa: A Clinical Approach* (Ophthalmology Monograph 9, 1996).

Mannis MJ, Smith ME. *Case Studies in Ophthalmology for Medical Students.* 2nd ed (1993).

Reeh MJ, Wobig JL, Wirtschafter JD. *Ophthalmic Anatomy* (Ophthalmology Manual, 1981).

Reinecke RD, Farrell TA. *Fundamentals of Ophthalmology: A Programmed Text* (1987).

Wilson FM II, ed. *Practical Ophthalmology: A Manual for Beginning Residents.* 4th ed (1996).

Slide-Script

Tang R. *Ocular Manifestations of Systemic Disease* (Eye Care Skills for the Primary Care Physician Series, 1996).

Continuing Ophthalmic Video Education

Keltner JL, Wand M, Van Newkirk MR. *Techniques for the Basic Ocular Examination* (1989).

Smelser G, Ozanics V. *Embryology of the Eye* (1977).

Ethics

AAO Ethics Committee. *The AAO Code of Ethics and You* (1987).

AAO Ethics Committee. *Clinical Trials and Investigative Procedures* (1992).

AAO Ethics Committee. *Code of Ethics* (reviewed annually).

AAO Ethics Committee. *The Ethical Ophthalmologist: A Primer* (1993).

AAO Ethics Committee. *Ethics in Ophthalmology: A Practical Guide* (reviewed annually).

> To order any of these materials, please call the Academy's Customer Service number at (415) 561-8540.

CREDIT REPORTING FORM

BASIC AND CLINICAL SCIENCE COURSE
Section 2

1999–2000

CME Accreditation

The American Academy of Ophthalmology is accredited by the Accreditation Council for Continuing Medical Education to sponsor continuing medical education for physicians.

The American Academy of Ophthalmology designates this educational activity for a maximum of 40 hours in category 1 credit toward the AMA Physician's Recognition Award. Each physician should claim only those hours of credit that he/she has actually spent in the educational activity.

If you wish to claim continuing medical education credit for your study of this section, you must complete and return the study question answer sheet on the back of this page, along with the following signed statement, to the Academy office. This form must be received within 3 years of the date of purchase.

I hereby certify that I have spent _____ (up to 40) hours of study on the curriculum of this section, and that I have completed the study questions. (The Academy, *upon request*, will send you a transcript of the credits listed on this form.)

☐ *Please send credit verification now.*

Signature _____
                                                                                    Date

Name: _____

Address: _____

City and State: _____ Zip: _____

Telephone: (_____) _____ *Academy Member ID# _____
                  area code

* Your ID number is located following your name on any Academy mailing label, in your Membership Directory, and on your Monthly Statement of Account.

Section Evaluation

Please indicate your response to the statements listed below by placing the appropriate number to the left of each statement.

1 = agree strongly
2 = agree
3 = no opinion
4 = disagree
5 = disagree strongly

_____ This section covers topics in enough depth and detail.

_____ This section's illustrations are of sufficient number and quality.

_____ The references included in the text provide an appropriate amount of additional reading.

_____ The study questions at the end of the book are useful.

In addition, please attach a separate sheet of paper to this form if you wish to elaborate on any of the statements above or to comment on other aspects of this book.

Please return completed form to: **American Academy of Ophthalmology**
P.O. Box 7424
San Francisco, CA 94120-7424
ATTN: Clinical Education Division

SECTION COMPLETION FORM

BASIC AND CLINICAL SCIENCE COURSE

ANSWER SHEET FOR SECTION 2

Question	Answer	Question	Answer
1	a b c d	22	a b c d e
2	a b c d	23	a b c d
3	a b c d	24	a b c d e
4	a b c d	25	a b c d e
5	a b c d	26	a b c d e
6	a b c d e	27	a b c d e
7	a b c d	28	a b c d e
8	a b c d	29	a b c d e
9	a b c d e	30	a b c d e
10	a b c d e	31	a b c d e
11	a b c d e	32	a b c d e
12	a b c d e	33	a b c d e
13	a b c d	34	a b c d e
14	a b c d	35	a b c d
15	a b c d e	36	a b c d e
16	a b c d	37	a b c d
17	a b c d e	38	a b c d e
18	a b c d	39	a b c d e
19	a b c d e	40	a b c d e
20	a b c d e	41	a b c d e
21	a b c d e	42	a b c d e

STUDY QUESTIONS

STUDY QUESTIONS

The following multiple-choice questions are designed to be used after your course of study with this book. Record your responses on the answer sheet (the back side of the Credit Reporting Form) by circling the appropriate letter. For the most effective use of this exercise, *complete the entire test* before consulting the answers.

Although a concerted effort has been made to avoid ambiguity and redundancy in these questions, the authors recognize that differences of opinion may occur regarding the "best" answer. The discussions are provided to demonstrate the rationale used to derive the answer. They may also be helpful in confirming that your approach to the problem was correct or, if necessary, in fixing the principle in your memory.

1. Considering the relationship of the paranasal sinuses to the orbital structures, an infection of which of the following sinuses is most likely to result in visual loss secondary to optic neuropathy?

   a. Frontal sinus
   b. Ethmoid sinus
   c. Maxillary sinus
   d. Sphenoid sinus

2. Which bone does the optic foramen pass through?

   a. Ethmoid
   b. Lesser wing of sphenoid
   c. Greater wing of sphenoid
   d. Palatine

3. Which nerve lies outside of the muscle cone?

   a. Optic nerve
   b. Inferior division of cranial nerve III (oculomotor)
   c. Superior division of cranial nerve III
   d. Cranial nerve IV (trochlear)

4. The short ciliary nerves contain the following:

   a. Sympathetic nerves to the iris dilator muscle
   b. Parasympathetic nerves to the iris sphincter muscle
   c. Trigeminal sensory fibers
   d. All of the above

5. Aneurysms of the anterior communicating artery are most likely to affect which cranial nerve?

   a. Oculomotor (cranial nerve III)
   b. Abducens (cranial nerve VI)
   c. Optic nerve
   d. Olfactory (cranial nerve I)

6. Which of the following muscles develop from neural crest–derived mesenchymal cells?

   a. Sphincter muscle
   b. Ciliary muscle
   c. Palpebral muscle of the eyelid
   d. None of the above
   e. All of the above

7. During normal closure of the embryonic fissure, all of the following are true *except:*

   a. The hyaloid artery becomes enclosed in the eye
   b. The process begins in the mid region
   c. A coloboma results
   d. The inner and outer layers of the optic cup meet and fuse

8. Differentiation of the neurosensory retina includes all of the following *except:*

   a. Begins with ganglion cells
   b. Is complete at birth
   c. Follows centraperipherally in the optic cup
   d. Involves mitosis and apoptosis

9. A mutation in the PAX6 gene manifests as

   a. Coloboma of the optic nerve
   b. Microphakia
   c. Microphthalmos
   d. Peters anomaly
   e. None of the above

10. Ocular malformations in the mouse model of fetal alcohol syndrome occur as a result of

    a. Persistent embryonic fissure
    b. Delayed detachment of lens vesicle
    c. Impaired migration of neural crest cells
    d. All of the above
    e. None of the above

11. Anomalies of the face, posterior embryotoxon, iris strands, and hypoplasia of the iris stroma are features of

    a. Axenfeld anomaly
    b. Rieger anomaly
    c. Peters anomaly
    d. Rieger syndrome
    e. Polycoria

12. The triad of cataracts, deafness, and cardiac anomalies is characteristic of

    a.   Rubella infection during the first trimester
    b.   Rubella infection after the first trimester
    c.   Trisomy 13
    d.   Deletion of short arm of chromosome 11
    e.   Lowe syndrome

13. The following are lists of X-linked ocular disorders. For which one grouping of disorder(s) are characteristic fundus findings frequently seen in the carrier females?

    a.   X-linked retinitis pigmentosa, Norrie disease
    b.   Choroideremia, retinoschisis, X-linked retinitis pigmentosa
    c.   Nettleship-Falls ocular albinism, choroideremia, X-linked retinitis pigmentosa
    d.   Norrie disease, retinoschisis, Nettleship-Falls albinism

14. Which of the following malignanacies is not caused by loss of activity of both copies, or alleles, of the gene but is the result of an autosomal dominant oncogene?

    a.   Retinoblastoma
    b.   Wilms tumor
    c.   von Hippel–Lindau syndrome
    d.   Multiple endocrine neoplasia, type 2B (MEN2B)

15. Which of the following has *not* been reported to occur as a result of haploinsufficiency from mutation of one of the alleles for the PAX6 gene?

    a.   Aniridia
    b.   Keratoconus
    c.   Autosomal dominant keratitis
    d.   Peters anomaly
    e.   Dominantly inherited macular hypoplasia

16. Which of the following statements is *not* true about the term *anticipation* as a genetic phenomenon?

    a.   Anticipation refers to the earlier and more severe expression (phenotype) of a dominant trait from one generation to the next.
    b.   Anticipation is an outmoded term that has no basis in genetic pathogenesis and should be abandoned.
    c.   Anticipation occurs with the expansion of a triplet repeat sequence, from replication slippage or unequal crossing over during meiosis.
    d.   Anticipation has been reported with myotonic dystrophy, Huntington disease, and fragile X syndrome.

17. If a recessive defect is observed in 1 out of every 10,000 persons, the chance of an individual's being a carrier is

    a. 1 in 100
    b. 1 in 50
    c. 1 in 25
    d. 1 in 1000
    e. 1 in 500

18. What components of the genes are translated into a protein?

    a. Exons
    b. Introns
    c. Promoter region
    d. Regulatory regions

19. Mutations of the gene for peripherin/*RDS* will cause which of the following phenotypes?

    a. Retinitis pigmentosa
    b. Pattern-like macular dystrophy
    c. Fundus flavimaculatus
    d. Choroidal atrophy
    e. All of the above

20. Which of the following statements about retinoblastoma is correct?

    a. Homozygous deletions within the 13p14 region have been noted in at least some retinoblastomas.
    b. All retinoblastomas arising from germinal mutations present as bilateral tumors.
    c. Almost half of nonocular second tumors associated with familial retinoblastomas are astrocytomas.
    d. A short arm chromosome 11 deletion is seen in some patients with familial retinoblastoma.
    e. There is evidence that the defect in familial retinoblastoma is recessive at the cellular level.

21. Which of the following presenting phenotypes has/have been reported in association with mutations of the Norrie disease gene (NDP)?

    a. Bilateral congenital exudative retinal detachment
    b. Bilateral posterior PHPV
    c. Bilateral pseudoglioma
    d. X-linked vitreoretinopathy
    e. All of the above

22. Which of the following inheritance types has *not* been reported to be associated with the phenotype of retinitis pigmentosa?

    a. Autosomal dominant
    b. Autosomal recessive
    c. X-linked recessive
    d. Maternal (mitochondrial)
    e. None of the above

23. The outer segment of the photoreceptor contains predominantly

    a. Palmitic acid (16:0)
    b. Linoleic acid (18:2)
    c. Docosahexaenoic acid (22:6)
    d. Arachidonic acid (20:4)

24. Lipid peroxidation is reaction of oxygen with
    1. Polyunsaturated fatty acids
    2. Saturated fatty acids
    3. Phospholipid headgroups
    4. Monounsaturated fatty acids

    a. 1, 2, and 3
    b. 1 and 4
    c. 1, 3, and 4
    d. 1 and 3
    e   All of the above

25. What is *not* a component of membranes?

    a. Phospholipids
    b. Proteins
    c. Nucleic acids
    d. Cholesterol
    e. Sugars

26. Which of the following are commonly used synonyms for the macular pigment?
    1. Yellow spot
    2. Xanthophyll pigment
    3. Carotenoids
    4. Antioxidants

    a. 1, 2, and 3
    b. 1 and 4
    c. 1, 3, and 4
    d. 1 and 3
    e. All of the above

27. Significant amplification occurs during visual transduction, and one bleached rhodopsin molecule leads to the hydrolysis of multiple molecules of cGMP. How large is this amplification?

    a. 100
    b. 1000
    c. 10,000
    d. 100,000
    e. 1,000,000

28. Vitamin E is concentrated in the
    1. Photoreceptors
    2. Horizontal cells
    3. Ganglion cells
    4. Retinal pigment epithelium

    a. 1, 2, and 3
    b. 1 and 4
    c. 1, 3, and 4
    d. 1 and 3
    e. All of the above

29. Characteristic(s) of latanoprost include(s)
    1. It is a $PGF_{2\alpha}$ agonist
    2. It is a PGE_2 agonist
    3. It reduces intraocular pressure by about 30%
    4. It releases arachidonic acid

    a. 1, 2, and 3
    b. 1 and 4
    c. 1, 3, and 4
    d. 1 and 3
    e. All of the above

30. Which vitamin A isomer is the rhodopsin chromophore?

    a. 11-*cis*-retinol
    b. 11-*cis*-retinaldehyde
    c. All-*trans*-retinol
    d. All-*trans*-retinaldehyde
    e. Retinyl ester

31. Functions of the retinal pigment epithelium include
    1. Vitamin A transport
    2. Phagocytosis of photoreceptor tips
    3. Promotion of retinal adhesion
    4. Absorption of stray light by melanin

    a. 1, 2, and 3
    b. 1 and 4
    c. 1, 3, and 4
    d. 1 and 3
    e. All of the above

32. The lipid layer of the tear film is secreted by
    1. Meibomian glands
    2. Glands of Henle and Manz
    3. Glands of Krause and Wolfring
    4. Glands of Zeis

    a. 1, 2, and 3
    b. 1 and 4
    c. 1, 3, and 4
    d. 1 and 3
    e. All of the above

33. Drugs showing zero order kinetics of elimination

    a. Are more common than those showing first-order kinetics
    b. Decrease in concentration exponentially with time
    c. Have a half-life independent of dose
    d. Show a plot of drug concentration versus time that is linear
    e. Show a constant fraction of the drug eliminated per unit time

34. Administration of a drug that acts to dilate arterioles would cause which one of the following?

    a. Increased output from the parasympathetic neurons
    b. Bradycardia
    c. Increased contractility of the heart
    d. No change in arterial blood pressure
    e. Activation of sympathetic and parasympathetic output to the heart

35. Administration of low doses of norepinephrine produces a decrease in heart rate. Which of the following statements best explains this observation?

    a. Norepinephrine decreases the peripheral resistance.
    b. Norepinephrine activates β_2 receptors.
    c. Norepinephrine directly decreases the heart rate.
    d. Norepinephrine activates a vagal reflex that decreases the heart rate.

36. Which of the following anesthetics exhibits the shortest induction time when each agent is administered at a concentration that ultimately produces anesthesia?

    a. Ethyl ether
    b. Halothane
    c. Methoxyflurane
    d. Nitrous oxide
    e. Benzodiazepine

37. Hyperkalemia is observed with which of the following diuretics?

    a. Chlorthiazide
    b. Furosemide
    c. Acetazolamide
    d. Spiranolactone

38. Which one of the following anti-infective agents is bactericidal?

    a. Erythromycin
    b. Penicillin
    c. Tetracycline
    d. Clindamycin
    e. Sulfonamide

39. Sulfonamides are agents of choice in the treatment of which of the following?

    a. Syphilis
    b. Cholera
    c. Nocardiosis
    d. Streptococcal pneumonia
    e. Rickettsial infections

40. Which one of the following adverse effects is *not* observed with administration of aminoglycosides?

    a. Anemia
    b. Nephrotoxicity
    c. Ototoxicity
    d. Respiratory paralysis
    e. Allergic reactions

41. All of the following statements about zidovudine (AZT) are correct *except:*

    a. It must be converted to the nucleotide form to express its antiviral activity.
    b. It is incorporated into growing viral but not mammalian nuclear DNA.
    c. It is currently used to treat severe herpesvirus and respiratory syncytial virus infections as well as AIDS.
    d. It is toxic to bone marrow and causes adverse hematological effects.
    e. It penetrates the CNS.

42. Which one of the following antiviral agents exhibits the greatest selective toxicity?

    a. Idoxuridine
    b. Amantadine
    c. Acyclovir
    d. Zidovudine
    e. Ribavirin

ANSWERS

1. Answer—d. Sphenoid sinus. The sphenoid sinus lies just medial to the optic nerves. In some individuals there is only mucosa separating the two with lack of bone.

2. Answer—b. Lesser wing of sphenoid.

3. Answer—d. Cranial nerve IV.

4. Answer—d. All of the above.

5. Answer—c. Optic nerve. The anterior communicating artery lies just above the intracranial portion of the optic nerves just as they join at the chiasm. An aneurysm here can cause a downward compression on one or both optic nerves.

6. Answer—b. Precursor ciliary muscle cells differentiate from neural crest–derived mesenchymal cells located between the primitive ciliary epithelium and the anterior scleral condensation at the margin of the optic cup. The sphincter muscle of the iris differentiates from the anterior layer of epithelium (the forward extension of the retinal pigment epithelium), and the palpebral muscle of the eyelid develops from mesodermal mesenchyme that infiltrates the skin folds of the eyelids.

7. Answer—c. A coloboma results from the abnormal closure of the embryonic fissure. Normal closure of the fissure, which begins in the mid region, involves fusion of the inner and outer layers of the optic cup. The process encloses the hyaloid artery within the eye.

8. Answer—b. Differentiation of the retina is incomplete at birth. Even though the fovea is the focal point for the centraperipheral development of the retina, relocation of the bipolar cells to the periphery of the foveal slope occurs by 4 months after birth, and remodeling of this region continues until nearly 4 years of age.

9. Answer—d. Patients with Peters anomaly (or with aniridia) have a mutation, often a deletion or insertion of a single nucleotide that causes a frame-shift in the coding region, in the PAX6 gene. A mutation in the PAX2 gene can produce an optic nerve coloboma. Microphakia and microphthalmos can result in fetal alcohol syndrome, although microphthalmos is also associated with many different chromosomal anomalies.

10. Answer—d. All these abnormalities occur in the mouse model of fetal alcohol syndrome as a primary event caused by faulty induction in the forebrain at the gastrula stage. History of alcohol abuse during the first trimester is associated with similar malformations in humans.

11. Answer—d. Inadequate regression of tissues or failure of cell differentiation results in Axenfeld, Rieger, or Peters anomalies. Anomalies of the face and of the umbilicus are additional features in Rieger syndrome. Polycoria results from local hypo- or hyperplasia of the iris stroma and pigment epithelium.

12. Answer—a. The classic triad of cataracts, deafness, and cardiac anomalies results from maternal rubella infection in the first trimester. Salt-and-pepper fundus may be the only residuum of infection in the second trimester. Aberrant cellular differentiation in trisomy 13 gives rise to many anomalies, including cloudy cornea and media as well as retinal dysplasia. Deletion of short arm of chromosome 11 produces nonfamilial aniridia, Wilms tumor, genitourinary anomalies, and mental retardation. In Lowe syndrome aberrations of amino acid metabolism are associated with congenital cataract, glaucoma, neuromuscular hypotonia, and developmental delay.

13. Answer—c. The carriers for retinoschisis and, typically, Norrie disease will have a normal fundus, whereas most, but not all, carriers for X-linked RP will show patchy pigmentary retinopathy or a tapetal sheen. Carriers for choroideremia will nearly always show patchy pigment epithelial disturbance and carriers for Nettleship-Falls ocular albinism will show alternating patches or palisades of normal and hypopigmented fundus coloration in the mid and far periphery.

14. Answer—d. MEN2B is the only one of the above that is not the result of loss of activity of both alleles of a tumor-suppressor gene. MEN2B results from the mutation of a single copy of the gene called RET, which is also associated with multiple endocrine neoplasia type 1, medullary thyroid carcinoma, and Hirschsprung disease.

15. Answer—b. Keratoconus is the only one of the above that has not been reported to occur with a PAX6 mutation.

16. Answer—b. Until recently, this statement would have been considered true. However, with the discovery of the molecular basis for myotonic dystrophy, Huntington disease, fragile X syndrome, and several other disorders associated with expansion of triple repeat sequences, anticipation as a true genetic phenomenon has been rejuvenated.

17. Answer—b. The correct answer is determined by calculating the square root of the frequency of defective individuals (1 out of every 10,000 persons) and multiplying by 2, since an individual can carry the defective gene on *either* of two homologous chromosomes.

18. Answer—a. Exons are segments of DNA that are transcribed into mature messenger RNA and eventually translated into protein. Introns are segments of DNA between exons that are spliced out of the mature mRNA and, hence, not translated into proteins. The promoter region is the site of binding of the RNA polymerase and, hence, the initiation of transcription. Regulatory regions exist both 5′ and 3′ to the open reading frame, or ORF (that portion of the gene translated into protein).

19. Answer—e. All of the above phenotypes have been reported with mutations of peripherin/*RDS,* in some instances with several phenotypes within the same family, indicating that factors, some presumably genetic, other than the original mutation, may play a role in pathogenesis.

20. Answer—e. Homozygous deletions within the 13q14 region (not 13p14) have been noted in patients with retinoblastomas. Not all germinal mutations present as bilateral tumors.

21. Answer—e. Although, classically, patients with Norrie present with pseudogliomas or retrolental masses, patients who have had otherwise typical Norrie disease have presented as having, or were originally thought to have, congenital exudative retinal detachments and bilateral posterior PHPV. Several families have been reported where the mutation of the gene produced an X-linked vitreoretinopathy rather than pseudoglioma in family members.

22. Answer—e. All of the inheritance types have been reported to cause the phenotype of retinitis pigmentosa.

23. Answer—c. All of the above are present in rod outer segments, but 22:6 is the predominant fatty acid.

24. Answer—b. Both poly- and monounsaturated fatty acids contain double bonds.

25. Answer—c. Nucleic acids are not a component of membranes.

26. Answer—a. Antioxidants is not a synonym for the macular pigment.

27. Answer—d. Two amplification steps exist that cause one moledule of bleached rhodopsin to lead to the hydrolysis of 100,000 cGMP molecules.

28. Answer—b. See Figure XVIII-6.

29. Answer—d. Latanoprost is a $PGF_{2\alpha}$ agonist that decreases IOP by about 30%.

30. Answer—b. 11-*cis*-retinaldehyde is the rhodopsin chromophore.

31. Answer—e. See Table XVII-1.

32. Answer—b. See Figure X-1.

33. Answer—d. In most clinical situations the concentration of a drug is much less than Michaelis-Menten constant K_m. Half-life increases with dose. A constant amount of drug is eliminated for unit time. Decrease in concentration is linear with time.

34. Answer—c. Dilation of arterioles activates the baroreceptor reflex, causing an increase in sympathetic output and decrease in parasympathetic activity. Increased sympathetic activity increases heart rate. Vasodilation also results in decrease in blood pressure.

35. Answer—d. Norepinephrine interacts with α receptors to produce peripheral vasoconstriction and an increase in peripheral resistance. In addition, norepinephrine has low affinity for β receptors. Vasoconstriction leads to an increase in blood pressure, which triggers a parasympathetic slowing of the heart.

36. Answer—d. Because of its low solubility, nitrous oxide rapidly saturates arterial blood reaching the brain.

37. Answer—d. Spiranolactone is a potassium-sparing diuretic that decreases the secretion of K^+ into urine, resulting in hyperkalemia. All other listed diuretics result in hypokalemia.

38. Answer—b. All the other drugs listed are bacteriostatic.

39. Answer—c. Penicillin is the drug of choice in syphilis and streptococcal pneumonia. Tetracycline is the drug of choice in cholera and rickettsial infections.

40. Answer—a. All other adverse effects are known to result from aminoglycosides.

41. Answer—c.

42. Answer—c. Acyclovir is monophosphorylated in the cell by the herpesvirus-coded enzyme, thymidine kinase. Thus, uninfected cells show little activation of the drug, and the toxicity is therefore highly selective for herpesvirus-infected cells.

INDEX

Alleles, 184, 251–252
  dominant, 187
  null, gene therapy and, 244
Allelic association. *See* Linkage
    disequilibrium
Allelic heterogeneity, 184, 249, 276
Allergic conjunctivitis, drugs for,
    422–423, 422*t*
Alomide. *See* Lodoxamide
Alpha-adrenergic agents, 404–407. *See
    also specific agent*
  antagonists, 407
  direct-acting, 404
  indirect-acting, 404–406
  for lowering intraocular pressure, 446
Alpha-adrenoceptors, effects mediated
    by, 405*i*
Alpha (α) crystallins, 331, 332*t*
Alternate splicing, 211
Alu repeat sequence, 184, 203
Amacrine cells, development of, 144
Amber codon, 184
Amide local anesthetics, 438, 439*t*, 440
Amikacin, 425*t*, 428–430
Amino acids, symbols for, 201*t*
ε-Aminocaproic acid, 443
Aminoglycosides, 428–430
Amniocentesis, 297
Amoxicillin, 426
Amphotericin B, 432, 432*t*
Ampicillin, 425*t*, 426
Anaerobic glycolysis, in glucose
    metabolism
  in lens, 335
  in retina, 364
Anaphase, 191
Anaphase lag, 206
  mosaicism caused by, 265
Anaphylaxis, slow-reacting substance of,
    319. *See also* Leukotrienes
Ancobon. *See* Flucytosine
Anemia
  aplastic, chloramphenicol causing, 428
  sickle cell, point mutation causing, 273
Anesthesia/anesthetics, local
    (topical/regional), 438–441, 439*t*
Aneuploidy, 184, 206
  autosome, 259–265
  sex chromosome, 265
Aneurysms, cranial nerve III, 109

Angelman syndrome, imprinting
    abnormalities causing, 213
Angular artery, 35
Animal cap, 125
  fibroblast growth factor affecting, 129
Aniridia, 125, 171
  homeobox gene mutations in, 130,
    271–272
  mutation rate of, 272
  short arm 11 deletion syndrome and,
    271–272
Anisocoria, 125, 171
Anlage, 125
Annulus of Zinn, 21, 101
Anomalies, congenital. *See* Congenital
    anomalies
Anophthalmos, 125, 163, 164*i*
Antagonist, 392
Antazoline, 421
Antazoline/naphazoline, 422*t*
Anterior chamber, 54–56
  anatomy of, 54–56
  congenital anomalies of, 169–171,
    170*i*, 171*i*
  development of, 153–154, 154*i*
Anterior chamber angle
  development of, 153–154, 154*i*
  gonioscopy of, 59–61
Anterior segment, developmental
    abnormalities of, 160, 161*i*, 162*i*
Antibiotics, 424–433, 425*t*. *See also
    specific type and specific agent*
Anticipation (genetic), 184, 274
Anticodon, 213
Antifibrinolytic agents, 443
Antifibrotic agents, 423–424
Antifungal agents, 431–433, 432*t*
Antihistamines, 421–423, 422*t*. *See also
    specific agent*
Anti-inflammatory agents, 414–424, 415*t*.
    See also specific agent
Antimetabolites, 423–424
Anti-oncogenes. *See* Tumor-suppressor
    genes
Antioxidants
  in lens, 375, 376*i*
  in retina and retinal pigment epithelium,
    377–379, 380*i*
Antisense DNA, 184, 202
Antisense oligonucleotides, in gene
    therapy, 245, 246*i*

Antisense primer, for PCR, 235
Antiviral agents, 433–437, 434t. *See also*
    specific agent
  systemic, 434–437
  topical, 433
Aphakia, vitreous changes associated with,
    341–342
Aplasia, definition of, 125
Aplastic anemia, chloramphenicol
    causing, 428
Aponeurosis, levator, 33
Apoptosis, 125, 184
Apraclonidine, 405–406
Aqueous humor, 55
  biochemistry and metabolism of,
      325–328
  carbohydrates in, 326
  carbon dioxide in, 328
  dynamics of, 316–317
  glutathione in, 326
  growth modulatory factors in, 327–328
  inorganic ions in, 325
  organic ions in, 325
  oxygen in, 328
  proteins in, 326–327
  separation of from blood. *See*
      Blood–aqueous barrier
  urea in, 326
Aqueous phase, of tear film, 306–307
Ara-A. *See* Vidarabine
Arachidonate, in vitreous, 341
Arachidonic acid, in eicosanoid synthesis,
    317, 318i
  nonsteroidal anti-inflammatory drugs
      and, 419
Arachnoid mater, optic nerve, 101, 102i
Arrestin, in rod outer segments, 348t
Artificial tears, 441
Ascertainment, 185
Ascorbate, osmotic diuretic effects of, 413
Ascorbic acid (vitamin C)
  antioxidant effect of
    in lens, 375
    in retina and retinal pigment
        epithelium, 379
  in aqueous humor, 325
ASO. *See* Allele-specific oligonucleotides
Aspirin, 420, 420t
Association (genetic), 227–228
Assortative mating, 185

Ataxia
  intermittent, enzyme defect and ocular
      findings in, 280t
  with neuropathy and retinitis
      pigmentosa, mitochondrial DNA
      mutations and, 225, 225i
ATM protein kinase, in DNA repair, 216
Atrophy, gyrate, enzyme defect and ocular
    findings in, 280t
Atropine, 321, 400
Aureomycin. *See* Chlortetracycline
Automated DNA sequencing, 237, 238i
Auto-oxidation, 373–374, 374i
Autophagy, in retinal pigment
    epithelium, 371
Autosomal dominant inheritance,
    283–284, 285t
Autosomal recessive inheritance,
    279–283, 283t
Autosomes, 185
  aneuploidy of, 259–265
Axenfeld anomaly, 168, 169, 170i. *See*
    also Neurocristopathy
Axenfeld-Rieger syndrome, 169–170, 170i
Azidodeoxythymidine. *See* Zidovudine
Azlocillin, 426
AZT. *See* Zidovudine

Bacitracin, 425t, 429t, 431
  with polymyxin B, 429t
Bacteriophage, 185
Bands, chromosome, 256–257, 256i,
    257i, 258i
Barr body, 185, 250, 288
Basal cells, conjunctival, 41
Basal lamina
  corneal, 47–49, 310i
  retinal blood vessel, 84
Base excision repair, 217
Base pair, 185, 199
  mutations of, 219
    conserved, 219
  repair of, 217, 218
Basic fibroblast growth factor, in aqueous
    humor, 327
Basic secretors, 308
Bathorhodopsin, 352
BAX gene, in DNA repair, 216
Benoxinate, 441
Bergmeister's papilla, 91, 175

Carrier (genetic), 185, 288
  heterozygote, 281–282
  ocular findings in, 289t, 290–291i
Carteolol, 409, 409t
Caruncle, 36
Catalase, antioxidant effect of, 375
  in retina and retinal pigment
    epithelium, 378
Cataract
  congenital and infantile, 172–174
  lens carbohydrate alterations and,
    234, 335
  oxidative lens damage and, 375–376
  removal of. See Cataract surgery
  "sugar," aldose reductase in
    development of, 335, 337
Cataract surgery
  extracapsular cataract extraction (ECCE)
    lens capsule and, 74
    lens epithelium and, 75
  intracapsular cataract extraction (ICCE),
    vitreous changes associated with,
    341–342
Cat's cry syndrome, 272
Cavernous sinus, 119–120, 119i
CCAAT box, 185
cDNA, 186, 199–200
cDNA clone, 185
cDNA library, 190, 233
Cefamandole, 427
Cefazolin, 425t, 427
Cefoperazone, 427
Cefotaxime, 427
Cefoxitin, 427
Ceftazidime, 425t
Ceftizoxime, 427
Cefuroxime, 427
Centimorgan, 185
Central retinal artery, 84, 105, 106i, 107i
Central retinal vein, 105, 106i
Centromere, 185, 205–206
  chromosome morphology determined by
    position of, 257
Cephalexin, 427
Cephalosporins, 427
  allergic reaction to, 425–426
  mechanism of action of, 424–426
  structure of, 424, 426i
Cephalothin, 427
Cephradine, 427

Cetamide. See Sulfacetamide
Chamber angle
  development of, 153–154, 154i
  gonioscopy of, 59–61
Chemical transmission, in retina, 361–363
Chiasm, anatomy of, 102–103
Chibroxin. See Norfloxacin
Chloramphenicol, 428, 429t
Chloride, in aqueous humor, 325
Chloromycetin. See Chloramphenicol
Chloroptic. See Chloramphenicol
Chlortetracycline, 429t
Cholinergic agents, 393–403. See also
    specific agent
  antagonists, 393
  direct-acting agonists, 393, 395i
  indirect-acting agonists, 393, 395i
Cholinergic neurons, 319
Cholinergic receptors, in iris–ciliary body,
    319, 320t
Cholinesterase inhibitors, 399–400, 403
  intermediate formation and, 399, 399i
  miotic action of, 397t
  toxicity of, 400
Chondroitin sulfate, 313, 442
Chondroitin sulfate proteoglycan, 358
Choriocapillaris, 68, 68i, 70–72, 72i,
    73i, 74i
  differentiation of, 148
Chorionic villus sampling, 185, 297–298
Choristoma, 125
Choroid, 52i, 68–72, 68i
  anatomy of, 68–72, 68i
  development of, 148–150
  gyrate atrophy of, enzyme defect and
    ocular findings in, 280t
  stroma of, development of, 150
Choroideremia, ocular findings in carriers
    of, 289t, 291i
Chromatid, 185, 205
Chromatin, 185, 204
Chromokinesins, 206
Chromosomal aneuploidy, 184, 206
  autosome, 259–265
  sex chromosome, 265
Chromosomal banding, 256–257, 256i,
    257i, 258i
Chromosome arm painting, 258–259,
    260i, 261i
Chromosome translocation, 197, 267

macular, 174
  optic nerve, 174–175
  Pax-2 mutation causing, 130
Color vision defects, red-green, ocular findings in carriers of, 289t
Combinatorial multi-fluor FISH, 258–259
Complementary DNA (cDNA), 186, 199–200
Complementary DNA clone (cDNA clone), 185
Complementary DNA library (cDNA library), 190, 233
Compound heterozygote, 186, 278
Cone outer segments. *See also* Cones
  development of, 143
  renewal of, 349, 350i
  shedding of, 350–351
Cone pedicle, 80, 83i
Cone pigments, 347–349
Cones, 80, 83i. *See also* Cone outer segments
  extrafoveal, 80
  foveal, 80, 88
Confocal scanning laser ophthalmoscopy, for optic disc evaluation, 99, 100i
Congenital, definition of, 186, 248. *See also* Genetics
Congenital anomalies, 160–179. *See also specific type*
  homeobox gene mutations causing, 130
Congenital rubella, cataracts caused by, 173–174
Congenital stationary night blindness, with myopia, ocular findings in carriers of, 289t
Conjunctiva, 39–41, 40i
  bulbar, 39, 40i
  forniceal, 39
  hyperemia of, latanoprost causing, 446
  palpebral, 34, 34i, 39
Conjunctivitis, allergic, drugs for, 422–423, 422t
Consanguinity, 186, 282
Consensus sequence, 186
Conservation (genetic), 186
Conserved base-pair mutations, 219
Contig, 186, 231
Contiguous gene deletion syndrome, 271
Copper, in aqueous humor, 325

Cornea
  anatomy of, 46, 47–51, 48i, 310i
  basal lamina of, 47–49, 310i
  biochemistry and metabolism of, 310–314, 315i
  central, 47
  congenital/developmental anomalies of, 167–168, 169i
  development of, 150–152, 151i, 152i
  endothelium of, 51, 52i, 310i, 314, 315i
  epithelium of, 47–49, 48i, 310i, 311
  innervation of, 311
  nonepithelial cells in, 49
  peripheral, 47
  stroma of
    anatomy of, 49, 310i
    biochemistry and metabolism of, 312–314
    development of, 150–152
  topographic features of, 46
Cornea shields, collagen, for drug administration, 391
Corneal pump, 314, 315i
Corneal storage medium, 443
Corneoscleral meshwork, 57
Corticosteroids (steroids), 415–418, 418t
  route of administration of in ocular inflammation, 419t
Cosmid, 186, 198
Counseling, genetic, 296–298
CPEO. *See* Chronic progressive external ophthalmoplegia
CpG island rescue, 231
Cranial nerve I (olfactory nerve), anatomy of, 93, 94i, 95i
Cranial nerve II. *See* Optic nerve
Cranial nerve III (oculomotor nerve)
  anatomy of, 94i, 107–110, 109i
  aneurysms of, 109
  course of, 10i, 109
  fascicular portion of, 109
  palsy of, eyelid fissure changes in, 26
  superior division of, 109
Cranial nerve IV (trochlear nerve), anatomy of, 94i, 111–112, 111i
Cranial nerve V (trigeminal nerve)
  anatomy of, 94i, 112–116
  interconnections of, 112, 113i
Cranial nerve V₁ (ophthalmic nerve), 94i, 113, 115

Cranial nerve V$_2$ (maxillary nerve), 94*i*, 113, 116
Cranial nerve V$_3$ (mandibular nerve), 94*i*, 113, 116
Cranial nerve VI (abducens nerve), anatomy of, 94*i*, 116, 117*i*
Cranial nerve VII (facial nerve)
  anatomy of, 116–119, 118*i*
  cervicofacial division of, 118–119
  labyrinthine segment of, 118
  mastoid segment of, 118
  palsy of, eyelid fissure changes in, 26, 27*i*
  temporofacial division of, 118–119
  tympanic segment of, 118
Cranial nerves. *See also specific nerve*
  anatomy of, 16, 93–119
  central and peripheral connections of, 93–119
Crest cells. *See* Neural crest cells
Cri du chat syndrome, 272
Crigler-Najjar syndrome, enzyme defect and ocular findings in, 280*t*
Crolom. *See* Cromolyn sodium
Cromolyn sodium, 421, 422*t*
Crossing over, 186, 254. *See also* Recombination
  unequal, 198
Cryptophthalmos, 125, 167, 167*i*
Crystallins, lens, 331–332, 332*t*
  development of, 146
CS. *See* Cockayne syndrome
CSPG. *See* Chondroitin sulfate proteoglycan
Cupping, optic disc, 99, 100*i*
Curare/curare-like drugs, 403
CVS. *See* Chorionic villus sampling
Cyanoacrylates, 446
Cyclic AMP, in signal transduction in iris–ciliary body, 322–324, 323*i*
Cyclic GMP, in signal transduction in retina, 355–358, 356*i*, 357*i*
Cyclin-dependent kinases, 216
Cyclo-oxygenase, nonsteroidal anti-inflammatory drugs affecting, 419, 420
Cyclopentolate, 321
Cycloplegia/cycloplegics, 125, 165, 165*i*, 400
  muscarinic antagonists causing, 321, 400–401, 401*t*

Cystic eye, 166
Cytogenetics/cytogenic markers, 227, 254
Cytokine gene transfer, 446
Cytoplasmic genes, 222
Cytovene. *See* Ganciclovir

D-penicillamine, for Wilson disease, 300
DAG. *See* Diacylglycerol
Dapiprazole, 321, 407
Dark-adapted sodium channels, 355
Dark current, 355
de Morsier syndrome, 174
Decadron. *See* Dexamethasone
Decamethonium, 403
Decongestants, ocular, 442
Defy. *See* Tobramycin
Degeneracy, of genetic code, 186
Deletion, 267
Demecarium, 397*t*, 399
Demodex folliculorum, cholinesterase inhibitors for treatment of, 400
Demulcents, 441
Denaturing gradient gel electrophoresis, 237
Deoxyribonucleic acid. *See* DNA
Dermatan sulfate/chondroitin sulfate, in corneal glycosaminoglycans, 313
Dermoids (dermoid cysts/tumors), 125, 168
  orbital, 178
Dermolipomas, 168
Descemet's membrane
  anatomy of, 49–51, 50*i*, 310*i*
  biochemistry and metabolism of, 314
  development of, 151
Dexamethasone, 415*t*, 418*t*
DFP. *See* Diisopropyl phosphorofluoridate
DGGE. *See* Denaturing gradient gel electrophoresis
DHA. *See* Docosahexaenoic acid
Diabetes mellitus, vitreous changes associated with, 342
Diacylglycerol (DAG), in signal transduction in iris–ciliary body, 322–324, 323*i*
Diagnostic agents, 442
Dichlorphenamide, 410*t*
Diclofenac, 319, 415*t*, 421
Dicloxacillin, 426
Didanosine, 437
Dideoxycytidine (DDC). *See* Zalcitabine

Dideoxyinosine (DDI). *See* Didanosine
Diet, in inborn errors of metabolism, 300
Diffusion, in aqueous humor
    dynamics, 316
Diflucan. *See* Fluconazole
Digenic inheritance, 186
Diisopropyl phosphorofluoridate, 399
Dilator muscle, 63–64
  miotics affecting, 320–321
  mydriatics affecting, 321
Dinucleotide repeats, 191
Dipivefrin, 389, 390*i*, 407–408, 408*t*
Diploid, definition of, 186
Diplotene phase of meiosis, 191
Direct sequencing, for mutation screening,
    237, 238*i*
Disomy, uniparental, 198
DNA, 187, 199
  analysis of, 233–239
  antisense, 184, 202
  complementary (cDNA), 186, 199–200
  creation of RNA from, 211
  damage to, 216–217
  dispersed repetitive, 186–187
  double-stranded, 199, 200
  free radical damage of, 375
  "junk," 203
  mitochondrial, 222–223
    diseases associated with mutation of,
      222–223, 225*i*
  molecular manipulation of, 233–239
  recombinant, 195, 233, 236*i*
  repair of, 216–218
  replication of, 195, 215–216
  satellite, 196
  sense, 196, 202
  sequencing of, 237, 238*i*
  structure of, 199, 200*i*
  telomeric, 197, 203
DNA libraries, 190, 233, 234*i*
  cDNA library, 190, 233
  genomic, 190, 233, 234*i*
DNA viruses, recombinant, for gene
    therapy, 447
Docosahexaenoic acid, in retina,
    346, 347*i*
Dominant inheritance (dominant gene),
    187, 278–279
  autosomal, 283–284, 285*t*

Dominant medical disorders, 187,
    278–279
  gene therapy for, 244–245, 246*i*
Donor corneas, storage of, 443
Donor splice site, 187
Dorzolamide, 410*t*
Down syndrome (trisomy 21),
    263–265, 264*t*
  pharmacogenetics and, 298–299
DPE. *See* Dipivefrin
Drugs, ocular, 383–450. *See also specific*
    agent
  for *Acanthamoeba* infections, 438
  adrenergic agents, 403–409
  anti-inflammatory agents, 414–424
  antibiotic, 424–433, 425*t*
  antifibrinolytic, 443
  antifungal agents, 431–433
  antiviral agents, 433–437
  carbonic anhydrase inhibitors, 409–412
  cholinergic agents, 393–403
  concentration of, absorption affected
    by, 386
  for corneal storage medium, 443
  decongestants, 442
  diagnostic agents, 442
  for dry eye, 441
  in eyedrops, 384–387, 385*i*, 387*i*
  fibrinolytic, 442
  for gene therapy, 446–448
  growth factors, 444–445
  intraocular injection of, 388
  intraocular pressure lowered by, 446
    apraclonidine, 405–406
    beta-adrenergic agonists, 407–408
    beta blockers, 408–409
    latanoprost, 421
    osmotic agents, 412–414
  intravenous administration of, 389
  investigational, 444–445
  for irrigation, 442
  legal aspects of use of, 450
  local anesthetics, 438–441
  methods of design and delivery
    of, 389–392
  new, 444–446
  in ointments, 387–388
  oral preparations of, sustained-
    release, 388
  osmotic agents, 412–414

periocular injection of, 388
pharmacodynamics of, 392
pharmacokinetics of, 384–392
pharmacologic principles and, 384–392
purified neurotoxin complex, 411
solubility of, absorption affected by, 386
systemic therapy and, 388–389
thrombin, 443
topical, 384–388, 385*i*, 387*i*. *See also*
  Eyedrops
viscoelastic, 442
viscosity of, absorption affected by, 386
Drusen, 79
Dry eye, medications for, 441
DS/CS. *See* Dermatan sulfate/chondroitin
  sulfate
Duchenne muscular dystrophy, mutation
  rate of, 273
Dulcitol (galactitol), 336
Duplication, chromosome, 267
Dura mater, optic nerve, 102*i*
Duranest. *See* Etidocaine
Dysautonomia, familial (Riley-Day
  syndrome)
  enzyme defect and ocular findings
    in, 280*t*
  racial and ethnic concentration of, 277
Dysgenesis, definition of, 125
Dysplasia, definition of, 125

ECCE. *See* Extracapsular cataract
  extraction
Echothiophate, 397*t*, 399
Econopred. *See* Prednisolone
Ectoderm, 125, 134, 135*i*
  ocular structures derived from, 132*t*
Ectropion
  physiologic, 63
  uveae, 63
Edinger-Westphal nucleus, 107, 109*i*
Edrophonium, 403
Edwards syndrome (trisomy 18), 262, 262*t*
Ehlers-Danlos syndrome, enzyme defect
  and ocular findings in, 280*t*
Eicosanoids
  ocular effects of, 317–319
  synthesis of, 317, 318*i*
Electrical transmission, in retina, 361–363
Electrolytes, in tear film, 306, 307*t*
Electrophoresis, denaturing gradient
  gel, 237

Electroretinogram, glucose metabolism in
  retina affecting, 364–365
Elevated intraocular pressure
  drugs for, 446
    apraclonidine, 405–406
    beta-adrenergic agonists, 407–408
    beta blockers, 408–409
    latanoprost, 421
    osmotic agents, 412–414
  glucocorticoids causing, 417
11p13 syndrome (short arm 11 deletion
  syndrome), 271–272
ELM. *See* External limiting membrane
Embryogenesis, 126, 133–134, 133*i*, 135*i*,
  136*i*, 137*i*
Embryology, 123–179. *See also* Congenital
  anomalies; Eye, development of
  terms used in, 125–127
Embryonic fissure, 136–137, 137, 142*i*
  persistence of, 160, 162
Embryonic nucleus, 146
Embryotoxon, posterior, 127, 168, 169,
  170*i*. *See also* Neurocristopathy
Emollients, ocular, 441
Encephaloceles, 166–167
Encephalopathy, Leigh necrotizing,
  enzyme defect and ocular findings
  in, 280*t*
Endoderm, 134, 135*i*
Endonucleases, 187
  restriction, for mutation screening, 237
Endothelium
  corneal, 51, 52*i*, 310*i*, 314, 315*i*
  retinal blood vessel, 84
Energy production
  glucose metabolism in lens and,
    334–337
  glucose metabolism in retina and,
    363–365
Enhancer, 187
Enoxacin, 430
Environmental agents, chromosomal
  aberrations caused by, 268
Enzymatic method, for DNA sequencing,
  237, 238*i*
Enzyme defects, disorders associated with,
  279–280*t*
  autosomal recessive inheritance of, 281
  management of, 300
Epiblast, 134
Epinephrine, 407–408, 408*t*

Globe
  realignment of, 158, 159*i*
  topographic features of, 46
Globulins
  in aqueous humor, 326
  in vitreous, 340
Glucocorticoids, 415–418, 418*t*. *See also*
    Corticosteroids
  route of administration of in ocular
      inflammation, 419*t*
Glucose
  in aqueous humor, 326
  metabolism of
    in cornea, 311, 312*i*
    in lens, 334–337
    in retina, 364
Glucose-6-phosphate dehydrogenase
    deficiency
  pharmacogenetics and, 298
  racial and ethnic concentration of, 277
Glutathione
  antioxidant effect of, in retina and
      retinal pigment epithelium, 378
  in aqueous humor, 326
Glutathione peroxidase, antioxidant effect
    of, 375, 376*i*
  in retina and retinal pigment
      epithelium, 378
Glutathione-S-transferase, antioxidant
    effect of, in retina and retinal pigment
    epithelium, 378
Glycerin/glycerol, 413, 413*t*
Glycogen, in cornea, 311
Glycolysis
  in corneal glucose metabolism,
      311, 312*i*
  in lens glucose metabolism, 335
  in retinal glucose metabolism, 364
Glycoproteins, in vitreous, 340–341
Glycosaminoglycans
  in Bowman's layer, 311
  in corneal stroma, 313
Glycosylation, protein, 215
GM₁ type I gangliosidosis (generalized
    gangliosidosis), enzyme defect and
    ocular findings in, 279*t*
GM₂ type I gangliosidosis (Tay-Sachs
    disease), enzyme defect and ocular
    findings in, 279*t*

GM₂ type II gangliosidosis (Sandhoff
    disease), enzyme defect and ocular
    findings in, 279*t*
Goblet cells, 31*i*, 31*t*, 39
  conjunctival, 41
  mucins produced by, 308
Goldenhar syndrome
    (oculoauriculovertebral dysplasia),
    dermoids in, 168
Gonioscopy, chamber angle, 59–61
Gramicidin, with polymyxin B and
    neomycin, 429*t*
Graves disease, eyelid fissure changes in,
    26, 27*i*
Gray line (intermarginal sulcus), 28, 305
Ground substance, of cornea, 49
Growth factors, 126, 444–445
  in aqueous humor, 327–328
  homeobox gene expression affected by,
      129, 130
  in ocular development, 128–129
Guanylate cyclase, in rod outer
    segments, 348*t*
Gyrate atrophy, enzyme defect and ocular
    findings in, 280*t*

Haploid, definition of, 188
Haploid insufficiency
    (haploinsufficiency), 188
  aniridia caused by, 271
  gene therapy for disorders caused
      by, 244
Haplotype, 188
Helix-loop-helix motif, 207, 208*i*
Helix-turn-helix motif, 207, 208*i*
Hemizygote/hemizygous, 188, 252
Hemorrhage, vitreous affected by, 342
Henle, fiber layer of, 85
  carotenoids in, 379, 380*i*
Hereditary, definition of, 189, 247. *See
    also* Genetics
Hermansky-Pudlak syndrome, racial and
    ethnic concentration of, 277
Herpes simplex viruses, keratitis caused
    by, topical antiviral agents for, 433
Herpex. *See* Idoxuridine
Heterochromatin, 204

Heterogeneity, 189, 249, 276–277
  allelic, 184, 249, 276
  clinical, 185, 249
  genetic, 249
  locus, 249, 276
Heteroplasmy, 189
Heterozygosity, loss of, 222
Heterozygote/heterozygous, 189, 251, 278
  carrier, 281–282
  compound, 186, 278
  double, 252
Hexose monophosphate shunt
  in corneal glucose metabolism,
    311, 312*i*
  in lens glucose metabolism, 335
Hexylcaine, 439*t*
Histones, 204
HIV infection, antiviral agents for, 437
HM crystallin, 332*t*
HMP shunt. *See* Hexose monophosphate
    shunt
HMS. *See* Hydroxymethyl progesterone;
    Medrysone
Holandric inheritance/trait, 189, 285
Holocrine glands, 28
Homeobox, 126, 189. *See also* Homeobox
    genes
Homeobox genes, 129–130, 189
  growth factors affecting expression of,
    129, 130
  mutations in, 130
  in ocular development, 129–130
Homeodomain, 129
Homeotic selector genes, 129, 189. *See
  also* Homeobox genes
Homocystinuria
  enzyme defect and ocular findings
    in, 280*t*
  vitamin B$_6$ replacement therapy for, 301
Homologous chromosomes, 189
Homoplasmy, 189
Homozygote/homozygous, 189, 251, 278
Horizontal cells, 80, 83*i*
Horner syndrome, eyelid fissure changes
    in, 26, 27*i*
Host cell, 189
HOX genes, 129, 130, 189
HPMPC. *See* Cidofovir
Human Genome Project, 298
Human immunodeficiency virus infection,
    antiviral agents for, 437

Humorsol. *See* Demecarium
Hunter syndrome, enzyme defect and
    ocular findings in, 279*t*
Hurler syndrome, enzyme defect and
    ocular findings in, 251, 279*t*
Hyalocytes
  in hyaluronic acid synthesis, 340
  in secondary vitreous, 148
Hyaloid artery, posterior, persistent,
    175, 177*i*
Hyaloid system
  development of, 156–157
  regression of, 148, 149*i*, 157
  remnants of, 175, 177*i*
Hyaluronate, 442
Hyaluronic acid, in vitreous,
    338–340, 340*i*
  ophthalmic surgery and, 342
Hyaluronidase, in aqueous humor, 327
Hybrid clones, segregation of cellular traits
    and chromosomes in, 227
Hybridization, 189
  fluorescence in situ, 258–259
Hydrocortisone, 418*t*
Hydrolytic enzymes, in retinal pigment
    epithelium, 368, 368*t*
Hydroxyamphetamine, for pupillary
    testing, 405
Hydroxymethyl progesterone, 421
Hydroxypropyl methylcellulose, 442
Hydroxytoluene, butylated, as
    antioxidant, 376
Hyperemia, conjunctival, latanoprost
    causing, 446
Hyperglycinemia, enzyme defect and
    ocular findings in, 280*t*
Hypertelorism, 126
Hypoblast, 134
Hypoplasia, definition of, 126

Ibuprofen, 420*t*
ICCE. *See* Intracapsular cataract extraction
Idoxuridine, 433, 434*t*
Ig. *See under* Immunoglobulin
IGF–1. *See* Insulin-like growth factor–1
IGFBPs. *See* Insulin-like growth factor
    binding proteins
Illegitimate transcripts, 190
ILM. *See* Internal limiting membrane
Ilotycin. *See* Erythromycin
Imidazoles, 432–433

Leber hereditary optic neuropathy,
mitochondrial DNA mutations and,
224, 225*i*
Leigh necrotizing encephalopathy, enzyme
defect and ocular findings in, 280*t*
Lens (crystalline)
anatomy of, 72–76, 74*i*, 329–330
biochemistry and metabolism of,
329–337
capsule of
anatomy of, 73–74, 75*i*, 329
formation of, 146, 147*i*
carbohydrate metabolism in, 334–337
chemical composition of, 331–333
congenital anomalies of, 172–174
cortex of, 330
development of, 146–148, 147*i*
epithelium of, 74–75, 329–330
nucleus of, 330
oxidative damage to, 375–376
transport functions in, 333–334, 334*i*
Lens fibers, 76, 76*i*, 330
chemical composition of, 331
Lens placode, 127, 136, 146
Lens proteins, 331–333, 332*t*
Lens sutures, 76
development of, 146
Lens vesicle, 136, 146
Lenticonus, 172
Leucine zipper motif, 207, 208*i*
Leukocoria, persistent hyperplastic primary
vitreous and, 175
Leukodystrophy
Krabbe, enzyme defect and ocular
findings in, 279*t*
metachromatic, enzyme defect and
ocular findings in, 279*t*
Leukomas, 126, 168
Leukotrienes, 317, 318*i*, 319
nonsteroidal anti-inflammatory drugs
and, 419
Levator disinsertion, eyelid fissure changes
in, 26, 27*i*
Levator palpebrae superioris muscle,
32–33
Levobunolol, 408, 409*t*
Levocabastin, 422, 422*t*
LHON. *See* Leber hereditary optic
neuropathy
Liability, in inheritance, 190

Library, DNA, 190, 233, 234*i*
cDNA, 190, 233
genomic, 190, 233, 234*i*
Lid margin. *See* Eyelid, margin of
Lidocaine, 439*t*, 440
Ligands, in signal transduction in
iris–ciliary body, 322
Light
photoreceptor plasma membrane
activities affected by, 355–358,
356*i*, 357*i*
rhodopsin changes caused by, 351–353,
351*i*, 352*i*
Limbus, 53–54, 54*i*
anatomy of, 53–54, 54*i*
Limiting membrane
external, 85
development of, 141
internal, 85
middle, 85
Linkage (gene), 190, 228–230, 230*i*, 232*i*,
250, 254
Linkage disequilibrium (allelic
association), 191
Linoleate
auto-oxidation of, 373–374, 374*i*
photo-oxidation of, 374–375, 374*i*
Lipid layer, of tear film, 305–306
Lipid peroxidation, 375
mechanisms of, 373–375
Lipid solubility
ocular medication absorption affected
by, 386, 387*i*, 388
Lipid strip, 305
Lipidation, protein (prenylation), 215
Lipids
in photoreceptor membranes,
344–346, 345*i*
in retinal pigment epithelium, 367
in tear film, 305–306
in vitreous, 341
Lipofuscin granules (wear-and-tear
pigment), 77
Liposomes
for drug delivery, 391
for gene therapy, 447, 447*t*
Lipoxygenase, nonsteroidal anti-
inflammatory drugs and, 419
Lissamine green, as diagnostic agent, 442
Livostin. *See* Levocabastin
Local anesthetics, 438–441, 439*t*

Lockwood
  suspensory ligament of, 41
  upper tendon of (superior orbital
    tendon), 21
Locus (gene), 191. *See also* Gene
Locus heterogeneity, 191, 249, 276
LOD score, in linkage, 229
Lodoxamide, 421–422, 422*t*
Lomefloxacin, 430
Long arm 13 deletion syndrome (13q14
    syndrome), 268–270, 270*t*
Loop of Meyer, 103
Lowe syndrome, 172
  ocular findings in carriers of, 289*t*
Lower tendon of Zinn (inferior orbital
    tendon), 21
Lumirhodopsin, 352–353
Lutein, 86
  antioxidant effect of, 379
  structure of, 380*i*
Lymphatics, eyelid, 36
Lyonization (X chromosome inactivation),
    191, 212, 250, 288–292
β-Lysin, in tear film, 307
Lysozyme
  in aqueous humor, 327
  in tear film, 307

Macula, 86–88, 87*i*
  anatomy of, 86–88, 87*i*
  carotenoids in, 379, 380*i*
  coloboma of, 174
  lutea, 86
Magnesium, in aqueous humor, 325
Main intrinsic polypeptide, 332*t*, 333
Mandibular nerve. *See* Cranial nerve V$_3$
Mannitol, 413, 413*t*
Mannosidosis, enzyme defect and ocular
    findings in, 279*t*
Maple syrup urine disease, enzyme defect
    and ocular findings in, 280*t*
Marcaine. *See* Bupivacaine
Marfan syndrome, spherophakia in, 172
Margin, lid. *See* Eyelid, margin of
Marginal tear strip, 305
Marker site, 229
Maternal age, Down syndrome incidence
    and, 263
Maternal inheritance, 288
Maxidex. *See* Dexamethasone
Maxillary nerve. *See* Cranial nerve V$_2$

MCM proteins, 216
Meckel's cave, 115
Medial rectus muscle, 21, 23*t*
Medications. *See* Drugs
Medrysone, 415, 415*t*
Megalocornea, 167, 168, 169*i*
Meibomian glands (tarsal glands), 28, 31*t*,
    34, 35*i*
  tear film lipids secreted by, 305
Meiosis, 191, 252–254, 253*i*
Melanin, in retinal pigment
    epithelium, 370
Melanocytosis, oculodermal (nevus
    of Ota), 175
Melanogenesis, 144, 150
Melanosomes
  differentiation of, 144, 150
  in retinal pigment epithelium, 77, 144
MEM. *See* Minimum essential medium
Mendelian disorder (single-gene disorder),
    191, 274
Mendel's law of independent
    assortment, 254
Meninges, optic nerve, 101, 102*i*
Mepivacaine, 439*t*, 440
Mesencephalic nucleus, of cranial nerve V
    (trigeminal), 112
Mesenchyme, 126
Mesoderm, 126, 134, 135*i*
  ocular structures derived from, 132*t*
Messenger RNA (mRNA), 126, 211
  processing of, 211
Metacentric chromosome, 257
Metachromatic leukodystrophy, enzyme
    defect and ocular findings in, 279*t*
Metarhodopsin, 353
Methacholine, 394–396
Methazolamide, 410*t*
Methicillin, 425*t*, 426
Methylation, 212
Metipranolol, 409, 409*t*
Meyer, loop of, 103
Mezlocillin, 426
Miconazole, 432, 432*t*
Microcornea, 167, 168*i*
Microphakia, 160
Microphthalmos, 126, 160, 161*i*, 162,
    163, 164, 164*i*
  microcornea with, 167, 168*i*
Microsatellite, 191, 229
Microspherophakia, 172

Nalfon. *See* Fenoprofen

Nanophthalmos, 126, 165

Naphazoline/antazoline, 422*t*

Naphazoline/pheniramine, 422*t*

Naphcon-A. *See* Naphazoline/pheniramine

Naprosyn. *See* Naproxen

Naproxen, 420*t*

NARP. *See* Neuropathy, with ataxia and retinitis pigmentosa

Nasal sinuses, 9, 10*i*

Nasociliary nerve, 115

Nasolacrimal duct, 16, 39, 40*i*
  occlusion of, ocular medication absorption and, 384, 385*i*

Natacyn. *See* Natamycin

Natamycin, 432, 432*t*

Necrotizing encephalopathy, Leigh, enzyme defect and ocular findings in, 280*t*

Neomycin, 425*t*
  with polymyxin B, 429*t*

Neosporin. *See* Polymyxin B/neomycin/bacitracin; Polymyxin B/neomycin/gramicidin

Neotal. *See* Polymyxin B/neomycin/bacitracin

Neovascularization, gonioscopic visualization of, 59

Nerve fiber layer, 85

Nervus intermedius, 116

Nettleship-Falls X-linked ocular albinism, ocular findings in carriers of, 289*t*, 291*i*, 292

Neural crest cells, 126
  in ocular development, 130–131, 132*t*, 134, 136*i*

Neural folds, 126, 134, 137*i*

Neural plate, 134

Neural tube, 126, 134

Neurocristopathy, 126, 131, 168

Neuroectoderm, 126
  ocular structures derived from, 132*t*

Neuromuscular blocking drugs, 403

Neuropathy
  with ataxia and retinitis pigmentosa, mitochondrial DNA mutations and, 225, 225*i*
  optic, Leber hereditary, mitochondrial DNA mutations and, 224, 225*i*

Neurosensory retina, 80–84. *See also* Retina
  anatomy of, 80–84
  development of, 140–144, 143*i*
  glial elements of, 81–82
  neuronal elements of, 80, 83*i*
  vascular elements of, 84, 84*i*

Neurotoxin complex, purified, 441

Neurotransmitters
  in iris–ciliary body, 319–322, 320*t*
  in retina, 363

Nevus
  congenital, 175
  of Ota (oculodermal melanocytosis), 175

NFL. *See* Nerve fiber layer

Nicotinic agents, 393, 403
  antagonists, 403
  indirect-acting agonists, 403

Niemann-Pick disease
  enzyme defect and ocular findings in, 280*t*
  racial and ethnic concentration of, 277

Night blindness, congenital stationary with myopia, ocular findings in carriers of, 289*t*

Nitrogen bases, 192

Nizoral. *See* Ketoconazole

Nondisjunction, 192
  aneuploidy caused by, 259
  in mosaicism, 265–266

Nonhistone proteins, 204

Nonpaternity, 192

Nonsteroidal anti-inflammatory drugs (NSAIDs), 415*t*, 419–421
  prostaglandins affected by, 319

Norepinephrine
  adrenergic receptor response to, 404
  synthesis and release of, 404, 406*i*

Norfloxacin, 429*t*, 430

Northern blot, 192, 235

Notochord, 134

NSAIDs. *See* Nonsteroidal anti-inflammatory drugs

Nuclear envelope, 203

Nuclear matrix, 204

Nuclear pores, 203

Nucleolus, 203

Nucleoside, 192

Nucleosome, 192

Optic pits, 126, 127, 174–175
Optic radiations, 103
Optic stalk, 134, 140*i*, 145
Optic sulcus, 127, 134, 139*i*
Optic tract, 103, 104*i*
Optic ventricle, 137
Optic vesicle, 127, 134
OptiPranolol. *See* Metipranolol
Ora serrata, 89, 90*i*
Oral medication, sustained-release
    preparations of, 388
Orbicularis oculi muscle, 28–29
Orbit
    anatomy of, 9–16
    bony, 9, 11*i*
    cysts of, 166–167, 166*i*
    dermoid cyst of, 178
    development of, 158
    fissures in, 16, 17*i*, 18–19*i*
    floor of, 14, 14*i*
        fracture of, 14
    foramina in, 16
    lateral wall of, 15, 15*i*
    margin of, 10, 12*i*
    medial wall of, 12, 13*i*
    optic nerve in, 95*t*, 101
        blood supply of, 105
    roof of, 10–12, 13*i*
    septum of, 32, 33*i*
    teratoma of, 166
    vascular system of
        anatomy of, 41–45, 42*i*, 43*i*, 44*i*
        development of, 156–157
    volume of, 9
Orbital gland, 37
ORC. *See* Origin replication/recognition
    complex
ORF. *See* Open reading frame
Organ transplantation, for enzyme
    deficiency disease, 300
Organogenesis, 127
    in eye, 134–159, 139*i*, 140*i*, 141*i*, 142*i*.
        See also specific structure
Origin of replication, 193, 215
Origin replication/recognition complex,
    193, 216
Orudis. *See* Ketoprofen
Osmitrol. *See* Mannitol
Osmoglyn. *See* Glycerin

Osmotic agents, 412–414. *See also*
    specific agent
Ota, nevus of (oculodermal
    melanocytosis), 175
Ouabain, 409
Outer segments. *See* Cone outer segments;
    Photoreceptor outer segments; Rod
    outer segments
Overlap, smallest region of, 196
Ovum, 252
Oxacillin, 426
Oxygen
    in aqueous humor, 328
    corneal supply of, 311
Oxygen radicals (free radicals)
    cellular sources of, 372–373, 373*i*
    in lens, 375–376
    retinal damage caused by, 376–377
Oxytetracycline, with polymyxin B, 429*t*

p53 gene, in DNA repair, 216
p arm, 193, 206, 257
Palmitate, in vitreous, 341
Palpebral conjunctiva, 34, 34*i*, 39
Palpebral gland, 37
Palpebral ligaments, 33, 34*i*
2-PAM. *See* Pralidoxime
Pancuronium, 403
Papillae, Bergmeister's, 91, 175
Para-aminoclonidine, 446
Parasympathetic nerves, cholinergic drug
    action and, 293, 394*i*
Paredrine. *See* Hydroxyamphetamine
Pars plana, 64
Pars plicata, 64
Patau syndrome (trisomy 13),
    259–261, 261*t*
PAX genes, 129, 189
    mutations in, 130, 209, 271
PCD. *See* Programmed cell death
PCR. *See* Polymerase chain reaction
Pedigree analysis, 293–295
    symbols used in, 295*i*
Penetrance (genetic), 193, 275, 285*t*
    familial, 282–283
    incomplete (skipped generation), 284
Penicillamine, for Wilson disease, 300
Penicillin, 425*t*
Penicillin G, 426
Penicillin V, 426

Penicillins, 426. *See also specific agent*
  allergic reaction to, 425–426
  mechanism of action of, 424–426
  penicillinase-resistant, 426
  structure of, 424, 426*i*
Pentose phosphate pathway, in lens
  glucose metabolism, 335
Perfloxacin, 430
Pericytes, retinal blood vessel, 84
Periocular injections, 388
Periocular tissues, development of, 158
Periorbital sinuses, 9, 10*i*
Peripherin, in rod outer segments, 348*t*
Peripherin gene mutation, in retinitis
  pigmentosa, 361
Peroxidation, lipid, 373–375
Persistent hyperplastic primary vitreous,
  175, 178*i*
Persistent posterior hyaloid artery,
  175, 177*i*
Peters anomaly, 168, 170, 171*i*. *See also*
  Neurocristopathy
  homeobox gene mutations in, 130
Petrosal nerve, greater superficial, 115
Phagocytosis, by retinal pigment
  epithelium, 371
Phagolysosomes/phagosomes, in retinal
  pigment epithelium, 78, 371
Pharmacodynamics, of ocular drugs, 392
Pharmacogenetics, 193, 298–299
Pharmacokinetics, of ocular drugs,
  384–392
Pharmacology, ocular, 383–450. *See also*
  specific agent and Drugs, ocular
  legal aspects of, 450
  principles of, 384–392
Phenethicillin, 426
Pheniramine/naphazoline, 422*t*
Phenocopy, 193, 274
Phenotype, 193, 273–274
Phenylalkanoic acid, 419. *See also*
  Nonsteroidal anti-inflammatory drugs
Phenylephrine, 404
Phenylketonuria, enzyme defect in, 281
Phosducin, in rod outer segments, 348*t*
Phosphate, in aqueous humor, 325
Phosphatidylcholine, in retinal pigment
  epithelium, 367
Phosphatidylethanolamine, in retinal
  pigment epithelium, 367

Phosphatidyl-inositol-4,5-bisphosphate
  (PIP_2), in signal transduction in
  iris–ciliary body, 322–324, 323*i*
Phosphodiesterase, in rod outer
  segments, 348*t*
Phospholine Iodide. *See* Echothiophate
Phospholipase A_2, in arachidonic acid
  release, nonsteroidal anti-
  inflammatory drugs and, 419
Phospholipase C, in rod outer
  segments, 348*t*
Phospholipids
  in retinal pigment epithelium, 367
  in tear film, 305–306
Phosphonoformic acid. *See* Foscarnet
Phosphoprotein phosphatase, in rod outer
  segments, 348*t*
Photo-oxidation, 374–375, 374*i*
Photoreceptor outer segments. *See also*
  Photoreceptors
  chemistry of, 344–349
  lipids of, 344–346, 345*i*
  proteins of, 346–347
  synthesis and turnover of, 349–351
Photoreceptors, 80, 83*i*. *See also* Cones;
  Photoreceptor outer segments; Rods
  development of, 142–143
Photorefractive keratectomy (PRK),
  312, 313*i*
Photorhodopsin, 352
PHPV. *See* Persistent hyperplastic primary
  vitreous
Physostigmine, 397*t*, 399
Pial septae, optic nerve, 101, 102*i*
Pigment epithelium
  ciliary body, 66, 66*i*
  iris, 63
  retinal. *See* Retinal pigment epithelium
Pigment granules, in retinal pigment
  epithelium, 370
Pigmentation
  congenital abnormalities of, 175–177,
    178*i*, 179*i*
  iris, latanoprost affecting, 446
Pigments, visual, 344, 347–349. *See also*
  specific type
  dynamics of, 351–355
Pilocarpine, 394, 396–397, 397*t*
  with cholinesterase inhibitors, 400
PIP_2. *See* Phosphatidyl-inositol-4,
  5-bisphosphate

signal transduction in, 355–358
stratification of, 85
Retinal arterioles, 105
Retinal artery, central, 84, 105, 106*i*
Retinal detachment, 77
rhegmatogenous, posterior vitreous
detachment and, 91, 91*i*, 92*i*
Retinal pigment epithelium (RPE)
anatomy of, 70*i*, 71*i*, 77–79, 366–367
antioxidants in, 377–379, 380*i*
autophagy in, 371
biochemistry and metabolism of,
366–371
as biologic filter, 369
composition of, 367–368, 368*t*
congenital abnormalities of, 174
congenital hypertrophy of, 177, 179*i*
development of, 144–145
functions of, 366*t*
phagocytosis by, 371
pigment granules in, 370
regional differences in, 77, 79*i*
subretinal space maintenance and,
369–370
in vitamin A metabolism, 368–369
Retinal vein, central, 105, 106*i*
Retinaldehyde, 351–353, 351*i*, 352*i*,
353, 355
in retinal pigment epithelium, 368–369
Retinitis pigmentosa
with neuropathy and ataxia,
mitochondrial DNA mutations
and, 225, 225*i*
point mutations in, 360–361
vitamin A supplementation in, 301
X-linked, ocular findings in carriers of,
289*t*, 290*i*
Retinoblastoma
genetics of, 268–270
long arm 13 deletion syndrome and,
268–270
mutation rate of, 272
Retinoic acid, 353
Retinoid binding protein,
interphotoreceptor, 358
Retinol, 353, 354, 355
Retinyl ester, 353, 354, 355
Retroposon, 195
Retrotransposition, 195
Retroviral vectors, in gene therapy, 244,
245*i*, 447

Rev-Eyes. *See* Dapiprazole
Reverse transcription, 195–196
RFLPs. *See* Restriction fragment length
polymorphisms
Rhodopsin
bleaching of, 351–353, 352*i*
cGMP hydrolysis and, 355–358, 357*i*
dynamics of, 351–355
light-evoked changes in, 351–353,
351*i*, 352*i*
molecular biology of, 359
in rod outer segments, 346–347, 348*t*
Rhodopsin kinase, in rod outer
segments, 348*t*
Ribavirin, 436–437
Ribonucleic acid. *See* RNA
Ribosomal RNA (rRNA), 211, 214
Ribosomes, protein synthesis in,
213–214, 214*i*
Rieger anomaly, 168, 169, 170*i*. *See also*
Neurocristopathy
Rieger syndrome, 170
Riley-Day syndrome (familial dysautonomia)
enzyme defect and ocular findings
in, 280*t*
racial and ethnic concentration of, 277
Rimexolone, 415*t*, 418
Ring chromosome, 267
Riolan, muscle of, 29
RNA, 199
creation of from DNA, 211
heteronuclear, 189, 211
messenger (mRNA), 126, 211
processing of, 211
ribosomal (rRNA), 211, 214
synthesis of, in retinal pigment
epithelium, 367
transfer (tRNA), 211, 213–214, 214*i*
RNA splicing, 196, 211
RNA viruses, recombinant, for gene
therapy, 447
Robertsonian translocation, 267
Rod outer segments. *See also* Rods
development of, 143
lipids of, 344–346, 345*i*
proteins in, 346–347, 348*t*
renewal of, 349, 350*i*
shedding of, 350–351
Rods, 80, 83*i*. *See also* Rod outer
segments
Rose bengal, as diagnostic agent, 442

Sphincter muscle, 63–64
  development of, 155
  innervation of, 319
  miotics affecting, 320–321
  mydriatics affecting, 321
Spinal nucleus and tract, of cranial nerve V
    (trigeminal), 112–114, 114*i*
Spindle plate, 206
Spiral of Tillaux, 21, 24*i*
Splice junction site, 196
Spliceosome, 196, 211
Splicing
  alternate, 211
  RNA, 196, 211
Sporadic, definition of, 197, 248
SRO. *See* Smallest region of overlap
SRS-A. *See* Slow-reacting substance of
    anaphylaxis
SSCP. *See* Single-stranded conformational
    polymorphism
Stationary night blindness, congenital,
    with myopia, ocular findings in
    carriers of, 289*t*
Statrol. *See* Polymyxin B/neomycin
Stearate, in vitreous, 341
Steroids. *See* Corticosteroids
Stop codon (termination codon), 197
Storage diseases, enzyme defect and
    ocular findings in, 279*t*
Streptokinase, 442
Streptomycin, 420
Stroma
  choroidal, development of, 150
  corneal
    anatomy of, 49, 310*i*
    biochemistry and metabolism
      of, 311–314
    development of, 150–152
  iris, 61
  scleral, anatomy of, 53
STRs. *See* Short tandem repeats
STS. *See* Sequence-tagged sites
Submetacentric chromosome, 257
Subretinal space (interphotoreceptor
    matrix/IPM), 358–359, 358*i*, 360*i*
  retinal pigment epithelium in
    maintenance of, 369–370
Succinylcholine, 403
  pharmacogenetics and, 299

"Sugar" cataracts, aldose reductase in
    development of, 335, 337
Sulamyd. *See* Sulfacetamide
Sulf-10. *See* Sulfacetamide
Sulfacetamide, 427–428, 429*t*
Sulfisoxazole, 429*t*
Sulfite oxidase deficiency, 280*t*
Sulfonamides, 427–428
Sulindac, 420*t*
Superior oblique muscle, 21, 23*t*
Superior orbital fissure, 16, 17*i*, 18–19*i*
Superior orbital tendon (upper tendon of
    Lockwood), 21
Superior rectus muscle, 21, 23*t*
Superoxide dismutase, antioxidant effect
    of, 375
  in retina and retinal pigment
    epithelium, 378
Supraorbital foramen/notch, 16
Suprofen, 319, 415*t*, 421
Surface ectoderm, ocular structures
    derived from, 132*t*
Surfactants, in eyedrops, 386–387
Suspensory ligament of Lockwood, 41
Sustained-release devices, for ocular
    medication administration,
    389–391, 390*i*
Sympathetic nerves, cholinergic drug
    action and, 293, 394*i*
Synaptic cleft, in signal processing in
    retina, 361
Synaptic vesicles, in signal processing in
    retina, 362
Synechiae, peripheral anterior, 60
Syneresis, 341
Synophthalmia, 127, 165
Syntenic traits, 254
Synteny, 197, 226–227
Systemic drug therapy, for ocular
    disorders, 388–389

Tandem repeats, short, 196, 229, 232*i*
Tarsal glands (meibomian glands), 28, 31*t*,
    34, 35*i*
  tear film lipids secreted by, 305
Tarsus, 33–34, 34*i*
TATA box, 197, 207–209
TATA-box binding protein, 209
Taurine, retinal pigment epithelium in
    transport of, 368

Tay-Sachs disease (GM$_2$ type I gangliosidosis)
  enzyme defect and ocular findings in, 279t
  racial and ethnic concentration of, 277
TBP. *See* TATA-box binding protein
Tear film, 305–309
  biochemistry and metabolism of, 305–309
  precorneal, 47, 305, 306i
  preocular, 305
  properties of, 307t
  solutes, 306
Tear meniscus, 305
Tear sac, 39
Tear strip, marginal, 305
Tearing, reflex, absorption of ocular medication affected by, 307
Tears. *See also* Tear film
  artificial, 441
  deficiency of, mucin, 308, 309, 309i
  dysfunction of, 309, 309i
    mucins in, 308, 309, 309i
  secretion of, 308
Telomerase, 207
Telomere, 206–207
Telomeric DNA, 197, 203
Temafloxacin, 430
Tenon's capsule, 41
Tensilon. *See* Edrophonium
Teratogen, 127
Teratoma, 127
  orbital, 166
Terminal deletion, 267
Termination codon (stop codon), 197
Terramycin. *See* Polymyxin B/oxytetracycline
Tetracaine, 439t, 441
Tetracyclines, 428, 429t
Tetrahydrotriamcinolone, 418t
TGF–β. *See* Transforming growth factor–beta
Third cranial nerve. *See* Cranial nerve III
Third nerve palsy, eyelid fissure changes in, 26
13q14 syndrome (long arm 13 deletion syndrome), 268–270, 270t
Threshold, genetic, 197
Thrombin, 443
Thromboxanes, 317, 318i
Thymoxamine, 321, 407

Thyroid disease, eyelid fissure changes in, 26, 27i
Ticarcillin, 425t, 426
Tight junctions, in retinal pigment epithelium, 77, 366
Tillaux, spiral of, 21, 24i
Timolol, 309t, 408
  sustained-release preparation of, 391
  systemic absorption of, 385i
Timoptic. *See* Timolol
Tissue plasminogen activator, 442
Tobramycin, 425t, 428–430, 429t
Tobrex. *See* Tobramycin
Tolectin. *See* Tolmetin
Tolmetin, 420t
Tonic pupil (Adie's pupil), pharmacologic testing for, 394–396
Topical medications. *See* Eyedrops; Ointments
Tosufloxacin, 430
tPA. *See* Tissue plasminogen activator
Trabecular meshwork, 54i, 55–61, 55i, 56i, 57i
  corneoscleral, 57
  development of, 153–154
  uveal, 57
Trait, 278
  holandric, 189, 285
  segregation of in clones of somatic cell hybrids, 227
Tranexamic acid, 443
Transcript domains, 205
Transcription, 197, 207–213, 210i
  reverse, 195–196
Transcription factors, 202, 207–209
  protein structures of, 207, 208i
Transcripts, illegitimate, 190
Transducin
  in cGMP hydrolysis, 356–358, 357i
  in rod outer segments, 348t
Transfer RNA (tRNA), 211, 213–214, 214i
Transferrin
  in aqueous humor, 327
  in vitreous, 340
Transforming growth factor–beta
  in aqueous humor, 327
  in ocular development, 128, 129
Transgenic animals, for genetic studies, 239, 242i
  of retina, 359–361
Transient nerve fiber layer of Chievitz, 141

ILLUSTRATIONS

The authors submitted the following figures for this revision. (Illustrations that were reproduced from other sources or submitted by contributors not on the committee are credited in the captions.)

Gerhard W. Cibis, MD: Fig VI-16

Randy H. Kardon, MD, PhD: Fig IV-18

Ramesh C. Tripathi, MD, PhD: Fig III-9, Fig III-11

F.J.G.M. van Kuijk, MD, PhD: Fig XI-3, Fig XII-3, Fig XVI-2, Fig XVI-4, Fig XVI-5, Fig XVI-8, Fig XVIII-1, Fig XVIII-2, Fig XVIII-3, Fig XVIII-4, Fig XVIII-5, Fig XVIII-6

Richard G. Weleber, MD: Fig IX-3